Reserved Keywords in Java

Data-declaration keywords:

byte	int	float	char	double

Loop keywords:

while	for	break	continue

Conditional keywords:

if	else	switch

Exception keywords:

throw	try	catch

Structure keywords:

class	extends	interface	implements

Access keywords:

public	private	protected

Specifying Character Literals

Description or Escape Sequence	Sequence	Output
any character	'y'	y
backspace BS	'\b'	backspace
horizontal tab HT	'\t'	tab
line feed LF	'\n'	linefeed
form feed FF	'\f'	form feed
carriage return CR	'\r'	carriage return
double quote	'\"'	"
single quote	'\''	'
backslash	'\\'	\
octal bit pattern	'0ddd'	(octal value of ddd)
hex bit pattern	'0xdd'	(hex value of dd)
Unicode character	'\dddd'	(actual Unicode character of dddd)

Arithmetic Operators

Operator	Operation	Example
+	Addition	g + h
-	Subtraction	g - h
*	Multiplication	g * h
/	Division	g / h
%	Modulus	g % h

Assignment Operators

Operator	Operation	Example	Meaning
+=	add to current variable	g += h	g = g + h
-=	subtract from current variable	g -= h	g = g - h
*=	multiply by current variable	g *= h	g = g * h
/=	divide by current variable	g /= h	g = g / h

Increment and Decrement Operators

Operator	Operation	Example	Meaning
++	increment by 1	g++	g = g + 1
--	decrement by 1	g--	g = g - 1

Comparison Operators (return true or false)

Operator	Operation	Example	Meaning
==	Equal	g == h	Is g equal to h?

!=	Not equal	g != h	Is g not equal to h?
<	Less than	g < h	Is g less than h?
>	Greater than	g > h	Is g greater than h?
<=	Less than or equal to	g <= h	Is g less than or equal to h?
>=	Greater than or equal to	g >= h	Is g greater than or equal to h?

Bitwise Operators

Operator	Operation
&	Bitwise AND
¦	Bitwise OR
^	Bitwise XOR
<<	Left shift
>>	Right shift
>>>	Zero fill right shift
~	Bitwise complement
<<=	Left shift assignment
>>=	Right shift assignment
>>>=	Zero fill right shift assignment
x&=y	AND assignment
x¦=y	OR assignment
x^=y	NOT assignment

Comment Indicators

Start	Text	End Comment
/*	text	*/
/**	text	*/
//	text	(everything to the end of the line is ignored by the compiler)

Primitive Data Type Keywords

boolean	char	byte	short	int	long	float	double

Integer Data Type Ranges

Type	Length	Minimum Value	Maximum Value
byte	8 bits	-128	127
short	16 bits	-32768	32767
int	32 bits	-2147483648	2147483647
long	64 bits	-9223372036854775808	9223372036854775807

Unary Operators

Operator	Operation
-	Unary negation
~	Bitwise complement
++	Increment
--	Decrement
!	Not

Operator Precedence

++	--	!	~	instanceof	*
/	%	+	-	<<	>>
>>>	<	>	<=	>=	==
!=	&	^	&&	¦¦	?:
=	op=				

Peter Norton's
Guide to
Java Programming

Peter Norton
&
William Stanek

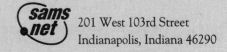
201 West 103rd Street
Indianapolis, Indiana 46290

To the dreamers of the world who dream the perfect dreams and then create wonderful things like Java.

Copyright © 1996 by Peter Norton

International Standard Book Number: 1-57521-088-6

Library of Congress Catalog Card Number: 96-67206

99 98 97 96   4 3 2 1

Interpretation of the printing code: the rightmost double-digit number is the year of the book's printing; the rightmost single-digit, the number of the book's printing. For example, a printing code of 96-1 shows that the first printing of the book occurred in 1996.

Composed in Goudy and MCPdigital by Macmillan Computer Publishing

Printed in the United States of America

Trademarks

President, Sams Publishing	*Richard K. Swadley*
Publishing Team Leader	*Greg Wiegand*
Managing Editor	*Cindy Morrow*
Director of Marketing	*John Pierce*
Assistant Marketing Managers	*Kristina Perry*
	Rachel Wolfe

Acquisitions Editor
Christopher Denny

Development Editors
Anthony Amico, L. Angelique Brittingham

Software Development Specialist
Steve Straiger

Senior Editor
Kitty Wilson

Production Editor
Kimberly K. Hannel

Copy Editor
Marilyn Stone

Indexer
Tom Griffin

Technical Reviewers
Karen Clere, Christopher Stone

Editorial Coordinator
Bill Whitmer

Technical Edit Coordinator
Lynette Quinn

Resource Coordinator
Deborah Frisby

Formatter
Frank Sinclair

Editorial Assistants
Carol Ackerman, Andi Richter, Rhonda Tinch-Mize

Cover Designer
Tim Amrhein

Book Designer
Alyssa Yesh

Copy Writer
Peter Fuller

Production Team Supervisor
Brad Chinn

Production
Mary Ann Abramson, Georgiana Briggs, Susan Knose, Ayanna Lacey

Overview

Contents

Acknowledgments

Creating the perfect book on Java programming required a great deal of effort—long hours, days without sleep, grueling research, and much more. I want to personally thank everyone who poured their heart into this book.

Special thanks to my wife and family, who continue to put up with the tappety-tap of my keyboard at all hours of the day and night. Without your support, this book wouldn't have been possible.

About the Author

William Robert Stanek (`director@tvp.com`) is the publisher and founder of The Virtual Press (`http://tvp.com/` and mirror site `http://www.tvpress.com/`), a non-traditional press established in March 1994. As a publisher and writer with over 10 years of experience on networks, he brings a solid voice of experience on the Internet and electronic publishing to his many projects. He was first introduced to Internet e-mail in 1988 when he worked for the government, and has been involved in the commercial Internet community since 1991.

His years of practical experience are backed by a solid education, including a Master of Science in Information Systems and a Bachelor of Science in Computer Science. While his press publishes electronic books under four imprints, the core business is shifting, and the time that isn't spent writing such runaway hits as Sams.net's *Web Publishing Unleashed* is spent consulting with corporate clients and developing hot new Web sites.

William served in the Persian Gulf War as a combat crew member on an Electronic Warfare aircraft. During the war, he flew on numerous combat missions into Iraq and was awarded nine medals for his wartime service including one of our nation's highest flying honors, the Air Force Distinguished Flying Cross. He has written many books, articles, and essays. His book-length projects include nine fiction titles and six nonfiction titles. Watch for the upcoming release of his *FrontPage Unleashed* from Sams.net in August 1996. When he's not writing or working, he spends time with his family, his favorite time of the day being when he reads to his youngest child.

Tell Us What You Think!

As a reader, you are the most important critic and commentator of our books. We value your opinion and want to know what we're doing right, what we could do better, in what areas you'd like to see us publish, and any other words of wisdom you're willing to pass our way. You can help us make strong books that meet your needs and give you the computer guidance you require.

Do you have access to CompuServe or the World Wide Web? Then check out our CompuServe forum by typing **GO SAMS** at any prompt. If you prefer the World Wide Web, check out our site at `http://www.mcp.com`.

Note: If you have a technical question about this book, call the technical support line at (800) 571-5840, ext. 3668.

As the team leader of the group that created this book, I welcome your comments. You can fax, e-mail, or write me directly to let me know what you did or didn't like about this book—as well as what we can do to make our books stronger. Here's the information:

FAX: 317/581-4669

E-mail: `programming_mgr@sams.mcp.com`

Mail: Greg Wiegand
Comments Department
Sams Publishing
201 W. 103rd Street
Indianapolis, IN 46290

Introduction

Peter Norton's Guide to Java Programming is the definitive guide to the Java programming language. It is designed to meet the needs of today's Web publishers and programmers by helping you set the pace for the future of Internet and object-oriented programming. Not only does this book provide the broadest and most extensive coverage of essential issues, it is the only book on the market of its kind.

Java represents the future of object-oriented programming, and *Peter Norton's Guide to Java Programming* is the key to this future. We have taken great care to provide invaluable tips and pour our expertise into every page. As you read this book, you will learn about everything the Java programming language has to offer.

For Internet developers, programmers, and Web publishers, now is the time to get in on the inside track to Java. Throughout much of 1995, Java was in Alpha and Beta testing. During this time, Java development was limited to the Solaris and Windows NT environments. But all this quickly changed as word about Java spread like wildfire. In January 1996, Sun Microsystems officially released Java 1.0, and you can now obtain free developer's kits for every major operating system including Solaris, AIX, Windows 95/NT, OS/2, and Macintosh.

For non-programmers, using a programming language such as Java may seem impossible, but nothing could be further from the truth. The simple fact is that if you can create an HTML, a SGML, or a VRML document, you should be able to create Java-powered documents and applications as well. You will find that Java is easy to learn and use because it eliminates or automates many of the problem areas of earlier programming languages.

The power of Java is that even the most basic Java programs can feature multimedia. This is primarily because the fundamentals of the Java programming language are easy to learn and use. Through a plain-English approach, I guide you from the fundamentals to advanced programming and beyond. Here are the major topics covered in this book:

- Getting started
- The fundamentals of the Java programming language
- Using the Java Developer's Kit
- A complete walk-through of the Java Application Programming Interface
- Developing Java applets for the Web
- Using applets in Web publications
- Reusing applets
- Developing stand-alone applications
- Using Java applications in the real world

- Application upgrades
- Developing advanced applets
- Developing advanced applications
- Advanced debugging and troubleshooting
- An inside look at the Java Virtual Machine
- Online resources for Java

Who Should Read This Book?

Peter Norton's Guide to Java Programming is for today's Web publishers and programmers. Although this book is intended for those with a casual to accomplished knowledge of programming or Web publishing, the plain-English approach makes this book perfect for just about anyone. I truly hope you find this book to be invaluable as you plot your course to success in Java programming.

How This Book Is Organized

This book is designed to be the most comprehensive resource on the Java programming language available anywhere. Chapter by chapter, you will learn everything you need to know to develop and design powerful programs using Java.

Part I, "Next Stop—Java," covers everything you need to know to get started. After introducing the Java programming language and the basic principles of object-oriented programming, Chapter 1 explores the evolution of programming languages and how Java came to be. Chapter 2 details everything the programmer or Web publisher needs to get started with creating Java programs, including installing the Java Developer's Kit. The chapter also provides insight into how C/C++ programmers can best make the transition to Java.

The primers in Part II, "Power Primers," are designed to give you a jump-start on Java development. In addition to being a primer on the World Wide Web, Chapter 3 demonstrates the power of Java through a discussion of the multimedia uses of Java on the Web. Chapter 4 provides a primer on the Java programming language. In this chapter, you create your first Java applet and a Java application. Chapter 5 discusses the essential tools for creating and developing Java programs and how to use them. Featured tools include the developer's tools in the Java Developer's Kit and Java WorkShop, a hot new graphical development environment.

Part III, "Anatomy of the Java Language," examines the inner workings of the Java programming language. Chapter 6 explores the fundamentals of the language including tokens, types, expressions, declarations, and control flow statements. In Chapter 7, everything discussed so far starts to come together as you learn that Java objects are built from classes that contain the fundamentals, a group of classes forms a package, and abstract classes called interfaces patch the structure together. Chapter 8 explores the key concepts of multithreading, error handling, and streaming. These concepts are essential to complete the final pieces of Java programming theories.

The Java Application Programming Interface contains a wealth of ready-to-use code that can save you development time and money. Part IV, "The Java Application Programming Interface," examines everything the API has to offer. In Chapter 9, you will find a list of all available API packages and their relation to one another. Chapter 10 examines the Applet and Language class libraries and their uses in Java programs. Chapter 11 examines the Abstract Windowing Toolkit library and its uses in Java programs. Chapter 12 examines the I/O and Utility libraries and their uses in Java programs. Chapter 13 examines the Net and Debug libraries and their uses in Java programs.

Part V, "Developing Java Applets for the Web," details everything you need to know to develop Java programs for use on the Web. Through example applets, Chapter 14 demonstrates the structure of basic and intermediate-level applets and provides steps for building your own applets. After creating and testing an applet, the next important step is incorporating the applet into an HTML document for use on the World Wide Web. Chapter 15 begins with a brief overview of HTML document structure and then explores HTML elements associated with Java applets. Finally, the chapter shows how the applet can be used in Web publications. An essential concept in object-oriented programming is reusing existing code, which saves development time and money. Chapter 16 discusses when and how to reuse code and provides real-world examples.

Part VI, "Developing Stand-alone Applications," details everything you need to know to develop stand-alone applications. Chapter 17 begins by examining how Java applications differ from applets and then demonstrates the structure of basic and intermediate-level applications. Because useful stand-alone applications are more difficult to create than applets, Chapter 18 provides insight into and examples of the features needed in applications. The chapter goes on to discuss how to increase the functionality of applications. In the real world, software applications have a development life cycle. Chapter 19 explains this life cycle in more detail than previous chapters and shows how to successfully implement application upgrades.

In Part VII, "Advanced Issues," you explore advanced design and development issues. Chapter 20 provides a hands-on example and complete walk-through of an advanced applet. You can use this chapter as a stepping stone for creating your own advanced applets. Chapter 21 provides a hands-on example and complete walk-through of an advanced application. You can use this chapter as a stepping stone for creating your own advanced applications. In Chapter 22, you learn how to use native programs and libraries with Java. These native programs can be in any other programming language including C, C++, and Smalltalk. Debugging and troubleshooting is another important part of programming. Chapter 23 explores advanced debugging issues and provides hands-on examples of using the Java debugger. The final chapter provides a detailed look at the Java runtime system and the Virtual Machine. Understanding the abstract specification of the Java Virtual Machine provides wonderful insight into how Java truly works.

The final section of the book puts key reference resources into your hands. Appendix A, "Java API Table Reference," is an invaluable at-a-glance resource for the Java API. Appendix B, "Java Terminology," is a glossary of terms you will use when working with Java.

Conventions Used in This Book

I have used the following conventions in this book.

Type Conventions

`monospace`	This computer font is used to represent code, whether onscreen or typed by you, and for filenames, directory names, and other nonstandard words.
`italic monospace`	I use italic computer font when the text is a placeholder or a variable rather than absolute code.
italic	Italic type is used to call your attention to new terms.

Icons

Note: Notes tell you about interesting facts that aren't really necessary to your understanding of Java; they're just for your information.

Tip: Tips contain tidbits of information that you might not learn elsewhere, or sometimes just tell you about a different way of doing something.

Warning: Warnings mean watch out—you can get into some trouble! Make sure you understand a warning before you follow any instructions that come after it.

Peter's Principle: I'll use the Peter's Principle icon to tell you about a rule that you might adopt as a standard operating procedure. It's like a tip that you can implement to improve general situations, and you can always use the principle as a rule to live by.

Looking Ahead: I include these boxes to give you a peek at what's coming up later and tell you how what you're currently reading will help you then.

The capability icon is intended to alert you to a situation or condition that you should track. It means that situation is dynamic and that better facilities are becoming available all the time.

Watch for the development issue icon to tell you how to implement or expand some function. In some ways it might be like the troubleshooting icon in that it tells you about a possible problem, but it will always offer some solution to the problem.

Each time you see the performance icon I'll be telling you about a technique you can use to make your product more efficient. I may offer some alternatives so that you can choose which method is best for you.

When you see this icon it means that there is a possibility for something to go wrong. The text shows you how to identify the problem and suggests a method for solving it.

I

Next Stop—
Java

1

Introducing Java

The Internet is the place where the little dynamo called Java was first set free. Now thousands of programmers, Internet developers, Web publishers, and software houses around the world are racing to learn everything they can about this tool for revolutionizing the Internet and the way programming is done. Anyone not connected to the Internet may be wondering what all the fuss is about. After all, C++ was supposed to revolutionize the software industry too, yet as you will soon learn, the major difference between C++ and Java is that Java delivers on all its promises. Java promises to bring revolutionary changes to the software industry and to the Internet; this chapter tells you how.

For Internet developers, programmers, and Web publishers, now is the time to get in on the inside track to Java. Throughout much of 1995, Java was in Alpha and Beta testing. During this time, Java development was limited to the Solaris and Windows NT environments, but all this quickly changed as word about Java spread like wildfire. In January 1996, Sun Microsystems officially released Java 1.0, and you can now obtain free developers kits for every major operating system, including Solaris, AIX, Windows 95/NT, OS/2, and Macintosh.

For nonprogrammers, using a programming language such as Java may seem impossible, yet nothing could be further from the truth. If you can create an HTML, an SGML, or a VRML document, you should be able to create Java-powered documents and applications as well. You will find that Java is easy to learn and use because it eliminates or automates many of the problem areas of earlier programming languages.

What Is Java?

JavaSoft, an operating company of Sun Microsystems, spent years developing a high-powered programming language for the '90s and beyond. Java delivers on this promise by being the most robust, easy-to-use, and versatile programming language available today. It includes the best aspects of earlier programming languages such as C and C++, allows you to create powerful applications, has features such as built-in multimedia capabilities that make creating multimedia presentations easier than ever, and leaves out those things we all hated about C and C++ like multiple inheritance, operator overloading, and pointers.

The best news about Java is that it is object oriented and architecture neutral. The promise of *object-oriented programming* (OOP) is the capability to reuse code. But, as C++ programmers will tell you (and if you are a C++ programmer, you probably already know this), good intentions do not mean a whole lot when it comes to reuse of C++ code. With Java, on the other hand, you can realize the benefits of code reuse immediately. You no longer have to develop separate applications for different platforms. With Java, you can develop a single application that is immediately usable on multiple platforms. Imagine the countless hours you will save by being able to develop a single application usable on Windows, UNIX, and Macintosh systems.

Considering that large corporations can use Java's platform independence to save millions of dollars on a single project, there is little wonder that Java is a buzzword in the software and Internet technology industries. Java has captivated much more than the imaginations of the techies. Companies from every business sector you can imagine—from finance to shipping—are examining ways to use Java.

For the entrepreneur or individual programmer, Java's platform independence allows you to develop powerful applications for operating systems you may never have worked with. This means that if you own a software-development or Internet-related business, whether it is a one-person operation or a conglomerate, you will be able to reach new customers and new markets. In an age when everyone is looking at the bottom line, a technology that allows you to sell more, do more, and reach larger audiences (potentially everyone who owns a computer) is certainly something worth investigating.

Furthermore, by allowing you to use the programming environment you are the most comfortable with, Java empowers you, the programmer. This is true whether you have limited technical skills or expert knowledge of computers. If you have a working knowledge of another programming language, you will find that Java is surprisingly easy to learn.

The developers of Java thought very carefully about the structure of their new language and by no mere coincidence modeled Java after C and C++. C is a favorite language for programmers doing procedural programming. C++ is a favorite language for programmers writing object-oriented programs. C and C++ have user and developer bases many times greater than their nearest competitors and could, in fact, be considered to be their own best competition.

Therefore, to ensure that Java is easy to understand and use, Java is modeled after C and C++. Java also borrows extensions from Objective C. These extensions allow for extremely dynamic method resolution. This makes it very easy for current C, Objective C, and C++ developers to transition to Java.

Any programmer who has ever had problems with pointers and memory management should rush to embrace Java with open arms. Java gets rid of pointers, automatically manages memory for you, and even features a garbage-collection routine that runs in the background.

In distributed environments, such as the World Wide Web, strict security mechanisms are essential —businesses simply cannot risk compromising their systems. The developers of the Java programming language knew this. They developed Java to be the most secure programming environment you will find anywhere. Java doesn't just fix security loopholes—it eliminates them, which makes Java the perfect language for programming on the Web.

Pointers are the biggest security problem with C/C++ programs. System crackers can use seemingly benign programs to forge pointers to memory, steal information from your system, and crash your system permanently. In Java, you can't forge pointers to memory because there are no pointers. Java eliminates many other security loopholes as well. For example, when Java programs are compiled and run, they are checked with a dynamic code verifier to ensure that the program has no malicious coding. Additionally, the Java runtime environment provides strict rules for programs started from remote hosts. These programs cannot access the local network, cannot access files on your local system, and cannot start programs on your systems either.

The Evolution of Java

As with many breakthroughs in science and technology, the Java programming language is the result of a concerted effort from a group of forward thinkers. Yet what you may find surprising—and perhaps shocking—about Java is that this truly ingenious technological development is not the result of a project that went perfectly from day one. Amazingly, if the project that began with the code name Green in the spring of 1991 had proceeded according to plan, Sun Microsystems would be in the commercial electronics business and the world would be without its jolt of Java. To understand the evolution and the true breakthrough Java represents, you have to roll the clock back to 1991.

In 1991 Sun Microsystems, Inc. was just beginning its climb to the position as the top producer of UNIX workstations. The company had revenues of nearly $2.5 billion for the previous fiscal year, up from a mere $210 million in 1986, and it seemed that the company was unstoppable. Sun's rise to fame was largely due to its pioneering efforts in open systems that enable businesses to build and maintain open network computing environments. Corporations raced to embrace Sun's open systems because they were fed up with the high costs and fees associated with closed network environments. Sun was climbing to the top of the mountain, and its executives knew it. Figure 1.1 shows Sun's site on the Web at http://www.sun.com/.

Figure 1.1.
Sun's Web site.

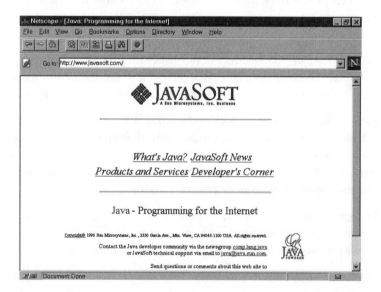

A movement began within Sun to develop new technologies that would sustain the corporation's phenomenal growth rate over the long term. A key area the company focused on was the commercial electronics market; the Green project was born as part of a larger project to develop advanced software for this market. The goal of the Green group was to establish Sun Microsystems as a player in the commercial electronics market. To achieve this goal, Sun's engineers and developers looked to microprocessors that would run on a variety of machines, particularly distributed real-time embedded systems that were both reliable and portable.

The key to Sun's success in this market would be the capability to easily port the system to multiple platforms. The plan was to develop the project in C++, but the developers ran into many problems as they tried to extend the C++ compiler. The developers ran into other problems as they tried to work in the constrictive framework of C++. Soon the developers realized that to succeed, they would have to try something bold and new. It was then that James Gosling began work on a new language he called Oak. Later, the new language would be called Java because in another twist of fate, Oak failed a trademark search.

Eventually, the developers created a PDA-like device to show off their efforts. Although the device used an early form of the Java programming language and a basic operating system and user interface, it was good enough to dazzle the executives at Sun. Around this time, the Green group developers incorporated under the name FirstPerson, Inc., which would later become JavaSoft. Figure 1.2 shows JavaSoft's site on the Web at `http://www.javasoft.com/`.

Figure 1.2.
JavaSoft's Web site.

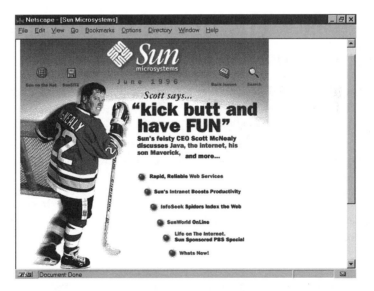

After that, it was a series of wrong turns for the Green group. A deal fell through with Time-Warner to develop set-top boxes that would be used for interactive television and video-on-demand. A deal fell through to develop an operating system for the 3DO. The public launch of the project was canceled, and much of the team left the Green group. By now it was early 1994, and the group of developers from Sun began looking to new areas once again.

It was about this time that a mass migration from the National Center for Supercomputing Applications (NCSA) to Silicon Valley began. A group of upstarts from NCSA created the company now called Netscape Communications Corporation. Silicon Valley was buzzing with thoughts of cyberspace, and this thing called the World Wide Web was starting to catch on like wildfire. By no coincidence, the Green group developers turned to the Internet and the Web as the answer to their problems. The Internet's distributed and multiplatform environment was perfect as a test bed for their project.

The rest, as they say, is history. Four years after the project began, those who hung in there got the gold ring. Java is currently the hottest topic on the Internet. Thousands of Web publishers and Internet developers want to learn how they can create high-powered Web documents complete with animation and multimedia. Millions of Web users want to learn where they can check out the latest Java-powered Web pages.

Sun Microsystems has done a wonderful job of keeping pace with this demand. They licensed Java technology to companies such as IBM, Microsoft, Silicon Graphics, Adobe, and Netscape. They continue to diligently update the Java language. And true to the ideal that made Sun Microsystems who they are today, Java and the Java Developer's Kit are provided free of charge to developers.

A Brief History of the Internet and the World Wide Web

As we look back on the evolution of Java and the evolution of the World Wide Web, it seems that the two technologies were on a parallel course. After all, Java was meant to be used in distributed environments and on open systems. The World Wide Web is an open-ended information system designed to be used in the Internet's distributed environment. Both Java and the Web are designed with portability, robustness, and ease of use in mind. Java also provides solutions for important security issues on the Web.

But how do the pieces fit together and why is Java so important to Internet development? To better understand how Java, the Internet, and the World Wide Web fit together, let's take a brief look at the history of the Internet and the World Wide Web.

The Early Days of the Internet

Although it may be hard to believe today, the Internet began as a U.S. government project. In 1969, four computers were linked over a long-distance connection in order to prove that such an outlandish concept could work. This early network was called the *ARPANET* (or Advanced Research

Projects Agency Network). The ARPANET slowly grew; by 1972, 50 universities and research facilities with military projects had connections. By the late 1980s, more than 80,000 computers were connected through a series of networks. Eventually, this collection of networks became the Internet.

From 1969 to 1991, the Internet was largely a private entity—the realm of researchers, scholars, and the military. Although commercial enterprises could connect to the Internet, the acceptable use policies pertaining to the use of the Internet prohibited them from conducting business. This all changed in 1991, when the ban on business activities was lifted. The ban was lifted primarily because of the formation of a parallel network backbone that allowed commercial transactions to flow separately from noncommercial transactions. This provided a way for businesses to conduct commercial activities without using areas restricted to research and education.

The Internet has been growing at a phenomenal rate ever since. Today, millions of computers and more than 50 million users are connected to the global Internet.

The Early Days of the Web

As we look back now, it's hard to believe that the Web was born only a few short years ago. Development on the World Wide Web project began at the European Laboratory for Particle Physics (CERN) in 1989. The Web is the brainchild of Tim Berners-Lee, who proposed the Web as a way for physicists around the world to collaborate using a networked information system based on hypertext.

The structure of hypertext documents was defined by a new language called the *Hypertext Markup Language* (HTML). Tim Berners-Lee based his new markup language on a subset of the *Standard Generalized Markup Language* (SGML). To transfer HTML documents to remote locations anywhere in the world, a new protocol was devised. This protocol, called the *Hypertext Transfer Protocol* (HTTP), offers a means of easily and quickly finding, retrieving, and displaying documents.

Hypertext allows you to navigate through networked resources at the touch of a button. Using a client application called a *browser*, you can select highlighted keywords or specified hot areas within a document to quickly and automatically navigate to a new document. The first browser was a text-only browser with limited capabilities, and it was because of these limitations that the Web did not catch on quickly in the Internet community.

In fact, in early 1993 there were only about 50 Web sites worldwide. Compare this tiny number to the thousands of Web sites available today, and it seems that the Web literally sprang to life overnight. Currently, there are more than 100,000 Web sites. The catalyst for this exponential growth rate was a browser called Mosaic. This browser, developed by NCSA, allowed users to exploit the Web's graphical capabilities, and that was exactly what the world wanted. Today, the Web is the fastest-growing segment of the Internet, and the browser that started it all, Mosaic, is only one of the dozens of available browsers.

The wild success of Mosaic inspired the 1994 migration of NCSA developers to Silicon Valley. A group of these developers formed the company now known as Netscape Communications Corporation. Netscape released its first browser, Netscape Navigator, which supported many proposed extensions to the HTML standard. These new features brought the Web one step closer to being a fully interactive multimedia feast for users and helped Netscape fuel another period of explosive growth for the Web.

1995 was a year of many firsts for the Web. Microsoft brought the world inline video as well as documents with soundtracks. Netscape delivered a new version of Navigator that supported frames, plugins, and many more unique features. Gavin Bell, Anthony Parisi, Mark Pesce, and others delivered the final 1.0 specification of the *Virtual Reality Modeling Language* (VRML), and Sun Microsystems delivered Java to the world on a silver platter.

In Java, Internet developers and Web publishers saw the means to finally create fully interactive multimedia presentations for the Web. This important step in the evolution of the Web was greeted with fanfare from the Internet community and is currently responsible for another period of explosive growth in Web development.

The Basics of Programming Languages

If you have seen Java in action, you should have little doubt of its importance to the development of the Web. Java is also important to the software industry. The Java programming language has many features that make it unique, powerful, and versatile. For example, most programming languages are either compiled or interpreted. Java is both, which is why it is so versatile. To understand how Java can be both compiled and interpreted, let's look at the basics of compiled and interpreted programming languages.

Interpreted Programming Languages

Although only a few programming languages are interpreted, they are generally the easiest to learn and use. An interpreted programming language that most people, even nonprogrammers, are familiar with or have at least heard of is BASIC. The BASIC programming language got its name because it is so rudimentary and easy to use.

You create a BASIC program using a simple, high-level language structure. When you are finished with the BASIC program, you can run it immediately. The BASIC interpreter reads the instructions in your code line by line. The BASIC interpreter translates these individual lines into sets of instructions the computer can understand. Because the lines of code must be translated into a form the computer understands as the program is executing, interpreted programs generally run more slowly than other programs and require more processor time.

Compiled Programming Languages

Compiled programming languages are generally more difficult to learn and use than interpreted programming languages. However, most programming languages are compiled. Compiled programming languages you may recognize include COBOL, FORTRAN, C, C++, and Pascal.

You create a program in a compiled language using a high-level language structure. When you are finished with the source code for the program, you compile it to a machine-readable and machine-executable form with a compiler. When you execute the program, the computer can directly interpret the instructions. Because the lines of codes do not have to be translated into a form the computer understands as the program is executing, compiled programs run very quickly compared to interpreted programs.

However, there is a trade-off to be made between speed and portability. Your code is compiled to such a low-level form that it can only be run on the platform for which it was compiled. This means that your code is not directly portable to other platforms.

Java: An Interpreted and Compiled Programming Language

As stated before, Java is both interpreted and compiled. You create a Java program using a simple, high-level language structure. When you are finished creating the Java program, you compile the source code to an intermediate level called *bytecode*. You can then run the compiled bytecode, which is interpreted by the Java runtime environment.

Bytecode is very different from machine code. Machine code is represented as a series of 0s and 1s. Bytecodes are sets of instructions that look a lot like assembler code. Although your computer can directly execute machine code, bytecodes must be interpreted before they can be executed. The trade-off between machine code and bytecode goes much deeper than what you may think. Machine code is usable only on the specific platform for which it was compiled. On the other hand, your program in bytecode form can run on any platform capable of using the Java runtime environment. This capability is what makes Java architecture neutral.

The Java runtime interpreter translates the bytecode into sets of instructions the computer can understand. Because the bytecode is in an intermediate form, there is only a slight delay in translating it to a form the computer understands. If you are familiar with how intermediate-level languages such as Assembler are used, you may see the true beauty in Java. Here's a language that allows you to compile the source code to a machine-independent and intermediate form that will execute nearly as quickly as if it were fully compiled.

If you are wondering how Java's architecture neutrality is achieved, you are not the only one; all compilers, even the Java compiler, compile source code for a specific machine. The trick to creating

Java bytecode is that the source code is compiled for a machine that does not exist. This machine is called the *Java Virtual Machine* and it exists only in nanospace, or within the confines of your computer system's memory. As amazing as creating a machine within the memory of your system is, Java is living proof that this concept is not only possible but powerful.

Fooling the Java compiler into creating bytecode for a nonexistent machine is only half of the ingenious process that makes Java architecture neutral. The Java Interpreter must also make your computer and the bytecode file believe they are running on a Java Virtual Machine. It does this by acting as the intermediary between the Virtual Machine and your real machine.

 Figure 1.3 illustrates how Java works on a typical computer. As you can see, the Virtual Machine is layered between your operating system and the Java object framework. Above the object framework are the user applications written in Java. (See Chapter 24, "The Java Virtual Machine," for detailed information on how the Java Virtual Machine works.)

Figure 1.3.
The layers of interaction for Java programs.

| User Applications |
| Java Objects |
| Java Virtual Machine |
| UNIX | Windows OS/2 | Macintosh |
| Operating Systems |

The Logical Evolution of C to C++

The C programming language has been popular ever since it was introduced in the early 1970s. The popularity of C stems largely from its relative ease of use, friendliness, and advanced features, which at the time appealed to both programmers and nonprogrammers. Considering that C's major competitors in those days were outdated and difficult-to-use programming languages such as COBOL and FORTRAN that ran primarily on mainframes, it is little wonder that C was called friendly and attracted a large following rather quickly.

Today's programmers would probably not find C to be the friendliest and most advanced programming language available. Primarily this is because even the best C programmers sometimes have problems tapping into C's advanced functions. If you are a C programmer and have ever had problems with pointers and memory management, you know what I am talking about. Pointers and memory management are difficult concepts for novices and experienced programmers alike. A single line of code pointing to the wrong location in memory can cause the application and the computer running the application to crash.

In the early 1980s, the personal-computer boom was beginning to hit the marketplace. To keep pace with the growth of the PC industry, software houses were developing programs as fast as they could. Key constraints for getting new applications to market were development time and the costs associated with the length of the development cycle. To cut costs and development time, software developers and programmers looked at ways to reuse existing code in future projects.

Although you can take segments of C code out of one project and use it in another project, code reuse in C is difficult and not always possible. To be successful, a section of code would have to pertain to a specific function or set of related functions such as file I/O or screen display. The section of code would also have to be generalized and contain no possibly conflicting assignments. However, depending on the complexity and type of new project you plan to code in C, it is often best to simply start from scratch. This is primarily because conflicts in the C code you are trying to reuse can take just as long to work out as it would to simply create new code.

The creative team at AT&T Bell Labs developed a possible solution to the problem of code reuse. They called this solution C++. C++ is an extension of C that allows you to create objects. *Objects* are separately defined code modules that are used to perform specific functions. Bjarne Stroustrup was the mastermind who had the creative vision to develop this extension of C that allows programmers to separate the functions specified within an application into generalized and reusable object modules. A decade after the introduction of C++, we can see it clearly as a logical evolution of C that was designed to address the needs of programmers, which is why C++ is the most widely used programming language.

The Great Leap Forward from C/C++ to Java

Although C++ is undoubtedly a powerful and popular programming language, it has its faults. These faults are rooted in its past as an extension of C. Like C, the most-difficult-to-understand-and-use aspects of C++ pertain to memory management and pointers. Furthermore, because C++ is an extension of C, it is very easy for C++ programmers to follow procedural coding habits they learned in other languages, especially in C. When you code a C++ application using procedural programming methods, you lose the benefits that object-oriented programming languages offer. This is where Java comes in.

Java is to programming in the '90s what C++ was to programming in the '80s—a giant leap forward. Like C++, Java is the next logical progression for programming languages and is strongly based in the most popular programming language of its day. With Java, you get the look and feel of C++ and the power of a language specifically designed for object-oriented programming. Unlike C++, Java completely severs the ties with procedural coding and forces you to follow sound object-oriented programming concepts.

The Java programming language features automated boundary checking that eliminates many of the problem areas of C and C++. With Java, there are no pointers, and memory management is automatic. The obvious benefits of this are that pointer problems and memory leaks are a thing of the past. No longer can you point to the wrong area of memory and crash the program. No longer can you make errors when freeing memory and cause a slow memory leak that will eventually cause the system to run out of memory.

Java has many other features that make it a joy to program in and a refuge for programmers who are tired of the difficulties associated with developing in C++. With Java, arrays are encapsulated in a class structure, which is another feature that facilitates Java's built-in boundary checking. Java performs automatic garbage collection, which is another feature that facilitates Java's built-in memory management.

The automatic garbage-collection routine also showcases Java's built-in multithreading capability. By running in the background routines that free up memory and provide general system clean-up functions, Java programs run more quickly and more efficiently.

Object-Oriented Programming Concepts and Java

Many first-time programmers and even experienced programmers who use procedural programming languages have problems grasping the basic concepts in object-oriented programming because OOP concepts are rather abstract and are designed under a different philosophy than traditional procedural programming languages. Concepts related to object-oriented programming include

- Objects
- Encapsulation and message passing
- Classes
- Libraries (packages in Java)
- Inheritance
- Access modifiers

Objects

The fundamental unit in object-oriented programming is the object. Languages that follow object-oriented concepts describe the interaction among objects. All objects have a state and a behavior.

The state of an object pertains to data elements and their associated values. Everything the object knows about these elements and values describes the state of the object. Data elements associated with objects are called *instance variables*.

The behavior of an object depends on the actions the object can perform on the instance variables defined within the object. In procedural programming, such a construct would be called a *function*. In object-oriented terminology, this construct is called a *method*. A method belongs to the class it is a member of, and you use a method when you need to perform a specific action more than once.

Thus, the state of an object depends on the things the object knows, and the behavior of the object depends on the actions the object can perform. If you create a software object that models your television, the object would have variables describing the television's current state, such as it is on, the current channel setting is 8, the current volume setting is 23, and there is no input coming from the remote control. The object would also have methods that describe the permissible actions, such as turn the television on or off, change the channel, change the volume, and accept input from the remote control.

> **Tip:** If you are having a hard time grasping what an object is, think of it as a chunk of code that performs a specific and generally related set of actions called methods.

Encapsulation and Message Passing

Objects encapsulate instance variables and related methods into a single, identifiable unit. Therefore, objects are easy to reuse, update, and maintain. You can quickly and easily do the following:

- Pinpoint the necessary input to the object and the output from the object
- Find variable dependencies
- Isolate the effects of changes
- Make updates as necessary
- Create subclasses based on the original object

Objects are as dynamic as you make them. An object can invoke one or more methods to accomplish a task. You initiate a method by passing a message to an object. A message must contain the name of the object you are sending the message to, the names of the methods to perform, and the values needed by those methods. The object receiving the message uses this information to invoke the appropriate methods with the specified values.

The benefit of encapsulation of instance variables and methods is that you can send messages to any object without having to know how the object works. All you have to know is what values a method will accept. Therefore, the software object describing your television could be extremely complex, but all you or the end user have to know to use the television is how to press the appropriate buttons on the remote control. The press of a button on the remote control sends a message to the television's software object, telling it which method to perform and the new input values for the method.

Classes

Classes encapsulate objects. A single class can be used to instantiate multiple objects. This means that you can have many active objects or instances of a class. The object describing the functions of your television is an instance of a class of objects called `television`.

Keep in mind that each object within a class retains its own states and behaviors. By encapsulating objects within a class structure, you can group sets of objects by type. The Java *Application Programming Interface* (API) describes many classes. Each class in the API specifies a set of objects that perform related functions and share common characteristics. Classes you create can serve a similar purpose.

> **Tip:** Think of a class as a unit of code that contains a set of specific and generally related code modules called objects.

Libraries

In C++ and other programming languages, a collection of related classes or functions is called a *library*. Java puts a twist on the concept of libraries by using the term *package* to describe a collection of related classes. Just as classes encapsulate objects, packages encapsulate classes in Java. As you will see in the section "Access Modifiers," this additional layer of encapsulation makes it easy to control access to methods.

Inheritance

Inheritance is a powerful aspect of object-oriented programming that allows you to easily reuse code and extend the functionality of existing classes. If you created a class to draw a shaded rectangle on the screen, you could extend the class to move the rectangle to specific locations on the screen without having to rewrite the original class. You could also extend the class for the shaded rectangle to display a series of user-selectable rectangles. In either case, the new class would inherit the methods that created the shaded rectangle and then extend the methods to perform the appropriate action.

Using this aspect of object-oriented programming, you can create a new class that inherits the functionality of an existing class. You can then extend the functions of the old class in ways that suit your current needs. The `television` class could have subclasses for black-and-white televisions, color televisions, and home-theater–style televisions. The new `television` subclass is not limited by the instance variables or methods of the superclass and can include instance variables and methods not defined in the superclass. The new subclass can also override inherited methods.

Access Modifiers

In object-oriented programming, access to methods and variables is controlled through access modifiers. The Java programming language defines four levels of access controls:

- Private methods and variables
- Protected methods and variables
- Friendly methods and variables
- Public methods and variables

Private Methods and Variables

Methods and variables that are controlled by an associated object and are not accessible to objects of different classes are generally considered to be *private*. The advantage of this is that only objects in a particular class can access the methods or variables without limitation. Java's private methods and variables are likewise accessible only by objects within the same class.

Protected Methods and Variables

Methods and variables that are controlled by an associated object and are accessible to objects in the current class or a subclass of the current class are generally considered to be *protected*. The advantage of this is that only objects in specific classes can access the variables without limitation. Java's protected methods and variables are likewise accessible only by methods in the same class or subclass.

Friendly Methods and Variables

Methods and variables that are accessible to other objects in most circumstances are considered to be *friendly*. By default, methods and variables you declare in Java are assumed to be friendly and are accessible by any class and objects in the same package. The advantage of this is that objects in a particular package (generally a set of related classes) can access each other without limitation.

Public Methods and Variables

Methods and variables that are accessible to all objects, even those outside the current class and package, are considered to be *public*. Java's public methods and variables are accessible by any object or class. Therefore, public methods and variables can be accessed without limitation.

Peter's Principle: Understanding the various access controls is easy if you think in terms of scope:

- Private—Accessible to objects within the current class
- Protected—Accessible to objects within the current class and subclasses of the current class
- Friendly—The default access, accessible by all classes within the current package
- Public—Accessible by all classes in any package

Programming with Java

Java is first and foremost an object-oriented programming language. Many programmers are surprised when they discover how easy it is to follow sound object-oriented design practices with Java. The following sections give you a better understanding of what Java offers.

The Primary Characteristics of Java

The ease with which you can transition to Java from C/C++ and Java's object-oriented capabilities are only the icing on the cake. Java has many powerful characteristics, most of which are discussed in previous sections of this chapter. Java is

Architecture-neutral
Distributed
Dynamic
Interpreted and compiled
Multithreaded
Network-ready and compatible
Object-oriented
Portable
Robust
Secure

These characteristics are the source of Java's power and the reason for Java's widespread popularity. As you begin to develop with Java, you will find that many of these characteristics are interrelated and are a direct outgrowth of Java's development for the following:

- Distributed networked environments
- High performance

- Easy reuse of code
- Security

A Design for Distributed Networked Environments

A key ingredient for a successful programming language designed for an environment as complex as the Internet is the capability to run on heterogeneous and distributed platforms. Java is able to do this because it is

- Architecture neutral, meaning that Java executables can run on any platform that has the Java runtime environment.
- Highly portable, meaning that Java has features that make it easy to use on heterogeneous platforms. To maintain portability, Java follows IEEE (Institute of Electrical and Electronics Engineers) standards for data structures, such as the use of integers, floating-point numbers, and strings.
- Distributed, meaning that it allows you to use objects located on local and remote machines.
- Network ready and compatible, meaning that it is ready to be used on complex networks and features direct support for common network protocols, such as FTP and HTTP, that make it compatible for use on networks.

A Design for High Performance

Another key ingredient for a successful programming language designed for complex network environments is performance. Java has many features that make it a high-performance language, including its compiler and runtime system. Java's interpreter is able to execute bytecode at speeds approaching that of code compiled to a purely machine-readable format because it is multithreaded.

Unlike many other programming languages, Java has built-in multithreading capabilities. *Multithreading* is the capability to run more than one process thread at a time. Multithreading allows Java's interpreter to run processes such as garbage collection and memory management in the background. Processes that run in the background take advantage of idle time for your computer's CPU. In the real world, many things occur simultaneously: The door bell rings, the phone rings, and your child runs into the kitchen screaming. You cannot answer the phone and the door and give Johnny a hug all at the same time. So what you do is grab Johnny with one arm, grab the phone with the other, and tell the person at the door to wait a moment.

To accomplish all three tasks in successive order, you prioritized. Your child was priority one. The phone call you have been waiting for all afternoon was priority two. The mail carrier delivering a package was priority three. Programs that are multithreaded are capable of prioritizing as well. When the computer is waiting for input from the user, background processes can be busily cleaning up memory, or when the computer pauses for an instant after crunching a number, a background process can squeeze in a few clock cycles to prepare a section of memory for use. Being able to run background processes while a foreground process waits for input from a user or pauses momentarily is essential for optimal performance.

A Design for Easy Reuse of Code

Although Java's object-oriented design is the key feature that makes code reuse possible, Java's designers knew that complex network environments tend to change rapidly. Therefore, to ensure that Java developers could easily reuse code even if the environment changed, Java was designed to be dynamic and robust. Java accomplishes this by delaying the binding of objects and through dynamic linking of classes at runtime, which avoids errors if the environment has changed since the program was compiled. Another way Java avoids errors is that it checks data structures at compile time and runtime.

Robustness and reliability go hand in hand. For Java to be robust, it must be reliable as well. As stated before, pointers and memory management are the source of many problems in C/C++ programs. Therefore, Java ensures robustness and reliability by not using pointers; by using dynamic boundary checking, which ensures that memory boundaries cannot be violated; and by providing for automatic memory management, which guards against memory leaks and memory violations.

A Design for Security

Security features in distributed networked environments are essential, especially in an automated world where computer viruses, trojan horses, and worms abound. Many of Java's characteristics ensure that it is extremely secure. For example, malicious programmers cannot access system heaps, stacks, or protected sections of memory because Java does not use pointers to memory and only allocates memory at runtime. This prevents malicious programmers from reaching restricted sections of the system.

Java also ensures system security at runtime by making the Java interpreter pull double duty as a bytecode verifier. Before the Java interpreter executes a program, it performs a check to make sure the program is valid Java code. Java proves the validity of code using a theorem prover that guards against the following:

- Access violations
- Forged pointers
- Illegal data conversions
- Incorrect values and parameters

- Malicious alteration or misuse of classes
- Overflow and underflow of the stack
- Suspicious or unwarranted activity

The Structure of the Java Language

The structure of the Java language is just as important as its characteristics. The following sections provide an overview of concepts related to the structure of Java programs.

Applets Versus Applications

Whether you first learned about Java through your excursions into cyberspace or by reading about it in the latest edition of *Dr. Dobbs' Journal*, you have probably seen references to both Java applets and Java applications. Unfortunately, technical writers both in cyberspace and in the real world sometimes assume that you know the difference between the two terms.

The term *Java applet* generally refers to a small application that is designed for use on the World Wide Web. Java applets require an external viewer program, so to use an applet, you need a Web browser or an applet viewer. Keep in mind that the smallness of an applet is entirely relative and that the key to an applet is its design for use with an external viewer.

The term *Java application* generally refers to an application that is designed for stand-alone use. A frequently used slang term for application is *app*. Java applications do not require an external viewer program. This means that you can execute a Java application directly using the Java interpreter. Keep in mind that some Java programs can run both as applets requiring an external viewer and as stand-alone applications.

Namespaces

The more complex the programs you create, the easier it is to accidentally reuse a variable or parameter name. In C++, a namespace conflict can take hours or days to fix, especially when you have large class libraries. Java has a unique naming system that avoids namespace conflicts by nesting the name at various levels.

Each component of a name is nested according to the following namespace levels:

- 0—Package namespace
- 1—Compilation unit namespace
- 2—Type namespace
- 3—Method namespace

- 4—Local block namespace
- 5—Nested local block namespace

The Java interpreter is responsible for maintaining and translating the namespace. The interpreter resolves object names by looking successively in each of the known namespaces. Each namespace is considered in precedence order from the highest level, the package namespace, to the lowest level, the nested local block namespace. Java generally uses the first match found.

The levels in the namespace represent a hierarchy that mirrors the actual structure associated with Java packages and classes. Names associated with each level are separated from the names in other levels by a period. The concept of namespace and levels within the namespace makes more sense when you see how they are actually used.

Java packages in the original package library have the `java` package name prepended and are generally followed by a class name within the package. The following is a declaration for the `BorderLayout` class type in the Abstract Windowing Toolkit (AWT) package:

```
java.awt.BorderLayout
```

The naming of function calls in Java programs follow the namespace conventions as well. The following is a declaration for a method called `println`:

```
System.out.println(str);
```

The full path to the `println` method within Java's namespace is as follows:

```
java.lang.System.out.println
```

Java resolves the location of the `println` method by searching for the unique occurrence of the `System` class in the currently defined namespace. When Java finds an occurrence of the `System` class, it looks for an occurrence of the `out` subclass, and finally it finds the `println` method.

Program-Naming Structures

The program file containing the actual instructions in the Java programming language is called the *source* or *source code*. You name source code files for Java with the `.java` extension. These files should be plain text files. When you compile the source using the Java compiler, `javac`, you compile the source to bytecode that can be executed.

In a procedural language such as Pascal, the complete executable code for a program is generally stored in one file. In an object-oriented language such as Java, the executable code is generally stored according to the class or library structure. After you compile your Java source code, you will have one file for each class you declared in the source. Each of these files will be named with the `.class` extension. These individual files are called *compilation units*.

Java compilation units contain package and import statements and declarations for classes and interfaces. These four components form the basic structure of Java programs.

Package Statements

The Java API includes a group of packages under the core `java` package. All classes and objects you create are assumed to be under this default package. Therefore, unless you state otherwise, Java uses the current path and generally assumes that your compiled code is in the current directory when you run a Java program. To tell Java where to look for packages, you use *package statements*.

Anyone experimenting with Java and not planning on full-scale Java development will probably want to follow the default package structure. However, if you plan to create applications in Java and want the classes and objects you create to follow a package-naming structure other than the default, you must include a package statement in the source code:

```
package PackageName
```

When defining new packages, you must follow Java's hierarchical naming structure. This means that levels within the package-naming structure should be separated from the package names in other levels by a period. This is a sample package statement for a multilevel package namespace:

```
package MyPackages.PackageSubName;
```

Your package names at each level of the namespace must mirror the actual directory structure on your file system. This is because Java transforms package names into pathnames to locate classes and methods associated with a package. It does this by replacing the periods with file system separators. So the package name `MyPackages.Gizmos` would be transformed into the following pathname for a UNIX system:

```
MyPackages/Gizmos
```

On a Windows 95/NT system, the package name `MyPackages.Gizmos` would be transformed into the following pathname:

```
MyPackages\Gizmos
```

Java finds the classes associated with a package using the pathname. Java would look for the `MyPackages.Gizmos` package and its associated classes and methods in the `\MyPackages\Gizmos` directory.

The Java language specification recommends that you use globally unique package names that pertain to your Internet domain when your packages will be available to nonlocal users. It is further recommended that you always capitalize the first component for the major domain, such as `COM`, `EDU`, or `GOV`.

Keeping in mind Java's precedence order, you reverse the order of the domain name, component by component. Thus, a globally available package called zoom associated with mcp.com would be named COM.mcp.zoom. This package name is transformed into the following pathname for a UNIX system:

COM/mcp/zoom

On a Windows 95/NT system, the package name COM.mcp.zoom is transformed into the following pathname:

COM\mcp\zoom

Import Statements

As with other languages, Java includes a core functionality that is globally accessible. In Java, these core functions are in the java.lang package. To access packages, classes, and objects that are not declared in this package library, you use *import statements*. Import statements help to define and re- solve the current namespace. They do this by allowing an imported package to be resolved using the name of its class component.

> **Note:** If you do not use import statements, you must specify the full package reference before each class name in your source code. Having to specify full package references can get tedious rather quickly, especially in long programs. Therefore, it is strongly recom- mended that you use import statements.

Import statements should appear before other declarations in the source code and generally follow package statements if they are used. The idea behind import statements is to help Java find the ap- propriate methods and to avoid namespace conflicts. To make Java's AWT class types available, you could use this import statement in your source code:

import java.awt;

This import statement allows Java to resolve the method awt.Button to java.awt.Button. Java also allows you to import only the class type you need. You can do this using a class type import state- ment such as

import java.awt.Button;

This import statement allows Java to resolve the method Button to java.awt.Button. A more effi- cient way to import packages is to import them on demand. You do this as follows:

import java.awt.*;

An asterisk in the last element of the import statement allows Java to import classes as necessary. This lets you dynamically add public types to the namespace, and as with class type import statements, Java can resolve the method `Button` to `java.awt.Button`.

> **Tip:** You will find that most Java programmers import classes on demand. Although this saves you a lot of typing, you should be as specific as possible about the packages you actually need. Specifically, you should rarely use an import statement that will make all classes in the Java language available. When two classes in two different packages have the same name, there will be a conflict unless you prepend the package name to the class name.

Class Declarations

In Java, all classes are derived from the system class named `Object`. This makes `Object` the root of the class hierarchy and means that all methods and variables in the `Object` class are available to all other classes. It is this class structure that makes code reuse in Java possible. All classes are by default private unless declared to be public.

Class declarations without modifiers follow this general format:

```
class name {
     //methods and variables associated with the class
}
```

Java supports single inheritance of classes. Therefore, each class except `Object` has only one superclass. This means that any class you create can extend or inherit the functions of only a single class. Although this may seem like a limitation if you have programmed in a language that allows for multiple inheritance of classes, Java supports multiple inheritance of class methods, which is accomplished through the class interface. As you will learn in the next section, you define the class interface with an *interface declaration*.

Interface Declarations

Interfaces are abstract classes. Through an interface, you can define the protocols for methods and final variables without having to worry about the specific implementation. This allows you to create what could be called *outlines* for programming structures that you will later define. Interfaces can also be extensions of one or more interfaces. While interfaces are by default private unless declared to be public, an interface's methods and constants are public.

> **Note:** Final variables are similar to the named constants used in other programming languages. The values associated with constants and final variables do not change.

Because you do not have to work out the full inner workings of methods associated with an interface, interfaces allow for rapid development. You can later implement the interface in a class declaration. Because a single class can implement more than one interface, it is possible to share the same interface with several classes or any instance of a class. This not only provides considerable flexibility, but it allows a class to inherit the properties of all method calls associated with multiple interfaces, and in turn with multiple classes.

A major difference between a class and an interface is that an interface cannot store data. Further, an interface does not provide an implementation for the methods; it only provides the declaration. Interface declarations without modifiers follow this general format:

```
interface name {
     //methods and static variables associated with the interface
}
```

Class declarations that use interfaces follow this general format:

```
class classname implements interfacename {
     //class body
}
```

Or they can take this format:

```
class classname implements interfacename1, … interfacenameN {
     //class body
}
```

The only bad thing about interfaces is that they require dynamic method binding, which reduces runtime performance. However, you should note that using interfaces to accomplish multiple inheritance actually reduces runtime overhead compared to the method of multiple inheritance used in C++.

The Java Specification and the API

Java was formally introduced to the world in May 1995 at SunWorld '95. Since then, Java has undergone an evolution of purpose and, as a result, the current specification for the Java programming language is a dramatically different language than what was first introduced.

The first version of Java released for general use on the Internet was Java Alpha. Alpha versions of software applications and programming languages are generally released to developers for review, comments, and bug fixes. The final Alpha implementation of Java is Java Alpha 3, which is used by the Alpha version of the HotJava Web browser.

HotJava was developed by Sun to showcase the features of Java and is written in the Java language. Despite the fact that the Alpha version of Java and HotJava have limited features, they enjoyed widespread use long after the release of Java Beta and Java 1.0. The Java Alpha release included HotJava, which put Java and HotJava in the hands of anyone who wanted to do Java development for the Internet and anyone who wanted to view Java-powered Web pages. Until late 1995, HotJava was the only browser available for viewing Java-powered Web pages.

Development for Java was in full swing by the time Sun released Java Pre-Beta 1. Java Pre-Beta 1 represented a major change in the structure of the Java language, which included the introduction of the applet AWT superclass. The AWT superclass is used to display graphical objects such as buttons and pop-up windows. These changes to the structure of the Java API made this revision and all future revisions incompatible with the Java Alpha. Pre-Beta 1 also introduced new Java tools such as the applet viewer and the Java debugger.

A few months after the release of Java Pre-Beta 1, Sun released Java Beta. Beta versions of software applications and languages are generally made available to wider audiences and generally concentrate on bug fixes. Although Java Beta had bug fixes and security improvements, the major changes to the Java language were again in the applet AWT superclass.

The final Beta version of Java was Java Beta 2. Java Beta 2 added functionality to all the Java packages. Although this in itself represented a major change to the Java API, Java Beta 2 was also a move to make the Java API compatible with the way the Netscape Navigator Web browser used Java Beta applets.

> **Looking Ahead:** Chapter 4, "The Java Language: A Primer," features a section on making the transition from Java prerelease versions to Java 1.0. Current Java Alpha and Beta programmers will find this section to be very helpful.

Because all versions of the Netscape Navigator since version 2.0 Beta 4 were able to display Java Beta applets, there was a major initiative by Internet developers to support and start creating Java Beta applets. For this reason, the Java Beta 2 API supports the Netscape <APPLET> tag and not the <APP> tag used previously. The <APPLET> tag is the standard for the official release of the Java 1.0 and later versions of the API.

Another far-reaching change to the Java language that Java Beta 2 introduced was the capability to load classes from zip files. Before this, when you installed Java on your file system, Java created a directory, subdirectory, and file structure that mirrored the structure of the Java API. Earlier discussions on how Java searches the namespace by translating the names into pathnames make clear why this was necessary. For example, to find the println method in previous versions of Java, Java would search the namespace along the full path to java.lang.System.out.println. It would do this by replacing the periods with the appropriate file system separator for your system. Java relied on the directory structure of your file system, and thousands of files were installed on your hard drive.

Support for loading classes from zip files makes it possible to compress the entire contents of the Java API into a single file, which saves space and gets rid of the clutter on your file system. When you install the current version of Java, you will find this single file, called `classes.zip`, in Java's `lib` subdirectory. So now when the Java runtime class loader and the Java compiler search the namespace, they first look along the appropriate file path. If the class file is not found, they look for the corresponding zipped file in `classes.zip`.

> **Looking Ahead:** Java allows you to zip packages and classes you create as well. Setting up the Java environment and creating zipped packages is discussed in Chapter 2, "Getting Started with the JDK."

In January 1996, Sun officially released Java version 1.0. The changes from Java Beta 2 to Java 1.0 are very minor and primarily relate to bug fixes. This means Java Beta 2 applets and Java 1.0 applets are compatible. It also means that the Netscape Navigator can display Java 1.0 applets as well as Java Beta applets.

Initially, Sun froze the Java API when they released the 1.0 version of Java. The Java API consists of pre-developed code that you can use in your applications. The code is organized into package libraries filled with useful classes and methods designed to make it easy to program with Java. The great thing about these packages is that they have all been thoroughly tested. You will find that these packages provide every core function you can think of and thus save you time and allow you to start developing applications in Java without having to reinvent the wheel.

To ensure that Java's security model was the best possible for the Internet, Sun asked the world to test it. Several months after the release of Java 1.0, the implementation of the security model in the Java bytecode verify was found to have a flaw. This flaw, identified by researchers at Princeton University, allowed sophisticated crackers to spoof an Internet Protocol address that allowed an applet to access a machine other than the one on which it was executing. Sun fixed the problem and immediately released Java 1.0.1.

Other security problems were found a short while later. In May 1996, Sun released Java 1.0.2. Not only did this release fix minor security problems, it also fixed minor bugs in the Java packages and introduced class interface changes. Another security bug found in June 1996 made it possible to manipulate the way objects are assigned and the way they work together in order to undermine the Java type system. After this bug was discovered by a researcher in the United Kingdom, Sun did a full security review to check for any bugs that may be related and again released an update to the JDK.

Because Sun and its partners for Java development have proclaimed that they intend to support the current API, one can reasonably expect that the Java programming language has finally reached a level of standardization. This is good news for anyone who wants to start developing with Java.

The progression of the Java language has not stopped. Sun will continue to develop Java and has already announced the next major release of Java. You may see the full release for JDK 1.1 late in 1996. Thankfully, the introduction of standardization ensures that programs you create today will be usable tomorrow.

The Java Virtual Machine

The Java Virtual Machine (JVM) is at the heart of the Java programming language. It is because of the Java Virtual Machine that Java is architecture neutral, dynamic, interpreted and compiled, network ready and compatible, portable, robust, and secure. The JVM makes these features possible by providing an abstract specification for which developers can design interpreters and programmers can design applications.

This abstract specification is a virtual machine that exists only in nanospace. Because the Java Virtual Machine exists only in memory, the Java developers were able to use object-oriented methodology to pass information—parameters, method calls, and other types of data—back and forth between the real machine and the virtual machine. After the developers mapped out the necessary interaction between the real machine and the virtual machine for things like standard I/O, file I/O, and memory management, they could create additional Java runtime environments for other systems.

Because the specification for the Java Virtual Machine is fully described for all to use and thus open for development, the Java programming language is free from the restrictions of proprietary languages. This means that any developer can create an interpreter for the Java Virtual Machine. (Chapter 24 provides a detailed look at the Java runtime system and the Java Virtual Machine.)

Summary

As you have seen in this chapter, the developers at Sun's JavaSoft division poured their hearts into the creation of a revolutionary programming language. No other programming language offers the power and versatility that Java offers. Java is the programming language for the '90s and beyond.

The Java language offers an easy-to-use structure that is modeled after two of the most widely used programming languages, C and C++. However, Java was engineered so that it does not have the problem areas inherent in C and C++. If you plan to develop Java applications, you will find that Java's object-oriented design is both friendly and familiar. You will also find that the Java API saves you hours of work and will help you to create better programs without having to reinvent the wheel.

2

Getting Started with the JDK

After reading about the features of the Java programming language in Chapter 1, "Introducing Java," you are probably eager to get started. Before you can dive into development for Java, you need to install a developer's environment on your computer. Although commercial vendors are racing to get Java development packages to the market, everything you need to get started creating hot new Java applications is available directly from JavaSoft. This free development environment straight from the creators of Java is called the *Java Developer's Kit*, or JDK.

To give you a jump start on Java development, this chapter details how to obtain, install, and configure the JDK on your computer. After you read the section on the Java environment, you might want to jump to the section detailing how to install a Java developer's environment on your particular computer system. In this chapter, you will find sections designed to give you a quick start no matter what operating system you use. You will find quick starts for UNIX platforms, including Solaris and AIX; Windows 95/NT; Macintosh; and OS/2.

If you are a current C/C++ programmer, insight into making the transition from C/C++ to Java is also essential for getting started with Java. For this reason, the chapter covers key concepts for making that transition.

The Java Developer's Environment

The development environment for Java is surprisingly rich, especially considering that the Java programming language is fairly new. Most Java developers and programmers find that the JDK contains everything they need to get started creating powerful Java programs. This is because the developer's kit includes the Java programming language core functionality, the Java Application Programming Interface (API) complete with multiple package sets, and essential tools for creating Java programs.

The Java Developer's Kit is currently available for most operating systems. You can obtain the Sun Solaris, Windows 95/NT, and Macintosh versions directly from JavaSoft. Because the JavaSoft FTP site is extremely busy, however, you might have to use a mirror site to obtain the source code for the JDK. Table 2.1 is a list of the main JavaSoft FTP site and mirror sites for the Solaris, Windows 95/ NT, and Macintosh versions of the JDK.

When you access one of the FTP sites listed in this section, you will want to use the directory path given instead of the full path to the JDK. This will allow you to see the entire contents of the associated directory. In this way, you can download the most current version of the JDK for your system.

Table 2.1. FTP sites for the Java JDK.

Site	URL Path to JDK	FTP Site
JavaSoft FTP	`ftp://ftp.javasoft.com/pub`	`ftp.javasoft.com`
USA mirror	`ftp://sunsite.unc.edu/pub/languages/java`	`sunsite.unc.edu`
USA mirror	`ftp://java.dnx.com`	`java.dnx.com`
UK mirror	`ftp://sunsite.doc.ic.ac.uk/packages/java`	`sunsite.doc.ic.ac.uk`
Sweden mirror	`ftp://ftp.luth.se/pub/infosystems/www/hotjava`	`ftp.luth.se`
German mirror	`ftp://sunsite.informatik.rwth-de/pub/mirror/` `➥java.sun.comaachen.de`	`sunsite.informatik.` `➥rwth-de`
Japan mirror	`ftp://ftp.glocom.ac.jp/mirror/java.sun.com`	`ftp.glocom.ac.jp`
Korea mirror	`ftp://ftp.kaist.ac.kr/pub/java`	`ftp.kaist.ac.kr`

Other versions of the JDK also are available. You will find versions for OS/2, AIX, and most UNIX platforms. The OS/2 and AIX versions of the JDK are available from IBM, but you have to register to use the IBM developers area. You can access IBM's online registration form at the following URL:

`http://www.hursley.ibm.com/javainfo/download/index.html`

There is, in fact, little difference in the actual workings of the developer's environment for most UNIX versions of the JDK. This means that once you obtain a JDK source for your computer, you can use most of the tips you will find in the Solaris section to help you get started. Because there are some key differences in the AIX configuration of the JDK, AIX users will find a section that outlines these differences.

Similarly, the OS/2 version of the JDK strongly relates to the Windows 95/NT version of the JDK. Therefore, although you will find a section for OS/2, you should first review the Windows 95/NT installation instructions.

The Java API and Core Language Functions

The heart of the Java programming language is contained in a set of packages called `java.lang`, which is a part of the Java Application Programming Interface. Although the `java.lang` package provides the core functionality of the Java programming language, it is not the only package included in the Java Developer's Kit.

The JDK includes the following packages: `java.applet`, `java.awt`, `java.awt.image`, `java.awt.peer`, `java.io`, `java.lang`, `java.net`, and `java.util`. These packages provide everything you need to start creating powerful Java applications quickly. The JDK also includes an additional package called `sun.tools.debug`, which is designed to make the application-debugging process easier.

Currently, you can also obtain the Java database connectivity application programming interface, which enables developers to write Java applications that access databases. The initial specification for the Java database classes was released in March 1996. A brief explanation of all packages currently available is shown in Table 2.2. (See Part IV, "The Java Application Programming Interface," for the complete inside scoop, including the hot new database classes.)

Table 2.2. Java packages.

Package	Package Name	Description
java.applet	Applet	A set of classes that relate to the applet environment and are generally used when viewing applets
java.awt	Abstract Windowing Toolkit	A set of classes that provide graphical interface tools such as buttons, controls, scrollbars, and windows
java.awt.image	AWT Image	A set of classes related to using images
java.awt.peer	AWT Peer	A set of classes for AWT peer classes and methods
java.sql	Database connectivity	A set of classes that enable developers to write Java applications that access databases
java.io	I/O	A set of classes that provide standard input/output and file I/O utilities
java.lang	Language	The core set of classes for the Java language that provide basic functions, such as string and array handling
java.net	Network	A set of classes that provide tools for accessing networks by protocols, such as FTP, Telnet, and HTTP
java.util	Utility	A set of classes that provide core utility functions such as encoding/decoding, hash tables, and stacks
sun.tools.debug	Debug	A set of classes that provide debugging functions and tools

Tools in the JDK

The Java Developer's Kit includes many terrific tools that make programming in Java a joy. You use these tools to create Java bytecode, to view your programs, and to debug your code. In the current version of the JDK, the Java interpreter and the Java compiler have been modified to load classes from zip files. Table 2.3 shows a brief description of these tools. (See Chapter 5, "Java Tools and the JDK: A Primer," for a detailed description of how to use these tools.)

Table 2.3. Tools in the JDK.

Executable	Tool Name	Description
appletviewer	The Java applet viewer	Used to view applets without a Web browser
java	The Java interpreter	Runs Java bytecode
javac	The Java compiler	Compiles Java programs into bytecode
javadoc	The Java API documentation generator	Creates API documentation in HTML format from Java source code
javah	The Java header and stub file generator	Creates C-language header and stub files from a Java class, which allows your Java and C code to interact
javap	The Java class file disassembler	Disassembles Java files and prints out a representation of Java bytecode
jdb	The Java language debugger	Helps you find and fix problems in your Java code

Power Start for Solaris

Solaris is the operating system used by most Sun Microsystems UNIX platforms. Because JavaSoft is an operating company of Sun Microsystems, the original Java developer's environment was created for Solaris version 2.3 or higher. Whereas the first developer's environment was very basic and included the HotJava browser and a limited API package set for the Alpha release of Java, the current developer's environment contained in the Java Developer's Kit is quite advanced and includes all the packages and tools discussed earlier in the chapter.

Note: The main operating system used on Sun Microsystems computers was originally called SunOS. When Sun moved to Solaris, the company tried to make a smooth transition to the new environment by calling the revisions of the old operating system Solaris 1.*x* and calling the new environment Solaris 2.*x*. The new naming scheme actually caused some confusion and continues to be a source of confusion today. To clear up your own understanding, keep in mind that when someone refers to Solaris 1.*x* they are referring to the old SunOS 4.*x*. When someone refers to Solaris 2.*x*, they are referring to SunOS 5.*x*. Consequently, Solaris 2.3 and SunOS 5.3 are essentially the same thing.

Because Solaris is a UNIX-based operating system, you should be able to use the tips and suggestions found throughout this section to help you install the JDK on any UNIX platform, providing that the JDK has been specifically compiled for your particular flavor of UNIX. Before installing the JDK, you should ensure that you have enough space on your hard drive for the installation. For Solaris, you retrieve a 4.5MB compressed file. When you install the JDK, you will need an additional 7.9MB of disk space. Although you can remove the compressed JDK file after a successful installation, you still need about 13MB of disk space initially.

Here are the steps to follow to set up a Java developer's environment on your computer:

1. Obtain the Java Developer's Kit
2. Install the Java Developer's Kit
3. Test the installation

Obtaining the Java Developer's Kit

The JDK for Solaris includes the complete set of tools for viewing, creating, and debugging Java programs and the precompiled code packages from the standard API. To obtain the source file for the JDK, you need to open an FTP session with one of the FTP sites listed in the "The Java Developer's Environment" section of this chapter.

Warning: If you have a pre-release version of the JDK installed on your system, you need to remove it before installing JDK 1.0 or later to remove files and directories that are no longer used with JDK 1.0 or later versions. However, before you do this, you should move any source code you created that is in the directories you will be deleting.

From the shell prompt, you can type the following to remove the previous installation of the JDK in its entirety:

```
rm -rf \file\path
```

> *file**path* is the actual path to the previous installation of Java, such as
>
> ```
> rm -rf \java
> ```
>
> For JDK 1.0 or later, you do not need to set Java-related environment variables for the base installation to work. You should check to see if you set Java-related environment variables when you last installed the JDK. You can do this by typing the following from the command line:
>
> ```
> env ¦ egrep "JAVA_HOME¦CLASSPATH¦LD_LIBRARY_PATH"
> ```
>
> If the `egrep` command returns no output, you did not set these variables and can continue with the installation. If the `egrep` command lists settings for these variables, you will want to consider unsetting them in your `.cshrc` or `.profile` files as appropriate. You will find a sidebar later in this chapter called "Creating Your Own Packages and Classes for UNIX" that can help you make these changes.

You can obtain the JDK source file from an FTP site in one of two ways:

- With your Web browser, enter the URL path to the FTP site as listed in the "URL Path to JDK" column of Table 2.1.

- From the shell prompt or Telnet session prompt, open an FTP session to the FTP site as listed in the "FTP Site" column of Table 2.1.

In the example that follows, the JDK source is downloaded from JavaSoft. If the JavaSoft FTP site is busy, you can obtain the source from any of the mirror sites listed in Table 2.1. Because file paths on the Internet tend to change, you should follow these steps in order:

1. Change to the directory where you want to install the JDK. When you uncompress and unpack the compressed JDK file later in the installation, you will be creating a directory called `java` under this directory.

2. Start the FTP session. You will be prompted to enter a user name and password. Use the name anonymous and a password as *youruserid@yourhostname*, such as `william@tvp.com`. Here is how you start an FTP session with the JavaSoft FTP server:

```
$ ftp ftp.javasoft.com
Connected to ftp.javasoft.com.
220 java3 FTP server ready.
Name (ftp.javasoft.com): anonymous
331 Guest login ok, send your complete e-mail address as password.
Password: userid@hostname.com
230-
230-     Welcome to the Java home site.
230-
230 Guest login ok, access restrictions apply.
Remote system type is UNIX.
```

3. The JDK binary file is generally located in a subdirectory called pub, so you want to change to the pub directory. On some mirror sites you will have to go through several subdirectories to get to Java's pub subdirectory. For example, on the Sunsite mirror (sunsite.unc.edu) you will have to change directories to pub/languages/java/pub. Start by listing the contents of the current directory and then changing to the pub directory:

```
ftp> ls
200 PORT command successful.
150 Opening ASCII mode data connection for /bin/ls.
total 24
lrwxrwxrwx   1 root      1    7 May 19 20:02 bin -> usr/bin
dr-xr-xr-x   2 root      1  512 May 19 21:09 dev
dr-xr-xr-x   2 nobody    1 1536 Jun 21 21:36 docs
dr-xr-xr-x   2 root      1  512 May 19 20:04 etc
dr-xr-xr-x   5 500       1  512 Jun 14 01:13 pub
drwx-wx-wx   2 root      1  512 Jun 22 00:56 tmp
dr-xr-xr-x   4 nobody    1  512 Jun 19 20:04 usr
-r--r--r--   1 root      1 1255 May 27 01:33 welcome.msg
226 Transfer complete.
ftp> cd pub
250 CWD command successful.
```

4. When you are in the publication directory for the Java programming language, you should list the contents of the directory. You want to download the most current version of the JDK. The most recent Solaris version in the example is JDK-1_1-solaris2-sparc.tar.Z. Download the appropriate source:

```
ftp> ls
200 PORT command successful.
150 Opening ASCII mode data connection for /bin/ls.
total 61148
-r--r--r--   1 root    1  4595974 Jan 23 16:35 JDK-1_1-solaris2-sparc.tar.Z
-r--r--r--   1 root    1  3720379 Jan 23 16:35 JDK-1_1-win32-x86.exe
-r--r--r--   1 root    1  2243968 Feb 14 00:56 JDK-1_1-mac.sea.bin
-r--r--r--   1 root    1  3049734 Feb 14 00:56 JDK-1_1-mac.sea.hqx
-r--r--r--   1 nobody  1  4508131 Dec 12 18:35 JDK-1_0-solaris2-sparc.tar.Z
-r--r--r--   1 nobody  1  3717250 Dec 12 18:36 JDK-1_0-win32-x86.exe
-r--r--r--   1 root    1    15868 Feb 14 00:56 README
-r--r--r--   1 nobody  1  5476531 Sep 11 02:05
➥hotjava-beta2-solaris2-sparc.tar.Z
-r--r--r--   1 nobody  1  3849659 Sep 11 02:06 hotjava-beta2-win32-x86.exe
226 Transfer complete.
ftp> bin
200 Type set to I.
ftp> get JDK-1_1-solaris2-sparc.tar
local: JDK-1_1-solaris2-sparc.tar remote: JDK-1_1-solaris2-sparc.tar
200 PORT command successful.
150 Opening BINARY mode data connection for JDK-1_1-solaris2-sparc.tar
➥(4595974 bytes).
226 Transfer complete.
4595974 bytes received
ftp>quit
```

Installing the Java Developer's Kit

After you obtain the source file, you should check to make sure the size of the file you downloaded matches the file size listed on the FTP site. If the file sizes are not identical, your file might have been corrupted during download. In that case, you want to delete the file from your system and try to download the JDK source file again.

Next, you need to uncompress and unpack the files. You can do this using the following command:

```
zcat JDK-1_1-solaris2-sparc.tar.Z ¦ tar xf -
```

> **Note:** The zcat command lists the contents of the compressed files and directories. The output of this is sent to the UNIX tape archive command tar, which extracts the files and directories but does not list the extraction to the screen. Although you should be able to use this command no matter which flavor of UNIX you are running, you can also uncompress and extract the files using the following series of commands:
>
> ```
> uncompress JDK-1_1-solaris2-sparc.tar
> tar -xf JDK-1_1-solaris2-sparc.tar
> ```

> **Note:** When you uncompress and unpack the compressed JDK file, you will be creating a directory called java under the current directory. If you are installing JDK 1.0 or later versions for Solaris on your system, the following files and subdirectories will be located under the java directory:
>
> ```
> -r--r--r--    1         2826 Jan 12 06:20 COPYRIGHT
> -r--r--r--    1         8195 Jan 16 16:45 README
> drwxr-xr-x    3         1024 Jan 12 11:09 bin
> drwxr-xr-x   25         1024 Jan 12 11:11 demo
> drwxr-xr-x    3         1024 Jan 12 11:09 include
> -r--r--r--    1         1017 Jan 16 16:49 index.html
> drwxr-xr-x    3         1024 Jan 12 11:10 lib
> -rw-rw-r--    1       372227 Jan 16 16:48 src.zip
> ```

The src.zip file contains the source code for some of the classes used in the JDK. Because these classes represent a good cross-section of the functionality introduced by the Java API and are written in the Java programming language, you can learn a lot by examining them. Therefore, I highly recommend that you unzip the src.zip file and make a note to go through some of the files after you read this book. By unzipping the src.zip file, you create the following directory structure on your file system:

```
src/
src/java/
src/java/lang/
src/java/util/
```

```
src/java/io/
src/java/net/
src/java/awt/
src/java/awt/peer/
src/java/awt/test/
src/java/awt/image/
src/java/applet/
src/sun/
src/sun/tools/
src/sun/tools/ttydebug/
```

All the executables—except for the Java source-level debugger, `jdb`—come in two forms. Executables with the suffix `_g` are for debugging and support all of Java's mechanisms for debugging. Executables without the suffix `_g` are optimized for normal use and support only limited debugging options. You will find the following executable files for the JDK tools in the `bin` directory:

```
java/bin:
total 5
-r-xr-xr-x    1          833 Jan 12 06:10 appletviewer
lrwxrwxrwx    1           13 Feb 23 01:09 java -> .java_wrapper
lrwxrwxrwx    1           13 Feb 23 01:09 java_g -> .java_wrapper
lrwxrwxrwx    1           13 Feb 23 01:09 javac -> .java_wrapper
lrwxrwxrwx    1           13 Feb 23 01:09 javac_g -> .java_wrapper
-r-xr-xr-x    1           71 Jan 12 06:16 javadoc
lrwxrwxrwx    1           13 Feb 23 01:09 javah -> .java_wrapper
lrwxrwxrwx    1           13 Feb 23 01:09 javah_g -> .java_wrapper
lrwxrwxrwx    1           13 Feb 23 01:09 javap -> .java_wrapper
lrwxrwxrwx    1           13 Feb 23 01:09 javap_g -> .java_wrapper
lrwxrwxrwx    1           13 Feb 23 01:09 jdb -> .java_wrapper
drwxr-xr-x    2         1024 Jan 12 11:09 sparc
-r-xr-xr-x    1         1911 Jan 12 06:10 upgrade
```

Most of the tools in the `bin` directory are symbolically linked to a Korn shell script called `.java_wrapper`. The function of the wrapper script is to set the environment variables Java needs if you forget to do it. It does this by finding the location of the Java tool you are trying to execute, backing up one directory, and setting this value to an environment variable called JAVA_HOME. The value for JAVA_HOME is the base directory where you installed the JDK.

The script then uses the value associated with the JAVA_HOME variable to set two other important environment variables: CLASSPATH and LD_LIBRARY_PATH. The CLASSPATH variable is used to find the Java class files. The wrapper script generally sets this path to

```
java/classes:java/lib/classes.zip
```

The default CLASSPATH tells the Java interpreter and compiler to look for your class files in the following order:

1. In the directory `java/classes` or the equivalent directory on your system

2. In the zipped file with a file path `java/lib/classes.zip` or the equivalent file path on your system

The LD_LIBRARY_PATH variable is used to find essential library files. The wrapper script generally sets this path to `java/lib/sparc`.

The final thing the wrapper script does is to locate and execute the tool you are trying to use. The compiled source for most of the Solaris JDK tools is actually located in java/bin/sparc. If you examine the files for the Java compiler and the Java debugger located in java/bin/sparc, you will also find that these are wrapper scripts.

Although it is good to know where the actual executables for the tools are located, you should only execute them via the wrapper script and from the java/bin directory. For this reason, you might want to add the full file path to java/bin to the search path specified in your .cshrc or .profile file. This will allow you to run the JDK tools without having to specify the full path to the binaries.

Peter's Principle: Creating Your Own Packages and Classes for UNIX

If you plan to create your own packages or to store Java classes you create in a directory other than the java/classes directory, you should set the CLASSPATH variable to the location you plan to use for your packages and class files. C shell users will want to do this by editing the .cshrc file in your home directory and adding a statement that sets the correct path to your Java classes, such as the following:

```
setenv CLASSPATH /myjavaclasses
```

The wrapper script is dynamic and will prepend the directories you specify for classes to the default CLASSPATH. This means that if you add the directory /myjavaclasses to the general CLASSPATH default by setting the environment variable as shown, the Java interpreter and compiler will search for Java class files on your system in the following order:

1. In the directory or directories you specified when you set the CLASSPATH environment variable

2. In the directory java/classes or equivalent directory on your system

3. In the zipped file with a file path java/lib/classes.zip or equivalent file path on your system

For these changes to take effect in the current command tool or shell environment, you will need to source your .cshrc file or type the setenv command at the shell prompt. This updates the current environment settings.

If you are using Bourne shell as your main UNIX shell, you can set the CLASSPATH in your .profile file. Do this by editing the .profile file in your home directory and adding statements that set and export the CLASSPATH variable's path, such as

```
CLASSPATH=/myjavaclasses
export CLASSPATH
```

For these changes to take effect in the current command tool or shell environment, you will need to set the CLASSPATH variable and export it from the command line, like this:

```
CLASSPATH=$HOME/java;export CLASSPATH
```

Another directory you will want to check is the demo directory. The demo directory contains many demonstration applets. By previewing these demos, you can see Java in action. The include directory contains C-language header and stub files. These files are primarily used to set paths and definitions needed by Java and that are essential to Java interaction with C.

The lib directory contains essential library files and the zip file for all classes included in the Java API, called classes.zip. Loading classes from zipped files makes it possible to compress the entire contents of the Java API into one file. The Java runtime class loader and the Java compiler extract any class files they need from classes.zip.

Warning: Although you can unzip the src.zip file, you should not unzip the classes.zip file. The classes.zip file contains all the classes and methods in the Java API. If you unzip this file, you will create hundreds of unnecessary files on your hard drive.

Testing the Installation

A great way to test your new Java developer's environment is to preview one of the demo applets included in the JDK. As you can see from the following code, each demo applet is located in the demo directory and has its own subdirectory:

```
demo:
total 23
drwxr-xr-x   4        1024 Jan 12 11:11 Animator
drwxr-xr-x   2        1024 Jan 12 11:11 ArcTest
drwxr-xr-x   2        1024 Jan 12 11:11 BarChart
drwxr-xr-x   2        1024 Jan 12 11:11 Blink
drwxr-xr-x   4        1024 Jan 12 11:11 BouncingHeads
drwxr-xr-x   2        1024 Jan 12 11:11 CardTest
drwxr-xr-x   2        1024 Jan 12 11:11 DitherTest
drwxr-xr-x   2        1024 Jan 12 11:11 DrawTest
drwxr-xr-x   2        1024 Jan 12 11:11 Fractal
drwxr-xr-x   3        1024 Jan 12 11:11 GraphLayout
drwxr-xr-x   2        1024 Jan 12 11:11 GraphicsTest
drwxr-xr-x   3        1024 Jan 12 11:11 ImageMap
drwxr-xr-x   3        1024 Jan 12 11:11 ImageTest
drwxr-xr-x   3        1024 Jan 12 11:11 JumpingBox
drwxr-xr-x   3        1024 Jan 12 11:11 MoleculeViewer
drwxr-xr-x   2        1024 Jan 12 11:11 NervousText
drwxr-xr-x   3        1024 Jan 12 11:11 ScrollingImages
drwxr-xr-x   2        1024 Jan 12 11:11 SimpleGraph
drwxr-xr-x   2        1024 Jan 12 11:11 SpreadSheet
drwxr-xr-x   4        1024 Jan 12 11:11 TicTacToe
drwxr-xr-x   3        1024 Jan 12 11:11 TumblingDuke
drwxr-xr-x   4        1024 Jan 12 11:11 UnderConstruction
drwxr-xr-x   3        1024 Jan 12 11:11 WireFrame
```

In the subdirectories for each demonstration applet, you will find all the files necessary to run the applet and to see how the applet was created. For example, the directory for the `TicTacToe` applet contains the following:

`TicTacToe.class`	The compiled class file for the `TicTacToe` applet
`TicTacToe.java`	The source code for the `TicTacToe` applet
`audio` directory	Contains AU sound files the applet uses
`example1.html`	A sample HTML document for viewing the applet
`images` directory	Contains the images the applet uses

To test the installation, you can view the applet by accessing the `example1.html` file with your Java-capable Web browser. You can also view the applet using the `appletviewer` tool that comes with the JDK. If you are currently in the `java` base directory, you can type the following to view the `TicTacToe` demo applet with `appletviewer`:

```
bin/appletviewer demo/TicTacToe/example1.html
```

The good news is that if you can run the demo applet, your base installation worked correctly. If you have any problems running the `TicTacToe` applet with `appletviewer`, check your current path by typing `pwd` at the shell prompt. You should change directories to the base `java` directory and try to run `appletviewer` again. Normally, the base `java` directory is `/java` or a subdirectory under your home directory called `java`.

If you get the error message `Exception in thread NULL` when running the Java interpreter, compiler, or `appletviewer`, you should check the setting for your `CLASSPATH` environment variable by typing the following from the command line:

```
env ¦ grep CLASSPATH
```

The current setting for `CLASSPATH` should not list the class directory from an older JDK release. For Java to run properly on your system, you must set the `CLASSPATH` variable correctly. If you do not plan to use packages and classes stored in a directory other than the `java` base directory, you will want to edit your `.cshrc` or `.profile` file and remove the line that sets the `CLASSPATH` variable. If you plan to use packages and classes stored in a directory other than the `java` base directory, you should update the setting for the `CLASSPATH` variable. Refer back to the sidebar titled "Creating Your Own Packages and Classes for UNIX" to see how to do this.

Anyone who wants to maintain a separate class directory should check to see if they have set the `CLASSPATH` environment variable correctly. An easy way to do this is to temporarily move one of the demonstration class files to the location where you plan to store your Java class files. The new location must be empty if you follow this example.

From the `java/demo/TicTacToe` directory, type

```
mv TicTacToe.class /destination/file/path
```

where `/destination/file/path` is the actual file path to the destination directory, such as

`mv TicTacToe.class /myclasses/new/TicTacToe.class`

You should now be able to run the `TicTacToe` demo on `appletviewer` without having to specify the path to the class file for the applet. From the `java/demo/TicTacToe` directory, type the following to test this:

`../../bin/appletviewer example1.html`

If you cannot view the applet, you should check your environment settings by typing the following from the command line:

`env ¦ grep CLASSPATH`

The `grep` should return your updated setting for `CLASSPATH`, such as

`CLASSPATH=/myclasses/new`

If the `grep` command returns no output or the `CLASSPATH` variable is set incorrectly, refer back to the sidebar "Creating Your Own Packages and Classes for UNIX" for helpful information.

Power Start for Windows 95/NT

Members of the Microsoft Windows family of operating systems are the most-used operating systems in the world. Windows 95 is the long-awaited enhancement to Windows 3.1, and Windows NT is a network-optimized version of Windows. After Sun Microsystems created the Solaris version of the Java Developer's Kit, it ported the JDK to Windows NT.

Because much of the inner workings of the Windows NT operating system are essentially the same as those of the Windows 95 operating system, the JDK was modified for use on both the Windows NT and Windows 95 platforms. The current developer's environment for Windows 95/NT is quite advanced and includes all the packages and tools discussed earlier in this chapter.

> **Note:** Although the friendly folks at IBM are working on a Windows 3.1 version of the JDK, at the time of this writing there is not a JDK for Windows 3.1 systems. However, because Windows 95/NT are Windows-based operating systems, you should be able to use the tips and suggestions you'll find throughout this section to help you install the JDK on systems running Windows 3.1 if a version of the JDK specifically compiled for use on Windows 3.1 systems is made available.

Before installing the JDK, you should ensure that you have enough space on your hard drive for the installation. For Windows 95/NT, you will retrieve a 3.7MB self-extracting archive file. When you install the JDK, you will need an additional 5.6MB of disk space. Although you can remove the self-extracting archive file after a successful installation, you still need about 10MB of disk space initially.

To set up a Java developer's environment on your computer, follow these steps:

1. Obtain the Java Developer's Kit
2. Install the Java Developer's Kit
3. Test the installation

Obtaining the Java Developer's Kit

The JDK for Windows 95/NT includes the complete set of tools for viewing, creating, and debugging Java programs and the precompiled code packages from the standard API. To obtain the source file for the JDK, you need to open an FTP session with one of the FTP sites listed in the section "The Java Developer's Environment" at the beginning of this chapter.

Warning: If you have a prerelease version of the JDK installed on your system, you want to remove it before installing JDK 1.0 or later to remove files and directories that are no longer used with JDK 1.0 or later versions. However, before you do this, you should move any source code you created that is located in the directories you will be deleting. From the MS-DOS prompt, you can type the following to remove the previous installation of the JDK in its entirety:

`deltree /Y C:\file\path`

`C:\file\path` is the actual path to the previous installation of Java, such as

`    deltree /Y C:\java`

You should also check to see if you set Java-related file paths when you last installed the JDK. You can do this by typing the following at the MS-DOS prompt:

`TYPE C:\AUTOEXEC.BAT`

This command lists the contents of your `AUTOEXEC.BAT` file to the MS-DOS prompt window. You should now check for Java-related file paths and environment variables. Java-related file paths include any file paths where the old version of the JDK was installed. Java-related environment variables include `JAVA_HOME`, `CLASSPATH`, and `LD_LIBRARY_PATH`.

If you did not set Java-related paths, you can continue with the installation. If you set Java-related paths, you want to check the validity of these settings when you follow the steps for setting and/or updating your paths as discussed in the sidebar titled "Setting Your Paths for Java in Windows 95/NT," found in the next section of this chapter.

You can obtain the JDK source file from an FTP site in one of two ways:

- With your Web browser, enter the URL path to the FTP site as listed in the "URL Path to JDK" column of Table 2.1.

- From the shell prompt or Telnet session prompt, open an FTP session to the FTP site as listed in the "FTP Site" column of Table 2.1.

In the following example, the JDK source is downloaded from JavaSoft. If the JavaSoft FTP site is busy, you can obtain the source from any of the mirror sites listed in Table 2.1. Because file paths on the Internet tend to change, you should follow these steps sequentially:

1. Start the FTP session. You will be prompted to enter a username and password. Use the name anonymous and a password as *youruserid@yourhostname*, such as william@tvp.com. Here is how you start an FTP session with the JavaSoft FTP server:

```
$ ftp ftp.javasoft.com
Connected to ftp.javasoft.com.
220 java3 FTP server ready.
Name (ftp.javasoft.com): anonymous
331 Guest login ok, send your complete e-mail address as password.
Password: userid@hostname.com
230-
230-    Welcome to the Java home site.
230-
230 Guest login ok, access restrictions apply.
Remote system type is UNIX.
```

2. List the contents of the current directory. The JDK binary file is generally located in a subdirectory called pub, so you want to change to the pub directory. On some mirror sites you have to go through several subdirectories to get to Java's pub subdirectory. For example, on the Sunsite mirror (sunsite.unc.edu) you have to change directories to pub/languages/java/pub. Start by listing the contents of the current directory and then changing to the pub directory:

```
ftp> ls
200 PORT command successful.
150 Opening ASCII mode data connection for /bin/ls.
total 24
lrwxrwxrwx   1 root      1   7 May 19 20:02 bin -> usr/bin
dr-xr-xr-x   2 root      1     512 May 19 21:09 dev
dr-xr-xr-x   2 nobody    1    1536 Jun 21 21:36 docs
dr-xr-xr-x   2 root      1     512 May 19 20:04 etc
dr-xr-xr-x   5 500       1     512 Jun 14 01:13 pub
drwx-wx-wx   2 root      1     512 Jun 22 00:56 tmp
dr-xr-xr-x   4 nobody    1     512 Jun 19 20:04 usr
-r--r--r--   1 root      1    1255 May 27 01:33 welcome.msg
226 Transfer complete.
ftp> cd pub
250 CWD command successful.
```

3. When you are in the publication directory for the Java programming language, you should list the contents of the directory. You want to download the most current version of the

JDK. The most recent Windows 95/NT version in the example is `JDK-1_1-win32-x86.exe`. Download the appropriate source:

```
ftp> ls
200 PORT command successful.
150 Opening ASCII mode data connection for /bin/ls.
total 61148
-r--r--r--   1 root     1    4595974 Jan 23 16:35 JDK-1_1-solaris2-sparc.tar.Z
-r--r--r--   1 root     1    3720379 Jan 23 16:35 JDK-1_1-win32-x86.exe
-r--r--r--   1 root     1    2243968 Feb 14 00:56 JDK-1_1-mac.sea.bin
-r--r--r--   1 root     1    3049734 Feb 14 00:56 JDK-1_1-mac.sea.hqx
-r--r--r--   1 nobody   1    4508131 Dec 12 18:35
➥JDK-beta2-solaris2-sparc.tar.Z
-r--r--r--   1 nobody   1    3717250 Dec 12 18:36 JDK-1_0-win32-x86.exe
-r--r--r--   1 root     1      15868 Feb 14 00:56 README
-r--r--r--   1 nobody   1    5476531 Sep 11 02:05
➥hotjava-beta2-solaris2-sparc.tar.Z
-r--r--r--   1 nobody   1    3849659 Sep 11 02:06 hotjava-beta2-win32-x86.exe
226 Transfer complete.
ftp> bin
200 Type set to I.
ftp> get JDK-1_1-win32-x86.exe
local: JDK-1_1-win32-x86.exe remote: JDK-1_1-win32-x86.exe
200 PORT command successful.
150 Opening BINARY mode data connection for JDK-1_1-win32-x86.exe
➥(3720379 bytes).
226 Transfer complete.
3720379 bytes received
ftp>quit
```

Installing the Java Developer's Kit

After you obtain the source file, you should check to make sure the size of the file you downloaded matches the file size listed on the FTP site. If the file sizes aren't identical, your file might have been corrupted during download. In that case, you want to delete the file from your system and try to download the JDK source file again.

To install the JDK from the MS-DOS prompt, follow these steps:

1. Open a DOS window.

2. Change to the directory that contains the JDK source file.

3. Move the JDK to where you want to install it. To install Java in `c:\java`, which is recommended, you can use the following command:

   ```
   move JDK-1_1-win32-x86.exe c:\
   ```

4. The self-extracting file will install itself if you type the name of the executable at the DOS prompt, like this:

   ```
   JDK-1_1-win32-x86.exe
   ```

When you run the self-extracting archive file, you will be creating a directory called `java` under the current directory. If you are installing JDK 1.0 or later for Windows 95/NT on your system, the following files and subdirectories will be located under the `java` directory:

```
 Directory of C:\java
BIN             <DIR>        02-23-96   2:32p bin
LIB             <DIR>        02-23-96   2:32p lib
DEMO            <DIR>        02-23-96   2:32p demo
COPYRI~1                2,826 01-12-96 10:11a COPYRIGHT
README                  8,237 01-16-96  1:46p README
INDEX~1   HTM           1,017 01-16-96  1:48p index.html
INCLUDE         <DIR>        02-23-96   2:32p include
SRC       ZIP         371,854 01-16-96  1:47p src.zip
```

The `src.zip` file contains the source code for some of the classes used in the JDK. Because these classes represent a good cross-section of the functionality introduced by the Java API and are written in the Java programming language, you can learn a lot by examining them. Therefore, I highly recommend that you unzip the `src.zip` file and make a note to go through the some of the files after you read this book.

Tip: The class files in the `src.zip` file are stored with Windows 95/NT long filenames. You will need an unzip utility, such as WinZip95 or EZ-Zip, that supports long filenames.

By unzipping the `src.zip` file, you create the following directory structure on your file system:

```
src\
src\java\
src\java\lang\
src\java\util\
src\java\io\
src\java\net\
src\java\awt\
src\java\awt\peer\
src\java\awt\test\
src\java\awt\image\
src\java\applet\
src\sun\
src\sun\tools\
src\sun\tools\ttydebug\
```

You will find the JDK tools in the `bin` directory. The `bin` directory contains the following executable and dynamic link library files:

```
 Directory of C:\java\bin
JAVAI     DLL         162,304 01-12-96  9:30a javai.dll
JAVA      EXE           4,608 01-12-96  9:30a java.exe
JAVAW     EXE           4,608 01-12-96  9:30a javaw.exe
JAVAP     EXE          72,192 01-12-96  9:30a javap.exe
JAVAH     EXE          40,448 01-12-96  9:26a javah.exe
JAVAI_G   DLL         265,216 01-12-96  9:35a javai_g.dll
JAVA_G    EXE           5,632 01-12-96  9:35a java_g.exe
JAVAW_G   EXE           6,144 01-12-96  9:35a javaw_g.exe
```

```
JAVAP_G   EXE      98,304   01-12-96   9:35a  javap_g.exe
JAVAH_G   EXE      54,784   01-12-96   9:31a  javah_g.exe
NET       DLL      14,336   01-12-96   9:37a  net.dll
NET_G     DLL      17,920   01-12-96   9:37a  net_g.dll
JAVAC     EXE       4,608   01-12-96   9:40a  javac.exe
JAVAC_G   EXE       6,144   01-12-96   9:40a  javac_g.exe
AGENT     DLL      14,848   01-12-96   9:41a  agent.dll
AGENT_G   DLL      18,432   01-12-96   9:42a  agent_g.dll
JDB       EXE       4,608   01-12-96   9:42a  jdb.exe
JDB_G     EXE       6,144   01-12-96   9:42a  jdb_g.exe
JAVADOC   EXE       4,608   01-12-96   9:43a  javadoc.exe
JAVADO~1  EXE       6,144   01-12-96   9:43a  javadoc_g.exe
AWT       DLL     139,264   01-12-96   9:45a  awt.dll
AWT_G     DLL     177,664   01-12-96   9:46a  awt_g.dll
JPEG      DLL      63,488   01-12-96   9:46a  jpeg.dll
JPEG_G    DLL      89,088   01-12-96   9:47a  jpeg_g.dll
MMEDIA    DLL       6,144   01-12-96   9:47a  mmedia.dll
MMEDIA_G  DLL       7,680   01-12-96   9:47a  mmedia_g.dll
APPLET~1  EXE       5,120   01-12-96   9:49a  appletviewer.exe
APPLET~2  EXE       7,168   01-12-96   9:49a  appletviewer_g.exe
MFC30     DLL     322,832   01-12-96   8:00a  mfc30.dll
MSVCRT20  DLL     253,952   01-12-96   8:00a  msvcrt20.dll
```

The executables and link libraries come in two forms. Those files with the suffix _g are compiled and linked with debugging information. Executables with the suffix _g support all of Java's mechanisms for debugging. Executables without the suffix _g are optimized for normal use and support only limited debugging options. Many of the files in this directory are used by the Java environment itself and are, in fact, the Windows 95/NT interface to Java. They include the following:

awt.dll   Java uses the `awt.dll` libraries to display graphics and to create graphical interfaces to buttons, scrollbars, and pop-up windows.

jpeg.dll   Java uses the `jpeg.dll` libraries to interpret and display JPEG images.

mmedia.dll   Java uses the `mmedia.dll` libraries to perform multimedia functions that include displaying GIF images and playing AU sound files.

net.dll   Java uses the `net.dll` libraries when you perform network operations.

Peter's Principle: Setting Your Paths for Java in Windows 95/NT

After installing the JDK, you should update your AUTOEXEC.BAT file so your computer can find the Java executables and class libraries. Follow these steps for updating your AUTOEXEC.BAT file:

1. Type the following:

   EDIT C:\AUTOEXEC.BAT

2. Add the full path to the Java executables to your PATH statement, which allows you to run the JDK tools without having to specify the full path to the binaries. If you

installed Java under the `c:\` directory, which is recommended, you would place the following line after your current PATH statement in your AUTOEXEC.BAT file:

```
PATH=%path%;C:\JAVA\BIN
```

3. Setting the CLASSPATH variable is optional. However, if you installed a previous version of the JDK, you should either remove the line that assigns the CLASSPATH variable or set the CLASSPATH environment variable to the location of the `classes.zip` file.

   If you installed Java under the `c:\` directory, you would add the following line to your AUTOEXEC.BAT file:

```
SET CLASSPATH=C:\JAVA\LIB\CLASSES.ZIP
```

   If you plan to create your own packages or to store Java classes in a private directory, you should prepend the directory path to the setting for the CLASSPATH variable. For example, if you wanted to store your class files in the directory `c:\myclasses`, you would set the CLASSPATH variable as follows:

```
SET CLASSPATH=C:\MYCLASSES;C:\JAVA\LIB\CLASSES.ZIP
```

4. Optionally, if you installed the JDK anywhere other than your file system's root directory and under a directory named `java`, you will have to set the JAVA_HOME environment variable. If you installed the JDK in `C:MYJAVA`, you would set this variable as follows:

```
SET JAVA_HOME=C:\MYJAVA
```

5. Save and close your AUTOEXEC.BAT file.

6. Reboot your computer. This sets the working environment for all future sessions. You can set your current working environment for use with Java. Your current working environment only applies to the MS-DOS prompt into which you enter the path setting. You must use the actual path to your Java executables. If you installed Java under the `c:\` directory, you would type the following at the MS-DOS prompt:

```
PATH=%PATH%;C:\JAVA\BIN;
```

Another directory you will want to check is the `demo` directory, which contains many demonstration applets. By previewing these demos, you can see Java in action. The `include` directory contains C-language header and stub files. These files are primarily used to set paths and definitions needed by Java and essential to Java interaction with C.

The `lib` directory contains essential library files and the zipped file for all classes included in the Java API, called `classes.zip`. Loading classes from zipped files makes it possible to compress the entire contents of the Java API into one file. The Java runtime class loader and the Java compiler extract any class files they need from `classes.zip`.

> **Warning:** Although you can unzip the `src.zip` file, you should not unzip the `classes.zip` file. The `classes.zip` file contains all the classes and methods in the Java API. If you unzip this file, you will create hundreds of unnecessary files on your hard drive.

Testing the Installation

A great way to test your new Java developer's environment is to preview one of the demo applets included in the JDK. As you can see from the following code, each demo applet is located in the `demo` directory and has its own subdirectory:

```
 Directory of C:\java\demo
WIREFR~1      <DIR>       02-23-96   2:32p  WireFrame
TICTAC~1      <DIR>       02-23-96   2:32p  TicTacToe
BOUNCI~1      <DIR>       02-23-96   2:32p  BouncingHeads
MOLECU~1      <DIR>       02-23-96   2:32p  MoleculeViewer
ARCTEST       <DIR>       02-23-96   2:32p  ArcTest
DRAWTEST      <DIR>       02-23-96   2:32p  DrawTest
CARDTEST      <DIR>       02-23-96   2:32p  CardTest
SPREAD~1      <DIR>       02-23-96   2:32p  SpreadSheet
BLINK         <DIR>       02-23-96   2:32p  Blink
TUMBLI~1      <DIR>       02-23-96   2:32p  TumblingDuke
NERVOU~1      <DIR>       02-23-96   2:32p  NervousText
FRACTAL       <DIR>       02-23-96   2:32p  Fractal
BARCHART      <DIR>       02-23-96   2:32p  BarChart
UNDERC~1      <DIR>       02-23-96   2:32p  UnderConstruction
JUMPIN~1      <DIR>       02-23-96   2:32p  JumpingBox
SCROLL~1      <DIR>       02-23-96   2:32p  ScrollingImages
DITHER~1      <DIR>       02-23-96   2:32p  DitherTest
IMAGEMAP      <DIR>       02-23-96   2:32p  ImageMap
GRAPHL~1      <DIR>       02-23-96   2:32p  GraphLayout
GRAPHI~1      <DIR>       02-23-96   2:32p  GraphicsTest
SIMPLE~1      <DIR>       02-23-96   2:32p  SimpleGraph
ANIMATOR      <DIR>       02-23-96   2:32p  Animator
IMAGET~1      <DIR>       02-23-96   2:32p  ImageTest
```

In the subdirectories for each demonstration applet, you will find all the files necessary to run the applet and to see how the applet was created. For example, the directory for the `TicTacToe` applet contains the following:

`TicTacToe.class`	The compiled class file for the `TicTacToe` applet
`TicTacToe.java`	The source code for the `TicTacToe` applet
`audio` directory	Contains AU sound files the applet uses
`example1.html`	A sample HTML document for viewing the applet
`images` directory	Contains the images the applet uses

To test the installation, you can view the applet by accessing the `example1.html` file with your Java-capable Web browser. You can also view the applet using the `appletviewer` tool that comes with the

JDK. If you are currently in the `java` base directory, you can type the following to view the `TicTacToe` demo applet with `appletviewer`:

```
appletviewer demo\TicTacToe\example1.html
```

If you are currently in the `java\demo\TicTacToe` directory, you can type the following to view the `TicTacToe` demo applet with `appletviewer`:

```
appletviewer example1.html
```

When you run `appletviewer`, the `TicTacToe` applet should display on your screen. Because the `TicTacToe` applet uses threads, `appletviewer` may write something similar to the following in the MS-DOS prompt area:

```
thread applet-TicTacToe.class find class TicTacToe
Opening stream to: file:/C:/java/demo/TicTacToe/TicTacToe.class to get TicTacToe
```

The good news is that if you can run the demo applet, your base installation worked correctly. If you have any problems running the `TicTacToe` applet with `appletviewer`, first make sure you are in the correct directory. Next, make sure your PATH statement and environment are set correctly. When you type PATH at the MS-DOS prompt, you should see the previous path settings and the updated path setting for Java. When you type SET at the MS-DOS prompt, you should see the previous environment settings and the setting for Java's CLASSPATH environment variable, providing that you set this variable.

If you get the error message `Exception in thread NULL` when running the Java interpreter, compiler, or `appletviewer`, you should check the setting for your CLASSPATH environment variable. You can do this by typing SET at the MS-DOS prompt. The CLASSPATH variable must specify the full path to the `classes.zip` file and should not list the class directory from an older JDK release.

Anyone who wants to maintain a separate class directory should check to see if they have set the CLASSPATH environment variable correctly. An easy way to do this is to temporarily move one of the demonstration class files to the location where you plan to store your Java class files. The new location must be empty if you follow this example.

From the `java\demo\TicTacToe` directory, type

```
mkdir c:\destination\file\path
move TicTacToe.class \destination\file\path
```

where `\destination\file\path` is the actual file path to the destination directory, such as

```
mkdir c:\myclasses
move TicTacToe.class c:\myclasses
```

You should now be able to run the `TicTacToe` demo on `appletviewer` without having to specify the path to the class file for the applet. From the `java\demo\TicTacToe` directory, type the following to test it:

```
appletviewer example1.html
```

If you cannot view the applet, you should check your environment settings. You can do this by typing SET at the MS-DOS prompt.

The SET command should return your updated setting for CLASSPATH, such as

`CLASSPATH=C:\MYCLASSES;C:\JAVA\LIB\CLASSES.ZIP`

If the CLASSPATH variable is set incorrectly, you should refer back to the sidebar "Setting Your Paths for Java in Windows 95/NT."

Power Start for Macintosh

The Macintosh has one of the friendliest operating systems available, and it is unfortunate that Mac owners had to wait so long for an initial implementation of the Java Developer's Kit. The first version of the Macintosh JDK released for general use was a limited-use Beta version that included the AWT and network packages but lacked many of the other packages found on other systems. Also, the Beta JDK only allowed you to create applets for use with external viewers.

The reasons for these limitations in the Beta JDK are many, but one of the major reasons is that the Macintosh operating system is fundamentally different from most other operating systems. The developers of the Beta JDK found that the folder hierarchy used in other JDKs did not make sense on a Mac. For example, on other systems the binary executables are stored in a bin directory. A "bin" folder on a Macintosh does not make much sense. Therefore, the developers moved the executables to the top-level folder.

Additionally, the command line used on other systems allows the tools in the JDK to be very basic and streamlined. Typing things at a command line, however, goes against the principles upon which the Mac is founded. Mac users like their drag-and-drop functionality, and that is what the developers of the Mac JDK set it to provide. However, graphical tools are inherently more complex than command-line tools, and that's why developing the Mac JDK was such a slow process.

The current Macintosh JDK is much more advanced and includes AWT, Networking, and Multimedia libraries. These three libraries provide the core functionality of the standard API on other systems. To run Java on your Mac, you should be running System 7.5 or higher on a Power Macintosh or a Macintosh with at least a 68030 processor.

Before installing the JDK, you should ensure that you have enough space on your hard drive for the installation. You will retrieve a 2.5MB compressed installer file. When you install the JDK, you need an additional 6MB of disk space. Although you can remove the compressed installer file after a successful installation, you still initially need about 9MB of disk space.

To set up a Java developer's environment on your Macintosh, follow these steps:

1. Obtain the Java Developer's Kit

2. Install the Java Developer's Kit

3. Test the installation

Obtaining the Java Developer's Kit

The JDK for Macintosh includes the complete set of tools for viewing, creating, and debugging Java programs and the precompiled code packages from the standard API. To obtain the source file for the JDK, you need to open an FTP session with one of the FTP sites listed in Table 2.1.

Warning: If a prerelease version of the JDK is installed on your system, you want to remove it before installing JDK 1.0 or later. This will remove files and directories that are no longer used with JDK 1.0 or later versions. However, before you do this, you should move any source code you created that is located in the directories you will be deleting. You can remove a previous installation by putting the top-level folder into the trashcan—don't forget to flush!

You can obtain the JDK source file from an FTP site in one of two ways:

- With your Web browser, enter the URL path to the FTP site as listed in the "URL Path to JDK" column of Table 2.1.

- Using an FTP tool, open an FTP session to the FTP site as listed in the "FTP Site" column of Table 2.1.

In the example that follows, the JDK source code is downloaded from JavaSoft. If the JavaSoft FTP site is busy, you can obtain the source from any of the mirror sites listed in Table 2.1. Because file paths on the Internet tend to change, you should follow the steps sequentially.

1. Start the FTP session using your FTP tool of your choice or a Web browser. The URL path to JavaSoft is

   `ftp://ftp.javasoft.com/pub`

   The FTP site you want to access with the FTP tool is `ftp.javasoft.com`. When you have successfully connected, you should see a listing of files and folders in the base directory.

2. Click on the `pub` directory. You should see a listing of the contents of the `pub` directory. You want to download the most current version of the JDK for Mac. Currently, the JDK is available in both Macintosh binary (`JDK-1_1-mac.sea.bin`) and Macintosh `hqx` format (`JDK-1_1-mac.sea.hqx`). Select and retrieve the version you want to download by clicking on it.

Installing the Java Developer's Kit

After you obtain the compressed installer file, you should check to make sure the size of the file you downloaded matches the file size listed on the FTP site. If the file sizes are not identical, your file might have been corrupted during download. In this case, you want to delete the file from your system and try to download the JDK source file again.

Before you can install the JDK, you need to decompress the installer file. You should use `Stuffit` to decompress the Macintosh binary file and `DeHQX` or `BinHex4` to decompress the `hqx` file.

> **Note:** If you used `Fetch` or `Anarchie` to download the files, the installer file was automatically decompressed when the download finished.

To install the JDK, simply run the installer program. You can change the name of the folder that will contain the JDK if you want. I prefer the folder name `Java` or `JDK` to the default. Folders and files created during the installation include the following:

`Java Compiler`	The Java compiler
`Applet Viewer`	An application used to view applets without a Web browser.
`Classes`	A folder for class files used by the compiler and `Applet Viewer`
`Java.shlb`	The Java runtime shared library for PowerPC
`lib`	A folder containing libraries for the Java interpreter and compiler
`Sample Applets`	A folder containing sample applets and source code

Testing the Installation

A great way to test your new Java developer's environment is to preview one of the sample applets included in the JDK. You can view the sample applets with your Java-capable Web browser or with the `Applet Viewer` tool that comes with the JDK.

To use the `Applet Viewer` tool, do the following:

1. Open the folder named `Sample Applets`.
2. Open the folder named `TicTacToe`.
3. Drop the file `example1.html` on the application Applet Viewer.

You should now be able to view the sample applet.

Power Start for OS/2

IBM's OS/2 operating system is a popular alternative to Microsoft Windows. The OS/2 version of the Java Developer's Kit is basically a port from the Windows 95/NT version. The first version of the OS/2 JDK released for general use was a Beta version. Because the Beta version was basically a direct port from the Windows 95/NT version, it had many problems. The current version of the JDK is much more advanced and features better support for the native OS/2 environment.

The OS/2 JDK requires OS/2 2.*x* or OS/2 Warp. IBM recommends a 486-class machine with 12MB+ RAM and OS/2 Warp for optimal performance, especially because you need OS/2 Warp to play Java audio files. You will also need an HPFS disk with at least 15MB of free space. Be forewarned that the JDK requires long-name support. Before installing the JDK, you should ensure that you have enough space on your hard drive for the installation. Additionally, to use the networking features of Java, you need TCP/IP software such as Warp IAK or TCP/IP 2.0+.

To set up a Java developer's environment on your computer, follow these steps:

1. Obtain the Java Developer's Kit
2. Install the Java Developer's Kit
3. Test the installation

Obtaining the Java Developer's Kit

The JDK for OS/2 includes the complete set of tools for viewing, creating, and debugging Java programs and the precompiled code packages from the standard API. To obtain the source file for the JDK, you have to register to use the IBM developers area on the Web.

Warning: If you have a pre-release version of the JDK installed on your system, you want to remove it before installing JDK 1.0 or later to remove files and directories that are no longer used with JDK 1.0 or later versions. However, before you do this, you should move any source code you created that is located in the directories you will be deleting. From the OS/2 command prompt, you can type the following to remove the previous installation of the JDK in its entirety:

```
deltree /Y C:\file\path
```

where C:\file\path is the actual path to the previous installation of Java, such as

```
deltree /Y C:\java
```

You should also check to see if you set Java-related file paths when you last installed the JDK. You can do this by typing the following at the OS/2 command prompt:

```
TYPE C:\CONFIG.SYS
```

The previous command should list the contents of your `CONFIG.SYS` file. You should now check for Java-related file paths. Java-related file paths include any file paths where the old version of the JDK was installed.

If you did not set Java-related paths, you can continue with the installation. If you set Java-related paths, you want to check the validity of these settings when you follow the steps for setting and/or updating your paths as discussed in the sidebar "Setting Up Your Java Environment in OS/2," which appears in the next section.

Obtaining the JDK source for OS/2 is as easy as 1, 2, 3:

1. With your Web browser, enter the URL path to IBM's Web site and follow the link from this index page to IBM's online registration form for software developers:

   `http://www.hursley.ibm.com/javainfo/download/index.html`

2. After you fill out and submit the form, you will receive an e-mail message verifying your username and password. This message should come back to you in a few minutes. After you receive a user ID and password, you will be able to access the private developers area and download the JDK source. You can click on the appropriate link on the index page listed earlier or try to access the OS/2 developers area directly at

   `http://www.hursley.ibm.com/javainfo/Developer/os2/index.html`

3. The developers page should have a link to a zip file containing the JDK source. Click on the link to download the JDK for OS/2.

Installing the Java Developer's Kit

Before you can install the JDK, you need to unzip the compressed source file. If you do not have an unzip utility that supports long filenames, Infozip's UNZIP version 5.12 or later works well.

To install the JDK, follow these steps:

1. From an OS/2 command prompt, change to the directory that contains the JDK source file.

2. Move the JDK to where you want to install it. To install Java in `c:\javaos2`, you can use the following command:

   ```
   move filename c:\
   ```

   where `filename` is the actual name of the zip file, such as

   ```
   move JAVAOS2.ZIP c:\
   ```

3. Unzip the file. Be sure to set the `-d` directories and subdirectories flag if your unzip utility requires it. If you are using Infozip's UNZIP, you can type the following:

   ```
   unzip javaos2.zip
   ```

When you unzip the JDK source file, you will be creating a directory called `javaos2` under the current directory. If you are installing the JDK for OS/2 on your system, subdirectories located under the `javaos2` directory include the following:

`.hotjava`	Directory containing network property files
`applet`	Output directory for applet viewer log files
`bin`	Directory containing the JDK tools
`classes`	Directory containing class files used by the compiler and applet viewer
`demo`	Directory containing demonstration applets and source code
`dll`	Directory containing dynamic linked library files needed by the Java compiler and interpreter
`include`	Directory containing `include` files for building native classes
`lib`	Directory containing library and Java property files
`src`	Directory containing the source for a subset of the classes from the API

The executables and link libraries come in two forms. Those files with suffix `_g` are compiled and linked with debugging information. Executables with the suffix `_g` support all of Java's mechanisms for debugging. Executables without the suffix `_g` are optimized for normal use and support only limited debugging options. The dynamic linked libraries are used by the Java environment itself and are, in fact, the OS/2 interface to Java.

The classes in the `src` directory represent a good cross-section of the functionality introduced by the Java API and are written in the Java programming language. You can learn a lot by examining them. Therefore, I highly recommend that you make a note to go through some of the files after you read this book.

Another directory you want to check is the `demo` directory, which contains many demonstration applets. By previewing these demos, you can see Java in action. The `include` directory contains C-language header and stub files. These files are primarily used to set paths and definitions needed by Java and essential to Java interaction with C. Finally, the `lib` directory contains essential library files.

Peter's Principle: Setting Up Your Java Environment in OS/2

After installing the JDK, you should update your `CONFIG.SYS` file so your computer can find the Java executables and class libraries. Follow these steps for updating your `CONFIG.SYS` file:

1. Type the following at the OS/2 command prompt:

   `EDIT C:\CONFIG.SYS`

2. Add the full path to the Java `dll` directory to the current path for the `LIBPATH` environment variable. This allows Java to find the DLL files. If you installed the JDK in `c:\javaos2`, the full path to the `dll` directory is

   ```
   c:\javaos2\dll
   ```

3. Add the full path to the Java `bin` directory to the current path setting. This allows Java to find the binary executables for Java. If you installed the JDK in `c:\javaos2`, the full path to the `bin` directory is

   ```
   c:\javaos2\bin
   ```

4. Optionally, if you installed the JDK in a directory other than `javaos2`, you will have to set the `HOME` and the `JAVA_HOME` environment variables. If you installed the JDK in `C:MYJAVA`, you would set these variables as follows:

   ```
   SET HOME=C:\MYJAVA
   SET JAVA_HOME=C:\MYJAVA
   ```

5. Save and close your `CONFIG.SYS` file.

6. Reboot your computer. Rebooting your computer sets the working environment for all future sessions. Optionally, you can type the following from the OS/2 command prompt to set your current working environment for use with Java. Your current working environment applies only to the OS/2 command prompt into which you enter the environment and path settings. You must use the actual path to your Java executables and dynamic link libraries. If you installed Java under the `c:\javaos2` directory, you would type the following at the OS/2 command prompt:

   ```
   SET PATH=%PATH%;C:\JAVAOS2\BIN;
   SET LIBPATH=%LIBPATH%;C:\JAVAOS2\DLL;
   ```

Testing the Installation

A great way to test your new Java developer's environment is to preview one of the demo applets included in the JDK. Each demo applet is located in the `demo` directory and has its own subdirectory. In the subdirectories for each demonstration applet, you will find all the files necessary to run the applet and to see how the applet was created. For example, the directory for the `TicTacToe` applet contains the following:

`TicTacToe.class`	The compiled class file for the `TicTacToe` applet
`TicTacToe.java`	The source code for the `TicTacToe` applet
`audio` directory	Contains AU sound files the applet uses
`example1.html`	A sample HTML document for viewing the applet
`images` directory	Contains the images the applet uses

To test the installation, you can view the applet by accessing the `example1.html` file with your Java-capable Web browser. You can also view the applet using the `appletviewer` tool that comes with the JDK. If you are currently in the `javaos2` directory, you can type the following to view the `TicTacToe` demo applet with the `appletviewer` tool:

```
start applet demo\TicTacToe\example1.html
```

If you are currently in the `java\demo\TicTacToe` directory, you can type the following to view the `TicTacToe` demo applet with the `appletviewer`:

```
start applet example1.html
```

When you run the `appletviewer` tool, you should see the applet and something similar to the following should be written to the `javaos2\applet` log files:

```
thread applet-TicTacToe.class find class TicTacToe
Opening stream to: file:/C:/javaos2/demo/TicTacToe/TicTacToe.class
➥to get TicTacToe
```

The good news is that if you can run the demo applet, your base installation worked correctly. If you have any problems running the `TicTacToe` applet with the applet viewer tool, first make sure you are in the correct directory. Next, make sure your PATH statement and environment are set correctly. When you type PATH at the OS/2 command prompt, you should see the previous path settings and the updated path setting for Java. When you type SET at the OS/2 command prompt, you should see the previous environment settings and the updated setting for the LIBPATH environment variable. Additionally, if you set the HOME and JAVA_HOME variables, you should see these settings as well when you type SET at the command prompt.

Performance Tuning for OS/2

A nice feature of the JDK for OS/2 is the capability to do additional performance tuning. In particular, the OS/2 JDK allows you to set three environment variables either permanently in your CONFIG.SYS or temporarily at the OS/2 command prompt.

Additional performance-tuning environment variables include the following:

JAVA_CONNECT_TIMEOUT=n	Used to adjust the time that Java will wait for a network connection before it reports a timeout. The default value for this variable is 30 seconds. Valid values for n are from 1 through 1,000,000.
JAVA_AUDIO_VOLUME=v	Used to adjust the audio volume from Java as a percentage of the maximum allowable volume. The default value for this variable is 50. Valid values for v are from 0 through 100.

JAVA_AUDIO_RATE=n   Used to set the preferred playback sample rate for audio. By default, Java first tries to play audio at 8,000 samples and then tries 11,025 samples. You can override this default by setting n to a specific value: 8 for 8,000 samples per second or 11 for 11,025 samples per second.

Power Start for AIX

One major flavor of UNIX for which the JDK is currently available is AIX. As you will see, the steps for installing the AIX version of the JDK are very similar to the steps for installing the Solaris version. This is because the underlying architecture for both Solaris and AIX is UNIX-based.

The AIX JDK requires AIX version 4.1.3 or higher. Before installing the JDK, you should ensure that you have enough space on your hard drive for the installation. For AIX, you will retrieve a 4.9MB compressed file. When you install the JDK, you will need an additional 9MB of disk space. Although you can remove the compressed JDK file after a successful installation, you still initially need about 15MB of disk space.

To set up a Java developer's environment on your computer, follow these steps:

1. Obtain the Java Developer's Kit

2. Install the Java Developer's Kit

3. Test the installation

Obtaining the Java Developer's Kit

The JDK for AIX includes the complete set of tools for viewing, creating, and debugging Java programs and the precompiled code packages from the standard API. To obtain the source file for the JDK, you have to register to use the IBM developers area on the Web.

> **Warning:** If you have a pre-release version of the JDK installed on your system, you want to remove it before installing JDK 1.0 or later to remove files and directories that are no longer used with JDK 1.0 or later versions. However, before you do this, you should move any source code you created that is located in the directories you will be deleting.
>
> From the shell prompt, you can type the following to remove the previous installation of the JDK in its entirety:
>
> ```
> rm -rf \file\path
> ```
>
> where \file\path is the actual path to the previous installation of Java, such as
>
> ```
> rm -rf \java
> ```

Obtaining the JDK source for AIX is as easy as 1, 2, 3:

1. With your Web browser, enter the URL path to IBM's Web site and follow the link from this index page to IBM's online registration form for software developers:

   ```
   http://www.hursley.ibm.com/javainfo/download/index.html
   ```

2. After you fill out and submit the form, you will receive an e-mail message verifying your username and password. This message should come back to you in a few minutes. After you receive a user ID and password, you will be able to access the private developers area and download the JDK source. You can click on the appropriate link on the index page listed earlier or try to access the AIX developer's area directly at

   ```
   http://www.hursley.ibm.com/javainfo/Developer/aix/index.html
   ```

3. The developers page should have a link to a zip file containing the JDK source. Click on the link to download the JDK for AIX.

Installing the Java Developer's Kit

The AIX JDK source file is compressed and packed. You need to uncompress and unpack the files. The following steps will guide you through the installation process:

1. Change to the directory that contains the JDK source file.

2. Move the JDK to where you want to install it. To install Java in /java, which is recommended, you can use the following command:

   ```
   mv filename /
   ```

   where filename is the actual name of the file, such as

   ```
   mv java1.1.tar.Z /
   ```

3. Uncompress and unpack the file. You can do this using the following command:

   ```
   uncompress filename | tar -xf -
   ```

   where filename is the actually name of the file, such as

   ```
   uncompress java1.1.tar.Z | tar -xf -
   ```

When you uncompress and unpack the compressed JDK file, you will be creating a directory called java under the current directory. If you are installing the JDK for AIX on your system, the following are some of the files and subdirectories that will be located under the java directory:

bin	Directory containing the JDK tools
classes	Directory containing the compiled class files for the Java API
demo	Directory containing demonstration applets and source code
include	Directory containing C-language header and stub files
lib	Directory containing runtime library and Java property files

lib/ums	Directory containing audio libraries for systems with audio hardware on the motherboard
lib/aix	Directory containing AIX-specific libraries and audio libraries for systems without audio hardware on the motherboard
java	Directory containing the source for a subset of the classes from the API

You will find the following executable files for the JDK tools in the bin directory. All the executables—except for the Java source-level debugger, jdb—come in two forms. Executables with the suffix _g are for debugging and support all of Java's mechanisms for debugging. Executables without the suffix _g are optimized for normal use and support only limited debugging options.

Another directory you want to check is the demo directory, which contains many demonstration applets. By previewing these demos, you can see Java in action. The include directory contains C-language header and stub files. These files are primarily used to set paths and definitions needed by Java and essential to Java interaction with C. Finally, the lib directory contains essential library files.

You should now add the full path to the java/bin directory to your search path. This will allow you to execute the JDK tools from any directory.

Testing the Installation

A great way to test your new Java developer's environment is to preview one of the demo applets included in the JDK. In the subdirectories for each demonstration applet, you will find all the files necessary to run the applet and to see how the applet was created. For example, the directory for the TicTacToe applet contains the following:

TicTacToe.class	The compiled class file for the TicTacToe applet
TicTacToe.java	The source code for the TicTacToe applet
audio directory	Contains AU sound files the applet uses
example1.html	A sample HTML document for viewing the applet
images directory	Contains the images the applet uses

To test the installation, you can view the applet by accessing the example1.html file with your Java-capable Web browser. You can also view the applet using the appletviewer tool that comes with the JDK. If you are currently in the java base directory, you can type the following to view the TicTacToe demo applet with appletviewer:

```
bin/appletviewer demo/TicTacToe/example1.html
```

The good news is that if you can run the demo applet, your base installation worked correctly. If you have any problems running the TicTacToe applet with appletviewer, check your current path by typing pwd at the shell prompt. You should change directories to the base java directory and try to run appletviewer again. Normally the base java directory is

```
/java
```

or a subdirectory under your home directory called

```
java
```

Making the Transition from C/C++ to Java

Since the release of Java Alpha in 1995, thousands of frustrated C/C++ programmers have chased the Java dream. From the hype surrounding Java and the rejoicing in the press, they expected to become expert Java programmers in no time. After all, like I said, Java is modeled after C and C++.

The problem is that you must always crawl before you walk. However, you will find that making the transition from C/C++ to Java is easy if you take the time to learn about the fundamental differences between C/C++ and Java. This section highlights these differences so you know what you can and cannot do in Java right from the start.

Java Has No Compile to Machine Code

C/C++ source code is compiled to machine code. This compiled source is usable only on the specific platform for which it was compiled. As you know, a compiled C/C++ program is directly executable. Java source code, on the other hand, is compiled to an intermediate form called *bytecode* that is neither machine code nor source code.

One benefit of compiling to bytecode is that Java bytecode is not platform specific and is usable on any platform to which the Java programming language has been ported. You execute Java source code using an interpreter that executes the bytecode and translates it to a machine-readable form.

Another benefit of compiling to an intermediate form is that no link step is required. The Java interpreter dynamically links in classes on demand.

Java Has No External C Syntax

In C++, you can get to existing C procedures and system calls using the extern C syntax that declares the C procedure to be outside the normal C++ namespace. In Java, there is no extern C syntax; as a result, you cannot use existing C or C++ code directly. In fact, it is rather difficult to use C++ code at all.

Before you abandon ship, you should realize that Java incorporates a wide range of functionality into the Java API. As specified earlier in this chapter, the API includes packages for graphics, multimedia, networking, system utilities, file I/O, and much more. This means that most of the common functions for which you would want to use your C/C++ libraries are already in the Java API.

Don't worry—for those C/C++ functions that you really need, there is a way to use them in Java. It is, however, indirect and not as easy as using the external C syntax. To use C functions in Java, you must define a method whose purpose is to interface to the C function. Within the method, you must specify how the C function will interact with Java. Using C++ programs in Java is a bit more convoluted. You must define a method whose purpose is to interface to a C class that invokes C++ functions and member functions from C.

> **Looking Ahead:** (See Chapter 22, "Integrating Native Programs and Libraries," for complete details on using C/C++ functions with Java.)

Generally, you will use C/C++ or another programming language when you want to implement platform-specific functionality or increase the speed of your application. Keep in mind that when you use other programming languages with Java, you may be sacrificing the platform independence of your application.

Java Has No Multiple Inheritance

An object that is a member of one class, a parent of another class, and needs to inherit the full functionality of both classes is one example of the need for multiple inheritance. Often when you are programming advanced object-oriented applications, you need to use classes that inherit the functionality of more than one class. In fact, the more advanced your application is, the more likely that you will need to use multiple inheritance.

Many experienced C++ programmers dig deep into their tool chests, find some old code they have written that uses multiple inheritance, and press on. In Java, this is not possible because Java does not support multiple inheritance. Java replaces multiple inheritance with *interfaces*. Current C++ programmers will find that the concept of interfaces is easier to understand and use than multiple inheritance, which is another plus for Java.

Interfaces allow you to define the protocols for methods and final variables without having to worry about the specific implementation. Once you declare an interface, other interfaces or classes can implement that interface. A class that implements an interface can have its own functionality. Additionally, both classes and interfaces can implement multiple interfaces. However, the one limitation to interfaces is that you must write code to reimplement the desired functionality in each class implementing an interface.

An interface guarantees that all objects inherited from it will provide the same methods as the interface. This allows for a more object-oriented approach to programming. Even classes that are inherited from multiple interfaces will always implement the methods of their interfaces. For example, a class derived from the television interface and the radio interface will have all the methods available to both interfaces.

Java Has No Namespace Problems

Anyone who has worked in a large C++ environment has probably encountered namespace problems. The simple fact is that when you have different programmers working on different sections of a project, someone is bound to create a class with the same name as a totally different class in some other part of the project. When this happens, you have namespace pollution and a big headache, especially if the overlap is not discovered until a late stage of the project—like when you are integrating the code modules for testing. Correcting a namespace problem costs time and money.

Java avoids namespace problems by creating a namespace with many levels that are considered in precedence order from the highest level, the package namespace, to the lowest level, the nested local block namespace. Each component level in the namespace is used to build a unique object name. Thus, two classes with the same name in different packages are unique.

Java Has No Pointers

Experienced C/C++ programmers know that most bugs in C/C++ code relate to problems with pointers and memory management. This is because practically everyone who has ever programmed in C or C++ has at one time or another had problems with pointers and memory management. These two areas of C/C++ programming are a trial by fire that you either learn flawlessly or have problems with forever after. As you know from Chapter 1, Java does not use pointers and automatically manages memory for you, which in itself is cause for celebration.

Technical Note: To be 100% technically accurate, Java does not actually eliminate the concept of pointers. Every instance of an object is referenced via a pointer. The only functionality that pointers have is to retrieve the value of the object to which it is pointing. Programmers and users cannot manipulate these pointers, which is a significant change from how pointers are used in C/C++. In C/C++, as most programmers know, you handle the pointers yourself and pray they don't go astray. Therefore, when you read that Java has no pointers, it means that, for all intents and purposes, Java eliminates pointers as most programmers know them.

Java Has No Separate Header Files

Header files are an important part of C++ programming. Many programmers use header files as impromptu documentation, primarily because header files can tell you at a glance how a particular class should be used. When you want to see the interface to a function, you bring up the header file and find the function. Java does not have header files. The signature of a method must appear simultaneously with its declaration. This means there is no convenient place to find answers quickly.

If having to wade through pages of code to learn how to use a particular class is not appealing, there is an upside. The Java Developer's Kit includes two tools that make this task easier: javap and javadoc. The Java disassembler, javap, can be used to print class signatures. The Java API documentation generator, javadoc, creates HTML documentation from comments embedded in source files. This means if you have good inline documentation, javadoc can be used to create documentation in a more traditional and easier-to-use form.

A lack of header files also has its advantages. Because the signature of a method must appear simultaneously with its declaration, it is more difficult to get a library that is missing the implementation of some member function. It is also more difficult to use files that are not in sync with the implementation.

Java Has No Stand-alone Functions

Something C++ programmers will need to get used to is that Java has no stand-alone functions. Java is first and foremost an object-oriented programming language. In Java, all Java applications are objects and all Java classes are derived from the primitive class Object.

Some Java Programs Have No `main` Function

Some Java programs, called applets, do not need a main function. However, each Java class may have a main method, and all Java applications include the equivalent of the main function. When a stand-alone application is executed, the main method is implemented and this is how parameters are passed into the application. When an applet is executed, initialization and start methods are implemented.

Java Has No Templates

In C++ you can write generic methods called *templates* that allow you to write one block of code that describes an implementation for several similar types of arguments. This enables you to create a method that accepts both integer and floating-point values, which saves you from having to write two methods that do essentially the same thing. You can also use templates to automatically generate classes, and that capability is a big plus.

Although Java's use of the `Object` class as the parent for all other classes could be construed as an implementation of templates, there is no functional equivalent of C++ templates in Java. Because of this, you would have to have separate methods for similar-type arguments. However, you can generally reuse methods simply by cutting, pasting, and making minor modifications as necessary.

Java Has Exception Handling

Error conditions that are not expected to occur under normal conditions are called *exceptions*. When an exception occurs, bad things happen. For example, a negative number is passed to a function that computes the square root of a number. The function expects all numbers it receives to be positive real numbers. It receives a negative number instead, and an exception occurs. Sometimes programs die right then and there; other times they do more insidious things, such as passing incorrect pointers that eventually access protected areas of the system.

Although there is no definitive way to handle exceptions in C++, many bleary-eyed C++ programmers will be happy to know that exceptions are a fundamental part of the Java programming language. In Java, if you call a method that could throw an exception, you must check to see if any of the possible exceptions occurred and handle them. Additionally, the Java compiler checks for exception handling and will tell you if you have not handled the exceptions for a particular method. As you will see in Chapter 8, "Tying It All Together: Threads, Exceptions, and More," building exception handling into your methods is easy. It also avoids yet another problem area in C/C++ programming.

Java Has Automated Garbage Collection

Keeping track of which chunks of memory are in use and which are not is a major headache in C++. Many C++ classes use destructors to free up chunks of memory that are no longer needed, but this does not always work. If you delete objects that are still in use, the program will crash. If you forget to delete objects that are no longer in use, the program will crash when your system runs out of memory. If you point to the wrong area of memory, you can overwrite essential data and crash the program.

Java avoids memory-related problems by automating garbage collection. To do this, the Java runtime environment tracks which chunks of memory are in use and which aren't. When a chunk of memory is no longer needed, the system automatically clears it. When a chunk of memory is needed, the system automatically allocates it.

As a result, you no longer have to worry about freeing memory when it's no longer in use. However, Java does not eliminate the need for destructors completely. You still might need destructors for certain classes, especially when you want to ensure that a process cleans up gracefully after it is terminated. Fortunately, Java provides an easy way to clean up processes gracefully using a finalize method. The `finalize` method can be used like a C++ destructor to do final cleanup on an object before garbage collection occurs. (See the section titled "The `finalize` Method," in Chapter 7, "Building Objects," for more information.)

Summary

The Java Developer's Kit contains everything you need to get started creating hot new Java applications. Versions of the JDK are currently available for Windows 95/NT, Macintosh, OS/2, and most UNIX platforms including Solaris and AIX. By installing the JDK on your system, you create a developer's environment complete with essential tools and precompiled code. For current C/C++ programmers, installing the JDK on your system is only the first step toward getting started. The next step is to review the differences between Java and C/C++, so you know exactly what you can and cannot do in the Java programming language.

II

Power
Primers

3

The Java Browser and the World Wide Web: A Primer

The Web is a powerful interface to everything the Internet has to offer. A few years ago, when people thought of the Internet, they equated it with the monotony of low-level protocols like FTP and Telnet. Today, when most people think of the Internet, they think of the dynamic environment that enables them to search through and access complex "webs" of text, graphics, sound, and video. In short, they equate the Web with the Internet—and that's because the Web has swallowed the Net.

Navigating the World Wide Web

 Navigating the Web can be as easy as activating a hypertext link. The power of hypertext is in its simplicity and transparency. Users can navigate through a global network of resources at the touch of a button. Hypertext documents are linked together through keywords or specified *hot areas* within the document. These hot areas could be graphical icons or even parts of indexed maps.

When a new word or idea is introduced, hypertext makes it possible to jump to another document containing complete information on the new topic. Readers see links as highlighted keywords or images displayed graphically. They can access additional documents or resources by selecting the highlighted keywords or images.

To look through hypertext documents, you need a browser. A *browser* is a software application that enables you to access the World Wide Web. When a hypertext document is loaded in your browser, you can activate a link by moving your mouse pointer to the area of the link and clicking the left mouse button.

Generally, text containing a hypertext link is underlined and displayed in a different color than other text on the page. By default, most browsers display links that you have not visited in blue and links that you have visited in purple or light red.

As you point-and-click your way through the Web, you probably do not think about the URLs you are using to access Web resources. However, if you plan to display Java applets on the Web, you should stop and think about the URLs you use. When you move your mouse pointer over a link, most browsers display the URL path to the file or object that will be retrieved when you activate the link. This is useful for identifying the type of file referenced by the link.

Most Web documents written in the *Hypertext Markup Language* (HTML) have the `.htm` or `.html` extension. For example, the URL path `http://www.tvp.com/idn/idnframe.html` tells the browser to use the *Hypertext Transfer Protocol* (HTTP) to obtain a file called `idnframe.html` in the `idn` directory on the `www.tvp.com` Web server.

Although following text-based links on Web pages is easy, following links embedded in graphic objects sometimes isn't. Some clickable images are displayed on the page with a distinctive blue border—this type is easy to identify. Other clickable images, however, have no borders around them at all, primarily because that Web publisher chose to use the extensions to HTML that enable the suppression of the border around images. So, how do you know when an image is clickable and when it is not if it has no distinct border?

One way to tell if the image is clickable is to move your mouse pointer over the image. If your browser shows that a URL (pronounced "you-are-el") path is associated with the image, you can click on it. Most images used on the Web are in either GIF or JPEG format. GIF images usually have a `.gif` extension. JPEG images usually have a `.jpg` or `.jpeg` extension. For example, the URL

```
http://www.tvpress.com/idn/idnttl.gif
```

tells the browser to use the hypertext transfer protocol to obtain a GIF image called `idnttl.gif` in the `idn` directory on the `www.tvpress.com` Web server.

URLs are much more powerful and complex than these simple examples suggest. The next section takes a closer look at the structure of URLs and how they are used on the Web.

Using URLs

Uniform resource locators (URLs) provide a uniform way of identifying resources that are available using Internet protocols. To better understand URLs, you should learn how they are defined and the formats for them.

How URLs Are Defined

URLs consist of characters defined by the ASCII character set. The URL specification allows for the use of uppercase and lowercase letters, but uppercase letters are generally not used. Not using uppercase letters avoids confusion when moving documents from a system that is case sensitive to one that isn't and vice versa.

Although URLs consist of characters defined by the ASCII character set, you cannot use all ASCII characters in your URLs. You can use the letters a–z, the numerals 0–9, and a few special characters. The special characters include asterisks, commas, dollar signs, exclamation points, hyphens, parentheses, periods, plus signs, single quotation marks, and underscores. You are limited to these special characters because other characters used in URLs have specific meanings. For example, the tilde character is used to map URLs to HTML directories in a user's home directory.

Note: A detailed look at URL formats, syntax, and reserved characters is beyond the scope of this book. For an authoritative plain-English look at URLs, I recommend *Web Publishing Unleashed* from Sams.net. Chapter 3, "Publishers' Tour of the Web," covers everything Web publishers should know about URLs.

URL Formats

The basic mechanism that makes URLs so versatile is their standard naming scheme. URL schemes name the protocol the client will use to access and transfer a particular file. Web clients use the name of the protocol to determine the format for the information that follows the protocol name. The protocol name is generally followed by a colon and two forward slashes (`//`). The colon is a separator. The double forward slash marks indicate that the protocol uses the format defined by the Common Internet Scheme Syntax.

The *Common Internet Scheme Syntax* is a common syntax for URL schemes that involve the direct use of Internet Protocol–based protocols. *IP-based protocols* specify a particular host on the Internet by a unique numeric identifier called an *IP address* or by a unique name that can be resolved to the IP address. The information following the double slash marks follows a format that is dependent on the protocol type referenced in the URL. Here are two general formats:

```
protocol://hostname:port/path_to_resource
```

```
protocol://username:password@hostname:port/path_to_resource
```

Hostname information used in URLs identifies the address to a host and is broken down into two or more parts separated by periods. The periods are used to separate domain information from the hostname. Common domain names for Web servers begin with www (for example, `www.tvp.com` identifies the Web server called `tvp` in the `commercial` domain).

Ports are rather like telephone jacks on the Web server. The server has certain ports allocated for certain things, such as port 80 for your incoming requests for hypertext documents. The server listens on a particular port. When it hears something, it—in essence—picks up the phone and connects the particular port.

Port information used in URLs identifies the port number to be used for the connection. If you do not specify a port number, a default value is used by your browser as necessary. Therefore, you do not have to specify port numbers in your URLs unless the connection will be made to a port other than the default.

By specifying the username and password information in a URL, you allow users to log into a system automatically. The two protocols that use both username and password information are FTP and Telnet. In an FTP session, the username and password information is often used to allow users to log into FTP servers anonymously. When a connection is made to an FTP server and the username and password information is not specified, the following default values are assumed: anonymous or guest for the username and the user's e-mail address as the password.

In Telnet, there are no default values. If you do not supply the username and password, the user will be prompted for this information, which is good because you don't want everyone to be able to remotely log into your server. You could allow users to log in automatically by specifying a user and password in your URL. However, you generally do not want to specify a personal password in a URL.

Therefore, if you want users to be able to log in automatically using Telnet, you should create a guest account with a generic password. In this way, you can strictly control the access guests have on your system.

The final part of a URL is the path to the resource. This path generally follows the directory structure from the root or slash directory to the resource specified in the URL.

Web Surfing with Java-Enhanced Browsers

Browsers are available for use on almost any computer operating system, including Amiga, Macintosh, OS/2, Windows 3.1, Windows 95/NT, and UNIX. You can think of a browser as your window to the Web; if you change your browser, you get a whole new view of what's out there. Use Lynx, and your window to the Web has only text. Text-only browsers are the original browsers for the Web. Although it might be hard to believe, several text-only browsers are still being developed.

Use NCSA Mosaic, and your window to the Web has text and graphics. Browsers that allow you to view Web documents containing text and graphics are the second generation of browsers, which are largely responsible for the phenomenal success of the Web.

Use HotJava, and your window has text, graphics, and live animation. Browsers that allow you to view Web documents containing text, graphics, inline multimedia, and live applications are the third generation of browsers that are driving the Web's transition to an extremely visual medium that rivals television for information content and entertainment value.

HotJava

The HotJava browser, developed by Sun Microsystems, Inc., is written entirely in Java. As the first browser to support Java applets, HotJava is extremely popular. Although the Alpha version of HotJava supports only Java Alpha, more recent versions of the browser support the 1.0 API. Versions of the browser are available for Macintosh, Windows 95/NT, and Sun Solaris.

Although HotJava is popular, it is not feature rich like some of the other Java-enhanced browsers; it has a rather plain interface and limited extras. Still, HotJava is currently in the testing stages and may yet evolve into a full-featured browser.

Figure 3.1 shows JavaSoft's HotJava page. To learn more about HotJava and to download an evaluation version, visit JavaSoft at the URL `http://www.javasoft.com/java.sun.com/HotJava/index.html`.

Figure 3.1.
JavaSoft's HotJava page.

Netscape Navigator

The Netscape Navigator is the most widely used Web browser; versions of it are available for Macintosh, Windows, and UNIX X Window systems. Driven by Netscape's rise as a commercial corporation worth hundreds of millions of dollars, all of Netscape's products are shifting to a commercial model. However, you can download free versions of Netscape Navigator at the Netscape Web site. Netscape's Web site is shown in Figure 3.2. The URL to this site is

```
http://home.netscape.com/
```

Figure 3.2.
Web surfing with Netscape Navigator.

Not only does Navigator support Java, but it is undoubtedly the most feature-rich browser available today. It supports HTML 3.0, plug-ins, JavaScript, and unique Netscape extensions to HTML, such as frames. With HTML 3.0, you get support for tables, figures, and all the advanced features of HTML. Plug-ins allow you to add modules for inline video, sound, and multimedia. JavaScript, a scripting language modeled after Java, enables you to do client-side scripting.

Before you download the Navigator, keep in mind that only versions 2.0 and later support Java. Furthermore, although Netscape Navigator is available for a wide variety of platforms, Java support is limited to those platforms to which the JDK has been ported.

Oracle PowerBrowser

PowerBrowser is everything you would expect in a browser created by the database giant Oracle. The PowerBrowser software package includes a local database called Blaze, which enables you store and manage large amounts of data efficiently. The browser also supports HTML 3.0 and extensions to the HTML standard including backgrounds, tables, embedded objects, and Java. Developers versions of Oracle PowerBrowser for Windows 95 are available free of charge for evaluation.

Figure 3.3 shows Oracle's site on the Web at `http://www.oracle.com/`. To learn more about PowerBrowser and download the free Beta, visit this site.

Figure 3.3.
Learning about the Oracle PowerBrowser.

Internet Explorer

One of the most powerful browsers currently available is the Internet Explorer from Microsoft. This full-featured browser took the Web by storm in 1995 and quickly moved to the number-two position in popularity. Versions of Internet Explorer are available for Macintosh, Windows 95, and Windows NT.

Internet Explorer supports HTML 3; all Netscape extensions; and powerful multimedia extensions including background sounds, scrolling marquees, and inline video movies. Versions 3.0 and later also feature support for Java, ActiveX controls, and VBScript. With the release of the Internet Explorer VR extension that enables full VRML capability, Internet Explorer is definitely the browser to watch. Microsoft is also developing an enhanced version of VRML called ActiveVRML, with which you can create animated VRML worlds that take advantage of Java.

Figure 3.4 shows the Internet Explorer home page at Microsoft. The URL for the Internet Explorer home page is `http://www.microsoft.com/ie/default.htm`. From this page, you can access the most current version of the browser and obtain upgrade modules like Internet Explorer VR.

Figure 3.4.
Learning about Internet Explorer.

Liquid Reality

Like Internet Explorer VR, Liquid Reality is a VRML add-on module for Web browsers. Because Liquid Reality supports the integration of Java and VRML, you can use Liquid Reality to view Java-enhanced VRML worlds that are rich in interaction and animation. Versions of Liquid Reality are available for Windows 95/NT and Sun Solaris.

Figure 3.5 shows the Liquid Reality page at Dimension X's Web site. This page can be found at the URL `http://www.dimensionx.com/products/lr/index.html`. From this page, you can access a wealth of information about Liquid Reality and upcoming enhancements.

Figure 3.5.
Liquid Reality: the marriage of Java and VRML.

Web Hot Spots for Java Developers

As you explore the Web in search of Java resources, you will quickly discover that Java is the most talked-about programming language on the Web. No other programming language has as many entire sites devoted to it. No other programming language has repositories that list almost everything that's ever been done in the language. No other programming language has attracted the fanfare Java has attracted.

> **Tip:** If you want to actively join in the Java revolution using a newsgroup, the newsgroup you want to look at is `comp.lang.java`, which is a terrific resource for the Java developer community. When you visit the newsgroup, watch the goings on for a few days before participating. This will help you understand the style of the newsgroup.

Sun's Web Site

Java was conceived by Sun Microsystems, so it seems fitting that your tour of Web hot spots begins with Sun's Web site at `http://www.sun.com/`. Sun maintains one of the top sites on the Web for information relating to client/server computing. The site is largely organized around Sun's monthly magazine, *SunWorld*, with cover stories, features, and much more.

Figure 3.6 shows Sun's Web site. As you can see, it features a polished and easy-to-use interface that leads directly to the online edition of *SunWorld*. Although the issues covered in SunWorld relate mostly to client/server computing, this is also a good place to find Java-related articles and industry news. Currently, SunWorld is provided free of charge to online readers.

Figure 3.6.
Sun Microsystems's Web site.

JavaSoft

JavaSoft's Web site is the best place on the Web to find Java-related information. Figure 3.7 shows JavaSoft's main page at `http://www.javasoft.com/`. All the images on the page are hot links to key areas of the site. As a Java developer, the places you will want to visit often are the What's New? page, the Developers Corner page, and the HotJava Browser page.

The What's New? page is where you will find the latest industry news, including same-day press releases. The Developers Corner page provides the best access to the Java Developer's Kit, full documentation for developers, and extensions to the API (for example, the Java Database Connectivity API). The HotJava Browser page provides information on the latest release of HotJava and allows you to download the browser as well.

Figure 3.7.
JavaSoft's Web site.

Gamelan

The Gamelan Web site is officially sanctioned by JavaSoft as the repository of Java resources. Gamelan is unlike any other software repository on the Web and can be likened to Yahoo for its pioneering efforts in cataloging networked information.

> **Note:** Yahoo was one of the first catalog sites on the Web, and this helped it gain name-brand recognition with Web surfers worldwide. Today, despite the fact that there are better catalog sites, Yahoo continues to be one of the most popular catalogs of the Internet.

In the early days, Gamelan was nothing more than a long list of Java resources. Gamelan has since transformed itself into the definitive place on the Web to find everything and anything related to Java—no other programming language in existence has such a wealth of information about it collected in one place.

At the site shown in Figure 3.8, you will find a list of thousands of applets and applications programmed in Java and where they can be found on the Web. You will find a What's New listing of new Java-related resources. You will find a Who's Who list for Java programmers that allows you to tout your skills to the world. You will also find a What's Cool listing of the Java-related resources that are frequently visited from the Gamelan site. The URL to the Gamelan site is

```
http://www.gamelan.com/
```

Figure 3.8.
*Gamelan: A repository of
Java resources.*

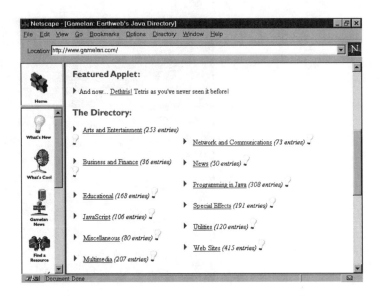

JARS

Although the *Java Applet Reviewing Service* (JARS) is a relative newcomer to the Web, it is my favorite for finding recent innovations in Java applet programming. Figure 3.9 shows the JARS Web site. As the name implies, JARS provides ratings for Java applets that are available on the Web. The top applets rated in any given time period are given awards in the following categories:

Top 1% Web Applet
Top 5% Web Applet
Top 25% Web Applet
Top 10 Web Applet
Top 100 Web Applet

You can search through listings of the top applets directly, by category, or by keyword. You can also find detailed reviews of applets and Java-powered Web pages that have been given the Judge's Pick award. The URL to the Java Applet Reviewing Service site is `http://www.jars.com/`.

Figure 3.9.
JARS: Rating Java applets.

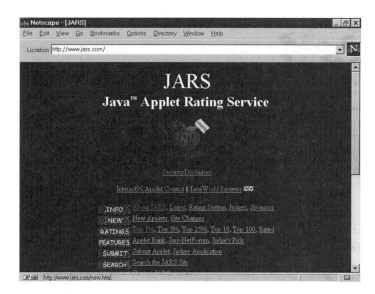

Third-Party Java Tools

Lots of third-party development tools are available for Java. This section focuses on the best of these tools. The speed with which industry giants, like Borland and Symantec, introduced Java development tools speaks volumes about Java's popularity and potential.

Borland C++ for Java Developers

Borland C++ for Java developers is a cutting-edge development environment for C/C++ and Java. To ease the transition for current C/C++ and Java programmers, Borland integrated its award-winning C++ development environment with Sun's Java Developer's Kit. The result is a graphical development environment that allows you to develop, test, and debug your applications without ever having to use command-line tools.

You can learn more about Borland C++ for Java developers by visiting Borland's Web site at

```
http://www.borland.com
```

Figure 3.10 shows a page at the Borland Web site dedicated to Borland C++ for Java developers. Key tools in the developer's kit include the following:

- Project Manager for Java—Helps you to organize C/C++ and Java source code and to track file dependencies.

- AppAccelerator—A just-in-time compiler for Java that compiles Java code to native code on the fly and increases the performance of Java applications by 5 to 10 times, compared to interpreted Java code.

- AppExpert for Java—Helps you get a fast start on Java projects by generating a custom application based on options you select.

- TargetExpert for Java—Helps with the build process.

Figure 3.10.
Borland C++ for Java developers.

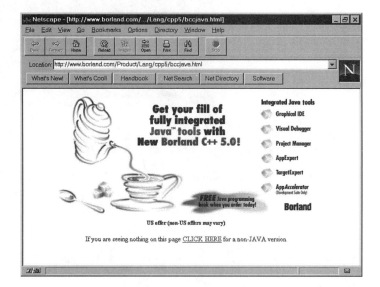

Symantec Café

Symantec Café is an integrated development environment for Java developers who use Windows 95/NT or the Power Mac. Like Borland C++, Symantec Café uses the tools in Sun's Java Developer's Kit as the basis for its graphical development environment. In fact, Café includes the entire release version of the JDK, which provides the Java class library source code and samples.

The integrated environment within which the program operates is called the Café Desktop. The desktop is a customizable interface to all the tools in Symantec Café. Because Café Desktop supports virtual desktop environments, you can access multiple viewing areas at the press of a button. You can learn more about Symantec Café by visiting the Web site shown in Figure 3.11. The URL to this site is http://www.symantec.com/.

Figure 3.11.
Symantec Café: An integrated development environment.

Symantec Espresso and Symantec Caffeine

Symantec Caffeine is a scaled-down version of Symantec Café for Java developers who use a Power Macintosh. As the first development environment for the Macintosh, Symantec Caffeine has a lot going for it. It provides a full-featured project-management system and powerful editing tools that boost productivity. To learn more about Symantec Caffeine, visit Symantec's Web site, shown in Figure 3.12, at the following URL:

```
http://cafe.symantec.com/caffeine/overview.html
```

Figure 3.12.
Symantec's Web site.

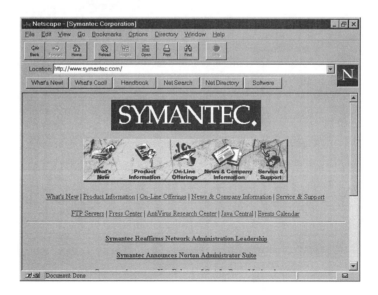

Symantec Espresso is a scaled-down version of Symantec Café for Java developers who use Windows 95/NT. It also provides a fully featured project-management system and powerful editing tools that will boost your productivity. You can learn more about Symantec Espresso at Symantec's Web site as well.

Rogue Wave's JFactory

JFactory by Rogue Wave is a graphical development environment designed to speed up the development process. The JFactory home page is shown in Figure 3.13. When you visit Rogue Wave, you should start on the company home page at `http://www.roguewave.com/`.

Figure 3.13.
JFactory on the Web.

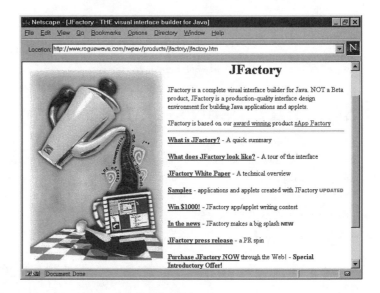

Visual application building and a core set of classes that extend the Java API are what make rapid development in JFactory possible. Although JFactory is limited in functionality as compared to Borland C++ for Java and Symantec Café, it offers a solid development environment without taxing your system. Figure 3.14 shows a sample session in JFactory.

Figure 3.14.
Rogue Wave's JFactory in action.

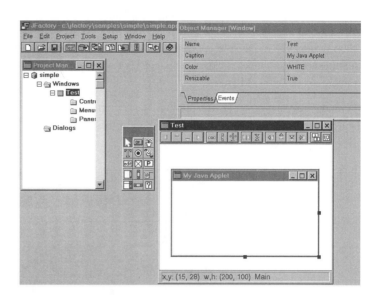

SunSoft's Java Workshop

Java Workshop is the kind of quality product you would expect SunSoft to produce. Figure 3.15 shows the area of Sun's Web site dedicated to Java Workshop at

`http://www.sun.com:80/sunsoft/Developer-products/java/Workshop/`

Figure 3.15.
Java Workshop on the Web.

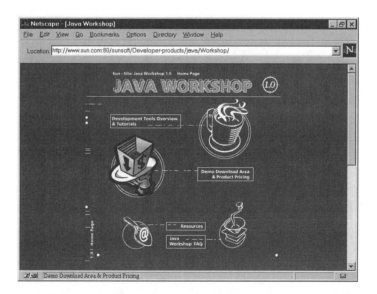

With the entire graphical development environment placed within a Webified desktop, Java Work-shop is as easy to use as your favorite Web browser and, like your Web browser, all the most-used features are accessible by clicking on an icon. A key feature is the extensive online help that is completely written in HTML format.

For more information on Java Workshop, see Chapter 5, "Java Tools and the JDK: A Primer." You will find an in-depth look at Java Workshop in the section called "Java Workshop: A Graphical Development Toolkit." Figure 3.16 shows Java Workshop's startup window.

Figure 3.16.
Java Workshop in action.

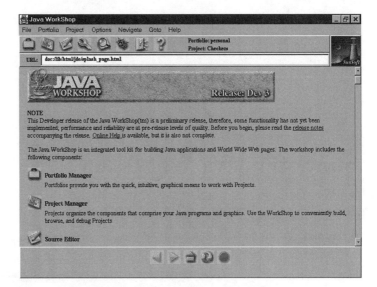

A Brief Tour of Live Applets on the Web

The best way to see applets is live on the Web. I hope that after reading this chapter and getting a look at what is possible with Java, you will get out your Web browser and join the millions of other Web surfers in search of the ultimate applet.

Dimension X Café

Dimension X is an outpost in cyberspace for cutting-edge products. One of these products is the Dimension X Café, where you can talk to other cybersurfers live and in real time. Figure 3.17 shows the beginning of a live chat with Dimension X Café. You can access the live chat area from this page at Dimension X: `http://www.dimensionx.com/products/cafe/index.html`.

Figure 3.17.
Live chat in the Dimension X Café.

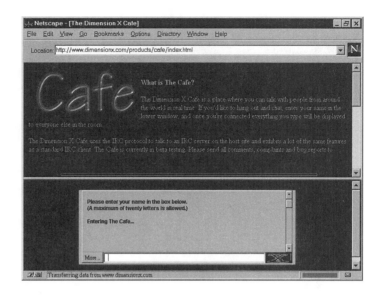

Although the Café has a long way to go before it can be declared the ultimate applet, it certainly is a start on one. By visiting any of the dozens of cybercafés, you can glimpse the Web of the future, where Web surfers will be immersed in real-time interaction.

WallStreetWeb

The WallStreetWeb applet is shown in Figure 3.18. Not only can the WallStreetWeb applet help you keep tabs on the stock market in real time—it also allows you to track a stock's history and trends at a glance while keeping pace with current data. This applet hints at what is to come as applets with real-time streaming become a part of everyday life on the Web.

To see the WallStreetWeb in action, visit BulletProof's Web site at the following URL:

```
http://www.bulletproof.com/WallStreetWeb/
```

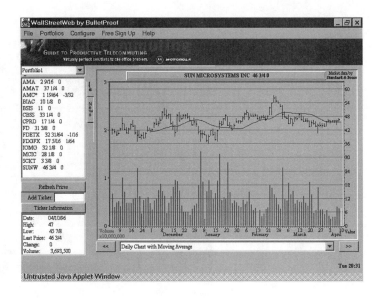

Figure 3.18.
Tracking the stock market with WallStreetWeb.

Celebrity Painter

The Celebrity Painter applet, shown in Figure 3.19, is a paint program with a twist. Instead of painting in a specific color, your brush paints with a palette based on a celebrity's picture. This allows you to paint in the hair of one celebrity, the eyes of another celebrity, the nose of another celebrity, and so on for some really comical masterpieces.

To see Celebrity Painter in action, visit the following home page:

```
http://www.demonsys.com/jorkin/CelebrityPainter
```

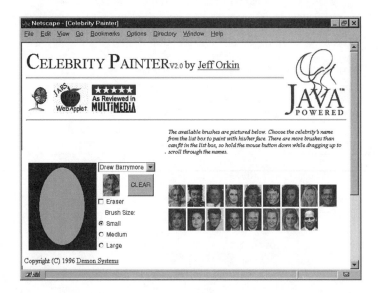

Figure 3.19.
Just having fun with Celebrity Painter.

DigSim

The DigSim applet, shown in Figure 3.20, is an advanced applet for creating digital simulations based on a set of schematics you can build right in the applet. Although downloading the applet to your system will take several minutes at best, DigSim is well worth the wait if only because every aspect of this feature-rich applet is well thought out and presented.

To see DigSim in action, visit the following home page:

`http://www.lookup.com/Homepages/96457/digsim/index.html`

Alternately, you can use this page: `http://www.lookup.com/Homepages/96457/digsim/load.html`.

Figure 3.20.
Advanced simulation with DigSim.

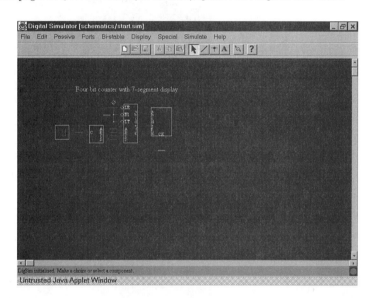

3D Netris

3D Netris from Earth Web is one of a growing number of game applets. (See Figure 3.21.) To say that Web surfers are fascinated by game applets would be an understatement—sites that feature game applets are some of the most visited on the Web.

To see 3D Netris in action, visit Earth Web's site at the following URL:

`http://www.earthweb.com/java/Netris/`

Figure 3.21.
Earth Web's 3D Netris.

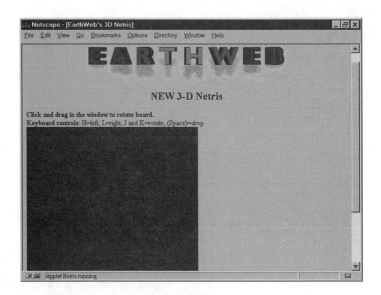

SGI Java-Powered Home Page

SGI's Java-powered home page is a joy to visit. The most recent version of the home page at

`http://www.sgi.com/`

contains applets that are used to create menus that activate when you move your mouse over them. As you can see from Figure 3.22, the globes on the left side of the page display submenus. What you cannot see is that the constellation of stars at the top of the screen turn into white dwarfs and that the control buttons at the bottom of the screen glow.

Figure 3.22.
SGI's hot Java-powered home page.

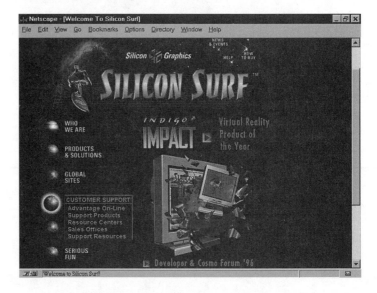

> **Note:** The SGI Web site is also a good place to find information about advanced graphics development and SGI's high-performance workstations.

SportsZone

Another hot Java-powered home page is maintained by ESPNET SportsZone. (See Figure 3.23.) One of the best Java enhancements is the live sports ticker applet called ScorePost. This applet lets you see the latest scores and has an interface that allows you to customize the way the scores look.

Figure 3.23.
ESPNET SportsZone on the Web.

A feature attraction at SportsZone is the Fantasy sports games programmed in Java. Because it was baseball season when I visited SportsZone, the Fantasy Baseball applet was available to create my dream team. This applet is shown in Figure 3.24. If you want to play fantasy baseball, visit SportsZone. I hope it will continue to provide access to the free demos long into the future.

When you visit SportsZone on the Web, you should start at `http://espnet.sportszone.com/`.

Figure 3.24.
The ultimate fantasy baseball game.

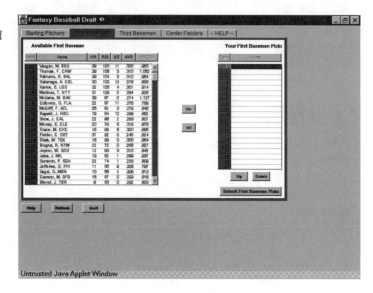

Summary

As you start on the journey to become a successful Java developer, you should visit the sites featured in this chapter. The Web has a wealth of Java-related resources to visit, study, and learn from. Navigating the Web is easy if you understand the principles of hypertext linking and URLs. Although hypertext references can be text or graphics based, they are all defined by URLs that specify the path to the resources to be accessed and retrieved. Because the Web provides a common interface to the Internet, you can use any Internet protocol to access and retrieve Web resources.

4

The Java Language: A Primer

After racing through cyberspace in Chapter 3, "The Java Browser and the World Wide Web: A Primer," you are probably ready for some hands-on experience with Java. Now you are going to dive right in to a primer for the Java programming language. The power of Java is that even the most basic Java programs can feature multimedia. This is primarily because the fundamentals of the Java programming language are easy to learn and use.

These fundamentals apply both to applets for use on the World Wide Web and to stand-alone applications. In this chapter, you create your first stand-alone application and your first applet. To show you how easy Java programming can be, one of these programs will use the built-in multimedia features of the language.

Don't worry—I'll stick to the basics. Even the most basic Java programs are useful in demonstrating the structure of Java programs. As you examine this structure, you will be able to see how classes, methods, and objects are used in Java programs.

Creating Your First Stand-alone Java Application

As long as the Java developer's environment is installed on your computer as discussed in Chapter 2, "Getting Started with the JDK," you are ready to create your first stand-alone application. To follow the examples in this section, you will need the Java compiler and the Java interpreter.

The Basic Structure of a Stand-alone Application

Your first Java program is a basic, stand-alone application called `FirstApp`. An important difference between Java applets and applications is the inclusion of a method called `main`. The `main` method is included in all Java applications.

Although all this simple application does is print the words "My first stand-alone application is a success," you will use this application as a stepping stone to more advanced programs and concepts. The great thing about Java is that all Java programs follow the same basic constructs. This is true no matter how complex or simple the program is.

The five-line application shown in Listing 4.1 is no different. It has all the features of more complex Java applications and all the features of an object-oriented program as well:

- It *is* an object
- It *uses* encapsulation and message passing

- It *defines* a class
- It *uses* inheritance
- It *uses* access modifiers

Listing 4.1. Your first Java application.

```java
class FirstApp {
    public static void main (String args[]) {
        System.out.println("My first stand-alone application is a success.");
    }
}
```

To understand how this simple five-line application uses five of the key object-oriented programming concepts, you can look at how these concepts relate to this application.

The Object and Encapsulation in `FirstApp`

Objects are the fundamental unit in object-oriented programming. All objects have a state and a behavior. Everything the object knows about its variables and methods describes its *state*. The actions an object can perform describe its *behavior*. The `FirstApp` program defines a single object that has

    A state that is unchanging or static

    A behavior that is to print out a statement

You can use objects to send messages to other objects without having to know how those objects work. This object-oriented programming concept is called *encapsulation*. In Java, objects, classes, and packages are all encapsulated.

Encapsulation allows you to use a Java object as long as you know what values the object will accept. The `FirstApp` program uses the concept of encapsulation to access a method called `println`. To use the `println` method, you do not have to know how it works. All you have to know is that if you pass the method a line of text, it will print the line of text to the screen.

Another thing you need to know to access an object is where it is in the namespace. Java allows you to access public methods and variables as long as you know where the methods and variables are in the namespace. The `println` method is one of dozens of methods in the `System` class. The `System` class is a part of the core Java language package of the *Application Programming Interface* (API).

Java knows how to find the `println` method because the path to the method is specified. Although you do not have to specify the full path to methods, the full path for the `println` method is

```
java.lang.System.out.println
```

You could translate this path into plain words. Here's how: `println` is a submethod of `out`, which is in the `System` class. The `System` class is a part of the `lang` package of the Java API.

Classes and Inheritance in `FirstApp`

In Java, classes encapsulate objects and serve to group a set of related methods and variables. Although most Java programs contain multiple class declarations, the `FirstApp` program has only one. This line of the `FirstApp` program declares it to be a class of objects called `FirstApp`:

```
class FirstApp {
```

Usually you will declare classes in Java using one of two general forms. The first general form of a class declaration is

```
class name {
        //body of class declaration
}
```

The second general form of a class declaration is

```
class name extends extendedclass {
        //body of class declaration
}
```

In both general forms, the open bracket signifies the beginning of the class and the close bracket signifies the ending of the class. Within the brackets, you define the methods and instance variables associated with the class.

You can extend all classes in Java with another class either implicitly or explicitly. By doing so, you can create a class that inherits the functionality of an existing class. This object-oriented programming concept is called *inheritance*. Inheritance allows you to reuse code and to extend the functionality of existing classes.

Like other Java classes that do not explicitly extend another class, the `FirstApp` class extends the `Object` class. By inheriting the functionality of the `Object` class, your programs can do many things that they otherwise would not be able to do. To put this in perspective, you could rewrite the first general form of class declarations as follows:

```
class name extends Object {
        //body of class declaration
}
```

Access Modifiers in `FirstApp`

In Java, access to methods and variables is controlled through *access modifiers*. The Java programming language defines four levels for access controls for methods and variables:

- Public   Accessible by any class without limitation
- Protected   Accessible only by methods in the same class or subclass
- Private   Accessible only by objects within the same class
- Default   Unless declared otherwise, assumed to be friendly or accessible by any class in the same package

The main method in `FirstApp` is declared to be public. This means the method is completely accessible to other methods and variables. Another program could access `FirstApp`'s `main` method by specifying the path to the method in Java's namespace.

Putting It All Together

Now that you have a basic understanding of how `FirstApp` uses object-oriented programming concepts, let's review the source code for `FirstApp` line by line.

The first line of the application declares the class as `FirstApp`. Because the declaration does not specify what class the application extends, by default `FirstApp` extends the `Object` class. The open bracket signifies the beginning of the `FirstApp` class:

```
class FirstApp {
```

The next line declares many things about a method called `main`:

```
public static void main (String args[]) {
```

You can break down the previous declarations item by item as follows:

public	The modifier `public` states that the method is accessible to other classes.
static	The modifier `static` states that the method is unchanging and implicitly final, meaning the method cannot be overridden.
void	The modifier `void` states that the method does not return a value.
main()	The word `main` specifies the `main` method for the application. Arguments for the method are placed between the open and close parentheses. The `main()` method is required in Java applications to tell the interpreter where to start. `main`, unlike `main()` in C/C++, does not return a value. Java handles its exceptions internally rather than sending them back to the system.
(String args[])	This specifies that the `main` method takes an argument that is an object of `String`.
{	The open bracket signifies the beginning of the method.

The next statement calls the `println` method of the `System` class and prints the sentence "My first stand-alone application is a success." As with other methods, the arguments to pass to the method are declared between open and close parentheses. Each statement in Java ends in a semicolon:

```
System.out.println("My first stand-alone application is a success.");
```

The final two lines of the `FirstApp` program are close brackets. The first close bracket completes the block of code associated with the `main()` method. The second close bracket completes the block of code associated with the `FirstApp` class.

Creating **FirstApp**

Now that you know what the `FirstApp` program looks like, you can create the program on your computer. Before you do this, there are two things you need to do:

1. Decide where on your file system you want to place your applications
2. Create an appropriately named file

Creating a File System Structure for Applications

When you installed the Java Developer's Kit on your system, you created a directory or folder to hold the files used by Java. Although you could store your personal Java applications in this directory, you might want to store them elsewhere so you can easily differentiate between the original programs and the ones you will create.

Peter's Principle: A good place to store your applications and all associated files might be in a directory called `java_apps`. You will find that the easier it is to get to the directory, the better—therefore, you should not place this directory too many levels deep in your directory structure. Depending on the complexity of your applications, you might want to create a separate subdirectory for each application.

For complex or multipart applications, storing each application in a separate subdirectory makes sense. If you searched through the files and directories you created when you installed the JDK, you saw that the demo applets included with the JDK are stored in separate subdirectories. In the base subdirectory for each applet, you will find the source code, the compiled code, and an HTML document used in displaying the applet. Usually, you will find additional directories for sound and image files associated with the applet as well.

Naming the Source File for the Application

After you have decided where you want to place your application and have created directories if necessary, you can create the source code for the application. Whenever you create source code files for Java, you must remember three rules:

- Java requires you to create source code files with the .java extension.
- Java requires that the source code file use the name of the primary or first class declaration.
- Regardless of whether your computer's operating system is case sensitive, the Java compiler is case sensitive, and your filenames must match the primary class name exactly.

Following these naming rules, you must store the FirstApp program in a file called FirstApp.java. Although you can use your favorite text editor or word processor to create this file, you must save the file as standard ASCII text. For the sake of simplicity and ease of use, many programmers prefer to use basic text editors as opposed to word processors. On UNIX systems, you can use a command-line editor such as vi or emacs. On Windows 95/NT systems, you can use the MS-DOS editor or the Windows Notepad. On Macintosh systems, you can use BBEdit or Simple Text.

After you finish entering the source code, you should check it line by line for accuracy. When you are sure the source code is accurate, save it to the directory you have designated for your applications.

Compiling **FirstApp**

To compile the application, you will use the Java compiler javac. When you compile the source, the Java compiler creates a separate file for each class in your program. If an application has more than one class file, you should always invoke the Java interpreter with the name of the class containing the main method. Because there is only one class declaration in FirstApp, the Java compiler will create only one class file.

Although compiling applications on the Macintosh is as easy as dragging the FirstApp.java file onto the compiler, other system owners should not be too envious. On other systems, javac is a command-line program. Because the command line offers a simplified interface and streamlined design, the version of javac for UNIX, Windows 95/NT, and OS/2 is actually much more versatile.

> **Looking Ahead:** If you like the ease of use associated with graphical tools and use a Windows-based or UNIX system, don't worry. Graphical tools for Java on all systems is something that is already here. Several third-party vendors have created compilers and interpreters that let you use graphical development environments. For more information on graphical development tools, see Chapter 5, "Java Tools and the JDK: A Primer."

Using a Graphical Compiler

Here are the steps you should use to compile FirstApp using a graphical compiler:

1. Drop the FirstApp.java file onto the compiler or select Open from the compiler's File menu.

2. The compiled output file, called FirstApp.class, is placed in the same directory as the source.

3. If an error window pops up, make sure you have typed the source correctly in the FirstApp.java file. If after correcting your mistakes you still cannot get the file to compile, refer to the section titled "Troubleshooting" at the end of this chapter.

Using a Command-Line Compiler

Here are the steps you should use to compile FirstApp using a command-line compiler:

1. Change to the directory containing the source code and type the following at the command prompt:

```
javac FirstApp.java
```

2. The compiled output file, called FirstApp.class, is placed in the same directory as the source.

3. If you get an error stating that the system cannot find javac, your path is not set up correctly. You will have to set your path correctly or type the full path to the compiler. If errors pertaining to the source code are listed to the command area, make sure you have typed the source correctly in the FirstApp.java file. If after correcting your mistakes you still cannot get the file to compile, refer to the section "Troubleshooting" at the end of this chapter.

Running FirstApp

When you compile an application, the compiler creates a separate file for each class declaration. Because the FirstApp program contains only one class declaration, only one class file is created. You run applications using the Java interpreter, java. On the Macintosh, using the Java interpreter is as easy as dragging the FirstApp.class file onto the interpreter. On other systems, the Java interpreter is a command-line program that is invoked with the name of the class you want to run.

Using a Graphical Interpreter

Here's what you should do to run FirstApp using a graphical interpreter: Drop the FirstApp.class file onto the interpreter icon or select Open from the interpreter's File menu.

You should see the sentence My first stand-alone application is a success. Congratulations—your first stand-alone application *is* a success. If the interpreter issues any errors, ensure that you tried to run the file with the .class extension. If you still have problems, refer to the section "Trouble-shooting" at the end of this chapter.

Using a Command-Line Interpreter

Here's what you should to do run FirstApp using a command-line interpreter: Change to the directory containing the compiled file with the .class extension and type the following at the command prompt:

```
java FirstApp
```

You should see the sentence My first stand-alone application is a success. Congratulations—your first stand-alone application *is* a success. If the interpreter issues errors, ensure that you typed FirstApp correctly and did not include the .class extension. If you still have problems, refer to the section "Troubleshooting" at the end of this chapter.

Your First Java Applet

If the Java developer's environment is installed on your computer, as discussed in Chapter 2, you are ready to create your first applet. To follow the examples in this section, you will need the Java compiler and the Java applet viewer.

The Basic Structure of an Applet

Your first Java applet is more complex than your first stand-alone application, yet still uses the same basic constructs and the same object-oriented programming concepts. This applet, called FirstApplet, uses Java's built-in multimedia features to display an image and play a sound file.

Listing 4.2 shows the FirstApplet program. Although the program is 17 lines long, four of these lines are used simply to make the program more readable.

Listing 4.2. Your first Java applet.

```
import java.awt.*;
import java.applet.*;

public class FirstApplet extends Applet {
Image NewImage;

  public void init() {
      resize(400,400);
```

continues

Listing 4.2. continued

```
      NewImage = getImage(getCodeBase(),"New.gif");
  }

  public void paint(Graphics g) {
      g.drawImage(NewImage,0,0,this);
      play(getCodeBase(),"New.au");
  }

}
```

Let's review the source code for FirstApplet line by line.

import statements allow the applet to use methods and classes from other packages:

```
import java.awt.*;
import java.applet.*;
```

By default, all Java programs import the java.lang package, which provides the core functionality of the Java language. The asterisk in the last element of the import statement allows Java to import classes dynamically. Here, the classes from the java.awt package and the java.applet package are imported dynamically.

This line declares a class called FirstApplet that extends the Applet class:

```
public class FirstApplet extends Applet {
```

By extending the Applet class, FirstApplet inherits the functionality of that class. The open bracket signifies the beginning of the FirstApplet class.

This line initializes the variable NewImage and declares it to be of type Image. Here, NewImage is a placeholder for the image the applet will display:

```
Image NewImage;
```

This line declares a method called init that overrides the init method of the Applet class:

```
public void init() {
```

Applet's init method is overridden so you can resize the window before you display the image. The modifier public states that the method is accessible to other classes. The modifier void states that the method does not return a value. Normally the arguments a method accepts are placed between the open and close parentheses. Because the init method accepts no arguments, nothing is placed between the parentheses.

Using the resize method, you can resize the display area for the applet. Here, the display area is resized to 400×400 pixels:

```
resize(400,400);
```

After you have declared a variable of a certain type, you can use it. This line of code sets a value for NewImage:

```
NewImage = getImage(getCodeBase(),"New.gif");
```

The getImage method is used to do this. The first argument for getImage is actually a call to a method called getCodeBase, which returns the location of the base or current directory on your hard drive. The base directory is the directory containing the class file you are running. The second argument is the name of the image that can be found at the specified location.

This line declares a method called paint that overrides the paint method of the AWT package:

```
public void paint(Graphics g) {
```

This method is overridden so the applet can draw the image to a specific location. The modifier public states that the method is accessible to other classes. The modifier void states that the method does not return a value. When the paint method is called, it needs to be sent an object of class Graphics. Graphics is the abstract base class for all graphic objects. The element g is the specified Graphics window.

This line invokes the Graphics object g, which displays the image called NewImage:

```
g.drawImage(NewImage,0,0,this);
```

All the actual work is done by a method called drawImage. The drawImage method accepts arguments that tell it what image to display and where to display it. Here, NewImage will be displayed at the x,y coordinate 0,0. The final argument is called an *observer*. The purpose of the observer is to notify whether the image is completely displayed.

As the name implies, the method play is used to play audio files. The first argument for play is a call to the getCodeBase method, which returns the location of the base or current directory on your hard drive:

```
play(getCodeBase(),"New.au");
```

The *base directory* is the directory containing the class file you are running. The second argument is the name of the sound file that can be found at the specified location.

Creating the Applet

Now that you know what the FirstApplet program looks like, you can create the program on your computer. Before you do this, you need decide where on your file system you want to place your applets. Then you need to create an appropriately named file.

> **Tip:** A good place to store your applets and all associated files might be in a directory called `java_applets`. Depending on the complexity of your applets, you may want to create a separate subdirectory for each applet. For complex or multipart applets, storing each applet in a separate subdirectory makes sense.

When you have decided where you want to place your applet and have created directories if necessary, you can create the source code for the applet. Whenever you create source code files for Java, you must remember three rules:

- Java requires you to create source code files with the `.java` extension.
- Java requires that the source code file use the name of the primary or first class declaration.
- Regardless of whether your computer's operating system is case sensitive, the Java compiler is case sensitive, and your filenames must match the primary class name exactly.

Following these naming rules, you must store the `FirstApplet` program in a file called `FirstApplet.java`. You must also save the file as standard ASCII text. After you finish entering the source code, you should check it line by line for accuracy. When you are sure the source code is accurate, you should save it to the directory you have designated for your applets.

Compiling `FirstApplet`

Compiling an applet is exactly the same as compiling an application. To compile the applet, you will use the Java compiler, `javac`. When you compile the source, the Java compiler creates a separate file for each class in your program. If an applet has more than one class file, you should always invoke the Java interpreter with the name of the class containing the primary method. Because there is only one class declaration in `FirstApplet`, the Java compiler will create only one class file.

Using a Graphical Compiler

Here are the steps you should use to compile `FirstApplet` using a graphical compiler:

1. Drop the `FirstApplet.java` file onto the compiler or select Open from the compiler's File menu.
2. The compiled output file called `FirstApplet.class` is placed in the same directory as the source.

3. If an error window pops up, make sure you have typed the source correctly in the `FirstApplet.java` file. If after correcting your mistakes you still cannot get the file to compile, refer to the section "Troubleshooting" at the end of this chapter.

Using a Command-Line Compiler

Here are the steps you should use to compile `FirstApplet` using a command-line compiler:

1. Change to the directory containing the source code and type the following at the command prompt:

   ```
   javac FirstApplet.java
   ```

2. The compiled output file called `FirstApplet.class` is placed in the same directory as the source.

3. If you get an error stating that the system cannot find `javac`, your path is not set up correctly. You will have to set your path correctly or type the full path to the compiler. If errors pertaining to the source code are listed to the command area, make sure you have typed the source correctly in the `FirstApplet.java` file. If after correcting your mistakes you still cannot get the file to compile, refer to the section "Troubleshooting" at the end of this chapter.

Creating an HTML File for Your Applet

Because applets are made for viewing with hypertext viewers such as Web browsers, you must create an HTML document before you can use an applet. Within the HTML document, you use a markup tag called `APPLET` to load and run the specified applet. In the `<APPLET>` tag, you refer to Java classes and not to the files containing the class that ends in the `.class` extension. The example HTML document contains an `<APPLET>` tag that refers to the `FirstApplet` class and not to the file named `FirstApplet.class`.

Using your favorite word processor or text editor, create a plain ASCII text file with the following contents:

```
<HTML>
<HEAD>
<TITLE>First Java Applet</TITLE>
</HEAD>
<BODY>
<APPLET CODE="FirstApplet" width=400 height=400></APPLET>
</BODY>
</HTML>
```

After you create the file, save it in the same directory as the compiled code for the `FirstApplet` program. Most HTML documents use the `.html` extension; you should save your HTML document with an appropriate name, such as `example.html`.

> **Looking Ahead:** See Chapter 15, "Creating Java-Powered Web Presentations with Applets," for complete details on using the `<APPLET>` tag.

Creating an Image for Your Applet

The Java API currently supports two image formats: GIF and JPEG, which are the most widely used image formats on the World Wide Web. The `FirstApplet` program displays a GIF image called `New.gif`, but you can create your own image to use instead. If you have published on the Web, you probably have a GIF image that `FirstApplet` can display. To use a GIF image you currently have on your computer, you will need to do the following:

1. Rename the image: `New.gif`.

2. Move the image to the directory containing the compiled code for the application.

If you do not have a GIF image you can use, don't worry. On the CD-ROM you will find a sample image in the directory for Chapter 4. You could also create an image using your favorite graphics program, such as CorelDRAW!. After you create the image, save the image to a file called `New.gif` and move it to the directory containing the source code for the application.

> **Note:** If you do not have a graphics program that will create GIF images and you plan to create applets for use on the World Wide Web, you should probably purchase one or download a shareware graphics program from a reliable archive site on the Internet. Here's how you can rewrite the `FirstApplet` program so that it uses a text string instead of an image:
>
> ```java
> import java.awt.*;
> import java.applet.*;
>
> public class FirstApplet extends Applet {
>
>   public void init() {
>       resize(400,400);
>   }
>
>   public void paint(Graphics g) {
>       g.drawString("My first Java applet.",50,50);
>       play(getCodeBase(),"New.au");
>   }
>
> }
> ```

Creating a Sound File for Your Applet

In order for sound files to play on your system, your system must be properly configured to play sound. At this time, the Java API supports only the Sun AU format. Fortunately, the AU sound format is one of the widely used formats on the World Wide Web. The `FirstApplet` program plays an AU sound file called `New.au`, but you can create your own sound file to use instead. If you have published on the Web, you might have an AU sound file that `FirstApplet` can use.

To use an AU sound file you currently have on your computer, you will need to do the following:

1. Rename the sound file: `New.au`.
2. Move the sound file to the directory containing the compiled code for the application.

Note: If you do not have an AU sound file, don't worry. The `FirstApplet` program will still run—it just won't play a sound file for you. Also, you will find a sample AU sound file on the CD-ROM in the directory for Chapter 4.

Running `FirstApplet`

After creating the necessary files for the `FirstApplet` program, you can run the applet using a hypertext viewer. The Java Developer's Kit includes a viewer called `appletviewer`. On the Macintosh, using `appletviewer` is as easy as dragging the HTML file that references the applet onto the AppletViewer icon. On other systems, `appletviewer` is a command-line program that is invoked with the name of the class you want to run.

Using a Graphical Applet Viewer

Here's what you should do to run `FirstApplet` using a graphical applet viewer: Drop your `.html` file onto the AppletViewer icon or select Open from `appletviewer`'s File menu.

You should now see a pop-up window for the applet viewer. Within a few seconds, you will see your GIF image and hear the audio file. If the viewer issues errors, ensure that you used the correct HTML document and that the document is in the same directory as your compiled code. If you still have problems, refer to the section "Troubleshooting" at the end of this chapter.

Using a Command-Line Applet Viewer

Here's what you should do to run `FirstApplet` using a command-line applet viewer: Change to the directory containing the compiled file with the `.class` extension and type the following at the command prompt:

```
appletviewer example.html
```

You should now see a pop-up window for the applet viewer. Within a few seconds, you will see your GIF image and hear the audio file. If the viewer issues errors, ensure that you used the correct HTML document and that the document is in the same directory as your compiled code. If you still have problems, see the next section, "Troubleshooting."

Troubleshooting

Troubleshooting is something of an art form. Some programmers can troubleshoot hundreds of lines of code in a few minutes. Others wade through the same code for hours. Thankfully, once the JDK is properly installed and tested on your system as outlined in Chapter 2, most of your errors at this stage should pertain to the code itself and your paths. Therefore, this is not an exhaustive list of all the errors that can occur during the running of Java programs. Rather, it is a list of pointers that should help you solve most problems and is divided into three parts:

- Compiler Errors
- Interpreter Errors
- Viewer Errors

Compiler Errors

Compiler errors are normally output directly to the command window. Whenever the Java compiler displays an error, it will not create the `.class` file. Consequently, you must fix errors before you can successfully compile and run the code. The Java compiler does a fair job of telling you where the errors are in your file. However, a single error can be the source of multiple errors later in the compilation. With this in mind, you should generally look to the earliest errors for the source of your problems. After you fix such an error, you should recompile the code and look for other errors.

Most of the mistakes in your code at this stage should be typing mistakes. Typos are often hard to find; you might have to check your code character by character. There are three problem areas in particular you should look for:

Semicolons	Statements should end with a semicolon.
Brackets	Each class and method should have an open bracket and a close bracket. This means that for every class and method declaration, you should have one open bracket and one close bracket. The `FirstApp` program has one class declaration and one method declaration. Thus, there should be two open and two close brackets. The `FirstApplet` program has one class declaration and two method declarations. Thus, there should be three open and three close brackets. The brackets must be placed properly. The open bracket follows the class or method declaration. The close bracket is the final item in the class or method.
Parentheses	Every method name should be directly followed by its arguments enclosed in parentheses. Even if a method has no parameters, it should have an open and a close parenthesis.

Ten Most Common Compiler Errors

The following is a list of the 10 most common errors you will see if there are typos in `FirstApp`. Each compiler error report is followed by a solution. Although `FirstApp` is a very basic program, you can use the logic involved in solving these errors to help solve problems with larger programs, including the `FirstApplet` program:

1. Compiler error report 1:

```
FirstApp.java:1: '{' expected.
class FirstApp
              ^
1 error
```

Solution: Add an open bracket to the class declaration on line 1 as follows:

```
class FirstApp {
```

2. Compiler error report 2:

```
FirstApp.java:3: ';' expected.
        System.out.println("First stand-alone application.")
                                                            ^
1 error
```

Solution: Add a semicolon to the end of the statement in line 4 as follows:

```
System.out.println("First stand-alone application.");
```

3. Compiler error report 3:

```
FirstApp.java:2: ')' expected.
    public static void main (String args[] {
                                           ^
1 error
```

Solution: Add a close parenthesis to the method declaration in line 2 as follows:

```
public static void main (String args[]) {
```

4. Compiler error report 4:

```
FirstApp.java:2: ')' expected.
        public static void main (String args]) {
                                             ^
1 error
```

Solution: In this case, the Java compiler gives a misleading error message. Line 2 is not missing a close parenthesis. It is missing an open square bracket. Although the error is misleading, it does help to pinpoint the source of the problem. Here the problem should be between the preceding open parenthesis and the next close parenthesis. The problem can be fixed as follows:

```
public static void main (String args[]) {
```

5. Compiler error report 5:

```
FirstApp.java:2: Class tring not found in type declaration.
        public static void main (tring args[]) {
                                 ^
1 error
```

Solution: Java is looking for a class called `tring` instead of a class called `String`, which can be fixed as follows:

```
public static void main (String args[]) {
```

6. Compiler error report 6:

```
FirstApp.java:2: Class vod not found in type declaration.
        public static vod main (String args[]) {
                      ^

FirstApp.java:2: Return required at end of vod main(java.lang.String[]).
        public static vod main (String args[]) {
                      ^

2 errors
```

Solution: The word `void` is entered incorrectly as `vod`. This causes the Java compiler to give one good error message and one misleading error message. To fix this problem, you only need to correct the typo:

```
public static void main (String args[]) {
```

7. Compiler error report 7:

```
FirstApp.java:2: Invalid method declaration; return type required.
        public static void (String args[]) {
                      ^

1 error
```

Solution: The method declaration is invalid because it is missing the name of the method. To fix this problem, you need to add the word `main`:

```
public static void main (String args[]) {
```

8. Compiler error report 8:

```
FirstApp.java:3: Method outprintln(java.lang.String) not found in
➥class java.lang.System.
        System.outprintln("First stand-alone application.");
                ^

1 error
```

Solution: The call to the `println` method has a typo that is causing the Java compiler to look for an invalid method called `outprintln`. Adding a period between the word `out` and the word `println` solves this problem:

```
System.out.println("First stand-alone application.");
```

9. Compiler error report 9:

```
FirstApp.java:3: ')' expected.
        System.out.println(First stand-alone application.);
                ^

1 error
```

Solution: The Java compiler gives a misleading error message. Line 3 is not missing a close parenthesis. It is missing double quotation marks. Although the error is misleading, it does help to pinpoint the source of the problem. Here the problem should be between the preceding open parenthesis and the next close parenthesis. The problem can be fixed as follows:

```
System.out.println("First stand-alone application.");
```

10. Compiler error report 10:

```
FirstApp.java:5: '}' expected.
}
 ^
FirstApp.java:5: '}' expected.
}
 ^
2 errors
```

Solution: The compiler is a bit confused because there is a problem in the way your open and close brackets are placed. In particular, you probably have an open bracket where a close bracket should be. Review the code and see where the close bracket should be placed. The best place to start is at line 5. Work your way backward from there.

Other errors you may encounter are related to your paths. Your paths aren't set up correctly if you see an error that says

```
javac:  Command not found
```

To fix this problem, you need to update your path so that it includes the directory where the Java binary executables are stored. Chapter 2 includes a section on testing the installation for each major operating system. You should refer to the section appropriate for your operating system.

Interpreter Errors

Sometimes a program will compile but still will not run with the Java interpreter. Unless redirected, interpreter errors are output directly to the command window. Most interpreter errors relate to either a missing main method or an incorrectly entered filename.

Three Most Common Interpreter Errors

The three most common errors you will see are listed in this section. Each interpreter error report is followed by a solution.

1. Interpreter error report 1:

```
In class FirstApp: void main(String argv[]) is undefined
```

Solution: All Java applications must have a main method. The class file you are trying to run is missing the main method. If there is only one class file for this application, add a main method to the source code and recompile. If there are more than one class file for this application, invoke the interpreter with the name of the class file containing the main method.

2. Interpreter error report 2:

```
Can't find class Firstapp
```

Solution: The Java interpreter cannot find the class file you have specified. This can be a result of an incorrectly typed class name or your path structure. First, check to make sure you have typed in the class name correctly. In this case, FirstApp was incorrectly entered as Firstapp. If you typed in the class name correctly, check your paths. You must either be in the directory containing the class file or have your paths set up correctly to look for the class file.

3. Interpreter error report 3:

```
Can't find class FirstApp/class
```

Solution: You have invoked the interpreter with the filename instead of the class name for your application, and the Java interpreter replaced the period with the appropriate directory separator for your system. When you invoke the interpreter again, do not use the .class extension—use the class name.

Other errors you may encounter are related to your paths. Your paths aren't set up correctly if you see an error that says

```
java:  Command not found
```

To fix this problem, you need to update your path so that it includes the directory where the Java binary executables are stored. Chapter 2 includes a section on testing the installation for each major operating system. You should refer to the section appropriate for your operating system.

Viewer Errors

Java's appletviewer introduces a new set of possible problems. This is primarily because to use appletviewer you need an HTML document with a correctly defined <APPLET> tag. Unless redirected, appletviewer errors are output directly to the command window.

Five Most Common Viewer Errors

The five most common errors you will see are listed in this section. Each viewer error report is followed by a solution:

1. Viewer error report 1:

```
I/O exception while reading: \C:\java_applets\new
```

Make sure that new is a file and is readable.

Solution: appletviewer does a good job of pinpointing the problem. You have entered the name of a file that either does not exist on your system or isn't at the location where Java expects to find it. If you typed in the name of the HTML document correctly, check your paths. You must either be in the directory containing the HTML document or have your paths set up correctly to look for the HTML document.

2. Viewer error report 2:

```
thread applet-FirstApplet.class find class FirstApplet
Opening stream to: file:/C:/java_applets/FirstApplet.class to get FirstApplet
load: class FirstApplet not found
```

Solution: The `appletviewer` was able to load the HTML document, but it cannot find the Java class you specified in the `<APPLET>` tag. View the contents of the HTML document and make sure you have correctly entered the class name. If you typed in the class name correctly, check your paths. Your HTML document must either be in the directory containing the Java class file, or the `<APPLET>` tag must specify the relative or full path to the class file.

3. Viewer error report 3:

```
Warning: No Applets were started, make sure the input contains an <applet> tag.
use: appletviewer [-debug] url¦file ...
```

Solution: `appletviewer` is trying to display the document, but the document does not contain an `<APPLET>` tag. Make sure you are invoking the `appletviewer` with the name of the HTML document and not the name of your Java class file. Then view the contents of the HTML document to make sure you have a fully qualified `<APPLET>` tag, such as

```
<APPLET CODE="FirstApplet" width=400 height=400></APPLET>
```

4. Viewer error report 4:

```
Warning: <applet> tag requires width attribute.
Warning: No Applets were started, make sure the input contains an <applet> tag.
use: appletviewer [-debug] url¦file ...
```

Solution: `appletviewer` is trying to display the document, but the document does not contain a fully qualified `<APPLET>` tag. In this case, the `<APPLET>` tag is missing the `WIDTH` attribute.

5. Viewer error report 5:

```
Warning: <applet> tag requires height attribute.
Warning: No Applets were started, make sure the input contains an <applet> tag.
use: appletviewer  -debug] url¦file ...
```

Solution: `appletviewer` is trying to display the document, but the document does not contain a fully qualified `<APPLET>` tag. In this case, the `<APPLET>` tag is missing the `HEIGHT` attribute.

Other errors you may encounter are related to your paths. Your paths aren't set up correctly if you see an error that says

```
appletviewer:  Command not found
```

To fix this problem, you need to update your path so that it includes the directory where the Java binary executables are stored. Chapter 2 includes a section on testing the installation for each major operating system. You should refer to the section appropriate for your operating system.

Summary

You have learned the basics of creating Java applications and applets. Applications are stand-alone programs designed to be invoked with an interpreter. Applets are programs designed to be viewed with an external viewer. Although applications and applets are very similar in design, one key difference between them is that applications require a `main` method and applets do not.

Through a simple application called `FirstApp`, you saw that even the most basic Java programs use key object-oriented programming concepts. This is because

- All Java programs define objects that have a behavior and a state.
- All Java programs use encapsulation and message passing, which allow you to use a Java object as long as you know what values the object accepts.
- All Java programs define one or more classes that group sets of related methods and variables.
- All Java programs use inheritance, which enables you to create classes that inherit the functionality of existing classes.
- All Java programs use access modifiers that control access to methods and variables.

The five-line program called `FirstApp` and the 17-line program called `FirstApplet` used the similar constructs as well. These constructs form the basis of the Java programming language. More complex Java programs that may be hundreds of lines long will also follow these basic concepts and constructs.

5

Java Tools and the JDK: A Primer

Programming in any language is easier if you have the proper tools. The Java Developer's Kit includes a complete toolkit for Java development. Beyond the JDK tools are tools featuring graphical interfaces. The more you understand about the tools used for Java development, the better prepared you will be to take advantage of everything the Java programming language has to offer. This chapter discusses the essential tools for creating, developing, and debugging Java programs with a focus on how to get the most out of them.

Tools in the Java Developer's Kit

A thorough understanding of the tools in the Java Developer's Kit is essential for your success in Java programming. Previous chapters discuss the basics of using some of these tools, but the focus in those early chapters is on how to use the tools and not on the features of the tools. As you will see in this chapter, each tool has unique features that are designed to help you do the following:

- Get more out of the Java programming language
- Troubleshoot problems in your programs
- Change environment defaults
- Optimize Java for your development or target system

Most versions of the JDK include seven tools for Java development:

- Java compiler
- Java API documentation generator
- Java header and stub file generator
- Java interpreter
- Java applet viewer
- Java class file disassembler
- Java debugger

As you saw in Chapter 2, "Getting Started with the JDK," the JDK is available for most operating systems. For Windows 95/NT, OS/2, and UNIX platforms, the developer's tools in JDK version 1.0 have a command-line interface. For Macintosh (and soon for other platforms as well), the developer's tools in JDK version 1.0 feature a graphical user interface. Graphical development environments for UNIX and Windows-based platforms are also available. Because you will get more out of this chapter if I break down the discussion according to the interface the tools use, it features two main sections. The first section is on command-line tools, and the second section is on graphical tools.

> **Looking Forward:** Because the Java debugger uses a separate API discussed in Chapter 13, "The Net and Debug Class Libraries," it is more appropriate to discuss using the debugger in a later chapter. For this reason, you will find a complete discussion on the Java debugger in Chapter 23, "Advanced Debugging and Troubleshooting."
>
> Similarly, the Java class file disassembler is used to examine Java bytecode, and a better place to discuss the disassembler is Chapter 24, "The Java Virtual Machine."

Command-line Tools in the JDK

For Windows 95/NT, OS/2, and UNIX platforms, the tools in the Java Developer's Kit version 1.0 execute from the command line. Although SunSoft and many third-party vendors have produced graphical developer's environments for Java, current programmers and system administrators may prefer the simplicity of the original command-line tools.

The advantage of using tools that do not have a graphical user interface is that they are streamlined, are generally more versatile, and use minimal system resources. Command-line tools also let you perform complex assignments and handle tasks with parameters easily.

The Java Compiler and Associated Environment Tools

Most discussions on compiling Java programs relate to the Java compiler, but there is a set of related tools you might want to use at compile time. These related tools include the Java compiler, the Java API documentation generator, and the Java header and stub file generator.

javac

When you compile Java programs, you use the Java compiler. The JDK includes two versions of the Java compiler. The first version, `javac`, is optimized for normal use and has only limited debugging capabilities. The second version, `javac_g`, is optimized for debugging and is intended for use with the Java debugger.

You run the Java compiler from the command line and pass it the full name of your Java source file. The Java compiler expects the source code to be in a file named with the `.java` extension. Additionally, when the source file contains multiple class declarations, the source file must be named after the primary class declaration. Therefore, it is best to always name your source files after the primary class declaration.

For each class declaration in the source file, the Java compiler creates a class file with a `.class` extension. Because the compiler is case sensitive, the first part of the class file will be named exactly as you typed it in the source file. By default, the class files are placed in the same directory as the source file. You can override this default with the `-d` option. The `-d` option of the Java compiler lets you specify the destination directory for your class files.

On UNIX platforms, you can specify a default destination directory as follows:

```
javac -d $HOME/jb_apps/myclasses QuizMaker.java
```

On Windows 95/NT and OS/2 platforms, you can specify a default destination directory as follows:

```
javac -d C:\jb_apps\myclasses QuizMaker.java
```

If the application you are compiling references any classes that are not stored in the current directory, you should either set the `CLASSPATH` environment variable or use the `-classpath` option. The `-classpath` option lets you specify a path for your class files that overrides the default or current `CLASSPATH` setting. Because this option takes precedence, you should set it to include the current directory, the location of your personal or third-party class files, and the location of the Java API classes.

On UNIX platforms, you can specify a path for class files as follows:

```
javac -classpath .:/usr/jb_apps/vendorclasses:java/classes:
➥java/lib/classes.zip QuizMaker.java
```

On Windows 95/NT and OS/2 platforms, you can specify a path for class files as follows:

```
javac -classpath .;C:\jb_apps;C:\java\classes;
➥C:\java\lib\classes.zip QuizMaker.java
```

You can generate debugging tables with the `-g` option. *Debugging tables* contain information about the program organized by line numbers. A similar and more useful option is the `-debug` option. This option generates a full trace of compiler activity that primarily relates to methods and declarations. If you change to the directory containing the source for the `FirstApp` program discussed in Chapter 4, "The Java Language: A Primer," and type the following,

```
javac -debug FirstApp.java
```

you will see output similar to this:

```
public static void main(java.lang.String[]);
{
    (method (System#0.out) println "My first stand-alone application
➥is a success.");
```

```
}
[check field FirstApp.main]
{
    (method (System#0.out) println "My first stand-alone application
is a success.");
}
{
    (method (java.lang.System.out) println "My first stand-alone application
is a success.");
}
[check field FirstApp.<init>]

{
}
{
    (method super <init>);
    {
    }
}
[inline field FirstApp.main]
[inlined field FirstApp.main]
(method (<empty>.out) println "My first stand-alone application
is a success.");
[code field FirstApp.main]
[inline field FirstApp.<init>]
[inlined field FirstApp.<init>]
(method super <init>);
[code field FirstApp.<init>]
```

As you can see, the `-debug` option generates an awful lot of output even for small programs. The output is useful, however, to get a line-by-line picture of what the compiler is doing with methods and declarations.

Tip: To capture the output of almost any Java tool to a file, redirect the output to a named file. For the Java compiler, you can do this using the following syntax:

`javac [options] filename.java > outputfile`

If you type the following,

`javac -debug FirstApplet.java > firstapp`

all debugging information from the compiler is directed to the file called `firstapp`.

Although the `-g` and the `-debug` options come in handy for advanced programs, you will find that for basic- to intermediate-level programs you really will not need to use them. Another option you might not need unless you are developing advanced programs is the `-nowarn` option. If you use this option, the compiler does not print out warnings. (Because warnings are not actual errors, you might sometimes want to stop the compiler's incessant displaying of them.) Typically, though, you will not see warnings anyway with basic- to intermediate-level programs.

One of the most useful command-line arguments for the compiler is the -0 option. With this option, you can optimize your source code so that it runs faster and uses fewer system resources. The compiler optimizes your code by creating inline references to static, final, and private methods.

Anytime when speed and system resources are a consideration, I highly recommend optimizing your code. However, there is a trade-off to be made between the compiled size of your program and the optimization of your program, which again primarily comes into play for advanced programs. Because optimized code contains inline references, it is sometimes—but not always—larger than non-optimized code. The Java compiler also takes longer to finish the compilation when you optimize the code.

Technical Note: To test the optimization, I ran some tests on my system. I compiled six Java programs of 100–300 lines in length with the -0 option and all the associated class files were actually smaller—by 300–800 bytes—than the non-optimized versions. I tried the same test with Java programs that were more than 1,000 lines in length. Although the size of one program did increase by 500 bytes, the optimized versions were usually smaller. Optimization actually reduced the size of one program from 18KB to 14.5KB.

Another useful compiler option is -verbose. With this option, you can turn on verbose messaging and see everything the compiler and linker are doing. Not only will verbose messaging tell you what source files are being read, but you can also see

- How long it took to parse each source file
- When and from where the compiler is loading each class
- When classes are being checked
- When the class file is being written to
- How long it took to complete the compilation

Because the -verbose option tells you what the compiler is doing to class and source files, you can use it in conjunction with the -debug option to get a complete picture of everything the compiler is doing. If you change to the directory containing the source for the FirstApplet program discussed in the previous chapter and type the following,

```
javac -verbose FirstApplet.java
```

you will see output similar to this:

```
[parsed FirstApplet.java in 500ms]
[loaded C:\JAVA\LIB\CLASSES.ZIP(java/applet/Applet.class) in 110ms]
[checking class FirstApplet]
[loaded C:\JAVA\LIB\CLASSES.ZIP(java/awt/Panel.class) in 0ms]
[loaded C:\JAVA\LIB\CLASSES.ZIP(java/awt/Container.class) in 110ms]
[loaded C:\JAVA\LIB\CLASSES.ZIP(java/awt/Component.class) in 160ms]
[loaded C:\JAVA\LIB\CLASSES.ZIP(java/lang/Object.class) in 0ms]
```

```
[loaded C:\JAVA\LIB\CLASSES.ZIP(java/awt/image/ImageObserver.class) in 0ms]
[loaded C:\JAVA\LIB\CLASSES.ZIP(java/awt/Image.class) in 60ms]
[loaded C:\JAVA\LIB\CLASSES.ZIP(java/awt/Graphics.class) in 60ms]
[wrote FirstApplet.class]
[done in 2030ms]
```

You can pass multiple parameters to the compiler, but you must precede each option with a hyphen. If you wanted to optimize the code and use the -verbose option, you would type the following:

```
javac -O -verbose QuizMaker.java
```

The command-line syntax for the compiler is

```
javac [options] filename.java
```

The compiler takes these options:

Option	Description
-classpath	Overrides the default or current CLASSPATH environment variable setting
-d	Specifies a destination directory for your class files
-debug	Generates a full trace of compiler activity for methods and declarations
-g	Adds debugging information, including line numbers
-nowarn	Turns off compiler warnings
-O	Optimizes source code by inlining static, final, and private methods
-verbose	Tells you what the compiler is doing to class and source files

javah

The Java C Header and Stub File Generator is an extremely useful environment tool. You will use it when you need to implement native methods. C header and stub files are necessary for Java and C programs to interact. As C programmers know, header and stub files are used by C programs to reference an object's instance variables. If you plan to interface your Java program to C or C++, you should generate header and stub files after compiling the Java source code.

The JDK includes two versions of this tool. The first version, javah, is optimized for normal use and has only limited debugging capabilities. The second version, javah_g, is optimized for debugging and is intended for use with the Java debugger.

You run the Java C Header and Stub File Generator from the command line and pass it the name of your Java class file without the .class extension. By default, javah creates a header file with the .h extension for each class name you pass to it and stores the file in the current directory. Header files are named with the class name and the .h extension. You can override this default with the -o option.

The -o option lets you specify a single output file for all generated source information. This is useful when you have Java programs that contain multiple class files and you want to store the associated header and stub information in one file. As javah stores the output in the exact file you name, you should always specify the .h extension in the destination filename. The following example creates a header file called concat.h for a Java program that has four classes associated with it:

```
javah -o concat.h RGBcanvas RGBcontrols HexInt RGB2Hex
```

Generated header files contain C struct definitions, define all the variables you might need, and create a handle for passing values back and forth between C and Java. The layout of the header file approximates the layout of the original class file with fields that correspond to instance variables. For every class you use in the Java program, there will be a struct definition with the package name prepended to the class name. Java replaces file path separators with the underscore character. Here are some examples:

```
struct Hjava_awt_peer_ComponentPeer;

struct Hjava_awt_Container;

struct Hjava_awt_Color;
```

Whereas header files are generated automatically, you must use the -stubs option to create a stub file with C declarations. Stub files are named with the class name and the .c extension—in the C programming language source files named with this extension. You can use this option as follows:

```
javah -stubs RGB2Hex
```

During the generation of header and stub files, javah builds temporary files. These files are generally stored in the \tmp directory on UNIX systems and on the c:\temp directory on Windows-based systems. If you are compiling all classes associated with an advanced application, these files can grow to be quite large. You can override the default directory with the -td option, which lets you specify the location of the temporary directory. Specifying a new location for the temporary directory is often useful, especially if your primary disk or the root partition doesn't have a lot of free space.

On UNIX platforms, you can set the location of the temporary directory as follows:

```
javah -td \usr\temp RGB2Hex
```

On Windows 95/NT and OS/2 platforms, you can set the location of the temporary directory as follows:

```
javah -td C:\windows\temp RGB2Hex
```

Note: On Windows and OS/2 platforms, javah stores temporary files in the directory specified by the TEMP environment variable, which on most systems is c:\temp. If the TEMP environment variable is not set on your system, javah checks for a TMP environment variable. Finally, if the TMP environment variable is not set, javah creates a temporary directory at c:\tmp.

Other options you can use include the -v option and the -classpath option. The -v option turns on verbose messaging, which lets you see what classes and temporary directory javah is using. The -classpath option lets you override the default and current CLASSPATH setting. If the program for which you are creating header and stub files makes use of any classes that are not stored in the current directory, you should either set the CLASSPATH environment variable or use the -classpath option.

The command-line syntax for the header and stub file generator is

```
javah [options] classname
```

or

```
javah [options] classname1 classname2 classname3 …
```

The header and stub file generator takes these options:

Option	Description
-classpath	Overrides the default or current CLASSPATH environment variable setting
-d	Specifies a destination directory for your header and stub files
-o	Specifies a single output file for all generated header and source information
-stubs	Creates stub files with C declarations in addition to the C header files
-td	Specifies a directory for temporary files and overrides the default
-v	Tells you what classes and temp directory javah is using

javadoc

The Java API Documentation Generator, as the name implies, is used to generate documentation from source files. Because the documentation is in the form of HTML documents, you can view it online with any HTML browser. The great thing about HTML documentation is that all object names are linked together. As a programmer, you will appreciate how thorough the documentation this tool creates is, especially if you are tired of having to write your own documentation. In fact, Sun used this tool to create the documentation files for the API.

You run the API Documentation Generator from the command line and pass it the full name of your Java source file. Here's an example:

```
javadoc FirstApplet.java
```

Caution: If you pass javadoc the name of your source file without the .java extension, it will create the documentation. However, javadoc will parse the source as it would a Java package. The result is a completely different set of documentation.

The API Documentation Generator expects the source code to be in a file named with the `.java` extension. You can also pass `javadoc` the name of a package and it will generate documentation for the entire package.

The only options you can use with the documentation generator are `-classpath`, `-d`, and `-verbose`. If the program for which you are creating documentation makes use of any classes that are not stored in the current directory, you should either set the `CLASSPATH` environment variable or use the `-classpath` option. The `-d` option lets you specify the destination directory for the HTML documentation. The `-verbose` option turns on verbose messaging and lets you see what classes and source files the compiler and linker are using.

The command-line syntax for the header and stub file generator is

```
javadoc [options] sourcefile.java
```

or

```
javadoc [options] packagename
```

The documentation generator takes these options:

Option	Description
-classpath	Overrides the default or current CLASSPATH environment variable setting
-d	Specifies a destination directory for your class files
-verbose	Tells you what the compiler is doing to class and source files

Using `javadoc`

The documentation generator parses declarations and document-style comments in Java source files and formats this into a set of HTML documents. For a source file containing class declarations, `javadoc` creates one documentation file for each class declaration. The name of the file is the class name plus the `.html` extension. These class documents contain a complete breakdown of the class. Three additional documentation files are always created as well:

- `packages.html`—Documentation file used for packages; is generally empty if you created documentation for a source file with class declarations.
- `AllNames.html`—Index file of all fields and methods used in the source file.
- `tree.html`—Documentation file that shows the class hierarchy used in the source file.

If you create documentation for packages, the `packages.html` file will contain an entry for each package. These entries will be linked to an appropriately named package file, such as `Package-PackageName.html`.

To better understand what `javadoc` does and how it does it, let's create documentation for the `FirstApplet` program. The first thing you will notice when you create documentation with `javadoc` is that it expects you to have the Java API documentation in HTML format installed on your system. It also expects you to have the source file in the base directory for the API documentation. Primarily, this is because of the way `javadoc` links object names back to the API documentation and because the documentation uses images from the API documentation.

To get around this problem, you could move your source file to the directory containing the API documentation and then run `javadoc`. However, by doing so you will overwrite the `packages.html` file that already exists in this directory. Also, if you generated any previous documentation with `javadoc`, you would overwrite the existing `AllNames.html` and `tree.html` files.

Avoiding Problems with the Documentation Generator

To avoid overwriting existing documentation and to be able to use the documentation with the API documentation, you might want to do the following:

1. Make a new directory.
2. Move the source file to the new directory.
3. Run `javadoc` in this directory on the source file.
4. If you are not creating documentation for a package, remove the `packages.html` file.
5. Using a text editor, edit the `tree.html` file. Prepend the name of your class for all references to the file `AllNames.html`. You could do this by searching on the keyword `AllNames.html` and replacing it with the appropriate name. There is generally only one reference you have to update.
6. Using a text editor, edit the `AllNames.html` file. Prepend the name of your class for all references to the file `tree.html`. You could do this by searching on the keyword `tree.html` and replacing it with the appropriate name. There is generally only one reference you have to update.
7. Move all remaining files to the directory containing the API documentation.

You can now use the documentation for your class with the API documentation and don't have to worry about it being overwritten the next time you create documentation.

To avoid overwriting existing documentation and to keep your documentation separate from the API documentation, you might want to do the following:

1. Make a directory for your documentation.
2. Change to your documentation directory and make a subdirectory called `images`.
3. Copy the contents of the `images` directory from the Java API documentation to the `images` directory you just made.

Then, each time you want to create documentation for a new class, you can do the following to update your personal documentation:

1. Move the source to a temporary directory.

2. Run `javadoc` in this directory on the source file.

3. If you are not creating documentation for a package, remove the `packages.html` file.

4. Using a text editor, edit the `tree.html` file. Prepend the name of your class for all references to the file `AllNames.html`. You could do this by searching on the keyword `AllNames.html` and replacing it with the appropriate name. There is generally only one reference you have to update.

5. Using a text editor, edit the `AllNames.html` file. Prepend the name of your class for all references to the file `tree.html`. You could do this by searching on the keyword `tree.html` and replacing it with the appropriate name. There is generally only one reference you have to update.

6. Move all remaining files to your documentation directory.

You can now use the documentation for your class and don't have to worry about it being overwritten the next time you create documentation.

Generating Documentation for `FirstApplet`

You can create documentation for the `FirstApplet` program following the steps listed in the previous section. Figure 5.1 shows what the resulting `AllNames.html` file should look like. Each of the underlined phrases is a hypertext link to key information within the document and to other documents.

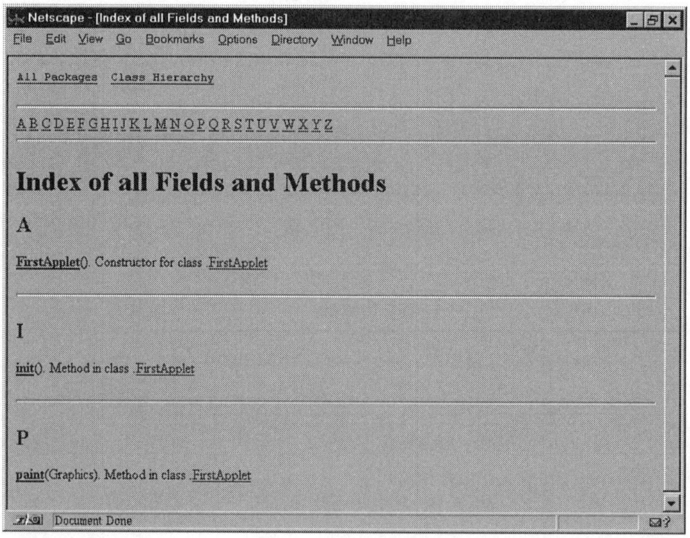

Figure 5.1.
An automatically generated index for `FirstApplet`.

The documentation generator puts a useful header on the document that allows you to quickly locate fields and methods alphabetically. Each of the entries in the main section of the document also contains hypertext links that let you quickly and easily navigate through lengthy documentation. You can access the tree.html file by clicking on the link titled "Class Hierarchy."

A partial view of the tree.html file is shown in Figure 5.2. This file contains a listing of every class used by the FirstApplet program. All class references are linked back to the Java API documentation.

Figure 5.2.

An automatically generated class hierarchy for FirstApplet*.*

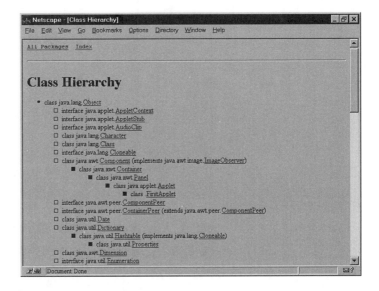

The most useful file in the documentation is the class file. For this example, the class file is named FirstApplet.html. The first section of this file is shown in Figure 5.3. From the class diagram shown at the top of the figure, you can see exactly where the FirstApplet class fits into the class hierarchy. As you can see, the FirstApplet class extends the Applet class, which in turn is an extension of other classes.

As shown in Figure 5.4, the next section of the document breaks the FirstApplet class into constructors and methods. Because this documentation is primarily for more advanced programs than this one, there is a constructor index and a method index that contain hypertext links to each constructor and method used in the program.

In the constructor section, each class is broken down by its class declaration. In the method section, each method is broken down by its method declaration and shows the relationship of your method to the methods in the API. Because the init() method of the FirstApplet class overrides the init() method of the Applet class, the FirstApplet class documentation contains the following definition for this method:

```
public void init()

    Overrides:
        init in class Applet
```

Figure 5.3.
An automatically generated overview of FirstApplet.

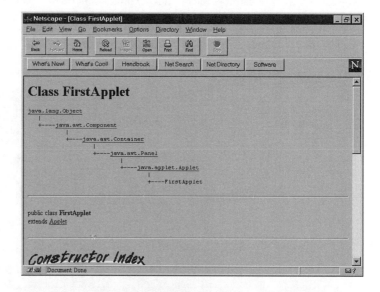

Figure 5.4.
Methods and constructors are broken down clearly in the documentation.

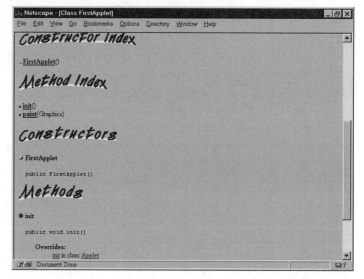

Enhancing the Documentation

You can enhance the documentation that javadoc creates using document-style comments. The most basic form of document-style comments allows you to add descriptions to the classes, methods, and variable declarations you use in your programs. You should always add comments just before the section or declaration to which the comments pertain. The documentation generator uses these comments to add a description to your classes, methods, and variables.

See Chapter 6, "Fundamentals of the Java Language," for a complete discussion about using comments in Java.

Add the following document-style comment to the FirstApplet program just before the class declaration:

```
/**
 * Peter Norton's Guide to Java Programming
 * The FirstApplet program creates a basic
 * applet with multimedia features.
 */
```

The documentation generator will include the description in the first section of the FirstApplet.html file. To support more advanced control over documentation, javadoc also lets you place markup instructions within the comments. There are two ways you can do this.

The first way is with HTML markup. To be useful, HTML markup should not interfere with tags and formatting that javadoc generates automatically. This means you should not use header tags, horizontal rules, or tags that denote head or body sections. One way to use HTML is to show code examples:

```
/**
 * The getImage() method is used to add an image to an applet
 * <PRE> NewImage = getImage(getCodeBase(),"New.gif"); </PRE>
 */
```

The documentation generator also supports a special set of documenting tags that are defined with the at symbol (@) and are always defined within document-style comments. With these tags, you can add many types of inline references including links to other documents, author entries, and version control. To use these tags, you specify the name of the tag followed by the reference text, like this:

```
/**
 * Peter Norton's Guide to Java Programming
 * The FirstApplet program creates a basic
 * applet with multimedia features.
 * @version     1.5 March 15, 1996
 */
```

When the documentation sees the version tag, it adds a version entry in the HTML document for the associated class. The entry would appear as follows:

```
Version:
    1.5 March 15, 1996
```

The six special tags that javadoc supports, as well as their corresponding entries in the documentation, are shown in Table 5.1. Your doc tags must be placed at the beginning of a line. Although you can use multiple tags of the same type within a document, you should keep tags of the same type together. For example, if there are multiple authors of the program, your entry should look something like this:

```
/**
 * Peter Norton's Guide to Java Programming
 * The FirstApplet program creates a basic
 * applet with multimedia features.
 * @author     Peter Norton
 * @author     William Stanek
 * @version    1.5 March 15, 1996
 */
```

Table 5.1. Doc tags and their uses.

Doc tag	Description	Displayed as
@author	Adds a reference for the author of the document. Used with construct-related comments.	Author: Author Name
@version	Adds a reference for the version of the document. Used with construct-related comments.	Version: X.X 01/01/99
@see	Adds a hypertext reference to an HTML document. You specify the name of the file without the .html extension. You can associate this tag with any valid class in the API simply by specifying the class name. If you associate this tag with variables or methods, you can add links to variables and parameters in other documents. To create a reference to a class's method, separate the class name and the method name with a pound sign, such as Applet#start.	See Also: filename.html
@param	Adds a parameter to the parameters section of the document. You specify the name of the parameter followed by a description of the parameter. Used with method-related comments.	Parameters: Name Description
@return	Specifies the value a method returns. Used with method-related comments.	Returns: Description
@exception	Specifies an exception a class throws. You specify the name of the exception followed by a description of the exception. Used with method-related comments.	Exception: Name Description

The Java Interpreter

The Java interpreter executes Java bytecode files. You will use the interpreter to run Java applications. Before the interpreter runs any program, it verifies that the classes associated with the program are valid and do not violate any language constraints.

The JDK includes two versions of the interpreter. The first version, `java`, is optimized for normal use and has only limited debugging capabilities. The second version, `java_g`, is optimized for debugging and is intended for use with the Java debugger.

You run the interpreter from the command line and pass it the name of your Java class file without the `.class` extension. For applications that include many classes, you will want to pass the interpreter the name of the class that declares the application's `main()` method. The interpreter executes the `main()` method and any threads specified in the `main()` method. If no threads are created by the `main()` method, the interpreter executes the `main()` method and then exits. If threads are created by the `main()` method, the interpreter exits when the last thread exits.

Because the interpreter expects the class file to contain a `main()` method, you generally cannot use the interpreter to run Java applets. If you want to run Java applets, you should use the Java applet viewer discussed in the next section of this chapter. The interpreter uses the following syntax:

```
java [options] classname [args]
```

Like other tools in the JDK, the Java interpreter accepts many options. Unlike other tools in the JDK, the interpreter also allows you to pass arguments to the class's `main()` method. You do this by putting the values for the arguments after the class name.

The `-classpath` option lets you specify a path for your class files that overrides the default or current `CLASSPATH` setting. Because this option takes precedence, you should set it to include the current directory, the location of your personal or third-party class files, and the location of the Java API classes.

On UNIX platforms, you can specify a path for class files as follows:

```
java -classpath .:\usr\jb_apps\vendorclasses:java\classes:
➥java\lib\classes.zip QuizMaker
```

On Windows 95/NT and OS/2 platforms, you can specify a path for class files as follows:

```
java -classpath .;C:\jb_apps\vendor;C:\java\classes;
➥C:\java\lib\classes.zip QuizMaker
```

An option of the interpreter that is sure to be a quick favorite in large development environments is `-checksource`. This option instructs the interpreter to make sure the compiled classes are current and to recompile the source files if they are not. The interpreter does this by comparing the modification date on the source files to the modification date on the class files. If any source file has a more recent date, that source file is recompiled before the interpreter uses the associated class. You can instruct the interpreter to check the source using either -checksource or -cs, like this:

```
java -cs FirstApp
```

Note: The -cs option serves the same purpose as the -checksource option. The primary reason for introducing the -cs option was to save keystrokes over the longer -checksource option.

Another useful option is -debug, which lets you attach the Java debugger tool to an interpreter session. When you use this option, the interpreter displays a password that must be used when starting the debugging session. The password is randomly allocated by session.

To track interpreter activity, you will want to use the -verbose or -v option. With this option, you can turn on verbose messaging and see what class files the interpreter is using. The classes the interpreter loads at runtime are very different from the classes used when the source is compiled. If you change to the directory containing the source for the FirstApp program discussed in Chapter 4 and type the following:

```
java -verbose FirstApp
```

Note: The -v option serves the same purpose as the -verbose option. The primary reason for introducing the -v option was to save keystrokes over the longer -verbose option.

You will see output similar to the following:

```
[Loaded java/lang/Cloneable.class from C:\JAVA\LIB\CLASSES.ZIP]
[Loaded java/lang/ThreadGroup.class from C:\JAVA\LIB\CLASSES.ZIP]
[Loaded java/lang/System.class from C:\JAVA\LIB\CLASSES.ZIP]
[Loaded java/io/BufferedInputStream.class from C:\JAVA\LIB\CLASSES.ZIP]
[Loaded java/lang/Thread.class from C:\JAVA\LIB\CLASSES.ZIP]
[Loaded java/lang/Object.class from C:\JAVA\LIB\CLASSES.ZIP]
[Loaded java/lang/Class.class from C:\JAVA\LIB\CLASSES.ZIP]
[Loaded java/lang/String.class from C:\JAVA\LIB\CLASSES.ZIP]
[Loaded java/lang/ThreadDeath.class from C:\JAVA\LIB\CLASSES.ZIP]
[Loaded java/lang/Error.class from C:\JAVA\LIB\CLASSES.ZIP]
[Loaded java/lang/Throwable.class from C:\JAVA\LIB\CLASSES.ZIP]
[Loaded java/lang/Exception.class from C:\JAVA\LIB\CLASSES.ZIP]
[Loaded java/lang/RuntimeException.class from C:\JAVA\LIB\CLASSES.ZIP]
[Loaded java/lang/Cloneable.class from C:\JAVA\LIB\CLASSES.ZIP]
[Loaded java/lang/ThreadGroup.class from C:\JAVA\LIB\CLASSES.ZIP]
[Loaded java/lang/System.class from C:\JAVA\LIB\CLASSES.ZIP]
[Loaded java/io/BufferedInputStream.class from C:\JAVA\LIB\CLASSES.ZIP]
[Loaded java/io/FilterInputStream.class from C:\JAVA\LIB\CLASSES.ZIP]
[Loaded java/io/InputStream.class from C:\JAVA\LIB\CLASSES.ZIP]
[Loaded java/io/FileInputStream.class from C:\JAVA\LIB\CLASSES.ZIP]
[Loaded java/io/FileDescriptor.class from C:\JAVA\LIB\CLASSES.ZIP]
[Loaded java/io/PrintStream.class from C:\JAVA\LIB\CLASSES.ZIP]
```

```
[Loaded java/io/FilterOutputStream.class from C:\JAVA\LIB\CLASSES.ZIP]
[Loaded java/io/OutputStream.class from C:\JAVA\LIB\CLASSES.ZIP]
[Loaded java/io/BufferedOutputStream.class from C:\JAVA\LIB\CLASSES.ZIP]
[Loaded java/io/FileOutputStream.class from C:\JAVA\LIB\CLASSES.ZIP]
[Loaded java/lang/StringBuffer.class from C:\JAVA\LIB\CLASSES.ZIP]
[Loaded java/lang/Integer.class from C:\JAVA\LIB\CLASSES.ZIP]
[Loaded java/lang/Number.class from C:\JAVA\LIB\CLASSES.ZIP]
[Loaded java/lang/NoClassDefFoundError.class from C:\JAVA\LIB\CLASSES.ZIP]
[Loaded java/lang/LinkageError.class from C:\JAVA\LIB\CLASSES.ZIP]
[Loaded java/lang/OutOfMemoryError.class from C:\JAVA\LIB\CLASSES.ZIP]
[Loaded java/lang/VirtualMachineError.class from C:\JAVA\LIB\CLASSES.ZIP]
[Loaded .\FirstApp.class]
[Loaded java/lang/Compiler.class from C:\JAVA\LIB\CLASSES.ZIP]
[Loaded java/util/Properties.class from C:\JAVA\LIB\CLASSES.ZIP]
[Loaded java/util/Hashtable.class from C:\JAVA\LIB\CLASSES.ZIP]
[Loaded java/util/Dictionary.class from C:\JAVA\LIB\CLASSES.ZIP]
[Loaded java/util/HashtableEntry.class from C:\JAVA\LIB\CLASSES.ZIP]
```

Another way to track interpreter activity is with the -t option. This option traces every instruction the Java virtual machine executes and is used only with the debugging version of the interpreter, java_g. Although this option is useful for advanced debugging, the listing is too lengthy for any other use. The instruction list for the five-line FirstApp program filled 175 pages.

If you want to check where your program is spending the most time during execution, you can use the -prof option. This option of the interpreter effectively replaced the profiler tool that was included in the Alpha release of the Java programming language. Using the -prof option, you can pinpoint areas of the code that are eating up more system time than they should. Often, you can rework the related section of code and improve the performance of the program.

When you run the interpreter with the -prof option, it dumps the profile information to a file called java.prof in the current directory. If you use the profile option on the FirstApp program, you will generate a file that fills three printed pages. Profiling information is broken down into sections. Each section is preceded by a comment statement that tells you the order of columns in the output. You can profile the FirstApp program using the following command:

```
java -prof FirstApp
```

The example that follows has two sections of profile information. The first section shows you the system count, the object called, the calling object, and the system time. The second section shows you how many handles were used, the number of free handles, the amount of heap used, and the amount of heap free. Here's the example:

```
# count callee caller time
4 java/lang/System.arraycopy(Ljava/lang/Object;ILjava/lang/Object;II)V
➥java/lang/String.getChars(II[CI)V 0
39 java/lang/System.arraycopy(Ljava/lang/Object;ILjava/lang/Object;II)V
➥java/lang/String.<init>([C)V 0
1 java/lang/Thread.getThreadGroup()Ljava/lang/ThreadGroup; java/lang/
➥ThreadGroup.<init>(Ljava/lang/String;)V 0
1 java/lang/String.valueOf(I)Ljava/lang/String; java/lang/StringBuffer.
➥append(I)Ljava/lang/StringBuffer; 10

# handles-used, handles-free heap-used heap-free
124 78518 5232 2511344
```

The interpreter includes a set of options for optimizing the runtime environment. Each program running on the Java runtime environment has a memory allocation pool assigned to it. The memory allocation pool is also referred to as the *garbage-collected heap* or simply the *heap*.

The `-mx` option lets you specify the maximum number of bytes to be allocated to the heap. All values you specify for the heap must be greater than 1,000 bytes and can be allocated in kilobytes or megabytes. By default, the interpreter sets this value to 16MB.

To set the maximum heap size in kilobytes, follow the value by k, with no intervening space, like this:

```
java -mx 900k FirstApp
```

To set the maximum heap size in megabytes, follow the value by m, with no intervening space, like this:

```
java -mx 1m FirstApp
```

You can set the startup size of the heap using the `-ms` option. All values you specify must be greater than 1,000 bytes and can be allocated in kilobytes or megabytes. By default, the interpreter sets this value to 1MB.

Java is a multithreaded programming environment. Each thread running on the Java runtime environment has two stacks associated with it. The first stack is used for Java code, and the second stack is used for C code. Memory used by these stacks draws from the total system memory pool. Whenever a new thread starts execution, it is assigned a maximum stack size for Java code and for C code.

The default maximum stack size for Java code is 400KB. You can override this default with the `-oss` option. All values you specify must be greater than 1,000 bytes and can be allocated in kilobytes or megabytes, such as

```
java -oss 100k FirstApp
```

The default maximum stack size for C code is 128KB. You can override this default with the `-ss` option. All values you specify must be greater than 1,000 bytes and can be allocated in kilobytes or megabytes, such as

```
java -ss 100k FirstApp
```

Note: If you set new values for stack size, you are specifying a maximum value that is assigned when new threads begin execution. Thus every thread that is spawned will inherit this value.

The interpreter provides you with control over garbage collection. Normally, garbage collection is performed automatically as a background thread, and the runtime environment goes about its business without telling anyone what it is doing. You can override this in two ways. You can either set the verbose flag for garbage collection using the -verbosegc option, which tells the runtime environment to print out messages whenever it frees memory, or you can turn off background garbage collection using -noasyncgc, the no asynchronous garbage-collection flag.

When you set the -noasyncgc option, no garbage collection takes place unless the program runs out of memory or explicitly tells the system to perform garbage collection. If it seems like a bad thing to let the program run out of memory before freeing memory, that's because it usually is. Garbage collection is a powerful feature of Java, and you should turn it off only in an extremely limited set of circumstances.

Before executing any program loaded over the network, the interpreter checks the validity of the class files. Part of the validation process is to ensure that the class file does not violate system security. This default option is called -verifyremote. The interpreter allows you to make verification more strict with the -verify option and to turn off verification completely with the -noverify option. Whereas the -verify option causes the interpreter to check the validity of all classes prior to execution, the -noverify option goes to the other extreme and tells the interpreter to never validate classes.

To override property values set in any program, you can use the -D option. This option redefines a named property value to a value you set. You can use the -D option to change the background color of text, windows, or buttons. The syntax for this option is

```
java -DpropertyName=newValue classname
```

The command-line syntax for the interpreter is

```
java [options] classname [args]
```

The interpreter takes the following options:

Option	Description
-classpath	Overrides the default or current CLASSPATH environment variable setting.
-cs, -checksource	Instructs the interpreter to make sure the compiled classes are current and to recompile the source files if they are not.
-ms	Sets the startup size of the heap.
-mx	Specifies the maximum number of bytes to be allocated to the heap.
-noasyncgc	Tells the runtime environment to perform no asynchronous garbage collection unless the program runs out of memory or the program explicitly tells the system to perform garbage collection.
-noverify	Turns off validity checking of class files.
-oss	Sets the maximum stack size used for Java code.
-prof	Dumps profiling information to a file called java.prof in the current directory.

continues

Option	Description
-ss	Sets the maximum stack size used for C code.
-t	Traces every instruction the Java Virtual Machine executes. Used only with the debugging version of the interpreter, java_g.
-v, -verbose	Tells you what class files the interpreter is loading.
-verbosegc	Tells the runtime environment to print out messages whenever it frees memory.
-verify	Checks the validity of all class files.
-verifyremote	Checks the validity of the class files before loading over the network (default for the interpreter).

The Java Applet Viewer

The Java applet viewer enables you to view applets without a Web browser. Because applets extend the Applet class and are made for viewing in Web documents, you must create an HTML document with the appropriate markup before you can use the applet viewer. After you have created such a document, you can use the applet viewer to view your applets.

You run the applet viewer from the command line by passing it the name or path to an HTML document that references one or more applets, such as

```
appletviewer example.html
```

Before displaying any applets, the applet viewer verifies that the HTML document contains an <APPLET> tag with three specific attributes: CODE, WIDTH, and HEIGHT. The CODE attribute tells the viewer what class file to load. The WIDTH and HEIGHT attributes tell the viewer what the size of the applet's canvas should be. The viewer also looks for the optional <PARAM> tag that sets input parameters for your applets. (See Chapter 15, "Creating Java-Powered Web Presentations with Applets," for a complete discussion on creating Java-enhanced HTML documents.)

The applet viewer does not make use of any other HTML tags within the document. This means your HTML document will not look the same as it would when viewed with a Java-capable Web browser. For each defined <APPLET> tag in the document, the applet viewer starts up a separate window, the height and width of which are determined by the attributes you set. This means that if you add three applets to a document, the applet viewer will place the applets in three separate windows. If you want to see how it looks to have three applets running in separate windows, view the Web presentation you create in Chapter 15 with the applet viewer.

The only option the applet viewer takes from the command line is the -debug option, which starts a debugging session with the Java debugger. With this option, you can debug your applets. (See Chapter 23 for more information on the Java debugger.)

The command-line syntax for the applet viewer is

```
appletviewer [option] document.html
```

The applet viewer takes the following option:

Option	Description
-debug	Starts a debugging session.

Additional Options Available While Running the Applet Viewer

When you are running an applet, an additional menu called Applets is available from the menu bar. After editing the HTML document associated with an applet, you can reload the document and the applet by selecting Reload from the Applets menu. Another useful option of the viewer is Clone. If you select Clone from the Applets menu, you can make a new copy of the applet window and restart the associated applet. This is useful if you are testing the behavior of the applet. Instead of reloading all the files associated with an applet or cloning an applet, you might want to restart the applet. To do that, you can select Restart from the Applets menu.

Two other options available from the menu can provide you information about an applet. The Tag option displays the <APPLET> tag associated with the currently running applet. The Info option shows additional information about the applet. Finally, the Close option closes the applet viewer window, and the Quit option exits the applet viewer.

When an applet is running in the applet viewer, these options are available from the viewer's menu:

Menu Option	Description
Clone	Allows you to make a new copy of the applet window and restart the associated applet.
Edit	Allows you to edit a document associated with the current applet.
Info	Allows you to see additional information about the current applet.
Properties	Allows you to set access options for the applet.
Quit	Allows you to quit the viewer.
Reload	Allows you to reload an applet and all associated files.
Restart	Allows you to restart an applet but does not reload the applet or its associated files.
Tag	Allows you to display the <APPLET> tag associated with the currently running applet.

Applet Viewer Security Mechanisms

The applet viewer loads local and remote applets using two different mechanisms. Applets that exist on the local file system and in a directory defined in the CLASSPATH environment variable are loaded by the file system loader. Applets downloaded from the network or that are not in a directory defined in the CLASSPATH environment variable are loaded by the applet class loader.

Applets loaded by the applet class loader are subject to the restrictions of the applet security manager. The security manager adds an additional layer of security controls to untrusted applets, which ensures the integrity of the client machine is not compromised when accessing remote information. These security controls place restrictions on what untrusted applets can and cannot do on the client system.

Specifically, untrusted applets cannot

- Read or write files
- Make directories
- List files in a directory
- Check file type, size, or modification date
- Start another program on the client
- Access other clients or IP addresses
- Access native code or libraries

Although applets loaded by the file system loader are trusted, the applet viewer still maintains security controls over them. These security controls can be relaxed by setting property values. You set property values in the file called, appropriately, properties. This file is located in the .hotjava directory under the Java installation directory and can be edited with a plain text editor.

Allowing Applets to Read Files and Directories

You can allow local applets to read files and directories by adding them to the access control list. To do this, set the property value acl.read equal to the files or directories you want applets to be able to read.

Reading Files on UNIX Systems

On a UNIX system, if you want applets to read a file called numbers.txt in the $HOME\java directory, edit the properties file and insert the following line:

```
acl.read=$HOME\java\numbers.txt
```

If you want applets to be able to access all the files in the $HOME\java directory, you can do this by setting the value for acl.read to

```
acl.read=$HOME\java
```

If you want applets to be able to read multiple directories or files, separate each entry by colons, like this:

```
acl.read=\java\applets\docs:\usr\images\gifs:\usr\temp
```

Reading Files on Windows and OS/2 Systems

On a Windows or OS/2 system, if you want applets to read a file called numbers.txt in the C:\java directory, edit the properties file and insert the following line:

```
acl.read=C:\java\numbers.txt
```

If you want applets to be able to access all the files in the C:\java directory, you can do this by setting the value for acl.read to

```
acl.read=C:\java
```

If you want applets to be able to read multiple directories or files, separate each entry by semicolons, like this:

```
acl.read=C:\java;C:\java\applets\docs
```

Allowing Applets to Write to Files and Directories

You can allow local applets to write to files and directories by adding them to the access control list. To do this, set the property value acl.write equal to the files or directories to which you want applets to be able to write.

Writing to Files on UNIX Systems

On a UNIX system, if you want applets to write to a file called numbers.txt in the $HOME\java directory, edit the properties file and insert the following line:

```
acl.write=$HOME\java\numbers.txt
```

If you want applets to be able to write to files in the $HOME\java directory, you can do this by setting the value for acl.write to

```
acl.write=$HOME\java
```

If you want applets to be able to write to multiple directories or files, separate each entry by colons, like this:

```
acl.write=\java\applets\docs:\usr\images\gifs:\usr\temp
```

Writing to Files on Windows and OS/2 Systems

On a Windows or OS/2 system, if you want applets to write to a file called `numbers.txt` in the `C:\java` directory, edit the `properties` file and insert the following line:

```
acl.write=C:\java\numbers.txt
```

If you want applets to be able to write to files in the `C:\java` directory, you can do this by setting the value for `acl.write` to

```
acl.write=C:\java
```

If you want applets to be able to write to multiple directories or files, separate each entry by semi-colons, like this:

```
acl.write=C:\java;C:\java\applets\docs
```

Applet Viewer Property Values

As you have seen, setting property values for local applets can be very useful. Many other property values are available to local applets as well. To access additional property values from within an applet, you can use the `getProperty()` method of the `System` class. Here's how:

```
String s = System.getProperty("valuename");
```

where `valuename` is the name of the property value you want to check, such as

```
String s = System.getProperty("java.version");
```

As shown in Table 5.2, local applets can access some property values by default. To remove access to these values, you can set them to `null` in the `.hotjava\properties` file, such as

```
os.arch=null
```

Table 5.2. Default system properties.

Property Value	Description
file.separator	The file separator for your operating system
java.class.version	Java class version number
java.vendor	Java vendor-specific information
java.vendor.url	URL of a particular vendor

Property Value	Description
java.version	Java version number
line.separator	The line separator for your operating system
os.arch	Operating-system architecture
os.name	Operating-system name
path.separator	The file path separator for your operating system

As shown in Table 5.3, there are other property values that local applets can access only if they are set to true in the .hotjava\properties file. You enter these values in the form valuename.applet=true. Here's how you could allow applets to read the user.name value:

```
user.name.applet=true
```

Table 5.3. Restricted system properties.

Property Value	Description
java.home	Java installation directory
java.class.path	Java CLASSPATH setting
user.name	User's account name
user.home	User's home directory
user.dir	User's current working directory

Graphical Developer's Tools

Graphical developer's tools for Java are available directly from Sun and from third-party vendors. This section examines the developer's tools available from Sun and its subsidiaries.

Macintosh Developer's Tools

The Macintosh has an entirely graphical user interface. For this reason, the JDK for Macintosh is much more than a simple port of the UNIX version. The first thing you will notice about the JDK tools is that they have a familiar look and feel. You can drag-and-drop files onto any of the tool icons to start them. You also can start the tools by clicking on their icons. After the tools are started, you can access pull-down menus that provide you with options and let you set or change defaults.

Key Differences in Java Tools for the Macintosh

Where the Java developer's tools differ from Macintosh applications is behind the scenes. Unlike the Solaris and Windows 95/NT operating systems, the Macintosh operating system is not inherently multithreaded. Because some multithreaded operations such as memory management are automatic in Java, the lack of built-in multithreading posed a major problem to the JDK developers.

The workaround was to perform multithreading at a higher level than on other systems. This provides Macintosh users with most of the advantages of a multithreaded environment. However, some operations that are controlled at the operating-system level or otherwise beyond Java's control block other threads. For example, when a menu is down, all other operations are blocked.

Memory management is an example of an operation that is sometimes blocking. Java is designed to automatically manage memory for you as a background task, yet on the Macintosh background memory management is not always possible. Periodically, Java tries to free memory by deleting objects that are no longer referenced. If Java cannot satisfy a request for memory, memory management moves temporarily from the background to the foreground. When this happens, you will see a busy cursor as Java searches for objects that can be freed.

You can avoid most memory problems by increasing the default settings for memory heaps to fit your needs and your system. On the Macintosh, Java maintains two memory heaps. The Macintosh Application Heap is used entirely for Macintosh allocations such as menus, windows, and buttons. The garbage-collected heap, or GC heap, is used by Java.

Whenever you start a new Java application, some memory is allocated to both the application heap and the GC heap. You can determine how much memory a Java application is allocated by checking the value associated with the largest unused block of memory before and after starting the application. This value can be found by clicking on About this Macintosh from the Finder.

Changing Heap Settings

You can change the heap settings in the Finder. To change the Macintosh Application Heap setting, follow these steps:

1. Access the Finder tool.
2. Click on the Get Info command.
3. Change the setting for the application heap in the space provided.

To change the garbage-collected heap setting, follow these steps:

1. Access the Finder tool.
2. Click on the Get Info command.
3. Change the setting for MultiFinder Temporary Memory.

> **Warning:** Before you change the heap settings, you should experiment with Java on your system.

The Java Compiler for Macintosh

When you compile Java programs, you will use the Java compiler. The Java compiler expects source code to be in a file named with the .java extension. Additionally, when the source file contains multiple class declarations, the source file must be named after the primary class declaration. Therefore, it is good to always name your source files after the primary class declaration. By default, the compiler uses between 800KB and 6000KB of temporary memory.

A handy feature of the compiler is the capability to link in a text editor that can be controlled by AppleEvents. This provides you with direct access to Java source files from within the compiler. Some of the text editors you can use include SimpleText, BBEdit 3.5 or later versions, and CodeWarrior IDE versions 7 or 8. You can set your preferred editor by selecting Preferences from the menu.

> **Note:** AppleEvents allow the text editor and the Java compiler to communicate by passing "events" back and forth. Events contain information that allows the compiler to start the text editor.

The Preferences submenu also lets you set compiler and debugging options. To better understand what these various options offer you, review the section on the command-line version of the Java compiler in this chapter.

The Java compiler automatically compiles your source code when you do one of the following:

- Drag-and-drop a source file with the .java extension onto the compiler icon.
- Click on the compiler icon. After the compiler is started, select Open from the File menu.

For each class declaration in the source file, the Java compiler creates a class file with a .class extension. Because the compiler is case sensitive, the first part of the class file will be named exactly as you typed it in the source file. By default, the class files are placed in the same directory as the source file.

When you start the compiler, a status window appears. From the status window you can determine

- The current free memory in the Java garbage-collected heap
- The current compiler activity
- The number of simultaneous compiles

Errors that occur during compiling are shown in a pop-up window. You can use the error report to pinpoint problems in the code. If you have set a preferred editor, you can go directly into an editor session by doing one of the following:

- Double-clicking on the errors shown in the error window
- Selecting Edit from the File menu

After you correct errors, save the file. You can now recompile the source file simply by selecting Rebuild from the File menu. The Rebuild option tells the compiler to recompile the last source file you tried to compile. If the source file still has errors, they will be listed to an error window.

To close pop-up windows started by the compiler, you can select the Close option from the menu. Each time you select Close, the frontmost window will close. If the status window is the frontmost window, the compiler will exit. You can also exit the compiler simply by selecting Quit from the menu. Because all current compiler actions are aborted when you quit, you generally should wait until the compiler completes what it is doing before exiting.

The compiler has the following menu options:

Menu Option	Description
Close	Allows you to close the frontmost window.
Edit	Allows you to edit a source file.
Open	Allows you to open a source file. The compiler automatically tries to compile any files you open.
Preferences	Allows you to set compiler options.
Quit	Allows you to quit the compiler.
Rebuild	Allows you to recompile the last source file you tried to compile.

The Applet Viewer for Macintosh

On the Macintosh, the Java applet viewer is designated by the AppletViewer icon. The applet viewer allows you to view applets without a Web browser. Because applets extend the Applet class and are made for viewing in Web documents, you must create an HTML document with the appropriate markup before you can use the applet viewer. After you have created such a document, you can use the applet viewer to view your applets.

To view an applet with the applet viewer, you can do one of the following:

- Drag-and-drop an HTML document with the .html extension onto the AppletViewer icon.
- Click on the AppletViewer icon. After the applet viewer is started, select Open Local from the File menu.

Before displaying any applets, the applet viewer verifies that the HTML document contains an <APPLET> tag with three specific attributes: CODE, WIDTH, and HEIGHT. The CODE attribute tells the viewer what class file to load. The WIDTH and HEIGHT attributes tell the viewer what the size of the applet's canvas should be. The viewer also looks for the optional <PARAM> tag that sets input parameters for your applets. (See Chapter 15 for a complete discussion on creating Java-enhanced HTML documents.)

The applet viewer does not make use of any other HTML tags within the document. This means your HTML document will not look the same as it would when viewed with a Java-capable Web browser. For each defined <APPLET> tag in the document, the applet viewer starts up a separate window, the height and width of which are determined by the attributes you set. This means that if you add three applets to a document, the applet viewer will place the applets in three separate windows. If you want to see how it looks to have three applets running in separate windows, use the applet viewer to view the Web presentation you create in Chapter 15.

By default, the applet viewer uses 300KB to 3000KB of temporary memory. When you start the applet viewer, a status window appears. From the status window you can determine

- The current free memory in the Java garbage-collected heap
- The number of applets currently running on the system

The Macintosh applet viewer lets you access applets on the Web. You can do this by selecting Open URL from the menu. If you type in the URL to an HTML document on the Web containing an applet, the applet viewer will display the applet. This lets any Mac user with the JDK installed on his system view applets even if his browser does not support them.

Just as you can configure a text editor for the compiler, you can configure a text editor for the applet viewer. Again, the text editor must be controllable by AppleEvents. You can set your preferred editor by selecting Properties from the menu. The Properties submenu also lets you set applet viewer options such as automatic verification of the class file and network access.

When you are running an applet, an additional menu called Applets is available from the menu bar. If you have set a preferred editor for the applet viewer, you can go directly into an editor session by selecting Edit from the Applets menu. You can use the editor session to edit the HTML document associated with the running applet. After you have made the necessary changes, save the HTML document. You can then reload the document and its associated applet by selecting Reload from the Applets menu.

Another useful option of the viewer is Clone. If you select Clone from the Applets menu, you can make a new copy of the applet window and restart the associated applet. This is useful if you are testing the behavior of the applet. Instead of reloading all the files associated with an applet or cloning an applet, you might want to restart the applet. To restart an applet, you can select Restart from the Applets menu.

Two additional options available from the menu can provide you information about an applet. The Tag option displays the <APPLET> tag associated with the currently running applet. The Info option shows additional information about the applet.

The applet viewer has the following menu options when no applets are running:

Menu Option	Description
Open Local	Allows you to load a local HTML document. The applet viewer automatically tries to display the applets defined by the <APPLET> tag within the document.
Open URL	Allows you to load an HTML document located on a remote host. The applet viewer automatically tries to display the applets defined by the <APPLET> tag within the document.
Properties	Allows you to set viewer options.
Quit	Allows you to quit the viewer.

When an applet is running in the viewer, these options are added under the Applets menu:

Menu Option	Description
Clone	Allows you to make a new copy of the applet window and restart the associated applet.
Edit	Allows you to edit a document associated with the current applet.
Info	Allows you to see additional information about the current applet.
Properties	Allows you to set viewer options.
Reload	Allows you to reload an applet and all associated files.
Restart	Allows you to restart an applet but does not reload the applet or its associated files.
Tag	Allows you to display the <APPLET> tag associated with the currently running applet.

The Java Interpreter for Macintosh

The Java interpreter executes Java bytecode files. You will use the interpreter to run Java applications. Before the interpreter runs any program, it verifies that the classes associated with the program are valid and do not violate any language constraints. For applications that include many classes, you will want to pass the interpreter the class file that declares the application's main() method.

The interpreter executes the main() method and any threads specified in the main() method. If no threads are created by the main() method, the interpreter executes the main() method and then exits. If threads are created by the main() method, the interpreter exits when the last thread exits. Because the interpreter expects the class file to contain a `main()` method, you generally cannot use the interpreter to run Java applets. If you want to run Java applets, you should use the Java applet viewer discussed in the previous section of this chapter.

To view a Java application with the interpreter, you can

- Drag-and-drop the class file with the `main()` method onto the interpreter icon.
- Click on the interpreter icon. After the interpreter is started, select Open from the File menu.

Most of the interpreter features are similar to those discussed in the previous sections of this chapter. You can set properties for the interpreter in the Properties menu. You can reload an application by selecting Reload from the File menu. To quit the current interpreter session, you select Quit from the File menu.

The interpreter has the following menu options:

Menu Option	Description
Edit	Allows you to edit a document associated with the current application.
Open	Allows you to open a class file. The interpreter automatically tries to run any files you open.
Properties	Allows you to set interpreter options.
Quit	Allows you to quit the current interpreter session.
Reload	Allows you to reload an application and all associated files.

Java WorkShop

The Java WorkShop is an integrated development environment that helps you develop and manage just about any type of programming project. Java WorkShop is a commercial product currently in development by SunSoft.

Java WorkShop is currently available for Solaris and Windows 95/NT. Free developers versions of Java WorkShop are available directly from SunSoft at

```
http://www.sun.com/sunsoft/Developer-products/java/
```

Navigating the WorkShop

Java WorkShop's entire graphical development environment is placed within a Webified desktop. This makes Java WorkShop as easy to use as your favorite Web browser. Figure 5.5 shows the main window for WorkShop. The navigation buttons depicted on the menu bar are accessible from any part of the desktop.

Figure 5.5.
Navigating the WorkShop.

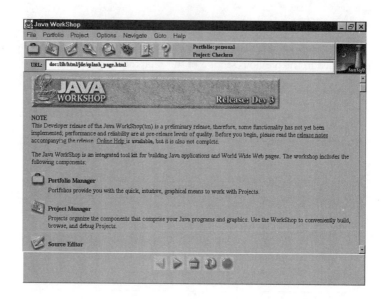

By clicking on a menu button, you can move quickly from tool to tool. The suitcase button takes you to a Portfolio Manager. The puzzle button takes you to a Project Manager. The pencil-and-notepad button takes you to the source editor. The wrench button takes you to a build session. The magnifying glass takes you to a source browser. The ladybug button takes you to the debugger. The light-switch button runs the current applet or application. The question-mark button takes you to WorkShop's online help.

Each tool in Java WorkShop displays in an HTML page that contains a specialized applet that performs a specific function such as debugging your code. Some applets launch an associated editor or browser. For example, the debugger applet starts a debugger browser. Let's look at each of the key tools in Java WorkShop.

Built-in Help

You can access Java WorkShop's online help system at any time by clicking on the Help button icon—the question mark on the main toolbar. The online help system is organized into eight subject areas:

- Contents—A list of all the help pages
- Index—A subject index of help topics
- Getting Started—An overview of Java WorkShop
- Debugging Applets—How to use Java WorkShop to debug Java programs
- Building Applets—How to use Java WorkShop to build Java programs
- Managing Applets—How to manage projects and portfolios using Java WorkShop

- Editing Source—How to use Java WorkShop to edit source files
- Browsing Source—How to use Java WorkShop to browse source files

You can access any of the help topics using the help toolbar. As you can see from Figure 5.6, the help toolbar is clearly labeled for easy navigation.

Figure 5.6.
Using the built-in help.

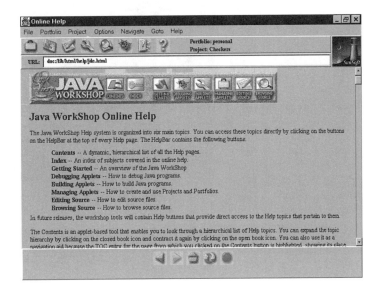

The Portfolio Manager

You can access Java WorkShop's Portfolio Manager at any time by clicking on the Portfolio Manager icon—the suitcase icon on the main toolbar. The purpose of the Portfolio Manager is to help you create and manage groups of projects called *portfolios*. Figure 5.7 shows the project-creation page in Java WorkShop. Your WorkShop projects can include local applets, remote applets, stand-alone applications, images, and Java packages.

By grouping projects into a portfolio, Java WorkShop allows you to quickly build, browse, and debug portfolio components. For example, each project in the portfolio is assigned an icon and a name. When you are on the Portfolio Manager page, you can compile all source files associated with a project by selecting its icon and then selecting the Build button on the main toolbar.

Editing Projects

When you create a project using the Portfolio Manager, you define attributes for the project—the puzzle icon on the main toolbar. These attributes can be changed with the Project Editor. You can access Java WorkShop's Project Editor at any time by clicking on the Project Editor icon—the puzzle icon on the main toolbar.

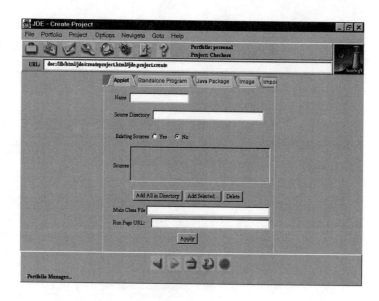

Figure 5.7.
Creating a new project with the Portfolio Manager.

As you can see from Figure 5.8, the Project Editor contains five folders in which you can assign default attributes for the project:

- General—Allows you to specify general information for the project including the name, type, and source directory of the project.
- Build—Allows you to specify information used when the project is compiled
- Debug/Browse—Allows you to specify information used when you debug and browse source files
- Run—Allows you to specify information used when you run an applet or stand-alone application
- Publish—Allows you to specify information used when you publish the project for others to use it.

You can access any of these folders simply by clicking on its associated tab. Whenever you change information in a folder, you should apply the changes before moving to another folder.

The Source Editor

When you want to create source files in Java WorkShop, you click on the Source Editor icon—the pencil-and-notepad icon on the main toolbar. The Source Editor in Java WorkShop is a stand-alone text editor. Although the features of the editor are very basic, it is easy to use and performs most of the tasks you would want a source code editor to do. Figure 5.9 shows the Source Editor.

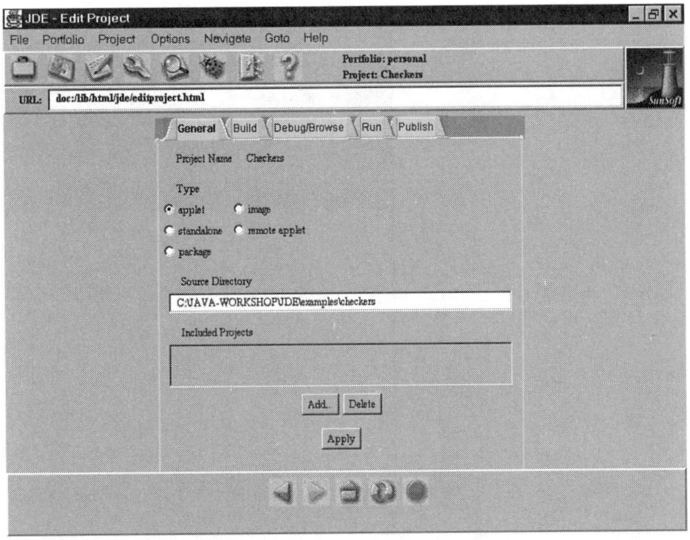

Figure 5.8.
Editing your Java projects.

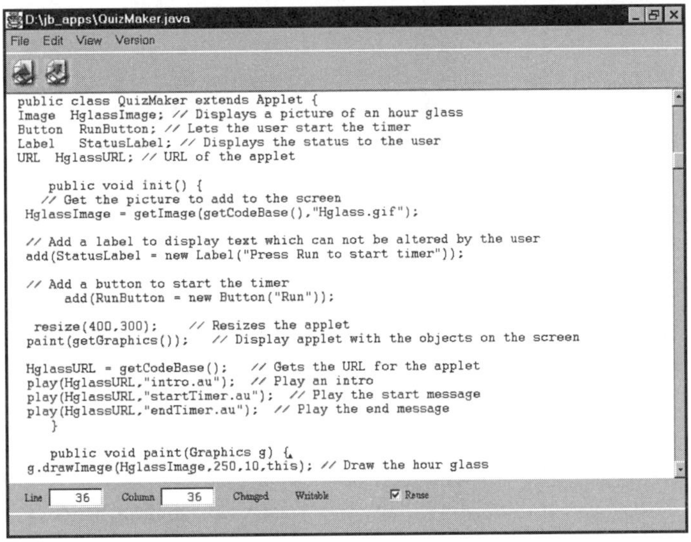

Figure 5.9.
The Source Editor in Java WorkShop.

Building Projects

Java WorkShop allows you to compile and build at any stage of a project. To start a build session, you simply press the Build button—the wrench icon on the main toolbar.

As you can see from Figure 5.10, the Program Builder allows you to compile entire projects or single files. If you build a project, the Program Builder uses the information you specified in the Project Manager or Project Editor information session. If you build a single file, the Program Builder uses the default settings for the current project to compile the file.

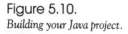

Figure 5.10.
Building your Java project.

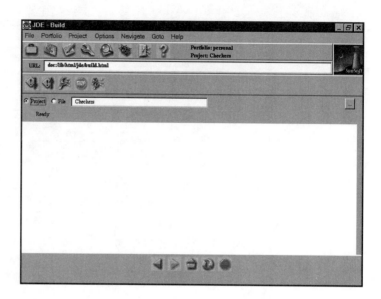

The Source Browser

When you want to view relationships in your source code, you will use the Source Browser. The Source Browser displays documentation for your WorkShop projects that resembles the documentation generated by the Java API documentation generator—javadoc. The advantage of the Source Browser is that you can view relationships at any time during or after the creation of a project simply by pressing the Source Browser button—the magnifying-glass icon on the main toolbar.

Figure 5.11 shows some of the classes used in the CheckersGame class, which is part of a demo applet that comes with Java WorkShop. To ensure this documentation is easy to use for programs of any size, the Source Browser includes a utility that allows you to search for references in specified source files.

The Debugger

To debug your code, you will use the WorkShop debugger, which is accessible at any time from the main toolbar. When you start a debugging session by clicking on the Debugger button—the lady-bug icon on the main toolbar—Java WorkShop moves to the debugger screen and starts a debugging browser. The purpose of the debugging browser is to let you see how specific changes affect the appearance of your Java program.

Debugging functions are organized into six folders. You can see the tabs for these folders in Figure 5.12, which also shows the debugging browser. Each folder provides you with control over a specific set of related functions. For example, the Thread/Stacks folder lets you view the current status of threads and stacks, start and stop threads, and add or remove items from the stack.

Figure 5.11.
The Source Browser.

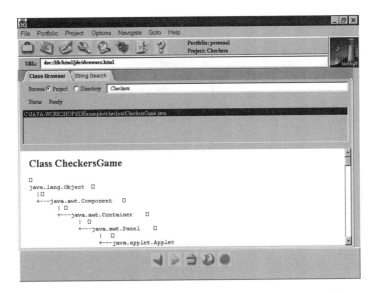

Figure 5.12.
The debugger and debugging browser.

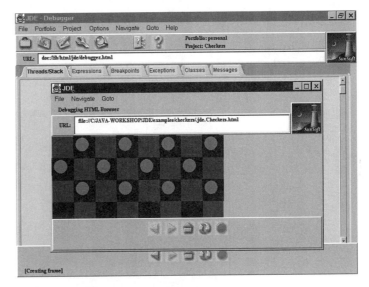

After you start a debugging session, Java WorkShop allows you to perform limited debugging functions in the Source Editor. To do this, the editor automatically displays a new toolbar with icons for common debugging functions. These functions allow you to stop at a breakpoint, clear breakpoints, resume execution of all threads, step into the program line by line, run to the current cursor location, move up the stack, and move down the stack.

Figure 5.13 shows the Source Editor with the debugging toolbar. If you compare Figure 5.13 with Figure 5.9, you can easily identify the changes.

Figure 5.13.
The Source Editor with the debugging toolbar.

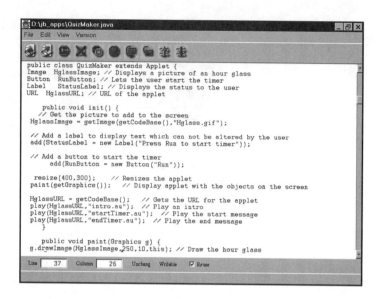

Running Projects in Java WorkShop

Running your project is as easy as clicking the Run button—the light-switch icon on the main toolbar. Depending on the type of project you are creating, WorkShop will either open a browser session or create a shell tool. Figure 5.14 shows the Checkers applet running in WorkShop's main window.

Figure 5.14.
Running the project.

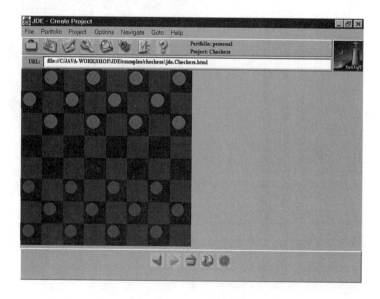

Summary

Whether you use a UNIX-based system or a Windows-based system, the Java Developer's Kit provides you with a complete toolkit for developing powerful Java programs. The tools you will use most often are the Java compiler, interpreter, and applet viewer. Other tools in the JDK have a more limited purpose but are useful as well. You can use the Java API documentation generator to create online documentation. You will use the Java header and stub file generator when you want Java classes to interact with C/C++ libraries. You will use the Java class file disassembler when you want to gain insight into the inner workings of class files.

III

Anatomy of the Java Language

6

Fundamentals of the Java Language

This book has been using broad terms to discuss the significance of Java as a programming language. It now digs deeper into Java to discuss the building blocks for writing programs. Those of you who are familiar with other languages such as C or C++ will find many familiar constructs in Java. However, you may have to "unlearn" some programming habits.

This chapter explains the fundamentals of Java programming language from broad concepts and logical program flow to specific keywords.

Tokens

The Java programming language has a term for its building blocks, or basic elements: *tokens*. Becoming familiar with these words and concepts is a prerequisite to programming in Java.

Chapter 4, "The Java Language: A Primer," explains the series of events surrounding compiling and running an application. This chapter explains the logic of the `javac` compiler.

At compile time, the `javac` compiler takes the code and pulls out specific information, called a *token*, for further processing.

First, `javac` takes out escape sequences from the raw byte codes. It determines if the escape sequences are line terminators or input characters. Next, `javac` takes out whitespace that is not internal to a string, including the ASCII space character, carriage return, line feed, and horizontal tab. Then the compiler gets down to the business of pulling out tokens.

There are several types of tokens: identifiers, keywords, literals, operators, separators, and comments.

Identifiers

The `javac` compiler needs to know the names of items in the program. For example, it must recognize the names of variables, methods, and component elements of classes. *Identifiers* are either Java reserved words or titles given to variables, classes, and methods. Reserved words are names that may be used only by Java. Using these words in any other way will cause a compile error.

Identifiers can be named anything as long as they begin with an alphabet character, a dollar sign, or an underscore. However, I do not recommend that you use the dollar sign or begin an identifier name with an underscore because these symbols are used by the Java libraries. This will help with debugging. Do use the underscore to connect words to make an identifier meaningful, as in `this_book`. As with all good programming, the more descriptive the identifier, the better.

Identifier Name Size

Java will often give a programmer just enough rope to get into interesting knots. For example, the `javac` compiler will accept uppercase or mixed-case words the same way it does keywords.

Java identifiers are case sensitive. For example, `char` is a reserved word in Java. This means that it is possible to assign a variable the identifier `Char`, `CHAR`, or variations thereof. However, this makes debugging difficult. You'll learn more on reserved words in the next section.

Keywords

Keywords are reserved words, which means that they cannot be used in any way other than how Java intends for them to be used. Keywords are, therefore, special tokens. They are always lowercase.

Java keywords are used as application flow controls, declarations, class identifiers, and expressions. Table 6.1 lists all the reserved keywords in Java. Keywords that pertain to the fundamentals of Java are explained in the appropriate section of this chapter.

Table 6.1. Reserved keywords in Java.

Data Declaration Keywords

boolean

byte

char

double

float

int

long

short

Loop Keywords

break

continue

do

for

while

Conditional Keywords

case

else

if

switch

continues

Table 6.1. continued

Exception Keywords

catch

finally

throw

try

Structure Keywords

abstract

class

default

extends

implements

instance of

interface

Modifier and Access Keywords

final

native

new

private

protected

public

static

synchronized

threadsafe

transient

void

Miscellaneous Keywords

false

import

null

package

return

```
super

this

true
```

The following keywords are reserved and are *not* being used in Java 1.0; they may be used in future releases:

```
byvalue
cast
const
future
generic
goto
inner
operator
outer
rest
var
```

Literals

Data is represented by *literals* in Java. Similar to literals in other programming languages, Java literals are based on character and number representations. The types of literals are integer, floating-point, boolean, character, and string.

Every variable consists of a literal and a data type. The difference between the two is that literals are entered explicitly into the code. Data types are information about the literals, such as how much room will be reserved in memory for that variable, as well as the possible value ranges for the variable. (Data types are discussed in the section "Using Data Types.")

Integer Literals

Integers are whole numbers, such as 1 and 5280. *Integer literals* can be decimal (base 10), octal (base 8), or hexadecimal (base 16).

Decimals can be positive, zero, or negative. Decimal literals cannot start with 0, as in 01234. After the beginning number, a decimal literal can consist of the numbers 0–9. Numbers beginning with 0 are reserved for octal and hexadecimal literals. Therefore, when using decimals, do not right-justify with leading zeros. The upper limit of a positive decimal integer is $2^{31}-1$, or 2,147,483,647. The lower limit is –2,147,483,648 or $–2^{31}$.

Octal literals start with 0 and can be followed by any number 0–7. They can be positive, zero, or negative. The maximum value of an octal literal is 017777777777, which is equivalent to $2^{31}-1$.

Hexadecimal integer literals start with 0x or 0X, followed by one or more hexadecimal digits. Letters A–F used in a hexadecimal integer can be uppercase or lowercase. Hexadecimal integers can be positive, zero, or negative. The upper limit of a positive hexadecimal literal is 0x7fffffff, which is, once again, equivalent to $2^{31}-1$. The values available are 1–9, A–F, and a–f.

A compile-time error will occur if any of these values is exceeded.

Floating-Point Literals

A *floating-point literal* represents a number that has a decimal point in it, such as 3.7. Java standards specify that floating-point numbers must follow the industry standard specification as written in IEEE-754.

Single-precision floating-point numbers consist of a 32-bit space and are designated by uppercase or lowercase *f*. Double-precision numbers are allotted a 64-bit space and are designated by uppercase or lowercase *d*. Double-precision floating-point numbers are the default. Therefore, 3.7 is a double-precision floating-point number, and 3.7f is a single-precision floating-point number.

How do you know whether to use a single- or double-precision floating-point number? It depends on the size of the number. If there is any possibility that a number could grow out of range or need to be of greater precision than single, declare it a double.

Compile-time errors will occur if a nonzero floating-point literal is too large or small.

The largest magnitude single-precision floating-point literal is ±3.40282347e+38f, and the smallest is ±1.40239846e–45f. The largest double-precision floating-point number is 1.79769313486231570e+308, and 4.94065645841246544e–324 is the smallest floating-point number.

> **Note:** Floating-point literals also can be expressed using exponents or scientific notation, as shown in the preceding paragraph. Uppercase or lowercase *e* is used to denote the exponent portion of a floating-point number. An example of this is 2.1e3f; this is a single-precision floating-point number representing 2100.

Boolean Literals

A boolean literal is either of the words *true* or *false*. Unlike other programming languages, no numeric value such as 0 or 1 is assigned. Therefore, the value of a boolean literal is, literally, true or false. Booleans are used extensively in program control flow logic.

Character Literals

Programmers often use a single character as a value. In Java, this is represented by *character literals*. The value of a character literal is enclosed by single quotes. An example is `'y'`.

Assigning a value to a character literal gets more interesting if the value must be a single quote, a backslash, or other nonprintable characters. A backslash (\) is used to designate certain nonprintable characters or characters that are properly part of the command. For example, assign the value `'\''` to characterize the single quote. Table 6.2 shows some examples of assigning values to character literals.

Table 6.2. Specifying character literals.

Description or Escape Sequence	Sequence	Output
Any character	`'y'`	y
Backspace (BS)	`'\b'`	Backspace
Horizontal tab (HT)	`'\t'`	Tab
Linefeed (LF)	`'\n'`	Linefeed
Formfeed (FF)	`'\f'`	Form feed
Carriage return (CR)	`'\r'`	Carriage return
Double quote	`'\"'`	"
Single quote	`'\''`	'
Backslash	`'\\'`	\
Octal bit pattern	`'\ddd'`	Octal value of *ddd*
Hex bit pattern	`'\xdd'`	Hex value of *dd*
Unicode character	`'\udddd'`	Actual Unicode character of *dddd*

Compile-time errors occur if anything other than a single quote follows the value designator or the character after `'\'` is anything but b, t, n, f, r, ", ', \, 0, 1, 2, 4, 5, 6, or 7.

String Literals

String literals are a sequence of characters enclosed in double quotes, such as `"This is a string literal"`. This could also be `"Hello World"` or even `""` for a null character string. The javac compiler does not strip out whitespace from within string literals.

String literals can be concatenated. For example, if one string contained `"This is the beginning"` and another string contained `" of a beautiful relationship"`, they could be concatenated together. The representation would be `"This is the beginning"` + `" of a beautiful relationship"`. (It is not necessary to have spaces on either side of the plus sign.)

A string literal cannot span more than one line; those that do so can be broken up at declaration time and then concatenated at use time. This also makes programs more readable and strings less likely to be mistaken for comments.

As with the character literal, the backslash is used to denote symbols that otherwise would not work. The double quote is represented by the string "\"".

Separators

Java uses the following separators: (), {}, [], ;, ,, and ..

The compiler uses these *separators* to divide the code into segments. They can also force arithmetic precedence evaluation within an expression. (You will learn more about precedence in the section "Using Operators in Expressions.") Separators are also useful as visual and logical locators for programmers.

Note the use of separators in the following code fragment:

```
if (location < 10) {
```

Here, the parentheses indicate to the compiler the boolean expression to be evaluated, which is whether the value of `location` is less than 10. The trailing { indicates the start of a block of code that will be executed if the boolean expression evaluates to `true`.

Operators

Operators are the symbols used for arithmetic and logical operations. Arithmetic symbols define operations that apply to numbers (for example, 2 + 3). Operators, except the plus sign (+), are used only for arithmetic calculations. The + operator can be used with strings as well, as shown in the previous example of string literal concatenation. Tables 6.3 through 6.7 list all the Java operators.

Table 6.3. The Java arithmetic operators.

Operator	Operation	Example
+	Addition	g + h
–	Subtraction	g – h
*	Multiplication	g * h
/	Division	g / h
%	Modulus	g % h

Table 6.4. The Java assignment operators.

Operator	Operation	Example	Meaning
=	Assign value	a = 7	a = 7
+=	Add to current variable	g += h	g = g + h
-=	Subtract from current	g -= h	g = g - h
*=	Multiply current	g *= h	g = g * h
/=	Divide current	g /= h	g = g / h
%=	Modulus current	g %= h	g = g % h

Table 6.5. The Java increment and decrement operators.

Operator	Operation	Example	Meaning
++	Increment by 1	g++ or ++g	g = g + 1
--	Decrement by 1	g-- or --g	g = g -1

Table 6.6. The Java comparison operators (which return **true** or **false**).

Operator	Operation	Example	Meaning
==	Equal	g == h	Is g equal to h?
!=	Not equal	g != h	Is g not equal to h?
<	Less than	g < h	Is g less than h?
>	Greater than	g > h	Is g greater than h?
<=	Less than or equal	g <= h	Is g less than or equal to h?
>=	Greater than or equal	g >= h	Is g greater than or equal to h?

Table 6.7. The Java bitwise operators.

Operator	Operation
&	Bitwise AND
¦	Bitwise OR
^	Bitwise XOR
<<	Left shift
>>	Right shift

continues

Table 6.7. continued

Operator	Operation
>>>	Zero fill right shift
~	Bitwise complement
<<=	Left shift assignment
>>=	Right shift assignment
>>>=	Zero fill right shift assignment
x&=y	AND assignment
x¦=y	OR assignment
x^=y	NOT assignment

Comments

Some programmers believe that if something is difficult to code, it should be difficult to maintain. There is a special place in the cosmos for them; let's hope that it's not on your project! Of course, *comments* should be used throughout code to explain the programmer's rationale. Comments also can be used to block out certain code sections for testing purposes.

Comments have an initial indicator (usually text) and an end indicator. Sometimes comments are used to separate logic, in which case there may be no text.

Table 6.8 illustrates three ways to indicate comments in Java.

Table 6.8. Comment indicators.

Start	Text	End Comment
/*	text	*/
/**	text	*/
//	text	(everything to the end of the line is ignored by the compiler)

The /* comment is familiar to C programmers. The /** comment is typically used for machine-generated comments. The third style is familiar to C++ programmers.

The following are examples of comments:

```
/* this is an example of a comment */

/** this is another example of a comment. I can
    go to multiple lines and the compiler will
```

```
    look at this as a comment until I do the proper
    end comment as in */

//  with this method I can't go to multiple lines unless
//  I start each line with the comment marker.
```

Comments can be used anywhere in code without affecting the code's execution or logic. Be sure to terminate the comment, or the compiler will get confused.

> **Warning:** If you forget to terminate a comment, you will see strange results when you try to compile or run the program. Basically, what happens is that the compiler interprets everything up to the next end-comment indicator as part of the comment, which can cut out entire sections of your program.

Tokens Summary

Tokens are the building blocks, the most basic parts of Java. An understanding of them is essential to successful programming in Java. The following sections give examples of the uses of tokens in Java.

Using Data Types

A *variable* is something that changes, or varies. In Java, a variable stores data. Data types define the kind of data that can be stored in a variable and the limits of the data.

An example of the use of a data type is

```
char my_letter;
```

This example demonstrates the two essential parts of a variable: the type (`char`) and the identifier (`my_letter`). The type notifies the compiler that the variable `my_letter` will be of type `char`. Recall that `char` is a reserved keyword, and data types are always designated by one of the reserved keywords. The variable name `my_letter` at this point has the value of `null`, which is the default value of type `char`. Finally, the semicolon tells the compiler that the defining of the variable is finished.

Another example of defining data types follows:

```
int no_of_albums, b, YellowRose, chair;
```

This code example has four variables: `no_of_albums`, `b`, `YellowRose`, and `chair`. Each of them is of type `int` (a reserved keyword). You can enter multiple variables of the same type on the same line when separated by a comma. The default value for integers is `0`. Once again, the semicolon ends the definition.

There are two major data types in Java: reference types and primitive types.

Data types can be stored in variables, passed as arguments, returned as values, and operated on.

Note: Remember, the definition or typing of a variable does not assign a value to the variable; it simply identifies the possible values of that variable.

Primitive Data Types

Primitive data types can have only one value at a time. They do not reference other data or indicate sequence in a group of data. They are primitive in that they are the simplest built-in forms of data in Java. All other data types are made up of combinations of primitive data types. The primitive data type keywords are shown in Table 6.9.

Table 6.9. Primitive data type keywords.

`boolean`
`char`
`byte`
`short`
`int`
`long`
`float`
`double`

Integer Data Types

There are four integer data types: `byte`, `short`, `int`, and `long`. Each can handle different ranges of numbers, as summarized in Table 6.10.

Table 6.10. Integer data type ranges.

Type	Length	Minimum Value	Maximum Value
`byte`	8 bits	-128	127
`short`	16 bits	-32768	32767
`int`	32 bits	-2147483648	2147483647
`long`	64 bits	-9223372036854775808	9223372036854775807

Java does some interesting things to integer values during operations. For example, a variable SmallNumber of type byte and a variable LargeNumber of type int are added together. The variables both automatically become type int, or 32 bits in length. SmallNumber widens to 32 bits for the operation. (The exception is if the result is boolean, in which case no variables are expanded.) So whenever two integers of varying length are operated on, the smaller of the integers becomes the same length in memory as the larger.

The only case in which ArithmeticException is called is when there is an attempt to divide by zero, so test for zero before attempting a divide operation.

In the section titled "Conditional Expressions" you will find examples of how to check numerical values.

Other interesting things happen in Java when the value of an integer exceeds its defined range. ArithmeticException will *not* occur. Instead, the value "wraps" around to the other end of the numeric range for that type. Here is an example:

```
class IntWrap {
public static void main (String args[])
    {
byte StartNumber = 120;
      byte SmallNumber;
      int  LargeNumber;
SmallNumber = StartNumber;
      for (LargeNumber=0; LargeNumber < 16; LargeNumber++) {
         System.out.println("StartNumber(" + StartNumber + ") + LargeNumber (" +
                           LargeNumber + ") = " + SmallNumber);
         SmallNumber++;
      }
   }
}
```

After you save the source code in a file called IntWrap.java, you can compile the source code by typing the following at the command line:

```
javac IntWrap.java
```

To run the program, type this:

```
java IntWrap
```

The output from the program should be as follows:

```
StartNumber(120) + LargeNumber (0) = 120
StartNumber(120) + LargeNumber (1) = 121
StartNumber(120) + LargeNumber (2) = 122
StartNumber(120) + LargeNumber (3) = 123
StartNumber(120) + LargeNumber (4) = 124
StartNumber(120) + LargeNumber (5) = 125
StartNumber(120) + LargeNumber (6) = 126
StartNumber(120) + LargeNumber (7) = 127
StartNumber(120) + LargeNumber (8) = -128
StartNumber(120) + LargeNumber (9) = -127
StartNumber(120) + LargeNumber (10) = -126
```

```
StartNumber(120) + LargeNumber (11) = -125
StartNumber(120) + LargeNumber (12) = -124
StartNumber(120) + LargeNumber (13) = -123
StartNumber(120) + LargeNumber (14) = -122
StartNumber(120) + LargeNumber (15) = -121
```

`char` Data Types

Type `char` is really a 16-bit unsigned integer that represents a Unicode value. In other words, it is possible to determine Unicode characters and escape codes by using a numeric representation. Remember, each printable and nonprintable character has a Unicode value. Because Java stores all characters as Unicode, it can be used with virtually any written language in the world. This is a prime strength for Java. Unfortunately, at this time there is little support for internationalization in the way of functions or methods to, for example, print dates, monetary denominations, time, or numbers according to locale.

> **Note:** *Unicode* is an international character set. By following the Unicode standard, Java can easily be used to print text in many different languages.

Floating-Point Data Types

Type `float` designates that the variable is a single-precision, 32-bit, floating-point number. Type `double` is a double-precision, 64-bit, floating-point number. Here are examples of declaring floating-point variables:

```
float SquareFootage;
```

```
double GrossNationalProduct;
```

`boolean` Data Types

Type `boolean` can only have a value of `true` or `false`. Internal to Java, a `boolean` value is a 1-bit logical quantity.

Other programming languages have `boolean` values of `0` for `false` and `1` for `true`. You can get Java to mimic this behavior if necessary: As in the C programming language, `x!=0` will convert the integer `x` to a `boolean` in which `0` equals `false` and anything else equals `true`. On the other hand, `y?1:0` will convert the `boolean` variable `y` to `0` for `false` and `1` for `true`.

It is best to think of `boolean`s in a new light if your "native" language is C or C++. It is a distinct data type best used to indicate success or failure.

Summary of Primitive Data Types

Primitive data types are the lowest-level objects in Java. Think of them as actual nongrouped pieces of data, such as numbers and single characters. Primitive data types can be only one value at a time in a specific application. Java initializes all primitive data types to default values if an initial value is not explicitly specified by the programmer. Integer and floating-point variables are initialized to 0. The char data type is initialized to null, and boolean data types are set to false.

Reference Data Types

There are situations in which variables must be logically grouped together for manipulation, possibly because they are going to be accessed in sequence or identifiers must point to dynamically allocated objects. These are called *reference data types*.

Recall that a primitive data type contains the actual value of a typed variable; a reference data type contains the address of a value rather than the value itself. The advantage is that reference data types can contain addresses that point to a collection of other data types. Those data types can themselves be of primitive or reference type.

There are three types of reference variables: array, class, and interface. Class and interface data types are covered in Chapter 7, "Building Objects."

Arrays

Arrays are single- or multidimensional groups of variables. Think of going grocery shopping with a partner who is as excited about it as you are. You say, "Honey, what is the third thing on the list?" (At my house, the reply is "I would tell you if I could read your handwriting." This is always good for a little aisle discussion.) The grocery list acts as the array. Each item on the list is an element, the smallest part of an array. It is referenced by its place in the array, as in the third item on the grocery list.

Elements can be of a primitive type, as in float, char, or int. Elements can also be a class or interface type. Arrays can consist of other arrays. Arrays can be a powerful and flexible Java tool if used appropriately.

You can declare an array without allocating it. In other words, the variable itself is created, but no space is allocated in memory for array objects until the array is initialized or values are assigned to the elements of the array. Arrays are generally initialized with the new command, which creates a new instance of a reference data type. It is conceptually similar to the malloc command in C or new in C++. In Java, declaring a reference type does not automatically create space for that type; it merely creates space for the address that points to that type.

The following code fragment shows the declaration of an array, its creation, and the assignment of values to an element of an array:

```java
class Array {
   public static void main (String args[])
   {

      int LISTSIZE = 5;
      String[] ShoppingList;
      int i = LISTSIZE;

      // create array

      ShoppingList = new String[LISTSIZE];

      // initialize array

      ShoppingList[0] = "carrots";
      ShoppingList[1] = "tofu";
      ShoppingList[2] = "rice milk";
      ShoppingList[3] = "onions";
      ShoppingList[4] = "pasta noodles";

      for (i=0; i < LISTSIZE; i++) {
         System.out.println(ShoppingList[i]);
      }
   }
}
```

After you save the source code in a file called `Array.java`, you can compile the source code by typing the following at the command line:

```
javac Array.java
```

To run the program, type this:

```
java Array
```

The output from the program should be as follows:

```
carrots
tofu
rice milk
onions
pasta noodles
```

More on Arrays

One-dimensional arrays are like the grocery list in the previous example. There is only one way to reference the items: by using a subscript to indicate which element number to access. The number used to reference the specific element of an array is called the *component*. This concept is represented in Java as

```
char ShowArray[] = new char[5];
```

In this example, ShowArray is the name of the array. The [5] declares that there are five elements in the array. All elements are of type char. The elements are referenced by ShowArray[0] to ShowArray[4]. In Java, the subscripts always start at zero and go to the length of the array minus 1. The new command initializes the array to null characters. Memory space is allocated to the array here so that values can be assigned to the array. Reference to elements in the array is by subscript or component. Therefore, ShowArray[1] = 'j' assigns the value of j to the second component in the array.

All the elements of an array must be of the same type.

> **Note:** In theory, all Java arrays are one dimensional. In fact, an array of arrays can be defined in Java, functioning as a two-dimensional array. (This characteristic of Java is noted here because the technical specification of Java states that all arrays are one dimensional.)

Two-dimensional arrays need two reference points because the data is stored in a grid of rows and columns. Think of a two-dimensional array as similar to the cells in a spreadsheet. An element is referenced by the row and column number of its location, as in [3][4]. This means that the current element being manipulated is in row 4, column 5 of an array. (Remember that arrays start at zero!)

Expressions

The main reasons that code is created are to manipulate, display, and store data. *Expressions,* or formulas, are Java's way of performing a computation. Operators are used in expressions to do the work of the program and to operate on variables. Expressions in Java are similar to, although a subset of, C and C++.

Variables must be declared before they are used. An error will occur if you try to operate on an undeclared variable.

The expression book = 4 uses the operator = to assign the value 4 to variable book. It is necessary to understand what Java expects of its operators and the correct syntax of its expressions to get anything accomplished in this language. So get ready to express yourself in Java!

Using Operators in Expressions

Every expression results in a value. The operators tell the javac compiler how to manipulate the variables and other data to give the appropriate result.

Unary Operations

An operator that manipulates a single value is called a *unary operator*. Binary operators act on two values.

The unary operation is useful to modify variables "in place." (C and C++ programmers may be familiar with this concept, but to COBOL and BASIC programmers it may be new.) That is, a variable can be operated on in some instances without an intermediate variable and then reassigned to the original variable. Whew! This operation is easy in Java. Table 6.11 summarizes the unary operators.

Table 6.11. Unary operators.

Operator	Operation
–	Unary negation
~	Bitwise complement
++	Increment
––	Decrement
!	Not

Increment and decrement operators are operators that actually change the value of the original variable. For example, after g++ is executed, the value of the variable g will have been incremented by one. Likewise, the decrement will actually decrement variable g by one. The other unary operators do not change the original variable but enable the coder to work with a "temporary" variable. For example, after !g is executed, the value of g will remain unchanged.

Incrementing increases the value by one, as in

```
GoUp++;    //GoUp is now incremented by 1
```

Decrementing decreases the value by one, as in

```
GoDown--;    //GoDown is now decremented by 1
```

The bitwise complement reverses the bit structure of a variable. It changes 1 to 0 and 0 to 1. Unary negation multiplies the variable by -1, in effect reversing the sign of an integer from positive to negative and negative to positive. However, the sign reversal is only in effect during the operation. The variable itself is not affected.

The following example demonstrates unary negation:

```
OppositeMe = -15;
CheckMe = -OppositeMe + 1;       //CheckMe has the value of 16
System.out.println(OppositeMe);  //OppositeMe still has the value of -15
```

Assignment Operations

An *assignment operator* stores a specific value in the memory area allocated to a variable. For example, in the expression g += 5;, 5 is added to the original value of variable g, and the old value is replaced. Here are more examples:

```
g = 5;      // assigns to g the value 5
g -=7;      // assigns to g the result of g - 7
g *=8;      // assigns to g the result of g * 8
g /=4;      // assigns to g the result of g / 4
g %=3;      // assigns to g the result of g % 3
```

Binary Operations

Unary operators act on only one variable, and *binary operators* act on two and return one value. Only the variable that receives the value as a result of the expression is changed.

Let's look at the simple expression c = b + 5. In this example, b + 5 is the binary operation. Only variable c is changed as it is assigned the value of whatever is in b plus 5. Variable b is unchanged. This seems to involve only common sense in a simple expression; however, more complex expressions do not appear so straightforward. It is possible to combine unary operations such as incrementing with binary operations to create a complex expression, changing more than one variable in the expression. Break these out in separate expressions if at all possible. This will help greatly in later debugging and maintenance.

Complex integer expressions require the use of separators to avoid unpredictable results. Separators such as parentheses notify the compiler of the order in which operations should be completed. In other words, separators set precedence. For example, the result of 2 * 3 + 4 is 10, but 2 * (3 + 4) is 14. In this situation, the separator overcomes the natural precedence of Java. This is a good time to discuss evaluation order.

Java's Evaluation Order

Java evaluates from left to right, as in the following:

```
class test {
   public static void main (String args [])
   {
      int ChangeYou, ChangeMe = 2;
ChangeYou = (ChangeMe+=2) * (ChangeMe+3);   //this is the important line
System.out.println("ChangeMe = " + ChangeMe);
      System.out.println("ChangeYou = " + ChangeYou);
   }
}
```

This is the output of this code:

```
ChangeMe = 4

ChangeYou = 28
```

In this expression, the variables ChangeYou and ChangeMe are declared to be type int and initialized to 2. Then the value of variable ChangeMe is incremented by 2, resulting in 4. The new value of ChangeMe is added to 3, resulting in 7. The results of the two values in parentheses, 4 and 7, are now multiplied. This value, 28, is assigned to ChangeYou.

This is a very poor example of code readability. It would be much better to break out the expression into multiple expressions. This shows that just because something is possible does not mean it is good. However, it is a demonstration of how Java fully executes expressions from left to right.

Another place to remember that Java evaluates from left to right is among operators of the same precedence value. In Java, + and – are evaluated at the same level of precedence. Therefore, if both a + and a – operation occur in the same expression, Java will resolve the expression from left to right.

Table 6.12 lists operators from highest to lowest precedence. Any operators that are on the same line are evaluated in the same order.

Table 6.12. Operator precedence, from high to low.

Highest			Lowest
[]	()		
--	!	~	instanceof
new (type) expression			
*	/	%	
+	–		
<<	>>	>>>	
<	>	<=	>=
==	!=		
&			
^			
&&			
||			
?:			
=	op=		

The separators [] and () change precedence. Everything within these separators will be computed before Java looks outside them. Java will evaluate the expression in separators using its regular rules of precedence, as in the following expression:

```
ConfuseMe = (3 * 2 + 3) + (6 + 4 / 2);
```

The value of `ConfuseMe` is 17. Multiplication is of a higher precedence than addition, so 3 * 2 is the first operation, which is then added to 3. In the next set of parentheses, division is of a higher precedence than addition, so 4 / 2 is the first operation, the result of which is then added to 6. The values from each set of parentheses, 9 and 8, are then added together and assigned to variable `ConfuseMe`. Let's just hope that variable `ConfuseMe` has been typed as an integer!

Using Arrays in Expressions

You can use arrays and elements of arrays in the same way as any other variable. It is not necessary to use any intermediate variable. Here are some examples:

```
TestArray[0] = 4

TestArray[1] = TestArray[0] * 1996;    //assigns the value of the first element
                                       // TestArray multiplied by 1996 to
                                       // the second element of array TestArray

TestArray[2]++                         // increments the value of the third element
                                       // of TestArray by one

AnotherArray[45] = "String data";      //  assigns a string of data to the 46th
                                       // element of AnotherArray
```

As you can see, arrays act as any other variable in an expression. The array structure is in place to group like items together for easy access.

Using `chars` in Expressions

Expressions are not just for numeric data types. Character variables are also assigned by means of an expression. Following is a code fragment that will get a character from the keyboard:

> **Note:** Many of the concepts in this code fragment have not been covered up to this point, but don't worry. We will get to them soon.

```
/*
    This is an example of getting a character from the keyboard and assigning
it to a variable
*/

//declares a new class of code
class GetCharFromKeyboard {

    //declares a method within the class
    public static void main ( String args[] )

    //exception that could be generated here
    throws java.io.IOException
```

```
//start block of code for this method
{

    //declares KeyboardChar type char
  char KeyboardChar;
    //assign keyboard input to KeyboardChar
  KeyboardChar = (char) System.in.read();
 //prints KeyboardChar to screen
  System.out.println(KeyboardChar);

 //ends block of code for method main
  }

//ends declaration of class GetCharFromKeyboard
}
```

Declarations

The *declaration statement* defines the type of variable. This section gives more code examples of declaration use.

Declarations can happen anywhere in sections of code, although it is best for readability to group them together in the beginning of a code section.

Blocks are sections of code beginning and ending with curly braces ({}). Think of a block as a logical unit of code that can call methods, perform expressions, display output, and so on. A variable declared in a block is valid for that block and all its sub-blocks; this is the *scope* of the identifier. However, the scope of a variable does not move outward to the enclosing block; that is, a variable that is declared in a block has no meaning in the area outside its curly braces.

With Java you can reuse identifier names between a block and sub-block of code. This means that in memory there may be more than one identifier of a given name. Be careful with this feature! The compiler does not check which variable is being called as long as the type is consistent.

Here is an example of *hiding* a variable by using a second declared variable of the same name:

```
class ShowHiding {
   public static void main (String args[])
   {
   int TableTop;
   TableTop = 2;
   ...
   switch  (AnyCommand) {
     case '1':
        int TableTop = 4;     // TableTop has just been declared again
                              // and assigned a value of 4
        break;
```

```
        ...
    }
    ....   /*return to the main loop
    System.out.println(TableTop);    /*TableTop still has a value of 2*/
}
```

In this situation, the second time variable TableTop has been declared as valid for the case command block only. Any values assigned to it are good only for the scope of that block. When program execution returns to the main block, any values assigned to the new variable are lost. The upshot is that there must be a compelling reason to use a variable name more than once in a program. And be careful not to declare two variables with the same name accidentally!

The previous example also shows the combination of a declaration and an assignment statement:

```
int TableTop = 4;
```

This declares a variable of type int, with identifier name TableTop and a value of 4.

Declaring **integer** Types

Variables of type integer are declared by the amount of memory space they will be allotted. (This is discussed more fully in the "Integer Data Types" section.) Following are examples of integer declarations:

```
byte ByteVar;       //8 bits
short ShortVar;     //16 bits
int IntVar;         //32 bits
long LongVar;       //64 bits
```

Declaring Floating-Point Types

Floating-point variables are 32 or 64 bits in length. Following are examples of floating-point declarations:

```
float FloatVar;     //32 bits
double DoubleVar;   //64 bits
```

Declaring **character** Types

A character type variable holds only one character. This is different from the Strings class, which contains groups of characters. Remember, the char type holds an integer that references the Unicode character. The following sample code declares two character types:

```
char MyChar;        // holds one character
char MyChar = 'y';  // declares variable MyChar and assigns y to it
```

Declaring Arrays

Arrays are covered in depth in the "Data Types" and "Expressions" sections of this chapter. Arrays are one-dimensional lists of objects that are referenced by component numbers or subscripts. They can consist of other arrays, resulting in classic multidimensional arrays.

Arrays are declared as follows:

```
char MyCharArray[];         //one-dimensional array
char AnotherArray[][];      //two-dimensional array
int IntegerArray[];         //one-dimensional array of integers
int []IntegerArray;         //equivalent to IntegerArray[]
```

Control Flow

This chapter has been explaining the basic elements of programming in Java: tokens, types, expressions, and declarations. Expressions, operators, and separators can be combined to manipulate data in a variety of ways. However, something is lacking: the ability to make decisions in the program. These decisions instruct the program which expression to solve or what data to assign to a variable. The solution to this problem is control flow. *Control flow* instructs the program how to make a decision and how further processing should proceed on the basis of that decision. Control flow gets your computer to start doing some of the thinking for you!

The building blocks of control flow are the { and } block delimiter characters and the if, while, do, for, and switch keywords. Each of these can be used to control how your program executes by determining if a condition is true and then executing a different section of code, based on the result. This is called a *conditional expression*.

Blocks and Statements

A *statement* is any line of code ending in a semicolon. A statement can be an expression, a method call, or a declaration. A *block* is a group of statements that form a single compound statement. Think of blocks as statements logically grouped together for program flow and readability.

How do you tell Java where a block starts and ends? The characters { and } group such sections together. For example, the following is considered a block of code:

```
{
   Store = "Grocery";
   Item[0] = "spinach";
   Item[1] = "tofu";
   Item[3] = "rice";
}
```

When the program runs and gets to this block of code, it will begin execution at the beginning { and will not continue execution elsewhere until leaving the final }. The opening {, the closing }, and all code in between is considered a *block*. The curly braces must be paired one with one another or Java will not know where a block begins and ends.

Conditional Expressions

Conditional expressions will generally execute one of several sections of code on the basis of a conditional test. This code can be as simple as a single statement, but more complex sections of code will be made up of many statements. Conditional expressions are used to make decisions in a program. They are used to evaluate whether a condition is true or false and will branch to different sections of code on the basis of the answer.

if

The simplest, but most important, conditional expression is the `if` statement. An `if` statement makes up a conditional expression of the form

```
if (expression) statement;
```

or

```
if (expression)
{
    statement(s);
}
```

If the expression in the parentheses evaluates to the boolean `true`, `statement` is executed. If the expression evaluates to `false`, `statement` is skipped and execution continues at the statement following the `if` statement. The following code fragment shows how this works:

```
int Number;                        // declare variable
Number = System.io.read();         // get character from keyboard
if ( (Number % 2) == 0 )
   System.out.println("even");     // test if number is even and
                                   // print "even" if it is
```

Note that `System.io.read` will retrieve only one character at a time, so this program actually will handle only single-digit numbers. Only the first character will be tested if you enter a multiple-digit number.

In this example, the program reads a number from the keyboard. It is then tested to determine if it is even. If it is, the `System.out.println` statement is executed and the program terminates or continues to the next statement block.

Here is how the previous example can be extended:

```
int Number;                        // declare variable
Number =System.io.read();          // get number from keyboard
if ( (Number % 2) == 0 )           // test if number is even
{                                  // begin block
```

```
    System.out.println("even");      // print message to screen
}                                    // end block
```

There is an optional companion to the if statement that can extend its usefulness: the else state-ment. The statement following the if expression is executed only if the expression evaluates to true. The statement following the else is executed only if the if expression evaluates to false:

```
int Number;                        // declare variable
Number = System.io.read();         // get character from keyboard
if ( (Number % 2) == 0 )           // test if number is even
   {                               // begin if block
       System.out.println("even");   // print message to screen
   }                               // end if block
else                               // else if number not even
{                                  // begin else block
   System.out.println("odd");      // print message to screen
}                                  // end else block
```

You can also nest if statements within each other if you need a more complex multiway branch:

```
char KeyboardChar;                         // declare variables
int Number;
System.out.print("Enter number> ");        // print prompt to screen
Number = System.in.read();                 // get character from keyboard
if ( (Number % 2) == 0 )                   // test if number is even
{    // begin if block
   if ( Number < 5 )
   {    // begin nested if block
       System.out.println("even & < 5");    // print message to screen
   }    // end nested if block
   else    // else if number not < 0
   {    // begin nested if block
       System.out.println("even & >= 5");    // print message to screen
   }    // end nested if block
}    // end if block
else    // else if number not even
{    // begin else block
   if ( Number < 5 )
   {    // begin nested if block
       System.out.println("odd & < 5");     // print message to screen
   }    // end nested if block
   else    // else if number not < 0
   {    // begin nested if block
       System.out.println("odd & >= 5");    // print message to screen
   }    // end nested if block
}    // end else block
```

if statements are powerful and are the underpinnings for much of programming. The if statement is a fundamental control structure, because almost anything can be tested with one.

switch

A variation on the if statement is the switch statement, which performs a multiway branch instead of a simple binary branch. switch statements are of the form

```
switch (expression)
{
   case value:
      statement(s);
      break;
   case value:
      statement(s);
      break;

         .
         .
         .

   default:
      statement(s);
      break;
}
```

The keyword `switch` begins the switch construct. The parentheses contain values that must evaluate to a `byte`, a `char`, a `short`, or an `int`. Next is a required {, followed by any number of constructs that begin with the keyword `case` and end with `break`, with any number of statements between. Next there is an optional section that begins with the keyword `default` and ends with `break`. Finally, a required } completes the `case` statement. This sounds complicated in description, but is obvious in usage, as demonstrated in the next example.

The `case` keywords are each followed by a *value*. This must also be of type `byte`, `char`, `short`, or `int`. The `case` statement itself works by evaluating the expression and then scanning down the `case` statements until an exact match is found. At this point the corresponding group of statements between the `case` and `break` will be executed. When the break is encountered, execution will resume at the first statement following the `switch` construct. If no matches are found and a default is present, the group of statements associated with `default` will be executed. If no `default` is present, execution will fall through the entire `switch` construct and do nothing, with execution again continuing after the end of the construct.

A `case` statement does not have to have a `break` associated with it. If `break` is not present, program execution falls through to the next `case` statement. It keeps executing that group of statements until a `break` is encountered, so be sure to place appropriate breaks if this is not the intended action.

Here is an example:

```
static void ParseChar (char KeyboardChar)
{
switch (KeyboardChar) {
      case 'l':
         System.out.println("left");
         break;
      case 'r':
         System.out.println("right");
         break;
      case 'q':         //note no break here, falls through
      case '\n':
         break;
      case 'h':         //note no break here either
      default
```

```
        System.out.println("Syntax: (l)eft, (r)ight, (q)uit");
        System.out.println("Please enter a valid character");
        KeyboardChar = '';
        break;
    }
}
```

In this example *expression* is a char type, and each case contains a corresponding char value.

> **Warning:** A common programming error is to forget to put in a break where it is needed; the result is that unintended codes are executed.

case statements cannot evaluate strings or objects, as is true with C and C++. Only items whose values can be evaluated as integers can be used in case statements. Remember, of course, that char is evaluated as an integer. Many times you will wish case statements could handle more complex objects. If you are working with one of the allowed expression types or can build some sort of index that uses one of these types, the switch statement can be an efficient and easily understood method for doing complex branching.

Looping Expressions

Looping expressions generally continue to loop through a section of code until a certain condition is met. Some looping expressions check the condition before executing the code. Other looping expressions check the condition after executing the code.

while

The while loop is a construct that repeatedly executes a block of code as long as a boolean condition remains true. The initial while expression is evaluated first. It is possible for the statements making up a while loop never to execute if the initial expression evaluates to false. while loops are of the form

```
while ( expression ) statement;
      or
while ( expression )
{
    statement(s);
}
```

The keyword while begins the while construct. The parentheses contain an expression, which must evaluate to a boolean. This is followed by a statement or a block.

When a while loop is encountered, the expression is evaluated first. If it evaluates to true, the statement or block following the while statement, known as the *body* of the while loop, is executed. When the end of the body is reached, the expression is evaluated again. If it is false, execution will continue with the next statement following the `while` loop. If it is `true`, the body of the `while` loop will be executed again. The body will continue to be executed until the expression evaluates to `false`.

Here is an example:

```
char KeyboardChar =(char)System.in.read();
while (KeyboardChar != 'q')
{
   ProcessChar(KeyboardChar);
   KeyBoardChar = (char)System.in.read();
}
```

This expression tests whether `KeyboardChar` is equal to the character q. If it is not, the body of the `while` loop will be executed, which will process the character and then read in another. This will continue until the character q is read in. Notice in this example that `KeyboardChar` has been initialized by reading a character before the loop is executed. If it was not explicitly set, the `while` loop might never be entered, depending on what value `KeyboardChar` had. This is another common programming error. Even if `KeyboardChar` were initialized to something, it would be processed before the user had a chance to type in a character.

A `while` loop continues to loop until the expression evaluates to `false`. It is possible for a `while` loop to execute forever if the expression never evaluates to `false`; this is known as an *infinite loop*. A common cause of infinite loops is that the programmer forgot to put a statement that changes part of the expression in the body of the loop. If the expression never changes, it will always evaluate the same and an infinite loop occurs.

do-while

The `do` loop enables your code to repeatedly execute a block of code until a boolean expression evaluates to `false`. It is almost identical to the `while` loop, except the expression is evaluated at the bottom of the loop rather than the top. This means that the contents of the loop will always be executed at least once. `do` loops are of the form

```
do statement; while ( expression );
      or
do
{
   statement(s);
} while ( expression );
```

The keyword `do` begins the `do` construct. This is followed by a statement or a block. Next is the keyword `while`, followed by the parentheses containing an expression that must evaluate to a boolean.

When a `do` loop is encountered, the statement or block following the `do` keyword is executed. When the `do` loop body completes, `expression` is evaluated. If it is `false`, execution will continue with the next statement following the `do` loop. If it is `true`, the body of the `do` loop will be executed again. The body will continue to be executed until the expression evaluates to `false`.

Here is an example:

```
do
{
   KeyBoardChar = (char)System.in.read();
   ProcessChar(KeyBoardChar);
} while (KeyBoardChar != 'q')
```

In this example, the body of the while loop is executed, which reads in a character and then processes it. The expression is then evaluated to determine if KeyBoardChar is equal to the character q. If it is, execution will continue with the first statement after the do loop. If it is not, the do loop body will be executed again. This will continue until the character q is read in.

Compare this version with the while loop version shown previously. It does not need an initialization of KeyBoardChar because the variable will be read in at the beginning of the loop. This is the most common reason for choosing a do over a while loop.

Like with the while loop, it is possible to create an infinite loop by forgetting to put in the body of the loop a statement that changes part of the expression.

for

The for loop enables code to execute repeatedly until a boolean expression evaluates to false. It is similar to a while loop but is more specialized. As in a while loop, the expression is evaluated at the top of the loop. However, it provides a more explicit means for initializing a loop variable and modifying it at the end of the loop. for loops are of the form

```
for (initialization; expression; modification) statement;
      or
for (initialization; expression; modification)
{
   statement(s);
}
```

The keyword for begins the for construct. The parentheses contain an *initialization*, an *expression*, and a *modification*. The *initialization* can be a statement of any kind, but typically its purpose is to initialize part of the expression. Initialization is followed by a semicolon (;), followed by an expression. Like the while and do loops, the expression must evaluate to a boolean. This is followed by another semicolon and then *modification*. *modification* also can be any statement, but again is typically used to modify part of the expression. Finally, this is followed by a statement or a block.

When a for loop is encountered, *initialization* is first executed, and then the expression. If it evaluates to true, the statement or block following the while statement is executed. This statement or block is known as the *body* of the for loop. When the end of the body is reached, *modification* is executed. The expression is then evaluated again. If it is false, execution continues with the next statement following the for loop. If it is true, the body of the for loop is executed again. The body continues to be executed until the expression evaluates to false.

Here is an example:

```
for (char KeyboardChar=ProcessChar(KeyboardChar); KeyboardChar != 'q';
KeyBoardChar=(char)System.in.read())
{
    ProcessChar(KeyboardChar);
}
```

In this example, KeyboardChar is initialized by reading in a character. expression is then evaluated to determine if KeyboardChar is equal to the character q. If so, execution will continue with the first statement after the for loop. If not, the body of the for loop will be executed, which will process KeyboardChar. Next, another character will be read in. This will continue until the character q is read in.

You can use for loops to move through a range of numbers. This is used in conjunction with arrays or other indexes. Here's an example:

```
int Array;
for (I=0; I < ArraySize; I++)
{
    if (Array[i] < 0)
    {
        System.out.println("ERROR: negative number encountered, index = " + I);
    }
    else
    {
        ProcessArray(Array[i]);
    }
}
```

This for loop will initialize I to a value of zero and then step through Array, checking for negative numbers before processing an entry. This is a compact, easily assimilated method of writing code.

Like with the while and do loops, it is possible to create an infinite loop by forgetting to put a statement that changes part of the expression in the body of the loop.

break

The break construct can be used to break out of the middle of a for, do, or while loop. (This chapter has already discussed how to use it to break out of a switch statement.) When a break statement is encountered, execution of the current loop immediately stops and resumes at the first statement following the current loop.

Here is how the previous for loop example could be extended:

```
int ix;
for (ix=0; ix < ArraySize; ix++)
{
    if (Array[ix] < 0)
    {
        System.out.println("ERROR: negative number encountered, index = " + ix);
        break;
```

```
   }
   ProcessArray(Array[ix]);
}
```

Again, this code will loop through Array looking for negative entries. However, by including the break statement, execution of this for loop will stop at the first negative entry. In this example, a negative entry might be considered so severe that no other processing should be done. Also notice that no else statement is needed because if an error occurs, execution will jump to the end of the loop, skipping the entry-processing code.

continue

The continue construct can be used to short-circuit parts of a for, do, or while loop. When a continue statement is encountered, execution of the current loop immediately resumes at the top, skipping all other code between it and the end of the loop.

The following for loop uses the continue construct:

```
int ix;
for (ix=0; ix < ArraySize; ix++)
{
  if (Array[ix] < 0)
    {
      System.out.println("ERROR: negative number encountered, index = " + ix);
      continue;
    }
    ProcessArray(Array[ix]);
}
```

Again, this code will loop through Array looking for negative entries. However, the inclusion of the continue statement means that execution of this for loop will not continue in the body of the loop if a negative entry is encountered. In this example, a negative entry might be considered illegal and should not be processed. However, it is not so severe that it stops processing other entries. Again, notice that no else statement is needed because if an error occurs, execution will continue at the top of the loop, skipping the entry-processing code.

Labeled Loops

If break and continue only take you to the end or beginning of the current loop, what do you do if you have nested loops and need to get out of more than just the current one? Java provides an extended version of break and continue for just this purpose. By adding a label to a loop and referencing it in a break or continue statement, you can make execution continue at the end or beginning of the loop of your choice.

Here's an example:

```
err:
for (ix=0; ix < ArraySize; ix++)
{
```

```
    for (j=0; j < ArraySize; j++)
    {
      if (Array[ix][j] < 0)
      {
          System.out.println("ERROR: negative number encountered, index = " + ix + "," +
j);
          break err;
      }
      ProcessArray(Array[ix][j]);
    }
}
```

In this example, Array is extended to two dimensions, and two for loops are used to step through all elements of the array. If a negative entry is encountered, execution will branch to the end of the for loop labeled err, rather than the normal inner one. Without this construct, you would need to set an additional flag variable and test it in the outer loop. The label itself must immediately precede the intended loop; if it is placed anywhere else in the code, a compile-time error will occur.

The capability to jump out of the middle of a loop is handled in C++ and some C implementations with a goto statement. The goto can branch anywhere in the code, which can lead to what is known as *spaghetti code*. Of course, spaghetti code is something we recognize in other people's code, but never our own! The labeled loop concept in Java provides breakout capability while limiting the scope. It is a good compromise.

Summary

This chapter covers the most basic parts of the Java programming language. It gives many examples of ways to use tokens, literals, data types, expressions, declarations, and control flow. Together these form the fundamentals of any program you write or application you develop in Java. This chapter is also a good reference for correct syntax. You will be well on your way to developing powerful applications in Java when you combine these fundamentals with the information covered in the next chapter.

7

Building Objects

Objects can be almost anything in Java. Everything in the language is designed to use small, somewhat self-contained pieces of code, or objects. Objects use the fundamentals such as declarations and expressions to do the real work of the language. The idea is to use these pieces of code in appropriate ways so you don't have to keep rewriting them for each use. This is why it's called "object-oriented" programming. (This concept is discussed in Chapter 1, "Introducing Java.")

The smallest logical unit of Java is the object. Everything else is merely a grouping of objects on a larger scale. This chapter describes how to create and use objects. It explores the structure of Java in greater detail than the previous chapter. Chapter 6, "Fundamentals of the Java Language," covers the smallest parts of objects, such as primitive data types and control flow keywords; this chapter shows you how to put the small pieces to work in a structural framework.

To create applications with Java, it is essential to understand how the parts fit together. Here you'll explore the grouping of objects into classes. Classes are given characteristics through inheritance. *Class libraries* are groups of classes. *Packages* are groups of class libraries. *Methods* are functions that perform activities within classes. Methods can have templates managed by interfaces.

These are abstract concepts. There is tremendous power for application flexibility in Java, but it is easy to get lost in terminology. This chapter is full of examples to make the concepts concrete and easy to understand. A conceptual example involving an apartment building is used throughout the chapter to demonstrate the structure of Java.

By the end of the chapter you should have a good idea of the relationships among the parts of Java and how to use them effectively.

An Introduction to Classes

Classes are made up of objects. This is easy to understand if you are familiar with object-oriented programming. If you are not, then what is an object? Think of an object as a unit that can be made up of other smaller units. Think of an apartment building, for example. It is made up of apartments. Each apartment probably has doors, windows, a kitchen, a bedroom, and a bathroom, among other things. Each apartment is a *unit*. Sometimes an apartment building is referred to as a *five-unit apartment building*.

The apartments do not all have to be exactly alike. Some may be on the first floor, some may be in the basement, some may face south, and some may be recently refurbished. One apartment may have two bedrooms and another, just down the hall, only one. Each apartment has its own mail slot with an individual address. Even though the apartments are not all identical, they are all apartments.

Apartments are the *objects* in this example. Even though they have smaller parts and are not identical, conceptually each is a unit. The apartment building is the *class*. It is made up of objects, or units. These objects are not all exactly alike, but they have enough similar characteristics that they can be *classed* together.

Another term useful in object-oriented programming is *instance*. Apartment building 3 is an *instance*, or actual apartment building. It is real. An instance is one specific object within the class of objects.

Each apartment has more interesting information. One might be empty. In this case, the empty status is the apartment's *state*. A rental-application program could keep track of available apartments on the basis of this state. A *method* would be associated with testing for the state of this apartment.

Now let's take these ideas to another level of abstraction. Have you ever driven by a huge apartment complex, say, outside a university? The complex is made up of apartment buildings, which are made up of apartment units. The whole complex can be referred to as Countrybrook or something else equally romantic and descriptive. The complex, then, is the conceptual gathering together of the apartment buildings in the area even though each apartment building is slightly different, with different addresses and other characteristics that make them unique.

The apartment complex is an example of one of the classes in a *class library*. A class library is a set of classes. Class libraries group classes that perform similar functions but are dissimilar enough to warrant their own classes. Recall that the apartment complex is one class. Suppose right down the street is a mall. The mall is made up of smaller units—stores. The mall is another class in the class library. It is a building, but it has quite a different structure and function than the apartment building. It could be set up as its own class.

Java comes with a set of class libraries that handle many tasks, such as input/output, screen painting, and mouse clicks. The class libraries of Java are its heart and strength. In fact, this is such an important subject that five chapters in this book are devoted to it. See Part IV, "The Java Application Programming Interace," for more information on the Java class libraries.

At this point it is important to begin to understand the concept of objects, libraries, class libraries, and packages. These concepts are the structure of Java.

Classes

Classes are made up of many different parts, such as methods and variables. Think back to the apartment example. The class is a template for information about a group of things, even though the individual things may be somewhat different. Classes also contain methods for obtaining information about the state of a member. Each real member of a class is referred to as an *instance*.

Methods are functions that report back a status. Methods can report back with a value such as an integer or a boolean. Methods can be called by other classes outside their own immediate class.

A *superclass* is the top-level class of every application. In Java, it is automatically the `Object` class. This means that if a class does not implicitly declare its superclass, or next higher class level, then it is a subclass of `Object`. (Declarations are discussed in the section "Declaring a Class.") Every instance of a class reimplements the definitions and logic created by the superclass.

Subclasses extend the superclass and create a new variation of the class. They inherit the characteristics of the preceding class.

Declaring a Class

A class must have a valid identifier name; it can begin with an alphabetic character, the underscore, or the dollar sign. When you think of an appropriate name, use this syntax for declaring a class:

```
class MySuperClass.MyClass {
    // class body
}
```

The class body is declared within curly braces. Notice that the name of the class has the superclass and . before the class name. (This is also how inheritance, discussed subsequently, is shown.) This is how the compiler knows where to go for information on the class.

The name associated with a class has the same restrictions that identifier names do; that is, they can be named anything as long as they begin with an alphabetic character, a dollar sign, or an underscore. By convention, however, a class name should begin with a capital letter. This makes the class easily distinguishable from methods, variables, and so on. Java itself follows this convention; it is highly recommended.

Overview of Application and Applet Classes

Java produces two program types: application and applet. *Applications* are stand-alone and can be run directly from the command line. *Applets* require an external program to provide an interface to the user. Web browsers and the Java Developer's Kit (JDK) applet viewer are examples of interfaces that support applets.

Applets are also more restricted in Java in what they can do. Because Web browsers are a common method for accessing applets, what the applet can do to the local system is a security concern. Therefore, applets are prevented from reading or writing local files to disk, accessing memory directly, and opening connections to other applets that do not reside on the same server as the current applet.

This provides basic security, such as preventing an applet on an unknown Web page from automatically getting a copy of your password file and sending it to the author of the applet. However, Java allows some of these restrictions to be reduced. Using the applet viewer, you can allow an applet to have read and write access to a particular directory or set of directories. This is potentially dangerous and should be used only with caution.

Note: The actual mechanism that provides security for applets is in the client application running the applet (for example, your browser or the applet viewer). This mechanism is usually the applet security manager. For more information on the applet security manager, refer to Chapter 5, "Java Tools and the JDK: A Primer."

Applications do not have these restrictions. Users running Java applications are allowed to access any files, memory locations, or network resources that they normally could.

Application Classes

Java applications are true applications, like those developed by any other language, such as C or C++. The idea of Java applets is popular at this writing, but Java applications have received little fanfare. Sun Microsystems is trying to change that perception. Sun anticipates the Java programming language to replace C++ as the development language of choice, for several reasons.

One reason is that it is a more streamlined language but still offers much of the power of C++. Java was developed by specifications in one organization; it has not just grown in an ad hoc manner like many other programming languages. Therefore, parts of Java fit together nicely. Java has eliminated some of the redundancy found in C++.

Another reason is that Java is platform independent with regard to programming and maintenance. An organization can write a Java application that will run on *every* platform for which a Java interpreter has been written. This is a huge win for companies that must support multiple platforms.

Think about the way companies run today. They probably support multiple platforms internally. They may want to sell applications to run externally on a client base that supports multiple platforms as well. It is not a rare occurrence to find users with multiple terminals on desks to support and access a variety of applications. Imagine being able to write one application that runs on a company's PCs, Macintoshes, mainframes, UNIX systems, and whatever else is available. You can do this with Java.

So, you ask, what is the drawback? The current problem is speed. Java can run significantly slower than a natively compiled application that converts source code into machine code. Performance relies on many factors. However, it is difficult for an interpreted language to compete with natively compiled code.

Performance issues will probably be overcome in the near future with optimized Java interpreters, or just-in-time compilers, which are slowly becoming available. There is also talk of writing native compilers that will allow code to reside on local systems. (Entrepreneurs, anyone?) The problem with this solution is the loss of the instant-updating features of Java. It's also possible that the performance hit will be acceptable because of the niceties of Java portability. Giving up the performance of machine code for the development ease of a higher-level language like C code was also deemed acceptable, although some purists complained. Now is the time to move to the next higher level of language instead of lamenting the loss of C.

> **Note:** A software toolkit for Java that includes a just-in-time compiler is Symantec Café. Many other software companies plan to include just-in-time compilers as well. Who knows—maybe the mainstream integration of Java into operating systems will bring with it the speedy just-in-time compilers.

Java applications are similar in structure to applets. The only major differences are method of declaration and program invocation. We have seen many examples of declarations. It may not have been obvious how the program began execution, though; this is handled by the method `main`.

main

Every Java application must define one method named `main`, which is similar to `main` in C and C++. When a Java application is invoked, the Java interpreter looks for the method named `main` and begins execution there. If `main` is not declared, the interpreter will complain.

`main` methods must always be declared public. It would be impossible for a program outside Java to even start the Java application if `main` were not declared public.

The `main` method itself must be declared in a fixed format:

```
public static void main (String args[]) {
   ...body of main...
}
```

The public declaration enables `main` to be accessed from external programs. `static` indicates that this method cannot be modified by subclasses. `void` means that this method does not return a value of any kind. `main` is the required name of the method. (`String args[]`) indicates that `main` will have command-line arguments consisting of an array of type `String`. This array contains the command-line arguments specified when this application was started.

Here is the standard Hello World! Java application:

```
public class HelloWorld {
  public static void main (String args[]) {
     System.out.println("Hello World!");
  }
}
```

To compile the example, type the following:

```
javac HelloWorld.java
```

When the compiler finishes, invoke the Java interpreter as follows:

```
java HelloWorld
```

The output from the application should be as follows:

```
Hello World!
```

Applet Classes

Applets are the most famous aspect of the Java programming language at this time. Java is associated with the World Wide Web; Java applets are powerful in that they can take a fairly static Web page and turn it into a highly interactive, animated multimedia extravaganza.

Applets in Java rely on an external program to interface with the user. They cannot be run by themselves. The Java-enabled Web browser and the applet viewer that comes with the Java Developer's Kit are two common examples of these programs.

Applets are an extension of an existing Java class, `java.applet.Applet`. An applet is really an example of a subclass. To declare an applet, you again use the `class` keyword, but the modifier `extends` is added. This notifies the compiler that an applet is a subclass of another class, in this case a subclass of `java.applet.Applet`. Here is an example declaration:

```
import java.awt.*;     //imports the class libraries*****library*****
import java.awt.image.*;
import java.applet.*;

public
class HelloWorldApplet extends Applet {
   public void paint (Graphics g){
     g.drawString("Hello World!", 10, 10);
   }
}
```

After compiling the source code for the applet, you will need to create an HTML document that will be used by your browser or the applet viewer to display the applet. Here is a sample HTML document for the `HelloWorldApplet` program:

```
<HTML>
<HEAD>
<TITLE>HelloWorldApplet</TITLE>
</HEAD>
<BODY>
<APPLET CODE="HelloWorldApplet" WIDTH=300 HEIGHT=300></APPLET>
</BODY>
</HTML>
```

Applets generally must be more "bulletproof" than applications because of the environment in which they run. Not only must they run, but they must be able to handle events like mouse clicks, repaints, suspensions, and others. Many things appear on the surface to be handled by the browser but in reality are handled by applet code.

An example of this is the following sequence of events: an applet prints an image on the screen. The user brings up another window that partially obscures the original image, and then removes the new window. Who is responsible for repainting the applet image? It is not the browser, but the applet. The browser will inform the applet that a repaint is needed, but it is then up to the applet to actually do the repaint or take other action.

Applets begin execution differently than applications. Applications begin program execution by calling method main. Applets instead use methods init and start. The browser will invoke the init method followed by the start method every time a Java applet is started. These do not have to be explicitly declared in the applet.

Look again at the HelloWorldApplet example. Notice that there is no call to invoke paint, yet the screen was painted anyway. Many things happen behind the scenes in a Java applet. This is an example of an applet beginning execution without an explicit declaration of methods init and start, instead relying on the default init and start methods. The default start method automatically calls the repaint method, which among other duties, invokes the paint method. paint must be explicitly declared for anything to be written to the screen.

This summarizes the series of events that occur when a viewer invokes an applet. It is important to understand this sequence if any of the applet startup methods are overridden. The applet will not execute to expectations if anything is left out. When a viewer calls an applet, first the applet calls init. This is either explicitly declared or it is the default. The viewer then calls start, which is once again either implicitly or explicitly declared. Within start is a call to repaint, which schedules a call to paint. The implicit paint method does not write anything to the screen, and therefore the method must be overridden.

init

The init method is only called the first time an applet is loaded into a viewer. One-time-only initializations take place in the call to method init. This is also a good place to get command-line arguments from the HTML page from which the applet was invoked. (Command-line arguments are discussed in the "Declaring a Package" section.)

The init method has a fixed format. It always must be named init, have a return type of void, be declared public, and have no arguments. An example of the init method follows:

```
public void init () {
    counter = 0;
}
```

The only action in this example of an init method is to set the variable counter to zero.

An init method is not required. It actually overrides an existing init method in class java.applet.Applet; this is why the name, return type, and other information are fixed.

start

The start method is called after the init method the first time an applet is loaded into a viewer or if an applet has been suspended and must be restarted. If the compiler can't find a start method explicitly declared in the applet, it will default to the start method in java.applet.Applet. An example of the start method follows:

```
public void start() {
  run = true;
  while (run == true) {
    count += 1;
    repaint();      //note that repaint is explicitly called
    try {Thread.sleep(1000); }
    catch(InterruptedException e) {}
  }
}
```

This start method sets variable run to true and then enters a while loop that will run as long as run is equal to true. The loop increments the counter that was initially set to zero in the init method. The repaint call causes the screen to be repainted after every increment. The try and catch lines cause the program to sleep for 1,000 milliseconds after every counter increment. (try and catch are exceptions covered in Chapter 8, "Tying It All Together: Threads, Exceptions, and More.")

A start method is not required. Like init, it actually overrides a default start method provided by the java.applet.Applet library. It also has a fixed format, as shown in the previous example.

stop

The stop method is called whenever an applet must be stopped or suspended. Without the method the applet continues to run, consuming resources even when the user has left the page on which the applet is located. There may be times when continued execution is desirable, but in general it is not. An example of the stop method follows:

```
public void stop() {
   run = false;
}
```

This stop method sets the run variable to false. This causes the loop in the start method from the previous example to exit the loop and fall through the end of the method. The result is that the application stops running. Note that only the run variable is changed.

Just as with init and start, a stop method is not required. It overrides a default stop method provided by the java.applet.Applet library. The stop method has a fixed format declaration, as shown in the previous example.

paint

The method `paint` is used to paint or repaint the screen. It is automatically called by `repaint` or can be called explicitly by the applet. The applet calls `paint` when the browser requires a repaint, such as when an obscured applet is brought to the front of the screen again.

`paint` has a fixed format. It always must be named `paint`, have a return type of `void`, and be declared public. However, unlike `init` and `start`, it does have an argument, of type `Graphics`. This is a pre-defined type in Java that contains many of the methods for writing graphics to the screen. Here is an example of a `paint` method:

```
public void paint(Graphics g) {
    g.drawstring("counter = " + counter, 10, 10);
}
```

This method writes the value of `counter` to the screen each time it is invoked. Combine this with the `start` and `repaint` methods. The `start` method increments `counter` and then calls `repaint`. The screen displays the new value of `counter` every time it is updated.

The compiler does not require a `paint` method. It overrides a default method provided by `java.applet.Applet`. However, if you do not override it, you will not be able to write anything to the screen.

An Example of `start`, `init`, `paint`, and `stop`

```
import java.awt.Graphics;
public class Counter extends java.applet.Applet {
  int counter;
  boolean run;
  public void init() {
    counter = 0;
  }
  public void start() {
    run = true;
    while (run == true) {
       counter++;
       repaint();
       try { Thread.sleep(1000); }
       catch(InterruptedException e) {}
    }
  }
  public void stop() {
     run = false;
  }
  public void paint(Graphics g) {
    g.drawString("counter = " + counter, 10, 10);
  }
}
```

This method will not yet run in this form; we still need threads and exceptions (discussed in Chapter 8).

Modifiers

Modifiers alter certain aspects of classes. They are specified in the declaration of a class before the class name. Several modifiers have been used in the examples in this chapter.

Class modifiers are used to specify two aspects of classes: access and type. *Access modifiers* are used to regulate internal and external use of classes. *Type modifiers* declare the implementation of a class. A class can be used as either a template for subclasses or a class in and of itself. (These modifiers are subsequently described in detail.)

Declaring Class Security

Classes can be declared with security so they can be accessed outside their package by using the `public` statement in the class declaration. If no explicit statement is made at declaration time, the class may be accessed only from within its own package. A compile error is generated if any other security modifier is used in the declaration, such as private or protected, which are reserved for methods.

The following are examples of declaring class security:

```
public class classname {    //able to be accessed outside of
                            //own package
}
class classname {           //only able to be accessed within
                            //own package
}
```

This is another example of code reuse in the same or different applications in Java. Java's structure makes this easy and allows for some protection if necessary.

Class Types: Abstract or Default

There are only two types available to classes: abstract or default. Abstract classes must be explicitly declared.

The `abstract` modifier is used to create template classes. These are classes that normally are used to provide a superclass for other classes. An abstract class can contain such things as variable declarations and methods but cannot contain code for creating new instances.

An abstract class can also contain abstract methods. These are methods that define return type, name, and arguments but do not include any method body. Subclasses are then required to implement those abstract methods in which they supply a body. If an abstract class contains only methods and no variables, it is better to use interfaces (covered in the "Interfaces" section). Here is an example of an abstract class declaration:

```
abstract class AClass {
    int globalVariable;
    abstract void isBlack (boolean) {
    }
}
```

This abstract class declares a global variable called globalVariable and defines a template for a method called isBlack. Notice that there is no body for the isBlack method. That is left to subclasses of AClass. The subclasses must implement isBlack or they will receive a compile-time error.

Class Variables

Chapter 6 discusses variables in a detached, stand-alone manner. This section shows how variables are used in a class.

Variables are used in classes to hold data to be used later. Good programming form places variables immediately following the class declaration statement, as in the following:

```
class ShowVariables {
    int Int1, Int2;        //declare some integer variables
    int Int3 = 37;         //declare and initialize a variable
    char OneChar;          //declare a character type variable;
    float FloatArray[];    //declare single dimensional array of floating-point
    boolean AmITrue;       //declare boolean variable
                           //here would be code to do something...
}
```

The variable declaration statements in this example just set up the variables to be used in this class. There are no methods or expressions set up to do anything at this point.

Every class can have variables associated with it. Variables fall into two categories: those that are particular to an instance, called *instance variables*, and those that are global to all instances of a particular class, known as *class variables*. The use of the variable determines its type.

Instance Variables

Instance variables exist only for a particular instance of an object. This means that different instances of a given class each have a variable of the same name, but Java stores different values for that variable in different places in memory. Each of these instance variables is manipulated individually. If an instance goes away, so does the variable. You can access instance variables from other instances, but the variable itself exists only in a particular instance.

Instance variables have been shown in the examples so far in this chapter. They are declared after a class declaration but before method declarations. Every instance of that class has a copy of this variable and can modify it as needed without affecting any other instance copies of the variable. Here is an example of an instance variable declaration:

```
class ACat {
    String[] name;
    String[] color;
    int weight;
}
```

Here every instance of class ACat has a name, color, and weight variable used to store information about a particular cat. If you had two cats and wanted to put them on your Web page, you could specify the name, color, and weight of each cat in individual instances without worrying about overwriting the information.

Static Variables

You can modify variable (and method) declarations with the static modifier. *Static variables* exist in only one location and are globally accessible by all instances of a class. A variable cannot be changed by a subclass if it has been declared static and *final*. Further, static variables have the same information in all instances of the class.

This is a valuable tool in situations in which a variable is shared by several instances of a class and/or subclasses. All instances will have the same value for the variable. All classes accessing that variable point to the same place in memory. This variable will remain there until the last instance accessing the variable is flushed from memory.

A static variable is declared in the same way as an instance variable but has the keyword static in front of it. In the following code, the variable animalType is declared static and is thus the same for all instances of class ACat:

```
class ACat {
    static String animalType[] = "cat";
}
```

In this way, all the instances can check this variable for the value of animalType. An external class can query this variable for the same information. Its value needs to be specified only once and stored in one location because the information is the same for all instances of class ACat.

Predefined Instances

Java comes with three predefined object values: null, this, and super. They are used as shortcuts for many common operations in Java.

null

What happens when the class being created is a superclass? A variable can be created that is simply a placeholder for subclasses to fill with values. In this situation, a variable can be declared null, meaning that no value is assigned to a variable, as in the following:

```
int PlaceHolder = null;    //PlaceHolder is an empty object
```

Following is a code fragment using null:

```
class ACat{
   static String name = null;
   public void main (String args[]) {
   ACat cat = new ACat();
   if (cat.name == null) {
      promptForName("Enter name> ");
   }
}
```

In this example the variable name is initialized to null. It is then tested in main to see if the variable is null. If so, the user is prompted to enter the cat's name. null cannot be used with primitive data types.

this

To refer to the current object, use the keyword this, which allows the current instance of a variable to be referenced explicitly. This is valuable when the current instance of a variable is to be passed to another class that will also use the variable:

```
void promptForName (String prompt){
   StringBuffer name;
   char ch = '\0';
   name = new StringBuffer();
   System.out.print(prompt);
   System.out.flush();
    While (ch != '\n') {
      try {ch = (char)System.in.read(); }
      catch (IOException e) {};
      name.append(ch);
   }
   this.name = name.toString();
}
```

The compiler understands implicitly that the current instance of a class variable is this. Do not explicitly reference it unless necessary.

super

super is a reference to the superclass. It is often used as a shortcut or explicit way to reference a member in the superclass of the current class. In the following code, a subclass named APersianCat uses the super keyword to reference the method promptForName in its superclass, ACat:

```
class APersianCat extends ACat {
   void getCatInfo {
      super.promptForName() :
   }
}
```

APersianCat would look for a method called promptForName in the current class if super were not used, generating a compile error.

Class Methods

We have been using methods throughout this chapter, but now a better definition of methods is in order. *Methods* are functionally similar to functions in C and C++. They provide a way to group a block of code together and then refer to it by name. You can use the block of code again simply by referring to the name of the method. Also, the code does not have to intrude into the middle of other code.

Methods do not have an explicit declaration keyword as classes do. They do have names but also have arguments and return types, which classes do not.

Arguments are parameters that are passed to the method when it is called so that a method can be made to do different tasks. The code internal to the method knows how to manipulate the input parameters.

Methods also have a *return type*. This is a value that can be returned to the code that called the method. Return values can be of any valid Java type, including strings and numeric values.

Methods can be called from not only the current class, but also from subclasses, superclasses, and even entirely unrelated classes. This is the structure internal to Java that makes it so flexible and time-effective.

An example of a method follows:

```
public static void main (String args[]) {
    ...body of method....
}
```

This method has been used many times in this book. It is the method `main`, which is the first method called when a stand-alone Java application is started. In this example, `public` and `static` are method modifiers, `void` is the return type, `main` is the name of the method, and `(String args[])` is the list of method arguments. This is followed by an opening { that marks the beginning of the body of the method. The method body can consist of any valid block of Java code. It can also include calls to other methods, even itself. Finally, the method body is followed by a final }.

Return Types

Methods can return any valid Java type. This could be a simple boolean, an array, an object representing an entire apartment complex—anything. The return type immediately precedes the variable name of a method. The following code declares a method named `isBlack` to return a variable with type `boolean`:

```
boolean isBlack (Color color) {
    if (color == black)
      return (true);
    else
      return (false);
}
```

The method body tests whether the color passed is black. If it is, the method uses the return keyword to specify that value to return to the calling method is boolean true. Otherwise, it will use return to return the boolean false.

void is a special return type in Java that indicates that there is no return type of any kind. This is used for methods that have no need to return anything to the calling program, or that modify only method arguments or global variables.

An example of a method that does not need to return anything is one that only prints output to the screen. There is no need to return anything because there is no further processing to be done. There is no need to use the keyword return anywhere in the method if the method is declared void.

Method Modifiers

The concept of modifiers presented with classes also can be applied to methods. Method modifiers control access to a method. Modifiers also are used to declare a method's type. However, methods have more modifiers available than do classes.

Declaring Method Security and Accessibility

Method-declaration statements provide information to the compiler about allowable access. In Java terms, accessibility is security. The five levels of access follow:

Level	Allowable Access
public	All other classes
private	No other classes
protected	Subclasses or same package
private protected	Subclasses only
<default>	Same package

private

The private modifier specifies that no classes, including subclasses, can call this method. This can be used to completely hide a method from all other classes. If no other classes can access the method, it can be changed as needed without causing problems. Here is an example of a method declared private:

```
private void isBlack (Color color) {
   ....
}
```

protected

The `protected` modifier specifies that only the class in which the method is defined or subclasses of that class can call the method. This allows access for objects that are part of the same application, but not other applications. Here is an example:

```
protected void isBlack (Color color) {
    ....
}
```

private protected

The `private protected` modifier is a special combination of `private` and `protected` access modifiers. This modifier specifies that only the class in which the method is defined or subclasses of the class can call the method. It does not allow package access as `protected` does but also allows subclasses as `private` does not. Here is an example:

```
private protected void isBlack (Color color) {
    .....
}
```

default

The method defaults to an access control in which the class itself, subclasses, and classes in the same package can call the method. In this case, no access type is explicit in the method-declaration statement. Here is an example:

```
void isBlack (Color color) {
    ....
}
```

static

The `static` modifier is associated only with methods and variables, not classes. The `static` modifier is used to specify a method that can only be declared once. No subclasses are allowed to implement a method of the same name. This is used for methods, such as `main`, that are entry points into a program. The operating system would not know which method to call first if there were two `main` methods. Static methods are used to specify methods that should not be overridden in subclasses. Here's an example:

```
static void isBlack (Color color) {
    ....
}
```

final

The `final` modifier indicates that an object is fixed and cannot be changed. When you use this modifier with a class-level object, it means that the class can never have subclasses. When you apply this modifier to a method, the method can never be overridden. When you apply this modifier to a variable, the value of the variable remains constant. You will get a compile-time error if you try to override a final method or class. You will also get a compile-time error if you try to change the value of a final variable.

Here is how you can use the `final` modifier:

```
class neverChanging {

    // a final variable
    final int unchangingValue = 21;

    // a final method
    final int unchangingMethod(int a, int b) {
    }
}
```

abstract

The `abstract` modifier is used to create *template methods*, which are very similar to function prototypes in C and C++. Abstract methods define return type, name, and arguments but do not include any method body. Subclasses are then required to implement the abstract method and supply a body. Here is an example of an abstract class:

```
abstract void isBlack (Color color) {
}
```

This defines a template for a method named `isBlack`. Notice that no body of `isBlack` is specified; that is left to subclasses of the class in which the abstract method is declared. The subclasses must implement a body for method `isBlack`, or they will cause a compile-time error.

Overloading Methods

The concept of *overloading* methods seems nonsensical at first. But when the idea seeps in, you will see that overloading adds to the power of Java. Why would anyone want to define methods with the same name but very different functionality? This is precisely what overloading does. You can define a method with the same name multiple times.

Java selects which method of the same name to call on the basis of the calling parameters. Every overloaded method must have a different and unique parameter list.

With Java you can overload any method in the current class or any superclass unless the method is declared static. For example, in the following code, method `isBlack` has been overloaded three times:

```
class CheckForBlack {
  public boolean isBlack (Color color) {
    if (color == black)
       return(true);
    else
       return(false);
  }
  public boolean isBlack (String desc) {
    return(desc.compareTo("black"));
  }
  public boolean isBlack (Paint paint) {
    if (paint.reflectedLight < .05)
       return(true);
    else
       return(false);
  }
}
```

Each method has the same name and return type, but each has a different argument list. The first checks to see if the color passed to the method is equal to the color black. The second method compares a string passed to the argument to see if it is equal to the string `"black"`. The last method determines if the `paint` object passed in to the method has a reflected light percentage of less than 5%. If it does, it is considered black.

In all these cases, the method name and return type are the same, but the arguments are different. The Java compiler automatically uses the method that matches the arguments passed in the call to determine the correct method. The Java compiler issues an error if no method call has arguments to match any of the methods.

Method overloading allows for flexible use of method calls. In the `isBlack` example, if you need another type of test, simply add it to the existing `CheckForBlack` class. A Java program can make `isBlack` calls using the new object.

In this way, you can cover multiple types of tests with only one method name. Overriding means that the programmer does not need to come up with different names for a method that accomplishes the same thing, but perhaps in a different way. The programmer can concentrate on readability and consistency without having to worry about method names. This also means that in a large project, a programmer does not need to worry about using a name that some other programmer has already used (as long as the arguments are different).

Working with Objects

Use of objects is one of the main differences between a procedural language such as C and an object-oriented language such as C++ or Java. In a procedural language, data is usually thought of as being distinct from the code. In object-oriented programming, the code is thought of as being one with the data.

Creating and Destroying Objects

Space is usually pre-allocated for data in procedural languages. The compiler knows the size, types, and number of variables and allocates space accordingly. The data-allocation space is fixed in memory and continues to be allocated until the application ends.

Data space is not pre-allocated in Java. Instead, it is created as needed. Space is used for as long as something is accessing the data, and then memory is automatically deallocated. This is similar to using the `malloc` and `free` system calls in C.

The biggest difference between Java and C is that there is no need to release memory explicitly after the program finishes with it. In Java, an automatic garbage-collection system finds any memory that is not in use and automatically frees it. This is a huge bonus for the programmer because "memory leaks" are a source of considerable problems in standard languages (and one of the reasons reboots are a regularly scheduled event on UNIX systems!).

Java and C++ have differences, also. In C++, constructor and destructor functions run whenever an object is created or destroyed. Java has an equivalent to the constructor function named `constructor`, but there is no exact equivalent to a C++ destructor. All objects in Java are removed using automatic garbage collection. There is no way to invoke destructors manually. There is a method named `finalize` that can be used like a C++ destructor to do final cleanup on an object before garbage collection occurs, but finalizers have several limitations.

Creating an Instance

Java allocates memory space similar to `malloc` in C using the keyword `new`. `new` creates an object of virtually any type, the exceptions being primitive data types. A variable is then assigned that points to that object. An example of this follows:

```
String desc;
desc = new String(10);
```

This allocates enough space in memory for a 10-character string and associates it with the variable `desc`. `desc` is now considered an object of type `String` and has all the methods associated with class `String`. `String` methods include methods to determine length, compare with other strings, obtain substrings, and many others.

Method invocation in Java differs from that in C. In a procedural language like C, the variable `desc` is normally passed as an argument to the appropriate function call. In Java, the object associated with the variable `desc` already has all the methods built into it. This is a result of the methods associated with type `String`. These methods became a part of object `desc` when it was created with `new`, as in the following example:

```
sizeOfString = desc.length              //gets the size of desc
if (desc.compareTo("black")       //tests to see if desc is equal to "black"
locOfSubString = desc.indexOf("black");   // returns index to substring
```

These examples focus on the object, not the functions; thus the name object-oriented programming.

Destroying an Instance

The destroy method is always called when an applet has completed or is being shut down. Any final cleanup takes place here. The destroy method always must be named destroy, have a return type of void, be declared public, and have no arguments. An example of a destroy method follows:

```
public void destroy() {
    counter = 0;
}
```

This destroy method only sets the variable counter to zero. destroy can accomplish many things, such as cleanly terminating network connections, logging information to files, and other final actions.

A destroy method is not required. It is actually overriding an existing destroy method in class java.applet.Applet; therefore, the name, return type, access security and arguments are fixed.

The Constructor Method

Recall that Java does not allocate memory for objects at application startup time but rather when the instance is created by keyword new. Several things occur when new is invoked. First, Java allocates enough memory to hold the object. Second, Java initializes any instance variables to default values.

Third, Java makes calls to any constructors that exist for that class. *Constructors* are special methods that are used to initialize an object. A constructor can do anything a normal method can, but usually is used simply to initialize variables within the object to some starting value.

Constructors do not have an explicit keyword to mark them as such. Instead, the constructor method name is the same as the name of the class in which the constructor is declared. In the following example, there is a method named ACat:

```
class. ACat {
    void ACat (String breed[]) {
        this.breed = breed;
    }
}
```

Constructor methods always have a return type of void and a name that matches the class in which they are defined.

When new is used to create a new object, the constructor in the previous example is invoked. For example, in the following code, the call to new passes the value Siamese to the constructor, which initializes the breed instance variable to that value:

```
ACat cat;
cat = new ACat("Siamese");
```

Constructors are like regular explicitly declared methods in that they can be overloaded by declaring them more than once with different arguments. Multiple constructors are created by declaring several methods with the same name as the class. Also, like overloaded methods, Java determines which constructor to use on the basis of the arguments passed to new, as in the following example:

```
class. ACat {
    void ACat (String breed[]) {
      this.breed = breed;
    }
    void ACat (Color color, int weight) {
      this.color = color;
      this.weight = weight;
    }
}
```

Here a second constructor with arguments of color and weight is declared in addition to the first constructor, which has an argument of breed. The second constructor is invoked as follows:

```
ACat cat;
cat = new ACat(black, 15);
```

This lends itself to great flexibility in the way a new object is constructed. Appropriate constructors are created on the basis of the needs of the application.

Constructors can call other constructors in the same class or a superclass. Java extends the constructor naming convention by using the this and super keywords to refer to constructors in the current or superclass, as in the following example:

```
class AMammal {
    anAnimal(String mammalType[]) {
}
class ACat extends AMammal {
    void ACat (String breed[]) {
      this.breed = breed;
    }
    void ACat (Color color, int weight) {
      this.color = color;
      this.weight = weight;
    }
    void ACat (Color color, int weight, String breed[]) {
      this(breed);
      this(color,weight);
      super("cat");
    }
}
```

The third constructor takes all the arguments that were used for the two other constructors. However, instead of duplicating the initialization code in the other two constructors, it simply calls them directly with the this() syntax. This example also shows a superclass named AMammal with a constructor that defines a mammal's type. The third ACat constructor uses this type using the super() syntax.

The `finalize` Method

When an object is no longer referenced by any objects, Java reclaims the memory space using garbage collection. Java calls a destructor method before garbage collection takes place. Unlike the constructor methods, destructor methods have a specific name: `finalize`. Here is an example:

```
void finalize() {
.....body of finalize method
}
```

Finalize methods always have a return type of void and override a default destructor in `java.object.Object`.

A program can call `finalize` directly just as it would any other method. However, calling `finalize` will not initiate any type of garbage collection. It is treated as any other method if called directly. When Java does garbage collection, `finalize` is still called even if it has already been called directly by the program.

The `finalize` method is like other methods in that it can be overloaded. Remember, however, that Java calls `finalize` automatically and does not pass any arguments at that time. If Java finds a `finalize` method with arguments at garbage-collection time, it will look for a `finalize` method with no arguments. If it does not find one, Java uses the default `finalize` method instead.

One difference between `finalize` and a C++ destructor is that the system only calls `finalize` when it is ready to reclaim the memory associated with the object. This is not immediately after an object is no longer referenced. Cleanup is scheduled by the system on an as-needed basis. There can be a significant delay between when the application finishes and when `finalize` is called. This is true even if the system is busy, but there is no immediate need for more memory. For these reasons, it may be better to call `finalize` directly at program termination rather than wait for garbage collection to invoke it automatically. It depends on the application.

Packages

How do packages fit into the hierarchy? Once again we return to the apartment example. In our town, there are several large complexes owned by a single company. This real estate company also owns malls, empty commercially zoned land, and warehouses. These are alike in that they are real property. Think of the company as the largest unit of reference for the properties. The company knows about each of the individual apartment units and can make use of them as needed.

In Java terms, the company is the *package*. The package groups together class libraries, such as the libraries containing information about different commercial properties, as well as tract land for suburbs. A package is the largest logical unit of objects in Java.

Packages in Java group a variety of classes and/or interfaces together. In packages, classes can be unique compared with classes in other packages. Packages also provide a method of handling access security. Finally, packages provide a way to "hide" classes, preventing other programs or packages from accessing classes that are for internal use of an application only.

Declaring a Package

Packages are declared using the `package` keyword followed by a package name. This must occur as the first statement in a Java source file, excluding comments and whitespace. Here is an example:

```
package mammals;
class AMammal {
    ...body of class AMammal
}
```

In this example, the package name is `mammals`. The class `AMammal` is now considered a part of this package. Including other classes in package `mammals` is easy: Simply place an identical package line at the top of those source files as well. Because every class is generally placed in its own source file, every source file that contains classes for a particular package must include this line. There can be only one package statement in any source file.

Note that the Java compiler only requires classes that are declared public to be put in a separate source file. Nonpublic classes can be put in the same source file. Although it is good programming practice to put each of these in its own source file, one package statement at the top of a file will apply to all classes declared in that file.

Java also supports the concept of package hierarchy. This is similar to the directory hierarchy found in many operating systems. This is done by specifying multiple names in a package statement, separated by a period. In the following code, class `AMammal` belongs to the package `mammal` that is in the `animal` package hierarchy:

```
package animal.mammal;
class AMammal {
    ...body of class Amammal
}
```

This allows grouping of related classes into a package and then grouping related packages into a larger package. To reference a member of another package, the package name is prepended to the class name. This is an example of a call to method `promptForName` in class `ACat` in subpackage `mammal` in package `animal`:

```
animal.mammal.Cat.promptForName();
```

The analogy to a directory hierarchy is reinforced by the Java interpreter. The Java interpreter requires that the `.class` files be physically located in a subdirectory with a name that matches the subpackage name, when accessing a member of a subpackage. If the previous example were located on a UNIX system, the class `promptForName` would be located as follows:

```
animal/mammal/ACat.class
```

Of course, the directory-naming conventions will be different for different operating systems. The Java compiler will happily place the `.class` files into the same directory as the source files. It may be necessary to move the resulting class files into the appropriate directory if the source files are not in the class files.

The class files can also be placed directly into the desired directory by specifying the `-d` (directory) option on the `javac` command line. To continue the example, the following code places the resulting output files in the subdirectory `animal/mammal/ACat` of the current directory:

```
> javac -d animal/mammal/ACat ACat.java
```

All classes actually belong to a package even if not explicitly declared. Even though in the examples used throughout most of this book no package name has been declared, the programs can be compiled and run without problems. As usual in Java, what is not explicitly declared automatically gets default values. In this case, there is a default unnamed package to which all such packages belong. The package does not have an explicit name, and it is not possible for other packages to reference an unnamed package. Therefore, no other package is able to reference most of the examples in this book as they are now. It is a good idea to place all nontrivial classes into packages.

Accessing Other Packages

Recall that you can reference packages by prepending a complete package name to a class. A shortcut—using the `import` statement—can be used when there are many references to a particular package or the package name is long and unwieldy.

The `import` statement is used to include a list of packages to be searched for a particular class. The syntax of an `import` statement follows:

```
import packagename;
```

`import` is a keyword and *packagename* is the name of the package to be imported. The statement must end with `;`. The `import` statement should appear before any class declarations in a source file. Multiple `import` statements can also be made. The following is an example of an `import` statement:

```
import mammal.animal.Cat;
```

In this example all the members (for example, variables, methods) of class `Cat` can now be directly accessed by simply specifying their name without prepending the entire package name.

This shortcut poses both an advantage and a disadvantage. The advantage is that the code is no longer cluttered with long names and is easier to type. The disadvantage is that it is more difficult to determine from which package a particular member came. This is especially true when a large number of packages are imported.

import statements can also include the wildcard character *. The asterisk specifies that all classes located in a hierarchy be imported, rather than just a single class. For example, the following code imports all classes that are in the mammal.animal subpackage:

```
import mammal.animal.*;
```

This is a handy way to bring all classes from a particular package.

The import statement has been used quite heavily in the examples in this book. It has typically been used to bring in various parts of the Java API. By default the java.lang.* set of classes is always imported. The other Java class libraries must be explicitly imported. For example, the following code brings in all the windowing toolkit graphic and image classes (see Part IV):

```
import java.awt.Graphics;
import java.awt.Image;
```

Package-Naming Conventions

Packages can be named anything that follows the standard Java naming scheme. By convention, however, packages begin with lowercase letters to make it simpler to distinguish package names from class names when looking at an explicit reference to a class. This is why class names are, by convention, begun with an uppercase letter. For example, when using the following convention, it is immediately obvious that mammal and animal are package names and Cat is a class name. Anything following the class name is a member of that class:

```
mammal.animal.Cat.promptForName();
```

Java follows this convention for the Java internals and API. The System.out.println() method that has been used follows this convention. The package name is not explicitly declared because java.lang.* is always imported implicitly. System is the class name from package java.lang.*, and it is capitalized. The full name of the method is

```
java.lang.System.out.println();
```

Every package name must be unique to make the best use of packages. Naming conflicts that will cause runtime errors will occur if duplicate package names are present. The class files may step on each other in the class directory hierarchy if there is duplication.

It is not difficult to keep package names unique if a single individual or small group does the programming. Large-group projects must iron out package-name conventions early in the project to avoid chaos.

No single organization has control over the World Wide Web, and many Java applications will be implemented over the Web. Remember also that Web servers are likely to include Java applets from multiple sources. It seems impossible to avoid duplicate package names.

Sun recognized this problem late in the development stage but before officially releasing Java. It developed a convention that ensures package-name uniqueness using a variation on domain names, which are guaranteed to be unique: to use the domain name in a reverse manner. Domain `mycompany.com` would prefix all package names with `com.mycompany`. Educational institute `city.state.edu` would prefix package names with `edu.state.city`. This neatly solves the naming problem and generates a very nice tree structure for all Java class libraries.

The **CLASSPATH** Environment Variable

The Java interpreter must find all the referenced class libraries when running a Java application. By default, Java looks in the Java install tree for the libraries. It is usually better when developing code to put your own class libraries someplace else. An environment variable named `CLASSPATH` can be used to tell Java where these libraries are located. `CLASSPATH` contains a list of directories to search for Java class library trees. The syntax of the list will vary according to the operating system being used. On UNIX systems, `CLASSPATH` contains a colon-separated list of directory names. Under Windows, the list is separated by `;`. The following is a `CLASSPATH` statement for a UNIX system:

```
CLASSPATH=/grps/IT/Java/classes:/opt/apps/Java
```

This tells the Java interpreter to look in the `/grps/IT/Java/classes` and `/opt/apps/Java` directories for class libraries.

Summary of Packages

Packages are used for grouping related classes together. They can be used to access related classes as well as to hide the internals of a package from outside programs.

Packages are declared using the `package` keyword, which must be located at the beginning of all source files that are to be a part of the same package. Package members can be accessed by prepending the complete package name separated by `.` to the needed member. The contents of packages can also be accessed by importing the package into a class using the `import` keyword. Doing so enables the code to specify package members directly without explicitly specifying the complete package name.

Package names by convention begin with lowercase letters. This distinguishes them from class names, which by convention begin with uppercase letters. Sun encourages programmers to use a reverse Internet domain name as the top level of a package name to keep package names unique on a global scale.

Packages can contain subpackages. Java requires that the resulting `.class` files reside in a directory structure that mirrors the package name hierarchy. By default, the Java interpreter looks for packages where the Java programs were installed. Use the `CLASSPATH` environment variable to list a set of additional directories to search.

Inheritance

One of the more powerful concepts in an object-oriented language is the concept of *inheritance*, which is a methodology whereby the code developed for one use can be extended for use elsewhere without having to make an actual copy of the code.

In Java, inheritance is done by creating new classes that are extensions of other classes. The new class is known as a *subclass*. The original class is known as a *superclass*. The subclass has all the attributes of the superclass, and in addition has attributes that it defines itself. A class can have only one superclass. This is known as *single inheritance*. A superclass can have multiple subclasses. To better clarify this concept, let's look at the apartment building example again.

Recall that an apartment building class is made up of individual apartments and may be part of a larger complex made up of other types of buildings such as schools, stores, and houses. One way to implement this in Java is to start with the concept of a building. All buildings share certain characteristics, including building size (height, width, depth), size of lot, and type of heating. Using these characteristics, we could build up a class that stores and manipulates these characteristics.

An apartment building can be thought of as being a more specialized version of a building. Apartment buildings are made up of a group of individual apartments, any of which might be empty at any given moment. These characteristics can be incorporated as part of the building class but would not apply to a school. Instead, an apartment building class is created that inherits characteristics of the building class but also adds its own particular characteristics. This creates a more specific version of building that is customized for describing an apartment building. More specialized versions of buildings could be created for a school, store, or house.

Declaring Inheritance

Declaring inheritance in classes is simply an extension of the class-declaration rules discussed earlier. This is done with the `extends` keyword:

```
class classname extends anotherclass {
   ... body of class
}
```

The `extends` keyword immediately follows the class name. It is followed by the name of the superclass from which this class will inherit characteristics. There can be only one class name following the `extends` keyword.

`Recall` from the examples in the "Applet Classes" section that the applets were declared as subclasses of `java.applet.Applet`. A declaration such as this provides an applet with all its inherent characteristics. There is no reason to code them because they are inherited from the superclass.

Let's use the apartment building analogy to demonstrate inheritance, starting with the building class:

```
public class Bldg {
    int height, width, depth, lotsize;
    String heatType;
    public String getHeatType () {
        return(heatType);
    }
}
```

In this simplistic version of a building class, variables for holding `height`, `width`, `depth`, and `lotsize` and a method for printing out the type of heating have all been declared. These are the characteristics that all buildings share.

The next step is to create an apartment building class that extends the previously declared building class:

```
public class AptBldg extends Bldg {
    int numApts;
    Apt apt[];
    public int findVacatApt () {
        int i;
        for (i = 0; i < numApts; i++) {
            if (apt[i].isVacant == true) {
                return(i);
            }
        }
        return(-1);
    }
}
public class Apt {
    boolean vacant;
    int aptNumber;
    public boolean isVacant() {
        return(vacant);
    }
}
```

In this example, two classes are declared: an apartment building class (`AptBldg`) and an apartment class (`Apt`). The apartment building class is declared using `extends Bldg`, which declares that `AptBldg` is a subclass of `Bldg`. By doing this, `AptBldg` inherits all the variables and methods declared in `Bldg`. `AptBldg` extends `Bldg` by declaring a variable for number of apartments and an array containing apartment objects. There is also a method that returns the first vacant apartment in the array of apartments.

The `Apt` class is a brand-new class and does not extend any other classes. It declares two variables, vacant and aptNumber, as well as method isVacant, which can be used to determine if the apartment is vacant. The next step is to use the classes that are now declared.

Using Inheritance

It is now time to create a program for apartment managers. This program must be able to do things such as find an empty apartment. The classes declared previously are used in a new Java program that can do this:

```
public AptManager {
    public findEmptyApt (AptBldg aptBldg) {
        int AptNum;
        String heatType;
        AptNum = aptBldg.findVacantApt();
        if (AptNum > 0) {
            heatType = aptBldg.getHeatType();
            System.out.println("Apartment " + AptNum + "is available for rent");
            System.out.println("Type of heat is" + heatType);
        }
    }
}
```

In this example, a method for finding an empty apartment has been created. It is passed an apartment building object as an argument. The method then calls the findVacantApt method in the aptBldg object to locate a vacant apartment. If one is found, a call to the method getHeatType is made to determine the type of heat in the building. Both of these pieces of information are then printed out.

Notice that although findVacantApt is explicitly declared in AptBldg, the getHeatType method is not. It is instead declared in the Bldg class. Because AptBldg is declared a subclass of Bldg, it automatically inherits all of Bldg's methods, including getHeatType. By using inheritance we have saved the effort of having to recode the method of determining the heat type. If other subclasses of Bldg, such as school or house, were declared, they would also inherit this same method. On a grander scale, you can save large amounts of coding effort.

Another important characteristic of Java is that it avoids the "fragile superclass" problem of C++; that is, a recompile of all subclasses must occur every time an upper-level class is changed. The very nature of Java is such that, because it is an interpreted language, no such recompile needs to take place. All superclass characteristics are passed down through inheritance. This is a great improvement over C++.

Summary of Inheritance

Inheritance is a method of reusing existing code while allowing for customization. When you're working with a group of objects that are similar to each other in some, but not all, ways, inheritance can be helpful.

Inheritance is used with class declarations. It is declared using the extends keyword. When a class extends another class, it is known as a subclass. The class it extends is known as the superclass. A class can have any number of subclasses but can have only one superclass. This is single inheritance.

With inheritance, a subclass can have full access to all the variables and methods declared in its superclass. This allows for items that are common to a group of classes to be placed in a single location. Other variables and methods can be declared in each subclass to add functionality or information as needed.

Inheritance provides a powerful mechanism for reusing existing code. This can be important in a large project. It also makes it simple to add new classes at any time.

Interfaces

Interfaces are Java's way of cutting down on the complexity of a project. Single inheritance makes it easy to find out method or class origins. However, this may be somewhat limiting. C++ permits multiple inheritance, which can be a breeding ground of needless complexity but does allow for ultimate flexibility. Java is less flexible but also less complex. It uses single inheritance for simplicity's sake but uses interfaces to bring in functionality from other classes.

A review of methods is in order before continuing. *Methods* are similar to functions in other languages. A method is a unit of code that is called and returns a value. Methods perform work on the variables and contain executable code. They are always internal to a class and are associated with an object.

The concept of interfaces is one of the main differences in project design between traditional C and Java application development. The C and other procedural programming language systems' development life cycle often begins with the definition of the application function names and their arguments as empty "black boxes." In other words, the programmers know the necessary argument parameters when programming code that calls these functions without knowing how they are implemented in the function. Thus they can develop code without first fully fleshing out all the functions. In C, this could be done by defining a function prototype for all the functions and then implementing them as resources and schedules permit. How is this accomplished in Java? Through interfaces.

An interface only defines a method's name, return type, and arguments. It does not include executable code or point to a particular method. Think of an interface as a template of structure, not usage.

Interfaces are used to define the structure of a set of methods that will be implemented by classes yet to be designed and coded. In other words, the calling arguments and the return value must conform to the definition in the interface. The compiler checks this conformity. However, the code internal to one method defined by the interface may achieve the intended result in a wildly different way than a method in another class.

The concept of using interfaces is a variation on inheritance used heavily in Java. The chief benefit of interfaces is that many different classes can all implement the same interface. This guarantees that all such classes will implement a few common methods. It also ensures that all the classes will implement these common methods using the same return type, name, and arguments.

Let's get theoretical. Say that a method is defined in the interface as boolean. The only argument is an input string. In the comments section, the method is said to test something to see if it is black and return `true` or `false`. Methods using this interface could be written to test cats, pavement, teeth, screen color—just about anything. The only thing these methods have in common is that they have the same definition. Any programmer seeing the method name knows the purpose of the method and the calling arguments.

Java, of course, does not require all classes that implement a method of a certain name to use the interface for argument verification. No language can make up for poor project management. It does, however, provide the structure for use.

Declaring an Interface

An interface is declared in much the same manner as a class, but instead uses the `interface` keyword instead of the `class` keyword:

```
interface name {
    ... body of interface
}
```

The interface body is declared between the curly braces. The body of an interface consists of declarations for variables and methods.

Modifiers

The same modifiers—`public` and `default`—available to classes can be applied to an interface's declaration. The default is `nonpublic`, which means accessible by any member of a given package. Most interfaces are `public` because interfaces are the only means to share variable and method definitions between different packages. Here is an example of a `public` interface declaration:

```
public interface AnInterface {
    ... //body of interface
}
```

Variables and methods declared inside an interface also have modifiers associated with them. However, the modifiers are limited to particular combinations for variables and methods.

Modifiers for variables are limited to one specific set: `public static final`. In other words, variables declared in interfaces can only function as constants. `public static final` are the default modifiers. It is not necessary to declare the modifiers explicitly, but it makes the code more self-documenting. Trying to assign other modifiers such as `protected` results in a compile-time error. Here are examples of variable declarations:

```
public static final int smtpSocket = 25;

public static final float pie = 3.14159;

public static final String = "The quick brown fox";
```

Modifiers for methods are limited to one specific set as well: `public abstract`, meaning that methods declared inside an interface can only be abstract. These are the default modifiers for methods. It is not necessary to declare them explicitly, but once again, it makes the code easier to read.

Trying to assign other modifiers, such as `protected`, results in a compile-time error. Here are example interface method declarations:

```
public abstract boolean isBlack(Color);

public abstract boolean isBlack(String);

public abstract StringBuffer promptForName(String);
```

As you can see in this example, overloaded methods can be declared in an interface just as in a class. An entire interface based on these examples follows:

```
public interface MyInterface {
   public static final int smtpSocket = 25;
   public static final float pie = 3.14159;
   public static final String = "The quick brown fox";
   public abstract boolean isBlack(Color);
   public abstract boolean isBlack(String);
   public abstract StringBuffer promptForName(String);
}
```

Interfaces also can extend other interfaces, just as classes can extend other classes, using the `extends` keyword. In the following code, the interface `AnInterface` declares a variable named `theAnswer`:

```
public interface AnInterface {
   public static final int theAnswer = 42;
}
public interface MyInterface extends AnInterface {
   public static final int smtpSocket = 25;
   public static final float pie = 3.14159;
   public static final String = "The quick brown fox";
   public abstract boolean isBlack(Color);
   public abstract boolean isBlack(String);
   public abstract StringBuffer promptForName(String);
}
```

The interface `MyInterface` specifies that it extends `AnInterface`. This means that any classes that use `MyInterface` will have access to not only the variables and methods declared in `MyInterface`, but also those in `AnInterface`.

You can also list multiple interfaces after the `extends` keyword. Multiple, possibly disparate, interfaces can be combined into a logical whole if desired, as in the following:

```
public interface YourInterface extends HerInterface, HisInterface {
   body of interface
}
```

Using an Interface

A continuation of the apartment example can be used to go into more detail on interfaces. Recall that an apartment building class AptBldg was defined previously. It contains all the information needed to define an apartment building.

Another piece of information that could be added to the apartment building class is address. Address can be manipulated after it is added to the class, one way to do this is simply to add address manipulation methods to the existing apartment building class. This limits the address information to just one class. If all the address-manipulation methods were placed in an interface, however, all classes would have access. Here is an example of such an interface:

```
public interface Address {
    public abstract void printAddress (anAddress);
    public abstract void setStreet (anAddress);
    public abstract String getState (anAddress);
}
```

The interface is a template for manipulating the address information through methods. The methods print the entire address, change the street name, and return only the state. Each of these methods is specific to manipulating addresses. So why place methods in an interface if it is easy to add to the existing class? Reusability is the hallmark of Java!

Now that the interface is defined, a class can make use of it with the implements keyword. Here is the syntax:

```
class name [extends classname ] implements interfacename [, interfacename] {
    ... body of class
}
```

The implements keyword follows the name of the class (or extends declaration) and in turn is followed by one or more comma-separated interface names. The capability to specify a list of interfaces enables a class to have access to a variety of predefined interfaces. In the building example, the class is declared as follows:

```
public class AptBuilding implements Address {
    ... body of class
}
```

Other classes can make use of these same methods by also implementing the same interface after it has been declared.

Suppose we decide to implement other classes, such as schools, stores, and high-rise office buildings. Each of these could use the same method definitions for manipulating addresses that were defined for class AptBldg. Not only does that save programming steps by reusing an existing template, it also enables all the different building classes to use the same methods for manipulating addresses. The call needed to look up a school's address is exactly the same as that needed for a store's address. This also means that the same method name is used. There is no need to come up with a unique name for every class's address. This is important in large projects.

This methodology covers the similarities between classes. What about the differences? Another application might need phone numbers in addition to addresses. This is easy in Java! Java does not specify that only methods derived from interfaces can be used. Any class is free to add methods for anything necessary. This customization only applies to one class, though. There is no need to worry about affecting other classes that also use the interface if an extension is used.

Summary

This chapter covers the concepts of classes, packages, inheritance, and interfaces. A solid knowledge of the relationships among these parts of Java is essential to creating applets and applications.

Classes in Java are used to define an object. Objects can consist of information and methods for manipulating that information. An instance is a specific implementation of an object.

Packages are groups of class libraries, which are made up of related classes. Packages can be used to control access security and make it easier to import an entire set of classes.

Inheritance allows for the reuse of existing code while providing a means for customization of new code. Java provides single inheritance between classes and subclasses. Subclasses always inherit the characteristics of their superclass. This is a building block of object-oriented programming.

Interfaces are templates of methods used to standardize method definitions. These are necessary due to Java's lack of multiple inheritance. Interfaces allow unrelated classes to share related methods.

8

Tying It All Together: Threads, Exceptions, and More

This chapter examines the final pieces of the Java programming language: threads, exceptions, and streams. Java uses these structures to create and control simultaneous activities and to perform error handling. These structures also perform interprocess communication among Java-controlled activities.

With threads, a single application in Java can easily run multiple concurrent code execution. This enables an application to do such powerful things as download a file, update a screen, and respond to user input all at the same time without the large amount of overhead incurred by the traditional fork used in languages such as C/C++.

Exceptions are Java's powerful and flexible method for handling errors, replacing the `return type` `error` code found in other languages. They are objects in Java and provide the same extensibility as any other object. Exceptions help to enforce Java's goal of being the safest language in which to program.

Streams are Java's way of communicating with the outside world. Streams enable a Java application to communicate with files, networks, devices, and other applications, and also allow for communication between threads within the same application. Streams are based on reading or writing a sequence of bytes from or to an outside source. Because the flow of data is a simple stream of bytes, specific knowledge of where the data comes from or is going to is not needed. This adds to Java's strength as a portable language.

There are several examples in this chapter that demonstrate these programming concepts. Try them yourself; you must see their output to appreciate and understand them. This is especially true because Java is not a procedural language, and it is difficult for most human minds to conceptualize nonsequentially. And you, the Java programmer-to-be, will have a lot more fun with Java when these powerful concepts are utilized.

These three structures are discussed in detail in the following sections. It is important to have a grasp of the uses of threads, exceptions, and streams to have powerful, pleasing Java applications and applets.

Threads

Threads enable a single program to run multiple parts of itself at the same time. For example, one part of a program can display an animation on the screen while another part builds the next animation to be displayed.

For advanced programmers, threads are a lightweight version of a process. Threads are similar to processes in that they can be executed independently and simultaneously, but are different in that they do not have all the overhead that a process does.

The `fork` command is used to create a new process in C or C++. A *forked process* is an exact copy of the original process, with exact copies of variables, code, and so on. Making this complete copy of all of the parent process makes using the `fork` resource expensive. When they are running, the child processes are completely independent of the parent process inasmuch as they can modify data without any effect on the parent process.

Threads do not make copies of the entire parent process. Instead, only the code needed is run in parallel. This means that threads can be started quickly because they don't have all of the overhead of a complete process. They do, however, have complete access to all data of the parent process.

Threads can read and/or write data that any other thread can access. This makes interthread communication simpler, but can lead to multiple threads modifying data in an unpredictable manner. Additional programming care is required with threads.

Uses of Threads

Threads are useful programming tools for two main reasons. First, they enable programs to do multiple things at one time. This is useful for such activities as letting a user do something while something else happens in the background.

Second, threads enable the programmer to concentrate on program functionality without worrying about the implementation of multitasking schemes. A programmer can simply spin off another thread for some background or parallel operation without being concerned about interprocess communications.

Declaring Threads

To create classes that make use of threads, you can extend the class `Thread` or implement the interface `Runnable`. Both yield the same result. By implementing `Runnable`, existing classes can be converted to threads without having to change the classes on which they are based.

Creating Threads by Extending `Thread`

An example of creating a thread by extending class `Thread` follows:

```
public class MyMain {
   public static void main          (String args[]) {
      CntThread cntThread;          //declare thread
      cntThread = new CntThread();  //create thread
      cntThread.start();            //start thread running
      try {System.in.read();}        //wait for keyboard input
      catch(java.io.IOException e){}
      cntThread.stop();             //stop thread
   }
}

class CntThread extends Thread {
   public void run() {
      int ix = 0;
      while (true) {
```

```
            System.out.println("running, ix = " + ix++);   //write count to screen
            try {Thread.sleep(1000);}                              //sleep 1 second
            catch(InterruptedException e){}
        }
    }
}
```

Note: To exit the program, press Ctrl+C.

In this example, a thread is created that will write an incrementing counter to the screen. It will continue to count until the main routine receives a character from the keyboard, at which time the counting thread stops. This means you can press any key on the keyboard followed by the Enter key or press only the Enter key to stop the thread from counting.

This is an excellent example of the concept of threads because it introduces the keywords try and catch (discussed in the "Exceptions" section in this chapter) and also demonstrates the creation and termination of a thread.

Creating Threads by Implementing **Runnable**

The second way to create a thread is by implementing the Runnable interface. Like the previous example, the following code creates a thread that increments a counter until a character is entered from the keyboard:

```
import java.applet.*;
import java.awt.*;

public class MyApplet extends Applet implements Runnable {

    int ix = 0;
    Thread mainThread;
    CntThread cntThread;

    public void start() {
        if (mainThread == null) {
            mainThread = new Thread(this);
            mainThread.start();                  //start main thread
        }
    }

    public void run() {
        cntThread = new CntThread(this);    //create CntThread instance
        cntThread.start();                  //start cntThread instance
    }

    public boolean keyDown(Event evt, int key) {    //process key press
        cntThread.stop();                           //stop cntThread instance
        return(true);
    }
```

```
    public void paint(Graphics g) {
       g.drawString("running, ix = " + ix, 10,20);   //write count to screen
    }
}

class CntThread implements Runnable {

    MyApplet parent;
    boolean loop;
    Thread cntThread;

    public CntThread(MyApplet p) {                    //constructor for CntThread
       parent = p;                                    //save parent instance
    }

    public void start() {
       if (cntThread == null) {
          cntThread = new Thread(this);               //create counting thread
          cntThread.start();                          //start counting thread
       }
    }

    public void stop() {
       loop = false;                                  //set value to exit main while loop
    }

    public void run() {
       loop = true;
       while (loop == true) {
          parent.ix++;                                //increment counter
          parent.repaint();                           //repaint screen
          try {Thread.sleep(1000);}                    //sleep 1 second
          catch(InterruptedException e) {}
       }
    }
}
```

Before you can view the applet in the applet viewer or your browser, you need to create an HTML document, such as the following:

```
<HTML>
<HEAD>
<TITLE>Using the Runnable Interface</TITLE>
</HEAD>
<BODY>
<APPLET CODE="MyApplet.class" WIDTH=400 HEIGHT=400>
<EM><B>You need a Java enabled Browser to see this cool applet</B><EM>
</APPLET>
</BODY>
</HTML>
```

This example also uses try and catch for exceptions. Look at the start and stop sections of the code. Starting and stopping threads are covered in detail later in the "Thread Methods" section of this chapter.

new and the Instantiation of Threads

Instances of threads are created using the standard new keyword. Arguments to new can either use the Thread class explicitly, as in

```
mainThread = new Thread(this);
```

or specify a class that is a subclass of Thread, like this:

```
mainThread = new MyThreadClass();
```

In the first example, the current instance, this, of an object is initialized as a thread. Any object, however, can be passed as an argument to the Thread class.

Note that the Thread class has few constructors. If additional constructor types are needed, creating a subclass of Thread with the needed constructors is quite useful. The second thread-creation example allows for these possibilities.

Destroying a Thread

You can control the execution of a thread in several ways using the stop, start, and destroy methods. The object remains in existence as long as the object is referenced somewhere, even if stop is invoked.

It is not necessary to explicitly destroy the thread object. Java's garbage collector takes care of this detail. If it is necessary to give the garbage-collection process a helping hand, make sure all references are removed to the thread object. The simplest way to do this is to assign the value null to all variables containing thread references, as in the following example:

```
Thread myThread = new Thread();
myThread.start();
myThread.stop();
myThread = null;
```

In this example, the thread object is instantiated with new. The thread is then started and stopped. Finally, null is assigned to the variable containing the thread instance. This last step ensures that Java's garbage collector will schedule a resource deallocation for that object.

Thread Methods

All Java threads implement four methods: init, run, start, and stop. These are default methods in the Thread class; if a class implements Runnable, these methods must be declared explicitly.

init

The init method is called the first time a thread is started. It is usually used for initialization of objects, but can be used in any way the programmer sees fit. Here is an example of an init method:

```
public void init() {
    index = 0;
}
```

This method simply assigns a value of zero to the index variable. Larger, more complex applications might include code that opens databases, creates display objects, or just about anything that should be done only the first time a thread is started.

start

The start method is called to start a thread execution. This method usually contains the code for actually creating and starting a thread. Here is an example of a start method:

```
public void start() {
    if (mainThread == null) {
        new mainThread = Thread(this);
        mainThread.start();
    }
}
```

This method checks to see if a thread has not yet been created by testing whether the thread object mainThread is null. If it is not, a new thread object is created using new, and then the thread itself is started by calling the object's start method.

stop

The stop method contains the code needed to stop a thread's execution, often in the form of generating a signal that will be caught by all threads and that causes them to exit. stop also can change an object that causes a calling loop in the run method to exit. Here is an example of a stop method:

```
public void stop() {
    loop = false; {
}
```

This method simply sets a variable to false. loop is used in a main loop run method for control flow.

run

The run method is similar in function to main in C or C++. run contains the main body of code to be executed by a thread. Here is an example of a run method:

```
public void run() {
    loop = true;
    while (loop == true) {
```

```
        System.out.println("index = " + index++);
        try {Thread.sleep(1000);}
        catch(InterruptedException e){}
    }
}
```

The body of this method consists of the initialization of the loop variable and a while loop that will continue executing until loop no longer has a value of true. The body of the loop prints out the value of the index variable to the screen and then sleeps for one second.

This method can be combined with the example from stop to control processing.

Named Threads

Java provides a means for assigning names to threads. Names can consist of any valid Java string. Naming threads makes it convenient to distinguish one thread from another and enables a parent process to query a thread for its name. A thread can be assigned a name at creation time or at any point thereafter. Threads can also be renamed at any time.

To assign a thread a name at creation time, simply use a Thread constructor that accepts a string as an additional argument, like this:

```
Thread myThread = new Thread(this."My first named thread");
```

In this example, the thread is instantiated by new and assigned a name of "My first named thread".

The getName Method

You can query a thread for its name using the getName method. getName returns the name associated with a specified thread object, as in the following example:

```
System.out.println("The name of this thread is " + myThread.getName());
```

This example prints out the name assigned to the thread object myThread. Using the previous example, this statement would print the following to the screen:

```
The name of this thread is My first named thread
```

A thread can also query for its own name in the same way:

```
System.out.println("My name is " + this.getName());
```

The setName Method

You can set or change a thread name after creation using the setName method. The parent process, the thread itself, or any other method that has access to the thread object can do this. Following is an example of changing a thread name using setName:

```
myThread.setName("My newly renamed first thread");
```

This example changes the name of the thread from "My first named thread" to "My newly renamed first thread".

Synchronization of Threads

Multiple threads can access the same object or method because threads are not independent processes with complete copies of data objects. However, there is no guarantee which thread will access an object at a given time, which can lead to unpredictable results. In situations when this is not acceptable, use the Java synchronization logic. The keyword that provides this logic is synchronized.

The synchronized Keyword

The synchronized keyword is used to lock an object long enough to execute a block of code. No other thread can make changes to the specified object while the block of code is being executed. Here is an example using synchronized:

```
public void printIndex() {
    syncronized(index) {
        index++;
        System.out.println("index = " + index);
    }
}
```

In this example, the printIndex method contains a synchronized block of code. In this block, the object index is locked while the block of code making up the body of the synchronized statement is executed. The increment of index and the printing of the value of index are contained inside the block. This ensures that the value of index is printed to the screen without having to worry that some other thread incremented index before it was printed.

synchronized also can be used as a modifier for methods, thus ensuring that only one thread at a time executes the method. The previous example could be rewritten using this construct as

```
public syncronized void printIndex() {
    index++;
    System.out.println("index = " + index);
}
```

Summary of Threads

Threads are Java's way of running multiple, parallel code segments simultaneously. They are a lightweight process that does not have all the overhead that a normal process has. Threads do not make complete new copies of variables in the way that the C/C++ fork command does, allowing for faster thread startup. It also means that threads have access to each other's data. This can make communication among threads easier, but synchronization of data access may be a problem.

Threads are based on the class `Thread` and can be implemented by either extending class `Thread` or using the interface `Runnable`. Using `Runnable`, you can add threading to existing classes.

All threads implement the `init`, `start`, `stop`, and `run` methods. You can explicitly define these in the code, or use the default methods that come with the `Thread` class. `init` is called the first time a thread is started, and it is a good place to put initialization code. `start` is called any time a thread is started. This is usually where thread initialization is done and the thread is actually started. `stop` is used to stop the execution of a thread and usually contains code that will terminate the main body of the thread. Finally, `run` is started by `start` and normally contains the body of the thread code.

The problem of multiple threads modifying the same variable can arise due to the structure of Java, which allows threads access to common variables. Also, the system is in control of scheduling the execution of threads, which may be a different schedule than the programmer had anticipated. You can control this situation by using `synchronized`. `synchronized` can be used on an object or on a method, and ensures that only one thread can execute a block of code at a given time.

Exceptions

So far, this book has presented the means by which a programmer can generate code correctly in Java. Correct code is, after all, is a valid programming goal. However, none but the simplest programs is error free; for example, simply not allowing enough space in an array for all needed elements results in an error.

There are problems that are beyond program control, and therefore also beyond the programmer's control. These include problems such as running out of memory. Other nonprogrammatic problems are the network being down or a hardware failure.

There are two main classes of problems in Java: *errors* and *exceptions*. Errors are caused by problems in Java itself and are generally of too detailed a nature for the program itself to solve. When an error is encountered, Java typically generates an error message to the screen and aborts the program.

Rationale for Java Exceptions

Java handles potentially recoverable errors through *exceptions*, a special object class that handles virtually all errors in Java. Java continues the idea of making code as reusable and error-free as possible by treating errors as objects. Exception-handling code resides in the `java.lang` package and is automatically included in all compiled code.

The reason Java treats exceptions as objects is to be able to handle various errors using a standard extensible interface. This manner of treating exceptions confers all the standard advantages that object-oriented design provides, such as reusability and customization.

Exceptions can be handled in Java in several ways: In some cases they can simply be ignored; they can be handled directly by the code in which they occur; or they can be passed on to the code that called the method containing the occurrence of the exception in the hopes that it will be handled there.

If an exception is not handled explicitly anywhere in the code, it is passed on to the Java interpreter. The Java interpreter might handle it in some way or might simply exit. In the case of an applet within a browser, this may result in the browser dying. This is not a desirable activity, so exception handling within a program is generally recommended.

As mentioned previously, some exceptions in Java can be completely ignored. The Java compiler requires others to be handled in one fashion or another to get a clean compile. This latter case is the reason you have seen some exception handling in the examples shown in Chapters 6, "Fundamentals of the Java Language," and 7, "Building Objects," such as in the example of the `sleep` method. This method can generate an exception that Java requires to be handled explicitly.

You can customize existing exceptions or create new ones. Remember, all exceptions are located in class `java.lang.Exception`. To customize an existing exception, the program simply overrides the existing methods or rewrites the existing variables. To create a new exception, create a new class that extends `java.lang.Exception`.

Exception Methods

Most Java exception handling is performed using the `try`, `catch`, `throw`, and `finally` methods. Of course, these methods can be extended if some unusual circumstance requires it.

Java uses the `try`, `catch`, and `throw` keywords to do actual exception handling. They are conceptually similar to a `switch` statement; think of `try` like the `switch` statement in terms of exactly identifying the condition to be tested.

`catch` is used to specify the action that should be taken for a particular type of exception. It is similar to the `case` part of a `switch` statement. There can be several `catch` statements in a row to deal with each of the exceptions that may be generated in the block specified by the `try` statement.

throw

Understanding exception handling in Java requires that you learn some new terminology. The first concept you need to grasp is that of *throwing* an exception, Java's name for causing an exception to be generated. For example, say a method was written to read a file. If the method could not read the file because the file did not exist, this would generate an `IOException`. In Java terminology, it is said that the method *threw* an `IOException`.

Think of it as a horse throwing a shoe: You must stop everything before real damage is done.

catch

The next term to learn in Java exception handling is `catch`. An exception *catch* is code that realizes the exception has occurred and deals with it appropriately. In Java terms, you say a thrown exception gets *caught*.

In the case of the `IOException` thrown because of the nonexistent file mentioned in the previous section, the `catch` statement writes an error message to the screen stating that the specified file does not exist. It then allows the user to try entering a different filename if the first was incorrect, or it may exit. In Java terminology, the `IOException` was caught.

try

`try` is the Java exception-handling term that means a Java program is going to try to execute a block of code that might generate (throw) an exception. The `try` is a way of telling the compiler that some attempt will be made to deal with at least some of the exceptions generated by the block of code.

finally

The `finally` statement is used to specify the action to take if none of the previous `catch` statements specifically deals with the situation. It is similar to the `default` part of a `switch` statement. `finally` is the big net that catches everything that falls out of the exception-handling statement.

An Example with try, catch, and finally

The following example is the standard structure for Java exception handling, incorporating `try`, `catch`, and `finally`:

```
try {
    statement that generates an exception
}
catch (ExceptionType1 e) {
    process exception type 1
}
catch (ExceptionType2 e) {
    process exception type 2
}
finally {
    process all other exception types
}
```

Using try in Exception Handling

`try` is used to inform Java that a block of code may generate an exception and that some processing of that exception will be done immediately following the `try`. The syntax of `try` is

```
try statement;
```

or

```
try {
   statement(s)
}
```

The keyword try begins the try construct and is followed by a statement or block containing the code that might generate an exception. This code could consist of several statements, one or more of which may generate an exception.

If any one statement generates an exception, the remaining statements in the block are skipped and execution continues with the first statement following the try construct, which must be a catch or finally statement. This is an important point to remember. It is an easy way to determine which block of code should be skipped if an error occurs. Here is an example:

```
public class MyMain {
   public static void main (String args[]) {
      int[] myArray = new int[10];
      try {
         System.out.println("Before valid array assignment");
         myArray[0] = 1;
         System.out.println("Before invalid array assignment");
         myArray[100] = 1;
         System.out.println("After array exception");
      }
   }
}
```

In this example, the array myArray is created with a length of 10. This is followed by a try statement that contains several statements. The first, third, and fifth statements simply write trace messages to the screen. The second statement contains a standard assignment statement that assigns the value 1 to array element 0. The third statement also assigns an array, but attempts to assign a value of 1 to element 100 of the array. Because the array is only 10 in size, this generates an ArrayIndexOutOfBounds exception.

In tracing the execution of the block of code following the try statement, the first three statements are executed normally. The fourth statement, the invalid assignment, will start to execute and then generate an exception, which causes execution to continue at the end of the block, skipping the fifth statement.

A compilation error will result if you attempt to compile this code as it stands because any try statement must be followed immediately by one or more catch or finally statements. No other type of statement is allowed after the end of the try statement and before the first catch or finally statement. (catch statements are explained in the next section.)

Using catch in Exception Handling

catch is used to handle a specific exception that has been generated in a try statement. The syntax is as follows:

```
catch (ExceptionType ExceptionObj) statement;
```

or

```
catch (ExceptionType exceptionObj) {
   statement(s)
}
```

The keyword catch begins the catch construct, followed by a parameter list that contains an exception type and an exception object. This in turn is followed by a statement or block containing the code used to process the exception.

Think of the catch construct as a method that will be called by the Java runtime interpreter if the particular exception type specified in the parameter list is generated. The object specified in the parameter list, exceptionObj, is a variable that contains the exception object generated and is local to the catch block. Within this block it can be manipulated as needed. The object must be assigned to a variable whose scope resides outside the block to use it outside the catch block, as in the following example:

```
public class MyMain {
   public static void main (String args[]) {
      int[] myArray = new int[10];
      try {
         System.out.println("Before valid array assignment");
         myArray[0] = 1;
         System.out.println("Before invalid array assignment");
         myArray[100] = 1;
         System.out.println("After array exception");
      }
      catch(ArrayIndexOutOfBoundsException e) {
         System.out.println("An array index error has occured");
      }
   }
}
```

This example continues the earlier try example in the "Using try in Exception Handling" section. The required catch statement has been added after the try statement. This catch statement will catch the ArrayIndexOutOfBoundsException specifically. If any other exception occurs, this catch statement is ignored. In this case, an ArrayIndexOutOfBoundsException is generated, so the body of this catch statement will be executed. This body simply generates an error message to the screen. Execution continues normally with the first statement following the catch block that is not a catch or finally block.

Additional catch statements can follow the first catch statement. They must immediately follow the try/catch statement; otherwise a compilation error will occur. When an exception in a try statement is generated, the Java interpreter will treat all the catch statements following the try statement as cases in a switch statement. The first statement that is matched will be executed, and the remainder will be skipped. (An example of this is provided in the introduction to the "Exceptions" section of this chapter.)

Note that Java does not require any processing of the exception at all. Simply having a catch statement for an exception with an empty block is sufficient to avoid program abortion. This has been used in several examples in Chapters 6 and 7 with the sleep method.

sleep is used to put a process to sleep for a specified period of time, during which an InterruptedException could be generated. This could result from some other process signaling this process to continue or quit, for example. In the examples used in this book, catching this type of exception is considered unimportant, and no processing is required. However, because in most cases the compiler generates an error if the exception generated by sleep is not caught, an empty catch statement is used, as in the following:

```
try {Thread.sleep(timePeriod);}
catch(InterruptedException e);
```

As you can see, the catch statement simply ends in a semicolon (;), which does nothing. The result is an InterruptedException error that is caught and then totally ignored.

Using **finally** in Exception Handling

finally is used to handle *any* exception generated within a try statement. The catch statement discussed previously can handle only one type of exception; the finally statement can handle any type of exception. Following is an example of the syntax:

```
finally statement;
```

or

```
finally {
   statement(s)
}
```

The keyword finally begins the finally construct, followed by a statement or block containing the code used to process the exception.

As with the catch statement, a finally block must follow immediately after a try or other catch statement or a compilation error results. A finally statement acts like a default case in a switch statement if it follows a series of catch statements. Anything that was not explicitly matched by an earlier catch statement is caught by the finally statement. A finally statement cannot be followed by another catch or finally statement or a compilation error will result. Because finally catches everything, additional statements would never be executed in any case. The following code fragment provides an example:

```
char readFile() {
   char ch = '\0';
   while (ch == '\0') {
      try {
         ch = myFile.read();
      }
      catch (EOFException e) {
         system.out.Println("End of file encountered");
         break;
      }
      catch (FileNotFoundException e) {
         promptUserForFileName(fileName);
         myFile = openFile(fileName);
       }
      finally() {
         system.out.Println("Unexpected error encountered while reading file");
         system.Exit(1);
      }
   }
   return(ch);
}
```

In this example, a `while` loop is used to read a single character from a file. The first statement in the loop is a `try` statement that attempts to read a character from a file. It is followed by two `catch` statements that look for two specific exception types. A `finally` statement follows that catches all other types of errors. The loop itself is followed by a return of the character read.

Many types of errors can occur when reading a file, including `End of file`, `File not found`, `Access permission errors`, and others. The first `catch` statement handles `End of file` exceptions by simply exiting the loop, resulting in the return of a `null` character. The second `catch` statement handles `File not found` errors by prompting the user for a new or correct filename, opening the file, and then allowing the `while` loop to try again. Lastly, the `finally` statement catches all other errors. It writes an error message to the screen and then causes the application to exit.

Using `throw` in Exception Handling

`throw` is used to cause the code itself to generate an exception. It is then up to calling routines to handle the exception. This is the preferred way of passing error information to calling routines in Java. The syntax follows:

```
throw(ExceptionObj);
```

The keyword `throw` begins the `throw` construct, followed by a parameter list containing a single item. This item is an *exception object*, an object that has been declared to be of the desired exception type.

The exception type can be any of those predefined in Java or one custom designed for the job. Most exceptions can be found in `java.lang.Exception`. To design a new exception, extend the class `java.lang.Exception`. Here is an example:

```
public class MyMain {
    public static void main (String args[]) {
        MalformedURLException e;
        e = new MalformedURLException("Are you a novice? Get your URL's right!");
        throw(e);
    }
}
```

In this example, an exception object (e) is declared. The object itself is then created with a standard new statement, in which the constructor allows replacing the standard error text for this exception. Finally, the exception object is thrown.

When an exception is thrown using the throw statement, current code execution stops. The exception is passed to the calling routine, and no other code is executed until the exception is caught somewhere. At that time, execution continues where the exception is caught. Keep this in mind when using the throw statement; it is usually a good idea to clean up as much as possible before throwing an exception. It is not a good idea to depend on the calling routines to clean up.

In some cases it may be desirable to catch a standard Java exception and then generate a customized exception by simply including a throw in a catch block, as in the following example:

```
public class MyMain {
    public static void main (String args[]) {
        int[] myArray = new int[10];
        try {
            myArray[100] = 1;
        }
        catch(ArrayIndexOutOfBoundsException e) {
            e = new ArrayIndexOutOfBoundsException("Please insure your array
            ➥index is within bounds.");
            throw(e);
        }
    }
}
```

This is a modified version of the earlier try and catch examples. In this version, a customized error message is generated regarding the array index problem by reassigning e to a new exception object that includes the customized message and then using throw to throw another exception that must be caught at a higher level. If a catch or finally statement followed this catch statement, it would be ignored. However, if this try statement were itself enclosed in a different try statement, the execution would catch the exception. In other words, it is possible to catch a self-generated exception by putting a throw statement inside a try statement. This is rather like playing catch with yourself!

The `java.lang.Exception` Class

Previously in the section titled "Exceptions," references were made to not only customizing existing exceptions, but creating new exceptions. These can be used to provide customized error codes for a particular application. Java does not provide a lot of numeric error-return codes as are found in other languages, so creating new exceptions falls right in with the Java philosophy.

Class `java.lang.Exception` is the superclass for all exceptions in Java. Creating your own extensions is simply a matter of extending this class just like extending any other class. For instance, to create a new exception called `MyOutOfRangeException`, the following implementation could be used:

```
public class MyOutOfRangeException extends Exception {
    public MyOutOfRangeException () {
        super();
    }
    public MyOutOfRangeException (String s) {
        super(s);
    }
}
```

In this example, a new class called `MyOutOfRangeException` has been created by extending the `Exception` class. It contains two constructors. The first one calls the exception superclass constructor. This creates a new exception, but does not provide a way for the calling routing to customize the message. The second constructor is the same, but enables the calling routine to specify the error message associated with the exception.

To use this exception, simply declare a variable of type `MyOutOfRangeException`, initialize it with one of the two constructors, and then throw it, as in the following example:

```
public class VerifyRange {
    MyOutOfRangeException e;
    public void verifyIntRange (int value, int low, int high)
    ➥throws MyOutOfRangeException {
        if ((value < low) || (value > high)) {
            e = new MyOutOfRangeException("number " + value + " out of range");
            throw(e);
        }
    }
}
```

In this example, a class called `VerifyRange`, to verify ranges of objects, has been created. The only method, `VerifyIntRange`, verifies that a value passed as an argument falls within the range also specified in the method's arguments. If the argument falls outside the range, a `MyOutOfRangeException` exception is created with `new` and then thrown with `throw`.

Notice that the method specifically declares that it throws this exception in the method declaration. Because of this, any calling routines are required to either provide an exception handler or explicitly declare that the method may pass on this exception. This would not be required if the `throw` portion of the declaration were left off. It is up to the programmer to determine whether an exception is important enough to require handling on the part of the calling routine.

Summary of Exceptions

Exceptions are Java's way of performing error handling. They are used in many ways as a replacement for the more standard return codes used by languages such as C and C++. Java itself makes heavy use of exceptions for error conditions, and any programs should be ready to handle them. Using instructions makes a program more robust, which makes for a better program.

Exceptions are handled using a combination of three statement types: try, catch, and finally. try is used to inform the compiler that exception handling will be performed on an associated block of code. catch is used for processing a specific exception generated in the try block of code. Several catch statements can be specified sequentially to handle specific exceptions in a specific order. The finally statement can be used to catch all exceptions not specifically caught by a catch statement.

A program can generate its own exceptions using the throw statement. The exception itself can be either preexisting or newly created. Even a preexisting exception can be customized by specifying a different message when creating the exception object.

If you need a new exception, you can create one by simply extending an existing exception class such as java.lang.Exception. Exceptions are usually simple and can be created using only two constructors. Everything else is done by the superclass that the new exception extended.

Judicious use of exceptions make the difference between a program and a truly user-friendly, good program. Nothing is less user-friendly than an aborted program.

Streams

You have probably noticed that the complexity of programming with Java has been slowly building in this book. The next subject is probably the most complex Java concept that must be mastered to complete your knowledge of Java: *streams*.

Streams in Java provide a way for two or more processes to send information to each other without any of the processes having to know anything about the others. This means that with streams you can write an application or applet that can then pass data to almost any other stream-based application or applet! It is even possible for multiple threads making up a single process to pass data to each other via streams.

Data Flow with Java Streams

At the highest level, streams work by simply sending information from a producer process to a consumer process. A *producer process* generates data for use by another process. A *consumer process* makes use of data produced by another process. Information that leaves a producer process is known as an *output stream*. Information that arrives at a consumer is known as an *input stream*. The information that makes up a stream is simply a sequence of data blocks sent one at a time from the producer process to the consumer process. The blocks themselves can be almost anything, from simple bytes to complex objects. Only the primitive data types are directly supported in Java, but any object can be sent as a data block by creating new stream classes.

Streams are *unidirectional*—that is, the data for a particular stream travels only from the producer to the consumer. The consumer cannot send any data back to the producer on this same stream.

However, there is nothing to prevent the consumer process from opening a different stream back to the producer process. In fact, a single process can have multiple streams that can be any combination of producers and consumers. These also can be opened between multiple other processes. This is one of the powerful attributes of streams.

Each stream has only a single producer and a single consumer. A single producer stream cannot feed multiple consumer streams, and a single consumer stream cannot be fed by multiple producer streams. This is not to say that a producer process could not feed multiple consumer processes; it's just that each consumer process must be fed by a different and unique stream. The same is true for a single consumer process that is fed by multiple producer processes.

Consumer processes do not have to blindly accept data from a producer, however. They can start and stop the flow of information, read as much or as little of a stream as desired, and in some cases even determine how much data is left in the stream. Consumer processes can also reset the stream to an earlier point. This control makes it sound like the consumer is communicating back to the producer process, but what is actually happening is that the consumer process is communicating with the Java internals that handle the stream.

If a consumer process pauses while receiving data from its end of the stream, the producer will not necessarily pause in sending data. The producer may continue to produce data, and the Java stream-handling code may buffer the data until the consumer process begins accepting data again. This is important to remember: *the producer and consumer do not communicate directly with each other over a streams interface*. Instead, the producer simply generates a stream of data at one end, which then goes into the Java stream-handling code. From there it is sent to the consumer. The producer and consumer have no knowledge of each other.

The Importance of Streams

Streams have many uses in Java and, in fact, are used quite heavily within Java itself. They are used to read and write information to devices, files, databases, network sockets, other processes—almost anything. All stream interfaces implement a basic set of methods that the programmer can use. These methods are common across all stream types, which makes using a new stream type simple.

There are a few stream methods found in some Java package extensions, but the standard ones are found in the `java.io` package. This package must be imported in all applications or applets that make use of threads.

There are some extended stream methods that are not always implemented, such as the capability to reset the stream to an earlier point. For these cases, there are other methods discussed in the following sections that you can use to check whether extended methods are supported. This makes it possible for a program to take advantage of these methods if they are available.

So how do you implement a stream? Let's find out!

Input Streams

Input streams are the data streams that are accepted and processed by a consumer process. As mentioned before, stream classes and their associated methods are found in the package java.io. Every application or applet that uses streams must explicitly import this package in the beginning of the code. You do this with a standard `import` statement:

```
import java.io.*;
```

There are many different classes of input streams. Each has its own purpose and can, of course, be extended or customized as needed by the programmer. Table 8.1 is a complete list of Java's input stream classes.

Table 8.1. Input stream classes.

BufferedInputStream	Reads data from the buffer to minimize number of actual reads needed
ByteArrayInputStream	Reads byte data into an array of bytes
DataInputStream	Reads data objects from a stream rather than bytes like most other input streams
FileInputStream	Reads data from a file
FilterInputStream	Allows a stream to connect to subclasses of itself that can be used to filter the data
InputStream	Abstracts the superclass to all InputStream classes
LineNumberInputStream	Reads an input stream that uses line numbers
PipedInputStream	Reads data from a pipe connected to another process
PushBackInputStream	Allows pushing a single character back onto input stream
SequenceInputStream	Treats multiple sequential input streams as single input stream
StringBufferInputStream	Reads character data into an array of characters (a string)

The methods associated with input streams are of two types: those that are guaranteed to work with all input streams (see Table 8.2) and those that are not (see Table 8.3).

Table 8.2. Input stream methods guaranteed to work.

read	Reads data from an input stream
skip	Skips past data in an input stream
markAvailable	Tests if the mark method is available on this input stream
close	Closes an input stream

Table 8.3. Input stream methods not guaranteed to work.

`available`	Amount of data available in an input stream
`mark`	Marks a point in an input stream to which to return
`reset`	Returns to a specified point in an input stream

The methods not guaranteed to work either may not be available as valid methods or may return inaccurate or inconsistent results because of the uncertain nature of a producer. Some producers send a consistent stream of data; others will not produce data until the intervening Java stream-handling code indicates it is ready. For these reasons, the results can be unpredictable.

read

The `read` method is the most basic of the input stream methods. This is the method an application uses to read data from a stream. It has several variations, mainly involving how much data is read, where in the stream the data starts and stops, and to where the data is written. Which `read` method you use depends on your application's needs.

All `read` methods are based on a *blocking read*, meaning that when a `read` method is called, it will not return until all the data requested has been received or an exception occurs. Recall that in some earlier examples, a read of the keyboard was done. In these cases, the `read` function did not return until a character was entered on the keyboard. This is an example of a blocking read. If the equivalent of a non-blocking read is needed, methods exist for checking if data is available before a read is executed.

All read methods also throw the `IOException` exception. This must be handled in an application's code, either by using a `try/catch/finally` structure or by adding a `throws` statement to the class declaration. The syntax of `read` follows:

```
int read();
int read(byte[] buffer);
int read(byte[] buffer, int offset, int length)
```

The first form of `read` simply attempts to read a single byte from the input stream. The byte `read` is returned by the function itself, cast as an `int`. The second form reads data into a *buffer*, an array of bytes. It attempts to read enough data to fill the buffer. The last version also attempts to fill a buffer, but starts at the indicated `offset` into the stream and will read only `length` bytes. All cases of `read` return an integer, which is used to indicate the number of bytes actually read. If there is nothing more to be read, it returns a -1, as in the following:

```
import java.io.*;

public class MyMain {
    public static void main (String args[]) {
        FileInputStream s;            //declare s to be a file input stream
        int rcode;                    //declare a variable for the read return code
        try {                         //use try to catch file open exceptions
```

```java
        s = new FileInputStream(args[0]);              //open the input stream
        rcode = 0;
        while (rcode != -1) {  //loop reading file until entire file is read
            try {                                  //use try to catch IO exceptions
                rcode = s.read();          //read character from file
                System.out.println("ch = " + (char)rcode);//print char to screen
            }
            catch (IOException e) {                 //handle IO exceptions
                System.out.println("Unknown IO error reading file " + args[0]);
                System.exit(2);
            }
        }
    }
    catch (FileNotFoundException e) {  //handle file not found exception
        System.out.println("File " + args[0] + " not found");
        System.exit(1);
    }
  }
}
```

In this example, read is used to read bytes from a file input stream. The name of the file to read is passed as the first argument on the command line when you run the application. Therefore, if you wanted the program to read from a file called sample.txt, you would invoke the MyMain application using the following:

```
java MyMain sample.txt
```

A stream object variable s is declared to be of type FileInputStream. It is then initialized by opening the file input stream using the new operator. This will result in the file actually being opened, so a File not found exception must be caught at this point if the file does not exist.

Next, a while loop is used to continuously read a single byte from the stream until the read method returns -1. The body of the while loop starts out by calling the read method to read a byte. read may return an IOexception, so it is also placed in a try statement. If the read succeeds, the byte is printed to the screen. If not, a catch statement writes an error and the application aborts.

This example shows the basics for handling a simple input stream. It shows how to open an input stream, read data from it, detect the end of it, and set up exception handling for both the open and the read of it.

skip

The skip method is used to bypass a fixed number of bytes of an input stream, thereby enabling the program to move quickly through the stream. It can be used to skip unneeded data or to move to a specific point in the stream. If used with a database input stream, it can be used to skip through a set of fixed-length records to get to the record needed. If used with a file input stream, it can provide some of the same functionality as the C/C++ lseek function.

The skip method works in a forward direction only. It cannot be used to skip backward to an earlier point in an input stream. Some input streams allow this functionality, but they use the mark and reset methods (covered later in their respective sections) to accomplish this.

The `skip` method throws the same `IOException` exception that `read` does. This must be handled in an application's code, either by using a `try/catch/finally` structure or by adding throws to the class declaration. The syntax of `skip` follows:

```
long skip(long num);
```

The `skip` method accepts a single argument of type `long`: the number of bytes to skip in the input stream. Because data streams do not have any fixed size, if more bytes than can be handled in a `long` must be skipped, use multiple `skip` statements.

There is a problem with large argument values in the implementation of `skip` as of this writing (Java 1.0). The `long` passed as an argument is internally cast to an `int` because `skip` is implemented using the `read(byte[])` method. The problem with this is that arrays in Java are constrained to be no larger than an `int`. If skips larger than `int` are required, they must be implemented as multiple `int` skips.

The `skip` method returns a `long` that is used to indicate the number of bytes actually skipped. If the end of the input stream has already been reached when `skip` is called, a `-1` is returned. The following code fragment provides an example:

```java
public long skipRecords (int num) {
    int recordSize = 512;                //size of a record in bytes
    long rcode = 0;
    try {
        rcode = s.skip(num*recordSize);  //skip num 512 byte records
        if (rcode > 0) {
            rcode /= recordSize;          //compute records skipped
        }
    }
    catch (IOException e) {              //handle IO exceptions
        System.out.println("Unknown IO error skipping " + num + " records");
    }
    return(rcode/recordSize);
}
```

In this example, `skip` is used in a method that indexes into an input stream by number of fixed 512-byte records. A `try` statement is used to catch an exception during the `skip` process. The `catch` statement prints an error message if an `IOException` exception is generated. The method returns the number of records skipped, a `-1` if the skip was at end of input, or `0` if an exception occurred. (This example is based on `s` being a stream object that has already been opened as a variable global to this method.)

close

The `close` method is used to close an input stream that an application or applet no longer needs. Java closes input streams automatically when an application or applet exits, which is why a `close` statement has not been used in the preceding stream examples. However, it is good programming practice to close any resources an application no longer needs.

The `close` method throws the same `IOException` exception that `read` and `skip` do. This must be handled in an application's code, either by using a `try/catch/finally` structure or by adding `throw` statement to the class declaration.

```
public long closeStream () {
   try s.close();                //close input stream
   catch (IOException e) {    //handle IO exceptions
      System.out.println("Unknown IO error closing input stream");
   }
}
```

In this example, close is used in a method that encapsulates the try and catch functionality into a single location. A try statement is used to catch an exception during the close process. The catch statement prints an error message if an IOException exception is generated. (As in the skip example used previously, this example is based on s being a stream object that has already been opened as a variable global to this method.)

available

The available method is used to determine if some amount of data is ready to be read without blocking in the input stream and to test whether enough data is available for processing before some other method such as read is called. However, available does not return valid information for all input streams. Some input streams always return 0, whereas others may return inconsistent numbers. This is due to the unknowns associated with the producer process and the implementation of the underlying Java code that handles the connection between the producer and consumer processes.

In other programming languages, the equivalent functionality of available is used to ensure that a required amount of data is available before issuing a read command. This is done because read often blocks until the read has completed. For applications that must continue doing other processing until all data needed is available, this is the only way to ensure that the application does not hang waiting for data.

In Java, threads can be used to handle this problem. By assigning a specific thread to do reading on an input stream, that thread can block, waiting for the required amount of input while other threads continue with needed processing. The easy availability of threads makes using available largely unnecessary. This is also why the incorrect or inconsistent results returned by available are not considered big problems. The syntax of available follows:

```
int available();
```

The available method simply returns an int indicating the number of bytes in the input stream that can currently be read without blocking. The available method does not have any parameters. Note that the return value is an int. Streams can be of unlimited size, so even if more than an int's worth of data is available, only an int's worth is reported. The following code fragment provides an example:

```
public boolean isRecordReady () {
   int recordSize = 512;                  //size of a record in bytes
   boolean rcode = false;
   try {
      //test if at least 512 bytes are available
      if (s.available >= recordSize) {
```

```
            rcode = true;
        }
    }
    catch (IOException e) {                    //handle IO exceptions
        System.out.println("Unknown IO error checking for record availability");
    }
    return(rcode);
}
```

In this example, available is used to determine if an entire fixed-length record of 512 bytes is available in the input stream. A try statement is used to catch an exception during the available test. The catch statement prints an error message if an IOException exception is generated. The method will return true if at least 512 bytes are ready or false if not. (As with skip and close, this example is based on s being a stream object that has already been opened as a variable global to this method.)

mark, markSupported, and reset

The mark method is used to mark a point in an input stream to which it may be necessary to return at a later time. This method is not available for all input stream types. A separate method called markSupported determines if a particular input stream supports this functionality. If mark is supported, you can use the reset method to return to the point indicated by mark.

The mark/reset methods have several limitations that make them useful only for specific applications. When mark is used, the program must specify a maximum amount of data that can go by before the reset method is called. If more than this amount of data goes by, reset will throw an exception. Also, there is no way to specify multiple marks on an input stream. If mark is called again before a reset is done, the mark is simply moved to the new location with the new limit on how much can be read before a reset occurs. The syntax of mark, markSupported, and reset follows:

```
void mark(int readLimit);
```

```
boolean markSupported();
```

```
void reset();
```

The mark method accepts a single parameter of type int that indicates how much data in the input stream can go by before calling the reset method. The markSupported method has no arguments and simply returns a boolean value indicating whether the mark function is available for a given input stream. reset has no calling arguments and no return value. It simply resets the input stream to the point at which mark was called. The following code fragment provides an example:

```
public static boolean checkForPostScriptHeader (int size) {
    byte buffer[];
    String txt;
    buffer = new byte[size];
    if (s.markSupported() == false) {
        System.out.println("Input Stream does not support mark");
        System.exit(1);
    }
    try s.read(buffer);
```

```
      catch (IOException e) {
         System.out.println("Unknown IO error reading data stream");
         System.exit(2);
   }
      try s.reset();
      catch (IOException e) {
         System.out.println("Unknown IO error reseting data stream");
         System.exit(3);
      }
      txt = new String(buffer,size);
      if ((txt.indexOf("\n%!") != -1) || (txt.indexOf("%!") == 0))
         return(true);
      else
         return(false);
}
```

This example is a method that checks a data input stream for a postscript header. If there is one, it will return true; otherwise it will return false. The mark and reset methods are used to return the data stream to its original location so that the calling routines can process the stream as needed.

The method starts by checking whether the mark method is available for this input stream using the markSupported method. If it is not, an application exit is forced. If mark is available, the input stream is marked with the passed-in size. This allows the calling application to specify how much data should be checked for a postscript header. After the input stream is marked, it is read into a buffer. If an IOexception occurs, a message is written to the screen and again the application exits. If the input stream is read successfully, it is then reset back to the location where the method was called. Again it tests for an IOException exception, and an error message and an exit occur if an exception is detected.

After the input stream is reset, the buffer is converted to a string value so that it can use the indexOf method to locate the postscript header. Finally, an if statement uses the indexOf method to locate the header. It is called twice: The first time it checks to see if any line begins with the necessary postscript header characters, and the second time it handles the special case at the beginning of the file where there is no newline character preceding the header. If a header is found, the method exits with a return value of true; otherwise, it exits with a return value of false.

Output Streams

Output streams are the data streams generated by a producer process. As mentioned previously, stream classes and their associated methods are found in the java.io package. Every application or applet that uses streams must explicitly import this package at the beginning of the code with a standard import statement:

```
import java.io.*;
```

As with input streams, there are many different classes of output streams. Each has its own purpose and can, of course, be extended or customized as needed by the programmer. Table 8.4 is a complete list of Java's output stream classes.

Table 8.4. Output stream classes.

BufferedOutputStream	Writes data to buffer to minimize the number of actual writes needed
ByteArrayOutputStream	Writes data to an array of bytes
DataOutputStream	Writes data objects to a stream rather than bytes like most other output streams
FileOutputStream	Writes data to a file
FilterOutputStream	Allows a stream to connect to subclasses of itself that can be used to filter the data
OutputStream	Abstracts the superclass to all output stream classes
PipedOutputStream	Writes data to a pipe connected to another process
PrintStream	Writes formatted data to the user's screen

Table 8.5 lists the three methods associated with output streams. Just like any other method in Java, these methods can be extended and customized as needed by the programmer.

Table 8.5. Output stream methods.

write	Writes data to an output stream
flush	Forces data to be written to pipe
close	Closes an output stream

write

The write method is the most basic of the output stream methods. This is the method an application uses to write data to a stream. As with the read method, there are several variations associated with it.

All write methods are based on a *blocking write*, meaning that when a write method is called, it will not return until all the data to be sent has been accepted or an exception occurs. When a call blocks, execution cannot continue until the call completes. This can cause problems if the programmer wants the application to continue if the write takes a significant amount of time. The solution, as with the input stream methods, is to use threads. If you put write into a separate thread, other executions can continue and the thread with write can take as long as it needs to complete the transaction.

All write methods also throw the IOException exception. This must be handled in an application's code, either by using a try/catch/finally structure or by adding throws to the class declaration. The syntax of write follows:

```
void write(int b);
void write(byte[] buffer);
void write(byte[] buffer, int offset, int length)
```

The variations on write almost exactly mirror those for read: The first simply writes a single byte to the output stream, and the second writes data to a buffer. The buffer is an array of bytes. The last version also writes a buffer, but will start at the indicated offset into the array and will only write length bytes. All cases of write have a return type of void. The only way to determine if an error occurred is to catch any exceptions that are thrown. Here is an example:

```
import java.io.*;

public class MyMain {

    public static void main (String args[]) {
        FileOutputStream s;                     //declare s to a file output stream
        int n,ix;                               //declare for loop variables
        try {                            //use try to catch file open exceptions
            s = new FileOutputStream(args[0]);     //open the output stream
            for (n=0; n < 20; n++) {               //outer for loop
               for (ix=0x30; ix < 0x7b; ix++) {    //inner for loop
                  try {                            //use try to catch IO exceptions
                     s.write(ix);                  //write character to output stream
                  }
                  catch (IOException e) {          //handle IO exceptions
                     System.out.println("Unknown IO error writing file " + args[0]);
                     System.exit(2);
                  }
               }                                   //bottom of inner loop
               try {
                  s.write('\n');
               }                    //write newline char to output stream
               catch (IOException e) {             //handle IO exceptions
                  System.out.println("Unknown IO error writing file " + args[0]);
                  System.exit(3);
               }
            }                                      //bottom of outer loop
        }
        catch (IOException e) {                  //handle file open exceptions
            System.out.println("Unknown IO error opening file " + args[0]);
            System.exit(1);
        }
    }
}
```

In this example, write is used to write bytes to a file output stream. The filename itself is passed as the first argument on the command line. A stream object variable s is declared to be of type FileOutputStream. It is then initialized by opening the file output stream using the new operator. This results in either the creation of a new file using the filename specified on the command line or the rewriting of an existing file. This results in the file being opened, so a file IOException exception must be caught at this point if the file is not accessible. Next, two nested while loops are used to write a series of characters to the stream.

The inner loop writes all ASCII characters between 0 and z. The body of this loop starts out by calling the write method to write a single character to the output stream. write may return an IOException exception, so it is placed in a try statement. If write fails, a catch statement writes an error and the application aborts.

The outer loop simply causes the inner loop to be run 20 times. However, after every inner loop completes, the outer loop writes a newline character to the output stream. This makes the resulting output file more readable.

This example shows the basics for handling a simple output stream. It shows how to open an output stream, write data to it, and set up exception handling for both open and write.

flush

The flush method is used to force any data buffered for the output stream to be written to the output device. Some streams may be connected to slow or even hung consumer processes, in which cases write may block for an overly extended period of time, if not forever. In these situations, the flush method can be used to force Java to accept the data. Java may simply buffer the data itself, waiting for the consumer process to begin accepting data again or to die, thus closing the pipe. Remember that if a write is blocked, the only way for an application to force the flush to occur is to call flush using a different thread. This is another example of why putting a stream I/O call into its own thread is a good idea. The syntax of flush follows:

```
void flush();
```

The flush method also throws the same IOException exception that write does. This must be handled in an application's code, either by using a try/catch/finally structure or by adding throws to the class declaration, as in the following example:

```
public void flushStream () {
   try {s.flush();}                  //close output stream
   catch (IOException e) {           //handle IO exceptions
      System.out.println("Unknown IO error flushing output stream");
   }
}
```

In this example, flush is used in a method that encapsulates the try and catch functionality into a single location. A try statement is used to catch any exceptions during the close process. The catch statement will print an error message if an IOException is generated. (This example is based on s being a stream object that has already been opened as a variable global to this method.)

close

The close method is virtually identical to the close used for input streams. It is used to close an output stream that an application or applet no longer needs. Java will automatically close output streams when an application or applet exits, which is why a `close` statement has not been used in the preceding stream examples. However, it is good programming practice to close any resources an application no longer needs. The syntax of `close` follows:

```
void close();
```

The `close` method throws the same `IOException` exception that `write` and `flush` do. This must be handled in an application's code, either by using a `try/catch/finally` structure or by adding a `throw` statement to the class declaration. The following is an example:

```
public void closeStream () {
    try {s.close();}                    //close output stream
    catch (IOException e) {             //handle IO exceptions
        System.out.println("Unknown IO error closing output stream");
    }
}
```

In this example, `close` is used in a method that encapsulates the `try` and `catch` functionality into a single location. A `try` statement is used to catch an exception during the `close` process. The `catch` statement will print an error message if an `IOException` exception is generated. (This example is based on `s` being a stream object that has already been opened as a variable global to this method.)

Summary of Streams

Streams are Java's way of reading and writing data to entities outside an application, such as files, networks, devices, or other processes. All streams in Java consist of a flow of 8-bit bytes. Some stream classes allow the writing of other object types, but internally they simply convert these objects to bytes. Streams can be broken into two main types: input streams and output streams.

Input streams accept data from an external source. Processes that accept input streams are known as consumers. You can use several methods with input streams: `read`, `skip`, `markSupported`, and `close` work with all input stream types; and `available`, `mark`, and `reset` only work with some input stream types. The `read` method is used to read data from an input stream. `skip` is used to skip over information in the input stream to get to data farther on. `close` simply closes an input stream. The `available` method can be used to determine if more data is available in an input stream, but the results returned by this method are not always accurate. The `markSupported` method is used to determine if a particular stream supports the `mark/reset` methods. These methods are used to mark a particular location in a stream and reset the stream back to that location.

Output streams produce data for an external destination. Processes that produce output streams are known as *producers*. You can use several methods with output streams: `write`, `flush`, and `close`. The `write` method is used to write data to an output stream. `flush` is used to force data to be written that may be buffered. `close` simply closes an output stream.

By using input and output streams, Java applications and applets can communicate with the rest of the world.

Summary

This chapter examines the final pieces of the Java programming language: threads, exceptions, and streams.

The section on threads covers concurrent execution of multiple sections of code. The methods to create, initialize, start, stop, and destroy a thread are also discussed. Threads are a powerful part of the Java programming language, and a programmer who becomes versed in their use can write more powerful, robust, and user-friendly programs.

The section on exceptions covers Java's use of exceptions in place of the more normal return-type error code. Exceptions provide a more robust and extensible way to do error handling. The methods for catching and handling an exception are explained, as well as generation of new, customized exceptions. Because exceptions are simply another object in Java, all the benefits regarding code reuse and customization apply.

Finally, the section on streams covers Java's use of this construct to communicate with the outside world. Streams are a sequence of bytes. By using such a simple data format, Java applications do not have to have specific knowledge of where data is coming from or being written to. This in turn lends itself to simpler, more reusable code. The methods to open, read, write, and close a data stream are covered, in addition to more complex concepts such as rereading a part of a stream. Streams in Java provide a flexible—but above all, standardized—method for external communication.

This concludes the basics of Java programming. With the tool sets covered to this point, you are now ready to create Java applications that will serve your needs. Part IV, "The Java Application Programming Interface," covers the class libraries in Java.

IV

The Java Application Programming Interface

9

Introducing
the Java API

For those of you impatiently waiting to put Java to use, this chapter will probably help with the frustration level a great deal. Java structure is presented in Part III, "Anatomy of the Java Language." Part IV, "The Java Application Programming Interface," begins the fun part. Now it is time to fill in the structure with some pretty fancy stuff, such as mouse clicks and graphics. This chapter and the next four explore in detail the capabilities of the prebuilt objects available in Java.

The *Application Programming Interface* (API) packages contain classes and interfaces for building applets and applications. This chapter provides an overview of all the packages available at this writing.

Another key skill presented here is how to read the Java API documentation online and know what to do with it. This chapter discusses how to create a library call using the documentation and how to interpret what the library call will do.

The Java API Packages

Java *libraries* are groups of prewritten classes available for programming. In other languages these procedures are called system service calls, system calls, or library calls and are used to access system time or date or to query the input device as to its type. Java libraries function as a rich resource of functionality for the programmer.

These libraries are gathered in *packages*—collections of class libraries or, sometimes, of other packages. (See Chapter 7, "Building Objects," for a discussion of packages and class libraries.)

This chapter presents the overall concept of the Java libraries and gives some idea of their use. Read on to get the details of each library in the next four chapters.

Think of this aspect of Java as a pyramid. The pyramid itself is the package, and the blocks that build it are libraries and classes.

The top block of the pyramid package is the `Object` class. This class is the superclass to all other classes. So we have a pyramid with the `Object` class at the top, and beneath it, side by side, are the class libraries that support the functionality of Java.

Java is designed to have great flexibility and to produce results quickly. Someone else has gone to the work of coding classes and interfaces to perform many feats of functionality, so why reinvent the wheel? In fact, you can create applications in which all the programmer needs to do is create variables and program logic through control flow. All other aspects of the application are performed by library calls, including painting the screen, performing input and output, manipulating data, and closing links.

Use library calls as much as possible to guarantee results across platforms. These classes and interfaces have been tested and, if not completely bulletproof, are close to it.

The Structure of the API Packages

Java packages are made up of class libraries. Java is made up of the following packages:

```
java.applet
java.lang
java.io
java.net
java.awt
java.awt.image
java.awt.peer
java.util
```

Recently, a new API has been added: The Java Database Connectivity API. This API can be used to connect to databases using SQL queries. It is not included in the base Java Developer's Kit (JDK) but can be downloaded from Sun's Web site. At the time of this writing this API was located at `http://www.javasoft.com/jdbc/`.

Packages are imported into program code using the following command:

```
import java.awt.*;   //imports the.package java.awt and all of its sub-packages
```

Java evaluates the `import` statements and the code. Only the libraries, classes, and interfaces used in the code are imported. Therefore, it is no waste of overhead if more classes are imported than are used. However, it is confusing to the programmer who must maintain the code later. Importing more packages or libraries than are needed also slows down the compile.

A brief description of the packages of Java and lists of the interfaces and classes from each package are in the following sections. The lists are included to give you a better understanding of the contents of the package. The rest of Part IV gives specifics of each package, including many examples of class usage.

java.lang

The `java.lang` package is imported by default into each class at compile time. There is no need to import it explicitly.

`java.lang` contains the classes that define the fundamental elements of Java. (These elements are covered in Chapter 6, "Fundamentals of the Java Language.") The lists of interfaces and classes shown in Tables 9.1 and 9.2 may look familiar after learning about primitive data types in Chapter 6.

Table 9.1. `java.lang` interfaces.

Interface	Usage
Clonable	Indicates object can be copied or cloned
Runnable	Indicates object can implement threads

Table 9.2. `java.lang` classes.

Class Name	Description
Boolean	Object wrapper for the primitive type `boolean`
Character	Object wrapper for the primitive type `character`
Class	Contains runtime representations of all class types
ClassLoader	Abstract class specifying how classes are loaded at runtime
Double	Object wrapper for the primitive type `double`
Float	Object wrapper for the primitive type `float`
Integer	Object wrapper for the primitive type `integer`
Long	Object wrapper for the primitive type `long`
Math	Library of standard mathematical functions
Number	Abstract superclass to all number types
Object	Superclass to all other class types
Process	Library of process control methods
Runtime	Library of runtime access methods
SecurityManager	Abstract class containing security policy method templates
String	Superclass for all string objects
StringBuffer	Superclass for all growable string objects
System	Library of system interface methods
Thread	Superclass for all thread objects and methods
ThreadGroup	Superclass for grouping multiple threads together
Throwable	Superclass for all exception-handling objects and methods

java.util

`java.util` is the library that contains objects used for system utilities. The `Date` class with its many methods is found here, as well as `Random`, a random number generator, and `Vector`, used to provide a growable array of objects. Tables 9.3 and 9.4 present a list of interfaces and classes found in `java.util`.

Table 9.3. `java.util` interfaces.

Interface	Usage
Enumeration	Indicates object can implement methods to count through a set of values
Observer	Indicates object can be tracked with class `Observer`

Table 9.4. `java.util` classes.

Class Name	Description
BitSet	Bit-manipulation library
Date	Date-manipulation library
Dictionary	Abstract parent to class hash table
Hashtable	Hash table–manipulation library
Observable	Observer-manipulation library
Properties	Persistent properties class
Random	Random number–manipulation library
Stack	Stack-manipulation library
StringTokenizer	String token–manipulation library
Vector	Vector-manipulation library

java.io

`java.io` is the library that contains objects useful in handling the input/output between Java and the keyboard, screen, printer, disk files, or network. It also provides interfaces for streams and files. Tables 9.5 and 9.6 present a list of `java.io` interfaces and classes.

Table 9.5. `java.io` interfaces.

Interface	Usage
DataInput	Template for classes implementing input stream methods
DataOutput	Template for classes implementing output stream methods
FilenameFilter	Template for classes implementing filename-filtering methods

Table 9.6. `java.io` classes.

Class Name	Description
BufferedInputStream	Buffered input stream allowing faster reads
BufferedOutputStream	Buffered output stream allowing faster writes
ByteArrayInputStream	Stream read from an array of bytes
ByteArrayOutputStream	Stream written to an array of bytes
DataInputStream	Generic byte-input stream
DataOutputStream	Generic byte-output stream
File	Platform-independent representations of filenames
FileDescriptor	Stream read from a file descriptor
FileInputStream	Stream read from a file
FileOutputStream	Stream written to a file
FilterInputStream	Abstract class for filtered input streams
FilterOutputStream	Abstract class for filtered output streams
InputStream	Superclass to all input stream classes
LineNumberInputStream	Input stream that is aware of line numbers
OutputStream	Superclass to all output stream classes
PipedInputStream	Stream for reading data from another process
PipedOutputStream	Stream for writing data to another process
PrintStream	Output stream for sending formatted data to output devices
PushbackInputStream	Input stream allowing a single byte to be pushed back onto the stream
RandomAccessFile	Input stream allowing random access to a file
SequenceInputStream	Input stream allowing multiple input streams to read in sequence
StreamTokenizer	Methods for converting an input stream into tokens
StringBufferInputStream	Stream read from a `StringBuffer`

java.net

`java.net` libraries contain routines that interact with network protocols. These objects interface with such protocols as sockets, Telnet, FTP, NNTP, and HTTP. Tables 9.7 and 9.8 present a list of `java.net` interfaces and classes.

Table 9.7. `java.net` interfaces.

Interface	Usage
ContentHandlerFactory	Template for classes implementing content handlers
SocketImplFactory	Template for classes implementing socket handlers
URLStreamHandlerFactory	Template for classes implementing URL handlers

Table 9.8. `java.net` classes.

Class Name	Description
ContentHandler	Class for creating objects from URLs
DatagramPacket	Class for representing network packets
DatagramSocket	Class for representing network sockets
InetAddress	Internet address–manipulation library
ServerSocket	Server socket–implementation library
Socket	Client socket–implementation library
SocketImpl	Abstract superclass for all socket classes
URL	URL-manipulation library
URLConnection	Abstract class for manipulating URL connections
URLEncoder	Methods for tokenizing URL strings
URLStreamHandler	Abstract class for opening URL connection streams

java.awt

AWT stands for *Abstract Windowing Toolkit*. As its name suggests, AWT libraries involve the GUI (graphical user interface) parts of Java, including such elements as boxes, buttons, borders, and menus. Tables 9.9 and 9.10 present a list of `java.awt` interfaces and classes.

Table 9.9. `java.awt` interfaces.

Interface	Usage
LayoutManager	Template for classes implementing layout containers
MenuContainer	Template for classes implementing menu containers

Table 9.10. `java.awt` classes.

Class Name	Description
BorderLayout	Methods for handling border layouts
Button	Methods for manipulating Button objects
Canvas	Generic template for implementing canvases
CardLayout	Methods for manipulating Rolodex-style card objects
Checkbox	Methods for manipulating Checkbox objects
CheckboxGroup	Methods for manipulating groups of Checkbox objects
CheckboxMenuItem	Methods for manipulating Checkbox-style menus
Choice	Methods for manipulating pop-up choice options
Color	Methods for manipulating colors
Component	Generic class for implementing AWT components
Container	Generic class for implementing AWT containers
Dialog	Methods for manipulating a pop-up dialog box
Dimension	Wrapper for representing width and height
Event	Methods for manipulating user input events
FileDialog	Methods for manipulating a file dialog box
FlowLayout	Methods for manipulating flow of Window objects
Font	Methods for manipulating fonts
FontMetrics	Methods for manipulating font characteristics
Frame	Methods for handling frames
Graphics	Abstract superclass to all Graphics objects
GridBagConstraints	Methods for placing restraints on GridBag layouts
GridBagLayout	Methods for placing objects in a window in a specified way
GridLayout	Methods for manipulating grid layout containers
Image	Abstract class for implementing platform-specific images
Insets	Methods for manipulating insets in containers
Label	Methods for manipulating labels
List	Methods for manipulating lists
MediaTracker	Methods for tracking media objects
Menu	Methods for manipulating menus
MenuBar	Methods for manipulating menu bars
MenuComponent	Superclass to all menu objects

Class Name	Description
MenuItem	Methods for manipulating menu items
Panel	Generic class for implementing panel containers
Point	Wrapper for representing points
Polygon	Wrapper for representing polygons
Rectangle	Wrapper for representing rectangles
Scrollbar	Methods for manipulating scrollbars
TextArea	Methods for manipulating text areas
TextComponent	Superclass to all text objects
TextField	Methods for manipulating single lines of text
Toolkit	Class used to bind the AWT to a specific implementation
Window	Methods for manipulating a Window object

java.awt.image

As is evident from the package title, java.awt.image is a subpackage of java.awt. java.awt.image's classes primarily involve the screen image as a whole, in contrast to java.awt, which involves the individual elements of a screen image. Tables 9.11 and 9.12 present the interfaces and classes found in java.awt.image.

Table 9.11. java.awt.image interfaces.

Interface	Usage
ImageConsumer	Template for receiving images from an image producer
ImageObserver	Template for receiving image-update information
ImageProducer	Template for producing images for an image consumer

Table 9.12. java.awt.image classes.

Class Name	Description
ColorModel	Abstract class for converting among color models
CropImageFilter	Methods for cropping images
DirectColorModel	Methods for translating color models
FilteredImageSource	Methods for applying filters to an image

continues

Table 9.12. continued.

Class Name	Description
ImageFilter	Methods for implementing an image filter
IndexColorModel	Methods for translating color models
MemoryImageSource	Methods for creating images using arrays of pixels
PixelGrabber	Methods to extract a subset of an image
RGBImageFilter	Methods for implementing an RGB filter

java.awt.peer

java.awt.peer is also a subpackage of java.awt. java.awt.peer consists only of interfaces. (See Table 9.13.) It is used in conjunction with java.awt to provide platform-dependent graphics for the window. The Java interpreter handles the call on a platform-specific basis.

Table 9.13. java.awt.peer interfaces.

Interface	Usage
ButtonPeer	Native template for manipulating Button objects
CanvasPeer	Native template for implementing canvases
CheckboxPeer	Native template for manipulating Checkbox objects
CheckboxMenuItemPeer	Native template for manipulating Checkbox-style menus
ChoicePeer	Native template for manipulating pop-up choice options
ComponentPeer	Native template for implementing AWT components
ContainerPeer	Native template for implementing AWT containers
DialogPeer	Native template for manipulating a pop-up dialog box
FileDialogPeer	Native template for manipulating a file dialog box
FramePeer	Native template for handling frames
LabelPeer	Native template for manipulating labels
ListPeer	Native template for manipulating lists
MenuBarPeer	Native template for manipulating menu bars
MenuComponentPeer	Superclass to all menu objects
MenuPeer	Native template for manipulating menus
MenuItemPeer	Native template for manipulating menu items
PanelPeer	Native template for implementing panel containers

Interface	Usage
ScrollbarPeer	Native template for manipulating scrollbars
TextAreaPeer	Native template for manipulating text areas
TextComponentPeer	Superclass to all text objects
TextFieldPeer	Native template for manipulating single lines of text
WindowPeer	Native template for manipulating a Window object

java.applet

The java.applet package contains an applet-specific class—Applet—and several interfaces. The Applet class contains the methods init, start, stop, and destroy (covered in Chapter 7). In other words, the java.applet package is used to control the structure and use of applets. Table 9.14 lists the interfaces for this package.

Table 9.14. java.applet interfaces.

Interface	Usage
AppletContext	Template for obtaining information about an applet's environment
AppletStub	Template used to implement an applet viewer
AudioClip	Template for implementing audio objects

sun.tools.debug

The sun.tools.debug libraries are used in conjunction with the debug-enabled Java binaries such as javac_g. These are used for debugging Java programs with tools such as the Java Debugger (jdb). The sun.tools.debug interface, DebuggerCallback, is a template for implementing communications between an application and a debugger. The classes in this package are listed in Table 9.15 for your reference.

Table 9.15. sun.tools.debug classes.

Class Name	Description
RemoteArray	Methods for debugging arrays
RemoteBoolean	Methods for debugging booleans
RemoteByte	Methods for debugging bytes

continues

Table 9.15. continued

Class Name	Description
RemoteChar	Methods for debugging chars
RemoteClass	Methods for accessing a class from a debugger
RemoteDebugger	Methods for instantiating a debugger
RemoteDouble	Methods for debugging doubles
RemoteField	Methods for accessing variables or methods via a debugger
RemoteFloat	Methods for debugging floats
RemoteInt	Methods for debugging ints
RemoteLong	Methods for debugging longs
RemoteObject	Methods for accessing objects via a debugger
RemoteShort	Methods for debugging shorts
RemoteStackFrame	Methods for accessing the stack frame of a suspended thread
RemoteStackVariable	Methods for accessing stack variables via a debugger
RemoteString	Methods for debugging strings
RemoteThread	Methods for debugging threads
RemoteThreadGroup	Methods for debugging threadgroups
RemoteValue	Methods for accessing variable values via a debugger
StackFrame	Wrapper for the stack frame of a suspended thread

Using the Java API

Now that we have flown over the packages at 30,000 feet, let's talk about ways these packages are useful to programmers. The Java class libraries provide a basis for most of the work that needs to be accomplished in an application. This includes painting a screen, getting information from the user, displaying it, allowing corrections, manipulating the input data, perhaps storing the data, and so on. It is up to the programmer to decide which class to use to get the job done.

It may appear to the Java beginner that it is easier to do all the coding, or to learn a few of the classes and ignore the rest, than to become familiar with the huge number of classes available in Java. This would be a very self-limiting course of action—part of learning Java classes is learning about constructors, methods, and variables.

Sun Microsystems's Web sites have a complete set of documentation covering Java's API. They are located at

```
http://java.sun.com
```

and

```
http://www.javasoft.com
```

The documentation is available as either browsable Web pages or PostScript files, which are simply screen shots of the Web pages. The browsable API documentation provides a fast way to look up specific information. (This section makes a lot more sense if you are looking at the appropriate online documentation at the same time you are reading the description.) The documentation is also available for downloading in a variety of formats, including PostScript, HTML, and PDF. At the time of this writing, this documentation could be found at

```
http://www.javasoft.com/java.sun.com/newdocs.html
```

API Web Reference Structure

This section is a short tutorial on how to use the Sun Web page based on Sun's Web site at this writing. Web sites change constantly, so do not be surprised if these instructions are less than correct when you read this. As always, your mileage may vary.

The first part of this section covers the structure of the package documentation. Just looking at the structure of the documentation can be very confusing the first few times. Still, it is important to understand where to look for information in the API documentation.

The second part of this section is a step-by-step instruction on getting information from Web pages and what to do with it. Code constructed from the examples demonstrates the implementation of this information.

The documentation is divided into packages:

```
java.lang
java.util
java.io
java.net
java.applet
java.awt
java.awt.image
java.awt.peer
sun.tools.debug
```

Package Documentation

The *package page* contains the interface index, the variable index, and the class index (see Figure 9.1). Some packages also have an exception index or an error index.

The *interface index* is a list of the interface names contained in the package. The *class index* is a list of class names contained in the package. The *exception index* is a list of exception names accessed by the classes in the package; the exceptions themselves are contained in the `java.lang` package. The *error index* is a list of error names accessed by the classes in the package.

Figure 9.1.

The `java.awt` *package reference page.*

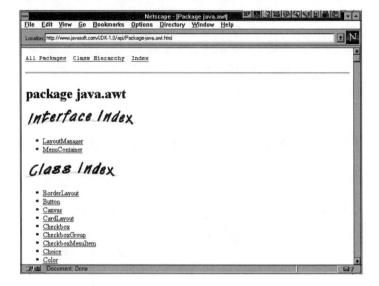

Interface Documentation

The *interface section* contains the actual reference information for each interface in the package. Multiple interfaces are broken out separately into an interface definition, a method index, and method definitions. Interfaces can also have a variable index. Remember, interfaces do not contain code (see Chapter 7); they are the structure of what must be implemented in either Sun- or programmer-written methods.

The *interface definition* contains basic information about the interface. It shows the interface declaration and a description of the interface's purpose. The declaration can include an `extends` keyword that shows other interfaces on which this interface is based. The interface definition also includes, in the *declaration section*, the declaration used to define the interface and a description of the possible uses of the interface.

There is usually a *method index*, which gives a brief index of all methods contained in the interface. (See Figure 9.2.) This includes the name of the method, the method parameter list, and a brief description of the method. The sections *method name* and *parameter list* list the method name and the parameter types the method accepts. It also includes a short description of the method's purpose.

The *methods definition* section of the interface is a more detailed description of each method in the interface. It includes a section on *method name*, which contains the name of the method and the *declaration* used in the interface to declare the method. This is the declaration that must be used when implementing the interface. Finally, it includes a description of the use of the interface.

The interface documentation also can contain a *variable index*. The variable index is a list of variables defined in the interface as well as a short definition of the variable. (See `java.awt.image.ImageConsumer` for an interface that uses several variables.)

Figure 9.2.
The method index from
`Java.applet.AppletContext`.

The *variables section* gives more detail on the variables defined in the interface. Figure 9.3 is an example from interface `java.awt.image.ImageConsumer`.

Figure 9.3.
The variable index from
`java.awt.image.ImageConsumer`.

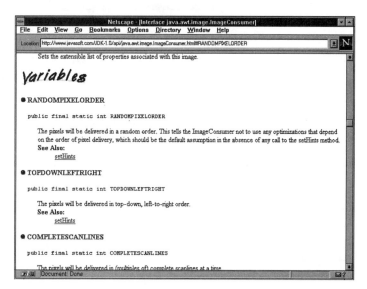

Class Documentation

The *classes section* contains the reference information for each class in the package. If a package contains multiple classes, each is broken out separately into inheritance, structure of class, class definition, the variable index, the constructor index, the method index, variables, constructors, and methods. (Some of these sections may be missing if the class does not use them.)

The inheritance class structure appears at the top of the page in classes. It is a visual and textual explanation of the inheritance structure of the class. An example of this structure is shown in Figure 9.4.

Figure 9.4.
Class documentation from `java.applet.Applet`.

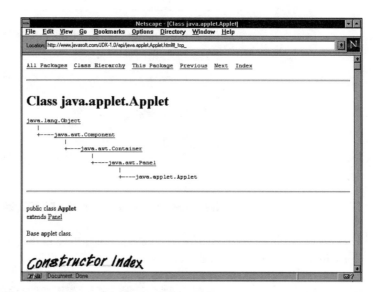

The visual reference shows the class and each of its superclasses until the top of the hierarchy is reached. Directly beneath this is a section that gives a brief definition of the class and possibly additional information such as cross-references. An example of the definition is

```
public class Button
   extends Component.
   A class that produces a labeled button component.
```

This is basic information showing how the class is declared and a description of its purpose. The declaration also can include an `extends` keyword that shows other classes on which this class may be based.

The *variable index* is list of appropriate variables for the class. For example, in the `java.awt.image.ColorModel` class, you will find this:

```
Variable Index
pixel bits
```

The *constructor index* is a list of the constructors for the method. It also contains a brief description of the constructor, as in the following example from `java.awt.Button`:

```
Button()
    Constructs a Button with no label.
Button(String)
    Constructs a Button with a string label.
```

Remember, constructors are used to create new objects.

The *method index* is a list of methods in the class. It also contains a brief description of the method, as in the following example from the `java.awt.Button` class:

```
addNotify()
    Creates the peer of the button.
getLabel()
    Gets the label of the button.
paramString()
    Returns the parameter String of this button.
setLabel(String)
    Sets the button with the specified label.
```

The *variable section* contains more detailed information about variables declared in the class. The following code fragment is from the `java.awt.image.ColorModel` class:

```
Variables
pixel_bits
protected int pixel_bits
```

`pixel_bits` is a variable that has access security of `protected`, is of primitive data type `int`, and is named `pixel_bits`. Therefore, any time this class is imported in a Java program, the `pixel_bits` variable is available.

The *constructors* section of the class lists the constructors contained in the library. This is shown in the following code fragment from `java.awt.Button`:

```
Button
    public Button()
    Constructs a Button with no label.
Button
    public Button(String label)
    Constructs a Button with a string label.
    Parameter:
      label - the button label.
```

The *methods definition* section lists the methods contained in the class and contains detailed information about their use. It lists the methods alphabetically and gives declaration syntax. The methods section also gives a detailed definition of the method, lists parameter information, lists overrides, and includes a "See Also" section. Each method may have a part or all of these elements, depending on applicability. Following is the `addNotify` method from `java.awt.Button`:

```
addNotify
    public synchronzed void addNotify()
    Creates the peer of the button.  This peer allows us to change the look of the
```

```
button without changing its functionality.
Overrides:
    addNotify is class Component
```

This method definition contains information about overrides. The following is the getLabel method from java.awt.Button:

```
getLabel
    public String getLabel()
    Gets the label of the button.
    See Also:
        setLabel
```

This definition has information about other methods in the class to cross-reference, in this case setLabel. The setLabel definition includes information on parameters, like this:

```
setLabel
    public void setLabel(String label)
    Set the button with the specified label.
    Parameters:
        Label - the label to set the button with
    See Also:
        getLabel
```

Exception Documentation

The *exception index* contains a list of exceptions used in a package. These exceptions are usually part of package java.lang, which is part of every Java program by default.

The *exception definition* shows the access security, the exact declaration of the exception, and other information such as cross references. The following example is from AWTException, which is called in java.awt:

```
AWTException
    public class AWTException
    extends Exception
    Signals that an Abstract Window Toolkit exception has occurred.
```

Exceptions are part of java.lang and are explicitly called as java.lang.Exception.

Constructing Code with Documentation Information

The previous section has given you an overview of the parts of the Java API documentation and what they mean. That is all well and good, but the larger issue is what to do with the information. This section constructs code using the information provided in the documentation.

Suppose you had a question about the method necessary to destroy an applet after its use.

Access to the Java API documentation is available at `http://www.javasoft.com`. This will bring up the home page for Sun's Java language. See Figure 9.5 for an example of this page as of this writing. Next, click `API documentation`.

Now click `Documentation`. Now click `Documentation for the n.n Release`.

Figure 9.5.
The `www.javasoft.com`
home page.

In `Package information`, click `java.applet`. This is the proper place to look for methods that control applets. In `Class information`, click `Applet`. Class information is displayed. See Figure 9.6 for an example of this page.

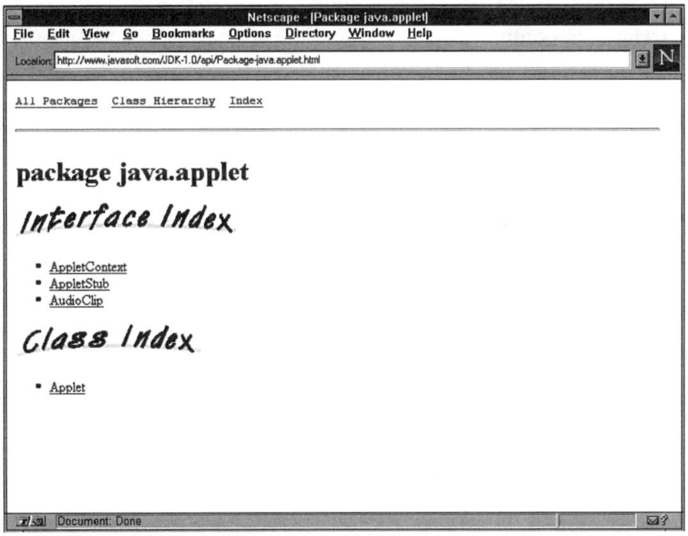

Figure 9.6.
The reference page for
`java.applet.Applet`.

In the `Method Index`, click `destroy`. This will bring up the reference page for the `destroy` method.

The following information is displayed:

```
destroy
   public void destroy()
   Cleans up whatever resources are being held.  If the applet is active it is
   stopped.
   See Also:
      init, start, stop
```

This is all the information you need to code the command. Following is a code fragment that creates and destroys an instance of an applet:

```
import java.applet.*;              //imports the java.applet library
public class MyApplet extends Applet {
   Applet anApplet;
   public void start() {
      anApplet = new Applet();    //create a new instance of MyApplet
      anApplet.destroy();         //stops the applet from executing
   }
}
```

The command that suits our purposes here is `anApplet.destroy();`. The method `destroy` is called from class `Applet` by the syntax

```
objectname.methodname;
```

Do not declare the `destroy` method, as in `public void destroy`. This part of the documentation just shows how the method is declared internally to class `Applet` and is provided for informational purposes only. In this case, the documentation shows that the method is void; therefore no information is returned from the `method` call. All the information about the methods in class `Applet` is imported with the `import` statement.

The next example is a bit more complex. This example is also from class `java.applet.Applet`, so get back into that online documentation. The method to look at this time is `getAppletInfo`. The online documentation looks like this:

```
getAppletInfo
   public String getAppletInfo()
   Returns a string containing information about the author, version and
   copyright of the applet.
```

This method should be defined in programs. The default applet returns `null`.

A code fragment using `getAppletInfo` follows:

```
import java.applet.*;                     //imports the java.applet library
public class MyApplet extends Applet {
   String owner;
   Applet anApplet;
   public void start() {
      anApplet = new Applet();           //create a new instance of MyClass
      owner = anApplet.getAppletInfo();  //returns applet information
   }
}
```

The information returned from the call to `getAppletInfo` is placed in variable `owner`. This information can now be displayed or manipulated in other ways.

This following example passes information to a method: `resize`, once again from `java.applet.Applet`. The online documentation is

```
resize
   public void resize(int width, int height)
   Requests that the applet be resized.
   Overrides:
      resize in class Component
```

`resize` is type `void`, so no information is returned from the method. It is necessary to supply the information `width` and `height` to the method to get it to do anything. This is how it could look:

```
String owner;
int howTall = 3, howWide = 7;
anApplet.resize(howTall, howWide);     //resizes the applet window
owner = anApplet.getAppletInfo();      //returns applet information
System.out.println("Applet information is "+owner);
```

Summary

This chapter introduces the Java API packages and demonstrates the process of retrieving API information from Sun's Web pages. When you know where to look for information and what to do with it, many, many things become possible with Java. The next four chapters go over the packages in more detail and give more examples on how to use the Java API.

10

The
java.lang
and
java.applet
Class
Libraries

The previous chapter gives an overview of the Java API. This chapter explores the `java.applet` and `java.lang` packages. The Applet class library—`java.applet`—controls applets. The Java language class library—`java.lang`—has two main purposes: to provide functionality for primitive data types and other Java structures and to provide exceptions.

Use this chapter as a guide to help locate more information and to understand the breadth and power of the Java API.

The `java.applet.Applet` Class

The Applet class is used to create, execute, and stop running applets. It is part of the format and structure that enables applets to run. The Applet class also provides applet-specific methods.

Most of the code in an applet is no different from that in an application. Both use `java.lang` classes, for example, to do arithmetic functions and string manipulations. Some methods, however, are applet specific and require the presence of a Java-enabled browser. For example, one of these methods is used to retrieve and play an audio clip from across the Net. All the Applet methods are described in the following sections.

More information on these methods can be found in the online API documentation. Be sure to "truth test" the information found in the documentation. Java is a young product, and its methods and classes are still undergoing revision.

destroy()

The `destroy()` method schedules with the Java interpreter to notify the garbage collector to sweep up unused resources.

getAppletContext()

The `getAppletContext()` method returns the environment in which the applet is running. This is usually the browser or applet viewer name. Listing 10.1 shows the use of the `Applet.getAppletContext` method.

Listing 10.1. The `Applet.getAppletContext` method.

```
import java.applet.*;
import java.awt.*;

public class AnApplet extends Applet {

    AppletContext myAppletContext;

    public void init() {
```

```
        //get context in which applet is running
        myAppletContext = this.getAppletContext();
        //disply status message using context
        myAppletContext.showStatus("entering init");
        sleep(2000);
    }

    public void start() {
        myAppletContext.showStatus("entering start");
        sleep(2000);
    }

    public void paint(Graphics g) {
        g.drawString("Hello World!", 10,20);
        sleep(2000);
    }

    public void sleep (int period) {
            try {Thread.sleep(period);}
            catch(InterruptedException e) {}
    }
}
```

getAppletInfo()

The getAppletInfo() method returns a string that was passed to it. It is called when the applet information is requested from the applet viewer. I recommend overriding the default information, which is a null value. Listing 10.2 is an example of overriding the getAppletInfo method of java.applet.Applet.

Listing 10.2. Overriding the getAppletInfo method of java.applet.Applet.

```
import java.applet.*;
import java.awt.*;

public class AnApplet extends Applet implements Runnable {

    Thread myThread;

    public void start() {
        if (myThread == null) {
            myThread = new Thread(this);
            myThread.start();
        }
    }

    public void stop() {
        if (myThread != null) {
            myThread.stop();
            myThread = null;
        }
    }
```

continues

Listing 10.2. continued

```
    public void run() {
       repaint();
    }

    public String getAppletInfo() {
       return("Applet:getAppletInfo;  Author:Mr. X; Version:1.0;
       ➡Copyright 1996, Macmillan");
    }

    public void paint (Graphics g) {
       g.drawString(getAppletInfo(),10,20);
    }
}
```

getAudioClip(URL) and getAudioClip(URL, String)

The getAudioClip(URL) and getAudioClip(URL, String) methods get an audio clip. Listing 10.3 is an example of the use of these methods. Be sure to read the notes about Java-recognized and -playable audio clips.

Listing 10.3. Retrieving and playing audio clips from across the Internet.

```
/*
    This example will retrieve two audio clips from the Internet.
    One it will play in a loop, the other it will play once.  They
    will play simultaneously.

    Notes:

       Java only understands how to play .au files that are recorded
       as 8Khz, 8bit, mono.  Many .au files on the web are 16 bit.
       These will not play, but no error messages are generated.

*/

import java.applet.*;
import java.awt.*;
import java.net.*;
import java.awt.image.*;

public class AnApplet extends Applet implements Runnable {

    Thread myThread;
    String aURL;
    URL myURL;
    AudioClip myAudioClip;
    String errTxt = "Initializing";
    int x,y,ix;
    MediaTracker mt;

    public void start() {
       if (myThread == null) {
```

```java
      myThread = new Thread(this);
      myThread.start();
   }
}

public void stop() {
   if (myThread != null) {
      this.showStatus("Applet stopped");
      myThread.stop();
      myThread = null;
   }
}

public void run() {
   resize(400,400);
   // set aURL to audioclip location string
   aURL = "http://www.geffen.com/beck/Sounds/paynomind.au";
   updateDisplay("running new URL");
   // generate URL object using aURL location
   try {myURL = new URL(aURL);}
   catch(MalformedURLException e) {
      updateDisplay("new URL Failure");
      this.stop();
   }
   updateDisplay("running getAudioClip");
   myAudioClip = getAudioClip(myURL);    // actually retrieve audioclip
   if (myAudioClip == null) {
      updateDisplay("getAudioClip returned null");
      this.stop();
   }
   updateDisplay("Playing "+aURL);
   myAudioClip.loop();  // play audioclip in endless loop
   updateDisplay("audo clip complete");
   // location of new audio clip
   aURL = "http://java.internetone.com/blimp.au";
   updateDisplay("running new URL");
   // generate URL object using new location
   try {myURL = new URL(aURL);}
   catch(MalformedURLException e) {
      updateDisplay("new URL Failure");
      this.stop();
   }
   updateDisplay("running play");
   // play audio clip once.  will mix in with already playing clip
   play(myURL);
   updateDisplay("play complete");
}

public void updateDisplay(String txt) {
   errTxt = new String(txt);
   this.showStatus(errTxt);
   repaint();
}

public void repaint(Graphics g) {
   paint(g);
}
```

continues

Listing 10.3. continued

```
    public void paint (Graphics g) {
        ix+=20;
        g.drawString(errTxt,10,ix);
    }


    public void sleep (int period) {
         try {Thread.sleep(period);}
         catch(InterruptedException e) {}
    }
}
```

getCodeBase()

The getCodeBase() method gets the base URL—that is, it returns the directory path in which the applet was started. The code shown in Listing 10.4 uses the Applet.getCodeBase method to return the CodeBase or directory in which the applet was started.

Listing 10.4. Using the **Applet.getCodeBase** method to return the **CodeBase**.

```
import java.applet.*;
import java.awt.*;

public class AnApplet extends Applet {

    public void paint(Graphics g) {
        g.drawString("This applet is URL - " + this.getCodeBase(), 10,20);
    }
}
```

getDocumentBase()

getDocumentBase gets the document URL. The code shown in Listing 10.5 uses the Applet.getDocumentBase method to print the document base for this applet to the screen.

Listing 10.5. Using the **Applet.getDocumentBase** method to print the document base.

```
import java.applet.*;
import java.awt.*;

public class AnApplet extends Applet {

    public void paint(Graphics g) {
        g.drawString("This applet is embedded in URL - " +
        ➡this.getDocumentBase(), 10,20);
    }
}
```

getImage(URL) and getImage(URL, String)

getImage gets an image retrieved from the URL argument location. Listing 10.6 demonstrates the use of the java.applet.Applet.getImage method.

Listing 10.6. Using the java.applet.Applet.getImage method.

```
/*
    This example retrieves a gif image from the Internet and displays it
    on the screen.  Height and Width return -1 until image has completely
    arrived.
*/

import java.applet.*;
import java.awt.*;
import java.net.*;
import java.awt.image.*;

public class AnApplet extends Applet implements Runnable {

    Thread myThread;
    Image myImage;
    URL myURL;
    String errTxt = "Initializing";
    int x,y;
    MediaTracker mt;

    public void start() {
        if (myThread == null) {
            myThread = new Thread(this);
            myThread.start();
        }
    }

    public void stop() {
        if (myThread != null) {
            myThread.stop();
            myThread = null;
        }
    }

    public void run() {
        // location of image
        try {myURL = new URL("http://www.tvp.com/vpttlb.gif");}
        catch(MalformedURLException e) {
            errTxt = new String("new URL Failure");
            this.showStatus(errTxt);
            this.stop();
        }
        myImage = getImage(myURL);// request retrieval of image
        if (myImage == null) {
            errTxt = new String("getImage returned null");
            this.showStatus(errTxt);
            this.stop();
        }
```

continues

Listing 10.6. continued

```
        else {
            // create MediaTracker object to monitor retrieval
            mt = new MediaTracker(this);
            mt.addImage(myImage,1);
            // wait for image to arrive
            try {mt.waitForID(1);}
            catch (InterruptedException e) {}
            x = myImage.getWidth(this);// get image width
            y = myImage.getHeight(this);// get image height
            if ((x != -1) && (y != -1)) {// insure image is complete
                resize(x,y);// resize screen to size of image
                repaint();
            }
        }
    }


    public void paint(Graphics g) {
        if (myImage != null) {
            g.drawImage(myImage,10,20,this);// draw image on screen
        }
        else {
            g.drawString(errTxt,10,20);
        }
    }

    public void sleep (int period) {
        try {Thread.sleep(period);}
        catch(InterruptedException e) {}
    }
}
```

getParameter(String) and getParameterInfo()

The getParameter() method gets a parameter or an array of strings describing the applet. This information should be overridden in applets so that other applets can access the specific information. Listing 10.7 demonstrates the use of the getParameterInfo method from java.applet.Applet.

Listing 10.7. Using the getParameterInfo method from java.applet.Applet.

```
/*
    This example can make use of several http parameters.  getParameterInfo
    is defined so that if an application queries this applet, it can
    find out what the parameters are.  The parameters that this applet
    accepts are window size (height and width) and a URL of an audioclip
    to play.

    Note:
        getParameterInfo is similar to getAppletInfo in that
        it is a method you should override in your class to return the
        appropriate information to others that wish to query your applet.
*/
```

```java
import java.applet.*;
import java.awt.*;
import java.net.*;

public class AnApplet extends Applet implements Runnable {

    Thread myThread;
    int height, width;
    String param, strURL;
    URL myURL;

    public void init() {
        height = 200;
        width = 400;
        strURL = "http://www.tvp.com/test/test.au";
    }

    public void start() {
        if (myThread == null) {
            myThread = new Thread(this);
            myThread.start();
        }
    }

    public void stop() {
        if (myThread != null) {
            myThread.stop();
            myThread = null;
        }
    }

    public void run() {
        param = getParameter("width");
        if (param != null) {
            width = Integer.parseInt(param);
        }
        param = getParameter("height");
        if (param != null) {
            height = Integer.parseInt(param);
        }
        param = getParameter("URL");
        if (param != null) {
            strURL = param;
        }
        resize(width,height);
        try {myURL = new URL(strURL);}
        catch(MalformedURLException e){}
        play(myURL);
        repaint();
    }

    public String[][] getParameterInfo() {
        String paramInfo[][] = {
            { "height", "int", "resize to height pixels" },
            { "width", "int", "resize to width pixels" },
            { "URL", "URL", "play audoclip located at URL" }
        };
```

continues

Listing 10.7. continued

```
        return(paramInfo);
    }

    public void paint (Graphics g) {
        g.drawString("now playing: "+strURL,10,20);
    }
}
```

After you compile the applet source code, you will need to create an HTML document to view the applet, such as the following sample document:

```
<HTML>
<HEAD>
<TITLE> The Audio Player Applet </TITLE>
</HEAD>
<BODY>
<APPLET CODE="AnApplet" width=300 height=300>
<PARAM NAME="width" VALUE="200">
<PARAM NAME="height" VALUE="200">
<PARAM NAME="URL" VALUE="http://tvp.com/hello.au">
</APPLET>
</BODY>
</HTML>
```

Note: To hear an actual sound file play on your system, you must specify a valid value for the URL parameter. Passing parameters to applets is explored in Chapter 15, "Creating Java-Powered Web Presentations with Applets."

init()

The init() method initializes the applet. This method is described in detail in Chapter 7, "Building Objects." Most of the examples in this chapter demonstrate its use as well. This method normally should be overridden in code, which allows you to specify precisely how the applet will be initialized.

play(URL) and play(URL, String)

The play() method plays an audio clip retrieved by getAudioClip. See Listing 10.3 for an example of the use of play.

resize(int, int) and resize(Dimension)

The resize() method resizes an applet. The dimensions are in pixels. Listing 10.8 is an example of resize.

Listing 10.8. Using the `resize` method.

```
/*
    This applet uses the Applet.resize method to resize the applet
    window to different sizes.  The first time it uses int,int as
    parameters, the second time it uses a dimension object as a parameter.

*/

import java.applet.*;
import java.awt.*;

public class AnApplet extends Applet implements Runnable {

    int x,y;
    Dimension d;
    Thread myThread;

    public void start() {
        if (myThread == null) {
            myThread = new Thread(this);
            myThread.start();
        }
    }

    public void stop() {
        if (myThread != null) {
            myThread.stop();
            myThread = null;
        }
    }

    public void run() {
        x = 10;
        y = 20;
        repaint();
        sleep(2000);
        this.resize(300,300);     // resize(int,int)
        x = 10;
        y = 40;
        repaint();
        sleep(2000);
        d = new Dimension();
        d.width = 200;
        d.height = 800;
        this.resize(d);       // resize(Dimension)
        x = 10;
        y = 60;
        repaint();
    }

    public void paint(Graphics g) {
        g.drawString("Hello World! - " + x + "," + y, x,y);
    }

    public void sleep (int period) {
        try {Thread.sleep(period);}
        catch(InterruptedException e) {}
    }
}
```

setStub(AppletStub)

The setStub() method sets the applet stub. Generally, this function is performed automatically by the system and you will not need to perform this function in your code.

showStatus(String)

The showStatus() method shows a status message in the applet's context. For example, in Netscape the status message shows up in the status area at the bottom of the browser window. See Listing 10.3 for an example of showStatus.

start() and stop()

The start() method starts the applet and the stop() method stops the applet execution. (These methods are discussed in Chapter 7.) The online documentation on start, as well as that on stop and destroy, is misleading. It states that it is not necessary to call these methods explicitly. I have had more predictable results when these methods *are* called explicitly. See the listings throughout this chapter for examples of the use of the start and stop methods.

isActive()

isActive() returns true if the applet is active. The status of the method is true immediately before start is executed. See Listing 10.9 for a demonstration of the use of isActive().

Listing 10.9. isActive() displays the boolean value of whether the applet is active.

```
import java.applet.*;
import java.awt.*;

public class AnApplet extends Applet {

    public void paint(Graphics g) {
        g.drawString("thisApplet is active = " + this.isActive(), 10,20);
    }
}
```

The java.lang Package and Its Classes

The java.lang package is so important that it would be just about impossible to do anything in Java without it. This is why it is imported automatically into all applets and applications at compile time. You never need to explicitly import java.lang. The following sections include information about all the first-level classes and a brief description of each. More detailed information about each class is available in the online documentation.

Boolean

Java's utility classes work with objects only when those objects are used as arguments. However, in Java, booleans are *not* objects. The Boolean class provides a format to "wrap around" boolean data values to make them acceptable to Java utility classes. This process is referred to as an *object wrapper*.

Here is an example of a method to convert strings to booleans:

```
Boolean myBool = Boolean.valueOf("True");    //convert string to Boolean
```

This declares a new Boolean variable and sets it to the boolean value represented by the string "True". Note two things about this line: First, the variable myBool is declared to be of type Boolean as opposed to type boolean; second, the Boolean class is called directly on the right-hand side of the assignment operator. This can be done when a method is needed without having or needing a corresponding object declared in the program code.

Here is another method that does the opposite: It converts a Boolean variable to a string:

```
System.out.println("myBool = " + myBool.toString()); //convert Boolean to string
```

Boolean is a simple class with a limited set of methods. These are probably the two most likely to be used by most programmers.

Character

The Character class works as an object wrapper for characters in the same way that the Boolean class wraps booleans. There are more methods available for this class than for Boolean.

Here is an example of the method used to convert characters to integers of any specified radix:

```
myInt = Character.digit('b',16);  //convert Character to int in specified radix
```

Because b is the hexadecimal value for 11, the previous example assigns myInt the value 11.

Here are examples of other methods in class Character:

```
myString = myChar.toString();                //convert myChar to String
if (Character.isLowerCase(myChar))           //test if char is lowercase
    myChar = Character.toUpperCase(myChar);  //convert to uppercase
if (Character.isUpperCase(myChar))           //test if char is uppercase
    myChar = Character.toLowerCase(myChar);  //convert to lowercase
if (Character.isSpace(myCharArray[i]))       //test if char is white space
    I++;                                     //go on to next character
```

Class

The Class class contains subclasses that return runtime information about classes. Each class instance automatically has Class descriptor objects associated with it.

Here are examples of methods for determining class names and functions:

```
System.out.println("Class name = " + myClass.getName());     //return class name
    //return class name with "class" or "interface" prependedSystem.out.println("Class
type/name = " + myClass.toString());

//get superclass of this class
mySuperClass = myClass.getSuperclass();
//test if class is an interface or not
if (myClass.isInterface() == "true")
   System.out.println("This object is an interface");
else
   System.out.println("This object is a class");

//return all interfaces associated with this class
myClassArray = myClass.getInterfaces();
```

ClassLoader

The ClassLoader class overrides the default structure of Java when loading in classes. The default is defined by the CLASSPATH environment variable and is platform dependent. ClassLoader requests that files and classes be loaded from remote areas such as across the network. It also contains methods for interpreting foreign classes created by defineClass() to be loaded as regular Java classes. ClassLoader is an abstract method and is not called if the default mechanisms are to be followed. This class is used mainly by Java interpreters and debuggers.

Compiler

Java uses the Compiler class at program compile time. This class includes the following methods:

```
command(Object)
compileClass(Class)
compileClasses(String)
disable()
enable()
```

The Java compiler invokes these methods when you compile a Java program.

Number, Float, Integer, Long

Number is an abstract superclass for all number classes. It includes the Integer, Long, Float, and Double number classes. Number contains the basic template methods for converting an arbitrary number into an instance of Integer, Long, Float, or Double. The primitive number classes are all based on this class.

Float, Integer, Double, and Long are all object wrappers used to make their respective data types acceptable to operations that require objects. All these data types contain basic methods for converting the corresponding primitive types to and from these classes. They also contain methods for converting between numeric data types as well as for converting to and from String types. The String type is useful for accepting text input of numbers and being able to easily convert the string to a number for processing.

Here are several examples of the various operations available for these data types:

```java
public class MyMain {
    public static void main (String args[]) {
        Integer myInteger;    //declare variables
        Double myDouble;
        Float myFloat;
        Long myLong;
        Number myNumber;
        String myString;

        //Integer constructor
        myInteger = new Integer(37);
        //Double constructor; conversion Integer to int
        myDouble = new Double((double)myInteger.intValue());
        //convert Double to string
        myString = myDouble.toString();
        myLong = Long.valueOf(myString);
        System.out.println(myLong);
    }
}
```

Many of the methods associated with these data types may seem extraneous. After all, why provide a method to convert an integer to a string when this is done automatically when using the + operator in conjunction with strings? The reason is that it may be necessary to treat an integer as an object and use an associated method. If a generic class for printing values of objects to a stream is needed, it may be easier to simply pass an object to all subclasses of that class, do the conversion to string, and then print to the stream. By converting a primitive type to an object, you can treat it just like any other possible object rather than make it a special case.

Math

The utility class Math contains the standard Java math library, including such math functions as absolute value, exponents, roots, and trigonometric functions. All methods in this class are *static*, which means they cannot be subclassed or instantiated. Some aspects of this class, such as out-of-range or immeasurable results, are platform dependent.

Here is an example of using the pow and sqrt functions to create a method that calculates the distance between two points:

```
static double calcDist(double x1,double y1,double x2,double y2) {
    double length;
    length = Math.sqrt(Math.pow((x1-x2),2) + Math.pow((y1-y2),2));
    return(length);
}
```

In addition to the standard math functions, there are routines for selecting a value on the basis of a numerical limit. This is done with the min/max and floor/ceil routines. The min and max routines provide a terse method to select the smaller or larger of two numbers, respectively, which can make for more compact code. The following two code fragments accomplish the same thing—setting x equal to the greater of a or b—but the second is obviously much more compact.

```
if (a > b) {          //determine if a > b
    x = a;            //a is greater, set x equal to a
}
else {
    x = b;            //b is greater, set x equal to b
}

x = Math.max(a,b);    //set x equal to greater of a and b
```

The floor and ceil routines offer similar compactness. These routines return the next higher or lower whole number for a given value. They are useful in working with graphic coordinates, such as screen displays, that typically require whole numbers.

Using floor and ceil routines allows for more specific control over how fractional numbers are handled. For example, if a calculation is done to draw a polygon, it is important that the lines making up the polygon actually have endpoints that are the same as the next connecting line. If some other method, such as rounding or casting to int, is used, the line coordinates may be off by a single pixel, resulting in an image that does not look quite right—or possibly downright sloppy.

Here is an example of how the floor method could be used:

```
void clipToRectangle(float x1,y1,int basex) {
    z1 = x1/y1

    //return the largest whole number less than or equal to z1
    z2 = Math.floor(z1);

    //insert body of message to make use of z2 value then return to caller

}
```

One last function worth mentioning in the java.lang.Math library is random(). This method generates random numbers, which are used in a variety of applications from quantum mechanics to shoot-em-up games. The random() function in Java returns a double-precision floating-point number between 0 and 1. By using this value as a multiplier, a random number between any two limits can be produced. Here is an example of a method that will produce an integer random number between any two specified limits:

```
public static int genRandomInt(int lowerLimit, int upperLimit) {
    double tmpNum;                         //declare temporary variable
    tmpNum = upperLimit-lowerLimit;   //calculate difference between high and low
    tmpNum *= Math.random();               //multiply random value times difference
    tmpNum = Math.round(tmpNum);           //round to nearest whole number
    tmpNum += lowerLimit;                  //add new value to lower limit
    return((int)tmpNum);              //cast resulting number to int and return value
}
```

This code fragment could have been rewritten in a single return but was broken out into several lines to show more clearly how the number was generated.

With random-number library functions, one question that should always be asked is, "How truly random are the numbers produced?" Many random-number generators do not produce very random numbers. So how accurate is the random-number generator in Java's math library? Not very, as it turns out.

Following is a small program to test the random() function. It tests a random number generator by calling it repeatedly to generate numbers between 0 and 99 using the method specified previously. It then stores in an array the number of times each number between 0 and 99 is generated. At the end, it prints out how many of each were actually generated. If random() generates truly random numbers, each number between 0 and 99 should be generated an equal number of times if random is called often enough. This program allows the number of iterations to be specified on the command line:

```
import java.util.Random;

public class MyMain {
    public static void main (String arg[]) {
        Random rnd = new Random();
        Integer cnt;
        int i,j;

        int arrIndex = 0;

        cnt = Integer.valueOf(arg[0]);
        int intArr[] = new int[cnt.intValue()];

        for (i=0; i<cnt.intValue(); i++) {
            for (j=0; j<100; j++) {

                arrIndex = Math.abs(rnd.nextInt() % cnt.intValue());
                intArr[arrIndex]++;
            }
        }
        for (i=0; i<cnt.intValue(); i++) {
            System.out.println("intArr[" + i + "] = " + intArr[i]);
        }
    }
}
```

Testing Java's random-number generator using this program shows that `random()` is not really very random. Running this with a command-line value of 10,000,000 did not yield very high consistency. This means that the `random()` function, while quite usable for applications such as games, should not be relied upon for any application in which security might be a concern, such as encryption of critical information.

Object

`Object` is the class from which all other objects in Java are derived. This class supports a basic set of methods that all subclasses should customize for their own needs. These methods are implemented in the `Java` class as actual routines, not simply as abstract methods. This is so all subclasses will inherit these routines, ensuring that the methods can be called without causing runtime exceptions. Again, most methods should be overridden in any objects the programmer declares. The methods themselves include methods for comparing, duplicating, and garbage collecting.

To clarify how these work, following is an example based on this simple class:

```
public class MyObject {
    int x,y;
}
```

This class simply holds two integer variables, x and y. Because all classes are automatically subclasses of the `Object` class, the base `Object` methods are inherited by default. Because the methods for comparing objects do not work as you might expect them to, these methods should be overridden, as is shown in the next example.

The first method to look at is the method for comparing two objects, called `equals`. It is used to determine if all values instantiated in each instance of an object are equal. The method included in the `Object` class simply checks to see if the two objects are actually the same instance. Any implementation of a class should include a method that compares two different instances to see if they are equal. The following example implements an `equals` method for class `MyObject`:

```
public boolean equals(Object obj) {
    return((obj != null) &&          //does obj point to an object?
           (obj instanceof MyObject) &&   //is obj an instance of MyObject?
           (((MyObject)obj).x == x) &&
           (((MyObject)obj).y == y));  //do values for x & y match?
}
```

This method simply returns the results of a series of statements that check various parts of the objects to determine whether they are equal. The first simply checks to ensure that the passed-in object is not null; the second checks that the passed-in object is of type `MyObject`; and the last tests check whether all variables held in `MyObject` are of equal value. If all of the checks are validated, the two objects are considered equal and `true` is returned. If any of these checks fails, `false` is returned.

The next base method is called `clone`. Its purpose is to allow the creation of a new instance of an object that is an exact duplicate of the original instance. The default method implemented in the `Object` class does absolutely nothing. The following example implements a `clone` method for the `MyObject` class:

```
public synchronized Object clone {
   MyObject m = new MyObject();    //create new instance of MyObject
   m.x = x;
   m.y = y;                        //set x & y values to the same values
   return(m);                      //return clone of object
}
```

This method creates a new instance of `MyObject` and then sets the values x and y in the new instance equal to the original values of x and y. Note that because an existing method is being overridden, the declaration must match the original; therefore, the `clone` method actually returns type `Object` instead of type `MyObject`. This method must be synchronized so that the values of x or y do not change in the middle of a call to this method.

The next method is called `toString`. This method provides a way to represent an object as a string. It is automatically called when an object is included in a print string with the + operator. How this is actually implemented is entirely up to the programmer. For simple objects, this can be as simple as returning a string representation of a few variables. More complex objects may need to print out something far more complex or may simply print out some subset of the data available. Like `clone`, the default method implemented in the `Object` class does nothing and should be overridden. The following example shows the implementation for `MyObject`:

```
public final synchronized String toString() {    //implement toString method
   return "[" + x + "," + y + "]";                //print out values of object instance
}
```

This method simply returns a string containing the values of x and y in square brackets.

The last method to be discussed is called `finalize`. It is called by the garbage-collection mechanism in Java just before the object is freed. This method should contain any final cleanup, such as closing files and signaling other processes, that an object should do at that time. Not all objects require this final cleanup and so do not necessarily have to implement this method.

The default `finalize` method implemented in the `Object` class does nothing, so it will work quite well if nothing special is needed. The class used as an example up to this point does not require a `finalize` method, but here is an example:

```
public void finalize() {
   x = -1;
   y = -1;    //set x & y to -1
}
```

This method simply sets the values of x and y to –1.

Process, Runtime, System

The Process class contains methods that control and manipulate subprocesses. It is an abstract class that can be used to get the stand input or stand output of a subprocess. The Process class can also be used to kill a subprocess, wait for a subclass to terminate, and retrieve the final exit value of the process.

Runtime is used by the Java interpreter at application runtime. The Runtime class contains classes and methods to get information about systems at runtime. One method is totalMemory, which returns the number of bytes in system memory. Runtime also has methods that apply to the application currently running. It has a method called gc that runs the garbage collector, but it is best to have the garbage collector run by default unless there are special circumstances.

System classes act as a platform-independent means to do system-level input and output as well as handle errors. The standard input streams are used to read character data. Standard output streams are used to print to the screen. The ubiquitous example of the use of System follows:

```
System.out.println("Hello World!");
```

System variables are static.

The following example contains a method named print that prints out the properties of the system it is running on, as well as the total and free available memory:

```
import java.util.*;
class MyEnv {
   public void print() {

      //declare properties object
      Properties p;
      //declare runtime object
      Runtime r;
      //get properties of system
      p = System.getProperties();
      //get runtime information
      r = Runtime.getRuntime();
      //list all properties available
      p.list(System.out);
      //print os version
      System.out.println(System.getProperty("os.version","unkn"));
      //print total memory
      System.out.println("Total memory = " + r.totalMemory());
      //print free memory
      System.out.println("Free  memory = " + r.freeMemory());
} }
```

The example class that follows contains a method called runCmd that will run a command passed in as a parameter. The runCmd method will then wait for the command to complete before continuing. If an error occurs during execution of either the exec or waitFor command, System.exit will be used to force the entire application to abort with the indicated exit codes:

```
import java.io.*;
class MyExec {
   public void runCmd(String cmd[]) {
      Process p;                           //declare process object
      Runtime r;                           //declare runtime object
      r = Runtime.getRuntime();            //get runtime information
      try {
         p = r.exec(cmd) ;                 //execute command
         try {
            p.waitFor();                   //wait for command to complete
         }
         catch(InterruptedException e) {   //handle waitFor failure
            System.out.println("ERROR: waitFor failure");
            System.exit(10);               //exit application with exit code 10
         }
      }
      catch(IOException e) {               //handle exec failure
         System.out.println("ERROR: exec failure");
         System.exit(11);                  //exit application with exit code 11
      }
   }
}
```

This application uses the classes described in this section to actually print information about the system to the screen and to run a command using the exec method. The command can be specified on the command line:

```
import java.util.*;
import java.io.*;

public class MyMain {
   public static void main (String arg[]) {
      MyEnv myEnv;                //declare MyEnv object
      MyExec myExec;              //declare MyExec object
      myEnv = new MyEnv();        //create MyEnv object
      myEnv.print();             //print system information to the screen
      myExec = new MyExec();      //create MyExec object
      myExec.runCmd(arg);    //call runCmd method using command line arguements
   }
}
```

SecurityManager

The SecurityManager class is an abstract class. You can create subclasses of it to implement a security policy, such as the one used to manage the security of applets. The applet viewer's security manager is used to restrict the functions of applets and guard against malicious coding.

The key thing to know about security managers is that client applications can have only one security manager. Generally, clients cannot reference or create their own security manager. The security manager is executed when the program starts and cannot be replaced, overridden, extended, or overloaded.

String

The `String` class provides methods for representing and manipulating character strings. String values cannot be changed after creation. Each character in a string can be accessed as an array. The following two statements are equivalent:

```
String string1 = "Ben";
   char string2[] = {'B', 'e', 'n'};
```

The second letter in the string can be extracted by the statement

```
    String e = string1.substring(1, 2);
```

There are other methods for string manipulation in this class, such as the following:

```
class StringFun {
    public static void main (String args[]) {
        String str = "Manipulating strings in Java is easier than you think.";
        System.out.println("The value of the string is: " + str);
        System.out.println("Length of the string is: " +str.length());
        System.out.println("The index of the character J: " +str.indexOf('J'));

        System.out.println("The index of the beginning of the substring \"easier\" is:
        ➥" + str.indexOf("easier"));
        System.out.println("The character at position 10: " + str.charAt(10));
        System.out.println("The substring from positions 14 to 20: " +
        ➥str.substring(14,20));
        System.out.println("The string in upper case: " + str.toUpperCase());
    }
}
```

StringBuffer

`StringBuffer` allows strings to be changed and created. Remember, strings normally cannot be changed. There are many methods and constructors used here to manipulate strings. One example follows:

```
benName = new StringBuffer().append("B").append("e").append("n").toString();
```

This is similar to using + for string concatenation.

Thread

`Thread` contains methods for creating, manipulating, and destroying threads. (See Chapter 8, "Tying It All Together: Threads, Exceptions, and More," for more detailed information on threads.)

ThreadGroup

`ThreadGroup` contains methods that create, manipulate, and destroy groups of threads.

Throwable

Throwable methods are used in conjunction with exceptions. This class provides information to trace back through the stack in case of exceptions. It also prints out exception messages.

java.lang Exception Classes

Remember that java.lang, with all its classes and subclasses, is imported into every program by default. One reason that exceptions are part of the java.lang library is that it is important to be able to test for exceptions in every program.

Exceptions are discussed in Chapter 8. The full list of exception classes is shown in Table 10.1. They are listed in hierarchical order, starting at the top of the pyramid.

Table 10.1. Exception classes in java.lang.

Exception	Extends	Purpose
ClassNotFoundException	Exception	Thrown when a requested class could not be found.
CloneNotSupportedException	Exception	Thrown when there has been an attempt to clone an unclonable object.
IllegalAccessException	Exception	Thrown when a requested method could not be accessed.
InstantiationException	Exception	Thrown when there has been an attempt to instantiate an abstract class or an interface. Interfaces are templates of methods and can never be instantiated. Abstract classes are also intended to be templates. They show the return value and argument types but must be overridden.

continues

Table 10.1. continued

Exception	Extends	Purpose
InterruptedException	Exception	Thrown when another thread has interrupted the currently running thread.
NoSuchMethodException	Exception	Indicates that a requested method could not be found.
RuntimeException	Exception	Traps for exceptions that occur during the execution of bytecode by the Java Virtual Machine.
ArrayStoreException	RuntimeException	Thrown during runtime when the user is trying to store the wrong type of object in an array.
ClassCastException	RuntimeException	Thrown when an invalid cast has occurred.
IllegalArgumentException	RuntimeException	Indicates that an illegal argument exception has occurred.
IllegalThreadStateException	IllegalArgumentException	Indicates that a thread is not in the proper state for a requested operation. For example, the thread may not be running when a request is made to it.
NumberFormatException	IllegalArgumentException	Thrown when an invalid number format has occurred, such as when the user attempts to use a decimal point with a number typed as an integer.
ArithmeticException	RuntimeException	Thrown when an exceptional arithmetic condition has occurred. This class would be invoked when dividing by zero.

Exception	Extends	Purpose
IllegalMonitorStateException	RuntimeException	Thrown when a monitor operation has been attempted and the monitor is in an invalid state. This could indicate permission problems.
IndexOutOfBoundsException	RuntimeException	Indicates that an index is out of bounds. This exception is fairly generic in nature. It has two subclasses that are more specific; see next two entries.
ArrayIndexOutOfBoundsException	IndexOutOfBoundsException	Indicates that an invalid array index has been used.
StringIndexOutOfBoundsException	IndexOutOfBoundsException	Indicates that a String index is out of range.
NegativeArraySizeException	RuntimeException	Thrown when there has been an attempt to create an array that is negative in size. In other words, the argument to size the array is not a positive integer.
NullPointerException	RuntimeException	Indicates that there has been an attempt to use a pointer with a null value. It is a good idea to do bounds checking on pointer values before use.
SecurityException	RuntimeException	Indicates that a security exception has occurred. This is usually an attempt to access classes, methods, or variables that are not public.

An Example of an Exception from `java.lang-exceptions`

Listing 10.10 is an example of a Java applet that uses the `ArrayIndexOutOfBoundsException` exception. It shows how the exception is generated, caught, and replaced with a new `ArrayIndexOutOfBoundsException`, which generates a custom error message.

Listing 10.10. Use of the `ArrayIndexOutOfBoundsException` exception.

```
import java.applet.*;
import java.awt.*;
import java.net.*;

public class AnApplet extends Applet implements Runnable {

    Thread myThread;

    public void start() {                      //start running the applet
        if (myThread == null) {                //create a thread if doesn't exit
            myThread = new Thread(this);
            myThread.start();
        }
    }

    public void stop() {                       //stop the applet from running
        if (myThread != null) {                //if the thread is running, stop it
            myThread.stop();
            myThread = null;
        }
    }

    public void run() {
        int[] arr = new int[10];               //create an array with 11 elements
        try {arr[11] = 1;}                     //access the 12th element in the array
        catch(ArrayIndexOutOfBoundsException e) {    //in case of this exception
            e = new ArrayIndexOutOfBoundsException("Idiot, didn't you do
            ➥bounds checking on your array accesses?");      //override exception
            throw(e);          //throw exception message and exit method
        }
    }
}
```

Summary

This chapter has explored the `java.applet.Applet` and `java.lang` packages from the Java API. The `java.lang` package contains classes associated with basic data structures in Java as well as Java-wide exceptions. Structures such as `Boolean` and `Integer` are included as classes in `java.lang`.

The `java.applet` package is used to create an applet instance and to perform applet-specific functions. Applets require the presence of a browser or applet viewer, and the `Applet` methods rely on this environment.

11

The AWT
Class
Library

This chapter covers the classes and interfaces of the Abstract Windowing Toolkit (AWT). Here you'll learn how the AWT classes and interfaces are used to create the graphical user interface (GUI) of applets and stand-alone applications. The listings in this chapter are sample programs that illustrate the use of these GUI components. When you are finished with this chapter, you will be able to use the AWT classes and interfaces in your own Java applets and applications.

Introduction to the AWT

The classes and interfaces of the *Abstract Windowing Toolkit* (AWT) are used to develop stand-alone applications and to implement the GUI controls used by applets. These classes support all aspects of GUI development, including event handling.

The Component and Container classes are two of the most important classes in the java.awt package. The Component class provides a common superclass for all classes that implement GUI controls. The Container class is a subclass of the Component class and can contain other AWT components. It is well worth your while to familiarize yourself with the API description of these two classes.

The Window class is a subclass of the Container class that provides a common set of methods for implementing windows. The Window class has two subclasses, Frame and Dialog, that are used to create Window objects. The Frame class is used to create a main application window, and the Dialog class is used to implement dialog boxes. Let's explore the Frame class first and then look at the Dialog class.

Using the **Frame** Class to Implement Application Windows

The Frame class is a subclass of Window that encapsulates an application window. A Frame object is capable of containing a menu bar and displaying a title. Listing 11.1 shows how a Frame object is used to implement a simple window program.

Listing 11.1. The **FrameExample** program.

```
import java.awt.*;

public class FrameExample extends Frame {
 public static void main(String args[]){
  FrameExample win = new FrameExample();
 }
 public FrameExample() {
  super("FrameExample");
  pack();
  resize(400,400);
  show();
 }
```

```
public void paint(Graphics g) {
 g.drawString("A Basic Window Program",100,100);
}
public boolean handleEvent(Event event) {
 if(event.id==Event.WINDOW_DESTROY){
  System.exit(0);
  return true;
 }else return false;
 }
}
```

After you create a Frame object within an application, you use the show() method to display the frame. The show() method is inherited from the Window class. Other methods used in the initial display of a Frame object are the pack() and resize() methods. The pack() method, like the show() method, is inherited from the Window class. It organizes the components contained in a Window object and determines the Window object's size. The resize() method is inherited from the Component class. It is used to resize a Window object to a particular dimension.

This small program introduces the basic structure of stand-alone applications. The main class of the program subclasses the Frame class and creates a single main() method like those used in console programs. The main() method uses the FrameExample() constructor to create a window for an application.

The FrameExample() constructor uses the superclass constructor to set the title of the window to FrameExample. The pack() method is typically used to pack the components of the window, which allows Java to organize the component objects on the window. The resize() method is invoked to resize the window to 400 pixels by 400 pixels. Finally, the show() method is invoked to cause the window to be displayed.

The paint() method is invoked by the runtime system to initially paint the contents of the application window and to repaint the window if it is moved, resized, or covered. The paint() method is passed an object of the Graphics class as a parameter. This object is used to update the window's display by drawing on its default canvas. The paint() method of FrameExample draws the text A Basic Window Program at the coordinates (100,100).

The handleEvent() method usually provides the primary event handling for AWT components. A handleEvent() method is typically provided with a program's Frame subclass. The handleEvent() method of FrameExample looks for a WINDOW_DESTROY event and shuts down the program using the exit() method of the System class. The Event class is covered in the section titled "Handling Events in Programs That Use Windows."

Figure 11.1 shows the window initially displayed by the FrameExample program.

Figure 11.1.
The FrameExample
program's initial display.

Using Menus and Menu Bars

The MenuBar class provides an implementation of the menu bar commonly attached to stand-alone applications. It is a subclass of the MenuComponent class, which provides a common set of methods for all menu-related classes. You attach a MenuBar object to a Frame object using the setMenuBar() method of the Frame class.

A MenuBar object contains one or more Menu objects that implement pull-down menus. The Menu class provides methods for adding MenuItem objects and separators to the pull-down menu implemented by a Menu object. It also provides methods for accessing the MenuItem objects contained in a Menu object. Because the Menu class is a subclass of the MenuItem class, a Menu object can contain another Menu object, thus allowing multiple levels of cascading menus to be created. The program shown in Listing 11.2 illustrates this concept.

Listing 11.2. The MenuExample program.

```
import java.awt.*;

public class MenuExample extends Frame {
 String menuSelection = "Select a menu item.";
 public static void main(String args[]){
  MenuExample win = new MenuExample();
 }
 public MenuExample() {
  super("MenuExample");
  pack();
  resize(400,400);
  addMenus();
  show();
 }
 void addMenus() {
  MenuBar menubar = new MenuBar();
  Menu file = new Menu("File");
  Menu edit = new Menu("Edit");
  Menu view = new Menu("View");
  file.add("Open");
```

```
    file.add("Save");
    file.add("Close");
    file.add("Quit");
    edit.add("Copy");
    edit.add("Cut");
    edit.add("Paste");
    view.add("Zoom");
    menubar.add(file);
    menubar.add(edit);
    menubar.add(view);
    setMenuBar(menubar);
  }
  public void paint(Graphics g) {
   g.drawString(menuSelection,100,100);
  }
  public boolean handleEvent(Event event) {
   if(event.id==Event.WINDOW_DESTROY){
    System.exit(0);
    return true;
   }else if(event.id == Event.ACTION_EVENT &&
     event.target instanceof MenuItem){
    if("Quit".equals(event.arg)){
     System.exit(0);
     return true;
    }else{
     menuSelection = "You selected "+event.arg.toString()+".";
     repaint();
     return true;
    }
   }else return false;
  }
}
```

The MenuItem class is a subclass of the MenuComponent class that is used to implement an item contained in a pull-down menu. It provides methods for enabling and disabling (graying out) the label associated with a MenuItem object and for setting and retrieving the label. The MenuItem class has two subclasses—Menu and CheckboxMenuItem. You have already been introduced to the Menu class; the CheckboxMenuItem class implements a menu item that can be checked or unchecked and provides methods that can be used to set and retrieve its checked status. To learn more about check boxes, see the section "Check Boxes and Radio Buttons."

The MenuComponent class is the superclass of these menu classes. Its methods are used to perform general menu-related operations, such as those used to create menu items.

The MenuContainer interface defines those methods that must be implemented by any class that contains a menu-related object. The MenuContainer interface is implemented by the Frame, Menu, and MenuBar classes.

The MenuExample program follows the same general structure as the FrameExample program shown in Listing 11.1. It invokes the addMenus() method in the MenuExample() constructor to set up the window's menus. Notice that the menuSelection variable is a String object and is declared as a field variable of the MenuExample class.

The addMenus() method creates a MenuBar object and some Menu objects and then adds menu items to the Menu objects. The Menu objects are then added to the MenuBar object, and the MenuBar object is set on the application window using the setMenuBar() method.

The paint() method is overridden to draw the menu item selected by the user on the window's default canvas. Note that you generally don't call the paint() method directly. The paint() method is invoked automatically when you use these methods: show(), repaint(), or update().

The handleEvent()method of the FrameExample program is expanded to check for an ACTION_EVENT object with a MenuItem as its target in order to handle the action of a user selecting an item from a menu. It updates the menuSelection object to identify the menu item selected by the user. The repaint() method is used to cause the window to be redrawn, which, as discussed, invokes the paint() method for you.

Figure 11.2 shows the window initially displayed by the MenuExample program.

Figure 11.2.
*The MenuExample program's
initial display.*

Handling Events in Programs That Use Windows

The Event class is central to the Java window event-generation and -handling mechanism. Event objects are generated by a user who interacts with a Java window program or applet and by the Java runtime system. User-generated events occur when users make selections on a menu or press a key. Events generated by the runtime system include errors and exceptions. They are handled by a set of predefined event-handling methods that are defined by the Component class and its subclasses. These methods are overridden to perform custom event processing.

The Event class defines numerous constants to identify the events that are defined for the AWT classes. It is important that you review these constants to become familiar with the types of events that may need to be handled by your programs. You'll become aware of the common event handling performed for the various window components by working through the example programs in this chapter.

Implementing Dialog Boxes with the **Dialog** Class

The Dialog class, like the Frame class, is a subclass of the Window class. Whereas the Frame class is used to implement a main application window, the Dialog class is used to implement dialog boxes that pop up to present information and interact with the user of a window program or applet. Two types of Dialog objects can be created. A *modal dialog box* is a Dialog object that must be acted on and closed before a user is able to access other application windows. A *non-modal dialog box* does not have this restriction.

The program shown in Listing 11.3 illustrates the use of the Dialog class.

Listing 11.3. The **DialogExample** program.

```
import java.awt.*;

public class DialogExample extends Frame {
 Dialog dialog;
 public static void main(String args[]){
  DialogExample win = new DialogExample();
 }
 public DialogExample() {
  super("DialogExample");
  pack();
  resize(400,400);
  addMenus();
  createDialog();
  show();
 }
 void addMenus() {
  MenuBar menubar = new MenuBar();
  Menu file = new Menu("File");
  Menu dialog = new Menu("Dialog");
  file.add("Quit");
  dialog.add("Show");
  dialog.add("Hide");
  menubar.add(file);
  menubar.add(dialog);
  setMenuBar(menubar);
 }
 void createDialog() {
  dialog = new Dialog(this,"Dialog Box",false);
  dialog.resize(200,200);
 }
 public boolean handleEvent(Event event) {
  if(event.id==Event.WINDOW_DESTROY){
   System.exit(0);
   return true;
  }else if(event.id == Event.ACTION_EVENT &&
    event.target instanceof MenuItem){
   if("Quit".equals(event.arg)){
    System.exit(0);
```

continues

Listing 11.3. continued

```
    return true;
  }else if("Show".equals(event.arg)){
   dialog.show();
   return true;
  }else{
   dialog.hide();
   return true;
  }
 }else return false;
 }
}
```

The DialogExample program follows the same structure as the FrameExample and MenuExample programs. It creates the dialog variable to refer to a dialog box that it creates and displays. The createDialog() method is invoked from the DialogExample constructor to create this dialog box.

The addMenus() method has been updated to support menu items for showing and hiding the dialog box.

The createDialog() method creates a non-modal dialog box and resizes it to a 200 pixel × 200 pixel size. The dialog box is not displayed until the Show menu item is selected and handled by the handleEvent() method.

The handleEvent() method handles the Show menu item by causing the dialog box to be displayed via the show() method of the Window class. It handles the Hide menu item by invoking the hide() method of the Component class.

> **Note:** The show() method of the Window class overrides the show() method of the Component class and is used to display Window objects. Unlike the show() method of the Component class, the show() method of the Window class does more than merely display the window; it will also bring the window to the front if the window is already visible.

Figure 11.3 shows the window initially displayed by the DialogExample program.

Figure 11.3.
The DialogExample
program's initial display.

Using the **FileDialog** Class to Access the Local File System

The FileDialog class is a subclass of the Dialog class and is used to provide the capability to select a file from a directory listing. The FileDialog class provides the capability to use separate dialog boxes for loading and saving files.

The program shown in Listing 11.4 illustrates the use of the FileDialog class.

Listing 11.4. The **FileDialogExample** program.

```
import java.awt.*;

public class FileDialogExample extends Frame {
 FileDialog dialog;
 public static void main(String args[]){
  FileDialogExample win = new FileDialogExample();
 }
 public FileDialogExample() {
  super("FileDialogExample");
  pack();
  resize(400,400);
  addMenus();
  createDialog();
  show();
 }
 void addMenus() {
  MenuBar menubar = new MenuBar();
  Menu file = new Menu("File");
  Menu dialog = new Menu("Dialog");
  file.add("Quit");
  dialog.add("Show");
  menubar.add(file);
  menubar.add(dialog);
  setMenuBar(menubar);
 }
 void createDialog() {
  dialog = new FileDialog(this,"File Dialog Box");
 }
 public boolean handleEvent(Event event) {
  if(event.id==Event.WINDOW_DESTROY){
   System.exit(0);
   return true;
  }else if(event.id == Event.ACTION_EVENT &&
    event.target instanceof MenuItem){
   if("Quit".equals(event.arg)){
    System.exit(0);
    return true;
   }else if("Show".equals(event.arg)){
    dialog.show();
    return true;
```

continues

Listing 11.4. continued

```
  }else{
   return false;
  }
 }else return false;
 }
}
```

The `FileDialogExample` program is very similar to the `DialogExample` program except that instead of creating and displaying a `Dialog` object, it displays a `FileDialog` object. Notice that the Hide menu item has been removed. This is because the File dialog box is modal and cannot be hidden after it is displayed.

The `createDialog()` method creates the `FileDialog` object and titles it with the text `File Dialog Box`.

Figure 11.4 shows the window initially displayed by the `FileDialogExample` program.

Figure 11.4.
The `FileDialogExample`
program's initial display.

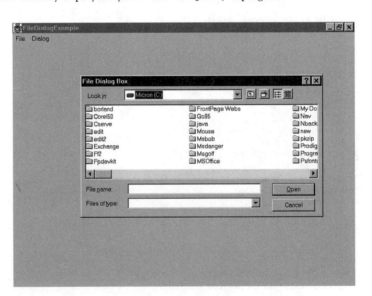

Organizing Components Using the `Panel` and `Layout` Classes

This section discusses the AWT classes that are used to organize components within applications and applets.

The `Panel` class is the most common class for organizing components within stand-alone applications. It is a subclass of the `Container` class and is displayed as a panel within a window. It inherits almost all of its methods from its Container and Component superclasses. The program shown in Listing 11.5 illustrates the use of the Panel class.

> **Note:** The Applet class is a subclass of the Panel class that is used to implement a panel within a Web browser's display window. It adds many useful methods that provide access to the capabilities of the browser.

Listing 11.5. The **PanelExample** program.

```java
import java.awt.*;

public class PanelExample extends Frame {
 public static void main(String args[]){
  PanelExample win = new PanelExample();
 }
 public PanelExample() {
  super("PanelExample");
  pack();
  resize(400,400);
  addMenus();
  addPanel();
  show();
 }
 void addMenus() {
  MenuBar menubar = new MenuBar();
  Menu file = new Menu("File");
  file.add("Quit");
  menubar.add(file);
  setMenuBar(menubar);
 }
 void addPanel() {
  Panel panel = new Panel();
  panel.add(new Button("one"));
  panel.add(new Button("two"));
  panel.add(new Button("three"));
  panel.add(new Button("four"));
  panel.add(new Button("five"));
  add("South",panel);
 }
 public boolean handleEvent(Event event) {
  if(event.id==Event.WINDOW_DESTROY){
   System.exit(0);
   return true;
  }else if(event.id == Event.ACTION_EVENT &&
    event.target instanceof MenuItem){
   if("Quit".equals(event.arg)){
    System.exit(0);
    return true;
   }else{
    return false;
   }
  }else return false;
 }
}
```

The PanelExample program follows the same structure of the programs you've studied so far in this chapter. It invokes the addPanel() method from its constructor to add a Panel object that contains Button objects. No event handling is provided for the buttons, so when you click on them, nothing happens. Buttons and button-related event handling is covered in the section "Labels and Buttons." It is included here to show how components can be added to a panel and then added to the main application window.

Figure 11.5 shows the window initially displayed by the PanelExample program.

Figure 11.5.
The PanelExample
program's initial display.

The LayoutManager interface defines methods that must be implemented by classes that are used to organize the way Component objects are laid out in a Container object. Five AWT classes implement this interface: BorderLayout, CardLayout, FlowLayout, GridBagLayout, and GridLayout. These classes are used to lay out objects that are instances of the Container class and its subclasses in the following manner:

- The BorderLayout class provides the capability to lay out a Container object along the border and in the center of the container.
- The CardLayout class provides the capability to lay out a Container object as a deck of cards.
- The FlowLayout class provides the capability to lay out a Container from left to right in a series of rows.
- The GridBagLayout class provides the capability to lay out a Container object according to a set of GridBagConstraints objects.
- The GridLayout class provides the capability to lay out a Container object in a grid.

The GridBagConstraints class is used to create objects that specify the size and positioning of an object that is controlled by a GridBagLayout object.

> **Note:** The Insets class provides the capability to add margins to the layout and can be used with the GridBagConstraints class.

The program shown in Listing 11.6 illustrates the use of the five layout classes.

Listing 11.6. The **LayoutExample** program.

```java
import java.awt.*;

public class LayoutExample extends Frame {
 public static void main(String args[]){
  LayoutExample win = new LayoutExample();
 }
 public LayoutExample() {
  super("LayoutExample");
  addMenus();
  addPanels();
  pack();
  resize(600,600);
  show();
 }
 void addMenus() {
  MenuBar menubar = new MenuBar();
  Menu file = new Menu("File");
  file.add("Quit");
  menubar.add(file);
  setMenuBar(menubar);
 }
 void addPanels() {
  setLayout(new GridLayout(3,2));
  Panel flow = new Panel();
  Panel border = new Panel();
  Panel card = new Panel();
  Panel grid = new Panel();
  Panel gridbag = new Panel();
  border.setLayout(new BorderLayout());
  card.setLayout(new CardLayout());
  grid.setLayout(new GridLayout(2,2));
  gridbag.setLayout(new GridBagLayout());
  addButtons(flow);
  addButtons(card);
  addButtons(border);
  addButtons(grid);
  addButtons(gridbag);
  add(flow);
  add(card);
  add(border);
  add(grid);
  add(gridbag);
 }
 void addButtons(Panel panel){
   if(panel.getLayout() instanceof BorderLayout) {
    panel.add("North",new Button("one"));
    panel.add("East",new Button("two"));
```

continues

Listing 11.6. continued

```
     panel.add("South",new Button("three"));
     panel.add("West",new Button("four"));
   }else if(panel.getLayout() instanceof GridBagLayout) {
    GridBagLayout layout = (GridBagLayout) panel.getLayout();
    GridBagConstraints constraint1 = new GridBagConstraints();
    constraint1.fill = GridBagConstraints.BOTH;
    constraint1.gridwidth = 1;
    constraint1.gridheight = 1;
    constraint1.gridx = 0;
    constraint1.gridy = 0;
    GridBagConstraints constraint2 = new GridBagConstraints();
    constraint2.fill = GridBagConstraints.BOTH;
    constraint2.gridwidth = 2;
    constraint2.gridheight = 1;
    constraint2.gridx = 1;
    constraint2.gridy = 0;
    GridBagConstraints constraint3 = new GridBagConstraints();
    constraint3.fill = GridBagConstraints.BOTH;
    constraint3.gridwidth = 2;
    constraint3.gridheight = 1;
    constraint3.gridx = 0;
    constraint3.gridy = 1;
    GridBagConstraints constraint4 = new GridBagConstraints();
    constraint4.fill = GridBagConstraints.BOTH;
    constraint4.gridwidth = 1;
    constraint4.gridheight = 1;
    constraint4.gridx = 2;
    constraint4.gridy = 1;
    Button button1 = new Button("one");
    Button button2 = new Button("two");
    Button button3 = new Button("three");
    Button button4 = new Button("four");
    layout.setConstraints(button1,constraint1);
    panel.add(button1);
    layout.setConstraints(button2,constraint2);
    panel.add(button2);
    layout.setConstraints(button3,constraint3);
    panel.add(button3);
    layout.setConstraints(button4,constraint4);
    panel.add(button4);
   }else{
    panel.add(new Button("one"));
    panel.add(new Button("two"));
    panel.add(new Button("three"));
    panel.add(new Button("four"));
   }
 }
 public boolean handleEvent(Event event) {
  if(event.id==Event.WINDOW_DESTROY){
   System.exit(0);
   return true;
  }else if(event.id == Event.ACTION_EVENT &&
    event.target instanceof MenuItem){
   if("Quit".equals(event.arg)){
    System.exit(0);
    return true;
```

```
    }else{
     return false;
    }
  }else return false;
 }
}
```

The `LayoutExample` program is twice as long as the programs you've looked at so far in this chapter because it performs quite a bit more setup in order to display panels that illustrate each of the five layout classes.

In this program, the `addPanels()` method sets the layout of the application window to a three-row by two-column grid. Five panels illustrating the five layout classes are added to this grid.

The `addButtons()` method is used to add buttons to the panels to show how each of the five different layouts causes the buttons to be displayed. Buttons are laid out along the edges and center of a `BorderLayout` object. A `GridBagLayout` object is laid out using `GridBagConstraints` objects. The field variables of these objects are updated to specify the position, size, and fill mode of the buttons that are added to the `GridBagLayout` object. The buttons added to `Panel` objects using the other layouts do not require any special setup.

Figure 11.6 shows the window initially displayed by the `LayoutExample` program.

Figure 11.6.
The `LayoutExample`
program's initial display.

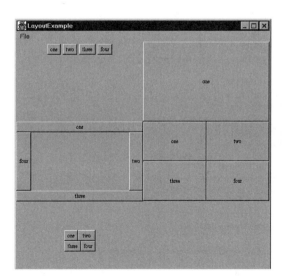

Using Common GUI Controls

This section introduces the common GUI controls provided by the AWT and shows how to handle the events associated with these controls. The controls covered are provided by the `Label`, `Button`, `Checkbox`, `Choice`, `List`, `TextField`, and `TextArea` classes. Other GUI controls are discussed later in this chapter.

Labels and Buttons

The Label class is used to display a line of read-only text. It provides methods to set and retrieve the text of a Label object and to align the text within the object's display.

The Button class provides the capability to use buttons within Java applications and applets. Button objects are labeled with a text string; using images with buttons is not currently supported by Java. The clicking of a button results in an Event object that is identified as an ACTION_EVENT object. The program shown in Listing 11.7 illustrates the use of the Label and Button classes.

Listing 11.7. The ButtonExample program.

```java
import java.awt.*;

public class ButtonExample extends Frame {
 Label label = new Label("Default Text");
 public static void main(String args[]){
  ButtonExample win = new ButtonExample();
 }
 public ButtonExample() {
  super("ButtonExample");
  addMenus();
  addButtons();
  pack();
  resize(400,400);
  show();
 }
 void addMenus() {
  MenuBar menubar = new MenuBar();
  Menu file = new Menu("File");
  file.add("Quit");
  menubar.add(file);
  setMenuBar(menubar);
 }
 void addButtons() {
  add("North",label);
  label.setAlignment(Label.CENTER);
  Panel panel = new Panel();
  panel.add(new Button("one"));
  panel.add(new Button("two"));
  panel.add(new Button("three"));
  panel.add(new Button("four"));
  add("Center",panel);
 }
 public boolean handleEvent(Event event) {
   if(event.id==Event.WINDOW_DESTROY){
    System.exit(0);
    return true;
   }else if(event.id == Event.ACTION_EVENT &&
     event.target instanceof MenuItem){
    if("Quit".equals(event.arg)){
     System.exit(0);
     return true;
    }else{
     return false;
```

```
    }
  }else if(event.id == Event.ACTION_EVENT &&
    event.target instanceof Button){
   label.setText((String) event.arg);
   return true;
  }else return false;
 }
}
```

The `ButtonExample` program illustrates the use of the `Button` and `Label` classes by displaying the label of the last button clicked by a user using a `Label` object. The `Label` object is initially labeled with the string `Default Text` upon program startup. The `addButtons()` method is invoked from within the `ButtonExample` constructor to set up the `Label` and `Button` objects.

The `handleEvent()` method checks for `ACTION_EVENT` events with a `Button` target to handle the user's button clicks. It handles the event by setting the `Label` object to the label of the button that was clicked.

Figure 11.7 shows the window initially displayed by the `ButtonExample` program.

Figure 11.7.
The ButtonExample
program's initial display.

Check Boxes and Radio Buttons

The `Checkbox` class provides the capability to implement radio buttons as well as check boxes. The `CheckboxGroup` class is used to group `Checkbox` objects and identify that they should be treated as radio buttons instead of as check boxes.

The `Checkbox` class provides methods for retrieving and modifying its checked state and label. The checking and unchecking of a check box or radio button causes an `ACTION_EVENT` `Event` object to be generated.

The program shown in Listing 11.8 illustrates the use of check boxes and radio buttons.

Listing 11.8. The CheckboxExample program.

```java
import java.awt.*;

public class CheckboxExample extends Frame {
 Label label = new Label("Default Text");
 Checkbox checkbox[] = new Checkbox[6];
 public static void main(String args[]){
  CheckboxExample win = new CheckboxExample();
 }
 public CheckboxExample() {
  super("CheckboxExample");
  addMenus();
  addComponents();
  pack();
  resize(400,400);
  show();
 }
 void addMenus() {
  MenuBar menubar = new MenuBar();
  Menu file = new Menu("File");
  file.add("Quit");
  menubar.add(file);
  setMenuBar(menubar);
 }
 void addComponents() {
  add("North",label);
  label.setAlignment(Label.CENTER);
  Panel panel = new Panel();
  Panel panel1 = new Panel();
  panel1.setLayout(new GridLayout(3,1));
  Panel panel2 = new Panel();
  panel2.setLayout(new GridLayout(3,1));
  checkbox[0] = new Checkbox("one");
  checkbox[1] = new Checkbox("two");
  checkbox[2] = new Checkbox("three");
  CheckboxGroup group = new CheckboxGroup();
  checkbox[3] = new Checkbox("four",group,false);
  checkbox[4] = new Checkbox("five",group,false);
  checkbox[5] = new Checkbox("six",group,false);
  for(int i=0;i<3;++i) panel1.add(checkbox[i]);
  for(int i=3;i<6;++i) panel2.add(checkbox[i]);
  panel.add(panel1);
  panel.add(panel2);
  add("Center",panel);
 }
 public boolean handleEvent(Event event) {
   if(event.id==Event.WINDOW_DESTROY){
    System.exit(0);
    return true;
   }else if(event.id == Event.ACTION_EVENT &&
     event.target instanceof MenuItem){
    if("Quit".equals(event.arg)){
     System.exit(0);
     return true;
    }else{
     return false;
    }
```

```
  }else if(event.id == Event.ACTION_EVENT &&
    event.target instanceof Checkbox){
   String text = "";
   for(int i=0;i<6;++i) {
    if(checkbox[i].getState()) text += checkbox[i].getLabel() + " ";
   }
   label.setText(text);
   return true;
  }else return false;
 }
}
```

The CheckboxExample program displays the results of user check box and radio button clicks by updating the text displayed by a Label object.

The checkbox[] array is used to store both check boxes and radio buttons. The addComponents() method is invoked by the CheckboxExample() constructor to add the check boxes and radio buttons to the application window.

The addComponents() method places the Label object to be updated in the top center of the application window. It then creates three Panel objects, two of which are placed on the third Panel object. Both of the second-level panels are set up using the grid-style layout with one column and three rows. The three check boxes are placed in one panel, and the three radio buttons are placed in the other. A CheckboxGroup object is used to organize the radio buttons into a common CheckboxGroup object.

The ACTION_EVENT event associated with a user checking on a check box is handled by determining which check boxes and radio buttons are checked and displaying their labels using the Label object at the top of the window. Play around with the program to see how check boxes are treated differently than radio buttons.

Figure 11.8 shows the window initially displayed by the CheckboxExample program.

Figure 11.8.
The CheckboxExample
program's initial display.

Choices and Lists

The Choice class implements a list of choices from which a single choice may be selected. Its methods provide the capability to update the list and query its status.

The List class implements lists from which a single or multiple selections may be made. Its methods provide the capability to update the elements of a list and query their selection status. The program shown in Listing 11.9 illustrates the use of the Choice and List classes.

Listing 11.9. The **ListExample** program.

```
import java.awt.*;

public class ListExample extends Frame {
 Label label = new Label("Default Text");
 Choice choice = new Choice();
 List list = new List(3,true);
 public static void main(String args[]){
  ListExample win = new ListExample();
 }
 public ListExample() {
  super("ListExample");
  addMenus();
  addComponents();
  pack();
  resize(400,400);
  show();
 }
 void addMenus() {
  MenuBar menubar = new MenuBar();
  Menu file = new Menu("File");
  file.add("Quit");
  menubar.add(file);
  setMenuBar(menubar);
 }
 void addComponents() {
  add("North",label);
  label.setAlignment(Label.CENTER);
  Panel panel = new Panel();
  Panel panel1 = new Panel();
  Panel panel2 = new Panel();
  try {
   choice.addItem("one");
   choice.addItem("two");
   choice.addItem("three");
  } catch (NullPointerException ex) {
  }
  panel1.add(choice);
  list.addItem("four");
  list.addItem("five");
  list.addItem("six");
  list.addItem("seven");
  list.addItem("eight");
  panel2.add(list);
  panel.add(panel1);
```

```
     panel.add(panel2);
     add("Center",panel);
  }
  public boolean handleEvent(Event event) {
    if(event.id==Event.WINDOW_DESTROY){
     System.exit(0);
     return true;
    }else if(event.id == Event.ACTION_EVENT &&
       event.target instanceof MenuItem){
     if("Quit".equals(event.arg)){
      System.exit(0);
      return true;
     }else{
      return false;
     }
    }else if(event.target instanceof Choice ||
       event.target instanceof List){
     String text = choice.getSelectedItem() + " ";
     for(int i=0;i<5;++i) {
      if(list.isSelected(i)) text += list.getItem(i) + " ";
     }
     label.setText(text);
     return true;
    }else return false;
  }
}
```

The ListExample program illustrates the similarities and differences between the Choice and List classes. The label, list, and choice variables are used to provide access to their related GUI components. These field variables are created and initialized in the beginning of the class description.

The addComponents() method adds a Label object at the top of the window and then creates three panels. The panel variable refers to the main Panel object and is added to the center of the application window. The panel1 and panel2 variables refer to Panel objects that are placed on the left and right sides of the area covered by the main panel. A Choice object is created and added to the left panel, and a List object is created and added to the right panel.

The handleEvent() method is updated to check for events related to the Choice or List classes and updates the Label object with the user's selections.

Figure 11.9 shows the window initially displayed by the ListExample program.

Text Fields and Text Areas

The TextField class provides the capability to enter a single line of text. To allow users to enter password information without revealing the password to onlookers, you can use the TextField class, which allows you to set an alternate character to display instead of the actual text. The alternate characters are used only to mask the characters and do not affect the actual data entered. Most programs set the echo character to an asterisk. To set an alternate character, you use the setEchoCharacter() method.

Figure 11.9.
The ListExample *program's initial display.*

The TextArea class provides the capability to enter multiple lines of text. It provides horizontal and vertical scrollbars to scroll the text that is entered.

The TextComponent class is the superclass of the TextField and TextArea classes and provides several methods that are common to both of these classes. The setEditable() method allows TextField and TextArea objects to be defined as read-only.

The program shown in Listing 11.10 illustrates the use of the TextField and TextArea classes.

Listing 11.10. The **TextExample** program.

```
import java.awt.*;

public class TextExample extends Frame {
 TextField textfield = new TextField("Enter text here.");
 TextArea textarea = new TextArea("And it will be inserted here!");
 public static void main(String args[]){
  TextExample win = new TextExample();
 }
 public TextExample() {
  super("TextExample");
  addMenus();
  addComponents();
  pack();
  resize(400,400);
  show();
 }
 void addMenus() {
  MenuBar menubar = new MenuBar();
  Menu file = new Menu("File");
  file.add("Quit");
  menubar.add(file);
  setMenuBar(menubar);
 }
 void addComponents() {
  add("North",textfield);
  add("Center",textarea);
```

```
}
public boolean handleEvent(Event event) {
  if(event.id==Event.WINDOW_DESTROY){
   System.exit(0);
   return true;
  }else if(event.id == Event.ACTION_EVENT &&
    event.target instanceof MenuItem){
   if("Quit".equals(event.arg)){
    System.exit(0);
    return true;
   }else{
    return false;
   }
  }else if(event.id == Event.ACTION_EVENT &&
     event.target instanceof TextField){
   textarea.insertText(textfield.getText()+"\n",0);
   return true;
  }else return false;
 }
}
```

The `TextExample` program creates a `TextField` object and a `TextArea` object and displays them in the North and Center regions of the application window. When the user enters text into the `TextField` object and presses the Enter key, the text is inserted at the beginning of the `TextArea` object.

The `TextExample` class creates and initializes the `TextField` and `TextArea` objects. Notice how the initial text to be displayed in these fields is specified in their respective constructors.

The `handleEvent()` method checks for an action event that is identified as a `TextField` object, and then updates the `TextArea` object with the text contained in the `TextField` object. The `getText()` method of the `TextComponent` class is used to retrieve the user's text from the `TextField` object. The `insertText()`method of the `TextArea` class is then used to insert this text at the beginning of the `TextArea` object.

Figure 11.10 shows the window initially displayed by the `TextExample` program.

Figure 11.10.
*The `TextExample` program's
initial display.*

Drawing with the **Canvas** and **Graphics** Classes

The Canvas class provides the capability to display a Graphics object within a window area. The paint() method of the Graphics class is used to update the Graphics object associated with a Canvas object. The Graphics class is an abstract class that provides numerous methods for drawing objects and displaying images. Access to a Graphics object is provided via the paint() method of the Canvas and Component classes. The program shown in Listing 11.11 illustrates the use of the Canvas and Graphics classes.

Listing 11.11. The **GraphicsExample** program.

```
import java.awt.*;

public class GraphicsExample extends Frame {
 LeftCanvas lcanvas = new LeftCanvas();
 RightCanvas rcanvas = new RightCanvas();
 public static void main(String args[]){
  GraphicsExample win = new GraphicsExample();
 }
 public GraphicsExample() {
  super("GraphicsExample");
  addMenus();
  addComponents();
  pack();
  resize(200,200);
  show();
 }
 void addMenus() {
  MenuBar menubar = new MenuBar();
  Menu file = new Menu("File");
  file.add("Quit");
  menubar.add(file);
  setMenuBar(menubar);
 }
 void addComponents() {
  setLayout(new GridLayout(1,2));
  add(lcanvas);
  add(rcanvas);
 }
 public void paint(Graphics g) {
  lcanvas.repaint();
  rcanvas.repaint();
 }
 public boolean handleEvent(Event event) {
  if(event.id==Event.WINDOW_DESTROY){
   System.exit(0);
   return true;
  }else if(event.id == Event.ACTION_EVENT &&
    event.target instanceof MenuItem){
   if("Quit".equals(event.arg)){
    System.exit(0);
```

```
    return true;
  }else{
   return false;
  }
 }else return false;
 }
}

class LeftCanvas extends Canvas {
 public LeftCanvas() {
  super();
 }
 public void paint(Graphics g) {
  g.setColor(Color.red);
  g.fillOval(10,10,50,50);
 }
}

class RightCanvas extends Canvas {
 public RightCanvas() {
  super();
 }
 public void paint(Graphics g) {
  g.setColor(Color.blue);
  g.fillRect(10,10,50,50);
 }
}
```

The GraphicsExample program declares two subclasses of the Canvas class: LeftCanvas and RightCanvas. An object from each of these classes is created and added to the main application window. The layout of the GraphicsExample window is set to a one-row by two-column GridLayout object. This accomplishes the same results as using multiple panels as you saw in the previous examples in this chapter. The paint() method of the GraphicsExample class is defined to invoke the repaint() methods of the LeftCanvas and RightCanvas objects, which causes these objects to update their respective screen areas.

The LeftCanvas class extends the Canvas class and uses the setColor() and fillOval() methods of the Graphics class to draw a red oval in the Graphics object associated with the canvas.

The RightCanvas class is defined in a manner similar to the LeftCanvas class. It draws a blue rectangle instead of a red oval.

Figure 11.11 shows the window initially displayed by the GraphicsExample program.

Figure 11.11.
*The GraphicsExample
program's initial display.*

Geometrical Classes

The AWT provides the Point, Rectangle, Polygon, and Dimension classes to support geometrical operations. The Point class encapsulates a point in a two-dimensional plane. The Rectangle class represents a rectangle by its upper-left corner and its height and width dimensions. The Polygon class represents a polygon as an array of its x coordinates and an array of its y coordinates. The Dimension class encapsulates the dimensions of a two-dimensional object. The program shown in Listing 11.12 illustrates the use of these classes.

Listing 11.12. The GeometryExample program.

```java
import java.awt.*;

public class GeometryExample extends Frame {
 Point p1 = new Point(0,0);
 Point p2 = new Point(100,100);
 Dimension dim = new Dimension(50,50);
 Rectangle rect = new Rectangle(p2,dim);
 int xcoord[] = {150,275,300,350,290,250,200,150};
 int ycoord[] = {150,125,50,150,175,250,350,150};
 Polygon poly = new Polygon(xcoord,ycoord,xcoord.length);
 public static void main(String args[]){
  GeometryExample win = new GeometryExample();
 }
 public GeometryExample() {
  super("GeometryExample");
  addMenus();
  pack();
  resize(400,400);
  show();
 }
 void addMenus() {
  MenuBar menubar = new MenuBar();
  Menu file = new Menu("File");
  file.add("Quit");
  menubar.add(file);
  setMenuBar(menubar);
 }
 public void paint(Graphics g) {
  g.drawLine(p1.x,p1.y,p2.x,p2.y);
  g.drawRect(rect.x,rect.y,rect.width,rect.height);
  g.drawPolygon(poly);
 }
 public boolean handleEvent(Event event) {
  if(event.id==Event.WINDOW_DESTROY){
   System.exit(0);
   return true;
  }else if(event.id == Event.ACTION_EVENT &&
     event.target instanceof MenuItem){
   if("Quit".equals(event.arg)){
    System.exit(0);
    return true;
```

```
    }else{
     return false;
    }
   }else return false;
 }
}
```

The `GeometryExample` class creates several geometrical objects in the class declaration. Two `Point` objects are created and assigned to the `p1` and `p2` variables. A 50 pixel × 50 pixel `Dimension` object is created and assigned to the `dim` variable. A `Rectangle` object is created using the `Point` object referenced by the `p2` and `dim` variables and assigned to the `rect` variable. A `Polygon` object is then created with vertices at the points (150,150), (275,125), (300,50), (350,150), (290,175), (250,250), and (200,350).

The `paint()` method is overridden to draw the geometrical objects on the `Graphics` object of the application window's default canvas. It draws a line from `p1` to `p2`, the `Rectangle` object specified by `rect`, and the `Polygon` object specified by `poly`.

Figure 11.12 shows the window initially displayed by the `GeometryExample` program.

Figure 11.12.
The `GeometryExample`
program's initial display.

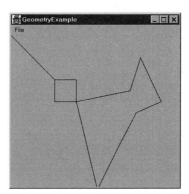

Using Fonts

The `Font` class encapsulates fonts in a system-independent manner by defining several system-independent fonts that are mapped to the fonts supported by the local operating and windowing system. This class also defines constants that allow a `Font` object to be displayed using a plain, bold, italic, or bold-italic style.

The `FontMetrics` class encapsulates the size parameters of a `Font` object. It provides several methods that return the pixel width of characters and character strings, as well as methods that return the height, ascent, descent, and leading pixel length of a `Font` object. The *ascent* and *descent* values measure the number of pixels that a `Font` object ascends above and descends below its baseline. The *leading* of a `Font` object is the minimum distance between the ascent of one line of text and ascent of the following line of text. The *height* of a `Font` object is the sum of its ascent, descent, and leading.

The program shown in Listing 11.13 shows how the Font and FontMetrics classes are used.

Listing 11.13. The **FontExample** program.

```
import java.awt.*;

public class FontExample extends Frame {
 public static void main(String args[]){
  FontExample win = new FontExample();
 }
 public FontExample() {
  super("FontExample");
  addMenus();
  pack();
  resize(150,400);
  show();
 }
 void addMenus() {
  MenuBar menubar = new MenuBar();
  Menu file = new Menu("File");
  file.add("Quit");
  menubar.add(file);
  setMenuBar(menubar);
 }
 public void paint(Graphics g) {
  Font font = new Font("Helvetica",Font.BOLD+Font.ITALIC,24);
  g.setFont(font);
  FontMetrics metrics = g.getFontMetrics(font);
  int ascent = metrics.getAscent();
  int height = metrics.getHeight();
  int leading = metrics.getLeading();
  int baseline = leading + ascent;
  for(int i=0;i<10;++i) {
   g.drawString("Line "+String.valueOf(i),10,baseline);
   baseline += height;
  }
 }
 public boolean handleEvent(Event event) {
  if(event.id==Event.WINDOW_DESTROY){
   System.exit(0);
   return true;
  }else if(event.id == Event.ACTION_EVENT &&
    event.target instanceof MenuItem){
   if("Quit".equals(event.arg)){
    System.exit(0);
    return true;
   }else{
    return false;
   }
  }else return false;
 }
}
```

The FontExample program creates a 24-point, bold, italic, Helvetica Font object and uses the FontMetrics object associated with this font to draw text on the window's default Graphics object.

Most of the processing is performed in the overridden paint() method. It creates the Font object and uses the getFontMetrics() method of the Graphics class to get the FontMetrics object associated with the font. It then retrieves the ascent, height, and leading parameters of the font via the FontMetrics object.

The baseline variable is used to keep track of the vertical coordinate of where a line of text should be displayed. The distance between subsequent baselines is the height metric of the font.

Ten lines of text are displayed to show how all of these methods come together to draw text on a Graphics object.

Figure 11.13 shows the window initially displayed by the FontExample program.

Figure 11.13.
The FontExample *program's
initial display.*

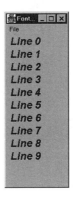

Image-related Classes

The Image and Color classes encapsulate graphical images and colors in a format-independent manner. The classes and interfaces of the java.awt.image package are used to implement image processing applications. The ImageProducer interface defines the methods that are implemented by classes that produce image data. The ImageConsumer interface defines methods that are used by classes that use image data. The ImageObserver interface defines constants and methods that are used to monitor the loading of an image.

The ColorModel, DirectColorModel, and IndexColorModel classes are used to implement portable color models. The FilteredImageSource, ImageFilter, RGBImageFilter, and CropImageFilter classes provide the capability to implement image-filtering algorithms. The PixelGrabber and MemoryImageSource classes are used to capture an image to a memory array and to generate an image from a memory array. The MediaTracker class provides the capability to track the loading of a list of images.

The program shown in Listing 11.14 illustrates the use of some of the image-related classes introduced in this section.

Listing 11.14. The `ImageExample` program.

```java
import java.awt.*;

public class ImageExample extends Frame {
 Image image;
 public static void main(String args[]){
  ImageExample win = new ImageExample();
 }
 public ImageExample() {
  super("ImageExample");
  addMenus();
  loadImage();
  pack();
  resize(400,400);
  show();
 }
 void addMenus() {
  MenuBar menubar = new MenuBar();
  Menu file = new Menu("File");
  file.add("Quit");
  menubar.add(file);
  setMenuBar(menubar);
 }
 void loadImage() {
  Toolkit toolkit = getToolkit();
  image = toolkit.getImage("test.gif");
 }
 public void paint(Graphics g) {
  g.drawImage(image,0,0,this);
 }
 public boolean handleEvent(Event event) {
  if(event.id==Event.WINDOW_DESTROY){
   System.exit(0);
   return true;
  }else if(event.id == Event.ACTION_EVENT &&
    event.target instanceof MenuItem){
   if("Quit".equals(event.arg)){
    System.exit(0);
    return true;
   }else{
    return false;
   }
  }else return false;
 }
}
```

The `ImageExample` program loads the `test.gif` file and displays it on the default `Graphics` object of the application window.

The `loadImage()` method gets the default `Toolkit` object of the application window and uses the `getImage()` method of the `Tookit` class to load the `test.gif` file into the `Image` object referenced by the `image` variable. The `Toolkit` class is covered in the section "The `Toolkit` Class and the Native Platform Window Implementation."

The paint() method performs the actual drawing of the image on the screen. You will probably notice some flickering of the image while it is being displayed. This occurs because the program is trying to display the image at the same time that it is loading it, much like the image display of a Web browser. The example in the next section shows you how to use the MediaTracker class to avoid this problem.

Figure 11.14 shows the window initially displayed by the ImageExample program.

Figure 11.14.
The ImageExample
program's initial display.

Using Scrollbars

Scrollbars provide the capability to scroll an object that is too large to fit in a window. Both vertical and horizontal scrollbars are supported by the AWT. Vertical scrollbars scroll an object up and down in a window, and horizontal scrollbars scroll an object left and right. Both types of scrollbars are implemented via the Scrollbar class.

Scrollbars generate events based on user interaction. A user can click on the end of a scrollbar to generate a SCROLL_LINE_UP or SCROLL_LINE_DOWN event, click between the scrollbar's tab and the end of the scrollbar to generate a SCROLL_PAGE_UP or SCROLL_PAGE_DOWN event, or move the scrollbar's tab with the mouse to generate the SCROLL_ABSOLUTE event.

Scrollbars are defined by their orientation, value, visible, minimum, and maximum parameters. The orientation parameter specifies whether a scrollbar is horizontal or vertical. The minimum and maximum parameters specify the minimum and maximum values associated with a scrollbar. The value parameter specifies the current value of a scrollbar. The visible parameter specifies the visible size of the area to be scrolled.

The program shown in Listing 11.15 illustrates the use of the Scrollbar class.

Listing 11.15. The **ScrollbarExample** program.

```
import java.awt.*;

public class ScrollbarExample extends Frame {
  Image image;
```

continues

Listing 11.15. continued

```
Scrollbar horiz = new Scrollbar(Scrollbar.HORIZONTAL,0,400,0,500);
Scrollbar vert = new Scrollbar(Scrollbar.VERTICAL,0,400,0,500);
public static void main(String args[]){
 ScrollbarExample win = new ScrollbarExample();
}
public ScrollbarExample() {
 super("ScrollbarExample");
 addMenus();
 loadImage();
 add("South",horiz);
 add("East",vert);
 pack();
 resize(400,400);
 show();
}
void addMenus() {
 MenuBar menubar = new MenuBar();
 Menu file = new Menu("File");
 file.add("Quit");
 menubar.add(file);
 setMenuBar(menubar);
}
void loadImage() {
 Toolkit toolkit = getToolkit();
 image = toolkit.getImage("bigtest.gif");
 MediaTracker tracker = new MediaTracker(this);
 tracker.addImage(image,7);
 try {
  tracker.waitForID(7);
 } catch(InterruptedException ex) {
 }
}
public void paint(Graphics g) {
 g.drawImage(image,0-horiz.getValue(),0-vert.getValue(),this);
}
public boolean handleEvent(Event event) {
 if(event.id==Event.WINDOW_DESTROY){
  System.exit(0);
  return true;
 }else if(event.id == Event.ACTION_EVENT &&
   event.target instanceof MenuItem){
  if("Quit".equals(event.arg)){
   System.exit(0);
   return true;
  }else{
   return false;
  }
 }else if(event.target instanceof Scrollbar) {
   repaint();
   return true;
 }else return false;
}
}
```

The ScrollbarExample program loads and displays a GIF image that is too large to fit in the application window. It uses scrollbars to allow the user to scroll through the image's display. The image is contained in the bigtest.gif file.

The horizontal and vertical scrollbars are created at the beginning of the class's declaration. These scrollbars are assigned to the horiz and vert variables. The handleEvent() method is updated to look for any scrollbar-related events and invokes the repaint() method to cause the screen to be redrawn in response to these events.

The paint()method is overridden to redisplay the loaded image based on the current values of the scrollbars. The getValue() method of the Scrollbar class is used to retrieve these values.

The loadImage()method uses a MediaTracker object to cause the program to wait for an image to be loaded before performing further processing.

Figure 11.15 shows the window initially displayed by the ScrollbarExample program.

Figure 11.15.
The ScrollbarExample program's initial display.

The Toolkit Class and the Native Platform Window Implementation

The Toolkit class provides access to the native platform window implementation via the peer interfaces of the java.awt.peer package. It also provides methods that return the parameters associated with the screen display.

The program shown in Listing 11.16 illustrates the use of the Toolkit class.

Listing 11.16. The ToolkitExample program.

```
import java.awt.*;

public class ToolkitExample extends Frame {
 public static void main(String args[]){
```

continues

Listing 11.16. continued

```
  ToolkitExample win = new ToolkitExample();
 }
 public ToolkitExample() {
  super("ToolkitExample");
  addMenus();
  TextField textfield = new TextField();
  add("South",textfield);
  Toolkit toolkit = getToolkit();
  int resolution = toolkit.getScreenResolution();
  Dimension dim = toolkit.getScreenSize();
  String text = "Screen Resolution (in dots per inch): "+
   String.valueOf(resolution);
  text += ", Screen Size: "+dim.width+"x"+dim.height;
  textfield.setText(text);
  pack();
  resize(400,200);
  show();
 }
 void addMenus() {
  MenuBar menubar = new MenuBar();
  Menu file = new Menu("File");
  file.add("Quit");
  menubar.add(file);
  setMenuBar(menubar);
 }
 public boolean handleEvent(Event event) {
  if(event.id==Event.WINDOW_DESTROY){
   System.exit(0);
   return true;
  }else if(event.id == Event.ACTION_EVENT &&
    event.target instanceof MenuItem){
   if("Quit".equals(event.arg)){
    System.exit(0);
    return true;
   }else{
    return false;
   }
  }else return false;
 }
}
```

The ToolkitExample program illustrates the use of the getScreenResolution() and getScreenSize() methods of the Toolkit class. The ToolkitExample constructor uses these methods to retrieve the dots-per-inch screen resolution and display size associated with your computer's display. These parameters are then displayed via a TextField object.

Figure 11.16 shows the window initially displayed by the ToolkitExample program.

Figure 11.16.
The ToolkitExample
program's initial display.

Summary

In this chapter you have learned about the classes and interfaces of the Abstract Windowing Toolkit. You have learned how the AWT classes and interfaces are used in applets and stand-alone applications and have examined several programming examples. You should now be able to use the AWT classes and interfaces in your own Java applets and programs.

12

The Java
I/O and
Utility Class
Libraries

This chapter continues our adventure of exploring the Java packages. Two packages are covered here: `java.io` and `java.util`. The `java.io` package contains interfaces, classes, and methods that facilitate input and output of data to applets and applications. The `java.util` package is a mixed bag of utilities useful in writing Java programs. Its classes are used to manipulate dates, create hash tables, and directly manipulate stacks of objects, among other things.

Introduction to the `java.io` Package

The Java input and output package—`java.io`—is used to implement streams. Streams are covered in Chapter 8, "Tying It All Together: Threads, Exceptions, and More;" refer to that chapter if you have difficulty with some of the examples or information in this chapter. Here I cover the classes and methods that manipulate streams.

Streams are used to move groups of data from point A to the Java application or from the Java application to point B. At its simplest, transmitted data is in the form of a stream of bytes without formatting or identification. It is up to the Java application to reformat and reinterpret it in such a way that the data makes sense to the application.

Data traditionally has been stored in files on a disk somewhere. Moving data was a simple matter of opening a file, copying the data to memory, copying the needed portions from memory, and moving the data from memory to a new disk location under a new filename on a system that controlled all the steps of the process.

That scenario is certainly not the case these days. Data can be generated by users on a local network and loaded on a distributed system. It can come from just about any system in the world over the Internet; and from disk, tape, CD-ROM, and so on. The source of the data may be running any number of operating systems, which means that the data might be in a format foreign to the system running the Java application. Therefore, Java must be able to interpret data in many formats from many sources. It must be adaptable enough to handle this data without requiring code changes if the data stream origin changes. The classes and methods in `java.io` help make this happen.

How Java's I/O System Works

Remember that the whole idea behind Java is to provide a non–platform-specific application language. This includes the movement and interpretation of data. The classes and methods in the `java.io` package allow great flexibility in sending and receiving data.

Java provides control over the flow of input streams using `mark` and `reset` (discussed in Chapter 8). However, not all forms of Java I/O allow the use of `mark` and `reset`.

The following sections discuss the various ways to move data in Java. Pick the one that best suits your needs, because each has advantages and disadvantages.

Java Input Streams

Input streams are streams of data that arrive from a source and are loaded into Java. Java doesn't care about the data's origins; it only cares about the data being available to send to the Java application. All the input stream classes throw the exception `IOException`. (Refer to the section in Chapter 8 called "Exceptions" for more information.)

All the input stream classes are based on the abstract class `InputStream`. The next section discusses the methods associated with that class.

The `InputStream` Class

`InputStream` is the abstract class that contains all the possible types of inputs to Java. Its subclasses use most or all of its methods. These methods are discussed in the "Input Streams" section of Chapter 8, but let's go over them again.

read

All of `InputStream`'s subclasses can read data from an input stream. These reads are based on *blocking*, which allows the Java application to wait if the input stream is not continuous.

skip

The `skip` method is used to bypass a fixed number of bytes of an input stream. This method is available to all of `InputStream`'s subclasses.

close

The `close` method is used to shut down an input stream that is no longer being used. Files are closed automatically when the Java garbage collector finalizes and closes them. However, it is important to manually close the stream if the file is going to be opened again soon. You can't know exactly when the garbage collector will finally close the stream, and Java will not reopen an already open file.

available

The `available` method is used to determine whether the data is ready to be sent. Remember, the program will block if the data is not ready but a `read` request has been sent. If you put the `read` request in a separate thread, it won't matter if the block occurs; in that case it is not necessary to use `available`. Make sure, however, that this makes sense in the application. Using separate threads is not advisable if the whole application relies on the data to be sent.

The `available` method is not available for all subclasses of `InputStream`.

mark, markSupported, and reset

The mark method marks a point in an input stream to return to later. The markSupported method makes sure that the type of input stream allows mark. The reset method returns to the point marked by mark. These methods are not supported in all the subclasses of InputStream.

More on the **InputStream** Class and Its Subclasses

The subclasses of InputStream are ByteArrayInputStream, FileInputStream, FilterInputStream, PipedInputStream, SequenceInputStream, and StringBufferInputStream. Each is discussed in detail in the following sections.

The **FilterInputStream** Class

FilterInputStream has four subclasses: BufferedInputStream, DataInputStream, LineNumberInputStream, and PushbackInputStream. These subclasses work in a unique way with FilterInputStream: They allow it to control the flow of a file to them. FilterInputStream does nothing by itself.

Think of FilterInputStream as providing the structure of the pipe for the flow of data while its subclasses chop the data up into small, usable bits. Picture FilterInputStream as the a pasta maker that squeezes out the dough while the subclass turns it into spaghetti or fettucine or lasagna noodles. The data is the dough. It is also possible to change the "mold," or subclass, midstream, just as you would change the form on the pasta maker. However, you don't have to stop the machine while changing the form; the data still flows through.

FilterInputStream's subclasses are widely used in writing Java programs. Following is a discussion of the subclasses. (Read the online documentation for a full list of each subclass's capabilities.)

The **BufferedInputStream** Class

BufferedInputStream is a subclass of FilterInputStream. It implements all the methods defined in the superclass InputStream.

> **Note:** BufferedInputStream is the *only* class that uses mark and reset correctly.

Another key attraction to using BufferedInputStream is that it creates a read *buffer*, which is an array of bytes. This read buffer smooths out the stream of data so that reading can be continuous, as opposed to waiting for the input to reach the stream. The size of the buffer and the size of the reads can be controlled through `BufferedInputStream`'s methods. Listing 12.1 is an example of `BufferedInputStream` and `BufferedOutputStream`.

Listing 12.1. An example of `BufferedInputStream` and `BufferedOutputStream`.

```
/* Notes:

        This class implements buffered file input/output streams by extending
        class BufferedInputStream.  This is not a complete implementation of all
        of FileInputStream (not enough constructors, or getFd()).

        The main example simply copies the first 128 bytes of file one to
        file two, then resets file one to the beginning and proceeds to copy
        all of file one to file two.  This has no practical purpose, but does
        demonstrate that a BufferedFileInputStream class has been created that
        implements mark and reset, which FileInputStream does not support.

        Syntax:
            MyMain <source file> <dest file>
*/

import java.io.*;

public class MyMain {

    public static void main (String args[]) {

        // declare buffered file input stream
        BufferedFileInputStream bfis;
        // declare buffered file output stream
        BufferedFileOutputStream bfos;

        // declare buffer
        byte buf[];
        int cnt;

// create 1024 byte buffer
        buf = new byte[1024];
        try {
            //create buffered file input stream using first argument
            //on command line
            bfis = new BufferedFileInputStream(args[0]);
            //create buffered file output stream using second argument
            //on command line
            bfos = new BufferedFileOutputStream(args[1]);
            // mark beginning of file to be buffered for 128 bytes
            bfis.mark(128);
            // read 128 bytes from source file
            bfis.read(buf,0,128);
            // write buffered bytes to dest file
            bfos.write(buf,0,buf.length);
            // reset to beginning of file
            bfis.reset();
            // loop through source file reading 1024 bytes at a time
```

continues

Listing 12.1. continued

```
        while (bfis.read(buf,0, 1024) != -1) {
          // write buffer to dest file
          bfos.write(buf, 0, buf.length);
        }

        // close source file
        bfis.close();
        // close source file
        bfos.close();

    }
    // catch file not found errors (do nothing)
    catch (FileNotFoundException e){}
    // catch IO errors (do nothing)
    catch (IOException e){}
  }
}

// declare new class that extends buffered input stream
class  BufferedFileInputStream extends BufferedInputStream {

// declare file input stream
  FileInputStream f;

// override buffered input stream constructor
  public BufferedFileInputStream(String filename) throws IOException {
    // create buffered input stream using file input stream
    super(new FileInputStream(filename));
  }
}

// declare new class that extends buffered output stream
class  BufferedFileOutputStream extends BufferedOutputStream {

  // override buffered output stream
  public BufferedFileOutputStream(String filename) throws
  IOException {
    // create buffered output stream using file output stream constructor
    super(new FileOutputStream(filename));
  }
}
```

The `DataInputStream` Class

`DataInputStream` is a subclass of `FilterInputStream`. It also implements the `DataInput` interface. Look at the following list of methods in `DataInputStream`, and the major use of the class becomes obvious (note that these same methods are used by the class `RandomAccessFile`):

```
readBoolean
readByte
readChar
readDouble
```

```
        readFloat
        readInt
        readLine
        readLong
        readShort
        readUTF
        readUnsignedByte
        readUnsignedShort
```

These methods are used to read primitive data types. Remember primitive data types from Chapter 6, "Fundamentals of the Java Language"? This class interprets primitive data types across platforms and makes them accessible to Java.

The `LineNumberInputStream` Class

`LineNumberInputStream` is a subclass of `FilterInputStream`. This class keeps track of line numbers, which could be used to mark and reset data streams. `LineNumberInputStream` also can be used to nest the handling of input streams so that it is possible to simultaneously read the stream for other purposes and keep track of line numbers.

The `PushbackInputStream` Class

`PushbackInputStream` is a subclass of `FilterInputStream`. It creates a one-byte input buffer that allows the input stream to retreat one byte after it has been read. This makes it possible to test the next byte before taking action. Listing 12.2 is an example of `PushbackInputStream`.

Listing 12.2. An example of `PushbackInputStream`.

```
/* Notes:

    This class implements a word search program. A word is defined as a
    character string.  It considered a word instead of a substring if the
    word is followed by a space.  The algorithm works its way through the
    input stream.  If it actually finds a word, it pushes the space
    that delimited the word back on the stream so that it can be processed
    if needed by other algorithms.

    The main example accepts a string to search for and a filename to
    search in as command line arguments.  It will print "Word found" if
    the word is successfully found, and "Word not found" if it does not.

    Syntax:
       MyMain <string to search for> <file to search>
*/

import java.io.*;
```

continues

Listing 12.2. continued

```java
public class MyMain {

    public static void main (String args[]) {

        // declare FindWord object
        FindWord f;

        try {
            // create FindWord object by passing it a FileInputStream object.
            //File opened in second argument on command line.
            f = new FindWord(new FileInputStream(args[1]));

            // find word specified as first argument on command line.
            if (f.find(args[0]))
                // print out found message if word is found
                System.out.println("Word found");
            else
                // print out not found message if word not found
                System.out.println("Word not found");
        }

        // handle file not found exceptions
        catch(FileNotFoundException e) {
            System.err.println("ERROR: File not found");
            System.err.println("   file = " + args[1]);
            System.exit(2);
        }
    }
}

// declare class FindWord
class  FindWord {

    // declare PushbackInputStreamObject
    PushbackInputStream pbs;

    // declare FindWord constructor
    public FindWord(InputStream in) {
        // create pushback stream using passed in input stream
        pbs = new PushbackInputStream(in);
    }

    // declare method to find word in stream
    public boolean find (String word) {
        // declare buffer to be used in stream reads
        byte buf[];
        int i = 0;
        // declare booleans for word found and end-of-file
        boolean found, EOF;
        // create one byte array needed by stream read
        buf = new byte[1];
        // initialize word found variable to false
        found = false;
        // initialize end-of-file variable to false
        EOF = false;

        // declare string buffer so a space can be appended to search word
```

```
        StringBuffer sbWord;
        // create string buffer initialized to search word followed by a space
        sbWord = new StringBuffer(word + " ");

    // label for labeled continue inside loop
    startOver:
        // loop waiting for word found or end of file
        while ((! found) && (! EOF)) {

            // loop for matching search word to chars in input stream
            for (i=0; i < sbWord.length(); i++) {
                try {
                    // read char from stream checking for EOF
                    if (pbs.read(buf,0,1) == -1) {
                        // set EOF boolean if EOF reached
                        EOF = true;
                    }

                    // compare stream char to search word char
                    if ((char)buf[0] != sbWord.charAt(i)) {
                        // if different continue in OUTER while loop
                        continue startOver;
                    }
                }
                // handle IO exceptions
                catch(IOException e){
                    // exit application if IO error occurred
                    System.exit(3);}

            }
            // word found if this point reached, push space back on stream
            try {pbs.unread(buf[0]);}
            // handle IO exceptions
            catch(IOException e){
                    // exit application if IO error occurred
                    System.exit(4);}
            // return true since word found
            return(true);
        }
        // return false since word not found
        return(false);
    }
}
```

The `ByteArrayInputStream` Class

The `ByteArrayInputStream` class extends the `InputStream` class. This class is used to create an input stream from a buffer. The input stream is accessed in the number of bytes set by the programmer. The flow of data to the input stream is controlled by three variables:

- `buf`—The buffer where data is stored

- `Count`—The number of bytes to use in the buffer

- `Pos`—The current position in the buffer

`ByteArrayInputStream` allows use of the `reset` method, which resets the input stream back to the beginning. There is no `mark` method to mark a specific place in the stream.

The `FileInputStream` Class

The `FileInputStream` class extends the `InputStream` class. This class allows Java to read files. This will work only with sequential files, not with hash tables or indexed files. The file itself must be accessible to Java.

Be sure to explicitly close the file input stream if there are to be subsequent accesses to it after the end of file has been reached. `mark` and `reset` are not available to `FileInputStream`. The only way to return to a position is to skip to it and then read to find a desired piece of data. There is no way to know exact positions in the file directly with `FileInputStream`.

Refer to the section in Chapter 8 titled "Input Streams" for an example of the use of `FileInputStream`.

The `SequenceInputStream` Class

`SequenceInputStream` allows multiple files to be read in sequence and converted into a single stream. The first input is read through to the end of file, then the next file is read, and so on. The output is a byte array. The only methods available are `read` and `close`.

One reason to use `SequenceInputStream` is to receive multiple inputs, create one input stream, and pass the stream off to another class that has more data-manipulation methods available.

The `StringBufferInputStream` Class

`StringBufferInputStream` is used to create an input stream from a buffer. The input stream is an array of string characters. The flow of data to the input stream is controlled by three variables:

- `buf`—The buffer where data is stored
- `Count`—The number of characters to use in the buffer
- `Pos`—The current position in the buffer

This is similar to `ByteArrayInputStream`; the only difference is that `ByteArrayInputStream` inputs the stream as an array of bytes, whereas `StringBufferInputStream` creates the input stream as an array of string characters. With `StringBufferInputStream`, you can use the `reset` method, which resets the input stream to the beginning. There is no `mark` method to mark a specific place in the stream.

Java Output Streams

Once again, refer to Chapter 8 for a detailed discussion of output streams. I will do only a quick review here. This section discusses the `java.io` package and its output stream classes.

Output streams are data streams generated by a Java application or applet for use elsewhere. There are several ways to format the data for output: It can be piped, buffered, printed to a screen, stored in an array of bytes, or output to a file. Output stream classes perform the output duty.

All the output stream classes are based on the abstract class `OutputStream`. The next section discusses the methods associated with `OutputStream`.

The **OutputStream** Class

`OutputStream` is the abstract class that contains all the possibilities of output from Java. Its subclasses are `BufferedOutputStream`, `ByteArrayOutputStream`, `DataOutputStream`, `FileOutputStream`, `FilterOutputStream`, `PipedOutputStream`, and `PrintStream`.

`OutputStream`'s subclasses use most or all of its methods. These methods are discussed in Chapter 8, but a quick review never hurts.

write

The `write` method is used to write data to a stream. It varies for each class in its output. All `write` methods are the same in that they block, or wait, for the receiving device to catch up. All `write` methods also throw the exception `IOException`.

See the section titled "Input Streams" in Chapter 8 for an example of `write`.

flush

The `flush` method is used to force any data buffered for the output stream to be written to the output device. This is the only way to override a block. This also may be the only way to write data if the receiving device requires it.

close

The `close` method closes an output stream. It is identical in logic to the `close` used for input streams. The Java garbage collector schedules a cleanup to the output streams when an applet or application closes. Be sure to manually call `close` if the application can't wait for the garbage collector.

The `FilterOutputStream` Class

`FilterOutputStream` has three subclasses: `BufferedOutputStream`, `DataOutputStream`, and `PrintStream`. These subclasses work in a unique way with `FilterOutputStream`; they allow it to control the flow of a file to them. `FilterOutputStream` does nothing by itself. (This is the output equivalent to `FilterInputStream`.)

Following is a discussion of the subclasses. Read the online documentation for a full list of each subclass's capabilities.

The `BufferedOutputStream` Class

`BufferedOutputStream` implements all the methods defined in superclass `OutputStream`. `BufferedOutputStream` uses `flush` and can create a nested stream to allow other output streams to flush.

Another key attraction to using `BufferedOutputStream` is that it creates a write buffer in the form of an array of bytes. This write buffer smooths out the stream of data so that writing can be continuous, as opposed to waiting for the output to reach the stream. The size of the buffer and the size of the writes can be controlled through `BufferedOutputStream`'s methods.

The `DataOutputStream` Class

`DataOutputStream` also implements the `DataOutput` interface. It is the inverse of `DataInputStream` and is used to write primitive data types. Following is a list of associated methods:

```
writeBoolean
writeByte
writeChar
writeDouble
writeFloat
writeInt
writeLine
writeLong
writeShort
writeUTF
writeUnsignedByte
writeUnsignedShort
```

`DataOutputStream` is used with `BufferedInputStream` to pull and push primitive data types across platforms.

The `PrintStream` Class

`PrintStream` is used to write formatted data to the user's screen. `PrintStream` is the actual class used to perform the printing in methods, like this:

```
System.out.print()
System.out.println()
```

It is possible to do autoflushing with `PrintStream`. The two constructors to use with `PrintStream` are

`PrintStream(OutputStream)`—Creates a new `PrintStream`

`PrintStream(OutputStream, boolean)`—Creates a new `PrintStream`, with autoflushing

`PrintStream` formats primitive data types for display to the screen. The following methods are used:

```
print(Object)
print(String)
print(char[])
print(char)
print(int)
print(long)
print(float)
print(double)
print(boolean)
println()
println(Object)
println(String)
println(char[])
println(char)
println(int)
println(long)
println(float)
println(double)
println(boolean)
```

See Listing 12.3 for an example of the use of `PrintStream`.

Listing 12.3. An example of the use of `PrintStream`.

```
/* Notes:

    This class implements a generic write class that can write any arbitrary
    object type to a file.  The constructor is used to open the file.  The
    resulting output stream is used as the constructor for the PrintStream
    class.  PrintStream is used because it can write arbitrary objects.
    PrintStreams implicitly use "toString" methods within objects to
    convert objects to strings.
```

continues

Listing 12.3. continued

```
        An arbitrary class called PhoneInfo is created simply for the purpose of
        demonstrating PrintStream's ability to write any type of object.

        The main example simply populates a PhoneInfo array and then uses the
        WriteObjToFile class to actually write the information to the file.  The
        filename to write to is specified on the command line.

        Syntax:
            MyMain <dest file>
*/

import java.io.*;

public class MyMain {

    public static void main (String args[]) {

        int i;
        // declare WriteObjToFile object
        WriteObjToFile w;
        // create info to populate phone info database
        String[] s =   {"Roy Rogers", "(111) 111-1111",
                        "Jesse James", "(222) 222-2222",
                        "Wyatt Earp", "(333) 333-3333"};
        // declare PhoneInfo array
        PhoneInfo[] p;

        // create PhoneInfo array
        p = new PhoneInfo[s.length/2];
        // loop through PhoneInfo array creating phoneinfo objects
        for (i=0; i<s.length; i+=2) {
           p[i/2] = new PhoneInfo(s[i],s[i+1]);
        }
        try {
           // create WriteObjToFile object
           w = new WriteObjToFile(args[0]);
           // loop through phone database passing objects to WriteObjToFile
           for (i=0; i<p.length; i++) {
              w.write(p[i]);
           }
        }
        // catch IO exceptions
        catch(IOException e) {
           System.err.println("ERROR: IO Exception");

           System.exit(2);
           }
       }
}

// declare PhoneInfo class
class PhoneInfo {

    // declare information variables
    String name, phoneNum;
```

```java
        // declare PhoneInfo constructor
        public PhoneInfo(String name, String phoneNum) {
            // initialize name based on constructor argument
            this.name = new String(name);
            // initialize phone number based on constructor argument
            this.phoneNum = new String(phoneNum);
        }

        // declare toString method for returning string representation of instance
        public String toString() {
            // return string
            return("Name: " + name + "\nPhone Number: " + phoneNum);
        }
    }

// declare WriteObjToFile class
class  WriteObjToFile {

    // declare PrintStream object
    PrintStream ps;

    // declare constructor
    public WriteObjToFile(String filename) throws IOException {
        try {
            // create printstream using FileOutPutStream as the stream to write to
            ps = new PrintStream(new FileOutputStream(filename));

        }
        // handle file not found errors
        catch (FileNotFoundException e) {

            System.err.println("ERROR: File not found");
            System.err.println("   File = " + filename);
            System.exit(2);
        }
    }

    // declare method to write arbitrary objects
    public void write (Object o) {

        // write object to output stream
        ps.println(o);

    }
}
```

The `ByteArrayOutputStream` Class

`ByteArrayOutputStream`, the counterpart of `ByteArrayInputStream`, is used to create an input stream from a buffer—that is, it pushes Java output into a buffer. The buffer grows as needed.

The flow of data to the output stream is controlled by two variables:

- `buf`—The buffer where data is stored
- `Count`—The number of bytes in the buffer

With `ByteArrayOutputStream`, you can use the `reset` method, which resets the output stream buffer so that the space of the buffer is not released and can be reused. There is no `mark` method to mark a specific place in the stream.

The `FileOutputStream` Class

`FileOutputStream`, the counterpart to `FileInputStream`, enables Java to write to files. The file and directory must be accessible to Java, which is a security issue.

> **Warning:** Be sure to explicitly close the file output stream if there are to be subsequent accesses to it after the end of file has been reached. Otherwise, the file will not be properly terminated with an end of file marker and you will get errors.

The only methods available to `FileOutputStream` are the following:

`close()`—Closes the stream

`finalize()`—Closes the stream when garbage is collected

`getFD()`—Returns the file descriptor associated with this stream

`write(int)`—Writes a byte of data

`write(byte[])`—Writes an array of bytes

`write(byte[], int, int)`—Writes a subarray of bytes

The `PipedOutputStream` Class

`PipedOutputStream` supports moving data to and from threads that are piped together using the `PipeInputStream`. Because `PipedOutputStream` is connected to the `PipeInputStream`, the two must work together.

The methods associated with these classes are

`close()`—Closes the stream

`connect(PipedInputStream)`—Connects this output stream to a receiver

`write(int)`—Writes a byte

`write(byte[], int, int)`—Writes a subarray of bytes

Miscellaneous I/O Classes

The `java.io` package includes two miscellaneous I/O classes for dealing with files: `File` and `RandomAccessFile`.

The `File` Class

The `File` class is used to represent a filename on a host system. It cannot read or write to the file, but it can get information about the file such as its name, path, and so on. It works as an abstract way of dealing with a platform-specific file.

The `RandomAccessFile` Class

`RandomAccessFile` implements both `DataInput` and `DataOutput` interfaces. It combines both input and output access to a file within the security confines of Java. The numerous methods associated with it read and write primitive data types, close the file, and locate the file. `RandomAccessFile` also allows `skip`.

The `java.util` Package

The `java.util` package is sort of a catch-all for handy utilities. It contains the following classes:

    BitSet
    Date
    Dictionary
    Hashtable
    Observable
    Properties
    Random
    Stack
    StringTokenizer
    Vector

As you can see, this is certainly a mixed bag of classes. Read on for a description of each one. See the online documentation for details on all the methods associated with each class.

The `Bitset` Class

The `Bitset` class creates a set of bits that can grow as needed. It has methods that can manipulate the bits in the set. Listing 12.4 is an example of how to use `Bitset`.

Listing 12.4. An example using `Bitset`.

```
/* Notes:
   This class does 7 bit even parity generation and checking.
*/
```

continues

Listing 12.4. continued

```java
import java.util.*;
public class MyMain {

    public static void main (String args[]) {

        Parity p;                       // declare parity object
        p = new Parity((byte)100);      // create parity object
        p.genParity();                  // generate parity bit
        if (p.chkParity())              // check for parity error
            System.out.println("no parity error");
        else
            System.out.println("parity error");
    }
}

class  Parity {                         // declare class parity

    BitSet b;                           // declare bitset object

    public Parity(byte data) {          // declare parity constructor
        int i;
        b = new BitSet(8);              // create new bitset object length 8
        for (i=0; i<7; i++) {           // copy input data bits to bitset
            if (((1 << i) & data) == 1) { // test if data bit is 1
                b.set(i);               // set corresponding bitset bit
            }
        }
    }

    public void genParity() {           // method to generate parity bit
        int i, cnt;
        cnt = 0;
        for (i=0; i<7; i++) {           // loop through bitset counting data bits
            if (b.get(i)) {
                cnt++;
            }
        }
if ((cnt % 2) == 0)              // test if even or odd number data bits set
            b.clear(7);                 // even, clear parity bit
        else
            b.set(7);                   // odd, set parity bit
    }

    public boolean chkParity() {        // method to check for parity errors
        int i, cnt, parityBit;
        cnt = 0;
        for (i=0; i<7; i++) {           // loop through bitset counting data bits
            if (b.get(i)) {
                cnt++;                  // increment count of set data bits
            }
        }
        if (b.get(7))                   // get setting of parity bit
            parityBit = 1;              // parity bit set
        else
            parityBit = 0;              // parity bit not set
        if (((cnt %2) ^ parityBit) == 0) // check if parity bit set correctly
            return(true);               // no parity error detected
```

```
        return(false);                    // parity error detected
    }
}
```

The **Date** Class

Date provides methods for examining and manipulating date and time. Time in Java is measured in milliseconds since January 1, 1970. Java attempts to handle time from the system with which it is interacting. UTC is Coordinated Universal Time, which seems to be the worldwide standard.

Note: The Date class does not work as documented in the Java API. Although you should be able to work with dates since 1900, dates before January 1, 1970 are generally not usable.

See Table 12.1 for a list of methods to see the full scope of this class.

Table 12.1. Methods available for the **Date** class.

Method	Purpose
UTC(int, int, int, int, int, int)	Calculates a UTC value from YMDHMS
after(Date)	Checks whether this date comes after the specified date
before(Date)	Checks whether this date comes before the specified date
equals(Object)	Compares this object against the specified object
getDate()	Returns the day of the month
getDay()	Returns the day of the week
getHours()	Returns the hour
getMinutes()	Returns the minute
getMonth()	Returns the month
getSeconds()	Returns the second
getTime()	Returns the time in milliseconds since the epoch
getTimezoneOffset()	Returns the time zone offset in minutes for the current locale that is appropriate for this time
getYear()	Returns the year after 1900

continues

Table 12.1. continued

Method	Purpose
hashCode()	Computes a number that is used when storing objects in hash tables.
parse(String)	Given a string representing a time, parses it and returns the time value
setDate(int)	Sets the date
setHours(int)	Sets the hours
setMinutes(int)	Sets the minutes
setMonth(int)	Sets the month
setSeconds(int)	Sets the seconds
setTime(long)	Sets the time
setYear(int)	Sets the year
toGMTString()	Converts a date to a String object using the Internet GMT conventions
toLocaleString()	Converts a date to a String object, using the locale conventions
toString()	Converts a date to a String object using the UNIX time conventions

It is important to remember that months start with 0, which is January, and end with 11, which is December. The days of the week also start with 0, which is Sunday, and go through 6, which is Saturday. Dates of the month are normal.

> **Note:** Dates that are not within the normal range parameters are interpreted through consecutive iterations of the date range. For example, 32 January is recognized as 1 February.

Listing 12.5 is an example of the use of the Date class.

Listing 12.5. Using **Date**.

```
/* Notes:

    Java's time handling utilities in java.util do not seem to handle
    dates before 1970 even though it is documented as 1900.
    Usage: date specified on the command line as first argument:
       MyMain "18 Apr 1972"
```

```
*/

import java.util.*;

public class MyMain {

    public static void main (String args[]) {

BDay b;                     // declare birthday object;
        b = new BDay(args[0]);      // create birthday object initialized
                                    // to first date specified on command line
        b.printBDayInfo();          // print out resulting birthday information
    }
}

class  BDay {                               // declare new class birthday

    String sign;                // declare string object to hold Astrological sign
    Date d;
// declare date object to hold date of birth

    public BDay(String date) {          // declare constructor for this class
        Date c;                         // declare date object used for comparisons
        int year;                       // declare int to hold year of birth

        d = new Date(date);
// create new date object initialized to birthday
        year = d.getYear();             // get year from birth date
        while (true) {                  // loop finding Astrological sign
            c = new Date("20 Jan " + year);
// create comparison date of end of capricorn period
            if (d.before(c)) {
// check if birth date came before capricorn
                sign = new String("Capricorn");     // if so, set sign to capricorn
                break;                               // break out of while loop
            }
            c = new Date("19 Feb " + year);     // repeat above for aquarius
            if (d.before(c)) {
                sign = new String("Aquarius");
                break;
            }
            c = new Date("21 Mar " + year);     // repeat above for pisces
            if (d.before(c)) {
                sign = new String("Pisces");
                break;
            }
            c = new Date("20 Apr " + year);     // repeat above for aries
            if (d.before(c)) {
                sign = new String("Aries");
                break;
            }
            c = new Date("21 May " + year);     // repeat above for taurus
            if (d.before(c)) {
                sign = new String("Taurus");
                break;
            }
            c = new Date("21 Jun " + year);     // repeat above for gemini
```

continues

Listing 12.5. continued

```
               if (d.before(c)) {
                  sign = new String("Gemini");
                  break;
               }
               c = new Date("23 Jul " + year);      // repeat above for cancer
               if (d.before(c)) {
                  sign = new String("Cancer");
                  break;
               }
               c = new Date("23 Aug " + year);      // repeat above for leo
               if (d.before(c)) {
                  sign = new String("Leo");
                  break;
               }
               c = new Date("23 Sep" + year);       // repeat above for virgo
               if (d.before(c)) {
                  sign = new String("Virgo");
                  break;
               }
               c = new Date("23 Oct " + year);      // repeat above for libra
               if (d.before(c)) {
                  sign = new String("Libra");
                  break;
               }
               c = new Date("22 Nov " + year);      // repeat above for scorpio
               if (d.before(c)) {
                  sign = new String("Scorpio");
                  break;
               }
               c = new Date("22 Dec" + year);       // repeat above for sagittarius
               if (d.before(c)) {
                  sign = new String("Sagittarius");
                  break;
               }
               c = new Date("31 Dec" + year);       // catch end case for capricorn
               if (d.before(c)) {
                  sign = new String("Capricorn");
                  break;
               }
            }
         }

// declare method for printing birthdate information
      public void printBDayInfo() {
         Date t,c;
// declare date objects for todays date and for comparisons
         t = new Date();                            // obtain todays date
         t.setHours(0);
// set hours of todays date to zero
         t.setMinutes(0);
// set minutes of todays date to zero
         t.setSeconds(0);
// set seconds of todays date to zero
         c = new Date(t.getYear(), (d.getMonth()-1), d.getDate());
// create date object for this years birthday
System.out.println("You were born on: " + (d.getMonth()+1) + "/" +
         d.getDate() + "/" + d.getYear());    // print out birth date
```

```
        System.out.println("Your sign is:      " + sign);
// print out Astrological sign
      if (c.before(t))
// check if birthday already occurred this year
          System.out.println("Your birthday has already occurred this year");
// print out birthday already occurred
      else
          if (c.after(t))
// check if birthday is yet to come this year
              System.out.println("Your birthday has yet to occur this year");
// print out birthday is yet to come
          else
              System.out.println("TODAY IS YOUR BIRTHDAY!");
// if neither before today or after today, it must be today
    }
}
```

As you can see, there are numerous ways to use Date's methods to manipulate and examine dates.

The **Dictionary** Class

Dictionary is an abstract class. Its only current subclass is Hashtable. Dictionary is used to create a way of organizing objects. (See the following "Hashtable" section for the implementation of Dictionary.)

The idea is to access objects nonsequentially. There are keys to identify and access objects. Think of Dictionary as storing objects in a structure similar to an indexed file.

The **Hashtable** Class

Hashtable extends Dictionary and is used to map keys to values. The methods associated with Hashtable enable the placing, locating, and retrieving of objects that are used as keys. The Properties class extends Hashtable.

The **Properties** Class

Properties is a class that loads an input stream into a hash table. It also allows saves and gets from the hash table.

The **Random** Class

Random contains methods that create pseudo-random numbers. These numbers can be either Gaussian, Double, Float, Int, or Long. The seed, or starting point, can be reset anytime using the appropriate method.

The **Vector** Class

Vector is the abstract parent class for **Stack**. You will use the vector class to implement a growable array of objects.

The **Stack** Class

Stack extends the **Vector** class. It creates a last in, first out (LIFO) stack of objects. See Listing 12.6 for an example using **Stack**.

Listing 12.6. An example using **Stack**.

```
/* Notes:

        Either java or NT java will not accept "-" as a command line argument.
        The user must specify "--" to get the program to simply see "-".
        This program works by specifying an RPN string on the command line.
*/

import java.util.*;

public class MyMain {

    public static void main (String args[]) {

        // declare RPN calculator object
        RPNCalculator c;
        // create RPN calculator passing command line arguments
        c = new RPNCalculator(args);
    }
}

// declare new RPN calculator class
class  RPNCalculator {

    // declare Stack object
    Stack s;
    // declare generic object
    Object o;

    // RPN Calculator constructor which also solves equation string passed to it
    public RPNCalculator(String args[]) {

        int i,j;
        int[] num;
        // declare object to hold current arithmetic operator
        Character operator;
        // create new stack
        s = new Stack();
        // create two integer array to hold operands
        num = new int[2];

        // loop through equation strings
        for (i=0; i < args.length; i++) {
```

```java
        // handle number format exceptions
        try {
          // try converting string to number and push on stack if successful
          s.push(new Integer(args[i]));
        }

        // string is not a number, must be an operator
        catch(java.lang.NumberFormatException e) {
          // convert string operator to character
          operator = new Character(args[i].charAt(0));
          // loop through operands operator will be used with
          for (j=0; j<2; j++) {

            // not enough operands on stack, generate error
            if (s.empty()) {
              System.err.println("ERROR: stack is empty");
              System.exit(2);
            }

            // extract operand from stack
            num[j] = ((Integer)s.pop()).intValue();
          }

          // switch based on operator
          switch (operator.charValue()) {

          // operator is "+", add operands
          case '+':
            s.push(new Integer(num[1] + num[0]));
            break;

          // operator is "-", subtract operands
          case '-':
            s.push(new Integer(num[1] - num[0]));
            break;

          // operator is "*", multiply operands
          case '*':
            s.push(new Integer(num[1] * num[0]));
            break;

          // operator is "/", divide operands
          case '/':
            s.push(new Integer(num[1] / num[0]));
            break;

          default:
            // unknown operator, print error message
            System.err.println("ERROR: invalid operator: " + operator);
            System.exit(3);
            break;
          }
        }
      }
      // value remaining on stack must be answer, print to screen
      System.out.println(((Integer)s.pop()).intValue());
  }
}
```

The **StringTokenizer** Class

The StringTokenizer class provides a set of methods for converting an input stream into a set of tokens. Methods are provided for specifying which characters make up a token, which characters serve as token delimiters, whether case should be considered, and whether numeric characters should be converted to numbers. The StringTokenizer class also understands the /* */ comment-naming conventions of C, C++, and Java as well as the // used in C++ and Java.

The StringTokenizer class specifies all the parts that determine a token and then retrieves a single token in its entirety piece by piece from an input stream. This can be used for anything from splitting a simple sentence into individual words to processing something as complex as Java source code. (See the online documentation for details of the individual methods.)

Summary

Java provides several ways to deal with moving data through its applications. The java.io package contains classes that handle the input and output of data. The data arrives in a stream and can be sliced and diced in various ways by the subclasses of the abstract classes InputStream and OutputStream.

The data stream may block, or wait, if the flow is not continuous. Both input and output classes provide buffers to smooth this flow. All input classes are able to skip a certain number of bytes forward in the stream; some classes can mark a spot and then reset the stream to that spot. Some classes store the data in byte arrays, and one class stores it in a character string array.

Data accessed or stored by Java must originate or be placed in an area that is Java accessible. Much of the Java security schema relies on the segmentation of Java data from other system data. Therefore, it would not be a good idea to put a copy of your password file in this area.

The java.io package doesn't care where data originates; it only cares about what the programmer wants to do with it. The data-manipulation classes enable Java to be truly non–platform-specific, even when manipulating data.

The java.util package contains classes that add functionality to Java. These classes include a date manipulator (Date) and a bitset creator and manipulator (Bitset). There are also classes that provide a mechanism for a hash table structure of an object file (Dictionary and Hashtable). There is a pseudo-random number generator (Random). Another class creates a stack of objects (Stack), and another turns a string of characters into tokens (StringTokenizer).

13

The Net and Debug Class Libraries

A discussion of the API for the Internet's premier programming language would not be complete without a look at the class library that makes networking possible—java.net. Although java.net is the final class library in the original Java API, new class libraries that extend the functionality of the Java programming language are continually being introduced. One such class library is the sun.tools.debug library, which was added to give Java built-in debugging support. Whenever you use the Java debugger, you are accessing this library.

Introduction to the Net Class Library

The Net class library, java.net, provides a high-level interface for connections over the Internet or any other kind of TCP/IP network. Using these interfaces makes it possible for a Java application to connect to existing network services, provide its own network services, and even allow for multiuser, network-aware games over the Internet. Whereas these can be quite complicated to program in other languages, the java.net package allows the basics of socket connection to be set up in as little as 10 lines of code. That's power!

The following sections describe the classes in the java.net package.

The **ContentHandler** Class

ContentHandler is used to read a stream of data that is generated by a network connection and produce an object. The exact content handler called depends on the MIME type of the remote data.

ContentHandler should not be called directly. This task is much better performed by URL.getContent() or URLConnection.getContent(), which simplify the process of reading a stream of data.

The **DatagramPacket** Class

DatagramPacket is used to both send and receive datagram packets. A *datagram packet* is a segment of data containing packet data, packet length, Internet address, and port. This allows programming at the IP packet level.

DatagramPacket methods are used to determine the address, length, and port of the datagram packet, as well as retrieve the data itself. See the online documentation for details.

The **DatagramSocket** Class

DatagramSocket is used for creating UDP-based connections over a network. Services such as Sun's *Network File System* (NFS) use UDP as the underlying protocol. Java applications can also create and/or use UDP-based network connections by making use of this class. Only the advanced programmer will use this class. See the online documentation for details.

The **InetAddress** Class

InetAddress makes an object of Internet addresses. This makes them able to be manipulated as String objects or within other network classes.

Listing 13.1 is an example of using the InetAddress class.

Listing 13.1. An example of class **InetAddress**.

```
/* Notes:

     The main example simply accepts a hostname as an argument and
     prints out the following information.
        Hostname and IP address of system application is running on.
        IP address of hostname
        Additional IP addresses associated with hostname
        (try www.microsoft.com)

     Syntax:
        MyMain <hostname>
*/

import java.net.*;

public class MyMain {

   public static void main (String args[]) {

      InetAddress inetAddr, inetAddrs[];
      int i;

      try {
         inetAddr = InetAddress.getLocalHost();
         System.out.println("Local System:");
         System.out.println("    " + inetAddr);
// print out hostname and IP address of local host
         inetAddr = InetAddress.getByName(args[0]);
// create an InetAddress object from a given hostname
         System.out.println(inetAddr.getHostName() + ":");
         System.out.println("    " + inetAddr);
// print out hostname and IP address in inetAddr
         System.out.println("Additional addresses:");
         inetAddrs = InetAddress.getAllByName(args[0]);
// get all addresses associated with a give hostname
         for (i=1; i < inetAddrs.length; i++) {
// loop through printing out all addresses
            System.out.println("    " + inetAddrs[i]);
         }
      }
      catch (UnknownHostException e) {
// handle unknown host exceptions
         System.err.println("ERROR: Hostname cannot be resolved");
         System.err.println("    hostname = " + args[0]);
      }
   }
}
```

Java Socket Handlers

Java has classes within its java.net package to govern the use of sockets. *Sockets* are a network-specific utility. Those of you who are familiar with UNIX network programming are probably well versed in sockets.

Sockets are network processes that connect two hosts and create a two-way "pathway" to carry data between the server and the client. Sockets communicate on a specific port (but which port is up to the programmer). The application notifies the operating system that it is listening for activity on a certain port. The application then goes into a waiting state until it is requested to wake up due to activity on the port. It is not necessary for it to constantly query the port; the operating system notifies the application when there has been activity. The application then wakes up, completes the connection, and does whatever the programmer told it to do.

Sockets are useful in Java for implementing communication streams between programs. Sockets are the primary method of communication on the Internet. Web pages, file transfers, and electronic mail all communicate with each other using sockets. Because of the Java socket interface, it is easy to create Java applications that can participate in this network connectivity.

Java uses three classes in java.net for sockets: ServerSocket, Socket, and SocketImpl. The first two are the classes most likely to be used by a programmer. The last, SocketImpl, is generally implemented by the Java-enabled operating system. In other words, most programmers will not have to delve into the inner workings of SocketImpl.

The ServerSocket Class

ServerSocket is the socket created for the server side. ServerSocket listens for a connection request from a client and accepts the connection for a port on the server side.

Two of the methods associated with ServerSocket are accept and close. accept is used to create the socket and attach it to a port on the server end. close is used to shut down the connection at the end of its useful life. It is best to manually shut down the socket as opposed to waiting for the Java garbage collector to shut it down.

Listing 13.2 shows the source code for a generic socket server.

Listing 13.2. A Java-based generic socket server or daemon.

```
/* Notes:

    This example implements a java based generic socket server or daemon.
    It uses a socket to communicate with a socket client.  It can be used as
    the basis for almost any type of socker server based application. This
    particular example includes logging of the connections accepted and
    will accept a filename as part of the constructor which will be used
    for this logging capability.
```

```
        To better demonstrate it's use, a prototype of a POP server has been
        implemented.  The POP server does not actually retrieve mail, but
        does accept a connection on port 110 and will respond to a quit
        command.

        The main program simply creates a new JPop object and then executes
        its start method.  JPop will then loop waiting for and processing
        connections.  MyMain accepts a filename as an command line arguement.
        This is used for logging of the connections.

        Syntax:
          MyMain <logfile name>

*/

import java.io.*;
import java.net.*;
import java.util.*;

public class MyMain {

    public static void main (String args[]) {

        int i;
        JPop jp;                   // declare JPop object

        jp = new JPop(args[0]);    // create JPop instance
        jp.start();                // starts the JPop daemon
    }
}


class Daemon {                     // declare Daemon class

    public DataInputStream is;     // declare input stream variable
    public PrintStream os;         // declare output stream variable
    public String remoteHost;      // declare variable to hold remote hostname

    Socket s;                      // declare socket object
    ServerSocket ss;               // declare server socket object
    PrintStream lf;                // declare printstream object
    String logFile;                // declare logfile name variable
    int port;                      // declare port number variable
    String name;                   // declare application name variable

    // constructor for class Daemon
    public Daemon(int port, String name, String logFile) {
        this.port = port;          // save port number
        this.name = name;          // save application name
        this.logFile = logFile;    // save logfile name
        try {
            lf = new PrintStream(new FileOutputStream(logFile));   // open logfile
        }

        // handle file not found exceptions
        catch(FileNotFoundException e) {
            System.err.println("ERROR: File not found");
            System.err.println("   File = " + logFile);
```

continues

Listing 13.2. continued

```
          System.exit(5);
      }

      catch(IOException e) {System.exit(6);}      // handle IO exceptions
writeLogEnt("daemon started");           // write daemon started log entry
   }

   void start() {                 // method to start daemon
      try {
         ss = new ServerSocket(port);   // create server socket
         s = ss.accept();               // wait for incoming connection

         // get name of remote host for logging
         remoteHost = (s.getInetAddress()).getHostName();

         // write log entry
         writeLogEnt("connection accepted: port = " + s.getLocalPort() + ",
         ➥host = " + remoteHost);
         // open a data input stream using the socket getInputStream method
         is = new DataInputStream(s.getInputStream());
         // open an output PrintStream using the socket getOutputStream method
         os = new PrintStream(s.getOutputStream());
      }
      catch(IOException e) {            // handle exceptions
         System.err.println("ERROR: IOexception(1) encountered");
         this.exit(7);
      }
   }

   void stop() {                       // declare stop method
      writeLogEnt("daemon stopped");    // log daemon stopped message
      try {
         if (is != null)               // test input stream is not null
            is.close();                // explicitly close input stream
         if (os != null) {             // test if output stream is not null
            os.flush();                // explicitly flush output stream
            os.close();                // explicitly close output stream
         }
         if (s != null)                // test if socket is null
            s.close();                 // explicitly close socket
      }
      catch(IOException e) {           // handle exceptions
         System.err.println("ERROR: IOexception(2) encountered");
         this.exit(8);
      }
   }

   String date() {                     // declare method for getting todays date
      Date d = new Date();
      return(d.getMonth()+"/"+d.getDate()+" "+d.getHours()+":
      ➥"+d.getMinutes()+":"+d.getSeconds());
   }

   void writeLogEnt(String entry) {    // delcare method for writing log entries
      lf.println(date() + " " + name + ": " + entry);
   }
```

```
    void exit(int errCode) {              // declare common exit method
        // log exit message
        writeLogEnt("daemon exited with error code " + errCode);
        if (s != null) {                  // test socket is not null
            try {s.close();}              // close socket
catch(IOException e) {
            System.err.println("ERROR: IOexception(3) encountered");
        }
    }
        System.exit(errCode);             // exit application
    }
}

class JPop {              // declare Java POP class

    Daemon d;             // declare Daemon object

    public JPop(String logFile) {         // constructor for class JPop
        d = new Daemon(110, "JPop", logFile);    // create new Daemon instance
    }

    void start() {        // declare start method
        int i;
        String resp;      // variable to hold response from client
        while (true) {    // loop forever handling incoming connections
            d.start();    // start daemon
            // send response to remote host
            write("+OK " + d.remoteHost + " JPOP server ready");
            procConnection();      // process POP connection
        }
    }

    // declare method to process POP connecitons
    public void procConnection() {

        // variable to hold response from client
        String resp;
        String cmd = "";

        // process commands until quit received
        while (! cmd.equalsIgnoreCase("quit")) {
            resp = read();                    // read response from client
            // tokenize client response for processing
            StringTokenizer st = new StringTokenizer(resp);
            cmd = st.nextToken();             // get command

            if (cmd.equalsIgnoreCase("quit")) {    // test for quit command
                // send server shutdown message to client
                write("+OK " + d.remoteHost + " JPOP server shutdown");
                d.stop();                     // stop connection to client
                continue;                     // go to top of loop
            }
            // send error message to client
            write("-ERR Invalid command; valid commands:  QUIT");
        }
    }

    void write(String cmd) {          // declare method to write string to client
```

continues

Listing 13.2. continued

```
    d.os.println(cmd);                  // send string to client
}

String read() {                    // declare method to read string from client
    String resp = "";
    try {resp = d.is.readLine();}      // read response from client
catch(IOException e) {              // handle exceptions
        System.err.println("ERROR: read IOException");
        this.exit(10);
    }
    return(resp);                      // return exit code
}
void exit(int errCode) {           // declare exit method
    d.stop();                          // close connection to client
    System.exit(errCode);              // exit application
}
}
```

When you start this program, on the command line, you must pass the name of the file that you want to log socket messages as an argument. You can do this as follows:

```
java MyMain socket.txt
```

In the example, the filename socket.txt is the name of the file that will log socket messages. While the program is running, you can test the socket connection and logging. To do this, start your browser and point to the IP address of your local system using port 110. If you are on a network-capable machine such as UNIX or Windows NT, you can use the local loopback IP address of 127.0.0.1 for testing. For example, the URL http://127.0.0.1:110 could be used to test port 110.

If you are able to start the program and test the socket connection, the text file will have entries similar to the following:

```
daemon started
connection accepted: port = 110,host = ppp-5.ts-4.dc.idt.net
```

The Socket Class

Socket is the class used to create network connections and processes. Socket is used in conjunction with SocketImpl to implement the actual socket operations. Socket and SocketImpl are separated so that the implementation can be changed depending on the kind of firewall being used. See Listing 13.3 for an example of using Socket.

Listing 13.3. A Socket usage example.

```
/* Notes:

    This example implements a java based version of the Unix "biff" utility.
    It uses a socket to communicate with a POP server to determine if there
    is any mail for the user.
```

The main program simply calls the JBiff class methods every 60 seconds
to determine if there is new mail present on the server or not. It
accepts three command line arguments specifying the host to connect
to, the username to use, and the password to use. Note that this
is intended as an example only. Specifying passwords on command
lines is never recommended. To make this fully functional, a separate
dialogue box should be implemented to prompt for the password.
That is beyond the scope of this chapter however.

```
    Syntax:
        MyMain <hostname> <username> <password>

    Historical note:
        Where does "biff" come from?  A program for checking mail was
        written many years ago for Unix systems.  The programmer
        decided to simply name it after his or her dog "biff".  Many other
        "biff" type programs have been written since then and many
        of these have carried on the historical fun of the "biff"
        name.  For this reason, the class implementing the "biff"
        functionality was called jbiff for Java biff.  On another
        note, I had thought about naming the class after one
        of our dogs, spot or buffy, but decided that a program that
        was constantly giving out false alarms was not a good idea.
*/

import java.io.*;
import java.net.*;
import java.util.*;

public class MyMain {

    public static void main (String args[]) {

        int i;
        JBiff jb;          // declare jbiff object

        // create jbiff instance
        jb = new JBiff(args[0], args[1], args[2]);

        // loop forever checking mail
        while(true) {

            // check for new mail
            if (jb.chkMail()) {
                // print out have NEW mail message
                System.out.println("You have NEW mail");
            }
            else {
                // print out have mail message
                System.out.println("You have mail");
            }
            try {Thread.sleep(60000);}                      // sleep for 60 seconds
            catch(InterruptedException e){};                // handle exceptions
    }
        }
    }
```

continues

Listing 13.3. continued

```java
class  JBiff {

    Socket s;                    // declare socket object
    DataInputStream dis;         // declare data input stream object
    PrintStream dos;             // declare printstream object
    // variables for hostname, username, and password
    String hostname, user, pass;
    int mailBoxCnt;              // variable to hold last count of mail messages
    boolean mailBoxFlg = false;  // variable to hold status of New mail flag

    // constructor for class jbiff
    public JBiff(String hostname, String user, String pass) {
        mailBoxCnt = 0;          // initialize mail message count to zero
        this.hostname = hostname; // save hostname
        this.user = user;        // save username
        this.pass = pass;        // save password
    }

    // declare method for open socket connection to pop server
    void openMailBox() {
        String resp;             // variable to hold response from server
        try {
            // open new socket connection to hostname on port 110
            s = new Socket(hostname, 110);
            // open a data input stream using the socket getInputStream method
            dis = new DataInputStream(s.getInputStream());
            // open an output PrintStream using the socket getOutputStream method
            dos = new PrintStream(s.getOutputStream());
        }

        // handle file not found errors
        catch(UnknownHostException e) {
            System.err.println("ERROR: Host not found");
            System.err.println("   Host = " + hostname);
            System.exit(2);
        }
        catch(IOException e){};              // catch general IO exceptions
        resp = read();                   // read first line from pop server
        resp = write("USER " + user);    // send username command to pop server
        resp = write("PASS " + pass);    // send password command to pop server
    }

    // declare method to check for mail on pop server
    public boolean chkMail() {
        // variable to hold response from server
        String resp;
        // variable to hold current mail message count on server
        int cnt;
        // return code for method
        boolean rcode;
        // call method to open new connection to pop server
        openMailBox();
        // use STAT command to get count of mail messages on server
        resp = write("STAT");
        // tokenize server response for processing
        StringTokenizer st = new StringTokenizer(resp);
        // skip leading OK/ERR token
```

```
      st.nextToken();
      // get count of messages on server
      cnt = (new Integer(st.nextToken())).intValue();
      // send QUIT to close connection to pop server
      write("QUIT");

      // if more mail messages since last time, set new mail flag
      if (cnt > mailBoxCnt) {
         mailBoxFlg = true;
      }

      // if fewer mail messages since last time, clear new mail flag
      if (cnt < mailBoxCnt) {
         mailBoxFlg = false;
      }
      mailBoxCnt = cnt;             // save number of messages for next comparison
      return(mailBoxFlg);                   // return status of new mail flag
   }
String write(String cmd) {   // declare method to write string to pop server
   dos.println(cmd);                     // send string command to pop server
   return(read());             // return string returned from read of pop server
}

String read() {              // declare method to read string from pop server
   String resp = "";                    // initialize response variable
   try {
      resp = dis.readLine();           // read response from pop server
      if (! resp.startsWith("+OK")) {        // test for acceptable response
         // report error returned by pop server
         System.err.println("ERROR: err returned by pop server");
         System.err.println("   resp = " + resp);
         System.exit(7);
      }
   }
   catch(IOException e) {             // handle exceptions
      System.err.println("ERROR: read socket error");
      System.exit(6);
   }
   return(resp);                        // return string read from pop server
   }
}
```

Note: If you cannot access your host using the IP address, try the fully qualified domain and hostname, such as www.tvp.com.

The `SocketImpl` Class

`SocketImpl` is an abstract class, which means the programmer must subclass it to make it work. `SocketImpl` is used in conjunction with `Socket` to successfully adapt to different environments. One of the main reasons this is an abstract class is that the actual socket communications via Java are platform or firewall specific.

`SocketImpl` can be used with either streams or datagrams. It contains methods that can set a boolean as to whether the socket data is in a stream or a datagram.

The class defines other methods that accept, connect, close, and bind sockets to a port. These methods manipulate and control the socket. Of course, because they are part of an abstract class, the programmer must fill in the necessary details like IP address, port, and hostname.

Java URL-Related Classes

Java has classes in the `java.net` package that allow manipulation and connection to other locations on the Internet. These locations are denoted by a unique *Uniform Reference Locator* (URL).

The URL is set up to perform certain activities when a connection is made to it, such as loading a Web page or downloading a file. You can include these interfaces in a Java applet or application.

These URL classes are similar to sockets in that they allow easy integration of network applications into a program. URLs are a bit more user-friendly to work with than are sockets.

> **Note:** Many of the examples in Chapter 10, "The `java.lang` and `java.applet` Class Libraries," use URLs to access files. Check out Listing 10.3, which shows a program that reads an audio file based on a URL.

The **URL** Class

The URL class transforms a URL string into an object that can then be manipulated using associated methods. These methods serve purposes such as getting the filename, protocol, and hostname.

URL also has methods that can open and maintain the data connection of an input stream. This is much easier to use than the socket classes.

The **URLConnection** Class

URLConnection is another abstract class used to create and control a connection to a platform- and firewall-specific location. It is a simplified version of connection interface for the URL class. See the online documentation for a full list of its methods.

The **URLEncoder** Class

URLEncoder takes a string of text and turns it into the into `x-www-form-urlencoded` format, which is a MIME format. This can then be used in conjunction with the URL class.

The **URLStreamHandler** Class

URLStreamHandler is an abstract class. Its purpose is to create a format for opening a stream connection to a specific URL. This class is concerned with the protocol of the URL. If a programmer wants to create a new URL stream protocol, it is necessary to implement the methods specified in this abstract class. This is most definitely only for advanced programmers.

Introducing the **sun.tools.debug** Library

The sun.tools.debug library provides the necessary framework for debugging Java programs. Whenever you use the Java debugger, you are accessing this library. If you accessed its classes directly, you could create your own debugger. Because most Java developers will not need to create their own debugger, this section provides only an overview of the classes the library contains to give you insight into the debugging process.

The **DebuggerCallback** Interface

The DebuggerCallback interface is a template for implementing communications between an application and a debugger. The basic syntax for the interface is as follows:

```
public interface DebuggerCallback {
    …
}
```

All communications between client applications and a debugger are *asynchronous*. Asynchronous communications are rather like the way you and I use e-mail: We send a message and the receiver responds to the message when he gets a chance. The sections that follow look at the abstract methods in the DebuggerCallback interface.

One of the key methods in this interface is breakpointEvent(), which is used to report when a breakpoint has been reached. The method accepts a RemoteThread object—the thread that reached the breakpoint—as a parameter. You use breakpoints during advanced debugging to help determine the behavior and state of the program at a certain point in the program's execution.

See Chapter 23, "Advanced Debugging and Troubleshooting" for more information on breakpoints.

Other key methods in this class include exceptionEvent(), printToConsole(), quitEvent(), and threadDeathEvent(). The exceptionEvent() method is used to report that an exception has occurred. It accepts a RemoteThread object and a String object as parameters.

The `printToConsole()` method is used whenever the `DebuggerCallback` interface prints messages to the console—which, as you will see when you use the Java debugger, is quite often. The `printToConsole()` method accepts a `String` object as a parameter.

The `quitEvent()` method is used to tell the debugger that the client has exited. Generally, clients exit either by returning from the main thread or by calling `System.exit()`.

The `threadDeathEvent()` is used to report that a thread has died. This method accepts a `RemoteThread` object, which is the thread that died, as a parameter.

Methods that Deal with Remote Objects

As you might expect, most of the classes in a debugging library for an object-oriented programming language are designed to handle the debugging methods associated with objects. A complete listing of the types of remote objects handled by the debugger is as follows: arrays, booleans, bytes, characters, classes, doubles, fields, floats, integers, longs, shorts, strings, threads, thread groups, and variable values.

Each of these object types is handled in a separate class. These classes include

```
RemoteArray
RemoteBoolean
RemoteByte
RemoteChar
RemoteClass
RemoteDouble
RemoteField
RemoteFloat
RemoteInt
RemoteLong
RemoteShort
RemoteString
RemoteThread
RemoteThreadGroup
RemoteValue
```

Most of the methods used with specific objects types are similar to the methods used in the `RemoteObject` class. For example, the `RemoteArray` class is one of many classes in the `sun.tools.debug` package that allow remote debugging of specific object types. As you can probably tell by the name of the class, the `RemoteArray` class allows remote debugging of arrays.

What you probably cannot tell from the class name is that the `RemoteArray` class uses an extensive list of methods that handle every facet of debugging array objects. Still, the methods in the `RemoteArray` class are similar to the methods in the more generic `RemoteObject` class. Therefore, by examining the methods in the `RemoteObject` class, you can gain an understanding of most of the other classes in the `sun.tools.debug` package.

Table 13.1 is a summary of the methods in the `RemoteObject` class.

Table 13.1. Methods in the `RemoteObject` class.

Method	Purpose
`description()`	Returns a description of the object
`finalize()`	Performs this code when garbage collection is run
`getClass()`	Returns the object's class
`getField()`	Returns an instance variable
`getFields()`	Returns the non-static fields of an object
`getFieldValue()`	Returns the value of an object's instance variable
`getId()`	Returns the ID of an object
`setField()`	Sets an instance variable, specified by slot or name
`toString()`	Returns the object as a string
`typeName()`	Returns the object type

The `RemoteStackFrame` Class

Using the `RemoteStackFrame` class, the debugger can examine a suspended thread's stackframe. As a Java developer, you will often use the debugger to call the methods of this class.

The *stackframe* provides a frame of reference for everything related to a thread's stack. You can think of it as a snapshot of a thread's internals, including the thread's program counter, local variables, referenced methods, referenced classes, and the current line number of execution. The methods used to retrieve this information follow a very basic syntax. For example, when you call the `getLineNumber()` method, the method returns the current line number of execution. This and other methods in this class are shown in Table 13.2.

Table 13.2. Methods in the `RemoteStackFrame` class.

Method	Purpose
`getLineNumber()`	Returns the current line number of execution
`getLocalVariable()`	Returns a named stack variable in the current stackframe

continues

Table 13.2. continued

Method	Purpose
getLocalVariables()	Returns an array of all valid local variables and method arguments for the stackframe
getMethodName()	Returns the method name that the stackframe references
getPC()	Returns the program counter that the stackframe references
getRemoteClass()	Returns the class that the stackframe references

The **RemoteStackVariable** Class

The RemoteStackVariable class is similar to the RemoteStackFrame class. Using this class, the caller can obtain information about a specific stack variable.

The class has three methods: getName(), getValue(), and inScope(). The getName() method is used to get the name of a variable on the stack. The getValue() method is used to get the value of a variable on the stack. The inScope method is used to tell whether the variable is accessible.

The **RemoteDebugger** Class

Because the RemoteDebugger class can instantiate a connection with the Java interpreter session being debugged, client applications use this class as an interface to the Java debugging classes. To create a client interface, you use a constructor. The RemoteDebugger class provides an overloaded constructor interface that allows for the two different ways the debugger can be instantiated.

The first constructor is used to attach the debugger to a current interpreter session. As you will learn in Chapter 23, you do this by first starting the Java interpreter with the -debug option. The interpreter passes back a password, which is then passed to the debugger when it is invoked. In addition to accepting the password as a parameter, the constructor accepts a String object that identifies

- The host running the current interpreter session
- The client using the DebuggerCallback interface to receive messages from the debugger
- A verbose flag to turn on internal debugger message text

Here is the syntax for the first constructor:

```
public RemoteDebugger(String host,
                      String password,
                      DebuggerCallback client,
                      boolean verbose) throws Exception
```

The second constructor is used to create a remote debugger that will start a client interpreter session. When you start the debugger directly, it in turn starts the Java interpreter with any parameters you passed on the command line. For this reason, the second constructor accepts arguments that are to be passed on to the interpreter. Other parameters allow the client using the `DebuggerCallback` interface to receive messages from the debugger, and others set a `verbose` flag to turn on or off internal debugger message text.

The syntax for the second constructor follows:

```
public RemoteDebugger(String javaArgs,
                      DebuggerCallback client,
                      boolean verbose) throws Exception
```

Methods in the `RemoteDebugger` class enable debugging techniques you will use when you debug your programs. These methods are shown in Table 13.3.

Table 13.3. Methods in the `RemoteDebugger` class.

Method	Purpose
addSystemThread()	Adds a system thread
close()	Closes the connection to the remote debugger
findClass()	Finds a specified class
freeMemory()	Gets a report of the free memory available to the Java interpreter being debugged
gc()	Frees all objects referenced by the debugger
get()	Gets an object from the remote object cache
getExceptionCatchList()	Gets the list of the exceptions on which the debugger will stop
getSourcePath()	Gets the source file path the client is currently using
itrace()	Turns instruction tracing on or off
listBreakpoints()	Gets a list of the current breakpoints
listClasses()	Gets a list of the currently known classes
listThreadGroups()	Gets a list of the currently known thread groups
run()	Loads and runs a runnable Java class
setSourcePath()	Sets the search path for source files
totalMemory()	Obtains a report of the total memory used by the Java interpreter being debugged
trace(boolean)	Turns method call tracing on or off

The **StackFrame** Class

The StackFrame class provides a wrapper for the stackframe of a suspended thread. This class has a very basic constructor and a single method, called toString(), that returns an object as a string.

Summary

The java.net package contains classes that provide an easy-to-use interface to basic network programming. By using these classes, you can enable your Java application or applet to participate in the world of network connectivity. Some classes provide an abstract framework for protocol-specific programming. These abstract classes may be implemented in the Java-enabled operating-system interface.

The sun.tools.debug class library adds built-in debugging support to the Java programming language. Examining the classes in this library should have given you insight into the debugging process.

The mail server and mail client examples in this chapter are good demonstrations of how easy it can be to write complex network programs in Java, enabling even novice programmers to develop working network applications. This is yet another example of the power that has been built into Java, making it *the* programming language to use today!

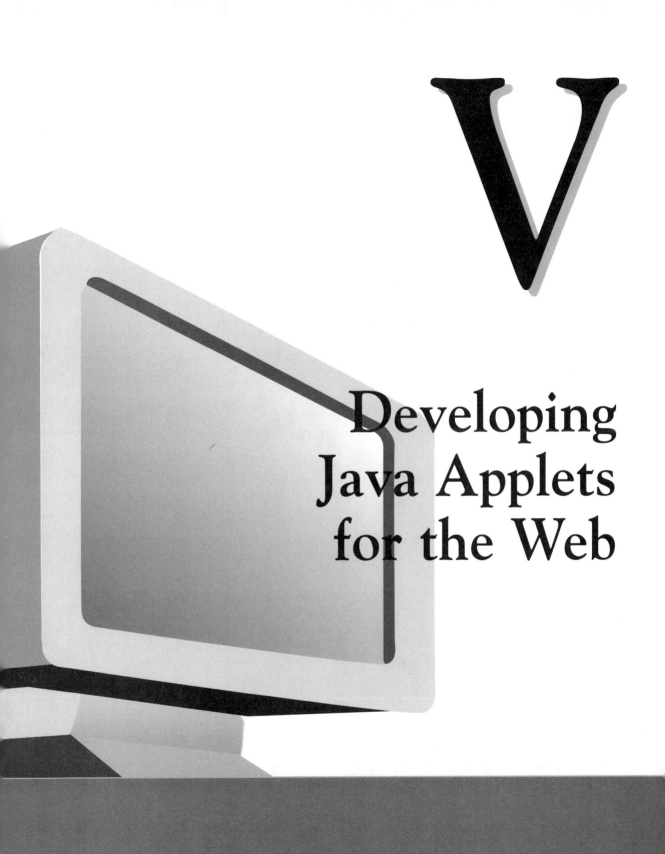

V

Developing
Java Applets
for the Web

14

Creating a Java Applet

Java is a powerful language that is just now coming into its own. If you've browsed the Web lately, you have probably seen applets in action. Stop by Sun Microsystems's home page, the Gamelan Web site, or thousands of other sites, and you will see applets come to life right before your eyes. Although applets using Java-based animation are great for their novelty and their capability to call attention to something, they do not fully demonstrate Java's power as a programming tool.

Beyond these beginning applets is the intermediate level of programming, which has multiple connotations. Some believe it begins when a programmer can write a program from scratch, while others contend that it begins with the ability to understand code and modify it to fit the circumstance.

For our purposes, the intermediate level begins when the programmer can allow interaction with the reader. This interaction is the key to distributed languages and the reason Java is getting so much attention. Formerly, the only way to allow for any degree of interaction across the Internet involved using CGI scripts written in languages native to the computer that stored them. Java is helping to change this while offering more power to a wider audience.

To create a CGI script, you must be able to write code in a language that the host computer can run. You also have to get permission to place the program on the host computer. Many Internet service providers (ISPs) have stopped giving this permission due to the computer resources these scripts require and security concerns. Java circumnavigates this issue by running its applets on the client computer instead of on the host, which reduces demands on the ISP's resources.

In this chapter you will construct two intermediate applets. These applets display features that can be found in larger applets without being overly lengthy or complex. The first applet, called `QuizMaker`, provides for a three-minute timer. Each step in building and testing the applet is described in detail. The second applet converts a color entered as three integers into a single number displayed in hexadecimal. The applet called `RGB2Hex` lets you preview the associated color. The end of this chapter gives some tips for debugging and provides a comparison of the two applets.

Conceptualization and Design of the `QuizMaker` Applet

The first step in designing an applet in Java or any other language is to have a good overall understanding of the tasks the applet will perform and for what purpose the applet will be used. Your goal is to create a detailed description of every object you will need to build the applet. This detailed description should specify the task or tasks the applet must perform without detailing how those tasks are to be accomplished.

When you complete the specification, it is easier to visualize how the applet will be presented to the user, what the applet will be used for, and what the user will be required to do to have the applet perform key tasks. Your specification may include a specific screen layout. Making a pencil drawing can help in determining all the pieces of information that need to be presented and deciding on an attractive layout.

After sketching the layout of the applet, describe each object in the applet in terms of its function. Many of these objects appear on the screen and can be defined from the screen layout. Other objects perform background tasks and are used to support the objects that appear in front of the user. These objects can be defined in terms of the tasks they perform. Don't worry if you do not recognize all the objects required while designing the applet. One of the advantages of an object-oriented language is the simplicity with which new objects can be added to provide functionality that was not considered during initial design.

The first applet you will build is called `QuizMaker`. The initial specification for `QuizMaker` follows:

The `QuizMaker` applet implements a simple timer to notify the user when three minutes are up. The user will press a button to start the timer. After the user starts the timer, the applet will provide a text display and a sound bite to indicate that the user should start the quiz. A different text and another sound bite will indicate that the user should stop. A picture will be included to enhance the visual appeal of the applet. The applet is simple to create and yet gives you experience working with the existing Java classes.

You can use the `QuizMaker` applet for the following:

- Letting readers take a timed quiz in one of your documents
- Letting readers track how far they can read in a certain time interval
- Letting readers stop and practice a task for a particular length of time before they continue reading
- Letting readers determine how long they have been working on something

Having described the tasks the applet will perform, you should now describe the layout of the applet. The layout doesn't have to be extravagant—a simple one drawn by hand is usually just fine. To lay out the `QuizMaker` applet, draw the key objects the user would see on a piece of paper:

- A picture of an hourglass
- A button the user can click on to start the timer
- An informational text label used to display messages, including `Start` and `Stop`, to the user

Figure 14.1 shows the initial layout for the applet. The picture of the hourglass is represented by the large rectangle on the right side of the figure. The start button is represented by the small rectangle in the lower left. Finally, the informational text is placed just above the start button.

Figure 14.1.
Layout of the `QuizMaker`
applet.

The next step is to describe the applet in terms of objects. For this example you will implement the applet using classes as they exist in the Java API. This will keep the code short and easy to follow. You implement the picture by creating an `Image` class object. The audio is provided using the `play()` method and supplying an appropriate audio file. The Java API also includes `Button` and `Label` classes, which are used for the button and the display, respectively.

Tip: Finding the appropriate class for a given function can be a matter of searching the API, your memory, and larger projects' libraries of objects created by others. Which class is appropriate for which function becomes more apparent as you work with the API and existing classes.

Defining the Applet Structure

Defining a class for each object is only part of determining the structure of the applet. Defining the applet structure also includes determining what objects are present when the applet starts, when new objects can be created, and how objects will communicate with each other. The `Object` super-class can be used to create new classes; however, for many programs there is a subclass already defined in Java that provides some or all of the functionality required.

The easiest way to create an applet is to extend the `Applet` class, which, as defined in the Java API, includes all the methods necessary for a working applet. The `QuizMaker` applet extends the `Applet` class to add the features described in the design. When the applet is started, it creates the objects such as the button, label, and picture. Because these objects are already defined by the Java API, you will not have to reinvent the wheel and can completely code the applet in only a few steps.

You still must define the communication between the objects. All communication is between these objects and the `QuizMaker` object. The event handler in the `Applet` class will be modified in the `QuizMaker` class to start tracking time when the button is pressed. Two new methods will be added to the `Applet` class: One will start the timer, and the other will stop it. When the timer expires, the `QuizMaker` object will direct the label to change its text.

The design of the `QuizMaker` applet is kept simple to provide experience in working with the `Applet` class. Chapter 16, "Applet Reuse," covers the redesign of the applet to take advantage of multiple threads.

Building the Applet

This section describes each step for building the QuizMaker applet. The comments before and after each section of code describe what the code does and important aspects of the syntax.

Step 1: Create an HTML Document to Test the Applet

The HTML document used to test the applet does not need to be extensive. However, it should include all the required HTML structure tags and display your applet prominently. Listing 14.1 is an example of an HTML document for the QuizMaker applet.

Listing 14.1. A sample HTML document.

```
<HTML>
<HEAD>
<TITLE> Quiz Maker</TITLE>
</HEAD>
<BODY>
<CENTER>
<H2> The QuizMaker Applet </H2>
<H3> Written with JAVA <H3>
<HR>
<APPLET CODE="QuizMaker" WIDTH=400 HEIGHT=300>
</APPLET>
</CENTER>
</BODY>
</HTML>
```

With this document available for testing, you can begin to define the classes in the QuizMaker applet. (See Chapter 15, "Creating Java-Powered Web Presentations with Applets," for complete details on creating HTML documents that use the <APPLET> tag.)

Step 2: Create a File Containing Included Classes

Java source files must be named with the .java extension and in a source file named for its class. For this reason, you should name the source code file for the new class QuizMaker.java.

Note: The Java compiler expects the source code to be in a file named with the `.java` extension. When the source file contains multiple class declarations, the source file must be named after the primary class declaration. For applications, the primary class is the class that contains the `main()` method. For applets, the primary class is the class that contains the `init()` and `run()` methods.

Because the `QuizMaker` applet uses existing Java classes, you must let the Java runtime environment know it must include these classes. This is done with the `import` statement. In all, the `QuizMaker` applet makes use of four packages: `java.applet`, `java.util`, `java.net`, and `java.awt`. The code to include these four packages follows:

```
import java.applet.*;
import java.util.*;
import java.net.*;
import java.awt.*;
```

Technical Note: Although you could be more specific and include only the classes you will actually be referencing, most applets make extensive use of the packages they import. For this reason, most programmers make the entire class available for importing on demand to prevent an extensive listing of classes. It is important to remember that the asterisk indicates that all classes in the package are to be made available and can be imported on demand. If you don't use the asterisk, the runtime environment will return an error indicating that the class to import could not be found. It is likewise important to include the semicolon at the end of each statement, or the compiler will generate an error.

Step 3: Declaring the **QuizMaker** Class

Now that all the existing classes you need are available, you can begin to create new classes. The following line of code creates the new class `QuizMaker` as an extension of the `Applet` class. The `Applet` class is public; the `QuizMaker` class will be as well. This means that other classes can create an instance of the `QuizMaker` class. It also allows the runtime environment to create an instance of the class. The code is as follows:

```
public class QuizMaker extends Applet {
```

The brace at the end of the line is significant. All the extensions to the `Applet` class must fall between the brace at the end of this line and its corresponding closing brace. In this case, the closing brace will be at the end of the applet code. In fact, you could put a brace on the following line, compile this code, and test it in your HTML file. It will appear as an empty box in the HTML document.

Step 4: Adding Class Variables

After declaring a new class, add code to the class so that it has some functionality beyond displaying an empty box. The applet should specify instance variables for each object you are adding to the class. Although instance variables must be declared outside the methods of the class and are usually placed at the beginning of the class, they can be placed anywhere before the method where they are used. The instance variable declaration lines for `QuizMaker` look like the following:

```
Image HglassImage; // Displays a picture of an hour glass
Button  RunButton; // Lets the user start the timer
Label   StatusLabel; // Displays the status to the user
URL HglassURL;  // URL of the applet
```

The first line declares an `Image` object to hold the picture to be displayed to the user. The second line declares a `Button` object, which enables the user to start the timer. The third declaration provides a read-only text area to display messages to the user. The final declaration provides a location for storing the URL of the applet.

The code can now be recompiled to test the syntax of these declarations. If you run the code again, note that there is no apparent change to the display. In the next step you will create methods that will modify the display.

Step 5: Define the Methods

All methods for a class must be included in the file prior to the closing brace that ends the class. This section details each method and recommends an order for coding and testing the methods used in the `QuizMaker` class. Several of the existing `Applet` class methods are overridden in the `QuizMaker` class. Two new methods, `runTimer` and `stopTimer`, are also added.

Step 5a: Define the `init()` Method

When the runtime environment loads the applet, it will run the `init()` method before executing the applet. This method is used to set up the screen size and create objects that are needed throughout the life of the applet. The `init()` method must be coded so that the other methods have objects with which to work. After the `init()` method is created, you can recompile and see the resulting changes when you run the applet. The code for the `init()` method is shown in Listing 14.2.

Listing 14.2. The `QuizMaker` class `init()` method.

```
public void init() {
 HglassURL = getCodeBase();   // Gets the URL for the applet

   // Get the picture to add to the screen
 HglassImage = getImage(HglassURL,"Hglass.gif");
```

continues

Listing 14.2. continued

```
// Add a label to display text which can not be altered by the user
add(StatusLabel = new Label("Press Run to start timer"));

// Add a button to start the timer
    add(RunButton = new Button("Run"));

 resize(400,300);    // Resizes the applet
paint(getGraphics());    // Display applet with the objects on the screen

play(HglassURL,"intro.au");  // Play an intro
play(HglassURL,"startTimer.au");  // Play the start message
play(HglassURL,"endTimer.au");  // Play the end message
    }
```

This `init()` method overrides the `init()` method that was originally defined for the `Applet` class and is public, so it can be called by other objects. Creating a public method is necessary so that the runtime environment can call it. `void` indicates that the method does not return a value.

The first action in this method is to get the base URL, or location on the file system, for the applet. The URL is stored because it is a required value for many of the methods used in `init()` and the other methods in this class. Using the URL, the `getImage()` method is invoked to create an `Image` object from the picture stored in the file `Hglass.gif`. The identifier for this `Image` object is `HglassImage`, which was declared as part of the class because the identifier will be needed when the class is drawn on the screen.

The next two lines of code use the `add()` method to add objects to the applet. This method is part of the API for the `Applet` class and makes it easy to add a new object to the applet. The first use of `add()` inserts a label object and sets the initial display to the string `"Press Run to start timer"`. The second use of `add()` inserts the button with the title Run. These objects are added at initialization so that they are presented to the user when the applet first appears. The objects will remain in existence for the life of the applet.

Because `QuizMaker` is an extension of the `Applet` class, the `resize` method of the `Applet` class is used in the next line to set the size of the applet to 400×300. This will have an effect only if the size is not set by the browser. The screen is then drawn using the `paint()` method. The `paint()` method will be overridden to draw the objects and images associated with the `QuizMaker` class, but it still must be passed the graphic on which to draw them. This is done by invoking the `getGraphic()` method. Notice that the methods can be combined.

The last three lines play an introductory audio clip and the two audio clips that will be used at the beginning and end of the timer. The `play()` method is available as part of the `Applet` class. It requires a URL and a filename. It looks for the file specified in the directory obtained from the URL. Playing all three audio clips is not really necessary, but the first time the audio clips are played there is a time delay that is inappropriate for use with the timer. Therefore, if you play them once in the introduction, they will sound appropriate when they are played later in the applet.

Step 5b: Define the `paint` Method

Like the `init()` method, the `paint()` method from the `Applet` class is overridden to provide different functionality for the `QuizMaker` class. The `paint()` method that you are creating is called in place of the one originally defined for the `Applet` class. Specifically, the `paint()` method is called when the program starts so that it can draw all the objects added during the initialization phase. In the `QuizMaker` class the `paint` method draws the `HglassImage` on the screen, as well as the button and the label. The code for this method is shown in Listing 14.3.

Listing 14.3. The `QuizMaker` class `paint()` method.

```
public void paint(Graphics g) {
 g.drawImage(HglassImage,250,10,this); // Draw the hour glass

 StatusLabel.resize(150,20);  // Resizes the label
 StatusLabel.move(10,10);   // Moves the label

 RunButton.resize(100,20);  // Resizes the button
 RunButton.move(20,40);   // Moves the button

   }
```

The methods used to draw the image and manipulate the button and label are all part of the Java API. Using the `drawImage()` method makes it easy to place the GIF image exactly where you want it on the applet. The other objects can be resized and moved to precise locations as well. So now you have completed the methods that affect the screen layout, but you need to create methods to run the timer.

Step 5c: Define the `runTimer()` Method

The timer itself is run from the `runTimer()` method. The `runTimer()` method is invoked when the user presses the button on the screen. When the button is pressed, a message indicating that the user should get ready is displayed and an audio clip telling the user to get ready and to start is played. When the audio clip stops, the displayed message is changed to indicate that the user should start.

The `runTimer()` method is responsible for storing the start time, which is created as a `date` object. The method converts the hours, minutes, and seconds of the start time to seconds. The value in seconds of the start time is stored in a local variable. This value is passed to the method that checks for the timer being expired. For more robustness, the day could be included in this value. The code for these activities is displayed in Listing 14.4.

Listing 14.4. The `QuizMaker` class `runTimer()` method.

```
/* Lets the user know to start,
 saves the start time and checks for time up */
   protected void runTimer() {
Date  StartTime;     // Holds the time the timer started
int  startSec;     // Start time in seconds

 // Let the user know to get ready
 StatusLabel.setText("Get the hour glass ready.");
 play(HglassURL,"startTimer.au");  // Play the start message
 StartTime = new Date();        // Get the starting time

 // Let the user know to start
 StatusLabel.setText("Time is slipping away.");

 // Calculate the start time in seconds
 // Get the number of seconds
 startSec = StartTime.getSeconds();
 // Convert minutes to seconds and add
 startSec += (StartTime.getMinutes() * 60);
 // Convert hours to seconds and add
 startSec += (StartTime.getHours() * 60 * 60);

 while (!stopTimer(startSec)) {}// Loop looking for the time up

 // Inform the user time is up
 StatusLabel.setText("The hour glass is empty!");
 play(HglassURL,"endTimer.au");
   }
```

The first line of the `runTimer()` method is protected so that it cannot be run by an arbitrary object; only the `QuizMaker` class and its subclasses have access to the `runTimer()` method. Currently, there are no other classes in the applet that use this method. However, if the applet is included as part of a larger project, creating the method as protected maintains the encapsulation expected in object-oriented programming. `void` following `protected` indicates that the method does not return any values. The next word, `runTimer`, is the name of the method.

The next two lines declare the instance variables `StartTime` and `startSec`. `StartTime` is a local instance of the `Date` object. It is declared locally because none of the other methods need to access these values, so there is no reason to share them. It is an object because that is what is returned by the `Date()` constructor. The variable `startSec` is declared as an integer value. This variable stores the time value of the `StartTime` object converted to seconds. This variable is created locally and then passed to the `EndTimer` method. The advantage of passing the variable as opposed to making it available to the entire class is that it prevents accidental manipulation of this important value.

The next line displays new text to the user using the `StatusLabel` object. The text of the label can be changed while the program is running using the `setText()` method of the `Label` class so that it can be used for displaying the computed value. To call this method for the correct object, the applet must have a name to reference the object.

The audio clip is played in the same manner as it was in the `init()` method. The URL object is defined at the class level, so it is available in this method. The audio clip instructs the user to get ready for the timer to start and then says Go.

The constructor `Date()` is used to create a new `Date` object. Used without parameters as it is here, constructor returns a `Date` object containing the current time and date. This object is then designated as `StartTime`.

Next, the text `Time is slipping away.` is displayed to the user on the `Label` object. The label displayed to the user is modified by the same means in several places. The text is modified using the `SetText(text)` method of the `Label` class. This method takes the new text as a parameter and causes the `StatusLabel` object to display it. Note that this does not create a new object, nor does it modify the text directly. `SetText(text)` instructs the `Label` object, in this case, `StatusLabel`, to change its own text.

The starting time in seconds is then calculated. First, the `getSeconds()` method of the `Date` class is used to get the seconds value in the starting time. This value is stored in the `startSec` variable. Second, the `getMinutes()` method returns the minutes value from the starting time. The number of minutes is multiplied by 60 to get the number of seconds, which is added to the value in `startSec` using the `+=` operator. This operator is used again to add the number of seconds to the starting time.

The method then loops, calling the `stopTimer(int)` method. This method returns `false` when the current time is less than three minutes after the time passed to it. It returns `true` if the current time is more than three minutes after the time passed to it. The loop continues until the `stopTimer(int)` method returns `true`. In Chapter 16 you will modify the `QuizMaker` applet so that it will pause and wait for time to pass, but this loop will suffice for the present example.

When the `stopTimer(int)` method returns `true`, the remainder of the `runTimer()` method is executed. It changes the label to indicate to the user that the hourglass is empty. It also plays an audio clip to the user to indicate that the timer has expired.

Step 5d: Define the `stopTimer()` Method

As described previously, the `stopTimer()` method checks to see if the current time is more than 180 seconds after the time passed in as a parameter. If this condition is true, the method returns `true`; otherwise, it returns `false`. The code for the `stopTimer()` method is shown in Listing 14.5.

Listing 14.5. The `QuizMaker` class `stopTimer()` method.

```
/* Checks the current system time to determine if 180 seconds has
 elapsed since start */
   protected boolean stopTimer(int startSec) {
 int stopSec;
```

continues

Listing 14.5. continued

```
Date StopTime = new Date();       // Get the new time
stopSec = StopTime.getSeconds(); // Get the number of seconds
// Convert minutes to seconds and add
stopSec += (StopTime.getMinutes() * 60);
// Convert hours to seconds and add
stopSec += (StopTime.getHours() * 60 * 60);
if ((stopSec - startSec) > 180) {
 return true;   // True means time has elapsed
} else {
 return false;   // False means time has not elapsed
}
   }
```

The stopTimer() method is protected because it would not make sense for another object to find out that the timer had expired. Only this object knows the start time, so only this object can do a valid comparison. The method returns a boolean value, so boolean is placed between protected and the method name.

After the method name, the type of the input variable is listed in parentheses. The integer input is expected to be the time, in seconds, when the timer was started. This could have been made a class variable of the QuizMaker class. However, that would have made it available to change by any method in the class, and only runTimer() really needs to change the value. Because only stopTimer() needs to read it, the value is passed in as a parameter.

In the lines after the declaration, stopTimer() gets the current time and converts it to seconds in the same manner as runTimer(). It then uses an if statement to determine when the difference in the number of seconds is greater than 180, meaning that more than three minutes have elapsed. Depending on the results of the if statement, the boolean value true or false is returned. Note that each must be stated explicitly and must follow the word return.

You have now finished all the methods that control the screen display and the timer. You still need to create a method that calls the runTimer() method. Keep in mind that the timer is started when the button is pressed. Pressing the button is a user event, so the next method you will define is the event handler.

Step 5e: Define the handleEvent() Method

The handleEvent() method is triggered by the runtime environment when a user, or other outside force, triggers an event. *Events* include activities such as a button being pressed or a window being resized. Events that are not handled by the method defined here will be handled by the handleEvent() method in one of the superclasses, such as the Applet class. In this sense the handleEvent() method is being extended, not overridden. The code for the method is shown in Listing 14.6.

Listing 14.6. The `QuizMaker` class `handleEvent()` method.

```
/* Event handler to detect when the button on the window is pressed */
    public boolean handleEvent(Event e) {
// If the window is closed end the program
 if (e.id == Event.WINDOW_DESTROY) {
     System.exit(0);
 }
// If the button is pressed start timer
 if (e.target instanceof Button) {
  runTimer();      // Start the timer
  return true;     // Return true so super does not act on event
 }
 return false;      // Return false so super can act on event
    }
  //The final brace ends the QuizMaker class
}
```

The `handleEvent()` method is public because this method will be invoked from the runtime environment. The method will return `true` if it successfully handles the event and `false` otherwise; therefore, a boolean return value is specified. The name `handleEvent` is followed by the input declaration. The event is passed an `Event` object named `e`.

In the first `if` statement, the event handler checks to see if `e` is caused by the window being closed by checking the `id` property of the `Event` object. If the window is being closed, this property will be equal to `WINDOW_DESTROY`, and the class exits using the `System.exit(0)` method. Otherwise, the `handleEvent()` method checks for the button being pressed.

The `handleEvent()` method determines that a button is being pressed by checking the target property of the `Event` object. If this property is a button, it means a button is being pressed. There is only one button in the `QuizMaker` applet, so the `runTimer()` method is triggered to run the timer. When it can handle the event, the `handleEvent()` method returns `true`. If an event other than the two events handled here should occur, the method will return `false` and allow the `handleEvent()` method in a superclass to respond to the event.

Step 6: Compile the Applet

Now that all the methods have been created, you can compile the completed applet. But before doing so, be sure that your path includes the directory containing the Java compiler, as specified in Chapter 2, "Getting Started with the JDK." When you compile the `QuizMaker.java` file, the Java compiler will create the `QuizMaker.class` file, which the runtime environment can load. When your applet has successfully compiled, you can view it using your World Wide Web browser or the Java applet viewer.

To compile `QuizMaker` using a graphical compiler, follow these steps:

1. Drop the `QuizMaker.java` file onto the compiler or select Open from the compiler's File menu.

2. Place the compiled output file called `QuizMaker.class` in the same directory as the source.

To compile `QuizMaker` using a command-line compiler, follow these steps:

1. Change to the directory containing the source code and type the following at the command prompt:

   ```
   javac QuizMaker.java
   ```

2. Place the compiled output file, called `QuizMaker.class`, in the same directory as the source.

Note: The `javac` command invokes the Java compiler. Note that you must pass the compiler the entire filename, including the `.java` extension. Also note that the name is case sensitive. If you do not pass the full filename with the correct extension in the correct case, the compiler will return an error saying it could not find your file.

The Finished Applet

Figure 14.2 shows the finished applet. Although this applet is a somewhat contrived example that extends only one class, it should give you practice in creating an applet and using some of the Java classes. The next applet example is more complex and will give you experience working with multiple objects in an applet.

Figure 14.2.
The `QuizMaker` *applet.*

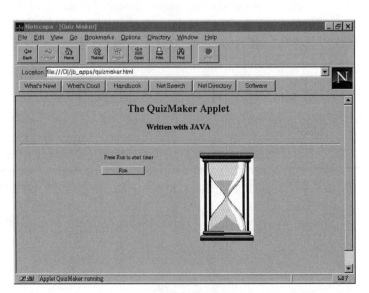

The full text of the completed applet is shown in Listing 14.7. After successfully compiling and running the QuizMaker applet, as shown earlier, try modifying some of the parameters to see the results. For example, lengthen or shorten the wait time, change the sizes of the objects, and move the objects to other locations. You might also try adding pictures, text, or buttons. This will give you practice in working with objects in Java before you move on to the next applet.

Listing 14.7. The QuizMaker applet.

```java
import java.awt.*;
import java.applet.*;
import java.util.*;
import java.net.*;

/**
 * Peter Norton's  Guide to Programming Java * The QuizMaker Applet
 * Acts as a three minute timer. Plays an audio message to start and
 * displays a start message. Plays an audio message at the end with
 * another display message.
 */

public class QuizMaker extends Applet {
Image  HglassImage; // Displays a picture of an hour glass
Button  RunButton; // Lets the user start the timer
Label   StatusLabel; // Displays the status to the user
URL  HglassURL; // URL of the applet

    public void init() {
    // Get the picture to add to the screen
 HglassImage = getImage(getCodeBase(),"Hglass.gif");

 // Add a label to display text which can not be altered by the user
 add(StatusLabel = new Label("Press Run to start timer"));

 // Add a button to start the timer
     add(RunButton = new Button("Run"));

  resize(400,300);      // Resizes the applet
 paint(getGraphics());    // Display applet with the objects on the screen

 HglassURL = getCodeBase();    // Gets the URL for the applet
 play(HglassURL,"intro.au");   // Play an intro
 play(HglassURL,"startTimer.au");  // Play the start message
 play(HglassURL,"endTimer.au");  // Play the end message
    }

    public void paint(Graphics g) {
 g.drawImage(HglassImage,250,10,this); // Draw the hour glass

 StatusLabel.resize(150,20);  // Resizes the label
 StatusLabel.move(10,10);   // Moves the label

 RunButton.resize(100,20);  // Resizes the button
 RunButton.move(20,40);    // Moves the button

    }
```

continues

Listing 14.7. continued

```java
    /* Lets the user know to start, saves the start time
       and checks for time up */
    protected void runTimer() {
Date  StartTime;     // Holds the time the timer started
int  startSec;      // Start time in seconds

// Let the user know to get ready
StatusLabel.setText("Get the hour glass ready.");
play(HglassURL,"startTimer.au");  // Play the start message
StartTime = new Date();   // Get the starting time

// Let the user know to start
StatusLabel.setText("Time is slipping away.");

// Calculate the start time in seconds
startSec = StartTime.getSeconds(); // Get the number of seconds
startSec += (StartTime.getMinutes() * 60); // Add # of minutes times 60

while (!stopTimer(startSec)) {} // Loop looking for the time up

// Inform the user the hour glass is empty
StatusLabel.setText("The hour glass is empty!");
play(HglassURL,"endTimer.au");
    }

    /* Checks the current system time to determine if 180 seconds
       has elapsed since start */
    protected boolean stopTimer(int startSec) {
int stopSec;

Date StopTime = new Date();  // Get the new time
stopSec = StopTime.getSeconds(); // Get the number of seconds
stopSec += (StopTime.getMinutes() * 60); // Add # of minutes times 60
if ((stopSec - startSec) > 180) {
 return true;    // True means time has elapsed
} else {
 return false;   // False means time has not elapsed
}
    }

    /* Event handler to detect when the button on the window is pressed */
    public boolean handleEvent(Event e) {
int myint;
// If the window is closed end the program
 if (e.id == Event.WINDOW_DESTROY) {
     System.exit(0);
 }
// If the button is pressed start timer
 if (e.target instanceof Button) {
  runTimer();     // Start the timer
  return true;    // Return true so super does not act on event
 }
 return false;     // Return false so super can act on event
    }
}
```

Creating a Second Applet

The second applet you create in this chapter is actually a new version of a CGI script that has been used on the Internet for some time. It converts a set of red, green, and blue (RGB) integer values into a single hex number. The conversion of RGB values to hex numbers is important on the World Wide Web because solid-color backgrounds are entered into HTML documents in hex. An added twist here is enabling readers to see the color displayed as a result of the RGB values they enter; this shows just some of what is possible with Java.

This applet, RGB2Hex, introduces several complexities not found in the QuizMaker applet. RGB2Hex shows how multiple classes can be extended in the same Java file and how multiple objects in the same applet can communicate with one another. RGB2Hex also shows how some of the objects you used in the previous example can be used in different ways. As you go along, feel free to add to or modify the RGB2Hex applet to suit your taste.

Conceptualization and Design of the Applet

As with the first applet, this section describes how to progress from an initial description of the applet to a complete design. The specification for the RGB2Hex applet is rather simple:

> The applet allows the user to enter values for the red, green, and blue components of a color. When the user finishes entering these values, the applet displays the corresponding color and the hexadecimal value for the color.

By expanding this definition, you will see that the applet has three fields for entering numbers, each with an appropriate label. The applet needs a place to display the hexadecimal result, and a portion of the screen must be available to display the color. The user must have a means to indicate that new numbers have been entered and that the applet should display the new color and hexadecimal value by using a button labeled Display. Given this information, you can construct a screen layout.

Figure 14.3 shows the initial layout for the applet. To keep the applet short, the screen layout is a simple rectangle with the top used for data entry and the bottom used to display the color. There is a button to indicate that the user has finished entering data in the middle with the display field for the hexadecimal value to the right of it.

Figure 14.3.
Screen layout for the
RGB2Hex *applet.*

The layout shown here could be divided into objects in many ways. In fact, you could create the entire applet as an instance of one object again. However, the code is easier to understand if you group the objects on the screen into an object containing controls and an object for the color display.

The field to display the results could be considered a separate object, but for simplicity it is created as part of the controls. This object also contains the labels, text entry fields, and display button, all of which are themselves objects. This completes the design of the applet, and you can move on to define the structure.

Defining the Applet Structure

As with the previous example, you must define which objects are present when the applet starts, when new objects are created, and how objects will communicate with each other. For the RGB2Hex applet, multiple existing Java classes are extended to provide the classes needed. Unlike the previous example, the RGB2Hex applet extends multiple classes, and the objects created must interface with one another.

The existing Canvas class is extended and used to display the color desired. Canvas supplies a constructor to create the object and a paint method to paint the background with the default background color. Canvas is generic and can be subclassed to provide a place to display the color the user has entered. It is extended so that the values entered by the user are stored as part of the object.

The paint method from the Canvas class is overridden. The new paint() method colors the object using the three internal values. A redraw method is added to update the internal values and call the paint method. The redraw method also returns the hexadecimal value for the color displayed.

The object for the controls is created by extending the Panel class, a generic container that can be used to hold other objects and display them in various ways on the screen. For the purpose of this applet, the object must hold three labels, three text entry fields, one button, and one display field. Each of these items is an object that will be created using existing classes. The objects are displayed in a standard grid layout. (The GridLayout is also an object defined in Java.)

Now that each object has been described, you must determine how they are created. The RGB2Hex applet is an extension of the Applet class. This class includes an init() method, which is called when the applet is created, as well as the canvas and the panel, which are created as part of the init() method for the applet. There is no need to create more than one instance of these objects as part of this applet.

The interactions between the objects are straightforward. When the button is pushed, the new color is displayed and the new hexadecimal value appears. To do this, the values entered in the text entry fields are passed to the canvas object. Either the canvas object or the control object could calculate the hexadecimal value; in this case, it is the canvas object. This value must be returned to the controls for display.

Building the Applet

Now that you have completed the structure of the applet, you can begin to actually build it. Although the construction of the code is not broken into separate steps as the first example, this section does provide a detailed description of each portion of the code. The RGB2Hex applet extends the Applet class and creates several accompanying classes. The code for each class is presented and a brief description of how the class works is given.

Creating the RGB2Hex Class

The Applet class is extended to create the RGB2Hex class, as shown in Listing 14.8. This class is responsible for creating additional objects and enabling the controls. The overall layout is the Java standard BorderLayout. This allows for placement of objects in North, South, East, West, and Center locations. The two objects you are creating for this applet will be in the North and Center locations. As part of initialization, the add() method is used to add the canvas and the controls to the frame. When the applet starts, it goes through initialization and then enables the controls. Then it adds itself to the frame and resizes the frame to 300×300.

Listing 14.8. The RGB2Hex class.

```java
public class RGB2Hex extends Applet {
    RGBcontrols controls;

    public void init() {
setLayout(new BorderLayout());
RGBcanvas c = new RGBcanvas();
add("Center", c);
add("North", controls = new RGBcontrols(c));
    }

    public void doColor() {
controls.enable();
    }

    public void stop() {
controls.disable();
    }

    public boolean handleEvent(Event e) {
if (e.id == Event.WINDOW_DESTROY) {
    System.exit(0);
}
return false;
    }
}
```

This completes the RGB2Hex class. However, this applet has been designed to use multiple classes. These classes can all be created in the same .java file. The remainder of this section describes the other classes.

Creating the RGBcanvas Class

The second class to create is the RGBcanvas class, as shown in Listing 14.9. This class is called in the second line of the init() method in the RGB2Hex class to create the object c. This object displays the color on the basis of the values entered by the user. The class is created by extending the Canvas class, which is part of the Java API.

The RGBcanvas class stores the three values the color is created from and the color value. The three RGB values are stored as integers. The color is stored as a Color object that is returned by the Java method Color(int, int, int) in the Color class, which encapsulates the RGB colors.

Three Color constructors can be used to create a Color object. The constructor used here takes the red, green, and blue values as separate integer parameters. The other constructors allow the red, green, and blue values to be specified as portions of a single integer or a floating-point value.

Two methods of the original Canvas are replaced. A new paint() method overrides the paint() method defined in the Canvas class. A new redraw() method replaces the existing Canvas class redraw() method.

The new paint() method colors the canvas using the three values, which are internal to the RGBcanvas class. It uses the bounds method for the Rectangle class to determine the size of the rectangle to color. The method creates a new color using the three values stored internally and then stores this value in the internal variable createColor. Then paint() sets the default color for the RGBcanvas to the newly created color and paints a rectangle the size of the RGBcanvas.

The redraw() method is created to load the numbers it receives as inputs into the internal values of the object. It then calls the repaint() method to color the object. repaint() is defined in the Component class and inherited by the Canvas class. It calls paint to repaint the Canvas. After calling the repaint() method, redraw() creates a hexadecimal value based on the values entered by the user and returns it to the calling method.

Listing 14.9. The RGBcanvas class first draft.

```
class RGBcanvas extends Canvas {
    int   RedValue = 12;
    int   GreenValue = 156;
    int    blueValue = 88;
    Color  createColor;
    String  HexString;
    String  HexFinal;

    public void paint(Graphics g) {
Rectangle r = bounds();

createColor = new Color(RedValue, GreenValue, blueValue);
g.setColor(createColor);
g.fillRect(0,0,r.width,r.height);
    }

    public String redraw(int red, int green, int blue) {
String HexString;
```

```
    this.RedValue = red;
    this.GreenValue = green;
    this.blueValue = blue;
    repaint();
    HexString = Integer.toString(red,16);
    while (HexString.length() < 2)
        HexString = "0" + HexString;
    HexFinal = HexString.toUpperCase();

    HexString = Integer.toString(green,16);
    while (HexString.length() < 2)
        HexString = "0" + HexString;
    HexFinal = HexFinal + HexString.toUpperCase();

    HexString = Integer.toString(blue,16);
    while (HexString.length() < 2)
        HexString = "0" + HexString;
    HexFinal = HexFinal + HexString.toUpperCase();

    return HexFinal;
        }
}
```

This code will work but is difficult to read because of the complicated conversion used to create the hexadecimal string. To simplify this code, the redraw method needs an easy way to convert from an integer in base 10 to hex. You could use the toString method of the Integer class to do the conversion, but this does not give the exact format desired. The redraw method must be sure the string returned has two characters and that the letters are uppercase.

Creating the HexInt Class

The simplest way to provide the conversion needed is to create a new class called HexInt, as shown in Listing 14.10. This class stores an integer and returns its value as a hexadecimal. The method toHexString(int) will return a string with the number of characters specified in the input parameter. The method uses the while statement to check that the string has fewer characters than the input.

Listing 14.10. The HexInt class.

```
class HexInt {
    int HInt;

    public HexInt(int AnInteger){
HInt = AnInteger;
}
    public String toHexString(int StrLen) {
String HexString;

HexString = Integer.toString(HInt,16);
```

continues

Listing 14.10. continued

```
while (HexString.length() < StrLen)
    HexString = "0" + HexString;
return HexString.toUpperCase();
    }
}
```

This class simplifies the redraw method in the RGBcanvas class. The HexInt class also allows the hexadecimal result to be calculated with a single assignment statement.

Error Handling for RGBcanvas

You can further enhance the RGBcanvas class by adding error handling. Despite the label giving the valid range, there is always the possibility that a user will enter values outside the valid range. If the values entered exceed the acceptable limits, the applet should return an error message.

Error checking could be added to the controls to prevent the applet from invoking the redraw() method when the user enters invalid values. However, the redraw() method could be invoked from some other location that could also supply an incorrect value. Therefore, error checking is added to the Canvas class in the redraw() method.

The redraw() method must check that each of its inputs is valid. In this case, valid inputs are numbers between 0 and 255. If redraw() receives an input outside this range, it must return an error string instead of the hexadecimal string and leave the color of the canvas unchanged. The error string used here is "Learn to count", but you can use any string. The method uses an if statement to check for integers outside the range. The double pipe symbols ¦¦ represent the logical OR operator. Here's the code for error checking the red color value:

```
if ((red < 0) ¦¦ (red > 255)) {
  return "Learn to count";
 }
```

All three error checks could be combined into one if statement. However, they are separated for clarity's sake. When the caller receives the message back from the Canvas object, it does not know whether the color changed. The caller simply displays the text string in the block provided and allows the user to decide what to do next. It is up to the user to determine that the input values were outside the specified range and to enter new values. However, incorrect values do not cause the program to abort, nor do they affect any other part of the program.

This method of error checking does not handle the possibility that the user may enter text instead of a number. If text is entered, the parseInt() method will generate an error. This will not be returned to the user, but because of the object-oriented nature of Java, this type of error will not cause a problem for the running applet. Although it is not needed for the users of this applet, code could be added to check each entry prior to converting it to an integer.

The final RGBcanvas class using the HexInt class and including error handling is shown in Listing 14.11.

Listing 14.11. The revised RGBcanvas class.

```
class RGBcanvas extends Canvas {
    int   RedValue = 12;
    int   GreenValue = 156;
    int   blueValue = 88;
    Color  createColor;

    public void paint(Graphics g) {
Rectangle r = bounds();

createColor = new Color(RedValue, GreenValue, blueValue);
g.setColor(createColor);
g.fillRect(0,0,r.width,r.height);
    }

    public String redraw(int red, int green, int blue) {
String HexString;

this.RedValue = red;
this.GreenValue = green;
this.blueValue = blue;
    if ((red < 0) || (red > 255)){
  return "Learn to count";
}
if ((green < 0) || (green > 255)){
  return "Learn to count";
}
if ((blue < 0) || (blue > 255)){
  return "Learn to count";
}
repaint();
HexString = new HexInt(red).toHexString(2) + new HexInt(green).toHexString(2)
+ new HexInt(blue).toHexString(2);
  return HexString;
    }
}
```

Now that the display on the canvas looks good, you must create a class to operate the controls you provide for the user.

Creating the RGBcontrols Class

The RGBcontrols class shown in Listing 14.12 provides a place for data entry and display. The control extends the existing Panel class. The class contains eight objects arranged in a grid pattern. GridLayout allows the developer to specify a certain number of rows and columns. In this case, there are four rows and two columns. The grid is filled from left to right and from top to bottom. Each of the objects it contains are instances of defined Java objects.

TextField enables the user to edit a single line of text. The class has four possible constructors. The constructor used here takes a single string parameter and uses it as the initialization string for the new field. The TextField class is a subclass of TextComponent, which supplies a getText() method that returns text in the TextComponent. Because each field must be referenced individually to retrieve the values the user enters, the objects are given identifiers that are internal to the Panel class: redField, greenField, and blueField.

The labels for the data entry fields are created using the Label class from the Java API. The Label class displays a single line of read-only text. The class allows for the alignment to be specified as LEFT, RIGHT, or CENTER. In this case, the default alignment, LEFT, is used. The labels for the text entry fields are placed to the left of the fields themselves. The applet does not need to update these objects, so they are not explicitly named. They are created using the new command when they are added to the RGBcontrols object.

The object used to display the hexadecimal code is called HexValue and is declared as part of the RGBcontrols class. It must be explicitly named so that it can be referred to and its setText() method invoked to change the display value. The value returned from the RGBcanvas class redraw() method is used as input to the setText() method.

The button used to signal that the user has finished entering new values and would like to see the results is created using the Button class from the Java API. This is another object that the applet does not need to update. Therefore, the object does not need a name and is created when it is added to the layout. Here, the button is created as an instance of the class Button. This class supplies a constructor, which takes a string parameter and uses it as the label for the button.

Only one method in the Canvas class must be overridden: the action() method, which is defined in the Component class and triggered any time an action occurs in a component. There is only one action to which the applet responds in this class—pressing the button. If there were multiple actions, you could use a switch statement to determine which action had occurred.

In this case, an if statement at the beginning of the method checks for the triggering event (pressing a button). There is only one button in the object, so there is no need to determine which button was pressed. If additional buttons were added, the method could use a switch statement to determine which button was pressed by checking the label of the button that triggered the event.

When the button is pressed, the action() method uses the getText() method to get the strings in the text fields. action() then uses the trim() method, defined as part of the String class, to remove any whitespace from around the text. Next, action() creates integers from the strings using the parseInt() method. To do this, it must create an instance of the Integer object for each string.

When the conversion is complete, action() passes the resulting integers to the redraw() method of the Canvas object. The string returned from redraw() is displayed by the HexValue object using the setText() method, defined as part of the TextComponent class, of which TextField is a subclass.

Listing 14.12. The **RGBcontrols** class.

```
class RGBcontrols extends Panel {
   TextField redField; /* Field to enter the value for red */
   TextField greenField; /* Field to enter the value for green */
   TextField blueField; /* Field to enter the value for blue */
   Label HexValue; /* Location to display the hex value */
    RGBcanvas canvas;

    public RGBcontrols(RGBcanvas canvas) { /* primary method declaration */
 setLayout(new GridLayout(4,2));
 this.canvas = canvas;
 add(new Label("RED        Enter 0 to 255"));
 add(redField = new TextField("12"));
 add(new Label("GREEN   Enter 0 to 255"));
 add(greenField  = new TextField("156"));
 add(new Label("BLUE       Enter 0 to 255"));
 add(blueField = new TextField("88"));
 add(new Button("Display"));
 add(HexValue = new Label(""));
    }

    public boolean action(Event ev, Object arg) {
 if (ev.target instanceof Button) {
    HexValue.setText(canvas.redraw(
 Integer.parseInt(redField.getText().trim()),
 Integer.parseInt(greenField.getText().trim()),
 Integer.parseInt(blueField.getText().trim())));

    return true;
 }

 return false;
    }
}
```

This completes the creation of the classes needed for the RGB2Hex applet. The next section provides all the code needed to create the applet in its final form.

The Finished Applet

Figure 14.4 shows how the RGB2Hex applet looks in the Netscape Navigator. For additional practice in modifying Java objects, you might move the display box for the hex number from the RGBcontrols object to the RGBcanvas object. Be sure to modify the paint of the canvas so the rectangle that changes color does not cover the text field displaying the hexadecimal number.

The complete text for the RGB2Hex applet is shown in Listing 14.13. When you compile the source code for the applet, one class file will be created for each declared class. To run the applet, name the RGB2Hex class in the <APPLET> tag of an HTML document. The RGB2Hex class calls the other class files when they are needed.

Figure 14.4.
The RGB2Hex *applet in Netscape.*

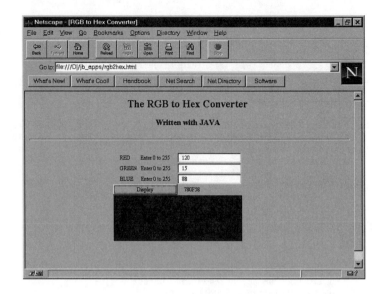

Listing 14.13. The **RGB2Hex** applet.

```java
import java.awt.*;
import java.applet.*;

/**
 * Peter Norton's  Guide to Java Programming * The RGB2Hex Applet
 * Converts Red, Green, and Blue values entered by the user to a
 * hexidecimal color code and displays the color. Can be run either
 * as a standalone application by typing "java RGB2Hex" or as an applet.
 */

public class RGB2Hex extends Applet {
    RGBcontrols controls;
    TextField test1;

    public void init() {
setLayout(new BorderLayout());
RGBcanvas c = new RGBcanvas();
add("Center", c);
add("North", controls = new RGBcontrols(c));
    }

    public void doColor() {
controls.enable();
    }

    public void stop() {
controls.disable();
    }

    public boolean handleEvent(Event e) {
if (e.id == Event.WINDOW_DESTROY) {
    System.exit(0);
}
```

```
    return false;
    }

    public static void main(String args[]) {
Frame f = new Frame("RGB2Hex");
RGB2Hex RGB2Hex = new RGB2Hex();

RGB2Hex.init();
RGB2Hex.doColor();

f.add("Center", RGB2Hex);
f.resize(300, 300);
f.show();
    }
}

/* Provides a hexidecimal representation of an integer */
class HexInt {
    int HInt;

    public HexInt(int AnInteger){
HInt = AnInteger;
    }

    public String toHexString(int StrLen) {
String HexString;

HexString = Integer.toString(HInt,16);
while (HexString.length() < StrLen)
    HexString = "0" + HexString;
return HexString.toUpperCase();
    }
}

/* Provides an object to display a color */
class RGBcanvas extends Canvas {
    int  RedValue = 12;
    int  GreenValue = 156;
    int   blueValue = 88;
    Color  createColor;

    public void paint(Graphics g) {
Rectangle r = bounds();

createColor = new Color(RedValue, GreenValue, blueValue);
g.setColor(createColor);
g.fillRect(0,0,r.width,r.height);
    }

    public String redraw(int red, int green, int blue) {
String HexString;

this.RedValue = red;
this.GreenValue = green;
this.blueValue = blue;
    if ((red < 0) ¦¦ (red > 255)){
 return "Learn to count";
}
```

continues

Listing 14.13. continued

```
if ((green < 0) || (green > 255)){
 return "Learn to count";
 }
if ((blue < 0) || (blue > 255)){
 return "Learn to count";
 }
repaint();
HexString = new HexInt(red).toHexString(2) + new HexInt(green).toHexString(2)
➥+ new HexInt(blue).toHexString(2);
 return HexString;
    }
}

/* Provides for user entry of RGB values and displays hexidecimal */
class RGBcontrols extends Panel {
   TextField redField; /* Field to enter the value for red */
   TextField greenField;/* Field to enter the value for green */
   TextField blueField; /* Field to enter the value for blue */
   Label HexValue; /* Location to display the hex value */
    RGBcanvas canvas;

    public RGBcontrols(RGBcanvas canvas) { /* primary method declaration */
   setLayout(new GridLayout(4,2));
   this.canvas = canvas;
   add(new Label("RED        Enter 0 to 255"));
   add(redField = new TextField("12", 4));
   add(new Label("GREEN    Enter 0 to 255"));
   add(greenField  = new TextField("156", 4));
   add(new Label("BLUE       Enter 0 to 255"));
   add(blueField = new TextField("88",4));
   add(new Button("Display"));
   add(HexValue = new Label(""));
    }

    public boolean action(Event ev, Object arg) {
   if (ev.target instanceof Button) {
      HexValue.setText(canvas.redraw(
    Integer.parseInt(redField.getText().trim()),
    Integer.parseInt(greenField.getText().trim()),
    Integer.parseInt(blueField.getText().trim())));

      return true;
   }

   return false;
    }
}
```

Comparing the **QuizMaker** Applet with the **RGB2Hex** Applet

The RGB2Hex applet has some similarities to the QuizMaker applet. Both are created by extending the Java Applet class. Some of the same classes, buttons, and labels are used in both applets, although they appear different on the display. Both applets depend on the init() method to create additional objects. Both applets trap and handle user events.

The applets each demonstrate different points. The first example illustrates that applets do not have to define multiple new classes. The second example shows that objects can be created, used, and displayed without being explicitly named. It also demonstrates how multiple objects in an applet can work together without one having to create the other.

The overall organization in each applet is different as well. The QuizMaker applet, containing a single class, leaves the handling of events up to that class. The RGB2Hex applet divides the work better because it has three classes. The controls can handle responding to user events while the Canvas handles the display. The RGB2Hex class is responsible for creating instances of the other two classes and handles the starting and stopping of the applet.

The only remaining challenge in creating the applets in this chapter is testing and debugging the code. Testing is important in creating software because errors can be costly in terms of performance and user confidence. The next section provides some suggestions for testing and debugging Java applets.

Testing and Debugging

A well-designed applet is easy to test and debug; the best check against logic problems is a well-thought-out design. Object-oriented languages, such as Java, assist with this by encapsulating information and preventing the programmer from making modifications that can have unexpected effects on other portions of the code. This does not mean that all code written in Java will be bug free. It is still possible to expect an object to behave in one manner and for its actual behavior be different.

The easiest type of problem to fix is a compiler error. Some of the basic problems that will cause the compiler to complain include the following:

- Lines missing the ending ;
- Mismatched braces—for example, a { without a matching }, or a } without a matching {
- Instance variables that are not declared
- Typos
- if statements missing ()s

The errors generated by the Java compiler often pinpoint the problems exactly, yet it is also common for one of the listed mistakes to generate several unrelated compiler errors. For example, not declaring an instance variable that is passed to a method could result in a compiler error saying the method is not defined for the type of parameters specified. Missing braces can result in other errors, including undefined variables.

Java is case sensitive: `TextField` and `textfield` are considered two different objects; therefore, verify the case of each letter of identifiers that are not recognized by the compiler.

There are several steps you can take to minimize both compiler and runtime errors:

- Keep methods short; this makes it easier to remember what the method is trying to accomplish and to create the code for it.

- Add one portion of code at a time; this increases your ability to determine where a particular problem is introduced.

- Compile after every change and run after any change that will be apparent to make it easier to see problems.

- Test as many possible combinations of scenarios as you can imagine, especially where user input is concerned.

Summary

In this chapter you have created two intermediate Java applets. You have gained experience in working with a variety of the objects supplied in the Java API and with extending classes. You have practiced designing applets and determining how a specification can be expanded into a complete object-oriented design. You have gained some experience in a step-by-step construction of applets and learned some techniques for debugging applets. You should now feel comfortable creating your own intermediate Java applets.

15

Creating Java-Powered Web Presentations with Applets

Applets are a driving force behind Java's widespread popularity. The World Wide Web and Java can help you reach a global audience of millions, yet before anyone can preview your dazzling new applets you must create a document that showcases what you've done. To do this, you use the *Hypertext Markup Language* (HTML) and Java-specific markup tags.

Although this chapter discusses HTML and HTML document structure, the focus is on using the unique Java-specific markup tags. You will use these tags to add applets to sample HTML documents in creative and powerful ways, and ultimately to create a Web presentation. After creating a Java-powered presentation, you will need to publish it on the Web. Enjoy this part, because this is when you get to show the world your work.

Basic HTML Document Structure

Many books have been written on the subject of HTML, and I recommend you buy a couple of them. It is not my intent to describe the creation of the more intricate documents that can be produced with HTML, but rather to show only the necessary steps to get a Web browser to display an HTML document.

Understanding URLs

The first thing to know about HTML is how to read a *Uniform Resource Locator*, or URL (pronounced you-are-el). URLs are the addresses of Internet resources and are used by the Web browser to find Web publications, sounds, graphics, and applets. The first part of a URL contains the information necessary to determine the protocol required to access and transfer the resource.

A protocol you may be familiar with is the *Hypertext Transfer Protocol* (HTTP). As discussed in Chapter 3, "The Java Browser and the World Wide Web: A Primer," HTTP is used to transfer Web documents. After the protocol specification, the URL lists the address of the resource, beginning with the Internet host and domain names. For example, look at the following URL, which specifies a hypertext document called `index.html` on JavaSoft's Web server:

`HTTP://java.sun.com/applets/index.html`

URLs follow this general pattern. Some contain a listing of directories and subdirectories, separated by slash marks, before the actual resource is named. No matter how long the URL is, the protocol is the first item and the actual resource is the last item. Everything between the protocol and the resource is the listing of the hostname followed by the directory path that leads to the resource.

You will need this basic understanding of how URLs work a little later in this chapter. After you have composed the HTML document and prepared the applet to be loaded onto a Web server, you will determine the URL where the Web publication will reside. When you know the URL, you can let others know where to find your page.

Introduction to HTML Tags

HTML provides Web browsers with information for formatting text, graphics, and other multimedia objects by using *markup tags*. Tags define the structure of HTML documents and include an element name enclosed by brackets—for example, <P>, which indicates a new paragraph.

Most tags are used in pairs. The *begin tag* tells the browser a document element is beginning, and the *end tag* tells the browser an element is ending. The only difference between the two is that the end tag contains a forward slash before the element name. For example, the begin document tag <HTML> is paired with the end document tag </HTML>.

Because HTML tags are based on standard ASCII text, all you need to create HTML documents is a text editor or word processor. You save your HTML documents as standard ASCII text with the .htm or .html extension.

> **Tip:** As you create your first Web page, keep in mind that ASCII text formatting is usually ignored by Web browsers. When your browser sees formatting such as tabs, spaces, paragraph returns, and page breaks—no matter how many times you repeat them—it interprets them as a single space. This primarily is because browsers rely on the HTML markup to specify the format of the page.

Although HTML is not case sensitive, it is important to use a consistent case in your tags. To clearly separate tags from text, it is a good practice to use either all uppercase or all lowercase and stick with it throughout the document. This is also important if you intend to use one of the many HTML editors available—they insert tags that are either all lowercase or all uppercase but do not mix the two in any single document.

The Header of an HTML Document

After the begin document tag <HTML>, the next tag to go into a Web page is the begin header tag, <HEAD>. This tag specifies the beginning of the document's header section and is used in a pair with the end header tag, </HEAD>. Although the HTML specification lists many tags for document headers, most document headers contain only a document title and its corresponding tags.

You specify the document title with the <TITLE> tag, which, with its corresponding end tag </TITLE>, should surround a well-thought-out title for your document. The title is significant because most Web browsers display the title prominently on their title bar. Browsers also store the title when readers save the location of the page as a bookmark or hotlist item. Both of these examples are good reasons for keeping the title as short and concise as possible. However, the title still must help the reader remember what it was about the page that caused him to mark its place. Other points to remember about the title are that there can be only one in each document and that it can contain only plain text.

The first Web presentation you will create in this chapter is for the RGB2Hex converter. Therefore, a good title might be something like the following:

```
<TITLE> RGB to Hex Converter </TITLE>
```

The title is short and to the point, but it clearly defines what the page contains. Having completed the header, you now must construct the body of the document.

The Body of an HTML Document

The document body begins with the next tag needed for defining the document structure, the body tag <BODY>. The remainder of the document, including all text, pictures, links, forms, tables, and Java applets, is contained within the begin and end tags in this pair. Your HTML document at this point should look like this:

```
<HTML>
<HEAD>
<TITLE> RGB to Hex Converter </TITLE>
</HEAD>
<BODY>
 . . .
</BODY>
</HTML>
```

Now that you have defined the basic document structure, you can add some features, such as headings that will be centered in the browser window. To center headings, use the center tag, <CENTER>, or add the attribute ALIGN=CENTER to the heading tag. Although the current HTML specification does not provide many options for allowing the document writer to perform true page layout, HTML does provide tags like these to help with the presentation.

Peter's Principle: The nice thing about the <CENTER> tag is that it is not just for headings. The tag can be used anywhere in the body of the document when you want text, graphics, or other multimedia objects to be centered in the browser window. The bad thing about the <CENTER> tag is that it is nonstandard HTML markup used by the Netscape Navigator browser or other browsers capable of using Netscape extensions to HTML. For this reason, I prefer to use the ALIGN attribute with the heading tags when I want to center text.

The heading tags come in six levels: <H1> through <H6>. The higher the number, the smaller the font size used in the heading. Heading tags are always used in pairs, meaning the <H1> tag specifies the beginning of a level-1 heading and the </H1> tag specifies the end of a level-1 heading.

In the RGB2Hex document, you will use the <H2> and <H3> heading tags. The text between the opening and ending heading tags can be of any length and can include multiple lines. This does not, however, mean that the header should be of great length. Looking at line after line of emphasized text can become annoying very quickly. Use the heading tags as titles for paragraphs or marquee signs for pictures, forms, tables, and applets. You can add the ALIGN attribute to any heading tag, as in the following:

```
<H1 ALIGN=CENTER> Heading text to center </H1>
```

To further enhance the appearance of the document, you can add horizontal rules, which are great for showing clear separation between headings and text or between different sections contained in a document. The tag for the horizontal rule is simply <HR> and is one of the few tags that does not require an ending tag. For each <HR> tag used, a single horizontal rule that extends the width of the page is produced. Inserting multiple adjacent <HR> tags will produce a double- or triple-line effect.

At this point the HTML document looks like this:

```
<HTML>
<HEAD>
<TITLE> RGB to Hex Converter </TITLE>
</HEAD>
<BODY>
<CENTER>
<H2> The RGB to Hex Converter </H2>
<H3> Written with JAVA <H3>
<HR>
</BODY>
</HTML>
```

Now that you have a document for presentation on the World Wide Web, you need to mesh together the document and the Java applet. To do so, you use the Java extensions to HTML, which are described in the next section of this chapter. These extensions are really just more tags that define for the browser what to look for, where to find the code for the applet, and how to display the applet when it is loaded. Although not all the Java extensions are exclusive to Java, they are included because of their usefulness in displaying an applet. When you finish the next section, the RGB2Hex applet will be an integral part of your Web page.

The Java Extensions to HTML

The APPLET and PARAM elements comprise what I refer to collectively as the Java extensions to HTML. I refer to them this way because they work much the same way that other extensions, such as Netscape's, have in the past—that is, they add to the value of the current HTML specifications. When the HTML 3.2 draft specification was released in May 1996, the APPLET and PARAM elements officially became a part of the HTML standard. HTML 3.2 is the next evolution of the Hypertext Markup Language and is designed to replace HTML 2.0.

You will find that the APPLET and PARAM elements have many attributes that serve different purposes, and that not all of them are required for each applet. Indeed, do not attempt to use all these attributes in every single instance of these elements. Trying to use all the Java extensions will only cause clutter and confusion if they serve no true purpose.

The following sections describe the attributes of the APPLET and PARAM elements and when it is appropriate to use each attribute.

The APPLET Element

When Java was first introduced, the APP element was added to HTML to indicate a Java applet. Recently, the APPLET element has taken its place, and with it came many changes. Most of these are subtle, so if you were writing Java code before the change you should have no problem picking them up. If you were not, forget that the APP element ever existed and just learn the APPLET element.

The APPLET element is similar to the former APP element in that it contains some required attributes and includes optional attributes. One major difference is that the APPLET element now has an opening tag <APPLET> and an ending tag </APPLET>. The updated HTML document that contains the APPLET element with the required fields is as follows:

```
<HTML>
<HEAD>
<TITLE> RGB to Hex Converter </TITLE>
</HEAD>
<BODY>
<CENTER>
<H2> The RGB to Hex Converter </H2>
<H3> Written with JAVA <H3>
<HR>
<APPLET CODE="RGB2Hex" WIDTH=300 HEIGHT=300>
</APPLET>
</CENTER>
</BODY>
</HTML>
```

Inside the APPLET element are the required attributes CODE, WIDTH, and HEIGHT. The CODE attribute has taken the place of the CLASS attribute found in the APP element. The CODE attribute is a required because it gives the name of the file that contains the applet's compiled Applet subclass. The CODE attribute is absolute and can contain only the filename for the applet, not a path to a filename. If the applet code resides in a directory other than the one the HTML document is in, the APPLET element must include the optional attribute CODEBASE to indicate the path to the applet.

The WIDTH and HEIGHT attributes define the initial width and height of the applet display area. The unit of measurement used by these attributes is the pixel. Remember that not everyone uses the same display resolution for their monitors; what may appear to be a large applet at a display resolution of 640×480 may appear small at 1024×768. However, it is impossible to account for every possibility.

Another important point to remember is that these attributes define only the initial display area for the applet and not any windows or dialog boxes that the applet might bring up. Now that you've learned about all the required attributes of the APPLET element, let's look at each of the optional attributes.

> **Tip:** You may find some applets that do not work with your Web browser. In all probability these applets will conform to the 1.0 Alpha API instead of API versions 1.0 and later that are reviewed in this chapter. Here is a quick conversion chart for rewriting these applets to conform to the current API:
>
> 1. Replace the APP element with the APPLET element.
> 2. Replace the CLASS attribute with the CODE attribute.
> 3. Replace the SRC attribute with the CODEBASE attribute.
> 4. ALIGN attribute remains.
> 5. HEIGHT and WIDTH attributes remain.
> 6. Place applet-specific attributes into <PARAM> tags.

If you know HTML or have published HTML documents, you may be wondering why the Java extensions specify begin and end APPLET tags. After all, all the necessary instructions are in the begin applet tag, <APPLET>, which makes the end APPLET tag seem unnecessary. Indeed, most Web publishers don't know why there are begin and end APPLET tags and don't place anything between them.

Between the begin and end APPLET tags, you can define an area of the document that will be displayed by browsers that are not capable of using Java applets. For example, if your applet is an animation, you can place an image reference in this area to allow readers who don't have Java-capable browsers to see something other than empty space. All Java-enhanced pages should contain a fully defined area of text, multimedia objects, and markup for such browsers. This will greatly expand the available audience for your Web presentations.

The HTML document you are creating can be extended using this concept, as shown in Listing 15.1. Readers who have a Java-capable browser see the RGB2Hex applet. Readers who don't see an image called RGB2Hex.gif and a message that tells them about the applet shown in the image. Figure 15.1 shows the document as displayed by a Web browser that cannot run Java applets.

Listing 15.1. Extending the document for wider audiences.

```
<HTML>
<HEAD>
<TITLE> RGB to Hex Converter </TITLE>
</HEAD>
<BODY>
<CENTER>
<H2> The RGB to Hex Converter </H2>
<H3> Written with JAVA <H3>
<HR>
<APPLET CODE="RGB2Hex" WIDTH=300 HEIGHT=300>
<IMG SRC="RGB2Hex.gif">
<BLOCKQUOTE>
```

continues

Listing 15.1. continued

```
The screenshot shows the RGB2Hex applet programmed in the Java
programming language. This applet lets you convert RGB color
values to hexadecimal values and see the corresponding color output.
</BLOCKQUOTE>
</APPLET>
</CENTER>
</BODY>
</HTML>
```

Figure 15.1.

Defining markup for users without Java-capable browsers.

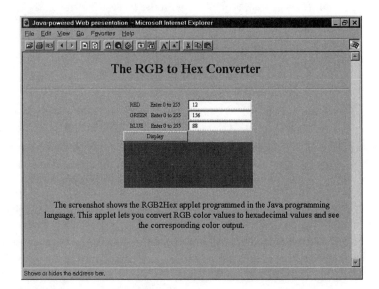

Optional Attributes for the **APPLET** Element

The optional attributes are every bit as important as the required ones. These attributes allow for much greater freedom in the use of applets and the layout of the Web presentation. This section reviews each optional attribute and gives details of how it is used.

ALIGN

Another feature that illustrates the attention to detail in the Java HTML extensions is the ALIGN attribute, which defines the alignment of the applet. Each of the possible values causes the applet or the text around it to line up differently. These values are the same as those for the <IMG> tag used for displaying images in HTML, as you can see from the following list:

- ALIGN=CENTER is similar to center justification in that it places the applet in the center of its line on the document.

- ALIGN=LEFT aligns the applet with the left side of the document.

- `ALIGN=RIGHT` aligns the applet with the right side of the document.
- `ALIGN=TOP` aligns the applet with the topmost item on its line, which can be anything from text to an image file.
- `ALIGN=TEXTTOP` aligns the applet with the top of the tallest text on the line.
- `ALIGN=MIDDLE` aligns the applet with the middle of the baseline of the text.
- `ALIGN=ABSMIDDLE` aligns the applet with the middle of the largest item on the line.
- `ALIGN=BASELINE` aligns the bottom of the applet with the baseline of the text.
- `ALIGN=BOTTOM` is actually the same as `ALIGN=BASELINE`.
- `ALIGN=ABSBOTTOM` aligns the bottom of the applet with the lowest item on the line. This can extend below the baseline of the text.

Note: The value `ALIGN=BASELINE` was introduced by Netscape Navigator. Although it is interchangeable with the value `ALIGN=BOTTOM`, the developers of Netscape felt the word `BASELINE` was a better description of the way the text would be aligned.

The `ALIGN` attribute determines how the text is arranged with regard to the applet, but it does not determine how much space there will be between the text and the applet. To adjust the whitespace around the applet, you use the `VSPACE` and `HSPACE` attributes.

HSPACE and VSPACE

The `HSPACE` and `VSPACE` attributes let you define, in pixels, the amount of whitespace around the applet. `VSPACE` defines the vertical space above and below the applet, and `HSPACE` defines the horizontal space on either side of the applet. These attributes also work the same as those used for the `<IMG>` tag in HTML and are used like the `WIDTH` and `HEIGHT` attributes. To have five pixels of space around the applet, you would use `HSPACE=5` and `VSPACE=5` in the `<APPLET>` tag.

These are all the attributes that affect how the applet will be displayed on the page. The next attribute is useful only when the applet cannot be displayed on the page.

Tip: Although the `ALIGN`, `VSPACE`, and `HSPACE` attributes are listed in the JDK, none of them seem to have been fully incorporated into Java-enabled Web browsers as of this writing. The `ALIGN` values `MIDDLE`, `TOP`, `TEXTTOP`, `ABSMIDDLE`, `BASELINE`, `BOTTOM`, and `ABSBOTTOM` do work, but the `LEFT`, `RIGHT`, and `CENTER` attributes did not at this writing. A practical workaround for this is to include a new paragraph tag (`<P>`) before each instance of an applet. Inside the braces of the new paragraph tag alignment, you can include instructions for the paragraph. `<P ALIGN=RIGHT>` will cause everything between it and the

</P> tag to align to the right margin of the document. Likewise, everything between a
<P ALIGN=CENTER> tag and its ending </P> tag will be center justified. A description of these
attributes is provided here in expectation that they will be incorporated into Web browsers
in the near future.

ALT

When you try to load a Java-enhanced document into a browser that does not support Java, the
applet will not be displayed. One alternative to a blank space in your page may be the alternative
text (or ALT) attribute. Using the ALT attribute, you can define alternative text to display when the
browser recognizes the <APPLET> tag but is not capable of running applets. In the <APPLET> tag, the
ALT attribute is used in this manner:

```
<APPLET CODE="RGB2Hex" WIDTH=300 HEIGHT=300
ALT="This JAVA applet is a utility to convert RGB
input to Hex values.">
```

Currently, this attribute is of dubious value solely because all Web browsers that recognize the <APPLET>
tag also automatically run Java applets. However, the HTML 3.2 specification includes the <APPLET>
tag, which means that browsers that claim to support HTML 3.2 must also support the <APPLET> tag.
Although these browsers may support HTML 3.2, they will not necessarily support Java.

CODEBASE

The optional attribute CODEBASE, mentioned previously, can be used in any HTML document to direct
the Web browser to look for an applet located someplace other than the current directory without
changing the current URL being viewed on the Web browser. With CODEBASE, anyone can use an
applet stored elsewhere. This could be important to someone who is allotted only a few megabytes
of storage space on his server, or perhaps to development teams that use separate servers and want to
save time by not having to transfer files before use.

If the applet's compiled Applet subclass resides anywhere other than the base document URL, CODEBASE
is needed to load the applet. CODEBASE is used to give the URL of the applet because the CODE attribute is absolute and can contain only the name of the Applet subclass. When CODE is used without
CODEBASE, the document's base URL is used.

A simple way to think of this is that if you use CODEBASE, you can tell the Web browser where to look
for the applet; otherwise, the browser looks in the current directory. Thus, using CODEBASE, you can
run an applet stored on a different server or in a different directory than your Web presentation.

CODEBASE is also valuable in that it assists in organization of the Web site and frees Java programmers from ties to a single directory, such as the cgi-bin directory normally used for CGI scripts. Creating subdirectories in your Web publication directory for applets can help you stay organized. In this way, Java applets can reside in their own directory, or applets for a particular page can be grouped into a directory on the basis of where they are used. CODEBASE enables an HTML document to refer to these directories without having to use a document located in the same directory as the applet. Attention to little details such as this is one reason for Java's popularity.

NAME

Another means of identifying an applet is the NAME attribute. It plays a key role in how applets interact with other applets on the same Web page. By naming an applet, you can target it from other applets on the page, which makes it possible for applets on the same page to find and communicate with each other. If, for example, a user activates one of three applets on a page and all three applets are named with the NAME attribute, the active applet can pass values to the other two applets that cause them to behave in new ways, display new images and text, or even start a new animation sequence.

The NAME attribute is also included in the braces of the <APPLET> tag. An example follows:

```
<APPLET CODEBASE="http://tvp.com/applets/HyperText"
CODE="NervousText" WIDTH=400 Height=75 ALIGN=middle NAME=appletA>
</APPLET>
<APPLET CODEBASE="http://java.sun.com/applets/applets/NervousText"
CODE="NervousText" WIDTH=400 Height=75 ALIGN=middle NAME=appletB>
</APPLET>
```

In this example, appletA can communicate with appletB. When message passing is used for communication in Java applets, using the correct name for the applet is important to ensure that messages go to their correct destination. The name of the destination can be passed to the sender as a parameter using the PARAM element (described next).

The PARAM Element

The PARAM element is used to pass general-purpose parameters to an applet. Without it, applets could not communicate with each other, and you could not pass general-purpose values to applets. This section looks at how parameters are referenced in HTML documents and Java code.

Parameters Referenced in HTML Documents

The PARAM element is one of the few elements in HTML that uses only a begin tag. You place the begin tag, <PARAM>, between the opening and ending <APPLET> tags. This is the only element between the APPLET tags that Java-capable Web browsers take advantage of when they run an associated applet.

Applets access the attributes in the <PARAM> tag by using the getParameter() method. This enables applets to look and behave differently when used in various Web documents.

The <PARAM> tag has two attributes that must be defined: the NAME attribute and the VALUE attribute. The NAME attribute assigns the name for which the getParameter() method in your applet searches. The VALUE attribute is used to pass a specific value to an applet. Here is an example using these attributes:

```
<HTML>
<HEAD>
<TITLE> Scrolling Text </TITLE>
</HEAD>
<BODY>
<APPLET CODE="ScrollText" WIDTH=800 HEIGHT=400>
<PARAM NAME=text VALUE= "Introducing the Java ScrollText Applet!">
<PARAM NAME=width value="800">
<PARAM NAME=height value="390">
</APPLET>
</BODY>
</HTML>
```

> **Note:** Do not confuse the NAME attribute of the <PARAM> tag with that of the <APPLET> tag. The name in the <PARAM> tag is the name that the getParameter() method searches for, as opposed to the <APPLET> attribute NAME, which is used to give each instance of an applet a name.

In the previous example, the applet ScrollText is being passed three separate parameters: The first is the text the applet will display; the second and third are the width and height again. The last two parameters are included because when an applet is displayed by a Web browser, the dimensions of the applet are taken from the HTML code. This can cause problems if the creator of the applet does not prepare for it.

Parameters from Inside Java Code

All of this seems easy from the outside, but to understand how this works in the Java code is another matter. Listing 15.2 shows the code for the ScrollText applet.

In the listing, the getParameter() method is used on lines 16, 17, and 30. These are the points where the Java code brings in the <PARAM> attributes listed in the HTML document. There can be as many <PARAM> attributes given as needed for the applet. For example, the ScrollText applet could be extended to receive other attributes such as the color of the text or the background. This would be a good project to undertake after you read Chapter 16, "Applet Reuse."

> **Note:** In Listing 15.2, code lines that use the `getParameter()` method are highlighted with bold text.

Listing 15.2. The `ScrollText` applet.

```java
import java.awt.Graphics;
import java.awt.Font;

/**
 * Peter Norton's Guide to Programming Java
 * The Java ScrollText Applet
 * This applet is used to scroll a text banner across the screen
 * The applet takes TEXT, WIDTH, and HEIGHT as parameters.
 */

public class ScrollText extends java.applet.Applet implements Runnable {

    int h;                         // Height of applet in pixels
    int w;                         // Width of applet in pixels
    char separated[];              // Output string in array form
    String s = null;               // Input string containing display text
    String hs = null;              // Input string containing height
    String ws = null;              // Input string containing width
    Thread ScrollThread = null;    // Thread to control processing
    int speed=35;                  // Length of delay in milliseconds
    boolean threadSuspended = false;
    int dist;

/* Setup width, height, and display text */
public void init() {
    ws = getParameter ("width");
    hs = getParameter ("height");
    if (ws == null){             // Read width as input
        w = 150;                 // If not found use default
    } else {
        w = Integer.parseInt(ws); // Convert input string to integer
    }
    if (hs == null){             // Read height as input
        h = 50;                  // If not found use default
    } else {
        h = Integer.parseInt (hs); // Convert input string to integer
    }
    resize(w,h);                 // Set font based on height
    setFont(new Font("TimesRoman",Font.BOLD,h - 2));
    s = getParameter("text");// Read input text, if null use default
    if (s == null) {
        s = " The Java ScrollText Applet at work.";
    }

    separated =  new char [s.length()];
    s.getChars(0,s.length(),separated,0);
}
```

continues

Listing 15.2. continued

```java
/* Start new thread to run applet */
public void start() {
    if(ScrollThread == null)
    {
        ScrollThread = new Thread(this);
        ScrollThread.start();
    }
 }

/* End thread containing applet */
public void stop() {
    ScrollThread = null;
 }

// While applet is running pause then scroll text
public void run() {
    while (ScrollThread != null) {
    try {Thread.sleep(speed);} catch (InterruptedException e){}
    scroll();
    }
    ScrollThread = null;
 }

// Scroll text by determining new location to draw text and redrawing
synchronized void scroll () {
    dist--;                // Move string to left
    // If string has disappeared to the left, move back to right edge
    if (dist + ((s.length()+1)*(h *5 / 11)) == 0){
    dist=w;
}
    repaint();
}

// Redraw string at given location
public void paint(Graphics g) {
    g.drawChars(separated, 0, s.length(), dist,4 *h / 5);
 }

// Suspend thread when mouse is pushed, resume when pushed again
public boolean mouseDown(java.awt.Event evt, int x, int y) {
        if (threadSuspended) {
            ScrollThread.resume();
        }
        else {
            ScrollThread.suspend();
        }
        threadSuspended = !threadSuspended;
    return true;
    }
}
```

To gain experience in working with parameter passing, type the applet as shown and then compile it. Refer to Chapter 14, "Creating a Java Applet," for complete instructions on compiling an applet.

Possible Problems with Parameters

There is one problem with using the <PARAM> tag: Unless all possible parameters are listed and used in the HTML document, there is no way—short of viewing the Java code—to know what parameters are set. To demonstrate this, look again at the ScrollText applet's HTML markup without some of the parameters listed:

```
<HTML>
<HEAD>
<TITLE> Scrolling Text </TITLE>
</HEAD>
<BODY>
<APPLET CODE="ScrollText" WIDTH=800 HEIGHT=400>
<PARAM NAME=text VALUE= "Introducing the Java ScrollText Applet!">
</APPLET>
</BODY>
</HTML>
```

In the previous example, the applet would default to the height and width listed in the Java code. Anyone attempting to use this applet would find it confusing when the attributes he set in the <APPLET> tag were overridden. Therefore, HTML authors should list all unused parameters for an applet in comments in the HTML document. A comment can be added to an HTML document by placing it between the begin comment tag (<!-) and the end comment tag (->).

You could create comments for the ScrollText applet as follows:

```
<!- Java applet ScrollText takes TEXT, WIDTH, and HEIGHT as parameters. ->
<APPLET CODE="ScrollText" WIDTH=800 HEIGHT=400>
<PARAM NAME=text VALUE= "Introducing the Java ScrollText Applet!">
</APPLET>
```

Adding Animation to Web Documents

Java-based animation is everywhere on the Web, and it might surprise you to learn that the source of most of it is a single applet called Animator. Animator is useful for creating powerful animation sequences. But best of all, the Animator applet is included as a demo in the JDK.

Overview of the **Animator** Applet

As the name implies, the Animator applet can be used to create animation sequences. You will find the source code in the demo/Animator directory under your base installation directory for Java. This directory contains the following files and directories:

```
 Directory of C:\java\demo\Animator
IMAGES         <DIR>        02-23-96  2:32p images
ANIMAT~1 JAV        21,410  10-13-95 10:23a Animator.java
ANIMAT~1 CLA        14,873  10-13-95  1:54a Animator.class
IMAGEN~1 CLA           706  10-13-95  1:54a ImageNotFoundException.class
PARSEE~1 CLA           410  10-13-95  1:54a ParseException.class
```

```
INDEX~1  HTM          3,411  10-13-95  1:54a index.html
AUDIO          <DIR>          02-23-96  2:32p audio
EXAMPL~1 HTM            428  10-13-95  1:54a example2.html
EXAMPL~2 HTM            477  03-07-96  8:32p example3.html
EXAMPL~3 HTM            419  10-13-95  1:54a example1.html
```

`Animator` is one of the most complex demos in the Java API. As you can see from the directory listing, the source code for the applet is in a file called `Animator.java`. When this file is compiled, three class files are created: `Animator.class`, `ImageNotFoundException.class`, and `ParseException.class`.

Look at the sample HTML documents in this directory. The file `index.html` provides a brief overview of using the `Animator` applet. The example documents—`example1.html`, `example2.html`, and `example3.html`—contain three different demos.

The audio files used in the examples are in the `audio` directory:

```
Directory of C:\java\demo\Animator\audio
SPACEM~1 AU         48,072  10-13-95  1:54a spacemusic.au
1        AU            946  10-13-95  1:54a 1.au
2        AU          1,039  10-13-95  1:54a 2.au
3        AU            993  10-13-95  1:54a 3.au
4        AU          1,006  10-13-95  1:54a 4.au
5        AU          1,016  10-13-95  1:54a 5.au
6        AU          1,048  10-13-95  1:54a 6.au
7        AU            980  10-13-95  1:54a 7.au
8        AU          1,064  10-13-95  1:54a 8.au
9        AU            989  10-13-95  1:54a 9.au
0        AU          1,010  10-13-95  1:54a 0.au
```

The file `spacemusic.au` provides a soundtrack example. The other files are sound sequences used with corresponding images you will find in the `images` directory. The `images` directory contains two directories:

```
Directory of C:\java\demo\Animator\images
LOADIN~1 GIF         1,518  10-13-95  1:54a loading-msg.gif
SIMPLE~1       <DIR>          02-23-96  2:32p SimpleAnimation
DUKE           <DIR>          02-23-96  2:32p Duke
```

The `loading-msg.gif` image is used in the `example3.html` demonstration document and provides an example of `startup image`. The directories `SimpleAnimation` and `Duke` contain the images used to create the demonstration animation sequences.

Using Parameters in the **Animator** Applet

The `Animator` applet presents an interesting use of the `<PARAM>` tag to pass many types of values. Parameters the applet accepts include the following:

- `background`—Name of background image to display, such as `<PARAM NAME=background VALUE="wallpaper.gif">`.

- `endimage`—Index number to end the animation sequence on, such as `<PARAM NAME=endimage VALUE="10">`.

- `images`—The images to display in succession with each image number separated by the pipe symbol, such as `<PARAM NAME=images VALUE="1¦2¦3¦4">`.

- `imagesource`—The URL path to the image files, such as `<PARAM NAME=imagesource VALUE="http://tvp.com/java/apps/images">`.

- `pause`—The delay time in milliseconds between images, such as `<PARAM NAME=pause VALUE="100">`.

- `pauses`—The delay time in milliseconds for each frame separated by the pipe symbol, such as `<PARAM NAME=pauses VALUE="100¦50¦¦100¦¦¦100">`.

- `positions`—The coordinate of each image frame, with the x coordinate separated from the y coordinate by @, such as `<PARAM NAME=positions VALUE="10@50¦10@60¦10@70">`.

- `repeat`—A boolean value set to `true` to repeat the animation sequence, such as `<PARAM NAME=repeat VALUE="true">U`.

- `sounds`—The sound files to play in succession with each filename separated by the pipe symbol, such as `<PARAM NAME=sounds VALUE="s1.au¦s2.au¦s3.au¦s4.au">`.

- `soundsource`—The URL path to the image files, such as `<PARAM NAME=soundsource VALUE="http://tvp.com/java/apps/sounds">`.

- `soundtrack`—The sound file to play in the background during the animation, such as `<PARAM NAME=pauses VALUE="soundtrack.au">`.

- `startimage`—Index number to start the animation sequence on, such as `<PARAM NAME=startimage VALUE="2">`.

- `startup`—Image to display at startup while the other images are loading, such as `<PARAM NAME=startup VALUE="startup.gif">`.

As you can see from the list of parameters and their uses, the `Animator` applet is quite versatile. Because most of the animation sequences you'll see on the Web use the `Animator` applet or a derivative of it, I highly recommend you look at the source code for this applet.

Creating a Java-Based Animation with `Animator`

Creating an animation with the `Animator` applet is easy. Just create a series of images and an HTML document, and add sound if you want to.

For your first animation, start small. If you want to create an original animation, use a series of only three or four images. You can also base your first animation on an existing one, such as the animation of JavaSoft's mascot, Duke, which is included in the demo. In this way, your first attempt at animation is sure to be a success.

Listing 15.3 shows a sample HTML document that uses the Animator applet and the Duke animation. Recall that because the CODEBASE attribute points to the Java demo directory, the compiled source code for the applet is actually obtained from this directory.

Listing 15.3. A sample document using the Animator applet.

```
<HTML>
<HEAD>
<TITLE> The Animator Applet </TITLE>
</HEAD>
<BODY>
<APPLET CODEBASE="file:///c:java\demo\Animator"
CODE="Animator" width=66 height=100 VSPACE=5 HSPACE=5 ALIGN=middle >
<PARAM NAME="imagesource" VALUE="file:///c:\java\demo\Animator\images\Duke">
<PARAM NAME="pause" VALUE="100">
<PARAM NAME="repeat" VALUE="true">
<PARAM NAME="endimage" VALUE="10">
</APPLET>
</BODY>
</HTML>
```

Note: Because the file paths in the CODEBASE and VALUE attributes reference the C drive, you may need to change the paths for use on your system. For example, if the JDK is installed on the D: drive, you would replace references to c: with d:. On a UNIX system, you would remove the references to c: entirely. You must change these references because the CODEBASE and VALUE attributes are used to point to the file's exact location on your file system.

Reducing Animation Flicker

A problem you will encounter whenever you use animation is *flicker*—that annoying wavering of the image or text as the applet redraws the screen. If you tested the ScrollText applet, you saw that the animated text flickered, and it probably annoyed you.

To fix the flickering of the ScrollText applet you need to draw the text first to a canvas that is off the screen. When that canvas has been drawn, it can be redisplayed on the screen in such a short period of time that no flicker is noticed. You will also need to modify the update() method so that it does not clear the screen between each drawing.

To create a canvas off the screen, you will need two containers. The first container is for the image or text you will draw to the screen. The second container is for the off-screen canvas. Here is the code you will need to add to the variable initialization section of the ScrollText applet:

```
Image offscreenImage;
Graphics offscreenGraphics;
```

Next, draw to the off-screen canvas and then move the animated text or graphics to the real canvas. To do this in the ScrollText applet, you will override the paint() method as follows:

```
public void paint(Graphics g) {
   Rectangle r = bounds();

   offscreenGraphics.clearRect(0,0,r.width,r.height);
   offscreenGraphics.drawChars(separated, 0, s.length(), dist, 4*h/5);
   g.drawImage(offscreenImage, 0, 0, this);
}
```

The final step is to override the update() method so that it does not clear the screen between each drawing. This is done as follows:

```
public void update(Graphics g) {
      paint(g);
}
```

The complete source code for the ScrollText applet with the flicker fix is shown in Listing 15.4.

Listing 15.4. The ScrollText applet with flicker fix.

```
import java.awt.Graphics;
import java.awt.Font;
import java.awt.Image;
import java.awt.Rectangle;

/**
 * Peter Norton's Guide to Java Programming
 * The Java ScrollText Applet With Flicker Fix
 * This applet is used to scroll a text banner across the screen
 * The applet takes TEXT, WIDTH, and HEIGHT as parameters.
 */

public class ScrollText extends java.applet.Applet implements Runnable {

   int h;              // Height of applet in pixels
   int w;              // Width of applet in pixels
   char separated[];        // Output string in array form
   String s = null;         // Input string containing display text
   String hs = null;        // Input string containing height
   String ws = null;        // Input string containing width
   Thread killme = null;     // Thread to control processing
   int speed=35;          // Length of delay between positions in milliseconds
   boolean threadSuspended = false;
   int dist;
   Image offscreenImage;
   Graphics offscreenGraphics;

/* Setup width, height, and display text */
public void init() {
   ws = getParameter ("width");
   hs = getParameter ("height");
   if (ws == null){          /* Read width as input, if not found use default */
      w = 150;
```

continues

Listing 15.4. continued

```java
    } else {
        w = Integer.parseInt(ws); // Convert input string to integer
    }
    if (hs == null){          /* Read height as input, if not found use default */
        h = 50;
    } else {
        h = Integer.parseInt (hs); // Convert input string to integer
    }
    resize(w,h);           /* Set font based on height */
    s = getParameter("text");   /* Read input text, if null use default */
    if (s == null) {
        s = " The Java ScrollText Applet at work.";
    }

    separated =  new char [s.length()];
    s.getChars(0,s.length(),separated,0);
    offscreenImage = createImage(w,h);
      offscreenGraphics = offscreenImage.getGraphics();
    offscreenGraphics.setFont(new Font("TimesRoman",Font.BOLD,h - 2));
}

/* Start new thread to run applet */
public void start() {
    if(killme == null)
    {
        killme = new Thread(this);
        killme.start();
    }
}

/* End thread containing applet */
public void stop() {
    killme = null;
}

/* While applet is running pause then scroll text */
public void run() {
    while (killme != null) {
    try {Thread.sleep(speed);} catch (InterruptedException e){}
    scroll();
    }
    killme = null;
}

/* Scroll text by determining new location to draw text and redrawing */
synchronized void scroll () {
    dist—;          // Move string to left
    if (dist + ((s.length()+1)*(h *5 / 11)) == 0){   // If string has disappeared
                        //to the left, move back
    dist=w;                    //to right edge
       }
    repaint();
}

/* Redraw string at given location */
public void paint(Graphics g) {
    Rectangle r = bounds();
```

```
    offscreenGraphics.clearRect(0,0,r.width,r.height);
    offscreenGraphics.drawChars(separated, 0, s.length(), dist, 4*h/5);
    g.drawImage(offscreenImage, 0, 0, this);
  }
public void update(Graphics g) {
    paint(g);
}

/* Suspend thread when mouse is pushed, resume when pushed again */
public boolean mouseDown(java.awt.Event evt, int x, int y) {
    if (threadSuspended) {
        killme.resume();
    }
    else {
        killme.suspend();
    }
    threadSuspended = !threadSuspended;
  return true;
  }
}
```

Publishing a Java Presentation on the Web

Now that you are familiar with the Java extensions to HTML, you can put together your first Java-powered Web presentation and publish it on the Web. But before you begin, there are some things you should consider as to when and where to use applets.

Using Live Applets

Determining when and where applets should be used in Web pages is not always easy. Prior to making the decision to fill your Web pages with applets, ask yourself if they are truly useful and if they enhance the page. If they do not, and only add to the load time of the page, perhaps it would be better not to use them. Sure, it's great to show off and display a visually exciting page, but consider how often someone will return to your page if it takes 10 minutes to load into the Web browser.

Journalists always talk about the five Ws. It should be no different in electronic publishing, except that instead of applying them to a story they are applied to the construction of a Web presentation.

The first W is Who—in this case, your target audience. There has been much ado in the press about the short attention span of today's youth, especially that segment often referred to as Generation X. If this is your target audience, what are the odds of them waiting through an extremely long page load when other places are just a click away? On the other hand, an extremely exciting visual display can be worth the wait. There is a trade-off.

The content of your page, the What, comes next. Think about what you are displaying. If it is a fan page that could be enhanced by the visual display of animation or use of sound, using Java applets left and right may be appropriate. If you are trying to sell something, scrolling messages will attract the eye. Perhaps using Java applets to demonstrate a sample of a software product would help sell more copies. Whatever the case, a few Java applets will more than likely make it all the more appealing, but overuse can kill the best of things.

The third W, When, is easy. Start using Java applets as soon as you are comfortable with your ability to create and incorporate a useful applet into your presentations. Java is experiencing tremendous growth right now. Internet users continually expect more interaction with the sites they visit. They expect sites to employ new technology as soon as it is available, and they are waiting to visit more Java-powered Web sites.

Where do you place the applets? Where they will achieve the effect you desire. If the applet is central to the design of the page, place it centrally on the page. Placing a small animation at the bottom of a page is usually a bad idea. If the applet is on the page just to serve as notification that you can use applets, then consider not using it at all. Remember that what is at the topmost center of a Web presentation will be the first thing users see. Do your best to use this space to grab their attention, because other Web presentations are always just a click of a mouse button away.

The last W, Why, is the hard part. I have pointed out several good reasons both for and against using Java applets. The best incentive I can think of for using Java applets is their capability to draw people in. A well-written applet will be noticed. Friends will tell friends about it, and some people will visit your Web presentation just to view the applet. However, a set of "been there, done that" applets will likewise keep people away unless your Web presentation provides something of value to them. A good rule of thumb is to use an applet if it provides additional value to your presentation.

The use of Java applets in and of itself will not guarantee a successful Web presentation. Using Java applets to enhance a good presentation will only make it better. Successful presentations come from organization, planning, and hard work. Plan your site before you develop and publish it. If an applet is not part of the original plan, design the modification to your site as carefully as you would plan a change to your software. This will save you a lot of time trying to fix the site later.

Putting Together the Presentation

After you consider when and where to use applets in your Web pages, you can start putting together your presentations. Your first Java-powered Web presentation incorporates everything I have discussed to this point in the chapter. Along with the RGB2Hex converter and the ScrollText applet, the presentation includes an animation featuring Duke that comes to life with the Animator applet. As you look over the markup in Listing 15.5, pay special attention to the CODEBASE locations.

Using CODEBASE, it is not necessary to physically locate the applets in the same directory as the HTML document. In fact, in this example, all the applets are in separate locations: RGB2Hex is in rgbconvert under the base directory; `ScrollText` is in `scrolltext` under the `base` directory; and `Animator` is in the animator directory.

Listing 15.5. A Java-powered Web presentation.

```
<HTML>
<HEAD>
<TITLE> Java-powered Web presentation </TITLE>
</HEAD>
<BODY>
<CENTER>
<H2> The RGB to Hex Converter </H2>
<HR>
<P>
<APPLET CODEBASE="rgbconvert" CODE="RGB2Hex" WIDTH=300 HEIGHT=300 >
<IMG SRC="RGB2Hex.gif">
<BLOCKQUOTE>
The screenshot shows the RGB2Hex applet programmed in the Java
programming language. This applet lets you convert RGB color
values to hexadecimal values and see the corresponding color output.
Other applets on the page display scrolling text and an animated image.
To see all this, you should get a Java-capable Web browser
such as the Netscape Navigator 2.0.
</BLOCKQUOTE>
</APPLET>
<HR>
<!- Java applet ScrollText takes TEXT, WIDTH, and HEIGHT as parameters. ->
<APPLET CODEBASE="scrolltext" CODE="ScrollText" WIDTH=800 HEIGHT=50>
<PARAM NAME=text VALUE=" The Java ScrollText Applet at work. ">
<PARAM NAME=width VALUE="800">
<PARAM NAME=height VALUE="50">
</APPLET>
<HR>
</CENTER>
</P>
<P ALIGN=right>
<STRONG>Powered by JAVA</STRONG>
<APPLET CODEBASE="animator"
CODE="Animator" width=66 height=100 VSPACE=5 HSPACE=5 ALIGN=middle >
<PARAM NAME="imagesource" value="images/Duke">
<PARAM NAME="pause" VALUE="100">
<PARAM NAME="repeat" VALUE="true">
<PARAM NAME="endimage" VALUE="10">
</APPLET>
</P>
</BODY>
</HTML>
```

Note: This example assumes that you've published all the necessary files for the presentation as outlined in the next section of this chapter. If you want to use the presentation on your local system, you will need to check and possibly update the file paths to the applets and image files.

The Web presentation is almost finished; but before we publish it, there are a few more things you should add. The first thing relates to the Duke animation. The caption above it says "Powered by Java", and, as unlikely as it may seem, there may be a few people browsing the Web who have not heard of Java. So, why not provide a link to the Java home page?

The best place to provide a link to the Java home page is on the word JAVA. The HTML code to provide this link uses the anchor tag (<A>) and is simple to add. The modified line in our Web document now looks like this:

```
<STRONG>Powered by <A HREF="http://java.sun.com">JAVA</A></STRONG>
```

Now the word JAVA will show up as a highlighted link to the JavaSoft home page. But if we can do that, why not modify the code like this:

```
<A HREF="http://java.sun.com">
<APPLET CODEBASE="animator"
CODE="Animator" width=66 height=100 VSPACE=5 HSPACE=5 ALIGN=middle >
<PARAM NAME="imagesource" value="images">
<PARAM NAME="pause" VALUE="100">
<PARAM NAME="repeat" VALUE="true">
<PARAM NAME="endimage" VALUE="10">
</APPLET>
</A>
```

After all, why not just make the applet itself the link to the home page? You cannot do this because it does not have the expected result of linking to the Java home page when the user clicks the applet. The applet traps the mouse-click event itself as opposed to allowing the HTML code to handle it. So, although applets may contain links or provide links, they cannot themselves be links.

The last thing I recommend adding to a Web presentation is another <A> tag, but this time it should include a mailto reference. This reference tells the reader's browser to open a create mail session that will be sent to the named user and provides a method for getting feedback on your Web presentation. The following mailto reference lets the reader send mail to the address for reporting bugs and making feature requests for Java:

```
<A HREF="mailto:java@java.sun.com">java@java.sun.com</A>
```

The finished presentation is shown in Figure 15.2. This sample presentation is quite basic, but it should help you envision how wonderful Java-powered presentations can be.

After all this, the Web publication looks pretty good. You have defined APPLET elements with their associated attributes and have incorporated them into an HTML document. The next step is to publish the presentation as a page on the World Wide Web. The page can be created to be viewed alone or as part of a group of related pages. Regardless of the number of pages, a display of information on the Web is considered a Web publication.

Figure 15.2.
The finished presentation.

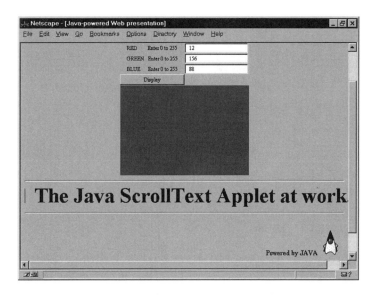

Publishing the Presentation on the Web

To publish your Java-powered presentation, you need access to a Web server through an Internet service provider, a commercial service provider, or another entity. Now you are ready to publish your presentation.

Step 1: Determine Where to Place Your Documents

The first step in publishing a Web document is to decide where it and all its supporting material will be stored. On many of the servers connected to the Internet, all materials set for publication on the Web must be stored in a specific subdirectory in the user's home directory. This subdirectory typically is named `public_html` on UNIX-based Web servers, but the best way to determine the directory for your HTML documents is to ask the Web server administrator.

> **Note:** Always turn to the server administrator if you have questions about directories or storage. The server administrator should understand the proper structure of the system you will be working with and can help prevent many mistakes.

Usually, Web servers map URL paths to the `public_html` subdirectory, and you can point to it using the tilde (~) followed by your system name. Thus, requests to `http://www.your_provider.com/~you` would be mapped to the subdirectory called `public_html` in your account, and a Web document called `present.html` could be accessed with the following URL:

```
http://www.your_provider.com/~you/present.html
```

Step 2: Create the Necessary Directory Structure

You should prepare your home directory for Web publishing by creating the appropriately named Web directory and any necessary subdirectories. From the command prompt in your home directory on a UNIX or Windows-based server, you can create a directory called `public_html` by typing the following command:

```
mkdir public_html
```

Make sure that the directory has the appropriately restricted mode for Web access, such as `705` on a UNIX system. The mode `705` means that the directory is readable, writeable, and executable by you, but only readable and executable by others. To change the mode of the `public_html` directory, type the following command:

```
chmod 705 public_html
```

Afterward, change to the `public_html` directory and create subdirectories as necessary. The use of subdirectories helps to keep everything clear and organized inside the `public_html` directory. As mentioned earlier, using `CODEBASE` frees you from having to keep the `.html` files with the `.java` or `.class` files. Create subdirectories for the `ScrollText`, `RGB2Hex`, and `Animator` applets by typing the following:

```
cd public_html
mkdir rgbconvert
mkdir scrolltext
mkdir animator
cd animator
mkdir images
```

> **Note:** Be sure the `CODEBASE` attribute for the `RGB2Hex` applet points to the subdirectory `rgbconvert`. Similarly, the `CODEBASE` attribute for the `ScrollText` applet should point to the subdirectory `scrolltext`.

Step 3: Move Your Documents

Next, use FTP or whatever protocol you are comfortable with to upload all files necessary for the presentation to the appropriate directories. The `RGB2Hex.java`, `ScrollText.java`, and `Animator.java` files are not necessary to run the Java applets. Therefore, they are not uploaded.

Upload the following files to the `rgbconvert` directory: `RGB2Hex.class`, `RGBcanvas.class`, `RGBcontrols.class`, and `HexInt.class`. Upload `ScrollText.class` to the `scrolltext` directory.

If you installed the JDK, you can find the `Animator` applet in the Java `demo` directory on your computer. Under this directory are subdirectories for the images. You will find the images for the `Duke` animation in the `images/Duke` directory. Upload the following files to the `animator` directory: `Animator.class`, `ImageNotFoundException.class`, and `ParseException.class`.

Now upload the following files to the `animator/images` directory: `T1.gif`, `T2.gif`, `T3.gif`, `T4.gif`, `T5.gif`, `T6.gif`, `T7.gif`, `T8.gif`, `T9.gif`, and `T10.gif`.

Next, save the HTML document for the presentation as `present.html` and upload it to the `public_html` directory. Some computer systems do not allow for file extensions beyond three characters. If this is the case on your system, save the document as `present.htm` and change the filename when it is on the Web server.

After uploading the files, ensure that the correct permissions are set on the files. File modes are similar to directory modes. On UNIX systems, the mode `705` is generally the appropriate access mode for your files. On other systems, you will want to ensure that the files are readable but not writeable.

Note: If you are interested in publishing on the Web, I highly recommend *Web Publishing Unleashed*, published by Sams.net. The book goes into great detail on every aspect of Web publishing and includes chapters on HTML, SGML, VRML, and much more. In particular, you may want to refer to Chapter 25, "Designing and Publishing a Web Document," which provides a complete walk-through of publishing a Web document, and Chapter 26, "Designing and Publishing a Web Site," which provides a complete walk-through of publishing a Web site.

Viewing the Presentation

To view your Java-powered presentation, you'll need to use a Java-enabled Web browser. These will automatically run any applets on a page when that page is first accessed. If you don't have a Java-enabled browser, refer to Chapter 3 to learn how to obtain and install a browser for your system.

As of this writing, browsers capable of running Java 1.0 applets include the following:

- Netscape Navigator version 2.0 and later
- HotJava browser Beta and later versions
- Oracle PowerBrowser version 1.5 and later releases
- Internet Explorer versions 3.0 Beta and later

When you have a Java-enabled browser, you can view your Web presentation. To do this, point your browser at the appropriate URL, such as the following:

`http://www.yourprovider.com/~yourid/present.html`

After downloading the document called `present.html`, your browser will download the necessary files to run the applets in the presentation. Therefore, you will notice a slight delay before the applets display. Now, all that's left is to wait for some feedback on your presentation.

How Does Java Compare to Other Available Products?

Java is a wonderful language and, for what it was designed to do, no other language comes close to it. However, this does not mean that it is a cure-all that does everything. Java as a programming language can be compared with other general-purpose programming languages, including the advantages of the different languages and the different ways they are used on the World Wide Web. The following sections perform this comparison. Although HTML is not considered a programming language, the boundaries between Java and HTML are also explored here.

Java Versus Perl

Perl has long been the preferred language of CGI programming. For server-based programs, few languages offer the power combined with ease of programmability to match Perl. Perl's true strength lies in its capability to perform rapid text parsing and its excellent string-manipulation features. When strictly dealing with text, Perl is often much faster than Java. However, Perl does not have Java's strong graphics capabilities.

Java is a *distributed language*, which means that it does not have to run on the server as Perl generally does. In addition to saving processing power on the server, Java applets can be moved from site to site more easily. Having Java run on the client means that Java can be stored on and run off any type of server without any change to the source or class files. Perl files can be moved from site to site, but they often require slight modifications after the move.

The biggest limitation of Java applets compared with Perl is that Java cannot write information to the server. However, this is a security issue, not a lack of programming power on Java's part. Look for problems such as this to be addressed within the next year.

Java Versus Other Programming Languages

Java can be compared with other languages besides Perl. Scripts can be written in the UNIX shell, C, or C++, which have the advantages of being well known and popular. They provide many low-level routines that Java does not supply. They enable the programmer to customize the application for a particular operating system or hardware. They also have been in use for many years, so there is a large quantity of existing routines for each. Therefore, don't expect Java to replace them in every area.

Java is a robust and powerful distributed language. Java's security also far surpasses the other languages discussed. However, this security is not needed in all applications. Java supports code reuse, but if large portions of the code already exist in another language, that may be the most appropriate language to use. Java's system independence is an advantage, but there is still an associated overhead. For areas that require a lot of numeric calculations, C may provide much faster response time. (See Chapter 18, "Using Java Applications in the Real World," for the inside scoop on using C and C++ routines with Java.)

Often, discussions about programming involve drawing analogies to carpentry or mechanics. These analogies are correct in stating that a programmer, like a carpenter, should use the right tool for the job at hand. A new nail gun will never be a reason to replace a trusty hammer, and a hot new programming language is no reason to abandon one with which you are comfortable.

Use the programming language that is appropriate for the job. If your project requires writing to a server, perhaps Perl or C++ would be your best choice. But for creating distributed applets or applications to run on the Internet, Java has no rival. Let the job dictate the proper tool. This is true for distributed software as well as for custom applications.

Java Versus Off-the-Shelf Software

Will distributed programs written in Java replace much of the off-the-shelf software of today? Although this might sound like a good selling point for Java, several technological advances will be required before this comes to fruition. Security and connection speeds, for example, must continue to improve.

Although Java is more secure than most general-purpose software-development languages, this security is not yet generally accepted. As the language becomes more widely used, there will be an increase in attempts to breach the security. Security will probably improve as the language develops, however, and the wider use of Java will help eliminate these concerns for many people.

Many of the speed concerns regarding transfer time for Java applets will be eliminated if ISDN or cable modems become the next standard for Internet connections. Using ISDN, you can connect at 64Kbps, 128Kbps, or more. Using cable modems, you can connect at speeds exceeding one megabit per second. However, to expect transfer rates for data across the Internet to approach the transfer rates of typical hard drives sounds a bit far-fetched at this time. Until these problems can be addressed, software manufacturers can remain confident that users will want to purchase and install local copies of most of their software.

Can Java produce software comparable in quality to what is seen on retailer's shelves? Yes. As an application-programming language, Java is quite competitive. In the upcoming chapters you will see how Java can be used for creating stand-alone programs as well as how it can support development by combining with other languages to produce robust programs. To complete this section, let's look at how Java works with HTML to meet user needs over the Internet.

Java Versus HTML

For several years, HTML has been the de facto language of the World Wide Web. Expecting Java to replace it is out of the question; all Web browsers make use of the markup tags inside HTML to display a Web publication. Java is an extension of this capability, not a replacement for it.

Some programmers believe that Java may assist in replacing the ever-expanding set of HTML tags. Instead of relying on HTML to format a Web document, they believe that Java can handle the formatting. However, because Java applets take significantly longer to transfer and run, I doubt that this will be put to use in the near future. For most sites, users would prefer to get rapid access to information. Because HTML files are transferred as plain text, they can be downloaded in very little time.

When HTML documents include images and sound clips, the transfer time is increased. In this case, Java might not significantly increase the time to load the page. However, if the images are static and can be successfully displayed using HTML tags, there might not be any reason to use Java. When the images would be more interesting if viewed one at a time, it might be advantageous to create an applet to display them. If the user would benefit by being able to start and stop the sound clip, a Java applet could enhance the page as well.

Java is best working with HTML, not trying to replace it. Java provides more capability for user interaction, but requires more patience on the part of the users. Java is an extension to HTML similar to the CGI scripts that first allowed users to enter data in response to HTML forms. Applets that allow storage of multiple URLs are actually a replacement of the CGI programs that do the same thing. Both CGI and Java still rely on HTML for display and distribution across the World Wide Web.

The future may well see faster data-transfer speeds across the Internet and thus make the viewing of multiple applets a less time-consuming event. If this happens, expect to see even more applets than are in use today, perhaps even Web presentations that are in fact an applet in and of themselves. In the meantime and for the foreseeable future, Java and HTML are partners.

Summary

In this chapter, the discussion has moved from placing Java applets on the World Wide Web to HTML tags to selecting the proper language for programming. Some of this might seem confusing until you have the experience of putting it into practice. When you begin to move applets from your computer to a server for display on the Internet, however, most of it will become clear. Just as with programming, the best way to learn is to practice.

The Internet is changing daily, but most of the change is merely growth and extension of protocols and methods that were already in place. What you have learned in this chapter is not final; it is only a jumping-off point into the Internet. Expect Java to continue to grow and expand alongside the Internet and, most of all, just have some fun with it as you go along.

16

Applet
Reuse

Software has become increasingly sophisticated and robust. The time allocated to develop it has decreased while its complexity has increased. To meet these conflicting demands, better tools for creating software were developed. Yet even with better tools, it is expensive and time-consuming to develop new software for every aspect of a project. Furthermore, often there are portions of a new project that are similar to work done on a preceding project. If the code from preceding projects is incorporated into the new project, time is saved not only on coding, but also on design and testing.

Because of the advantages of reusing code, modern languages have attempted to make code reuse easier. The object-oriented paradigm helps to encapsulate implementation details and promote reuse. Because Java is object-oriented, reuse of existing applets is an important consideration when creating new applets with similar features.

Java applets can be extended without modifying the existing code by merely extending the original classes and adding new ones. The advantage of adding code is the minimized chance of breaking any working applet. Although there is no guarantee that the extension will work the first time, there is no chance that the original applet will cease to operate or that other applets extending the original will be affected.

There are, however, times when it is advantageous to rewrite existing code to include new features rather than simply extending it, such as when there are fundamental changes to the understanding that led to the original design of the applet. The ramifications of such a change will depend on how widely the applet is used. Sometimes it is easier to release a completely new applet under a different name than simply leverage code from the existing applet.

The beginning of this chapter covers how to determine when reuse is appropriate based on the existing applet and the new requirements. Several examples of reusing code by extending applets are included. The chapter then presents an example in which rewriting is preferable to reuse.

Adding Functionality to Existing Applets

One of the biggest advantages to an object-oriented programming language such as Java is the ease with which existing code can be reused. The capability to reuse code increases the programmer's ability to modify both applets and applications.

Applets can be extended by creating a new applet as an extension of an existing one. Adding functionality to existing applets decreases design and coding time, resulting in modifications being released faster. The decrease in time between requirements analysis and applet release increases the likelihood that the applet will meet user needs.

Adding functionality to existing applets makes it easier to have several related products or different versions of the same product. Each product or version can be the result of different extensions.

Deciding Between Reusing and Rewriting Code

Reuse, in general, includes extending classes, adding new methods, overriding existing methods, or creating new classes to increase functionality. Reusing an applet implies that you will create a new class that is an extension of the original class. This extension is not a replacement; therefore, it must have a new name. However, because it is created by extending the original class, it will inherit portions of its functionality from that class.

Class reuse allows you to build larger, more complex, more sophisticated applets because you do not need to build the same pieces each time you start a new project. Benefits of class reuse include less code to develop, less code to maintain, and not having to redesign the same items repeatedly. As programmers learn more about the existing Java classes and increase their understanding of these classes, better ways to combine classes to provide the desired functionality will become apparent.

Using the same tools repeatedly, rather than switching regularly, enables the programmer to become thoroughly familiar with the classes. Reuse enables developers to create classes from a common base set so that many classes can be developed with the same features without having to recode the features.

Reuse is a benefit when it is easier to locate and include existing objects than it is to create new objects. Object-oriented programming languages in general make it easier to include existing code because objects are encapsulated and only interact with each other in well-defined ways. Now that you have learned how reusing and rewriting can be employed to add functionality to existing applets, you need to learn when it is appropriate to use each option.

Rewriting an applet means modifying one or more of the existing class definitions in the applet. This type of change can take many forms, including adding new class variables, changing the algorithm in a method, changing the interaction between methods of the class, or altering any underlying design decisions. When an applet is rewritten, it will have the same name as the original but will function differently. The original functionality may be enhanced or decreased, or may remain the same in the new applet. When you rewrite code, there is the potential of introducing errors in working applets and the danger of breaking classes that are an extension of the rewritten class.

Rewriting might not seem like a problem, but if the class has been used in several places, modifying it has the potential to affect several applets. Methods that are overridden in the extensions might no longer function as expected. Class-level variables used in the extension might be eliminated. New algorithms that improve the functioning of the class might be incompatible with the design of the class extensions.

The amount of challenge involved in rewriting an applet depends on how extensively the classes involved have been reused. For a single developer, there might be little risk in rewriting an existing applet. The developer can easily determine all the places where the applet has been used. However, for a multi-person development team with common object classes, changing a class can be a major undertaking. The team must locate all the places the class has been used and determine how the rewrite will affect those objects.

Changes that can be isolated and do not affect the overall design of the class are best made by extending the class. Changes that affect the core functionality of the class are best accomplished by rewriting. It may be prudent to rewrite using a new class name so that classes that are extensions of the existing one will continue to function correctly. Deciding between reusing an applet and rewriting it begins by accurately assessing the needs of the users.

Just as the first step in any development project is to determine the needs the program must fulfill, the beginning of any modification or enhancement is determining the requirements. This includes determining new functionality to be added, areas that could be improved, and perhaps some features that can be eliminated altogether. It is important to accurately understand the changes that are desired. A project that successfully implements unwanted changes is not truly successful.

Some questions to consider in determining the needs for a particular applet with regard to reusing or rewriting are

- What functionality does the applet currently provide?
- How could the existing features be enhanced?
- What functionality is missing at this time?
- Are all the features being used?
- What functionality may be desired in the future?

These questions are significant because they provide insight into the true requirements of the new applet. An understanding of all the existing functionality is needed so that all of it can be incorporated into any rewrite and tested in the test plan for the rewritten applet.

Studying ways to enhance the features of an applet to fulfill new needs can help determine which classes you need to extend. Asking about missing functionality indicates other ways the applet needs to be extended. Similarly, noting unused features allows for simplified redesign of an applet; unused features can be eliminated altogether.

Looking at these needs helps to determine if an applet should be extended or entirely rewritten. Suppose you have an applet that allows a user to enter two numbers, sums the two numbers, and displays the results. It is easy to imagine extending the applet to display the average of the two numbers as well. However, if you want an applet to sum a list of three or four numbers, it might be more appropriate to rewrite the applet because there will probably be modifications to the user input, code for checking when the input is complete, changes to the summation routine, and possibly changes to the display of the results to show how many numbers were added. As part of the rewrite, the applet could be made flexible enough to sum an arbitrarily long list of numbers as well.

> **Tip:** Although the coding effort involved in modifying an existing applet might not be as extensive as an initial development project, the analysis of requirements is as important and should be as extensive.

When you have answered the questions about the current needs, you can begin to look at ways to design and implement the new features. Design is as important when extending an applet as it is when creating a new one. When making these changes, it is often helpful to find existing applets with functionality similar to the features you plan to add. This is why a working knowledge of a variety of Java objects is beneficial.

The best way to learn about the objects supplied with Java is to examine existing applets and applications. You can look at the ones supplied with this book, work through them, and then download more applets from the Internet. You should also review the API to determine existing classes that can make developing your applet easier.

Carefully examine existing classes and look at functionality from an object-oriented point of view. An applet that plays sound clips when a user presses a button is not very different from an applet that displays images or plays MPEG clips when the user presses a button. You might be able to convert an existing applet to a new task with just a few minor changes.

It is important to gain a thorough understanding of the classes that make up the existing applet to determine how to incorporate the changes. Be sure to examine how the objects in the applet communicate with one another and how a new object will affect that communication. For example, if you reduce the size of the applet, you might need to change the size of some of the objects it displays. Part of understanding the classes used in an applet is determining how objects are placed on the screen. Then you can see what must be done to add a new object or change the layout.

When adding a new method, look at all the objects it might encounter and think of all the ways it might be invoked. Consider the possible side effects of changes to class variables or objects. Although you can never take all possibilities into account, you might want to consider where future enhancements are likely to occur and how things can be structured now to incorporate them easily later.

You should consider whether parts of another existing applet are similar to parts of the enhancement. Perhaps the controls and user-input areas are similar to something that exists and only the display needs to change, or vice versa. If code can be leveraged from an existing applet, writing the extended applet will be faster and easier.

The challenge in analyzing existing objects lies in the sheer volume of objects from which to choose. You have all of the API at your disposal, plus all the applets you have written, plus the many applets that are available at no cost through the Internet. One way to simplify your first attempt at a development project is to search for an applet similar to the one you want to create and to modify it.

Appearance is the most obvious way to analyze existing objects. Does this object display the way I want? Does it have all the parts I need? This is somewhat deceiving because the actual appearance of the object is the easiest to change. If you like the functionality of an object but do not like the image it displays or the shape it has, you can extend the object and rewrite only the method(s) that affect the display. Normally, all of the display will be isolated in one or two methods, such as `draw()` or `paint()`.

Besides appearance, consider the functionality of the object. Look for desired features an object possesses and determine if several objects working together are needed to create them. Study any features in the object that are unnecessary or unwanted to determine if they can be easily eliminated. Then determine any additional functionality you will need before the object can be used in the applet.

When studying the objects in an applet and considering new ones, you should also consider flexibility. Would it be better to rewrite an existing class at this time because it does not include enough options to allow for future expansion?

The hardest part in extending an existing object is being sure that your extensions are sufficient to bring about the changes you want without introducing any unwanted side effects. To do so, carefully examine the source code for the object. Pay close attention to when it creates its own methods and when it is using methods from a superclass. When you replace a method, you might want to use a call to the superclass to include the existing method as well as the one you create. Then again, it might be that you don't want the method of the object you are extending, but you do want the method of its superclass. Java is flexible enough to allow you to make that decision.

When to Reuse

In most development efforts, even when creating a new applet, you will reuse existing classes. Indeed, it would be exhausting and pointless to create all the objects by extending the `Object` class directly. The capability to reuse existing objects makes Java a powerful language.

Rather than creating an object by extending the `Object` class, you should extend an existing object when it meets the following criteria:

- It meets most of your requirements
- It can be easily extended to meet all of your requirements
- It can be incorporated into your design without extensive changes

Note: Because applets are just a particular type of object, these same guidelines can be applied to them.

There are four challenges to using existing objects:

- Locating the most appropriate object
- Assessing the merits of the existing object
- Modifying the object to the exact needs of the applet
- Maintaining an accumulation of objects

Java assists with all four of these areas. It makes it easy to locate existing objects by supplying the developer with the API documentation in HTML form, including links to related objects and an easy-to-search index. Because the documentation is electronic, it can be extended to include new objects as they are developed. The widespread popularity of the Java language and its portability across platforms increase the possibility of a particular object existing. Searching for suitable objects available on the Net is simplified by the platform independence and object-oriented nature of the language.

Java's documentation features enable developers to supply comments that can help assess an object's applicability to a given situation. The encapsulation of objects makes it easier to determine if an existing object supplies all the functions needed or if new methods must be added to the object for the new applet. Java also makes it easy to create a simple applet and test the class to determine its robustness and suitability.

It is particularly easy to adapt existing Java classes to specific needs by extending them. There is no limit on the number of extensions to a class, so existing classes can be extended many times. Therefore, it is reasonable to create most new classes by extending existing ones rather than extending the `Object` class. This means that more code can be reused and customized to fit your needs.

Java's ability to extract documentation from the comments included in the class definition eases the task of maintaining a large collection of useful objects. Its packaging features enable developers to group related classes. Its object-oriented nature and encapsulation features mean that a particular class can be stored without worry that it will be "missing something" if it is used again somewhere else.

The Java language is clearly meant to assist with all four of the challenges of code reuse. Because it is so conducive to reusing code, you might wonder when it is appropriate to rewrite a Java object. This topic is discussed in the next section.

When to Rewrite

Because rewriting code is inherently more costly than reusing it, even more consideration should be given to the decision to rewrite an applet. Rewrite an applet in the following situations:

- When you are altering its core functionality.
- When the changes you are making will affect more methods and classes than they will leave alone.

- When you are making a change in an assumption that was fundamental to the creation of the applet.

Rewriting is appropriate if the core functions of the applet have changed, if the assumptions on which the applet is based have changed, or if a better method of accomplishing the applet's task is found. Rewriting also may be necessary if the applet is communicating with another program and the interface is modified.

An applet is just a particular type of object, so it is not surprising that rewriting a single object is as challenging as rewriting an entire applet. Before rewriting an applet, it is important to isolate all the places that the object is used. Determine how the changes will affect each applet where the object appears and if the changes are desired in all of them. If the changes are desired only in some of the applets, you are better off copying the code to a new object class, making the changes there, and modifying only the applets that need the change so they point to the new class. This is the safest and often best way to modify any existing class.

Before presenting an example of rewriting an applet, the following sections illustrate several examples of applet extension. This demonstrates the ease with which applets can be extended. It also assists in establishing the circumstances when extending is better than rewriting and vice versa.

Extending an Applet

The steps for extending an applet are similar to the steps for constructing a new one. You must design the modification, code it, and test it. Testing is even more important when modifying existing applets because you must ensure that no existing functionality is lost, so it is discussed in detail in the "Testing the Extended Applet" section in this chapter.

You must take care when extending classes, and when creating them in the first place, to choose new class names that do not conflict with other classes in use. This potential can be reduced by carefully choosing names and by grouping classes into appropriate packages. Classes in the same package must have unique class names.

> **Note:** When considering the possibility of naming conflicts, keep in mind the five levels of the namespace used by Java. If two packages exist with classes having the same name, the package name is used to differentiate between the classes in an applet.

This section presents three increasingly complex examples of extending existing applets. It concludes with an example of an applet rewrite. Notice that the amount of work involved in the extension does not necessarily depend on the complexity of the initial applet.

Reusing ScrollText

The first example shows how simple extending an applet can be. You will add another parameter to the ScrollText applet to allow the HTML document to specify the background color of the applet. With this enhancement, the applet can run with the same background color as the document and the text will appear to be scrolling without a rectangular box around it.

The design of this modification is straightforward. The extended applet will read the new parameter and set the new background color at initialization. If the background parameter is not passed from the HTML file, the applet will set the background to white. For simplicity, the applet accepts input as a single integer in base 10. However, the program could easily expect three integers, three floats, or a single hex number such as HTML uses.

To create this extension, you will extend the existing ScrollText class to create a new class called ScrollText2. You need to create a .java file containing the code for the new class. This file must go in the same directory as the existing ScrollText file so that the Java compiler can find the original ScrollText class. The Java compiler needs to read the ScrollText.class file before extending the class.

> **Technical Note:** When extending a class, the Java compiler needs to locate the original class file. If it cannot locate the original class file but can locate the original source file, it will attempt to compile the original source code before compiling the new source code file. Therefore, if the ScrollText.java file containing the original class and the ScrollText2.java file containing the extended class are in the same directory, the Java compiler will first compile the ScrollText.java file to obtain the necessary class file and then compile the ScrollText2.java file. The result of this is a ScrollText.class file and a ScrollText2.class file.

In the new class, you will use the Color class, so you must import java.awt.Color. This is shown at the top of Listing 16.1. The new class will have two new class-level variables. The first will hold the string containing the input value of the new parameter, and the second is an object in the Color class.

The new class only has one method, init(). This method overrides the init() method in ScrollText. However, the first line of code in the new init() method calls the init() method of its superclass. This means the init() method in the original ScrollText class is used to read and store the parameters that are defined there. When that is completed, the init() method for ScrollText2 reads the parameter supplied under the name background. If the value of this parameter is null, the backColor object is set to a default background color of white. If the parameter is not null, it is converted to an integer and used to define a new color in the backColor object. In the final line of the method in Listing 16.1, the backColor object is used by the method setBackground(), thereby setting the new background color.

> **Note:** For simplicity's sake, the applet accepts color input as a single integer in base 10. This means the value for the background parameter may be any integer between 0 and 16,777,216, which is the range of colors on Java's 16.7 million–color palette.

Listing 16.1. The `ScrollText2` applet.

```java
import java.awt.Color;

/**
 * Peter Norton's Guide to Java Programming
 * The ScrollText2 Applet
 * This applet is used to scroll a text banner across the screen
 * and is an extension of the ScrollText Applet
 * The applet takes BACKGROUND, TEXT, WIDTH, and HEIGHT
 * as parameters.
 */

public class ScrollText2 extends ScrollText {

        String bs = null;                // Input string containing background color
        Color backColor;                 // Background color

/* Setup width, height, and display text */
public void init() {
        super.init();                    // Do original initialization

        bs = getParameter("background");
        if (bs == null){                 // Read color as input, if not found use default
            backColor = Color.white;
        } else {
// Convert color string to color
                backColor = new Color(Integer.parseInt(bs));
        }
        setBackground(backColor);        // Set the background color according to input

    }
}
```

As you can see, the code for this example is quite short; however, although the change is small, it is reasonable to extend the existing class rather than to modify it. By extending the class, you eliminate the risk of breaking working HTML pages that use the applet as defined. You also provide two different versions of the applet, so the Web-page designer can select the most appropriate version.

To compile the applet, save it to the file `ScrollText2.java` in the same directory as `ScrollText.java`. Then change to the directory containing the `ScrollText2.java` file and type the following at the command prompt:

```
javac ScrollText2.java
```

The new ScrollText2 class can be used in an HTML file by including the following:

```
<APPLET CODE=ScrollText2 WIDTH=400 HEIGHT=200></APPLET>
```

This example and the next both modify the screen displayed to the user. The third example is somewhat more complex because it involves multiple classes and requires that several methods be modified.

Reusing RGB2Hex

In this section, you will extend the RGB2Hex applet by adding a color wheel in the middle of the applet's canvas. Having a color wheel will provide a means of contrasting the color the user has entered with other existing colors and will assist your users in picking values for the color they want.

This new functionality meets the criteria for applet reuse because most of the existing applet remains the same. The core functionality of the applet is unchanged, as is its overall operation. Although you must make changes in several parts of the code, these sections are easily isolated and extended.

There are tradeoffs in any software-construction or -modification project. In this case, you could have created the color wheel as a separate class and included a component of that class on the RGBcanvas. Alternatively, you could modify the paint() method of the RGBcanvas class to paint the color wheel after it colors the canvas. In this case, because the color wheel is not required to perform any task, the second option is best. However, you will isolate the additions by creating a new method, paintwheel(), which will display the color wheel. The code for the new method follows:

```
public void paintwheel(Graphics g,int wheel_size,int wheel_x,int wheel_y){
    g.setColor(Color.red);
    g.fillArc(wheel_x, wheel_y, wheel_size, wheel_size, 0, 60);
    g.setColor(Color.orange);
    g.fillArc(wheel_x, wheel_y, wheel_size, wheel_size, 60, 60);
    g.setColor(Color.yellow);
    g.fillArc(wheel_x, wheel_y, wheel_size, wheel_size, 120, 60);
    g.setColor(Color.green);
    g.fillArc(wheel_x, wheel_y, wheel_size, wheel_size, 180, 60);
    g.setColor(Color.blue);
    g.fillArc(wheel_x, wheel_y, wheel_size, wheel_size, 240, 60);
    g.setColor(new Color(150,0,150));
    g.fillArc(wheel_x, wheel_y, wheel_size, wheel_size, 300, 60);
}
```

The paintwheel() method requires that the caller supply the Graphics object on which the wheel will be drawn. This works because the paint() method calling the paintwheel() method will have a Graphics object to pass. paintwheel() also requires that the caller supply the x and y coordinates at which to draw the wheel and the size of the wheel.

The method uses the setColor() and fillArc() methods from the Graphics class to draw a color wheel with six colors at the location specified. The setColor() method requires a Color object as a parameter. It sets the default color to the value it is passed. The `fillArc()` method creates an arc on the screen using the default color that was set by `setColor()`. The arcs are drawn in a circle using the same x,y coordinates. Six 60-degree angles are used to create a full circle. The colors used are all defined colors in the `Color` class of the Java API, except for the purple arc because purple is not part of the existing `Color` class. Purple is created as a new color in the `paintwheel()` method and then passed to the `setColor()` method.

Another alternative would be to create a `Color` class that includes a `Color.Purple` variable. To keep the extended applet as short as possible, however, this option was not chosen. It is sometimes faster and easier to define an instance of an object with a specific property, such as the color purple, than to extend the entire class to include that property. On the other hand, if you were to create several applets using a specific color scheme that included shades of purple, you might want to define a class called `ShadesOfPurple` that would include variables such as `PalePurple`, `LightPurple`, `MediumPurple`, and `DarkPurple`. The class `ShadesOfPurple` would have to be formed by extending the `Object` class because the `Color` class is declared as final in the API, meaning that it cannot be extended directly.

The `paintwheel()` method draws a color wheel, but it must be incorporated into the applet. The method is included in a new class formed by extending the `RGBcanvas` class. The new class is called `RGBcanvas2` and is declared as follows:

```
class RGBcanvas2 extends RGBcanvas {
```

The new class's one new method is `paintwheel()`, which overrides the `paint()` method from `RGBcanvas` and inherits the remainder of its features. If you had created the color wheel as a separate object, you would have had to redraw the wheel each time you painted the canvas so that the wheel would remain on top of the canvas. This would have meant changing the controls to draw both the canvas and the wheel. Sometimes the best way to incorporate a change is the one that involves changing the fewest methods.

In this case, you want the color wheel to appear on the canvas. Furthermore, the color wheel should appear no matter how many times the canvas is redrawn. Otherwise, the `paint()` method of the `RGBcanvas2` class should perform all the tasks the `paint` method in the original `RGBcanvas` class performs. Therefore, the `paint()` method in the new class contains the code from the `paint()` method in the `RGBcanvas` class. Following that, it will call the method defined previously to paint the color wheel on the display using the following line of code:

```
paintwheel(g, r.height/2, r.width/2 - r.height/4, r.height/4);
```

This is a complicated-looking line of code. Let's examine it more closely to see what it accomplishes. The `paintwheel()` method defined earlier takes four parameters. The first is the `Graphics` object on which to paint. This is supplied by the `paint()` method in the `RGBcanvas` class and is the first parameter passed on the code line.

The next parameter specified is the diameter of the color wheel. Because the area of the RGBcanvas object is wider than it is tall, use one-half the height as the diameter of the wheel. Conveniently, the paint() method of RGBcanvas already calls the bounds() method to determine its size. It stores this information in the rectangle object r that is referenced in the code line. The height of the rectangle is r.height. The wheel should have a diameter of half the height, so pass r.height/2 as the size of the wheel.

The last two parameters are the x and y coordinates for the lower-left corner of the region where you want the wheel drawn. This is required to accommodate the drawArc()method used in the paintwheel() method. You want the wheel to be centered from top to bottom and from left to right, and you know that its diameter is half the height of the box. Therefore, the y coordinate of the lower-left corner is set at one-quarter of the height of the box, or r.height/4.

The x coordinate is a little more complicated because the box is wider than it is tall. First, you determine the center of the box, r.width/2. Then subtract half the width of the circle you will draw. The total height of the circle is r.height/2, so half the height of the circle is r.height/4. Therefore, the x coordinate for the paintwheel() method is r.width/2−r.height/4.

The complete paint() method appears as follows:

```
public void paint(Graphics g) {
Rectangle r = bounds();

createColor =
    new Color(super.RedValue, super.GreenValue, super.blueValue);
g.setColor(createColor);
g.fillRect(0,0,r.width,r.height);
paintwheel(g, r.height / 2, r.width/2 - r.height/4, r.height/4);
```

The method as defined raises two questions: First, why wasn't a call to the superclass used, as in the last example, to use the paint() method in RGBcanvas? Primarily because you needed the values r.height and r.width to pass to the paintwheel() method. Because you cannot access these values from the superclass, you had the option of re-creating the entire procedure or repeating the work of creating the rectangle. Second, why was this complex formula created rather than giving paintwheel explicit x and y coordinates? The formula ensures that the color wheel will be centered in the RGBcanvas2 no matter how the canvas is sized. Using the formula means that the class is flexible enough to handle small and large sizes.

Having added this new class, you can compile and test it. Notice that there is no resulting change to the applet. You still must use the new class somewhere in the existing code. To do this, you must extend the applet itself. The new applet will be an extension of RGB2Hex, just as the new canvas is an extension of RGBcanvas.

Select a new name for the extended applet, in this case, RGB2Hex2. This applet is stored in a separate file, and the class RGB2Hex2 is created as an extension of RGB2Hex. Remember, in extending the applet the existing class will remain the same. The declaration for the new class appears as follows:

```
class RGB2Hex2 extends RGB2Hex {
```

This completes the changes required to add the color wheel to the applet. Figure 16.1 shows the applet with the color wheel.

Figure 16.1.
The RGB2Hex2 *applet.*

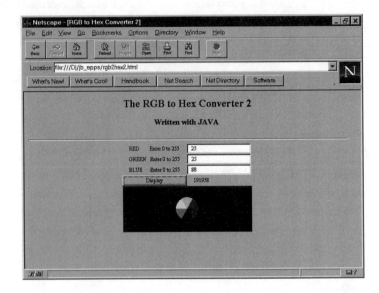

The changes made in this example do not differ in most respects from adding a function in a conventional programming language. However, the original applet, without the color wheel, remains intact for others to use. To illustrate the size of the extended applet in comparison to the code for the original applet, the complete code listing for the extended applet is shown in Listing 16.2.

Listing 16.2. The RGB2Hex2 **applet.**

```
import java.awt.*;
import java.applet.*;

/**
 * Peter Norton's Guide to Programming Java  * The RGB2Hex2 Applet
 * Converts Red, Green, and Blue values entered by the user
 * to a hexidecimal color code and displays the color.
 * This applet extends the RGB2Hex applet.
 * To help you better correlate colors the extended applet
 * displays a color wheel.
 */

public class RGB2Hex2 extends RGB2Hex {
    public void init() {
     setLayout(new BorderLayout());
     RGBcanvas c = new RGBcanvas2();
     add("Center", c);
     add("North", controls = new RGBcontrols(c));
        resize(300,300);
     }
}
```

```
/* Provides an object to display a color and colorwheel*/
class RGBcanvas2 extends RGBcanvas {
    public void paint(Graphics g) {
      Rectangle r = bounds();

      createColor =
          new Color(super.RedValue, super.GreenValue, super.blueValue);
      g.setColor(createColor);
      g.fillRect(0,0,r.width,r.height);
      paintwheel(g, r.height / 2, r.width/2 - r.height/4, r.height/4);
    }

/* Paints color wheel on the graphics object at the location specified */
public void paintwheel(Graphics g,int wheel_size,int wheel_x,int wheel_y){
    g.setColor(Color.red);
    g.fillArc(wheel_x, wheel_y, wheel_size, wheel_size, 0, 60);
    g.setColor(Color.orange);
    g.fillArc(wheel_x, wheel_y, wheel_size, wheel_size, 60, 60);
    g.setColor(Color.yellow);
    g.fillArc(wheel_x, wheel_y, wheel_size, wheel_size, 120, 60);
    g.setColor(Color.green);
    g.fillArc(wheel_x, wheel_y, wheel_size, wheel_size, 180, 60);
    g.setColor(Color.blue);
    g.fillArc(wheel_x, wheel_y, wheel_size, wheel_size, 240, 60);
    g.setColor(new Color(150,0,150));
    g.fillArc(wheel_x, wheel_y, wheel_size, wheel_size, 300, 60);
    }
}
```

The code for this applet should reside in the same directory as the code for the RGB2Hex applet so the Java compiler can locate the classes defined in RGB2Hex. The compiler must be able to locate those classes because all the classes defined in RGB2Hex2 are extensions of classes in RGB2Hex. The command to compile the new applet follows:

```
javac RGB2Hex2.java
```

The results of this compilation are two new files: RGB2Hex2.class and RGBcanvas2.class. The applet can be added to an HTML file as follows:

```
<HTML>
<HEAD>
<TITLE> RGB to Hex Converter 2</TITLE>
</HEAD>
<BODY>
<CENTER>
<H2> The RGB to Hex Converter 2</H2>
<H3> Written with JAVA <H3>
<HR>
<APPLET CODE="RGB2Hex2" WIDTH=300 HEIGHT=300>
</APPLET>
</CENTER>
</BODY>
</HTML>
```

Both of the examples so far have added to the display of the applet but have not significantly added to its capabilities. The next example increases the functionality of the applet so that it provides an interactive service that was not present in the original applet.

Reusing the `QuizMaker` Applet

In this example, you will modify the `QuizMaker` applet to allow the user to specify the length of time for the timer. After all, not everyone wants to take a three-minute quiz. This is an example of extending an applet to increase its functionality without changing how the applet performs its task. Although the change may seem more extensive than in the first example, the basic functioning of the `QuizMaker` applet remains the same.

One of the key design concepts for the extended applet is the need for somewhere to store the time for which the timer will run. This storage place must be accessed by both the method checking for the expiration of the timer and the method that displays it to the user. Therefore, this value should be stored at a class level.

The applet will also need to display this value to the user and be able to read a new value from him or her. For now, let's assume the applet will read the new value at the same time the button is pressed to start the timer. You can add a text input field to display the initial value and allow the user to modify it. However, if the user sets it to zero or to an invalid value such as text, you do not need to start the timer when the button is pressed.

Should the timer length be stored as an object or as a variable? Well, the value has no meaning apart from the timer that is using it. It would not make sense to have a timer length without a timer. Therefore, this is a property of the timer and not a separate object. So you should store the timer length as a class-level variable named `TimerLength`. This will be an integer value to store the number of seconds the timer will run.

The text input field used to display and retrieve information from the user can be created using a class, supplied in the API, named `LengthEntry`. It must be present when the timer starts, so adding it to the applet will be the responsibility of the `init()` method. This is done using the same `add()` method used by other objects. The line of code to add the text field and initialize its value follows:

```
this.add(LengthEntry = new TextField("180"));
```

This example initializes the value in the display to three minutes. The `StopTimer()` method must be modified to check the class-level object instead of using the value `180` that was hard-coded originally. The modified line appears as follows:

```
if ((stopSec - startSec) > TimerLength) {
```

The most interesting design decision is to determine when and where to set the new value in the class variable. It must be done after the button is pressed but before the start time is calculated. It could be done as part of the event handler or as part of the start() method. It could be coded into the existing methods, or a new method could be created for this task.

To decide where to place the code that sets the timer length, consider how the timer works. The decision to set the length of the timer is really made by the user. The applet is reading in the value in response to an action by the user. You could even modify the timer at some point to provide a second button just to accept new values for the timer length. This means that setting the timer value is associated more with the user event than with the starting of the timer. You might even want to modify the timer to include an automatic restart, and you probably would not want to have to reset the timer length every time. Therefore, a good way to set this value is via the event handler. To keep the event handler from becoming too long or complicated, create a new method to handle this task and call the method from the event handler.

The new method appears as follows:

```
protected void setTimer() {
      try {
         TimerLength = Integer.parseInt(LengthEntry.getText());
      } catch (NumberFormatException e) {
         TimerLength = 0;          // If error occurs set length to 0
      }
      if (TimerLength < 0)
         TimerLength = 0;          // If length is invalid set to 0
   }
}
```

This method sets the timer if the value in the text field is a valid integer greater than zero. If it is not an integer or is less than zero, it will set the length to zero.

This completes all the modifications to the applet. Figure 16.2 shows how the resulting changes will appear to the user.

Figure 16.2.
The QuizMaker *applet allowing the user to set the timer interval.*

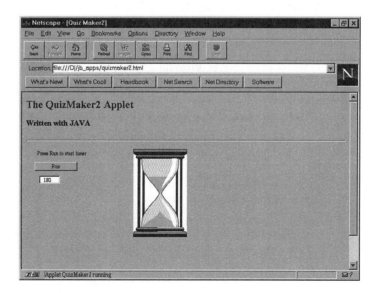

The complete code for the extension is shown in Listing 16.3. Notice how few lines of code are necessary to complete the entire extension.

Listing 16.3. The `QuizMaker2` applet.

```java
import java.awt.*;
import java.applet.*;
import java.util.*;

/**
 * Peter Norton's Guide to Java Programming
 * The QuizMaker2 Applet
 * Acts as an arbitrary length timer. Plays an audio message to start and
 * displays a start message. Plays an audio message at the end with
 * another display message.
 * This applet extends the QuizMaker applet.
 */

public class QuizMaker2 extends QuizMaker {
    int TimerLength;
    TextField LengthEntry;

    public void init() {
      this.add(LengthEntry = new TextField("180"));
      super.init();
    }

    public void paint(Graphics g) {
      super.paint(g);
      LengthEntry.resize(50,20);
      LengthEntry.move(30,70);
    }

    /* Checks the current system time to determine
        if 180 seconds has elapsed since start */
    protected boolean stopTimer(int startSec) {
      int stopSec;

      Date StopTime = new Date();            // Get the new time
      stopSec = StopTime.getSeconds();       // Get the number of seconds
      stopSec += (StopTime.getMinutes() * 60); // Add # of minutes times 60
      if ((stopSec - startSec) > TimerLength) {
          return true;                       // True means time has elapsed
      } else {
          return false;                      // False means time not elapsed
      }
    }

    /* Event handler to detect when the button on the window is pressed */
    public boolean handleEvent(Event e) {
// If the button is pressed start timer
      if (e.target instanceof Button) {
          setTimer();          // Set the length of time to run the timer
          runTimer();          // Start the timer
          return true;         // Return true so super does not act
      }
      return false;            // Return false so super can act on event
    }
```

```
protected void setTimer() {
    try {
      TimerLength = Integer.parseInt(LengthEntry.getText());
    } catch (NumberFormatException e) {
        TimerLength = 0;            // If error occurs set length to 0
    }
    if (TimerLength < 0)
        TimerLength = 0;            // If length is invalid set to 0
    }
}
```

This applet is significantly more versatile than the original QuizMaker applet. However, there are always ways to improve software, and there are always additional features desired by users. Not all of these features are best added by extending an applet. The last example shows why it may be appropriate to rewrite this particular applet.

Rewriting the QuizMaker Applet

The QuizMaker applet is more flexible now that the user can set the timer, but it still stops all the other functions of the computer while waiting on the timer. On a modern multitasking computer, this is an inordinate waste of resources. The user might want to run another application while the timer is running. Therefore, it would be nice to have a timer that runs in a single thread and allows the computer to perform other functions.

This is a change to the basic underlying assumptions around which the QuizMaker applet was created, altering the basic algorithm by which the applet functions. Therefore, it would make sense to take the existing applet and rewrite it. The new QuizMaker applet will make use of multithreading so that the computer is free to perform other tasks while the timer is running.

To use threads in the applet, your applet must implement the interface Runnable. The resulting declaration appears as follows:

```
class QuizMaker extends Applet implements Runnable {
```

The applet is declared as implementing Runnable; therefore, it must include a run() method. The run() method that follows is short and basically just enables the applet to run while waiting on the user to shut it down:

```
/* Run the applet */
public void run() {
    while (killme != null) {}
}
```

The run method enables the QuizMaker applet to run as long as the killme thread is not set to null. Now you need something to start the run() method and something else to set killme to null when it is time to end the applet. Because the start() method is called by the runtime environment each time a new instance of the applet is created, the start() method is used to create a new killme thread, passing the applet object as a parameter. start() will then start this new thread. Starting the new thread calls the run() method for the thread and—presto!—the applet is running in its own thread. The code for the start() method follows:

```
/* start new thread to run timer */
public void start() {
    if (killme == null)
    {
        killme = new Thread(this);
        killme.start();
    }
}
```

Now you need a way to stop the thread when the applet is closed. The stop() method is perfect for this. The value of the class variable killme, which is checked in the run() method, is changed in the stop() method. The stop() method is called only when the user leaves the page. The code for this short method follows:

```
/* End thread containing timer */
public void stop() {
    killme = null;
}
```

Could you have created a threaded timer by simply extending the existing QuizMaker class? Of course! After all, you are simply adding a variable, an object, and a few methods to the QuizMaker class. However, because you now have a thread for your timer, it would be convenient to use the sleep() method that is available as part of the thread class to implement the timer. This saves on computation by removing the empty while loop. Eliminating the date manipulation can also reduce computation costs and results in more readable code.

There are trade-offs here. If you use the sleep() method that is part of the Thread class, the code becomes easier to understand and you do not need the stopTimer() method. However, if you eliminate the stopTimer() method, the extension you built in the previous section will not work. You would have to rewrite the extension to provide the flexibility of allowing the user to enter the time. Of course, you are rewriting the applet anyway, so you could incorporate that flexibility into the timer.

Let's allow the user to select the length of the timer in the rewritten applet. Remove the StopTimer() method and replace the call to it with the following line:

```
try {Thread.sleep(TimerLength);} catch (InterruptedException e) {}
```

This calls the sleep() method, passing it the TimerLength. The value passed to sleep() is the time to suspend the thread in milliseconds. You must add the setTimer method you created to extend the applet but must modify it to convert the value the user enters from seconds into milliseconds. You also must include the LengthEntry object in the init() method, just as you did for the applet extension.

The final version of the QuizMaker class is shown in Listing 16.4. As you can see, the display resulting from this code is exactly the same as the display resulting from extending the class in the previous section. Could you have made all the changes as extensions and not had as much code in the class? You could have, but it would have been unreasonably hard to follow with methods being used in superclasses and then defined away in subclasses. This difficulty justifies the decision to rewrite the applet rather than extending it.

Listing 16.4. The revised QuizMaker applet with multithreading.

```java
import java.awt.*;
import java.applet.*;
import java.util.*;
import java.net.*;

/**
 * Peter Norton's Guide to Java Programming
 * Revised QuizMaker Applet
 * Acts as an arbitrary length timer. Plays an audio message to start and
 * displays a start message. Plays an audio message at the end with
 * another display message.
 * This applet is a multithreaded version of the original QuizMaker applet.
 */

public class QuizMaker extends Applet implements Runnable{
Image          HglassImage;      // Displays a picture of an hour glass
Button         RunButton;      // Lets the user start the timer
Label          StatusLabel;      // Displays the status to the user
URL            HglassURL;      // URL of the applet
Thread killme = null;      // Thread for timer processing
int            TimerLength;// Number of seconds the timer should run
TextField      LengthEntry;// User entry for number of seconds

    public void init() {
       // Get the picture to add to the screen
      HglassImage = getImage(getCodeBase(),"Hglass.gif");

       // Adds a label to display text which can not be altered by the user
       add(StatusLabel = new Label("Press Run to start timer"));

       // Adds a button to start the timer
            add(RunButton = new Button("Run"));
       this.add(LengthEntry = new TextField("180"));

       resize(400,300);                    // Resizes the applet
       paint(getGraphics());               // Displays applet

       HglassURL = getCodeBase();              // Gets the URL for the applet
       play(HglassURL,"intro.au");             // Play an intro
       play(HglassURL,"startTimer.au");        // Play the start message
       play(HglassURL,"endTimer.au");          // Play the end message
    }

    public void paint(Graphics g) {
       g.drawImage(HglassImage,180,10,this); // Draw the hour glass
```

continues

Listing 16.4. continued

```
    StatusLabel.resize(150,20);          // Resizes the label
    StatusLabel.move(10,10);             // Moves the label

    RunButton.resize(100,20);            // Resizes the button
    RunButton.move(20,40);               // Moves the button

    LengthEntry.resize(70,20);           // Resizes the entry box
    LengthEntry.move(30,70);             // Moves the box
}

/* Lets the user know to start, saves the start time
   and checks for time out */
protected void runTimer() {
    Date      StartTime;                 // Holds the time the timer started
    int       startSec;                  // Start time in seconds

    // Lets the user know to get ready
    StatusLabel.setText("Get the hour glass ready.");
    play(HglassURL,"startTimer.au");         // Play the start message
    StartTime = new Date();              // Get the starting time

    // Lets the user know to start
    StatusLabel.setText("Time is slipping away.");

    // Calculate the start time in seconds
    startSec = StartTime.getSeconds();   // Get the number of seconds
    startSec += (StartTime.getMinutes() * 60);//Add # of minutes times 60

    try {Thread.sleep(TimerLength);} catch (InterruptedException e) {}

    // Informs the user the hour glass is empty
    StatusLabel.setText("The hour glass is empty!");
    play(HglassURL,"endTimer.au");
}

/* Event handler to detect when the button on the window is pressed */
public boolean handleEvent(Event e) {
    int myint;
    // If the window is closed end the program
    if (e.id == Event.WINDOW_DESTROY) {
        System.exit(0);
    }
    if (e.target instanceof Button) {    // If the button is pressed start timer
        setTimer();                      // Set the length of time to run the timer
        runTimer();                      // Start the timer
        return true;                     // Return true so super does not act
    }
    return false;                        // Return false so super can act
}

/* Reads value from user if valid multiply by 1000 to convert */
/* to seconds otherwise set timer to 0                       */
protected void setTimer() {
    try {
        TimerLength = Integer.parseInt(LengthEntry.getText());
        TimerLength = TimerLength * 1000;
```

```
        } catch (NumberFormatException e) {
            TimerLength = 0;
        }
        if (TimerLength < 0)
            TimerLength = 0;
    }

    /* starts new thread to run timer */
    public void start() {
     if (killme == null)
     {
         killme = new Thread(this);
         killme.start();
     }
    }

    /* Ends thread containing timer */
    public void stop() {
     killme = null;
    }

    /* Runs the applet */
    public void run() {
     while (killme != null) {}
    }
}
```

This concludes the coding examples for this chapter. The next section addresses testing the extended applets.

Testing the Extended Applet

Software testing in general is one of the most important and yet most neglected aspects of software development. Testing code modifications is often even more hurried than initial software testing, generally due to time and budget constraints. Yet failure to adequately design and implement tests can increase the total amount of time and money spent on a project. Testing is also critical to providing high-quality software. Although Java increases the amount of code that can be reused, thereby decreasing the amount of new development, it does not eliminate the necessity of testing.

Regression testing the extended applet involves testing not only the new, but also the existing functionality. Your changes should not have affected any of the existing features; there is little risk of this if you are reusing an applet. However, you must verify that there are no unexpected side effects generated in the extension.

To ensure that you have tested all aspects of the applet and all the areas of change, you should have a written test plan to provide a methodical means of ensuring that all the tests are performed. It can also ensure the tests are run in an orderly fashion. If, while testing, you find a problem and make a correction, try to rerun all the tests from the beginning of the test plan.

If possible, it is best to run the entire test plan and document all the problem areas before making any changes. Often problems in one area will be related to problems in another. Addressing these problems as they occur in the test plan may result in an incomplete understanding of the problem. Waiting until all the problems are documented is best to reduce the amount of reworking and re-testing.

Although the need for a documented testing strategy is obvious on large projects with several developers, it is just as helpful on small projects. However, the documentation does not need to be fancy binders with sophisticated forms. Yellow notepads can work well for individuals testing their own applets. The next sections present sample test plans for each of the modifications described in this chapter.

Testing the `ScrollText2` Applet

A suggested test plan for the ScrollText2 applet follows:

1. Create an HTML document and run ScrollText2, passing only the parameters required in ScrollText. Does the applet run and scroll text as expected?

2. Modify the HTML document to pass an additional parameter with the name background and the value 121690. Does the text now scroll on a green background?

3. Modify the HTML document to set the value for the background parameter to 0. Does the applet now appear to be a solid black box?

In reading this test plan, note that the expected outcome is listed for each test. In creating a test plan, you are trying to confirm that the software does what is expected, not determine expected behavior.

In the last test, black text on a black background may not be the most desirable behavior. If changes such as these are being made at the request of a user, it is reasonable to confirm with the user that this type of danger is acceptable. The user may request an additional change to create white text when the background color is dark. These considerations are best made at design time, but it is better to review them when testing than to surprise the user at delivery.

This example is short, yet includes some important features of test plans. The plan includes testing for error, normal, and boundary conditions. The next test plan, for the RGB2Hex2 applet, includes the same types of tests. Because the user has more options available at runtime from the RGB2Hex2 applet, a larger test plan is necessary to test each option.

Testing the `RGB2Hex2` Applet

Applets that receive numeric input such as the RGB2Hex2 applet must be tested for correct results using both random-input and specific test cases. The test cases should include boundary conditions.

They also should include changes in each of the text entry fields. When retesting after making a change, all the original test cases should be performed again. In addition, new test cases must be added so that applets are not created specifically to meet the needs of the test case.

A suggested test plan for the RGB2Hex2 applet follows:

1. Create an HTML document and run RGB2Hex2. Does the applet with the color wheel appear as expected?

2. Enter a new value for the Blue component and press the button. Does the color wheel still display? Does the hexadecimal value still display? Check that the background behind the color wheel displays the color entered by the user.

3. Enter zeros for all three color values. Does the background turn black? Does the color wheel display? Does the hexadecimal value appear as 000000?

4. Enter all values as 255. Does the background turn white? Does the color wheel display? Does the hexadecimal value appear as FFFFFF?

This test uses the same strategy used in the ScrollText2 example. You test first for the normal conditions of the applet, and then for the boundary conditions of 0 and 255. This strategy is also used to test the QuizMaker applet. However, in testing QuizMaker you must verify the timer accuracy as well as the display.

Testing the Extended QuizMaker Applet

The test plan for the QuizMaker applet must include tests for invalid input and timer accuracy as well as verify that the original display and audio features were not affected by the enhancements. The following test plan incorporates all these situations:

1. Create a new HTML document to load the QuizMaker2 applet. Display the page and verify that the audio clips play in the beginning and that the image is displayed as expected.

2. Verify that the time default is 180 seconds.

3. Start the timer for the default time and verify that the audio messages play at appropriate times. Verify that the text display changes at the end of three minutes.

4. Change the timer value to 300 seconds and press the button. Verify that the text message changes back to Time is slipping away. and the audio clip plays.

5. Test that the timer runs for five minutes. Verify that the text message changes to done at the end and that the other audio clip plays.

6. Enter a text value into the input field. Does the timer run for zero seconds?

7. Enter a negative value into the input field. Does the timer run for zero seconds?

8. Enter the value 99 into the input field. Does the timer run for 99 seconds?

This test plan is more extensive than the previous plans and will take more time to complete. The testing process may proceed faster if the test plan is divided between several people; however, the results from different testers should be compared before any corrections are made.

Testing the Rewritten `QuizMaker` Applet

In addition to the tests listed previously, the test plan for the rewritten applet must test for problems resulting from the introduction of threads. The extended test plan will verify that the applet runs correctly even when other programs are loaded and unloaded:

1. Run the tests in the test plan for the extended `QuizMaker` applet. Does the applet perform correctly for all of them?

2. Start the applet and set the timer for 300 seconds. Start another program. Does the timer still run for the correct length of time?

3. Set the timer for 200 seconds. Close the other program. Does the timer still run for the correct length of time?

If there were other pieces of functionality in the applet, you would want to test those as well. If you had a test plan from the original version of the applet, it would be reasonable to repeat all the tests on it to verify that they still run correctly. Clearly, there are more tests you could run for this particular applet, but those listed here should be enough to instill a basic level of confidence in the performance of the applet.

Creating Tests for Your Own Applets

After looking at the test plans for each of the applets modified in this chapter, you now must consider how to create such test plans. The most important thing to remember is that it will require time to create a good plan, but you will reap more benefits. Well-crafted test plans can be modified and reused much like applets can be.

Take care in creating test plans to be sure they are as comprehensive and detailed as possible. The following list summarizes some of the items to include in a well-written test plan:

- Create at least one test for every piece of functionality included in the design of your applet.
- Test all normal working conditions.
- Include one test for each object on the screen, including each button, text entry, and check box.
- Include one test for each input from an HTML document.
- Test all boundary conditions. Create one test for each boundary condition.

- Test all error handling. Create one test for every error condition.
- State the expected results as part of the plan. Do not test just to determine what the results are.
- State expected results explicitly. State everything that will appear on the screen, as opposed to stating that the screen will appear as normal.
- If possible, provide a picture for screen appearance.
- Create several tests to determine performance under all conditions.
- Suppose the applet is resized or moved; does it still work as expected?

Often you can begin creating the test plan as soon as the requirements are understood. At that point, the plan should include basic tests for the functionality described in the requirements. The plan then can be modified during the design phase as new objects are added. The modifications would include specific tests for each object. The plan may be updated again during the coding phase to be sure all error handling is included and all boundary conditions are tested. A plan developed over time in this manner is generally more comprehensive than one developed after coding and before testing.

In general, remember that the more extensive the testing, the more likely it is that potential problems will appear during testing instead of after release. Testing is an important part of software construction and should not be taken lightly.

Summary

This chapter explores some of the ways you can extend existing applets. It covers when it is appropriate to extend an applet and when it is best to rewrite it. It provides several examples of extending applets and one example of rewriting an applet. You should now feel comfortable with modifying and extending existing applets to use in your own presentations.

The chapter also explains the importance of testing, providing many examples of test plans for applets and describing some important aspects of creating your test plans. You should now be able to create robust test plans for testing your own applets or those supplied to you.

VI

Developing Stand-alone Applications

17

Creating a Stand-alone Application

So far, all the chapters in this book have discussed Java development with applets that run in external viewers. These applets can be transferred across the Web or reside locally on the user's PC. Either way, they cannot be run without a Java-enabled browser or viewer.

This chapter introduces *stand-alone applications*. These are Java programs that can be run independent of a browser or external viewer. Unlike code that is compiled for a specific operating system, Java applications require the Java interpreter to be loaded each time they are run. They are run by calling the Java interpreter and passing it the name of the class file containing the application.

Until recently, few developers understood the benefits of Java beyond its usefulness to Internet development; therefore, few stand-alone applications were written in Java. This is rather unfortunate, because the true power of Java is in its usefulness to developing software for multiple platforms regardless of whether those platforms are connected to the Internet.

How Stand-alone Applications Differ from Applets

Although applications have many similarities to applets, they have some important differences as well. The similarities arise because both applets and applications are constructed using the Java API. The differences stem from the distinct environments in which the applets and applications run.

Differences in the Code

The most obvious way that stand-alone applications differ from applets is the static `main()` method. This method is ignored when a class is run as an applet, but is required to start the program if the class is run as an application. The difference is based on the environment that starts the class. This enables the same class to function as either an applet or an application.

Unlike C++, the `main()` method in Java must be part of the public class that defines an application. The method cannot be created separately from a class because it is used to create the initial classes used in the application.

The `main()` method is required for a class to be run as an application because this is the method the Java interpreter looks for when it starts. The entire application can be stored in this method; however, that is not a recommended practice. Generally, the `main()` method should create instances of objects and let the objects control the execution of the program.

Neither the `init()` method nor the `start()` method called by the browser for applets is automatically called by the Java interpreter when an application runs, so if an applet is converted to a stand-alone application, these methods must be explicitly called in `main()`.

There are also differences in the expectations users have for applets and applications. Applets are associated with a browser, and the browser handles starting and exiting, so applets usually are not expected to have menus or dialog boxes. Applications are generally larger, more robust, and specialized to serve a particular need. They usually contain multiple windows and a sophisticated user interface.

Differences in Performance

Applets are meant to be run in an external viewer, such as a Web browser, and are expected to operate across a network. Therefore, applets inherit all the overhead of the viewer in which they are running. So, even if your applet needs only 100KB of memory, you are still constrained by the memory needs of the Web browser, which could be an additional 4, 8, or 16MB of memory. On a system that's already running multiple applications, such as a word processor and a spreadsheet program, the additional memory needs of the browser can seriously affect performance.

Applications, on the other hand, are meant to be run in the Java interpreter on a local machine. Without the overhead associated with Java applets, Java applications can provide users with better performance. Better performance translates to improved response times and, possibly, increased productivity.

Differences in Security

There are benefits to using applets that are not directly available in applications. Browsers and other external viewers load local and remote applets using two different mechanisms. If an applet exists on the local file system and is in a directory defined in the CLASSPATH environment variable, the applet is loaded by the file system loader. These local applets are allowed to read and write files and can access native code.

Non-local applets are loaded by the applet class loader and are subject to the restrictions of the applet security manager. To ensure that the integrity of the client machine isn't compromised when accessing remote information, Java adds a layer of security controls that places restrictions on what applets loaded over the network can and cannot do.

To prevent non-local applets from gaining access to or destroying information on the client machine, applets are generally restricted from gaining access to the client's file system. This means applets cannot manipulate files or directories on the client in any way. They cannot read or write files. They cannot make directories. They cannot check file type, size, or modification date. They also cannot start another program on the client.

Although code written in another programming language, such as C or C++, can be called from within Java applications, this cannot be done from within applets loaded over the network. Again, this is because of security concerns: Any program that can invoke native code on a remote machine could also gain direct access to protected areas of the system.

Note: Most of the security controls for applets are provided by the applet security manager. Obviously, you could create similar security controls for applications, but why create what already exists?

Conceptualization and Design of the Application

Conceptualizing and designing an application is similar to what you would do with an applet. However, there are more options available when working with an application, and often applications require an extensive user interface. This implies there is more to consider during the design of an application.

Applets may include pop-up windows, but they are not trusted windows and appear with large warnings to the user. These warnings are produced by the Java-enabled browser and are not present with applications that often use dialog boxes to collect information from the user. When you design an application, you must build all the windows used in the application and define the manner in which the windows are opened and closed.

Note: Because windows are generally associated with applications that are not restricted by the security manager, Java labels windows used by applets as untrusted. This means that the windows are subject to the rules of the security manager.

Applications also can include menus for controlling windows and features. These menus must be included as part of the design. Applets may include menus, but this is uncommon because the applets are being run in the browser.

Recall from Chapter 14, "Creating a Java Applet," that the first step in designing an applet is to have a good overall understanding of the tasks it will perform. This applies to applications as well. This chapter demonstrates how to develop an application that sums an arbitrarily long list of numbers. The development is done in stages to illustrate different concepts that are important to applications.

Here's the initial specification for the application:

> Initially, the application will read a list of numbers from the command line and display the sum. You will then allow the user to enter additional values while the application is running. Finally, you will add a title and improve the display of the application.

To meet these requirements, you must create several objects in the application:

- An object to store and display the sum
- An object to allow data entry
- A container to hold the objects
- A title to describe the application

Before you define the structure of the application, remember that applications do not always require a sophisticated user interface. Indeed, some applications may be created to run on a server communicating across a network with another application. This type of application could write to a log file and not have any user interface at all.

The application that follows reads in arguments from the command line and returns the sum of the arguments. The purpose of this example is to demonstrate a simple application that does not require a graphical interface.

This application is short, so it is contained in the `main()` method. No functionality from any class already defined in the API is needed, so it inherits directly from the `Object` class. This is the default class; it is not necessary to explicitly state the inheritance.

Both the `Integer` and `String` classes are used for conversion, so import both into the application. The command-line arguments are read as a string. Each argument must be converted to an integer before it can be added to the sum. The sum is stored internally as an integer and converted to a string for display.

The conversions, shown in the following code fragment, cause the code to appear more complex than it actually is:

```
import java.lang.Integer;
import java.lang.String;

// Application to add numbers entered on the command line
class SumIt {
    public static void main(String args[]) {
        int theSum=0;          // the sum of the inputs
        int loopCounter;       // the current itteration

        for (loopCounter=0;loopCounter<args.length;loopCounter++)
            theSum = theSum + Integer.parseInt(args[loopCounter]);
        System.out.println("The sum is "+String.valueOf(theSum));
    }
}
```

This is a complete application in and of itself. Store it in the file `SumIt.java`. It can be compiled by typing

```
javac SumIt.java
```

When the application is compiled, you can run it from the command line by typing

```
java SumIt 20 35 5
```

where 20, 35, and 5 are the arguments passed to the application. The output appears as

```
The sum is 60
```

This style of application may be sufficient because some tasks do not require user interaction. However, even then it would make sense to divide the application into objects and methods that are then called by the main() method.

The next section discusses structuring the application into objects and methods. Some of the code from the SumIt example is used as you continue to develop the application.

Defining the Application Structure

As applications grow larger, it is cumbersome to work with them entirely in main(). Applications can use multiple objects just as applets can, so applications must be structured around objects just as applets are. To describe the application structure fully, define each of the objects, when the objects are created and destroyed, and how the objects communicate. Recall that these same characteristics are defined for each object in the applets.

Objects do not necessarily have to have separate displays. As the previous example shows, an application does not have to have a display at all. So if the display is not used to divide applications into objects, how does one divide them? There is no simple answer to this question.

Generally, grouping similar functionalities together will help define useful objects. Creating objects that mirror real-world objects is often useful. Objects also can be created to encapsulate particularly complex algorithms or to hide portions of code that should not be modified. Other objects are created strictly to assist with display to the user or output to a file.

The ability to define generic, reusable objects improves with practice. There is no particularly correct manner for determining the objects that compose an application. There can be many correct sets of objects, just as there can be many correct C programs with the same functionality.

In general, the main() method is used to create objects, which are responsible for doing the actual work of running the application. Defining separate objects for each task that the application performs and enabling the objects to perform these tasks provides more flexibility for reusing classes and modifying code.

A Nongraphical Example

A more flexible way to structure the application developed in the first section is to create a separate class to hold the sum. The remainder of the application must be able to interact with this class in specific, well-defined ways. It must be able to create a new sum, include a new number in the sum, and retrieve the sum. It does not have to subtract from the sum or, for our purposes here, clear the sum back to zero.

The following class defines methods appropriate for the object that computes the sums:

```
// Class to store a sum that is independent of the display mechanism
class ASum {
    int theSum;

    public ASum() {theSum = 0;}      // Constructor sets instance var to 0
    public void incSum(int toAdd) {
        theSum = theSum + toAdd;    // Add to instance variable
    }
    public int getSum(){
        return theSum;                // Return the value of the instance variable
    }
}
```

Just as you defined new classes in applets to isolate and encapsulate functionality, you do the same in applications. A `main()` method that utilizes the class defined here would appear as follows:

```
// Application to sum numbers entered on the command line
// this application uses a separate class to store the sum
class SumObj {
    public static void main(String args[]) {
        ASum theSum = new ASum();     // the sum of the inputs
        int loopCounter;               // the current iteration

        for (loopCounter=0;loopCounter<args.length;loopCounter++)
            theSum.incSum(Integer.parseInt(args[loopCounter]));
        System.out.println("The sum is "+String.valueOf(theSum.getSum()));
    }
}
```

Now there is no way that the value of the sum could be accidentally reset in the `main()` method. This type of structuring also means that if you want a graphical front end, you can add it without changing the class that stores the sum.

The capability to create an object in another class that displays it may not seem important for this example, but suppose the needed calculations were more complex. For example, instead of computing a sum, what if the application required a method that took several inputs and then did some abstract modeling or other complex calculations? In this circumstance, the capability to use the same method and add several different user interfaces is a large advantage. It reduces the risk that new interfaces would introduce errors in the model or calculations. This is the advantage of separating the user input from the back-end processing.

A Graphical Example

Adding a graphical front end to an application means adding some objects to the application. The application does not run in the browser, so it must have its own frame in which to run. This frame is created in the `main()` method.

In addition to the frame, the application needs an object to display the results. Because the results are not directly modifiable by the user, a label is used to display them. Therefore, both the Label and Frame classes must be imported for the application to use. The ASum class can be used exactly as it is in the previous example. The new SumGraph class follows:

```
import java.lang.Integer;
import java.lang.String;
import java.awt.Label;
import java.awt.Frame;

// Application that sums inputs from the command line and displays
// the result in a graphical interface. This application makes use
// of the ASum object for storing the sum.
class SumGraph {
    public static void main(String args[]) {
        Frame f;
        Label sl;      // Creates a new object to display the result
        ASum theSum = new ASum();      // the sum of the inputs
        int loopCounter;               // the current iteration

        for (loopCounter=0;loopCounter<args.length;loopCounter++)
            theSum.incSum(Integer.parseInt(args[loopCounter]));
        sl = new Label("The sum is "+String.valueOf(theSum.getSum()));

        f = new Frame("Sum");          // Creates frame for applicaton
        f.add("Center",sl);            // Puts the Sum object in frame
        f.resize(300, 300);            // Resizes the frame
        f.show();                      // Displays the frame
    }
}
```

Although the application now has a graphical user interface, all the control still resides in the main() method. The key to improving the design is to make the main() method responsible for creating objects that can then hold and display the sum. Furthermore, it is currently possible to modify the main() method so that it updates the sum but does not update the label. This results in a display that does not reflect the true value of the sum.

To avoid the problem of the display and the storage object becoming out of sync, make the storage object, theSum, accessible only by the Label class. Then all other objects that attempt to update the sum must do so via that class, so the Label class can adjust itself in response to each update.

To accomplish this, extend the Label class so that it can handle creating the sum as part of its constructor. Then all the main() method has to do is create a frame and display the new class in the frame.

The new class is called SumLabel and is defined as follows:

```
// Class used to display a Sum in as a Label
// This class makes use of ASum as an object to hold the sum
// The sum is created from an array of strings passed to the constructor
class SumLabel extends Label{
    public SumLabel(String args[]) {
        super();
```

```
ASum theSum = new ASum();      // the sum of the inputs
int loopCounter;               // the current itteration

for (loopCounter=0;loopCounter<args.length;loopCounter++)
    theSum.incSum(Integer.parseInt(args[loopCounter]));
super.setText("The sum is "+String.valueOf(theSum.getSum()));
    }
}
```

Notice that the constructor for the new class must be passed the argument list from the `main()` method. The new `main()` method is shown in the following code fragment:

```
// Application that sums inputs from the command line and displays
// the result in a graphical interface. This application makes use
// of the SumLabel object for displaying and storing the sum.
class SumGraph {
    public static void main(String args[]) {
        Frame f;
        // Create a new object to display the result
        SumLabel sl = new SumLabel(args);

        f = new Frame("Sum");        // Creates a new frame
        f.add("Center",sl);          // Puts the Sum object in the frame
        f.resize(300, 300);          // Resizes the frame
        f.show();                    // Displays the frame

    }
}
```

This method is shorter and easier to follow than the previous `main()`. A considerable amount of the functionality has been moved to the new class. It is also easier to see how another class that displays the average of the values entered, such as `AvgLabel`, could be added to this method.

Save all three of these classes—`ASum`, `SumLabel`, and `SumGraph`—in the file `SumGraph.java` and compile it using the command

```
javac SumGraph.java
```

When you run the application, you can pass the parameters on the command line as follows:

```
java SumGraph 23 54 1
```

The application displays the result in the frame titled `Sum`. The minimize and maximize buttons can be used to resize the window. However, there is one small problem with the user interface: The Close button on the window does not work. The only way to close the application is to press Ctrl+C with the cursor in the window where it was started.

What's going on here? The window resizes and iconifies correctly, but it does not close when the user presses its Close button. If this were an applet, the browser would take care of closing the applet when the user exits the window, but because this is an application, it is essential to test for the user closing the window and exiting the application. You could also add a Close button to the application. However, even if a separate Close button exists, the application must handle exiting when the window is closed.

The Frame class has an event handler that reacts when the user changes the size of the window, but it does not handle closing the window. There are two methods of solving this problem. First, you could extend the Frame class to a class myFrame, in which case the event handler in the new class would check for the window closing. The other option is to make the SumGraph class itself an extension of Frame. Either way, you should then add an event-handling method to respond to the window closing: a WINDOW_DESTROY event. If you use this event, the application must import the java.awt.Event class.

The following code shows the SumGraph class as extension of the Frame class. The event handler is extended to provide for the window being closed by the user:

```
import java.lang.Integer;
import java.lang.String;
import java.awt.Label;
import java.awt.Frame;
import java.awt.Event;

// Application that sums inputs from the command line and displays
// the result in a graphical interface. This application makes use
// of the SumLave object for displaying and storing the sum.
class SumGraph extends Frame {
    SumGraph() {
        super("Sum");
    }
    public static void main(String args[]) {
        SumGraph f = new SumGraph();           // Instantiate self
        // Creates a new object to display the result
        SumLabel sl = new SumLabel(args);

        f.add("Center",sl);            // Puts Sum object in the frame
        f.resize(300, 300);            // Resizes the frame
        f.show();                      // Displays the frame

    }
    // Event handler to allow for the closing of the window
    public boolean handleEvent(Event evt)
     {
         if (evt.id == Event.WINDOW_DESTROY)
          {
               System.exit(0);
             return true;
          }
         return super.handleEvent(evt);
    }
}
```

Okay, you need just two more objects for the application: an object to allow data entry, for which you can use a standard TextField object, and a heading or title across the top of the display. Although you could do this with an ordinary label with a large font, it is more interesting to use an object, such as the ScrollText applet from the previous chapter. You'll add these objects in the next section.

Building the Application

Although it seems the application is nearly complete, it does not yet interact with the user while it is running, nor does it write the result to a file. This section demonstrates how to add a text box to allow the user to add numbers while the application is running. This section then discusses how to write the result to a file and how to add enhancements such as menus and dialog boxes.

Allowing Interactive Updates to the Application

To allow interactive updates, there must be a way for the user to update the display. Currently, the text of the label used for display is set when the label is created with no provision to update it. In fact, there is no method available to the SumGraph class that will update the sum.

The label and the sum must be updated in the same method, which must be available to the SumGraph class. To accomplish this, create a method in the SumLabel class that updates both the sum and the label. Update the sum using the incSum() method from the ASum object created earlier. The new method follows:

```
public void updateSum(String newVal) {
    theSum.incSum(Integer.parseInt(newVal));
    super.setText("The sum is "+String.valueOf(theSum.getSum()));
}
```

For this method to work correctly, it must be able to access the same ASum object used in the constructor of the SumLabel. However, the object was created locally to the constructor. Therefore, the class SumLabel is modified to make the ASum object available to the entire class.

The declaration of theSum is taken out of the constructor and made into an instance variable. It is declared as protected so that no other objects can modify it. This prevents other objects from modifying the sum directly because other objects may modify theSum variable and not change the label appropriately.

You may want other objects to be able to retrieve the stored sum. In this case, create a method in the SumLabel class that will return the current sum. Use this method, getSum(), when creating a method that writes the sum to a file. The final version of the SumLabel class follows:

```
// Class used to display a Sum in as a Label
// This class makes use of ASum as an object to hold the sum
// The sum is created from an array of strings passed to the constructor
class SumLabel extends Label {
    protected ASum theSum;

    //Create the initial sum from an array of strings
    public SumLabel(String args[]) {
        super();                        // must go first in constructor
        int loopCounter;                // the current iteration
```

```
        theSum = new ASum();           // the sum of the inputs
        for (loopCounter=0;loopCounter<args.length;loopCounter++)
            theSum.incSum(Integer.parseInt(args[loopCounter]));
        super.setText("The sum is "+String.valueOf(theSum.getSum()));
        super.setAlignment(Label.CENTER);
    }
    // Allow other classes to view the sum, but not modify it
    public int getSum(){
        // Return the value of the protected object
        return theSum.getSum();
    }
    // Allow other classes to update the sum while also updating label
    public void updateSum(String newVal) {
        theSum.incSum(Integer.parseInt(newVal));
        super.setText("The sum is "+String.valueOf(theSum.getSum()));
    }
}
```

Now the application must include a call to the `updateSum` method. The user is expected to enter data into a `TextField` object created by the `main()` method. To create this object, the application needs to import the `java.awt.TextField` class.

When the user is finished adding a new number to the field, he or she is expected to press Enter. Pressing Enter triggers what is called an ACTION EVENT that can be handled either by the `action()` method or by the `handleEvent()` method. An `action` method is shown in the following example:

```
public boolean action(Event evt, Object arg) {
    if (evt.target instanceof TextField) {
        sl.updateSum(tf);
        return true;
    }
    else return false;
}
```

Instead of using the `action()` method, modify the existing `handleEvent()` method in the `SumGraph` class so that all the event handling in the `SumGraph` class occurs in one place and is easy to locate. Event handlers are more generic than action handlers, so it is not a problem for the `handleEvent()` method to contain all the responses. Actions occur when users press buttons or the Enter key when the cursor is in a text field. Events occur when the program senses a change in the environment. Events include moving the mouse, pressing a key, or leaving a text field in any manner.

Therefore, in the event handler, the programmer must be careful to react only when the user presses Enter in the entry field. The event handler must test that the event occurs in the `TextField` object and that the event is triggered by the user pressing Enter.

Pressing Enter is an `action event`. Therefore, an `event id` being equal to `ACTION_EVENT` indicates that Enter was pressed if the user is in a `TextField`. `ACTION_EVENT` is a static variable defined in the event class. The `event id` is automatically set to this value when an action event is triggered.

The event handler tests whether the user is in the entry field by testing for the event target being an instance of the TextField object. The complete handleEvent() method follows:

```
public boolean handleEvent(Event evt)
{
    // Allow for the closing of the window
    if (evt.id == Event.WINDOW_DESTROY)
     {
         System.exit(0);
        return true;
    //Allow for new values being entered in input field
    } else if (evt.target instanceof TextField &&
 evt.id == Event.ACTION_EVENT) {
        sl.updateSum(((TextField)evt.target).getText());
        return true;
    } else
     return super.handleEvent(evt);
}
```

Notice that it is not necessary to make the name of the TextField object available throughout the class. The event handler can act by using the object of the event. In fact, it is not essential to give a name to the TextField, although a name is created in main() for clarity.

The event handler calls the updateSum() method using sl, an instance of SumLabel that is available to the entire SumGraph class. From the object of the event, the event handler gets the text string to pass to updateSum. The event handler knows that the object of the event is a TextField object, and it can use the getText() method to retrieve the text from that field. The handler must be careful to cast the object to the correct object type so that all the methods associated with that type are available before it calls getText(). Pay careful attention to the parentheses on this line of code.

Writing to the Local Hard Drive

The security concerns that necessitate restricting an applet's capability to write to files are not present when working with applications. Although only the final sum is written to a file for the example, similar code could be used to write repeatedly to a file or multiple files.

A new method, writeSum(), handles writing to the file and is created as part of the SumGraph class. The writeSum() method uses a RandomAccessFile object to create a random-access file and write to it. For this method to compile correctly, the application should import the class java.io.RandomAccessFile.

The methods that write to the file all could throw an exception called IOException when they encounter an error writing to the file. The writeSum() method may either catch the exception or have the method throw the exception back to the caller. To keep the caller isolated from the details and problems of writing to the file, the method is defined to catch the exception. If an exception occurs, the method will print an error message to the screen, indicating that there was a problem writing to the file.

If everything proceeds normally, the method will open the file, get the sum from the `SumLabel` object, write the sum and appropriate text to the file, and close the file. The method will not return a status. The code for this method follows:

```
//Write a sum contained in the object sl to a file
public void writeSum(){
    RandomAccessFile    SumFile;

    try {
        SumFile = new RandomAccessFile("SumResult.txt","rw");
        SumFile.writeBytes("The sum is "+sl.getSum()+".\n");
        SumFile.close();
    } catch (java.io.IOException e) {
        System.out.println("Could not write to SumResult file.");
        System.out.println(e);
    }
}
```

The final step is to call the `writeSum()` method from an appropriate point in the application. The method should execute at the end of the program to write the final sum. How do you determine that the program is exiting? Well, the application currently exits when the user closes the window. The call to the `writeSum()` method is added just prior to the `System.exit()` call to ensure that the sum is written when the application closes.

The application now has most of the required functionality, but it still needs some type of title. The next section describes how to add the `ScrollText` applet to provide a scrolling title for the application.

Including an Applet in an Application

Applets are objects. Therefore, it seems reasonable that they could be included in applications. They can be, but certain modifications are necessary because the application does not include all the environment variables that the applet often expects. However, if the application happens to define all the objects included in a Java-enabled browser, the applet should run without modification.

The basic problem with including `ScrollText` in its existing form is that you can't define the parameters used in the `init()` method. The `init()` method uses `getParameter` to determine the height and width of its display and to get the text it will scroll. The application being built does not have a means of setting these parameters.

This can be solved by overloading the `init()` method. In the new `init()` method the values for width, height, and text are passed as parameters to the method. The internal values of the `ScrollText` applet are then set in the same manner as in the original `init()` method using the values passed to the method. With this one change, the `SumGraph` application can then make use of the `ScrollText` applet. The new `init()` method appears as

```
//Init() method to allow parameter passing from an application
public void init(String inWidth, String inHeight, String inText) {
    ws = inWidth;
    hs = inHeight;

    if (ws == null){          // Read width as input, if not found use default
        w = 150;
    } else {
        w = Integer.parseInt(ws); // Convert input string to integer
    }
    if (hs == null){          // Read height as input, if not found use default
        h = 50;
    } else {
        h = Integer.parseInt (hs); // Convert input string to integer
    }
    resize(w,h);                    // Set font based on height
    setFont(new Font("TimesRoman",Font.BOLD,h - 2));
    s = inText;                     // Read input text, if null use default
    if (s == null) {
        s = " The Java ScrollText Applet at work.";
    }

    separated =  new char [s.length()];
    s.getChars(0,s.length(),separated,0);
}
```

There are certainly many times when it is appropriate to use classes defined as applets within an application. It is important to be aware of all resources available in the browser that the application has to mimic or avoid.

Tip: Many existing applets can also be turned into applications. To do this, create a `main()` method for the applet. Within the `main()` method, create a frame for your application and then instantiate the applet. Because the applet is not running in the normal applet environment, you must make explicit calls to `init()` and `start()` within `main()`. Finally, place the applet in a frame and display the frame. Because you are using the `Frame` class, be sure to import `java.awt.Frame`.

Additional Needs

Up to this point the focus of the chapter has been on the organization and functionality of the application, but not its general appearance. Currently, the application appears as shown in Figure 17.1. This section reviews ways of improving the visual appeal of the application without changing the functionality.

Figure 17.1.

The SumGraph *application before formatting.*

Visual Enhancements

Improving an application's appearance generally does not involve a lot of code. Small coding changes can have large effects. However, changing the appearance can involve a lot of time. You may want to try several different changes to note their effects and experiment with different layouts and fonts until you find a combination that is visually pleasing.

To begin, change the layout of the frame to GridLayout instead of the default border layout. The grid is created with one column and three rows. There is only one column, so don't worry about the spacing between the columns. However, it is reasonable to set some space between the rows. The command is

```
f.setLayout(new GridLayout(3,1,0,10));
```

This results in a screen with three sections of the same size. The layout must be set before you start adding objects to the display.

The ScrollText applet is placed in the top section, the data entry field in the middle section, and the results in the bottom section. You can do this by explicitly stating where each will go, but it is easier to simply add them in this order. To use the GridLayout() method, import the class java.awt.GridLayout.

Next, modify the font for the frame to make the SumLabel and the TextField display larger. Set the font for the frame to a larger font size, say 16 points. The command is

```
f.setFont(new Font("TimesRoman",Font.BOLD,16));
```

Put this line before the line that creates the objects so that the new font will be applied to the objects. To use the setFont method, import the java.awt.Font class.

Tip: You may have realized that a large portion of formatting the screen lies in importing the correct classes to affect the display the way you want. It should be noted here that TimesRoman is one of several fonts known to Java. The supported fonts vary from platform

to platform. You can get a `String` array of the fonts supported on your platform using the following command:

```
String[] fonts= Toolkit.getDefaultToolkit().getFontList()
```

Now that the fonts are easier to read, the next change is to modify the `TextField` so that it appears as a single-line entry. Currently, the `TextField` takes up the entire space allocated to it in the grid. To change this, create a panel in the middle section of the layout. The `TextField` is placed on the new panel, which in turn is placed in the grid. This requires importing the class `java.awt.Panel` and making minor adjustments to `main()` as follows:

```
Panel pl = new Panel();          // Create panel for text field
f.add(pl);                       // Puts the panel for entry in the frame
pl.add(tf);                      // Puts the entry field in the panel
```

These changes merely affect the display, not the ability to access the `TextField` object.

The results would look better if they were centered in the layout. Do this by centering the `Label` in its grid component. Modify the `SumLabel` class to have the constructor set the alignment as follows:

```
super.setAlignment(Label.CENTER);
```

Another feature to include in the application is a set of insets. *Insets* are border areas of blank space that surround the grid layout. To create an inset, override the `insets()` method for the `SumGraph` class with the following method:

```
public Insets insets() {
    return new Insets(40,10,10,10);
}
```

This provides an inset of 40 pixels at the top and 10 pixels on the bottom and on each side. The application as it now appears is shown in Figure 17.2.

Figure 17.2.
The SumGraph *application after formatting.*

Formatting and layout are important parts of application development that you can do as part of the design before any of the application has been implemented. With an object-oriented language such as Java, the exact location of the display can be modified easily. Therefore, it may be easier to delay some aspects of the layout until the application has been created. This enables you to gain a better understanding of the objects needed for the application and the functionality desired.

Menus

The application as it currently exists fulfills the functionality explicitly stated in the specification. However, there are some general expectations about applications that you should consider.

Most users expect graphical applications to have a menu and an explicit Exit option. They usually expect a Help option to give explicit help or state some additional information about the program. They also expect a pop-up window to prompt them before they write output to disk. This section and the following describe how to add these features to the example application.

To add a menu to the application, create an instance of the MenuBar object from the Java API and use the setMenuBar() method in the Frame class to attach the menu bar to the frame. This is done in the constructor for the SumGraph class. It is also necessary to add menu items to the menu. You can create a separate method to add the items so that the constructor does not get too complex. Our constructor now appears as

```
SumGraph() {
    super("Sum");
    InitializeMenu();
    setMenuBar(mbar);
}
```

Tip: It is good practice to use a separate method to create your menu and call the method from the constructor. This keeps your constructor short and easy to understand.

In the InitializeMenu() method, two items need to be added to the menu bar. Each is an instance of the class Menu: the File menu, with the Save and Quit items; and the Help menu, with the About item.

To create the menus, the application should import three new classes, java.awt.MenuBar, java.awt.Menu, and java.awt.MenuItem. The InitializeMenu() method is created as private because no other class needs to initiate the menu for the application. The code for the method follows:

```
// Creates the menu and attaches it to the MenuBar
private void InitializeMenu()
{
    mbar = new MenuBar();
    Menu m = new Menu("File");
    m.add(new MenuItem("Save"));
    m.addSeparator();
    m.add(new MenuItem("Quit"));
    mbar.add(m);

    m = new Menu("Help");
    m.add(new MenuItem("About..."));
    mbar.add(m);
}
```

So, if you add these methods and recompile the application, the menu will appear on your application with all the items needed. However, the menu is not functional yet; you must associate a response with each of the items using the event handler. Check for an event target that is an instance of MenuItem; then determine which menu item triggered the event and respond accordingly. Here is the expanded handleEvent() method:

```
public boolean handleEvent(Event evt)
    {
        // Allow for the closing of the window
        if (evt.id == Event.WINDOW_DESTROY)
        {
            writeSum();
            System.exit(0);
            return true;
        //Allow for new values being entered in input field
        } else if (evt.target instanceof TextField &&
                    evt.id == Event.ACTION_EVENT) {
            sl.updateSum(((TextField)evt.target).getText());
            return true;
        //Allow for reaction to menu items
        } else if(evt.target instanceof MenuItem) {
            if (evt.arg.equals("Save")) {
                writeSum();
                return true;
            } else if (evt.arg.equals("Quit")) {
                writeSum();
                System.exit(0);
                return true;
            } else if (evt.arg.equals("About...")) {
                AboutBox ab = new AboutBox(this);
                ab.show();
                return true;
            }
        }
        return super.handleEvent(evt);
    }
```

Now the menu is just about done. You still need to define the AboutBox class that is used to create the About box displayed by the About menu item. This class is a dialog box that the user must close after viewing. The next section defines this class.

Dialog Boxes

Dialog boxes are simple windows that provide information to the user or ask easy questions. Dialog boxes are also appropriate for accessing files in the file system. Java provides a class, FileDialog, for that purpose. In this section, a read-only dialog box is added to provide information about the application.

Dialog boxes can be *modal*. A modal dialog box does not allow input to any other windows in the application while that dialog box is present. This type of dialog box is useful when you want the user to verify a particular operation before continuing with that operation.

In this section you will create a class to provide a basic dialog box. This dialog box displays a short description of the application and remains on the screen until the user presses the OK button on the dialog box. It will be modal, so the user will not be able to enter any additional numbers until the dialog box is closed.

The Java API provides a basic dialog box class that you will extend to create the dialog box. The new class is named AboutBox because it will be displayed from the About menu item.

The current frame is passed to the constructor of the new class. The constructor in turn passes the frame to the constructor of the Dialog class. The frame is used as the parent for the dialog box. In addition, the constructor for the Dialog class takes a string that is used as the title of the dialog box. The final parameter is a boolean value set to true. This indicates that the dialog box is modal and should prevent input to other windows. So far, the code for the dialog box appears as

```
class AboutBox extends Dialog
{
     public AboutBox(Frame parent)
     {
         super(parent, "About Dialog", true);
```

Next, display fields are added to the dialog box. BorderLayout is used for the dialog box, so the application must import java.awt.BorderLayout. After setting the layout, the About box adds a Label containing text that describes the program. To create a more generic About box, you can pass the text to the constructor as a parameter.

The About box also must have an OK button so the user can close the window. If the OK button is added directly to the window in the South position, it will spread across the entire bottom of the window. To prevent this, create a new panel to hold the button. This is similar to what you did for the TextField object in the main display window. The About box adds the OK button to the new panel and then adds the panel to the South position in the dialog box.

The last line in the constructor resizes the dialog box so that it is somewhat smaller than the main window. The constructor does not actually display the box. The caller is expected to use the show() method to display the dialog box on the screen. The remaining code for the constructor is

```
setLayout(new BorderLayout());
add("Center",new Label("Interactive Summation Program",Label.CENTER));
Panel pp = new Panel();
pp.add(new Button("OK"));
add("South",pp);
resize(300,200);
}
```

One more method is needed for the dialog box to work: The class must handle the action that occurs when the user presses the OK button. To account for this, add an action method to the AboutBox class. This method simply checks that the argument for the event is the OK button and then closes the dialog box. The code appears as

```
public boolean action(Event evt, Object arg)
    {
    if("OK".equals(arg))
    {
        dispose();
        return true;
    }
    return false;
    }
}
```

The box is closed using the `dispose()` method available to all dialog boxes and windows. This method closes the dialog box and releases its resource, which can then be collected by Java's garbage-collection mechanism.

The Finished Stand-alone Application

Sections of the `SumGraph` application have been mentioned throughout the discussion of different topics in this chapter. Listing 17.1 is the code for the complete application. The long list of imports could be shortened by importing `java.awt.*`. The individual list is shown to demonstrate the many different classes that are required to create even a simple application.

Listing 17.1. The enhanced **SumGraph** application.

```
/**
 * Peter Norton's Guide to Java Programming
 * The SumGraph Application
 * This application sums inputs and displays the result
 * in a graphical interface. You can pass inputs from the
 * command line as arguments or enter them individually in
 * a popup window. The application makes use of the SumLave
 * object for displaying and storing the sum.
 */

import java.lang.Integer;
import java.lang.String;
import java.awt.Label;
import java.awt.Frame;
import java.awt.Event;
import java.awt.TextField;
import java.io.RandomAccessFile;
import java.awt.GridLayout;
import java.awt.Font;
import java.awt.Insets;
import java.awt.Panel;
import java.awt.Menu;
import java.awt.MenuBar;
import java.awt.MenuItem;
import java.awt.Dialog;
import java.awt.Button;
import java.awt.BorderLayout;
```

continues

Listing 17.1. continued

```
// Class to store a sum that is independent of the display mechanism
class ASum {
    int theSum;

    public ASum() {theSum = 0;}      // Constructor sets instance var to 0
    public void incSum(int toAdd) {
        theSum = theSum + toAdd;   // Add to instance variable
    }
    public int getSum(){
        return theSum;                 // Return the value of the instance variable
    }
}
// Class used to display a Sum in as a Label
// This class makes use of ASum as an object to hold the sum
// The sum is created from an array of strings passed to the constructor
class SumLabel extends Label {
    protected ASum theSum;

    //Create the initial sum from an array of strings
    public SumLabel(String args[]) {
        super();                       // must go first in constructor
        int loopCounter;               // the current iteration

        theSum = new ASum();                    // the sum of the inputs
        for (loopCounter=0;loopCounter<args.length;loopCounter++)
            theSum.incSum(Integer.parseInt(args[loopCounter]));
        super.setText("The sum is "+String.valueOf(theSum.getSum()));
        super.setAlignment(Label.CENTER);
    }
    // Allow other classes to view the sum, but not modify it
    public int getSum(){
        // Return the value of the protected object
        return theSum.getSum();
    }
    // Allow other classes to update the sum while also updating label
    public void updateSum(String newVal) {
        theSum.incSum(Integer.parseInt(newVal));
        super.setText("The sum is "+String.valueOf(theSum.getSum()));
    }
}


// The main class for the application.
// This class extends the Frame class and sets up the menu bar
// and events.
class SumGraph extends Frame {
    static SumLabel sl;
    private MenuBar mbar;

    // Constructor that creates frame and menu
    SumGraph() {
        super("Sum");
        InitializeMenu();
        setMenuBar(mbar);
    }

    // Creates the menu and attaches it to the MenuBar
```

```
    private void InitializeMenu()
    {
        mbar = new MenuBar();
        Menu m = new Menu("File");
        m.add(new MenuItem("Save"));
        m.addSeparator();
        m.add(new MenuItem("Quit"));
        mbar.add(m);

        m = new Menu("Help");
        m.add(new MenuItem("About..."));
        mbar.add(m);
    }

    //Main method used to start application
    public static void main(String args[]) {
        SumGraph f = new SumGraph();             // Instantiate self
        f.setLayout(new GridLayout(3,1,0,10));
        f.setFont(new Font("TimesRoman",Font.BOLD,16));

        // Create new instances of needed objects
        sl = new SumLabel(args);
        Panel pl = new Panel();          // Create panel for text field
        TextField tf = new TextField("0",8);
        ScrollText st = new ScrollText();

        st.init("280","85","Sums are fun !");
        st.start();

        f.add(st);          // Puts the scrolling text in the frame
        f.add(pl);          // Puts the panel for entry in the frame
        f.add(sl);          // Puts the panel for sum in the frame
        pl.add(tf);         // Puts the entry field in the panel

        f.resize(300, 300);         // Resizes the frame
        f.show();                   // Displays the frame

    }
    public Insets insets() {
        return new Insets(40,10,10,10);
    }

    //Write a sum contained in the object sl to a file
    public void writeSum(){
        RandomAccessFile     SumFile;

        try {
            SumFile = new RandomAccessFile("SumResult.txt","rw");
            SumFile.writeBytes("The sum is "+sl.getSum()+".\n");
            SumFile.close();
        } catch (java.io.IOException e) {
            System.out.println("Could not write to SumResult file.");
            System.out.println(e);
        }
    }
    public boolean handleEvent(Event evt)
     {
```

continues

Listing 17.1. continued

```
                //Allow for new values being entered in input field
                if (evt.id == Event.WINDOW_DESTROY)
                 {
                    writeSum();
                      System.exit(0);
                    return true;
                 //Allow for new values being entered in input field
                } else if (evt.target instanceof TextField &&
                            evt.id == Event.ACTION_EVENT) {
                    sl.updateSum(((TextField)evt.target).getText());
                    return true;
                //Allow for reaction to menu items
                } else if(evt.target instanceof MenuItem) {
                    if (evt.arg.equals("Save")) {
                        writeSum();
                        return true;
                    } else if (evt.arg.equals("Quit")) {
                        writeSum();
                        System.exit(0);
                        return true;
                    } else if (evt.arg.equals("About...")) {
                        AboutBox ab = new AboutBox(this);
                        ab.show();
                        return true;
                    }
                }
                 return super.handleEvent(evt);
        }


}
// Class used to create an about box for the SumGraph application
class AboutBox extends Dialog
{
        // Constructor used to create window including information
        public AboutBox(Frame parent)
        {
            super(parent, "About Dialog", true);
            setLayout(new BorderLayout());
            add("Center",new Label("Interactive Summation Program",
                                    Label.CENTER));
            Panel pp = new Panel();
            pp.add(new Button("OK"));
            add("South",pp);
            resize(300,200);
        }
        //Action handler used to close window
        public boolean action(Event evt, Object arg)
        {
            if("OK".equals(arg))
            {
                dispose();
                return true;
            }
            return false;
        }
}
```

Before you can compile the SumGraph application, you need to make the changes recommended for the ScrollText applet. The revised ScrollText applet with the overloaded init() method can be used in applets and applications. The complete code for the revised ScrollText applet is shown in Listing 17.2.

Listing 17.2. The revised ScrollText applet.

```java
import java.awt.Graphics;
import java.awt.Font;
import java.awt.Frame;

/**
 * Peter Norton's Guide to Programming Java * The ScrollText applet
 * has been reworked so it can be used with applications
 * This object is used to scroll a text banner across the screen
 * and takes TEXT, WIDTH, and HEIGHT as parameters.
 */

public class ScrollText extends java.applet.Applet implements Runnable {

    int h;                        // Height of applet in pixels
    int w;                        // Width of applet in Pixels
    char separated[];             // Output string in array form
    String s = null;              // Input string containing display text
    String hs = null;             // Input string containing height
    String ws = null;             // Input string containing width
    Thread ScrollThread = null;      // Thread to control processing
    int speed=35;                 // Length of delay in milliseconds
    boolean threadSuspended = false;
    int dist;

//Init() method to allow parameter passing from an application
public void init(String inWidth, String inHeight, String inText) {
    ws = inWidth;
    hs = inHeight;
    if (ws == null){              // Read width as input, if not found use default
        w = 150;
    } else {
            w = Integer.parseInt(ws); // Convert input string to integer
    }
    if (hs == null){              // Read height as input, if not found use default
        h = 50;
    } else {
            h = Integer.parseInt (hs); // Convert input string to integer
    }
    resize(w,h);                  // Set font based on height
    setFont(new Font("TimesRoman",Font.BOLD,h-2));
    s = inText;                          // Read input text, if null use default
    if (s == null) {
        s = " The Java ScrollText Applet at work.";
    }

    separated =  new char [s.length()];
    s.getChars(0,s.length(),separated,0);
}
```

continues

Listing 17.2. continued

```
/* Start new thread to run applet */
public void start() {
    if(ScrollThread == null)
    {
        ScrollThread = new Thread(this);
        ScrollThread.start();
    }
}

/* End thread containing applet */
public void stop() {
    ScrollThread = null;
}

// While applet is running pause then scroll text
public void run() {
    while (ScrollThread != null) {
    try {Thread.sleep(speed);} catch (InterruptedException e){}
    scroll();
    }
    ScrollThread = null;
}

// Scroll text by determining new location to draw text and redrawing
synchronized void scroll () {
    dist—;                   // Move string to left
    // If string has disappeared to the left, move back to right edge
    if (dist + ((s.length()+1)*(h *5 / 11)) == 0){
    dist=w;
}
    repaint();
}

// Redraw string at given location
public void paint(Graphics g) {
    g.drawChars(separated, 0, s.length(), dist,4 *h / 5);
}

// Suspend thread when mouse is pushed, resume when pused again
public boolean mouseDown(java.awt.Event evt, int x, int y) {
        if (threadSuspended) {
            ScrollThread.resume();
        }
        else {
            ScrollThread.suspend();
        }
        threadSuspended = !threadSuspended;
    return true;
    }
}
```

Save the updated ScrollText applet to a file named ScrollText.java and run the Java compiler using the command

```
javac ScrollText.java
```

After compiling the ScrollText applet, you can compile the SumGraph application. If you haven't already saved the SumGraph application to a file named SumGraph.java, do so now. Then you can run the Java compiler using the command

```
javac SumGraph.java
```

Now you can run the SumGraph program by typing

```
java SumGraph
```

You can also pass the SumGraph program a list of numbers to sum from the command line, such as

```
java SumGraph 25 30 45
```

The program will save the final sum to a file named SumResult.txt in the directory where it runs.

> **Tip:** Testing a stand-alone application is very important. Follow the suggestions described in Chapter 14 for testing applets to create a test plan for your stand-alone application.

Summary

Applications have many similarities to applets and some important differences. Applications require a main() method. Applets do not. Applications have full access to the local file system and can access native code. Applets loaded over the network cannot access the client's file system in any way.

Although applets provide better security, applications are more flexible and generally have better performance. This increased flexibility and performance provides you with more options when creating applications. Most applications access the local file system and include graphical interfaces such as pop-up windows and pull-down menus.

18

Using Java
Applications
in the Real
World

Real-world applications differ from the simple stand-alone applications, such as SumGraph, in their size, complexity, and usefulness. This chapter introduces you to many of the techniques used to develop large applications.

This chapter works through a single example of an intermediate Java application and introduces additional tools and objects that are useful in building larger applications in Java. The chapter ends with a test plan for the application.

Bigger, Better, Faster Applications

Real-world applications are expected to have rapid response times; user-friendly help screens; attractive, well-thought-out layouts; and an easy-to-understand organization. Many features that are not necessary in applets are expected in applications.

Adding the features expected for applications increases the amount of programming required. Some features, such as menu layout and frame appearance, are expected to appear similarly among programs running on the same operating system. Most applications include an About box giving version, copyright, and authoring information. Applications also may include registration screens, graphical toolbars, pop-up information windows, and many other tools.

Java can be used to develop programs with all these features, although some are easier to include than others. The basic technique for developing applications remains the same as the programs grow. However, greater care must be taken with the design to allow for the additional features and to provide sufficient robustness to meet the needs of sophisticated users. A well-designed program can be easily broken into pieces so that a different person or team can work on each section. The sections then can be seamlessly joined to produce a working program in a short time period.

As more tools and utilities become available for Java, development time will be reduced. Because Java is object-oriented, incorporating existing utilities into Java programs is straightforward; recall how easy incorporating the ScrollText applet into the application was in Chapter 17, "Creating a Stand-alone Application."

With the java.awt package, you can create a program whose appearance reflects the operating system on which it runs. Therefore, programmers can incorporate features into their applications without worrying about how it will look on each platform.

Looking Ahead: In this chapter you will be working through the development of a more complex application. The application includes several features common in real-world applications. Many of these features are introduced in the sample application in Chapter 17, but the examples given here are significantly more robust. The discussions here will help prepare you for the advanced programs presented in Part VII, "Advanced Issues."

Conceptualizing a Real-World Application

Chapter 17 shows how the design of a simple application can be modified as it is created. This chapter develops a more complex example with more of the features found in real-world applications.

The design of a large application is generally an iterative breakdown process: The application is divided into smaller pieces and a design is constructed for each piece. One of the key engineering decisions is where to divide the pieces, which is not always obvious from the specification. It is not necessary that the pieces be of equivalent size or complexity, but it is necessary that they be well defined and have distinct boundaries.

Useful Online Resources

In developing larger applications, you can realize significant time savings if you use utilities that have already been developed. One of the greatest advantages of Java is the ease with which utilities can be shared among developers.

Some of these utilities are available through sites on the Internet. You can find counters, parsers, string tokenizers, and URL verifiers, just to name a few.

Some likely online sources for Java utilities include

`http://www.yahoo.com/Computers_and_Internet/Languages/Java/Utilities/`

`http://www.gamelan.com/`

`http://www.blackdown.org/~kbs/`

Try these sites and others to find useful utilities to incorporate into your applications.

Determining Requirements

The specification for the `SlideShow` application to be developed in this chapter is simply this:

> The application will display a slide show of multiple GIF images with related text.

Although this specification does not mention menus or controls, it is safe to assume these are expected. It is also reasonable to expect to provide a means of loading a show from a file and a graceful mechanism to exit the application.

Expanding on this definition, `SlideShow` must perform the following tasks:

- Load a show from a file
- Display images

- Display text
- Advance forward to the next slide
- Return to the previous slide
- Go to the last slide
- Go to the first slide
- Enable/disable the display of slides
- Enable/disable the display of text
- Provide help
- Provide authoring information
- Exit the program

Designing a Real-World Application

In this section the entire application is divided into objects, resulting in actual objects to be implemented in Java. In some cases, the objects are composed of other objects that you must define and implement. The process stops when all the components necessary to complete the tasks listed in the requirements are defined. These components will be either implemented as new classes in Java or created using existing Java class definitions.

Overall Design and Layout

First, you need to define the main features of the application. Applications are usually designed around one main viewing area with additional tools provided in separate windows. The main viewing area is where the user focuses when running the application; therefore, it should be well designed and pleasant to the viewer.

The application's viewing area can be made up of many components grouped into one container to simplify handling. The container is responsible for providing the methods that can be used to modify the display to the user. It does so using methods provided by each of the objects it contains. It groups the methods provided by its contents so that related events are always handled in the same manner, even when they are called by different controls.

The main screen will be more than a simple display window. The user must be able to move through the slides in the display. It also would be nice to provide controls on the display for moving through the pictures. These controls would function similar to VCR controls, enabling the user to move forward and backward through the slides.

> **Note:** Screen appearance is an important part of any commercial application. Customers will decide to purchase a product on the basis of the way they react to its appearance. They will spend a great deal of time interacting with your application; it should be a pleasant experience.

In considering screen layout for an application, you also need to consider fonts, icons, and text size. Some applications require a more modern font; others may require a larger or smaller text size. Java allows you to pick a particular icon and assign it to each window, so your application can be iconified to a graphic that is familiar to your users. The icon is set using the `setIconImage()` in the `Frame` class.

In creating the structure of the program, I made some decisions that reflect an idea of how the screen will be laid out. The program will have one area for display and another for controls. It will include a menu. The display area will be divided into two sections, one for text and the other for graphics. This is not all the information you would need to determine a screen layout, but it is a good starting point.

Design for the Main Window

The main window provides a frame for the application. Other objects in the display appear in the main window. In general, an application's main window will set its colors, fonts, layout, and other display aspects. It then adds the objects it is responsible for displaying, such as an event handler and the `main()` method used to start the application.

In the `SlideShow` application, two display aspects must be set: The background color will be defined to be light gray, and the layout will be set to a border layout.

Three objects should display in the main window: the menu bar that will display across the top of the frame, the display panel that consists of graphics and text objects, and a set of controls used to direct the slide shows.

Design for the Menu Bar

The menu bar is a separate object that is attached to the frame for the application. If there are multiple frames in an application, each one should have its own menu bar; but if the main window can control events in the other windows, those windows don't need a menu bar. If there are multiple menu bars, you must decide which features to include on each one. In the `SlideShow` application there is only one main window, and it will have a menu bar. The Help windows will not be given a menu bar.

> **Note:** Adding a menu bar to an application is not a trivial task. There are decisions about what to include on the menu bar, how to group choices on menus, when to make certain menu items visible, and how to connect each menu to the various activities it invokes.

In most applications you want all the activities of the application to be available on the menu because users will look at the menu when it is not obvious how to perform a certain activity on the screen. Your menu also must include an option to exit the application. If you are providing help screens with your application, they should be available from the menu as well.

For the `SlideShow` application, all the actions available on the control panel are duplicated on the menu. In addition, the menu will provide the capability to load a new show. Two check boxes will be added to the menu to enable the user to turn off the video or the text display. The menu also will allow the user to display help, display an About box, or exit the application.

After selecting the activities to include in the menu, you need to organize these options into groups on the menu. The first item on most application menus is the File menu, which includes options that involve loading and saving files. Generally, options to print a file, control the printer, close a particular window, and exit the application are also located here.

For the `SlideShow` application, the File menu will have two items: Load, which provides the option to load a new show; and Exit, which allows the user to exit the program.

The Help menu is usually the last item on the application menu. Items found here commonly involve providing assistance to the person using the application. This help may come in many different forms. The Help menu will provide one item for each type of help available.

The `SlideShow` application will provide a simple screen to describe the use of each of the controls. It will also have an About box that displays copyright, version, and authoring information. Each of these screens is accessible from the Help menu.

The remaining functions on the `SlideShow` menu bar will be grouped into the Display menu, which provides the items to move through the show and to turn off parts of the display.

The menu bar for the `SlideShow` application is summarized in Table 18.1.

Table 18.1. Menu bar features of the `SlideShow` application.

Category	Item	Description
File	Load	Loads slides into the application
	Exit	Exits `SlideShow`
Display	Forward	Moves forward to the next slide
	Back	Moves backward to the previous slide

Category	Item	Description
	Beginning	Moves to the first slide in the show
	End	Moves to the last slide in the show
	No Text	When checked, the text is hidden
	No Slides	When checked, the pictures are hidden
Help	Help Topics	Provides a description of the controls
	About	Provides authoring information

For some applications, menu items may be pertinent at some times but irrelevant at others. It makes sense to make these items invisible when they are not available. In Java, menu items can be made invisible only by removing them from the menu. However, it is perfectly legal to change the items on a menu at runtime.

Tip: There are times when it might make sense to dim certain menu items, such as those that are available under certain circumstances but are not currently available. This feature is not used in this application. The most common example of this technique is the Cut, Copy, and Paste commands on an Edit menu. The Java method to dim a menu item is `disable()`. These menu items can be made available again using the `enable()` method.

For the `SlideShow` application, there is no need to make any of the items invisible. However, the check boxes will be checked only if a particular option has been selected by the user.

Design for the **SlidePanel** Object

You need to define a new class, `SlidePanel`, to provide the display object. The new class is an extension of the `Panel` class and will contain two new classes: `SlideCanvas`, which will control the display of slides, and `SlideText`, which will control the display of the text.

Note: `SlideCanvas` and `SlideText` are the real performers of the application. These classes provide the features that are available to other objects in the application.

The `SlidePanel` class must include methods to provide the following functions:

- Advance to the next slide
- Revert to the previous slide
- Go to the first slide

- Go to the last slide
- Disable the display of slides
- Enable the display of slides
- Disable the display of text
- Enable the display of text
- Load a new show

The `SlidePanel` methods encapsulate the calls to the methods provided by the objects contained in the panel and are used by both the menu and the controls. `SlidePanel` is also responsible for confirming that the text being displayed corresponds to the slide being shown.

Design for the `SlideCanvas` Object

The `SlideCanvas` class will contain an array of images to display. This class is responsible for reading the `.gif` files that contain the images and for building the array, as well as for displaying the picture to the user and providing methods to control that display. It maintains the total number of slides stored in the array, the current slide, and a flag to indicate whether slides are currently being displayed to the user.

Design for the `SlideText` Object

The `SlideText` class is quite similar to the `SlideCanvas` class. The difference is that `SlideText` contains text strings rather than pictures. The text strings are read from `.txt` files containing descriptions of the slides in the `SlideCanvas` object.

The `SlideText` class will have the same list of internal reference variables and must provide methods similar to those provided by `SlideCanvas`. Instead of methods to enable and disable the display of slides, `SlideText` will provide methods to enable and disable the display of text.

Design for the Controls

Most applications will have some type of graphical controls on the screen in addition to a menu. Selecting appropriate controls and determining their layout are important design considerations. Controls can be grouped and included as a toolbar or a palette. An application may have large buttons for a user to indicate they are done with a certain task, or it may have a picture with different areas taking a user to different tasks. The application may provide scroll boxes, drop-down list boxes, or radio buttons. Java provides mechanisms for supplying many types of controls.

You can create controls as instances of existing objects in the `java.awt` package, or by extending and combining those objects to provide custom controls. *Controls* are separate objects that can be grouped together on an application. They are usually separated from the display area of the application, but they do not have to be. Each control or group of controls should have an event handler so that it can react appropriately when the user selects the control.

The controls for the `SlideShow` application will be constructed as a `Panel` object containing instances of the `Button` class. The controls will provide buttons to enable the user to move forward or backward through the show and to move to the first or last slide.

Design for the Dialog Boxes

Three dialog boxes will be provided in the `SlideShow` application. The first will appear off the Load item on the File menu and will enable the user to select a filename to load. The other two dialog boxes will appear off the Help menu.

Create the Load dialog box using the existing `FileDialog` class. The `FileDialog` class is an example of a *utility*, a class that is useful across many applications. To be useful, a utility must be self-contained and easy to understand. The Java Developer's Kit provides several good utilities, and other resources exist for gathering more Java utilities, such as the official Java reference resource at Gamelan. Utilities that are developed for one application can be easily transferred to another.

The other two dialog boxes will be created as extensions to the `Panel` class. The title of each dialog box and its contents will be coded into the extension. To make the window easy to close, the extensions will provide an OK button that closes the window.

File I/O

One of the biggest differences between developing applets and developing applications is the availability of local files for reading and writing. Chapter 17 presents a brief example of writing to a file. This section relates some additional details on reading from files and accessing them on the local disk.

The `SlideShow` application reads several different files. It initially reads a file to determine which slides are part of the show, and then reads the files containing those slides. Finally, it reads the text files containing a description or comment about each picture.

In the first file access, the application will read the names of the files without the extension so that the same filenames can be used for both slides and comments. The slides are stored in `.gif` files and the comments in `.txt` files.

Although there are several types of streams that can be used to read a file, the easiest method of performing file I/O is with a `RandomFileAccess` object. This object encapsulates many of the file-access mechanisms, reducing the complexity of the code used to read the file.

The `RandomFileAccess` methods may encounter errors when reading or writing a file such as missing files, corrupt files, files that are read-only, and similar problems related to file storage and access. Although the class may be able to handle some of these problems, many of them must be reported back to the user. Therefore, the methods in this class may throw an `IOException` error.

> **Note:** The `Exception` objects are a graceful way of handling error conditions. Any code that calls a method capable of throwing an exception must either catch the exception or throw back the exception to its caller. It is possible for a single method to throw multiple exceptions. (See Chapter 8, "Tying It All Together: Threads, Exceptions, and More," for a discussion of throwing and catching exceptions.)

If the method elects to catch the exception, it must provide code to do so. The code to catch exceptions uses the following syntax, with the method or methods being called within the braces after the keyword `try`:

```
try {...} catch (ExceptionType exceptionname) {...}
```

The exception handling is placed in the braces following the keyword `catch`. The `Exception` object that is caught is assigned a name so that it can be referenced. The way the exception is handled depends on the problem and the context in which it occurred.

Some exceptions can be ignored. In this case, the space between the braces is left blank. Other exceptions can be displayed with or without an error message to the user. Some can be displayed in their own pop-up window. Others can be written to a log file. Some may even cause the program to shut down. In the `SlideShow` application, file I/O exceptions result in an error message being displayed on the standard output—that is, the window where the application was started, not the window where the application is running.

Relationships Among Objects

After you have decided on the major pieces of your application, the relationships among them must be established. Some pieces may not have any interaction with other pieces. Other pieces will affect the display of the screen they appear on, while still others will affect the display of multiple screens. The menu must interact with many of the objects in the application.

For the application being created, the dialog boxes will be displayed via the menu. The menu will also be used to load a new show into the main window. The controls that have been defined must call methods in the display panel to change the display on the screen. The functions available on the controls should be duplicated on the menu; therefore, these methods also must be available to the menu.

The relationships among objects and the users of the program indicate the events that must be handled by the objects. The actions that occur on the menu must be handled in the event handler of the SlideShow class. The actions that occur in dialog boxes are handled by the event handler for the dialog box. The controls have an event handler to respond to user actions in the controls.

> **Peter's Principle:** In the real world, designing an application is hampered by the changing nature of the user's needs. The design process will start in one direction, only to have new needs or new constraints appear. The flexibility of Java helps to ease this problem; however, skilled project management is still important to successfully bring applications to completion.

Implementing a Real-World Application

In the implementation of the application, you will create the classes that were designed in the previous section as well as instances of these and other classes as needed to perform the tasks required for the application. Seven new classes must be defined to create the SlideShow application.

Building the Main Window

The first class to define is an extension of the Frame class named SlideShow. The main window is built in this class, as is the main() method used to start the application. After declaring the new class, two key containers are defined to create instances of the MenuBar and SlidePanel objects. These declarations appear as follows:

```
public class SlideShow extends Frame {
    protected MenuBar mbar;              // Menu for the slideshow
    protected SlidePanel displayPanel;   // Panel to display the show
```

To help you visualize these objects as they are discussed, Figure 18.1 shows the main window for the application.

The SlideShow() Method

Following a top-down methodology, you should construct the high-level objects before the low-level objects. For this reason, you now need to define the layout and style of the application and instantiate the key objects used to build the window. This is handled in a method called SlideShow(), which is shown in Listing 18.1.

Figure 18.1.
The main window of the
`SlideShow` *application.*

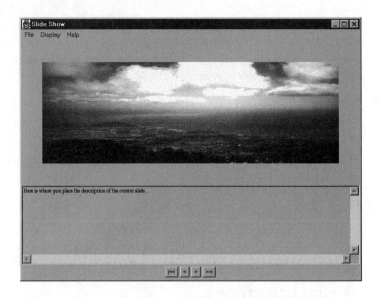

The `SlideShow()` method builds the main window in a few easy steps. It calls a method used to build the menu and then sets the menu bar on the frame. Afterward, it sets the color of the background and defines the layout style for the display panel and controls. Its final step is to create new instances of the display panel and the controls and add them to the frame. The display panel is instantiated and added to the center of the frame using a single line of code. Likewise, the controls are instantiated and added to the South portion of the frame using a single line of code.

Listing 18.1. The `SlideShow()` method.

```
public SlideShow(String args) {
    InitializeMenu();
    setMenuBar(mbar);

    setBackground(Color.lightGray);
    setLayout(new BorderLayout());
    add("Center",displayPanel = new SlidePanel(args));
    add("South",new ShowControls(displayPanel));
}
```

Creating the Menu Bar

The `SlideShow` class is also used to build the menu bar, which is an instance of the class `MenuBar` from the `java.awt` package. Compared with all the thought that goes into setting up a menu, the code to create it is short. For clarity, the code is placed in its own method called `InitializeMenu`. This method, shown in Listing 18.2, is called by the `SlideShow()` method.

To ensure that the menu bar is easy to use, menu items are logically grouped into menu categories. The SlideShow application's menu bar has three menu categories: File, Display, and Help, which are defined using the Menu class. Items on the menus are defined as MenuItem or CheckBoxMenuItem objects from the same package.

Just as you group menus into categories, you should also logically group menu items. If a particular menu can be grouped into subcategories, you can use the addSeparator() method to add a graphical rule to the menu to visually separate the categories of menu items.

After you define all the menu items for a particular menu, you need to add the menu to the menu bar using the add() method.

Listing 18.2. The `InitializeMenu()` method.

```
// Creates the menu and attaches it to the MenuBar
    private void InitializeMenu()
    {
        mbar = new MenuBar();
        Menu m = new Menu("File");
        m.add(new MenuItem("Load..."));
        m.addSeparator();
        m.add(new MenuItem("Exit"));
        mbar.add(m);

        m = new Menu("Display");
        m.add(new MenuItem("Forward"));
        m.add(new MenuItem("Back"));
        m.add(new MenuItem("Beginning"));
        m.add(new MenuItem("End"));
        m.addSeparator();
        m.add(new CheckboxMenuItem("No Text"));
        m.add(new CheckboxMenuItem("No Slides"));
        mbar.add(m);

        m = new Menu("Help");
        m.add(new MenuItem("Help Topics"));
        m.addSeparator();
        m.add(new MenuItem("About SlideShow"));
        mbar.add(m);
    }
```

Figure 18.2 shows the Display menu in the SlideShow application. The menu contains each of the menu items listed in the code with a separator between the menu subcategories.

Handling Events

The event handler of the SlideShow class is used to respond to the menu events in this application. The code for the event handler is shown in Listing 18.3. Notice that the item name is used to determine the user's selection. Therefore, the item names in the event handler must exactly match the item names listed on the menu.

Figure 18.2.
Using the menu.

The event handler is responsible for displaying the three dialog boxes created in the previous section. In each case, it creates the dialog box and assigns a name to the instance. It then uses the name to display the dialog box. When the Load dialog box closes, it passes the name of the file to the display panel so the appropriate file is loaded.

For events in the Display menu, the event handler calls the appropriate method on the display panel. When the user selects Exit or destroys the window, the event handler causes the application to exit.

Listing 18.3. The event handler for `SlideShow`.

```
// Event handler responds to events in the window and
    // events on the menu
    public boolean handleEvent(Event evt) {
        if (evt.id == Event.WINDOW_DESTROY &&
            evt.target instanceof SlideShow)
        {
            System.exit(0);
            return true;
        } else if(evt.target instanceof CheckboxMenuItem) {
            if (evt.arg.equals("No Text")) {
                if (((CheckboxMenuItem) evt.target).getState() == true)
                    displayPanel.NoText();
                else
                    displayPanel.ShowText();
                return true;
            } else if (evt.arg.equals("No Slides")) {
                if (((CheckboxMenuItem) evt.target).getState() == true)
                    displayPanel.NoSlides();
                else
                    displayPanel.ShowSlides();
                return true;
            }
```

```
        } else if(evt.target instanceof MenuItem) {
            if (evt.arg.equals("Load...")) {
                String FileName;
                FileDialog fd =
                    new FileDialog((Frame) this,
                                "Get New Slide Show",
                                FileDialog.LOAD);
                fd.show();
                FileName = fd. getDirectory() + fd.getFile();
                displayPanel.LoadShow(FileName);
                return true;
            } else if (evt.arg.equals("Forward")) {
                displayPanel.ShowNextSlide();
                return true;
            } else if (evt.arg.equals("Back")) {
                displayPanel.ShowPrevSlide();
                return true;
            } else if (evt.arg.equals("Beginning")) {
                displayPanel.ShowFirstSlide();
                return true;
            } else if (evt.arg.equals("End")) {
                displayPanel.ShowLastSlide();
                return true;
            } else if (evt.arg.equals("Exit")) {
                System.exit(0);
                return true;
            } else if (evt.arg.equals("About SlideShow")) {
                AboutBox ab = new AboutBox(this);
                ab.show();
                return true;
            } else if (evt.arg.equals("Help Topics")) {
                HelpBox ab = new HelpBox(this);
                ab.show();
                return true;
            }
        }
        return super.handleEvent(evt);      // Let parent handle event
    }
```

Starting the Application

The final method defined in the `SlideShow` class is the `main()` method. In any application, `main()` is the first method called when the application starts. Listing 18.4 shows this method.

The `SlideShow` application's `main()` method expects a filename to be passed as an argument from the command line. If this does not happen, the application prints a usage message and exits the application. If a filename is passed as an argument, the `main()` method does the following:

- Creates a new instance of the `SlideShow` object
- Sets a title on the main frame
- Resizes the application's frame to the current window size
- Shows the objects built when the `SlideShow()` method was invoked

Resizing your application's main frame to the current window size is a key design concept. In this way, you ensure that the main frame always fits in the user's screen.

Listing 18.4. The `main()` method.

```
// main method used to start application
public static void main(String args[]){

    // Verify that there is a filename to attempt to load show
    if (args.length <= 0) {
        System.out.println("Usage: java SlideShow filename.");
        System.exit(0);
    }

    // Create instance of this object
    SlideShow ss = new SlideShow(args[0]);
    ss.setTitle("Slide Show");          // Set the title of the frame
    ss.pack();                          // Pack components

    //resize frame to current window size
    Dimension d;
    d = Toolkit.getDefaultToolkit().getScreenSize();
    ss.resize(d.width, d.height);
    ss.show();                          // Display the frame
}
}
```

Adding the `SlidePanel` Class

The `SlidePanel` class added in the `SlideShow()` method is implemented next. This class defines the main viewing area for the application. The viewing area is divided into two parts: the picture and the text. This parallels the two objects that are placed in the `SlidePanel` class.

The two parts must change in coordination with one another. Therefore, these objects are protected in `SlidePanel`, and all events that modify the contents of these objects must occur through `SlidePanel`. This becomes important when you look at the code for the controls. The declaration and constructor for `SlidePanel` appear in Listing 18.5.

Listing 18.5. The `SlidePanel` constructor.

```
/**
 * SlidePanel class holds objects participating in the slideshow
 * Objects are arrays displaying one at a time to the user
 */
class SlidePanel extends Panel {
    protected SlideCanvas displayCanvas;    // Canvas to display .gifs
    protected SlideText displayText;        // Text area to display text

    // Constructor adds objects to the panel
```

```
      // Gives each object the filename to get load its array from
      public SlidePanel(String ShowName) {
            super();
            setLayout(new BorderLayout());
            add("Center",displayCanvas = new SlideCanvas(ShowName));
            add("South",displayText = new SlideText(ShowName));
      }
```

All the features that act on the display in the main viewing area must use methods defined in the object providing the main display. For custom controls, the name of the object providing this display is passed to each control. For menu options, the main event handler is used to activate the correct method.

In the `SlidePanel` object, you define methods for each of the functions listed in the design. The body of these methods consists of calling similar methods for each of the two objects on the display. (See Listing 18.6.) These methods will be implemented when you define the `SlideCanvas` and `SlideText` objects.

Listing 18.6. Methods for the `SlidePanel()` class.

```
public void ShowNextSlide() {
        displayCanvas.ShowNextSlide();
        displayText.ShowNextText();
    }
    public void ShowPrevSlide() {
        displayCanvas.ShowPrevSlide();
        displayText.ShowPrevText();
    }
    public void ShowFirstSlide() {
        displayCanvas.ShowFirstSlide();
        displayText.ShowFirstText();
    }
    public void ShowLastSlide() {
        displayCanvas.ShowLastSlide();
        displayText.ShowLastText();
    }
    public void NoSlides(){
        displayCanvas.NoSlides();
    }
    public void ShowSlides(){
        displayCanvas.ShowSlides();
    }
    public void NoText(){
        displayText.NoText();
    }
    public void ShowText(){
        displayText.ShowText();
    }
    public void LoadShow(String ShowName) {
        displayCanvas.LoadShow(ShowName);
        displayText.LoadShow(ShowName);
    }
```

Adding the **SlideCanvas** Object

Create the SlideCanvas class used to display images first. The information contained in this object is held in variables that are implemented as protected. The complete declaration appears as

```
/**
 * SlideCanvas is an extension of Canvas
 * It provides a means to display slides to the user
 */
class SlideCanvas extends Canvas {
    protected Image im[] = new Image[20];//Array of Images to display
    protected int NumSlides;       // Number of images in the array
    protected int CurrentSlide;    // Number of image currently displayed
    protected boolean showslide;   // False to turn off display
```

The constructor for this class takes one parameter: the name of the file containing the list of images the show will display. The constructor for the class is just three lines: the first calls the constructor for the Canvas class; the second calls the method (described in the "File I/O" section in this chapter) to load the array from the given filename; and the final line sets the showslide variable to true, indicating that slides are shown, not hidden, by default. The code for the constructor is

```
public SlideCanvas(String ShowName) {
        super();
        LoadShow(ShowName);      // Load internal array
        showslide = true;        // Enable the display of slides
    }
```

The class draws the image on the screen by overriding the paint() method. The new method will draw a blank rectangle if the display is currently disabled. Otherwise, it will determine the current size of the display and draw an appropriately sized image:

```
public void paint(Graphics g) {
        Rectangle r = bounds();
        if (showslide)
            g.drawImage(im[CurrentSlide],50,50,
                        r.width-100,r.height-100,this);
        else {
            g.setColor(Color.lightGray);
            g.fillRect(0,0,r.width,r.height);
        }
    }
```

The access methods needed for these variables are defined in the "Designing a Real-World Application" section in this chapter. These methods ensure that an instance of the class is repainted any time the current slide is altered. Again, you can see the advantages of protected variables. If the variable containing the current slide number could be accessed directly, there would be no guarantee that the slide would be repainted when the current slide is altered.

The first access methods are those that enable the user to move through the slide show. The methods that move forward or backward one slide must check for the array bounds. If the method encounters an array boundary, it simply remains on the same slide. The methods operate by setting a new current slide and then calling repaint() to display the slide, as in the following code fragment:

```
public void ShowNextSlide() {
        if (CurrentSlide < (NumSlides - 1)) {
            CurrentSlide = CurrentSlide + 1;
            repaint();
        }
    }
    public void ShowPrevSlide() {
        if (CurrentSlide > 0) {
            CurrentSlide = CurrentSlide - 1;
            repaint();
        }
    }
    public void ShowFirstSlide() {
        CurrentSlide = 0;
        repaint();
    }
    public void ShowLastSlide() {
        CurrentSlide = NumSlides - 1;
        repaint();
    }
```

To enable and disable the display of slides, access methods must be provided for the boolean variable showslide. These methods will change the value of the variable and then force a repaint of the screen so that the new value becomes effective immediately:

```
public void NoSlides(){
        showslide = false;
        repaint();
    }
    public void ShowSlides(){
        showslide = true;
        repaint();
    }
```

The last method to be defined for SlideCanvas is the one that loads the array. This code must open the file specified by the user, read each line from the file, store the line in the array, close the file, and handle any exceptions. These functions are shown in the following code:

```
public void LoadShow(String LoadFile) {
        RandomAccessFile     ListFile;
        String[] imgFile = new String[20];   // name of image to display
        int i;                                // Loop counter

        // Create an array of images and load the images
        i=0;
        try {
            // Open the file
            ListFile = new RandomAccessFile(LoadFile,"r");
            // Read until the end of the file is reached
            while (ListFile.getFilePointer() != ListFile.length() ) {
                // Store each line from the file in an array element
                imgFile[i] = ListFile.readLine() + ".gif";
                i++;
            }
            //Close the file
            ListFile.close();
```

```
        // Trap any errors which occur while reading the file
        } catch (java.io.IOException e) {
            System.out.println("Could not read from file.");
            System.out.println(e);
        }
```

 RandomAccessFile is a class that implements two different interfaces, DataOutput and DataInput. Therefore, objects that are instances of this class can be used for both reading and writing. The SlideShow application currently does not need to write to a file. However, writing to a file in an application works in a manner analogous to reading.

This type of file access will handle reading from and writing to text files. Something different is needed to read an image file. In applets, the getImage() method is used to get an image from a file or a URL. This method cannot be used in an application because it loads relative to the applet's URL. The application does not have a URL, so it needs another mechanism to load the image.

For applications, the image can be loaded using the getImage() method from a Toolkit object. To do this, the application first must get the current Toolkit object and then get the image. The getImage() method in the Toolkit object encapsulates all the details of reading the file and storing the image. The code to load the images for the slide show is

```
NumSlides = i;
        for (i=0; i<NumSlides;i++) {
            im[i] = getToolkit().getImage(imgFile[i]);
        }
    CurrentSlide = 0;
    }
}
```

Adding the SlideText Object

The SlideText class is similar to the SlideCanvas class except that it contains an array of text strings. The modified declaration appears as

```
/**
 * SlideText is an extension of TextArea
 * It provides a means to display text descriptions to the user
 */
class SlideText extends TextArea {
    protected String str[] = new String[20];//Array of Strings to display
    protected int NumTexts;        // Number of strings in the array
    protected int CurrentText;     // Number of strings currently displayed
    protected boolean showtext;    // True if text is not being displayed
```

The constructor for the SlideText class is just a little longer than the constructor for the SlideCanvas class. In addition to the tasks performed in the constructor for SlideCanvas, SlideText must set its Editable attribute to false to prevent viewers from modifying the slide descriptions:

```
public SlideText(String ShowName) {
        super();
        LoadShow(ShowName);     // Load internal array
```

```
        setEditable(false);     // Prevent editing of text
        showtext = true;        // Enable the display of text
    }
```

There is no `paint()` method for text classes. The normal `setText()` method takes a string as a parameter and sets the text of the object to that string. To prevent another object from accidentally setting the display text, you override this method and call a new implementation of `setText()` that does not require a parameter, as in the following code fragment:

```
// Override normal setText so text can not be reset accidentally
    public void setText(String str){
        setText();
    }
```

The new implementation of `setText()` will set the text based on the current text element in the array. Therefore, you do not need a parameter. If text is not being displayed, set the text to an empty string, which must be done using the version of `setText()` in the superclass because `setText(String)` was overridden for this class. The new implementation of `setText` is

```
public void setText(){
        if (showtext)
            super.setText(str[CurrentText]);
        else
            super.setText("");
}
```

The `SlideText` class is responsible for providing the same access methods as the `SlideCanvas` class. These methods are similar to those implemented for `SlideCanvas`. Note that the array boundaries must be checked in these methods as well:

```
public void ShowNextText() {
        if (CurrentText < (NumTexts - 1)) {
            CurrentText = CurrentText + 1;
            setText();
        }
    }
    public void ShowPrevText() {
        if (CurrentText > 0) {
            CurrentText = CurrentText - 1;
            setText();
        }
    }
    public void ShowFirstText() {
        CurrentText = 0;
        setText();
    }
    public void ShowLastText() {
        CurrentText = NumTexts - 1;
        setText();
    }
```

Hiding and displaying text is done by providing accessor methods for the boolean variable. Instead of forcing a repaint of the screen to cause the new value to become effective, these methods call `setText()` directly:

```
public void NoText(){
        showtext = false;
```

```
            setText();
      }
      public void ShowText(){
            showtext = true;
            setText();
      }
```

The load method follows the same algorithm as that for SlideCanvas; however, a new method is implemented to provide for reading an entire file into an element in the array of text strings. This method, called getText, will make use of the RandomAccessFile class in a manner similar to how filenames are read. However, instead of reading a line looking for a null terminator, this method will read the entire file into a string. The new method appears as

```
// Read text for an item from a file
      protected String getText(String LoadFile){
            RandomAccessFile      ListFile;
            byte b[] = new byte[1024];
            int numbytes;

            try {
                  ListFile = new RandomAccessFile(LoadFile,"r");
                  numbytes = (int)ListFile.length();
                  ListFile.read(b,0,numbytes);
                  ListFile.close();
            } catch (java.io.IOException e) {
                  System.out.println("Could not read from file.");
                  System.out.println(e);
            }
            return (new String(b,0));
      }
}
```

Using this method, the load method for the SlideText class can be implemented as follows:

```
// Load the text array based on filename in the LoadFile
      public void LoadShow(String LoadFile) {
            RandomAccessFile      ListFile;
            String[] strFile = new String[20];    // name of image to display
            int i;                                 // Loop counter

            // Create an array of strings and load the strings

            i=0;
            try {
                  ListFile = new RandomAccessFile(LoadFile,"r");
                  while (ListFile.getFilePointer() != ListFile.length() ) {
                        strFile[i] = ListFile.readLine() + ".txt";
                        i++;
                  }
                  ListFile.close();
            } catch (java.io.IOException e) {
                  System.out.println("Could not read from file.");
                  System.out.println(e);
            }
            NumTexts = i;
            for (i=0; i<NumTexts;i++) {
                  str[i] = getText(strFile[i]);
            }
```

```
        CurrentText = 0;
    }
```

Adding the Controls

Now that you can display images and text, you can turn your attention to creating the controls to navigate through the show. The controls are created using four buttons. These buttons are then grouped into a single object that is an extension of the Panel class.

The controls must reference a particular SlidePanel where they will cause slides to change. Therefore, the constructor for the controls takes an instance of SlidePanel as a parameter. This value is stored as an internal variable and is used by the event handler for this class. The declaration and constructor for the controls appear as

```
/**
 * Control bar for moving through a slide show
 */
class ShowControls extends Panel {
    static SlidePanel ss;        // Panel controls are attached to

    // Constructor requires a SlidePanel to which the
    // controls are attached
    public ShowControls(SlidePanel theShow) {
        ss = theShow;
        setLayout(new FlowLayout(FlowLayout.CENTER));
        add(new Button("¦<<"));
        add(new Button("<"));
        add(new Button(">"));
        add(new Button(">>¦"));
    }
```

When the user interacts with the controls, an event is triggered. The controls must react to this event and perform the desired operation. The action() method for the controls is triggered by the runtime environment when an action event, such as pressing a button, takes place on the control panel. This method determines whether a button was pressed by examining the event target. If the event target is not a button, it calls the action method for its superclass, which enables the runtime environment to react to other defined actions:

```
public boolean action(Event evt, Object arg) {
        if (evt.target instanceof Button) {
            handleButton((String)arg);
            return true;
        } else return super.action(evt,arg);
    }
```

When the action method determines that a button is the target of the action, it calls the handleButton method. This method determines which button is pressed and calls an appropriate method in the SlidePanel that this object controls:

```
// Determine which button was pressed and act accordingly
// Actions will refer to the Slide panel to which the
```

```
// control bar is attached
public void handleButton(String bname) {
    if (bname.equals(">")) {
        ss.ShowNextSlide();
    } else if (bname.equals("<")) {
        ss.ShowPrevSlide();
    } else if (bname.equals("¦<<")) {
        ss.ShowFirstSlide();
    } else if (bname.equals(">>¦")) {
        ss.ShowLastSlide();
    }
}
```

Adding the Dialog Boxes

Dialog boxes in their general form are introduced in Chapter 17. This section shows you how to implement the three dialog boxes that appear in response to the Load, Help Topics, and About SlideShow menu items.

The File Dialog Box

The File dialog box is a specific kind of dialog box. Implemented in the java.awt package, these boxes enable the user to select a particular file located on his or her system. By default, the dialog box displays the listing of the directory where the application is launched. However, the directory the dialog box displays can be modified by the application.

The dialog box can be supplied with a default filename so that it will display only files that match that filename. If the filename contains wildcards, all files matching the expression are displayed. In this manner, the File dialog box can be used to display only files of a certain type.

The dialog box is implemented so that its appearance depends on the operating system on which the application is running. This means the user has the look and feel of a familiar platform, but the application has all the advantages of platform independence. Thankfully, the difference in appearance of the dialog box is transparent to the programmer.

The constructor for the File dialog box is passed three parameters: the current frame as the parent of the new window; a title for the dialog box, in this case Get New Slide Show; and an indicator that this is an Open dialog box, not a Save dialog box. For the SlideShow application, the call to the file dialog box is

```
new FileDialog((Frame) this,"Get New Slide Show",FileDialog.LOAD);
```

The dialog box as it appears on a Windows system is shown in Figure 18.3.

Figure 18.3.
A file dialog box under Windows.

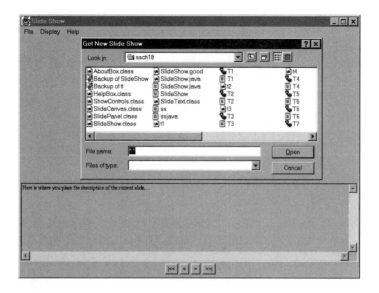

The `HelpBox` Class

The Help dialog box is designed as an extension to the `Panel` class and is constructed with a grid layout. Each of the help items is added as a label. The constructor for the dialog box takes care of resizing the box, but does not actually display it. The method that creates the dialog box will determine when to display it.

The OK button specified in the design is added at the bottom of the dialog box. The OK button is placed in its own panel so that it is displayed in a standard button shape instead of occupying the entire width of the grid item where it is displayed. Listing 18.7 shows the code for the `HelpBox` constructor.

Listing 18.7. Creating the Help dialog box.

```
/**
 * Basic Help window to explain the slide controls
 */
class HelpBox extends Dialog
{
    public HelpBox(Frame parent)
    {
        super(parent, "Help Topics", true);
        setLayout(new GridLayout(6,1));
        add(new Label("The controls work as follows:",Label.LEFT));
        add(new Label("    |<<    returns to the first slide",
            Label.LEFT));
        add(new Label("    <     returns to the previous slide",
            Label.LEFT));
```

continues

Listing 18.7. continued

```
        add(new Label("     >        advances to the next slide",
           Label.LEFT));
        add(new Label("     >>¦      advances to the last slide",
           Label.LEFT));
        Panel pp = new Panel();
        pp.add(new Button("OK"));
        add(pp);
        resize(250,300);
    }
}
```

Figure 18.4 shows the Help box for the SlideShow application.

Figure 18.4.
The Help box for
SlideShow.

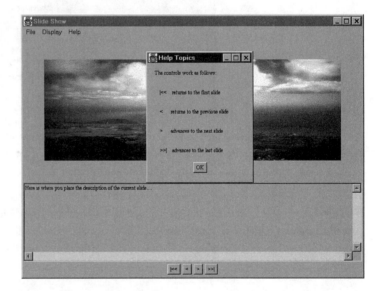

The dialog box must have an event handler to respond to user events in the dialog box. The user can click the OK button to close the dialog box or close the window where the dialog box is displayed. In either case, the application will dispose of the dialog box, indicating that it is done with the resource the object used. The event handler appears in Listing 18.8.

Listing 18.8. The HelpBox() event handler.

```
    // Event handler closes the window if the user
    // hits the OK button or the window close button
    public boolean handleEvent(Event evt) {
        if (evt.id == Event.WINDOW_DESTROY &&
            evt.target instanceof HelpBox) {
             dispose();
            return true;
```

```
        } else if("OK".equals(evt.arg)) {
            dispose();
            return true;
        }
        return false;
    }
}
```

The **AboutBox** Class

The About box is similar to the Help Topics dialog box. However, because it has different contents, it uses a different layout. At the center of the panel, a grid layout is used to display the authoring information. The OK button goes in its own panel in the South portion of the layout. The entire listing for the AboutBox class is shown in Listing 18.9.

Listing 18.9. Creating the About dialog box.

```
/**
 * Creates an about box for the Slideshow
 */
class AboutBox extends Dialog
{
    public AboutBox(Frame parent)
    {
        super(parent, "About SlideShow", true);
        setLayout(new GridLayout(3,1));
        add(new Label("SlideShow",Label.CENTER));
        add(new Label("by Peter Norton and William Stanek",Label.CENTER));
        Panel pp = new Panel();
        pp.add(new Button("OK"));
        add("South",pp);
        resize(250,200);
    }
    // Event handler closes the window if the user
    // hits the OK button or the window close button
    public boolean handleEvent(Event evt) {
        if (evt.id == Event.WINDOW_DESTROY &&
            evt.target instanceof AboutBox) {
            dispose();
            return true;
        } else if("OK".equals(evt.arg)) {
            dispose();
            return true;
        }
        return false;
    }
}
```

Figure 18.5 shows the About box for the SlideShow application.

Figure 18.5.
The About box for
`SlideShow`.

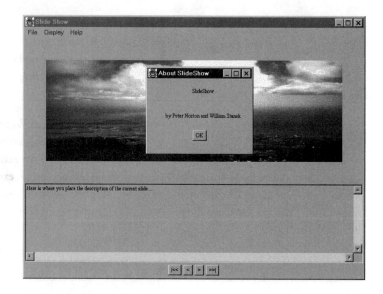

The Complete Project

To test the application, you must be able to run the application correctly. The stand-alone application can be run from the command line using the command

```
java SlideShow filename.txt
```

where `filename.txt` is the name of the file containing the list of slides to display. This file can be created using a standard text editor, provided that null characters are inserted between the filenames. The same type of text editor can be used to create the descriptions supplied with each slide.

For example, you could create a slide show file named `Hawaii.txt` containing a list of pictures from your vacation to Hawaii. The pictures are named

- `Mountain1.gif`
- `Mountain2.gif`
- `Beach1.gif`
- `Beach2.gif`
- `Luau1.gif`
- `Luau2.gif`

The file `Hawaii.txt` would appear as

```
Mountain1□Mountain2□Beach1□Beach2□Luau1□Luau2
```

where the symbol □ represents the null character. If you have difficulty including the null in a text editor, you can create a simple Java program to read filenames from the command line and insert them in a file. After each filename, append the string \n to get the null character. This allows you to use the simple `readline()` method in the program rather than adding code to parse the file.

> **Tip:** The ASCII code for the null character is `010`. In Microsoft Word, you can generate the null character that Java expects as an end-of-line marker by holding the Alt key and typing `010`. Unfortunately, when Word saves a text file, it puts an extra carriage return at the end of the file. Although `SlideShow` will run, it will look for an extra file and generate an error. Chapter 19, "Application Upgrades," demonstrates how to create a long-term fix for this problem by building slide shows within the application.

To continue the Hawaiian vacation slide show, you need six text files with the names `Mountain1.txt`, `Mountain2.txt`, `Beach1.txt`, and so on. These files will explain more about each picture. For example, `Mountain1.txt` might read

> View looking south from Ka Ala on the leeward coast of Oahu. Taken at 3 p.m. after an enjoyable all-day hike.

Text files such as these help you to remember more about each picture. They can be particularly helpful if you are going to keep the pictures for any length of time.

The finished application is shown in Listing 18.10. This example has demonstrated the possibilities of Java applications. Now you should be able to put the techniques discussed in this chapter to use to build original Java programs.

After working through this example, try to modify the application to increase your experience with Java. For example, you could rewrite the `Aboutbox` class so that the constructor takes two arguments, the title and the author. The class would then know exactly how to display the information and could be reused in other applications.

You could use a similar technique to create standard Help boxes. The argument to the constructor could be a string or list of strings containing the information to be displayed in the help window. These types of utilities are in the process of being developed for Java.

Listing 18.10. The complete **SlideShow** application.

```
import java.awt.*;
import java.applet.*;
import java.io.RandomAccessFile;

/**
 * Creates Window with panel for the slideshow
 * plus a Menu and controls for the SlideShow
```

continues

Listing 18.10. continued

```java
*/
public class SlideShow extends Frame {
    protected MenuBar mbar;                    // Menu for the slideshow
    protected SlidePanel displayPanel;         // Panel to display the show

    public SlideShow(String args) {
        setBackground(Color.lightGray);
        setLayout(new BorderLayout());
        add("Center",displayPanel = new SlidePanel(args));
        add("South",new ShowControls(displayPanel));

        InitializeMenu();
        setMenuBar(mbar);
    }
    // Creates the menu and attaches it to the MenuBar
    private void InitializeMenu()
    {
        mbar = new MenuBar();
        Menu m = new Menu("File");
        m.add(new MenuItem("Load..."));
        m.addSeparator();
        m.add(new MenuItem("Exit"));
        mbar.add(m);

        m = new Menu("Display");
        m.add(new MenuItem("Forward"));
        m.add(new MenuItem("Back"));
        m.add(new MenuItem("Beginning"));
        m.add(new MenuItem("End"));
        m.addSeparator();
        m.add(new CheckboxMenuItem("No Text"));
        m.add(new CheckboxMenuItem("No Slides"));
        mbar.add(m);

        m = new Menu("Help");
        m.add(new MenuItem("Help Topics"));
        m.addSeparator();
        m.add(new MenuItem("About SlideShow"));
        mbar.add(m);
    }
    // Event handler responds to events in the window and
    // events on the menu
    public boolean handleEvent(Event evt) {
        if (evt.id == Event.WINDOW_DESTROY &&
            evt.target instanceof SlideShow)
          {
              System.exit(0);
            return true;
        } else if(evt.target instanceof CheckboxMenuItem) {
            if (evt.arg.equals("No Text")) {
                if (((CheckboxMenuItem) evt.target).getState() == true)
                    displayPanel.NoText();
                else
                    displayPanel.ShowText();
                return true;
            } else if (evt.arg.equals("No Slides")) {
```

```java
            if (((CheckboxMenuItem) evt.target).getState() == true)
                displayPanel.NoSlides();
            else
                displayPanel.ShowSlides();
            return true;
        }
    } else if(evt.target instanceof MenuItem) {
        if (evt.arg.equals("Load...")) {
            String FileName;
            FileDialog fd =
                new FileDialog((Frame) this,
                            "Get New Slide Show",
                            FileDialog.LOAD);
            fd.show();
            FileName = fd. getDirectory() + fd.getFile();
            displayPanel.LoadShow(FileName);
            return true;
        } else if (evt.arg.equals("Forward")) {
            displayPanel.ShowNextSlide();
            return true;
        } else if (evt.arg.equals("Back")) {
            displayPanel.ShowPrevSlide();
            return true;
        } else if (evt.arg.equals("Beginning")) {
            displayPanel.ShowFirstSlide();
            return true;
        } else if (evt.arg.equals("End")) {
            displayPanel.ShowLastSlide();
            return true;
        } else if (evt.arg.equals("Exit")) {
            System.exit(0);
            return true;
        } else if (evt.arg.equals("About SlideShow")) {
            AboutBox ab = new AboutBox(this);
            ab.show();
            return true;
        } else if (evt.arg.equals("Help Topics")) {
            HelpBox ab = new HelpBox(this);
            ab.show();
            return true;
        }
    }
    return super.handleEvent(evt);       // Let parent handle event
}

// main method used to start application
public static void main(String args[]){

    // Verify that there is a filename to attempt to load show
    if (args.length <= 0) {
        System.out.println("Usage: java SlideShow filename.");
        System.exit(0);
    }

    // Create instance of this object
    SlideShow ss = new SlideShow(args[0]);
    ss.setTitle("Slide Show");              // Set the title of the frame
    ss.pack();                              // Pack components
```

continues

Listing 18.10. continued

```
                //resize frame to current window size
                Dimension d;
                d = Toolkit.getDefaultToolkit().getScreenSize();
                ss.resize(d.width, d.height);
                ss.show();                              // Display the frame
        }
}

/**
 * SlidePanel class holds objects participating in the slideshow
 * Objects are arrays displaying one at a time to the user
 */
class SlidePanel extends Panel {
        protected SlideCanvas displayCanvas;        // Canvas to display .gifs
        protected SlideText displayText;            // Text area to display text

        // Constructor adds objects to the panel
        // Gives each object the filename to get load its array from
        public SlidePanel(String ShowName) {
                super();
                setLayout(new BorderLayout());
                add("Center",displayCanvas = new SlideCanvas(ShowName));
                add("South",displayText = new SlideText(ShowName));
        }
        public void NoText(){
                displayText.NoText();
        }
        public void ShowText(){
                displayText.ShowText();
        }
        public void NoSlides(){
                displayCanvas.NoSlides();
        }
        public void ShowSlides(){
                displayCanvas.ShowSlides();
        }

        public void LoadShow(String ShowName) {
                displayCanvas.LoadShow(ShowName);
                displayText.LoadShow(ShowName);
        }
        public void ShowNextSlide() {
                displayCanvas.ShowNextSlide();
                displayText.ShowNextText();
        }
        public void ShowPrevSlide() {
                displayCanvas.ShowPrevSlide();
                displayText.ShowPrevText();
        }
        public void ShowFirstSlide() {
                displayCanvas.ShowFirstSlide();
                displayText.ShowFirstText();
        }
        public void ShowLastSlide() {
                displayCanvas.ShowLastSlide();
                displayText.ShowLastText();
        }
}
```

```java
/**
 * SlideCanvas is an extension of Canvas
 * It provides a means to display slides to the user
 */
class SlideCanvas extends Canvas {
    protected Image im[] = new Image[20];  // Array of Images to display
    protected int NumSlides;        // Number of images in the array
    protected int CurrentSlide;     // Number of image currently displayed
    protected boolean showslide;    // False to turn off display

    public SlideCanvas(String ShowName) {
        super();
        LoadShow(ShowName);
        showslide = true;
    }
    public void NoSlides(){
        showslide = false;
        repaint();
    }
    public void ShowSlides(){
        showslide = true;
        repaint();
    }

    public void paint(Graphics g) {
        Rectangle r = bounds();
        if (showslide)
            g.drawImage(im[CurrentSlide],50,50,
                        r.width-100,r.height-100,this);
        else {
            g.setColor(Color.lightGray);
            g.fillRect(0,0,r.width,r.height);
        }
    }
    public void ShowNextSlide() {
        if (CurrentSlide < (NumSlides - 1)) {
            CurrentSlide = CurrentSlide + 1;
            repaint();
        }
    }
    public void ShowPrevSlide() {
        if (CurrentSlide > 0) {
            CurrentSlide = CurrentSlide - 1;
            repaint();
        }
    }
    public void ShowFirstSlide() {
        CurrentSlide = 0;
        repaint();
    }
    public void ShowLastSlide() {
        CurrentSlide = NumSlides - 1;
        repaint();
    }
    public void LoadShow(String LoadFile) {
        RandomAccessFile      ListFile;
        // name of image to display
```

continues

Listing 18.10. continued

```
            String[] imgFile = new String[20];
            int i;           // Loop counter

            // Create an array of images and load the images

            i=0;
            try {
                ListFile = new RandomAccessFile(LoadFile,"r");
                while (ListFile.getFilePointer() != ListFile.length() ) {
                    imgFile[i] = ListFile.readLine() + ".gif";
                    i++;
                }
                ListFile.close();
            } catch (java.io.IOException e) {
                System.out.println("Could not read from file.");
                System.out.println(e);
            }
            NumSlides = i;
            for (i=0; i<NumSlides;i++) {
                im[i] = getToolkit().getImage(imgFile[i]);
            }
        CurrentSlide = 0;
        }
}

/**
 * SlideText is an extension of TextArea
 * It provides a means to display text descriptions to the user
 */
class SlideText extends TextArea {
    protected String str[] = new String[20];//Array of Strings to display
    protected int NumTexts;        // Number of strings in the array
    protected int CurrentText;     // Number of string currently displayed
    protected boolean showtext;    // True if text is not being displayed

    public SlideText(String ShowName) {
        super();
        LoadShow(ShowName);
        setEditable(false);
        showtext = true;
    }
    public void NoText(){
        showtext = false;
        setText();
    }
    public void ShowText(){
        showtext = true;
        setText();
    }
    // Override normal setText so text can not be reset accidentally
    public void setText(String str){
        setText();
    }
    public void setText(){
        if (showtext)
            super.setText(str[CurrentText]);
        else
```

```java
            super.setText("");

    }
    public void ShowNextText() {
        if (CurrentText < (NumTexts - 1)) {
            CurrentText = CurrentText + 1;
            setText();
        }
    }
    public void ShowPrevText() {
        if (CurrentText > 0) {
            CurrentText = CurrentText - 1;
            setText();
        }
    }
    public void ShowFirstText() {
        CurrentText = 0;
        setText();
    }
    public void ShowLastText() {
        CurrentText = NumTexts - 1;
        setText();
    }
    // Load the text array based on filename in the LoadFile
    public void LoadShow(String LoadFile) {
        RandomAccessFile    ListFile;
        String[] strFile = new String[20];   // name of image to display
        int i;                                // Loop counter

        // Create an array of strings and load the strings

        i=0;
        try {
            ListFile = new RandomAccessFile(LoadFile,"r");
            while (ListFile.getFilePointer() != ListFile.length() ) {
                strFile[i] = ListFile.readLine() + ".txt";
                i++;
            }
            ListFile.close();
        } catch (java.io.IOException e) {
            System.out.println("Could not read from file.");
            System.out.println(e);
        }
        NumTexts = i;
        for (i=0; i<NumTexts;i++) {
            str[i] = getText(strFile[i]);
        }
        CurrentText = 0;
    }
    // Read text for an item from a file
    protected String getText(String LoadFile){
        RandomAccessFile    ListFile;
        byte b[] = new byte[1024];
        int numbytes;

        try {
            ListFile = new RandomAccessFile(LoadFile,"r");
            numbytes = (int)ListFile.length();
```

continues

Listing 18.10. continued

```
                        ListFile.read(b,0,numbytes);
                        ListFile.close();
                } catch (java.io.IOException e) {
                    System.out.println("Could not read from file.");
                    System.out.println(e);
                }
                return (new String(b,0));
        }
}

/**
 * Control bar for moving through a slide show
 */
class ShowControls extends Panel {
    static SlidePanel ss;        // Panel controls are attached to

    // Constructor requires a SlidePanel to which the
    // controls are attached
    public ShowControls(SlidePanel theShow) {
        ss = theShow;
        setLayout(new FlowLayout(FlowLayout.CENTER));
        add(new Button("|<<"));
        add(new Button("<"));
        add(new Button(">"));
        add(new Button(">>|"));
    }
    // Determine which button was pressed and act accordingly
    // Actions will refer to the Slide panel to which the
    // control bar is attached
    public void handleButton(String bname) {
        if (bname.equals(">")) {
            ss.ShowNextSlide();
        } else if (bname.equals("<")) {
            ss.ShowPrevSlide();
        } else if (bname.equals("|<<")) {
            ss.ShowFirstSlide();
        } else if (bname.equals(">>|")) {
            ss.ShowLastSlide();
        }
    }
    public boolean action(Event evt, Object arg) {
        if (evt.target instanceof Button) {
            handleButton((String)arg);
            return true;
        } else return super.action(evt,arg);
    }
}

/**
 * Creates an about box for the Slideshow
 */
class AboutBox extends Dialog
{
    public AboutBox(Frame parent)
    {
        super(parent, "About SlideShow", true);
        setLayout(new GridLayout(3,1));
```

```java
        add(new Label("SlideShow",Label.CENTER));
        add(new Label("by Peter Norton and William Stanek",Label.CENTER));
        Panel pp = new Panel();
        pp.add(new Button("OK"));
        add("South",pp);
        resize(250,200);
    }
    // Event handler closes the window if the user
    // hits the OK button or the window close button
    public boolean handleEvent(Event evt) {
          if (evt.id == Event.WINDOW_DESTROY &&
              evt.target instanceof AboutBox) {
               dispose();
              return true;
        } else if("OK".equals(evt.arg)) {
              dispose();
              return true;
        }
          return false;
    }
}


/**
 * Basic Help window to explain the slide controls
 */
class HelpBox extends Dialog
{
    public HelpBox(Frame parent)
    {
        super(parent, "Help Topics", true);
        setLayout(new GridLayout(6,1));
        add(new Label("The controls work as follows:",Label.LEFT));
        add(new Label("    |<<    returns to the first slide",
            Label.LEFT));
        add(new Label("    <      returns to the previous slide",
            Label.LEFT));
        add(new Label("    >      advances to the next slide",
            Label.LEFT));
        add(new Label("    >>|    advances to the last slide",
            Label.LEFT));
        Panel pp = new Panel();
        pp.add(new Button("OK"));
        add(pp);
        resize(250,300);
    }
    // Event handler closes the window if the user
    // hits the OK button or the window close button
    public boolean handleEvent(Event evt) {
          if (evt.id == Event.WINDOW_DESTROY &&
              evt.target instanceof HelpBox) {
                 dispose();
              return true;
        } else if("OK".equals(evt.arg)) {
              dispose();
              return true;
        }
          return false;
    }
}
```

Testing and Debugging

Although you did not develop a test plan for the simple application created in Chapter 17, you should do so for this more complex application. The test plan is written using the components stated in the design. The overall question is, "Does the application perform as expected?"

The following questions are related to the main frame of the application:

- Does the frame containing the application work as expected?
- Does the application start as expected?
- Does the application start and display a slide with text?
- Does the application close when the user presses the Close button on the frame?
- Does the application resize when the user presses the resize buttons on the frame?

Next there are some basic questions about the appearance of the application:

- Does each slide appear?
- Does the text for each slide appear?
- Are the controls visible?
- Is the menu present?

The following questions relate to the menu. Although some menu items are similar, it is important to test each one individually. The purpose of testing is to verify how the application will appear to the user. Therefore, be sure to verify each of the following items:

- Does the Exit option on the menu shut down the application?
- Does the Load option on the menu work?
- Does the File dialog box open?
- When a show is selected in the File dialog box, is it displayed to the user?
- If the user cancels in the File dialog box, does the same slide show remain?
- Does the About box appear when the About menu item is selected?
- Does the Help box appear when the Help Topics menu item is selected?
- Does the Forward menu item move to the next slide in the show?
- Does the Backward menu item move to the previous item in the show?
- Does the Beginning menu item move to the first slide in the show?
- Does the End menu item move to the last slide in the show?
- Does the No Text menu cause the text to disappear when it is selected?
- Is the No Text menu item checked after it has been selected?
- Does selecting the No Text menu item a second time cause the text to reappear?

- After the No Text menu item is selected a second time, is the checkmark removed from the menu item?

- Does the No Slides menu cause the slide to disappear when it is selected?

- Is the No Slides menu item checked after it has been selected?

- Does selecting the No Slides menu item a second time cause the slide to reappear?

- After the No Slides menu item is selected a second time, is the checkmark removed from the menu item?

In addition to testing that the menu displays the Help and About windows, there are a few specific questions pertaining to the windows themselves:

- Is all the text visible when the Help window is displayed?

- Does the Help window close when the user presses the OK button?

- Does the Help window close when the user presses the Close button on its frame?

- Is all the text visible when the About window is displayed?

- Does the About window close when the user presses the OK button?

- Does the About window close when the user presses the Close button on its frame?

Specific tests are also needed for the controls. This may seem redundant because you have tested the methods during the menu test; however, it verifies that each control is connected to the correct method and is using the method correctly. Here are some of the tests you would perform for the SlideShow application:

- Does the control marked >>| move to the last slide in the show?

- Does the control marked |<< move to the first slide in the show?

- Does the control marked > move forward one slide?

- Does the control marked < move backward one slide?

This completes the test plan. There are tests for each piece of functionality provided by the application. There are certainly more questions that could be asked about the functioning of this application, but these tests are sufficient to verify the decisions made in the application design and to alert programmers to any unexpected occurrences.

Summary

This chapter demonstrates how to develop a complex, useful application. It pulls together concepts that are introduced in preceding chapters and applies them to the development of the application. The chapter covers several techniques for developing larger applications. The ideas presented here will assist you as you develop your own Java applications.

At this point, you should have an understanding of the Java language that will enable you to follow the discussions of advanced applications in Part VII. You also should fully understand the application presented in this chapter so that you can follow the discussion in Chapter 19.

19

Application Upgrades

Delivered code is not necessarily finished. This chapter covers application upgrades and maintenance, an important topic because almost every application continues to evolve after its initial delivery. The chapter begins with a discussion of the software life cycle. Then several enhancements are proposed for the SlideShow application developed in Chapter 18, "Using Java Applications in the Real World." The remainder of this chapter walks you through the tasks involved in working on these upgrades.

The Software Development Cycle

Software proceeds through several phases from its first inkling as an idea in someone's mind to a robust application fully installed on a user's system. At each stage the concept of the software is clarified, modified, and expanded. This section begins with a brief review of the software process.

The Development Process

There are many ways in which the software development process can be broken into stages. For our purposes, consider that software must be analyzed, designed, implemented, tested, and delivered. When these steps are completed, additional changes to the application are considered as upgrades or maintenance.

During *analysis*, user needs are defined and clarified. For Java applications, this means creating a concrete specification and then expanding it with the details that will be needed to create a complete design.

During the *design* phase, a means of accomplishing the user needs with appropriate hardware and software is defined. In Java applications, the conceptualization and design process includes the definition of the major classes that will be implemented and any inheritance between those classes.

Implementation refers to the process of actualizing a design by producing code. In Java, this means creating the classes and instances in a manner that can be run by the Java interpreter.

Testing means verifying that the software as implemented meets the design criteria and user specifications. Java applications must have a concrete test plan so the code can be reconciled with the requirements.

Delivery means supplying the user with the software. Java requires that the runtime environment be supplied along with the classes necessary for the implementation.

The Maintenance Process

Software development does not freeze at the moment of delivery. Usually, software must grow and change over time. These activities are collectively referred to as *software maintenance*. Application upgrades are part of the normal maintenance phase of the software life cycle. A modification effort is actually a mini project and must proceed through all the phases of the development process.

> **Peter's Principle:** Some maintenance projects are more "mini" than others. Small maintenance/upgrade projects may proceed quickly and informally through all the steps in the development process. For example, modifying a program that calculates loan amortization to run for a 15-year loan instead of a 30-year loan is probably a minor change. However, modifying the same program to allow for a 30-year adjustable-rate loan with an adjustment cap of 2 percent per year, a lifetime cap of 10 percent, and a user-specified yearly index figure is most likely a major change. The second instance requires input and calculations that do not currently exist in the program. The first change merely requires changing some of the variables in the program.

Large maintenance/upgrade projects require careful management and can include plans, designs, and code as large as the initial development effort. At times, the upgrade project may be larger than the original implementation project, yet the upgrade is still called maintenance because it starts with existing code.

There are many reasons for software modification and continued development after the first release. All products evolve, and software is no exception. Applications may need additional features not discovered during the original analysis and design. The software may need fixes to correct problems not discovered during initial development and testing, or the user's needs or environment may change over time.

Applications also can be delivered in increments. In fact, when projects are delivered in increments, they are easier to manage and generally more successful than those for which programmers attempt to deliver the entire project at one milestone. Delivered applications may need to be altered for reasons besides planned incremental releases, and the business reasons governing these changes may affect the modification process.

Java is a new language, so it is still evolving. As new releases come out, you may have to recompile or even reimplement code. Designs may be reworked to take advantage of new features in later releases. Functionality that is currently not available to users may become available. Features implemented in other ways may be incorporated into Java applications—for example, database access using the Java Database Connectivity API.

As new utilities are developed both in-house and externally, they can be incorporated into existing programs. However, portions of applications may have to be reworked to accommodate or match the new utilities.

Suggestions to Facilitate Modifications

Ease of maintenance is a part of every step in development. If the analysis is complete, users will find the most important features in the first release of the software. If the design is well thought out, modifications will be easier to include. If the code is easy to read and follow, it will be easier to maintain. Some suggestions to ease the modification process follow:

- Try to group changes and deliver another release rather than make incremental changes. Although a new release generally will involve a longer time period than will incremental changes, this gives you time to gain a better understanding of the proposed changes and assess their impact on the application. Having an entire release to work on will help to ensure that the analysis and design phases are done thoroughly. It is easier to assess the impact of minor changes if the entire application is being reviewed for a new release.

- Document all requested changes and the impact of any proposed change. The documentation process will force you to be more thorough about your research. The documentation will also help to point out conflicts among requests by different users. The documentation should supply an idea of the number of hours needed to complete the changes. It also should supply the impact of the request on the existing application and users.

- Have all users involved and in agreement about any modifications before making changes. If this doesn't happen, you may find yourself in the "change it and change it back" syndrome. It is less time-consuming to resolve conflicting opinions while the ideas for changing the application are still on paper.

- Have users assign a priority to each modification. You can reduce stress and conflict if you work on the most critical changes first and save the minor items for later. However, what is critical and what is minor to you may not be the same as what is critical or minor for your user. Sometimes screen design and layout are more critical to users than adding features they are not ready to use or error checking for errors they seldom encounter.

- Some changes may not be possible given current technology, time, and budget constraints. Talk the users through the reasons certain changes are not being implemented. Show them the cost of attempting to implement the change. Provide any information about when the tools might be available to enable you to make the change. For example, at this writing Java does not provide mechanisms for communicating directly with a database server. Although custom scripts could be written to enable a Java application to interact indirectly with a database server, this solution is very time-consuming. However, several people are at work creating this functionality. In a few months, it should be possible to use Java to access a database. So it would probably make sense to delay for a few months any change involving database connectivity.

- The value of experience with code modification cannot be overemphasized. It takes time to gain practice in working with conflicting needs and integrating new code with existing code. The modification process is easier if you work with experienced project managers.

The remainder of this chapter works through modifications to the SlideShow application developed in Chapter 18. Several requests for new features in the application are grouped into one new release.

Conceptualizing Application Upgrades

Before you begin any project, carefully analyze the development requirements to uncover hidden assumptions and resolve conflicts. This process is equally important when enhancing existing applications.

Looking Ahead: In this section, several new requests for the SlideShow application are presented and expanded. At the end of this section you should have a good idea of the new tasks that will be added to the application. This will enable you to create a comprehensive design for the modifications.

The following is a prioritized list of change requests for the SlideShow application:

- Adding a mechanism to build and save slide shows
- Adding check boxes to controls to turn on and off pictures or text
- Making it possible to read a show consisting of multiple files
- Adding a mechanism to enable continuous play on a timer
- Increasing the possible number of slides that can be stored
- Adding audio
- Adding radio buttons or list boxes to turn audio on and off

The items that are most important to the users are listed at the top of the list. Each item is discussed in more detail in the sections that follow.

The Build-and-Save Capability

Currently it is tricky to edit the slide show because of the null character that must be used to separate the entries and because the designers of the show are not able to see the show while they are working on it. It would be easier to create a slide show if you could look at the slides and pick and choose which slide to include. It also would be helpful to be able to rearrange the order of slides with a simple cut-and-paste menu similar to that found in word processors.

Changing the State of the Check Boxes

The options available on the first part of the display menu mirror the options on the control panel at the bottom of the display screen. However, the No Slides and No Text check box menu items are not reproduced on the control panel. It would enhance the design to implement these on the controls. The new items could be check boxes so that the current setting would be displayed to the user as part of the control. This seems like a straightforward addition to the controls because the same methods that are accessed from the menu should be usable by the controls.

Reading Multiple Files

In the original SlideShow application, a show consists of one list of names contained in a single text file. However, there may be times when users will want to load several shows, back to back. Currently, this can be done only by creating a new list of names containing all the slides in the order desired. It would be convenient to be able to list several files on the command line and have the pictures from each loaded.

Tip: If you wanted to load multiple files in the program, this modification would be more complex. In that case, changes would have to be made to the windows controlling the file loading. The current modification, however, does not require any changes to the display. It deals strictly with changes to the handling of the command-line arguments.

Currently, only the first command-line argument is passed to the methods that load the files. The remaining arguments are ignored. To complete this modification, the remaining arguments are passed to the load methods. Then as many slides as will fit in the array are added.

Continuous Play

The users want the entire slide show to redisplay at regular intervals. The display of the slides should run one at a time after the user presses one button. The user must have a button to stop continuous play and remain on the same slide. The play mechanism will start from the current slide and proceed forward. That way if the user stops the play, he or she can restart it from the same location.

Increasing the Number of Possible Slides

Okay, so 20 slides may not be enough for your whole trip to Europe. The application could be rewritten to use a linked list. Then you could increase the number of slides until they meet the memory limits on the computer. However, the easy approach for this one is to increase the size of the array. The array will be increased to hold up to 100 slides.

Final Task List

Now that you have a good understanding of each of the modifications, you can put together a list of the new tasks that the application must handle. Assuming the modifications will be grouped together and released as an upgrade to the application, you can create one task list for all the desired changes, such as the following:

- Cutting the current slide
- Copying the current slide
- Pasting a slide that has been cut or copied
- Inserting a new slide from a `.gif` file
- Saving a show to a new filename
- Adding check boxes to the controls
- Reading multiple files at startup
- Starting continuous play
- Ending continuous play
- Displaying up to 100 slides in a show
- Playing audio
- Disabling audio
- Enabling audio

In the next section, the objects and methods needed to accomplish these tasks are designed.

Designing Application Upgrades

At the end of the design you will have a list of new objects to be implemented. Because you are modifying an existing application, your design also should include a list of changes to existing objects. You must clearly define each of these changes.

Build-and-Save

The build-and-save enhancement is composed of several small changes to the existing application. The first three tasks involve editing the slide show. The design for these tasks is presented subsequently as one topic. The next topic is the design of the insert task. After the show can be edited, a mechanism must be developed to save the files involved in the modified slide show.

Editing the Slide Show

The users have been helpful in creating a specification that starts us down the path to design. You know to add a new menu, Edit, that will allow the users to cut, copy, and paste slides. This menu will be used to insert new slides into the slide show.

You must add Cut, Copy, and Paste methods to both SlideCanvas and SlideText. SlideCanvas will need an Image object to hold the image most recently cut or copied from its internal array, and SlideText will need a String object for the same reason.

The Cut method will copy a slide to the new object and remove it from the array. The Copy method will copy the slide to the new object but will leave it in the array. The Paste method will create a new slide in the array and paste the contents of the new object into the new position. However, the Paste method will not copy over an existing slide.

The user can delete all the slides in a show, in which case the application has nothing to display. To solve this problem, the paint() method for SlideCanvas is modified to display a blank rectangle when no slides are present. The setText() method for SlideText will display an empty string in this case.

Inserting New Slides

In addition to rearranging existing slides, the modified application will enable users to add a new slide to the show. The Insert menu item will be added in the Edit menu. This item will provide a dialog box to the user where he or she can enter the filename of the slide to add.

A File dialog box will be used to get the filename to add. The file must be in the same directory as the executing program. The filename will be passed to an Insert method in the SlidePanel class in the same manner that the load and save filenames are passed. The method in SlidePanel will remove the file extension and pass the filename to an Insert method for each of its two components.

The SlideCanvas object's Insert method will read a file using the filename and the .gif extension. It creates a new Image object based on the contents of the file and stores it in the current location in the array. The other items in the array are shifted forward to accommodate the new image.

The SlideText Insert method will read a file using the filename and the .txt extension. It will create a new String object and shift the contents of its array forward to accommodate the new object for text.

Saving the Modified Show

To save the modified show, you need the filenames for the .gif and .txt files. Currently, they are loaded when the show is loaded, but they are not stored. Part of this modification will be to modify the code so that updates are stored. This is done by making the arrays that hold the filename's instance arrays in the class rather than local to the Load method.

The filenames must be kept in the same order as the slides so that saved shows can be loaded in the proper order. Because slides can be rearranged within the array using the Edit menu items, you must provide a mechanism to rearrange the filenames. Another string is provided to act as a clipboard for the filenames so that they can be manipulated as the slides are manipulated.

The list of filenames must be passed to a method in `SlidePanel`, so you will create an accessor method called `getSlideFiles()` that returns the array of filenames. Another accessor method that returns the number of files currently in the show also will be provided, and the `saveShow` method in `SlidePanel` will be triggered from the menu.

The menu option will open a File dialog box to retrieve the filename where a list of slides in the show will be stored. The filename entered by the user then will be passed to the method in `SlidePanel`.

By default, the slide show names should be saved to a text file. This default can be established by setting the file name to `*.txt` before displaying the dialog box.

> **Tip:** When working with opening and closing files, it is often helpful to review the `FileDialogBox` methods available in the `java.awt` package to remind yourself of details that may be helpful to your users. These methods are reviewed in Chapter 12, "The Java I/O and Utility Class Libraries."

As an added feature, the filename setting for text files can be applied to the Load dialog box. Verify with the users that a filename restriction such as this will be helpful. The restriction makes it much easier to locate the proper file in the dialog box because only files with the `.txt` extension are displayed.

Check Boxes

The next enhancement involves a single task adding check boxes at the end of the existing controls. The first check box will have the text "Slides"; the second will have the text "Text." Both will be set by default.

When the Slide check box is cleared, the method `NoSlides()` method in the `displayPanel` is called. Similarly, when the Slide check box is checked, the `setSlides()` method in the `displayPanel` object is called. A corresponding set of method calls is used for the Text check box.

The state of the display can be changed on either the control panel or the menu bar. The menu must inform the controls if it changes the setting of this option, and vice versa. This implies that the menu and the controls each must be informed of the existence of the other.

The event handler for the menu is modified to notify the controls when the display state is changed through the menu. To accomplish this, the event handler must have a means to reference the controls object; therefore, an instance variable is added to store a reference to the controls.

Similarly, the controls are modified to indicate to the menu that a change of state has occurred. To notify the controls, the event is posted to the event handler for the menu. To post the event, the controls must know about the Menu object. Therefore, the constructor for the SlideControls class is modified to accept a reference to the MenuBar object and store the value in an instance variable.

Reading Multiple Files

Currently, when the application starts, the main() method passes only the first argument from the command line to the SlideShow constructor. This will be altered so that all the command-line arguments are passed. The constructor in SlideShow then passes the same array to the constructor for SlidePanel.

The constructor for SlidePanel will be modified to loop through an array of filenames and load each one. The first should go in the front of the array and be loaded normally. The loads of the remaining files need a mechanism to indicate to LoadShow that they should be loaded into the array after any existing slides and not on top of them. To provide this mechanism, a boolean argument is added to the LoadShow method. When this argument is false, the slides are loaded normally. When the argument is true, the slides are appended to the current show.

The LoadShow methods in both SlideText and SlideCanvas will be rewritten to accommodate multiple input files. There are two changes in the LoadShow() methods: The array counter, which stores the number of files in the array, must account for multiple load files; and the boolean parameter must be checked to determine whether the new slides should be appended to the slides already loaded or should start loading at the first position.

Because it is possible that multiple files will be loaded, the total number of slides in the array is not necessarily the number of slides loaded during a particular call to LoadShow. Therefore, the internal counter should not be initialized to zero each time this method is called but rather when an instance of the object is created. For this reason, the initialization is moved to the class level, and the LoadShow method sets its internal counter from the instance variable. The counter should be reinitialized when the user selects Load from the File menu.

Currently, there is no difference between the call to LoadShow from the main() method and the call from the menu. All the existing calls to this method could be modified to pass the second argument, or the method could be overloaded. In this case, if the second argument is not present, it is assumed to be false. Using the second option, there is no need to make changes to the existing code; you can be secure that the new functionality will not affect the existing objects. You now have a well-thought-out design for loading multiple files into one slide show.

Continuous Play

To implement the continuous-play mechanism, you will set up a timer that calls the ShowNextSlide() method when it expires. The timer will be part of the SlidePanel class, so it can be called from the menu, the controls, or both. It will run in its own thread so the user can make changes on the controls, such as canceling continuous play, while it is running.

An instance variable is added to the `SlidePanel` class to determine if the continuous play is currently set. A method will be provided to set this variable and start the timer, and another will clear this variable. The timer will check the variable each time it changes a slide. It will not change the slide and will stop looping if the instance variable indicates that continuous play has been canceled.

It also would be convenient for the timer to recognize when it is at the end of the show and stop looping. Therefore, a method is added in the `SlideCanvas` and `SlideText` classes that returns `true` if the current slide is the last slide and `false` otherwise. The timer will call one of these methods to determine if it is at the last slide.

Increasing the Number of Possible Slides

Currently, the maximum number of slides that can be stored in the show is 20, based on an array index of 10. This will be increased to allow for a maximum of 100 slides.

Unfortunately, the array index is used in several places throughout the `SlideCanvas` and `SlideText` objects. A global replacement of 20 with a higher number will solve the problem, unless there is a place where the code checks for a number less than or equal to 19 instead of less than 20. In the `SlideShow` application created in Chapter 18, all references are to the number 20. Still, we can prevent possible future problems by assigning a name to the array index.

The array index will be replaced with a static final variable named `ArrayMax`. The variable is static so that all instances of the class use the same value, and final so that its value cannot be changed after initialization. The value is initialized to 100, thus increasing the number of possible slides.

Adding Audio

It would enhance the appeal and usability of the application to have audio clips of the text messages. Then the user could study the picture while listening to the description instead of having to read the description and then examine the picture. Unfortunately, at this writing, the `play()` and `getAudio()` methods in Java are part of the `Applet` class. It can only be used to play a script if it is given a `baseURL`. Because of time constraints for the project, this request will remain unimplemented until a workaround for this problem is discovered.

Note: If audio support were essential to the application, you would have to create a class of objects for handling audio in applications. As with any other programming language, you would have to create the code for this object from scratch or modify the existing `play()` or `getAudio()` methods to work outside of applets.

Summing Up the Object Changes

Now that you have an understanding of the upgrade, you can modify the original design documentation for the upgrade. The modified menu categories are shown in Table 19.1.

Table 19.1. Menu features.

Category	Item	Description
File	Load	Loads slides into the application
	Save	Saves filenames of the current slides
	Exit	Exits `SlideShow`
Edit	Cut	Removes current slide and adds to clipboard
	Copy	Adds current slide to clipboard
	Paste	Copies from clipboard, creating a new slide
	Insert	Adds a new slide from a file
Display	Forward	Moves forward to the next slide
	Back	Moves backward to the previous slide
	Beginning	Moves to the first slide in the show
	End	Moves to the last slide in the show
	No Text	When checked, the text is hidden
	No Slides	When checked, the pictures are hidden
Help	Help Topics	Provides a description of the controls
	About	Provides authoring information

The design process includes taking the changes that have been described for each modification and reorganizing them according to the objects that are affected. Two lists are necessary, one for new objects to implement and one for existing objects to modify.

On the basis of the design discussion, you must implement the following objects:

- An `Image` object to store cut slide image
- A `String` object to store cut slide text
- An Edit menu item
- A Cut menu item
- A Copy menu item
- A Paste menu item
- An Insert menu item

- A dialog box for Slide Insert
- An array of image filenames
- An array of text filenames
- A string to store the cut image filename
- A string to store the cut text filename
- A Slide check box
- A Text check box

The many modifications to the existing classes are listed in Table 19.2.

Table 19.2. Changes to existing classes.

Class Name	List of Changes
SlideCanvas	Add Cut method
	Add Copy method
	Add Paste method
	Add Insert method
	Add method to return the current slide names
	Add method to return the current number of slides
	Modify LoadShow to allow multiple input files
	Increase the number of possible slides to 100
SlideText	Add Cut method
	Add Copy method
	Add Paste method
	Add Insert method
	Modify LoadShow to allow multiple input files
	Add a method to return true at the end of the show
	Increase the number of possible slides to 100
SlidePanel	Add Cut method
	Add Copy method
	Add Paste method
	Add Insert method
	Add a Save method
	Modify constructor to allow loading of multiple files

continues

Table 19.2. continued

Class Name	List of Changes
	Add a variable to determine if continuous play is on
	Add a method to start continuous play
	Add a method to stop continuous play
	Add a `Run` method
SlideControls	Add Slide check box
	Add Text check box
	Modify constructor to accept and store a `MenuBar` object
	Modify event handler to notify `MenuBar` if state changes via controls
SlideShow	Modify menu to include all items in Table 19.1
	Modify event handler to handle new items
	Add an instance variable referring to the current controls
	Modify event handler to notify controls when state is changed via the menu
	Modify the `main()` method to pass all input arguments to the constructor
	Modify the constructor to pass the input arguments to `SlidePanel`

Implementing Application Upgrades

This section demonstrates how to implement the changes described in the design section. Here, each of the new objects and the modifications for existing objects are implemented.

Changes to `SlideCanvas`

Given the list of changes created for the `SlideCanvas` class as part of the design, you could just go through and make each of the changes. However, it is important to study how some of the changes affect one another. For example, adding the array to maintain filenames means that this array must be dealt with when the position of images in the image array is changed.

Changes to Declarations

Several new components are added to the `SlideCanvas` class. They are protected containers used to store information used by `SlideCanvas`. The declaration for these objects appears as follows:

```
// Image object to store cut slide image
protected Image SlideClip;
// Array of image filenames
protected String[] imgFile = new String[20];
// String to store cut image filename
protected String FileClip=new String();
```

The declarations for the NumSlides and CurrentSlide variables are also changed so that they are initialized when they are declared. The new declarations are

```
protected int NumSlides=0;      // Number of images in the array
protected int CurrentSlide=0;   // Number of image currently displayed
```

Adding the cutSlide Method

You implement the cutSlide method by taking a reference to the current slide; storing it to the internal clipboard, SlideClip; and then removing the slide from the array. The complete cutSlide() method is shown in Listing 19.1.

Listing 19.1. The cutSlide() method.

```
public void cutSlide(){
        int i;
        //Check that there is an element to cut
        if (NumSlides < 0)
             return;
        //Copy element and its filename to buffer
        SlideClip = im[CurrentSlide];
        FileClip = imgFile[CurrentSlide];
        //Decrease the number of elements in the array
        NumSlides = NumSlides - 1;
        //Shift the array to close the gap
        for (i=CurrentSlide;i<NumSlides;i++) {
             im[i] = im[i+1];
             imgFile[i] = imgFile[i+1];
        }
        if (CurrentSlide == NumSlides)
             CurrentSlide = NumSlides - 1;
        repaint();
    }
```

Before cutting a slide, the cutSlide() method ensures the slide is present in the array. If no slides are present, it returns to its caller. If a slide is present, it copies to the SlideClip object, decreases the number of slides present, and shifts the array contents.

In most cases, when the user cuts a slide, the following slide becomes the current slide. However, if the last slide is clipped—meaning there is no following slide—the current slide is set to the previous slide. This check is made at the end of the cutSlide method by comparing the CurrentSlide variable and the NumSlides variable.

Because you have modified the filename array so it is available to the entire class, you can cut the filename associated with the current slide and save it to `FileClip`. In this way, the two arrays are kept parallel to one another through the cutting and pasting.

Adding the `copySlide` Method

You implement the `copySlide` method by copying the current slide into the internal clipboard. Recall that when you copy an object, you do not remove it from the array. The `copySlide()` method is shown in Listing 19.2.

Listing 19.2. The `copySlide()` method.

```
public void copySlide() {
        //Check that there is an element to copy
        if (NumSlides < 0)
            return;
        SlideClip = im[CurrentSlide];
    }
```

Adding the `pasteSlide` Method

The `pasteSlide` method creates a new slide in the array and then copies the slide from the internal clipboard to the array. The `pasteSlide()` method is shown in Listing 19.3.

Listing 19.3. The `pasteSlide()` method.

```
public void pasteSlide() {
        int i;
        //Check that there is an element to paste
        if (SlideClip == null)
            return;
        //Check that there is room to paste an element
        if (NumSlides == 20)
            return;
        //Make a space in the array and the file array
        for(i=NumSlides;i>=CurrentSlide;i--) {
            im[i+1]=im[i];
            imgFile[i+1]=imgFile[i];
        }
        // Increase the number of slides in the show
        NumSlides = NumSlides + 1;
        // Store the items in the clipboard to the new slot
        im[CurrentSlide] = SlideClip;
        imgFile[CurrentSlide]=FileClip;
        repaint();
    }
```

Adding the `insertSlide` Method

The `insertSlide` method loads a new image using its filename and stores the image in the internal array. If the internal array is full, the method simply returns. If the array is not full, each image is moved forward and the new image is inserted behind the current image. Listing 19.4 shows the code for this method.

Listing 19.4. The `insertSlide()` method.

```
public void InsertSlide(String FileName) {
        int i;
        //Check that there is room to paste an element
        if (NumSlides == 20)
            return;
        //Make a space in the array and the file array
        for(i=NumSlides;i>=CurrentSlide;i--) {
            im[i+1]=im[i];
            imgFile[i+1]=imgFile[i];
        }
        // Increase the number of slides in the show
        NumSlides = NumSlides + 1;
        // Store the items from the file to the new slot
        imgFile[CurrentSlide]=FileName;
        im[CurrentSlide] = getToolkit().getImage(imgFile[CurrentSlide]+".gif");;
        repaint();
    }
```

Adding Accessor Methods

The `SlideCanvas` class needs two methods to allow other classes to read, but not write, its protected variables. These methods allow the `SlidePanel` class to save the filenames in the current show. The first method returns the number of slides currently in the show, and the second returns the array containing the names of the slides:

```
public int getNumSlides() {
        return NumSlides;
    }
public String[] getSlideFiles() {
        return imgFile;
    }
```

Modifying `LoadShow` to Allow Multiple Input Files

The existing `LoadShow()` method is modified to take a boolean as a second parameter. If the parameter is passed as `true`, the method appends the slides it loads to the slides already in the array. If the parameter is set to `false`, the method overwrites the existing slides with the new slides.

To avoid modifying the existing calls to LoadShow(), you will overload the method by adding another LoadShow() method that just takes the filename as a parameter. This method simply calls the newly defined LoadShow(filename, boolean) method with the second parameter set to false. This causes any existing show to be overwritten when a new show is loaded, exactly as these calls worked before you made any changes.

The new LoadShow methods for the SlideCanvas class appear in Listing 19.5. If you compare this with the original methods, you will notice that the basic operation is the same; the only difference is in the statements that control how the local variable is initialized.

Listing 19.5. The **LoadShow()** methods.

```
public void LoadShow(String LoadFile){
    LoadShow(LoadFile,false);
}
// Load the text array based on filename in the LoadFile
public void LoadShow(String LoadFile,boolean addfile) {
    RandomAccessFile      ListFile;
    int i;              // Loop counter

    // Create an array of images and load the images
    if (addfile)
        i=NumTexts;
    else
        i=0;
    try {
        ListFile = new RandomAccessFile(LoadFile,"r");
        while (ListFile.getFilePointer() != ListFile.length() ) {
            strFile[i] = ListFile.readLine();
            i++;
        }
        ListFile.close();
    } catch (java.io.IOException e) {
        System.out.println("Could not read from file.");
        System.out.println(e);
    }
    NumTexts = i;
    for (i=0; i<NumTexts;i++) {
        str[i] = getText(strFile[i]+".txt");
    }
}
```

Increasing the Number of Possible Slides to 100

The simplest way to increase the number of slides allowed is to replace all instances of 20 with 100. However, you must then check the class carefully to ensure that there are no cases in which checks are made for the previous counter value, such as i 19 instead of i<20.

Cases like this present a problem that can be solved in other languages using constants, but you can't use constants for this in Java. In Java you can create a variable that is both static and final. Therefore, I will create a variable that can hold the value for the number of slides.

The new variable `ArrayMax` is declared in the `SlideCanvas` class. The declaration looks like this:

```
static final int ArrayMax = 100;                    // Size of array
```

All references to the value `20` as an array maximum are then replaced with the name `ArrayMax`.

The Complete `SlideCanvas` Class

You have made numerous changes to the `SlideCanvas` class. A complete listing, including all the changes and all the original code, is shown in Listing 19.6.

Note: As you start to work with the classes of the new `SlideShow` application, keep in mind that the new classes represent changes to the existing program. You will find the updated program in its entirety on the CD-ROM. Still, the best way to learn what is happening is to make the changes to each class individually. Before you start, you should copy the existing `SlideShow` application to a new directory on your hard drive. Next, replace the classes that have changed in their entirety with the new code for the class. The `import` statements in the original program should be included in the new application. These `import` statements should read as follows:

```
import java.awt.*;
import java.applet.*;
import java.io.RandomAccessFile;
```

Listing 19.6. The complete `SlideCanvas` class.

```
/**
 * SlideCanvas is an extension of Canvas
 * It provides a means to display slides to the user
 */

class SlideCanvas extends Canvas {
    // Size of array
    static final int ArrayMax = 100;
    // Array of Images to display
    protected Image im[] = new Image[ArrayMax];
    // name of image to display
    protected String[] imgFile = new String[ArrayMax];
    // Number of images in the array
    protected int NumSlides=0;
    // Number of image currently displayed
    protected int CurrentSlide=0;
```

continues

Listing 19.6. continued

```
// False to turn off display
protected boolean showslide;
// Image for cutting & pasting
protected Image SlideClip;
// String for cutting & pasting filename
protected String FileClip=new String();

public String[] getSlideFiles() {
    return imgFile;
}
public int getNumSlides() {
    return NumSlides;
}
public boolean endOfShow() {
    if (CurrentSlide == (NumSlides-1))
        return true;
    else
        return false;
}
public void cutSlide(){
    int i;
    //Check that there is an element to cut
    if (NumSlides < 0)
        return;
    //Copy element and its filename to buffer
    SlideClip = im[CurrentSlide];
    FileClip = imgFile[CurrentSlide];
    //Decrease the number of elements in the array
    NumSlides = NumSlides - 1;
    //Shift the array to close the gap
    for (i=CurrentSlide;i<NumSlides;i++) {
        im[i] = im[i+1];
        imgFile[i] = imgFile[i+1];
    }
    if (CurrentSlide == NumSlides)
        CurrentSlide = NumSlides - 1;
    repaint();
}
public void copySlide() {
    //Check that there is an element to copy
    if (NumSlides < 0)
        return;
    SlideClip = im[CurrentSlide];
}
public void pasteSlide() {
    int i;
    //Check that there is an element to paste
    if (SlideClip == null)
        return;
    //Check that there is room to paste an element
    if (NumSlides == ArrayMax)
        return;
    //Make a space in the array and the file array
    for(i=NumSlides;i>=CurrentSlide;i--) {
        im[i+1]=im[i];
        imgFile[i+1]=imgFile[i];
    }
```

```
                // Increase the number of slides in the show
                NumSlides = NumSlides + 1;
                // Store the items in the clipboard to the new slot
                im[CurrentSlide] = SlideClip;
                imgFile[CurrentSlide]=FileClip;
                repaint();
        }
    public void InsertSlide(String FileName) {
            int i;
            //Check that there is room to paste an element
            if (NumSlides == ArrayMax)
                return;
            //Make a space in the array and the file array
            for(i=NumSlides;i>=CurrentSlide;i--) {
                im[i+1]=im[i];
                imgFile[i+1]=imgFile[i];
            }
            // Increase the number of slides in the show
            NumSlides = NumSlides + 1;
            // Store the items from the file to the new slot
            imgFile[CurrentSlide]=FileName;
            im[CurrentSlide] = getToolkit().getImage
➥(imgFile[CurrentSlide]+".gif");;
repaint();
        }
    public SlideCanvas(String ShowName) {
            super();
            LoadShow(ShowName);
            showslide = true;
        }
    public void NoSlides(){
            showslide = false;
            repaint();
        }
    public void ShowSlides(){
            showslide = true;
            repaint();
        }
    public void paint(Graphics g) {
            Rectangle r = bounds();
            if ((showslide)&&(NumSlides>0))
                g.drawImage(im[CurrentSlide],50,50,r.width-100,r.height-100,this);
            else {
                g.setColor(Color.lightGray);
                g.fillRect(0,0,r.width,r.height);
            }
        }
    public void ShowNextSlide() {
            if (CurrentSlide < (NumSlides - 1)) {
                CurrentSlide = CurrentSlide + 1;
                repaint();
            }
        }
    public void ShowPrevSlide() {
            if (CurrentSlide > 0) {
                CurrentSlide = CurrentSlide - 1;
                repaint();
            }
```

continues

Listing 19.6. continued

```
      }
      public void ShowFirstSlide() {
          CurrentSlide = 0;
          repaint();
      }
      public void ShowLastSlide() {
          CurrentSlide = NumSlides - 1;
          repaint();
      }
      public void LoadShow(String LoadFile){
          LoadShow(LoadFile,false);
      }
      public void LoadShow(String LoadFile, boolean addfile) {
          RandomAccessFile     ListFile;
          int i;             // Loop counter

          // Create an array of images and load the images
          if (addfile)
              i=NumSlides;
          else
              i=0;
          try {
              ListFile = new RandomAccessFile(LoadFile,"r");
              while (ListFile.getFilePointer() != ListFile.length() ) {
                  imgFile[i] = ListFile.readLine();
                  i++;
              }
              ListFile.close();
          } catch (java.io.IOException e) {
              System.out.println("Could not read from file.");
              System.out.println(e);
          }
          NumSlides = i;
          for (i=0; i<NumSlides;i++) {
              im[i] = getToolkit().getImage(imgFile[i]+".gif");
          }
      }
  }
}
```

Changes to `SlideText`

The changes for `SlideText` are similar to the changes for `SlideCanvas`. Again, you can go through the list of changes to this object that are the result of the changes discussed in the "Designing Application Upgrades" section.

Changes to Declarations

So that the `SlideText` class is not dependent on the `SlideCanvas` class for any of its functionality, you need to program it to implement its own array of filenames. It also must declare a string to serve as a clipboard for the cut or copied text. These declarations appear as follows:

```
// name of file containing image to display
protected String[] strFile = new String[20];
// String for cutting & pasting
protected String StringClip=new String();
// String for cutting & pasting filename
protected String FileClip=new String();
```

The initialization of the NumText and CurrentText variables is also moved to the declaration and appears as follows:

```
protected int NumTexts=0;     // Number of strings in the array
protected int CurrentText=0;  // Number of string currently displayed
```

Now that you have added all the new objects you will need, you can add the new methods.

Adding the cutString Method

The cutString() method is added to remove the current text string from the array and store it in the newly declared StringClip object. The method must remove the corresponding filename for the strFile array and store it in FileClip. The code to perform these functions is similar to cutImage and is shown in Listing 19.7.

Listing 19.7. The cutString() method.

```
public void cutString(){
        int i;
        //Check that there is an element to cut
        if (NumTexts < 0)
            return;
        //Copy element and its filename to buffer
        StringClip = str[CurrentText];
        FileClip = strFile[CurrentText];
        //Decrease the number of elements in the array
        NumTexts = NumTexts - 1;
        //Shift the array to close the gap
        for (i=CurrentText;i<NumTexts;i++){
            str[i] = str[i+1];
            strFile[i] = strFile[i+1];
        }
        if (CurrentText == NumTexts)
            CurrentText = NumTexts - 1;
        setText();
    }
```

Adding the copyString Method

Before copying a text slide, the Copy method ensures there is a slide available for copying. It then copies the text to the StringClip variable and the filename to the FileClip variable. It does not affect the contents of the arrays. Listing 19.8 is the complete code for this method.

Listing 19.8. The `copyString()` method.

```
public void copyString() {
        //Check that there is an element to copy
        if (NumTexts < 0)
            return;
        StringClip = str[CurrentText];
    }
```

Adding the `pasteString` Method

Listing 19.9 shows the `pasteString()` method that is created to copy the text from the `SlideText` class's internal clipboard to a new location in the array. Before pasting the text slide, the `pasteString()` method ensures that a string exists to copy and that there is room to insert another string in the array. If both these conditions are true, the method shifts the array forward and creates the new string. The filename where the string is stored is pasted into the filename array so that the show can be saved accurately.

Listing 19.9. The `pasteString()` method.

```
public void pasteString() {
        int i;
        //Check that there is an element to paste
        if (StringClip == null)
            return;
        //Check that there is room to paste an element
        if (NumTexts == 20)
            return;
        //Make a space in the array and the file array
        for(i=NumTexts;i>=CurrentText;i--){
            str[i+1]=str[i];
            strFile[i+1]=strFile[i];
        }
        // Increase the number of slides in the show
        NumTexts = NumTexts + 1;
        // Store the items in the clipboard to the new slot
        str[CurrentText]=StringClip;
        strFile[CurrentText]=FileClip;
        setText();
    }
```

Adding the `insertSlide` Method

The purpose of the `insertSlide()` method is to read the text for a new slide from a file on the user's file system. To read a file and return its contents as a text string, the method makes use of the same `getText()` method used by `LoadShow`. Although the filename is passed by the caller, the `insertSlide()` method appends the file extension `.txt` so that only files with the `.txt` extension are read. The new method is shown in Listing 19.10.

Listing 19.10. The `insertSlide()` method.

```java
public void InsertSlide(String Filename) {
        int i;
        //Check that there is room to paste an element
        if (NumTexts == 20)
            return;
        //Make a space in the array and the file array
        for(i=NumTexts;i>=CurrentText;i--){
            str[i+1]=str[i];
            strFile[i+1]=strFile[i];
        }
        // Increase the number of slides in the show
        NumTexts = NumTexts + 1;
        // Read item from the file into the new location
        strFile[CurrentText]=Filename;
        str[CurrentText]=getText(strFile[CurrentText]+".txt");
        setText();
    }
```

Modifying the `LoadShow()` Method

The `LoadShow()` method for `SlideText` is overloaded just as is `SlideCanvas`. The new overloaded methods are shown in Listing 19.11.

Listing 19.11. The `LoadShow()` methods.

```java
// Overload LoadShow so existing calls don't need to be modified
public void LoadShow(String LoadFile){
    LoadShow(LoadFile,false);
}
// Load the text array based on filename in the LoadFile
public void LoadShow(String LoadFile,boolean addfile) {
    RandomAccessFile     ListFile;
    int i;            // Loop counter

    // Create an array of images and load the images
    if (addfile)
        i=NumTexts;
    else
        i=0;
    try {
        ListFile = new RandomAccessFile(LoadFile,"r");
        while (ListFile.getFilePointer() != ListFile.length() ) {
            strFile[i] = ListFile.readLine();
            i++;
        }
        ListFile.close();
    } catch (java.io.IOException e) {
        System.out.println("Could not read from file.");
        System.out.println(e);
    }
    NumTexts = i;
```

continues

Listing 19.11. continued

```
    for (i=0; i<NumTexts;i++) {
        str[i] = getText(strFile[i]+".txt");
    }
}
```

Adding the `EndOfShow()` Method

When the automatic-play feature is implemented, the `SlideShow` application must be able to detect when the end of the slide show is reached. To do this, an `endOfShow()` method is added to the `SlideText` class. This method returns `true` to the caller when the last slide is displayed. Listing 19.12 shows the `endOfShow()` method.

> **Note:** `CurrentText` is the index of the current string, and the index values start at zero. `NumTexts` is the total number of strings stored, counting from one. When the `CurrentText` value is one less than the `NumTexts` value, the last slide is in the display window.

Listing 19.12. The `endOfShow()` method.

```
public boolean endOfShow() {
        if (CurrentText == (NumTexts-1))
                return true;
        else
                return false;
    }
```

Increasing the Number of Possible Slides

The new static final variable `ArrayMax` also must be declared in the `SlideText` class. The declaration looks like this:

```
static final int ArrayMax = 100;              // Size of array
```

All references to the value `20` as an array maximum in the `SlideText` class are then replaced with the name `ArrayMax`.

The Complete `SlideText` Class

Listing 19.13 shows the complete `SlideText` class with all the new methods and the modifications to the existing methods.

Listing 19.13. The `SlideText` class.

```
/**
 * SlideText is an extension of TextArea
 * It provides a means to display text descriptions to the user
 */

class SlideText extends TextArea {
    // Size of array
    static final int ArrayMax = 100;
    // Array of Strings to display
    protected String str[] = new String[ArrayMax];
    // name of file containing image to display
    protected String[] strFile = new String[ArrayMax];
    // Number of strings in the array
    protected int NumTexts=0;
    // Number of string currently displayed
    protected int CurrentText=0;
    // True if text is not being displayed
    protected boolean showtext;
    // String for cutting & pasting
    protected String StringClip=new String();
    // String for cutting & pasting filename
    protected String FileClip=new String();

    public SlideText(String ShowName) {
        super();
        LoadShow(ShowName);
        setEditable(false);
        showtext = true;
    }
    public void cutString(){
        int i;
        //Check that there is an element to cut
        if (NumTexts < 0)
            return;
        //Copy element and its filename to buffer
        StringClip = str[CurrentText];
        FileClip = strFile[CurrentText];
        //Decrease the number of elements in the array
        NumTexts = NumTexts - 1;
        //Shift the array to close the gap
        for (i=CurrentText;i<NumTexts;i++){
            str[i] = str[i+1];
            strFile[i] = strFile[i+1];
        }
        if (CurrentText == NumTexts)
            CurrentText = NumTexts - 1;
        setText();
    }
    public boolean endOfShow() {
        if (CurrentText == (NumTexts-1))
            return true;
        else
            return false;
    }
    public void copyString() {
        //Check that there is an element to copy
```

continues

Listing 19.13. continued

```
            if (NumTexts < 0)
                return;
            StringClip = str[CurrentText];
    }
    public void pasteString() {
        int i;
        //Check that there is an element to paste
        if (StringClip == null)
            return;
        //Check that there is room to paste an element
        if (NumTexts == ArrayMax)
            return;
        //Make a space in the array and the file array
        for(i=NumTexts;i>=CurrentText;i--){
            str[i+1]=str[i];
            strFile[i+1]=strFile[i];
        }
        // Increase the number of slides in the show
        NumTexts = NumTexts + 1;
        // Store the items in the clipboard to the new slot
        str[CurrentText]=StringClip;
        strFile[CurrentText]=FileClip;
        setText();
    }
    public void InsertSlide(String Filename) {
        int i;
        //Check that there is room to paste an element
        if (NumTexts == ArrayMax)
            return;
        //Make a space in the array and the file array
        for(i=NumTexts;i>=CurrentText;i--){
            str[i+1]=str[i];
            strFile[i+1]=strFile[i];
        }
        // Increase the number of slides in the show
        NumTexts = NumTexts + 1;
        // Read item from the file into the new location
        strFile[CurrentText]=Filename;
        str[CurrentText]=getText(strFile[CurrentText]+".txt");
        setText();
    }
    public void NoText(){
        showtext = false;
        setText();
    }
    public void ShowText(){
        showtext = true;
        setText();
    }
    // Override normal setText so text can not be reset accidentally
    public void setText(String str){
        setText();
    }
    public void setText(){
        if ((showtext) && (NumTexts>0))
            super.setText(str[CurrentText]);
        else
```

```
                    super.setText("");

    }
    public void ShowNextText() {
        if (CurrentText < (NumTexts - 1)) {
            CurrentText = CurrentText + 1;
            setText();
        }
    }
    public void ShowPrevText() {
        if (CurrentText > 0) {
            CurrentText = CurrentText - 1;
            setText();
        }
    }
    public void ShowFirstText() {
        CurrentText = 0;
        setText();
    }
    public void ShowLastText() {
        CurrentText = NumTexts - 1;
        setText();
    }
    public void LoadShow(String LoadFile){
        LoadShow(LoadFile,false);
    }
    // Load the text array based on filename in the LoadFile
    public void LoadShow(String LoadFile,boolean addfile) {
        RandomAccessFile      ListFile;
        int i;              // Loop counter

        // Create an array of images and load the images
        if (addfile)
            i=NumTexts;
        else
            i=0;
        try {
            ListFile = new RandomAccessFile(LoadFile,"r");
            while (ListFile.getFilePointer() != ListFile.length() ) {
                strFile[i] = ListFile.readLine();
                i++;
            }
            ListFile.close();
        } catch (java.io.IOException e) {
            System.out.println("Could not read from file.");
            System.out.println(e);
        }
        NumTexts = i;
        for (i=0; i<NumTexts;i++) {
            str[i] = getText(strFile[i]+".txt");
        }
    }
    // Read text for an item from a file
    protected String getText(String LoadFile){
        RandomAccessFile      ListFile;
        byte b[] = new byte[1024];
        int numbytes;
```

continues

Listing 19.13. continued

```
        try {
            ListFile = new RandomAccessFile(LoadFile,"r");
            numbytes = (int)ListFile.length();
            ListFile.read(b,0,numbytes);
            ListFile.close();
        } catch (java.io.IOException e) {
            System.out.println("Could not read from file.");
            System.out.println(e);
        }
        return (new String(b,0));
    }
}
```

Changes to `SlidePanel`

The `SlidePanel` class is responsible for using the new methods provided by the `SlideCanvas` and `SlideText` classes. The changes presented for the `SlidePanel` class are from the list completed in the "Designing Application Upgrades" section.

Changes to Declarations

To include the autoplay feature, the `SlidePanel` class implements the `Runnable` interface so it can run a timer in a separate thread. This necessitates a change to the class declaration. The thread to run the timer and the boolean variable described in the design are declared as follows:

```
class SlidePanel extends Panel implements Runnable{
    protected boolean keepPlaying;        // True when in autoplay
    protected Thread lt;                   // Local thread for autoplay
```

Adding the `cutSlide`, `copySlide`, and `pasteSlide` Methods

The `cutSlide`, `copySlide`, and `pasteSlide` methods for the `SlidePanel` class are responsible for calling the corresponding methods of the `SlideCanvas` and `SlideText` objects. The methods containing these calls are shown in Listing 19.14.

Listing 19.14. The `cutSlide()`, `copySlide()`, and `pasteSlide()` methods for `SlidePanel`.

```
public void cutSlide(){
        displayCanvas.cutSlide();
        displayText.cutString();
    }
    public void copySlide() {
        displayCanvas.copySlide();
```

```
        displayText.copyString();
    }
    public void pasteSlide() {
        displayCanvas.pasteSlide();
        displayText.pasteString();
    }
```

Adding the `InsertSlide` Method

The `InsertSlide` method is only slightly more complex than the `Cut`, `Copy`, and `Paste` methods. The `Insert` method must remove the file extension from the filename it receives so it can pass just the filename to the `Insert` methods for `SlideCanvas` and `SlideText`. To do this, it uses the `indexOf` method found in the `String` class to locate the period (`.`) serving as the separator between the filename and the extension. It then creates a new string from the substring that appears before that character. The complete code is given in Listing 19.15.

Listing 19.15. The `InsertSlide()` method.

```
public void InsertSlide(String SlideFile) {
        String FilePrefix;
        int     sepIndex;

        sepIndex = SlideFile.indexOf(".");
        if (sepIndex < 0 )
            return;
        FilePrefix = SlideFile.substring(0,sepIndex);
        displayCanvas.InsertSlide(FilePrefix);
        displayText.InsertSlide(FilePrefix);
    }
```

Adding the `saveShow()` Method

The two new methods provided by `SlideCanvas` are used in the `saveShow()` method: The `saveShow` method opens a new file with the filename it is passed and writes the names of the current slides to the file, one per line. Listing 19.16 shows the code for this method.

Listing 19.16. The `saveShow()` method.

```
public void saveShow(String SaveFile) {
        RandomAccessFile       ListFile;
        String[] fileNames;
        int NumFiles;
        int i;

        NumFiles = displayCanvas.getNumSlides();
        fileNames = displayCanvas.getSlideFiles();
```

continues

Listing 19.16. continued

```
        try {
            ListFile = new RandomAccessFile(SaveFile,"rw");
            for (i=0;i<NumFiles;i++)
                ListFile.writeBytes(fileNames[i]+"\n");
            ListFile.close();
        } catch (java.io.IOException e) {
            System.out.println("Could not write to save file "+SaveFile);
            System.out.println(e);
        }
    }
```

Modifying the Constructor

The constructor of the SlidePanel class is modified to allow an array of strings as input. The constructor first calls the SlideCanvas and SlideText constructors with the first element in this array and then adds a new loop. The loop makes additional calls to SlideCanvas and SlideText using both the remaining values in the argument list and a second parameter set to true. The parameter indicates that the slides in these files should be loaded in addition to the existing slides. The new constructor is shown in Listing 19.17.

Listing 19.17. The constructor for SlidePanel.

```
// Constructor adds objects to the panel
// Gives each object the filename to load its array from
public SlidePanel(String ShowName[]) {
    super();
    setLayout(new BorderLayout());
    add("Center",displayCanvas = new SlideCanvas(ShowName[0]));
    add("South",displayText = new SlideText(ShowName[0]));
    int i=1;
    while (i < ShowName.length) {
        displayCanvas.LoadShow(ShowName[i],true);
        displayText.LoadShow(ShowName[i],true);
        i++;
    }
}
```

Adding Methods to Start and Stop Continuous Play

The startPlay() method sets the instance variable keepPlaying and starts a new thread. This creates the first call to the run method that will then loop through the slide show. The stop method just sets the instance variable keepPlaying to false and allows the run() method to fall out of the loop, terminating the thread. Both of these methods are shown in Listing 19.18.

Listing 19.18. The `StartPlay()` and `StopPlay()` methods.

```
public void StartPlay(){
    keepPlaying=true;
    lt = new Thread(this);
    lt.start();
}
public void StopPlay(){
    keepPlaying=false;
}
```

Adding the `run()` Method

The `run()` method added to the `SlidePanel` class implements the timer and loop. It uses the `sleep()` method with an interval of 4,000 milliseconds (4 seconds) to provide a pause between the display of each slide. The method is shown in Listing 19.19.

Listing 19.19. The `run()` method.

```
public void run(){
    while (keepPlaying && !displayCanvas.endOfShow()) {
        ShowNextSlide();
        try {lt.sleep(4000);}
        catch ( InterruptedException e ) {
            System.out.println("Continous play interrupted by");
            System.out.println(e);
        }
    }
}
```

The Complete `SlidePanel` Class

Listing 19.20 shows the complete `SlidePanel` class. The new variables, the new constructor, all the new methods, the old variables, and all the old methods are contained in this listing.

Listing 19.20. The `SlidePanel` class.

```
/**
 * SlidePanel class holds objects participating in the slideshow
 * Objects are arrays displaying one at a time to the user
 */

class SlidePanel extends Panel implements Runnable{
    protected SlideCanvas displayCanvas;     // Canvas to display .gifs
    protected SlideText displayText;          // Text area to display text
    protected boolean keepPlaying;            // True when in autoplay
    protected Thread lt;                      // Local thread for autoplay
```

continues

Listing 19.20. continued

```java
// Constructor adds objects to the panel
// Gives each object the filename to get load its array from
public SlidePanel(String ShowName[]) {
    super();
    setLayout(new BorderLayout());
    add("Center",displayCanvas = new SlideCanvas(ShowName[0]));
    add("South",displayText = new SlideText(ShowName[0]));
    int i=1;
    while (i < ShowName.length) {
        displayCanvas.LoadShow(ShowName[i],true);
        displayText.LoadShow(ShowName[i],true);
        i++;
    }
}
public void StartPlay(){
    keepPlaying=true;
    lt = new Thread(this);
    lt.start();
}
public void run(){
    while (keepPlaying && !displayCanvas.endOfShow()) {
        ShowNextSlide();
        try {lt.sleep(4000);}
        catch ( InterruptedException e ) {
            System.out.println("Continous play interrupted by");
            System.out.println(e);
        }
    }
}
public void StopPlay(){
    keepPlaying=false;
}
public void InsertSlide(String SlideFile) {
    String FilePrefix;
    int    sepIndex;

    sepIndex = SlideFile.indexOf(".");
    if (sepIndex < 0 )
        return;
    FilePrefix = SlideFile.substring(0,sepIndex);
    displayCanvas.InsertSlide(FilePrefix);
    displayText.InsertSlide(FilePrefix);
}
public void saveShow(String SaveFile) {
    RandomAccessFile     ListFile;
    String[] fileNames;
    int NumFiles;
    int i;

    NumFiles = displayCanvas.getNumSlides();
    fileNames = displayCanvas.getSlideFiles();

    try {
```

```
                    ListFile = new RandomAccessFile(SaveFile,"rw");
                    for (i=0;i<NumFiles;i++)
                        ListFile.writeBytes(fileNames[i]+"\n");
                    ListFile.close();
            } catch (java.io.IOException e) {
                System.out.println("Could not write to save file "+SaveFile);
                System.out.println(e);
            }
        }
        public void cutSlide(){
            displayCanvas.cutSlide();
            displayText.cutString();
        }
        public void copySlide() {
            displayCanvas.copySlide();
            displayText.copyString();
        }
        public void pasteSlide() {
            displayCanvas.pasteSlide();
            displayText.pasteString();
        }
        public void NoText(){
            displayText.NoText();
        }
        public void ShowText(){
            displayText.ShowText();
        }
        public void NoSlides(){
            displayCanvas.NoSlides();
        }
        public void ShowSlides(){
            displayCanvas.ShowSlides();
        }

        public void LoadShow(String ShowName) {
            displayCanvas.LoadShow(ShowName);
            displayText.LoadShow(ShowName);
        }
        public void ShowNextSlide() {
            displayCanvas.ShowNextSlide();
            displayText.ShowNextText();
        }
        public void ShowPrevSlide() {
            displayCanvas.ShowPrevSlide();
            displayText.ShowPrevText();
        }
        public void ShowFirstSlide() {
            displayCanvas.ShowFirstSlide();
            displayText.ShowFirstText();
        }
        public void ShowLastSlide() {
            displayCanvas.ShowLastSlide();
            displayText.ShowLastText();
        }
    }
```

Changes to **SlideControls**

Now modify the controls to add two new check boxes. The controls must now communicate with the menu bar when the state of either of the check boxes is changed. As with the other classes, the modifications are made as listed in the "Designing Application Upgrades" section.

Adding Storage for a **MenuBar**

To notify the menu that a check box changed on the control panel, the controls must know about the Menu object. Therefore, the constructor for the SlideControls class is modified to accept a MenuBar and store the value in an instance variable. This line appears as

```
static MenuBar mb;        // Menubar for the show
```

The value stored here is loaded in the constructor and used in the event handler.

Adding Check Boxes and New Buttons to the Controls

Before you can add check boxes and new buttons for AutoPlay and Stop to the ShowControls class, you must modify the constructor for the class to accept a MenuBar object and store the value in the new mbar object. In this way, the controls know when changes occur on the menu bar.

Next, add the new check boxes to the constructor. A local reference to each control is kept when it is added. This reference is used to set the control's state to checked. The final step is to add the AutoPlay and Stop buttons to the constructor.

Listing 19.21 shows the new constructor for the ShowControls class.

Listing 19.21. The constructor for the **ShowControls** class.

```
// Constructor requires a SlidePanel to which the
// controls are attached
public ShowControls(SlidePanel theShow) {
    Checkbox cbSlides;
    Checkbox cbText;

    ss = theShow;
    mb = mbar;
    setLayout(new FlowLayout(FlowLayout.CENTER));
    add(new Button("¦<<"));
    add(new Button("<"));
    add(new Button(">"));
    add(new Button(">>¦"));
    add(cbSlides = new Checkbox("Slides"));
    cbSlides.setState(true);
    add(cbText = new Checkbox("Text"));
    cbText.setState(true);
    add(new Button("AutoPlay"));
    add(new Button("Stop"));
}
```

Modifying the Event Handler

Implementing the radio buttons involves modifying the existing event handler for two new event types. The event handler will pass `Checkbox` events to a new method named `handleCheckbox()` and look for `CheckboxMenuItem` events. These events are passed to a new method called `handleCheckboxMenuItem()`. The new event handler appears as follows:

```
public boolean action(Event evt, Object arg) {
        if (evt.target instanceof Button) {
            handleButton((String)arg);
            return true;
        } else if (evt.target instanceof Checkbox) {
            handleCheckbox(((Checkbox) evt.target).getLabel(),(Boolean) arg);
            return true;
        }if(evt.target instanceof CheckboxMenuItem) {
            handleCheckboxMenuItem(evt);
            return true;
        }
        return super.action(evt,arg);
    }
```

> **Note:** Each class that has actions can have its own type of argument. Notice in the `handleEvent` method that the argument value for a check box is a boolean. This is unlike the `Button` class, in which the argument value in the action method is a string.

The `handleCheckbox` method responds to all `Checkbox` events in the `SlideControls` object. This method uses the instance variable in the `SlideControls` object to access the `SlidePanel`. It then shows or hides the slides for that `SlidePanel` depending on the state of the check box.

The method also posts the event to the event handler for the menu using the `postEvent()` method for the `MenuBar` object stored at the class level. This means the menu is notified when the state changes on the controls.

The `handleCheckbox()` method appears as follows:

```
public void handleCheckbox(Event evt, String cbname,Boolean cbstate){
    if (cbname.equals("Slides")) {
        if (cbstate.equals(Boolean.TRUE)) {
            ss.ShowSlides();
            mb.postEvent(evt);
        } else {
            ss.NoSlides();
            mb.postEvent(evt);
        }
    } else if (cbname.equals("Text")) {
        if (cbstate.equals(Boolean.TRUE)) {
            ss.ShowText();
            mb.postEvent(evt);
        } else {
            ss.NoText();
            mb.postEvent(evt);
```

```
        }
    }
}
```

The `handleCheckbox()` method changes the state of the check boxes on the controls in response to events that occur on the menu. When the state changes on the menu, the state of the check boxes must be changed. To do this, a `CheckBoxMenuItem` event is posted to the `ShowControls` object from the method handling the change in the menu. The method to handle these events appears as follows:

```
// Change state of checkboxes if state is different on menu
    public void handleCheckboxMenuItem(Event evt) {
        if (evt.arg.equals("No Text")) {
            if (((CheckboxMenuItem) evt.target).getState() == true)
                ((Checkbox) this.getComponent(5)).setState(false);
            else
                ((Checkbox) this.getComponent(5)).setState(true);
        } else if (evt.arg.equals("No Slides")) {
            if (((CheckboxMenuItem) evt.target).getState() == true)
                ((Checkbox) this.getComponent(4)).setState(false);
            else
                ((Checkbox) this.getComponent(4)).setState(true);
        }
    }
```

The event handler can now process state changes from either the controls or the menu. It must also be modified to react to the two new buttons, AutoPlay and Stop, that were added to the controls. The event handler in the `SlideControls` class passes all button-related events to the method `handleButton`. Modify this method to check for either of these buttons and to trigger the appropriate method in the `SlidePanel`. The new `handleButton` method appears as

```
public void handleButton(String bname) {
        if (bname.equals(">")) {
            ss.ShowNextSlide();
        } else if (bname.equals("<")) {
            ss.ShowPrevSlide();
        } else if (bname.equals("¦<<")) {
            ss.ShowFirstSlide();
        } else if (bname.equals(">>¦")) {
            ss.ShowLastSlide();
        } else if (bname.equals("AutoPlay")) {
            ss.StartPlay();
        } else if (bname.equals("Stop")) {
            ss.StopPlay();
        }
    }
```

Figure 19.1 shows the updated controls on the `SlideShow` application. Because both text and graphics are displayed in the figure, the check boxes for slides and text are checked.

Figure 19.1.
The updated controls for
`SlideShow`.

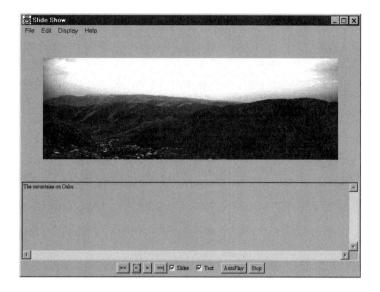

The Complete `ShowControls` Class

Although the changes to `ShowControls` are not as extensive as for other classes, a complete code listing, shown in Listing 19.22, can help to clarify them.

Listing 19.22. The `ShowControls` class.

```
/**
 * Control bar for moving through a slide show
 */

class ShowControls extends Panel {
    static SlidePanel ss;    // Panel controls are attached to
    static MenuBar mb;       // Menubar for the show

    // Constructor requires a SlidePanel to which the
    // controls are attached
    public ShowControls(SlidePanel theShow, MenuBar mbar) {
        Checkbox cbSlides;
        Checkbox cbText;

        ss = theShow;
        mb = mbar;
        setLayout(new FlowLayout(FlowLayout.CENTER));
        add(new Button("|<<"));
        add(new Button("<"));
        add(new Button(">"));
        add(new Button(">>|"));
        add(cbSlides = new Checkbox("Slides"));
        cbSlides.setState(true);
        add(cbText = new Checkbox("Text"));
```

continues

Listing 19.22. continued

```
            cbText.setState(true);
            add(new Button("AutoPlay"));
            add(new Button("Stop"));
    }
    // Determine which button was pressed and act accordingly
    // Actions will refer to the Slide panel to which the
    // control bar is attached
    public void handleButton(String bname) {
        if (bname.equals(">")) {
            ss.ShowNextSlide();
        } else if (bname.equals("<")) {
            ss.ShowPrevSlide();
        } else if (bname.equals("¦<<")) {
            ss.ShowFirstSlide();
        } else if (bname.equals(">>¦")) {
            ss.ShowLastSlide();
        } else if (bname.equals("AutoPlay")) {
            ss.StartPlay();
        } else if (bname.equals("Stop")) {
            ss.StopPlay();
        }
    }
    public void handleCheckbox(Event evt, String cbname, Boolean cbstate) {
        if (cbname.equals("Slides")) {
            if (cbstate.equals(Boolean.TRUE)) {
                ss.ShowSlides();
                mb.postEvent(evt);
            } else {
                ss.NoSlides();
                mb.postEvent(evt);
            }
        } else if (cbname.equals("Text")) {
            if (cbstate.equals(Boolean.TRUE)) {
                ss.ShowText();
                mb.postEvent(evt);
            } else {
                ss.NoText();
                mb.postEvent(evt);
            }
        }
    }
    // Change state of checkboxes if state is different on menu
    public void handleCheckboxMenuItem(Event evt) {
        if (evt.arg.equals("No Text")) {
            if (((CheckboxMenuItem) evt.target).getState() == true)
                ((Checkbox) this.getComponent(5)).setState(false);
            else
                ((Checkbox) this.getComponent(5)).setState(true);
        } else if (evt.arg.equals("No Slides")) {
            if (((CheckboxMenuItem) evt.target).getState() == true)
                ((Checkbox) this.getComponent(4)).setState(false);
            else
                ((Checkbox) this.getComponent(4)).setState(true);
        }
    }
    public boolean action(Event evt, Object arg) {
```

```
            if (evt.target instanceof Button) {
                handleButton((String)arg);
                return true;
            } else if (evt.target instanceof Checkbox) {
                handleCheckbox(evt, ((Checkbox) evt.target).getLabel(),
➡(Boolean) arg);
                return true;
            }if(evt.target instanceof CheckboxMenuItem) {
                handleCheckboxMenuItem(evt);
                return true;
            }
            return super.action(evt,arg);
        }
}
```

Changes to `SlideShow`

The changes to the SlideShow class complete the necessary modifications. The SlideShow modifications supply the new menu with a corresponding event handler and allow all command-line arguments to be supplied to the SlidePanel class.

Modifying the Menu

You can modify the InitializeMenu() method so that Edit appears on the menu bar. On the Edit menu you add Cut, Copy, Paste, a separator, and Insert. Because the Paste option is not available until a slide has been cut or copied, you must ensure that its menu item is disabled when the menu is first displayed. The event handler then must enable this menu option after a Cut or Copy event occurs.

The line to disable the Paste item looks like this:

```
m.getItem(2).disable();
```

The InitializeMenu() method with the new menu items is shown in Listing 19.23.

Listing 19.23. The `InitializeMenu()` method.

```
private void InitializeMenu()
    {
        mbar = new MenuBar();
        Menu m = new Menu("File");
        m.add(new MenuItem("Load..."));
        m.add(new MenuItem("Save..."));
        m.addSeparator();
        m.add(new MenuItem("Exit"));
        mbar.add(m);

        m = new Menu("Edit");
```

continues

Listing 19.23. continued

```
        m.add(new MenuItem("Cut"));
        m.add(new MenuItem("Copy"));
        m.add(new MenuItem("Paste"));
        m.addSeparator();
        m.add(new MenuItem("Insert"));
        m.getItem(2).disable();
        mbar.add(m);

        m = new Menu("Display");
        m.add(new MenuItem("Forward"));
        m.add(new MenuItem("Back"));
        m.add(new MenuItem("Beginning"));
        m.add(new MenuItem("End"));
        m.addSeparator();
        m.add(new CheckboxMenuItem("No Text"));
        m.add(new CheckboxMenuItem("No Slides"));
        mbar.add(m);

        m = new Menu("Help");
        m.add(new MenuItem("Help Topics"));
        m.addSeparator();
        m.add(new MenuItem("About SlideShow"));
        mbar.add(m);
    }
```

Figure 19.2 shows the new Edit menu for the SlideShow application. Because there are no objects on the buffer, the Paste option is dimmed.

Figure 19.2.
The Edit menu for
SlideShow.

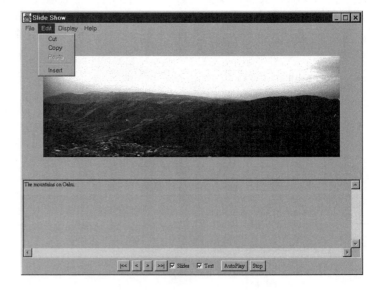

Modifying Declarations

The event handler must communicate with the controls to inform them of state changes on the menu, so a reference to the controls must be available to the event handler. This reference is declared at the class level and set in the constructor for the class. The declaration appears as follows:

```
protected ShowControls SlideControl;// Controls to move through show
```

Modifying the Constructor

The SlideShow constructor is modified to set the SlideControl object when it creates the controls. The controls are created using the new constructor for the ShowControls class. The ShowControls constructor requires a menu bar as a parameter; therefore, the creation of the menu bar is moved to the beginning of the constructor.

The SlidePanel constructor is now expecting an array of arguments instead of a single string. Therefore, the SlideShow constructor is modified to accept an array of arguments and pass them to SlidePanel.

The new version of the SlideShow constructor with these three changes appears in Listing 19.24.

Listing 19.24. The **SlideShow** constructor.

```
public SlideShow(String args[]) {
    InitializeMenu();           // Menu creation moved to the top
    setMenuBar(mbar);           // Menu attached to frame

    setBackground(Color.lightGray);
    setLayout(new BorderLayout());
    add("Center",displayPanel = new SlidePanel(args));
    // Set instance variable for controls so it may be called in event handler
    // Pass the controls a reference to the menu
    add("South",SlideControl = new ShowControls(displayPanel, mbar));

}
```

Modifying the **main()** Method

The only alteration to the main() method is that it should pass the entire array of input arguments instead of only the first item in the array. This amounts to changing the line

```
SlideShow ss = new SlideShow(args[0]);
```

to the following:

```
SlideShow ss = new SlideShow(args);
```

Modifying the Event Handler

Several modifications must be made to the event handler for the SlideShow class. The handler must accommodate events for each of the new menu options and the events from the check boxes on the controls.

This is an appropriate time to consider breaking the event handler into smaller objects. Perhaps it would be appropriate to have one method for each type of component as is done in the SlideControls object. However, for the frame most of the events involve menu items. Therefore, divide the event handler for SlideShow into pieces based on the four menus on the menu bar. A fifth method will handle the state changes from the controls. The event handler still exits the application in response to the WINDOW_DESTROY event.

The event handler checks the event target to determine if it is an instance of a menu item or of a check box. If it is neither of these, the event handler for the parent class is called. If the target is a menu item, the event handler must determine the menu where the item appears. The explicit casting makes this check look more complex than it is. For example, the line

```
if (((Menu) ((MenuItem) evt.target).getParent()).getLabel().equals("File")) {
```

casts the event target to a menu item and then gets the parent of that menu item. The parent is cast as a menu, and the getLabel() method of the menu class is used to get the name of the menu. If the name is File, the statement returns true, indicating this is an item on the File menu.

The new event handler appears in Listing 19.25.

Listing 19.25. The event handler for SlideShow.

```
// Handles events in main window
// Even handlers are supplied for each menu on the menu bar
public boolean handleEvent(Event evt) {
      if (evt.id == Event.WINDOW_DESTROY &&
          evt.target instanceof SlideShow)
        {
            System.exit(0);
          return true;
      } else if(evt.target instanceof MenuItem) {
          if (((Menu) ((MenuItem) evt.target).getParent()).
➡getLabel().equals("File")) {
              return handleFileEvent(evt);
          } else if (((Menu) ((MenuItem) evt.target).getParent()).
➡getLabel().equals("Edit")) {
              return handleEditEvent(evt);
          } else if (((Menu) ((MenuItem) evt.target).getParent()).
➡getLabel().equals("Display")) {
              return handleDisplayEvent(evt);
          } else if (((Menu) ((MenuItem) evt.target).getParent()).
➡getLabel().equals("Help")) {
              return handleHelpEvent(evt);
          }
      } else if (evt.target instanceof Checkbox) {
          return handleCheckbox(evt, (Checkbox) evt.target);
```

```
        }
            return super.handleEvent(evt);      // Let parent handle event
    }
```

You can now create each of the new methods called in the event handler. These are reviewed in the order they are listed in the event handler.

The `handleFileEvent()` method must allow saves in addition to the loads and exits that were in the original event handler. When the Save item is selected on the menu, the event handler responds by creating a new File dialog box. The parent for this box is the current frame, the title is Save Slide Show, and the type is a Save dialog box. After the box is created, the `setFile()` method is used to set the extension for the file to `.txt`. This encourages the user to save the show as a text file. When the user has selected the filename, the new filename and directory are passed to the `saveShow()` method in the `SlidePanel` class.

The complete `handleFileEvent()` method is shown in Listing 19.26.

Listing 19.26. The `handleFileEvent()` method.

```
// Event handler responds to events from the File menu
    public boolean handleFileEvent(Event evt) {
        if(evt.target instanceof MenuItem) {
            if (evt.arg.equals("Load...")) {
                String FileName;
                FileDialog fd =
                    new FileDialog((Frame) this,
                              "Get New Slide Show",
                              FileDialog.LOAD);
                fd.setFile("*.txt");
                fd.show();
                FileName = fd. getDirectory() + fd.getFile();
                displayPanel.LoadShow(FileName);
                return true;
            } else if (evt.arg.equals("Save...")) {
                String FileName;
                FileDialog fd =
                    new FileDialog((Frame) this,
                              "Save Slide Show",
                              FileDialog.SAVE);
                fd.setFile("*.txt");
                fd.show();
                FileName = fd.getDirectory() + fd.getFile();

                displayPanel.saveShow(FileName);
                return true;
            } else if (evt.arg.equals("Exit")) {
                System.exit(0);
                return true;
            }
        }
            return super.handleEvent(evt);      // Let parent handle event
    }
```

The `handleEditEvent()` method is used to respond to the items on the edit menu. The Paste item should be enabled only when the Cut or Copy command is selected. The line to do this appears as follows:

```
((Menu)((MenuItem) evt.target).getParent()).getItem(2).enable();
```

This line casts the event target as a menu item and uses the `getParent()` method for the `MenuItem` class to get the menu where the item is listed. This an instance of the Edit menu. The Paste command that you want to enable is the third item on this particular Edit menu, but because the index for the menu item starts at zero, the third item has an index of 2. This item is enabled with the `enable` command. Each of these steps could have been written out separately, as in the following code:

```
MenuItem targetItem;
Menu     targetMenu;

displayPanel.copySlide();
targetItem = (MenuItem) evt.target;
targetMenu = (Menu) targetItem.getParent();
targetMenu.getItem(2).enable();
```

The event handler is modified to handle the new items that have been added to the menu. The rewritten event handler appears in Listing 19.27.

Listing 19.27. The `handleEditEvent()` method.

```
// Event handler responds to events from the Event menu
    public boolean handleEditEvent(Event evt) {
        if(evt.target instanceof MenuItem) {
            if (evt.arg.equals("Cut")) {
                displayPanel.cutSlide();
                ((Menu)((MenuItem) evt.target).getParent()).
➥getItem(2).enable();
                return true;
            } else if (evt.arg.equals("Copy")) {
                ((Menu)((MenuItem) evt.target).getParent()).
➥getItem(2).enable();
                displayPanel.copySlide();
                return true;
            } else if (evt.arg.equals("Paste")) {
                displayPanel.pasteSlide();
                return true;
            } else if (evt.arg.equals("Insert")) {
                String FileName;
                FileDialog fd =
                    new FileDialog((Frame) this,
                                "Get New Slide Show",
                                FileDialog.LOAD);
                fd.setFile("*.gif");
                fd.show();
                FileName = fd.getFile();
                displayPanel.InsertSlide(FileName);
                return true;
            }
```

```
            }
            return super.handleEvent(evt);      // Let parent handle event
    }
```

The `handleDisplayEvent()` method responds to the items on the Display menu. The items to maneuver through the show are handled in the same manner as in the original application. The response to the `CheckboxMenuItems` is modified to post the event to the control panel. The response to the AutoPlay and Stop menu items is to call the appropriate method in the `SlidePanel` class. Listing 19.28 shows the complete `handleDisplayEvent()` method.

Listing 19.28. The `handleDisplayEvent()` method.

```
// Event handler responds to events from the Display menu
    public boolean handleDisplayEvent(Event evt) {
        if(evt.target instanceof CheckboxMenuItem) {
            if (evt.arg.equals("No Text")) {
                if (((CheckboxMenuItem) evt.target).getState() == true){
                    displayPanel.NoText();
                    SlideControl.postEvent(evt);
                } else {
                    displayPanel.ShowText();
                    SlideControl.postEvent(evt);
                }
                return true;
            } else if (evt.arg.equals("No Slides")) {
                if (((CheckboxMenuItem) evt.target).getState() == true) {
                    displayPanel.NoSlides();
                    SlideControl.postEvent(evt);
                } else {
                    displayPanel.ShowSlides();
                    SlideControl.postEvent(evt);
                }
                return true;
            }
        } else if(evt.target instanceof MenuItem) {
            if (evt.arg.equals("Forward")) {
                displayPanel.ShowNextSlide();
                return true;
            } else if (evt.arg.equals("Back")) {
                displayPanel.ShowPrevSlide();
                return true;
            } else if (evt.arg.equals("Beginning")) {
                displayPanel.ShowFirstSlide();
                return true;
            } else if (evt.arg.equals("End")) {
                displayPanel.ShowLastSlide();
                return true;
            }
        }
        return super.handleEvent(evt);      // Let parent handle event
    }
```

The response to the items on the Help menu does not change. However, because the event handler is divided into several methods, a new method, shown in Listing 19.29, is created to handle these events.

Listing 19.29. The `handleHelpEvent()` method.

```
// Event handler responds to events from the Help menu
public boolean handleHelpEvent(Event evt) {
    if(evt.target instanceof MenuItem) {
        if (evt.arg.equals("About SlideShow")) {
            AboutBox ab = new AboutBox(this);
            ab.show();
            return true;
        } else if (evt.arg.equals("Help Topics")) {
            HelpBox ab = new HelpBox(this);
            ab.show();
            return true;
        }
    }
    return super.handleEvent(evt);      // Let parent handle event
}
```

The `SlideShow` object modifies the state of the check boxes on the menu in response to changes on the controls. These are `Checkbox` events that are handled in the new method `handleCheckbox()`. This method checks the name and state of the check box and modifies the current state of the menu accordingly. The new method appears in Listing 19.30.

Listing 19.30. The `handleCheckbox()` method.

```
public boolean handleCheckbox(Event evt, Checkbox cb) {
    boolean cbstate = cb.getState();
    String cbname = cb.getLabel();
    if (cbname.equals("Slides")) {
        if (cbstate == true)
            ((CheckboxMenuItem) mbar.getMenu(2).getItem(6)).setState(false);
        else
            ((CheckboxMenuItem) mbar.getMenu(2).getItem(6)).setState(true);
        return true;
    } else if (cbname.equals("Text")) {
        if (cbstate == true)
            ((CheckboxMenuItem) mbar.getMenu(2).getItem(5)).setState(false);
        else
            ((CheckboxMenuItem) mbar.getMenu(2).getItem(5)).setState(true);
        return true;
    }
    return super.handleEvent(evt);
}
```

The Complete `SlideShow` Class

The `SlideShow` class now includes all the changes discussed in this section. Listing 19.31 shows the code for the complete class.

Listing 19.31. The `SlideShow` class.

```
/**
 * Creates Window with panel for the slideshow
 * plus a Menu and controls for the SlideShow
 */

public class SlideShow extends Frame {
protected MenuBar mbar;                     // Menu for the slideshow
    protected SlidePanel displayPanel;      // Panel to display the show
    protected ShowControls SlideControl;// Controls to move through show

    public SlideShow(String args[]) {
        InitializeMenu();
        setMenuBar(mbar);

        setBackground(Color.lightGray);
        setLayout(new BorderLayout());
        add("Center",displayPanel = new SlidePanel(args));
        add("South",SlideControl = new ShowControls(displayPanel, mbar));

    }
    // Creates the menu and attaches it to the MenuBar
    private void InitializeMenu()
    {
        mbar = new MenuBar();
        Menu m = new Menu("File");
        m.add(new MenuItem("Load..."));
        m.add(new MenuItem("Save..."));
        m.addSeparator();
        m.add(new MenuItem("Exit"));
        mbar.add(m);

        m = new Menu("Edit");
        m.add(new MenuItem("Cut"));
        m.add(new MenuItem("Copy"));
        m.add(new MenuItem("Paste"));
        m.addSeparator();
        m.add(new MenuItem("Insert"));
        m.getItem(2).disable();
        mbar.add(m);

        m = new Menu("Display");
        m.add(new MenuItem("Forward"));
        m.add(new MenuItem("Back"));
        m.add(new MenuItem("Beginning"));
        m.add(new MenuItem("End"));
        m.addSeparator();
        m.add(new CheckboxMenuItem("No Text"));
        m.add(new CheckboxMenuItem("No Slides"));
        mbar.add(m);
```

continues

Listing 19.31. continued

```
            m = new Menu("Help");
            m.add(new MenuItem("Help Topics"));
            m.addSeparator();
            m.add(new MenuItem("About SlideShow"));
            mbar.add(m);
    }
    // Event handler responds to events from the File menu
    public boolean handleFileEvent(Event evt) {
        if(evt.target instanceof MenuItem) {
            if (evt.arg.equals("Load...")) {
                String FileName;
                FileDialog fd =
                    new FileDialog((Frame) this,
                                   "Get New Slide Show",
                                   FileDialog.LOAD);
                fd.setFile("*.txt");
                fd.show();
                FileName = fd. getDirectory() + fd.getFile();
                displayPanel.LoadShow(FileName);
                return true;
            } else if (evt.arg.equals("Save...")) {
                String FileName;
                FileDialog fd =
                    new FileDialog((Frame) this,
                                   "Save Slide Show",
                                   FileDialog.SAVE);
                fd.setFile("*.txt");
                fd.show();
                FileName = fd.getDirectory() + fd.getFile();

                displayPanel.saveShow(FileName);
                return true;
            } else if (evt.arg.equals("Exit")) {
                System.exit(0);
                return true;
            }
        }
        return super.handleEvent(evt);      // Let parent handle event
    }
    // Event handler responds to events from the Event menu
    public boolean handleEditEvent(Event evt) {
        if(evt.target instanceof MenuItem) {
            if (evt.arg.equals("Cut")) {
                displayPanel.cutSlide();
                ((Menu)((MenuItem) evt.target).getParent()).getItem(2).enable();
                return true;
            } else if (evt.arg.equals("Copy")) {
                ((Menu)((MenuItem) evt.target).getParent()).getItem(2).enable();
                displayPanel.copySlide();
                return true;
            } else if (evt.arg.equals("Paste")) {
                displayPanel.pasteSlide();
                return true;
            } else if (evt.arg.equals("Insert")) {
                String FileName;
                FileDialog fd =
```

```
                        new FileDialog((Frame) this,
                                    "Get New Slide Show",
                                    FileDialog.LOAD);
                fd.setFile("*.gif");
                fd.show();
                FileName = fd.getFile();
                displayPanel.InsertSlide(FileName);
                return true;
            }
        }
        return super.handleEvent(evt);      // Let parent handle event
    }
    // Event handler responds to events from the Display menu
    public boolean handleDisplayEvent(Event evt) {
        if(evt.target instanceof CheckboxMenuItem) {
            if (evt.arg.equals("No Text")) {
                if (((CheckboxMenuItem) evt.target).getState() == true){
                    displayPanel.NoText();
                    SlideControl.postEvent(evt);
                } else {
                    displayPanel.ShowText();
                    SlideControl.postEvent(evt);
                }
                return true;
            } else if (evt.arg.equals("No Slides")) {
                if (((CheckboxMenuItem) evt.target).getState() == true) {
                    displayPanel.NoSlides();
                    SlideControl.postEvent(evt);
                } else {
                    displayPanel.ShowSlides();
                    SlideControl.postEvent(evt);
                }
                return true;
            }
        } else if(evt.target instanceof MenuItem) {
            if (evt.arg.equals("Forward")) {
                displayPanel.ShowNextSlide();
                return true;
            } else if (evt.arg.equals("Back")) {
                displayPanel.ShowPrevSlide();
                return true;
            } else if (evt.arg.equals("Beginning")) {
                displayPanel.ShowFirstSlide();
                return true;
            } else if (evt.arg.equals("End")) {
                displayPanel.ShowLastSlide();
                return true;
            }
        }
        return super.handleEvent(evt);      // Let parent handle event
    }
    // Event handler responds to events from the Help menu
    public boolean handleHelpEvent(Event evt) {
        if(evt.target instanceof MenuItem) {
            if (evt.arg.equals("About SlideShow")) {
                AboutBox ab = new AboutBox(this);
                ab.show();
                return true;
```

continues

Listing 19.31. continued

```
                } else if (evt.arg.equals("Help Topics")) {
                    HelpBox ab = new HelpBox(this);
                    ab.show();
                    return true;
                }
        }
          return super.handleEvent(evt);      // Let parent handle event
    }
    public boolean handleCheckbox(Event evt, Checkbox cb) {
        boolean cbstate = cb.getState();
        String cbname = cb.getLabel();
        if (cbname.equals("Slides")) {
            if (cbstate == true)
                ((CheckboxMenuItem) mbar.getMenu(2).
➡getItem(6)).setState(false);
            else
                ((CheckboxMenuItem) mbar.getMenu(2).
➡getItem(6)).setState(true);
            return true;
        } else if (cbname.equals("Text")) {
            if (cbstate == true)
                ((CheckboxMenuItem) mbar.getMenu(2).
➡getItem(5)).setState(false);
            else
                ((CheckboxMenuItem) mbar.getMenu(2).
➡getItem(5)).setState(true);
            return true;
        }
        return super.handleEvent(evt);
    }
    // Handles events in main window
    // Even handlers are supplied for each menu on the menu bar
    public boolean handleEvent(Event evt) {
        if (evt.id == Event.WINDOW_DESTROY &&
            evt.target instanceof SlideShow)
          {
             System.exit(0);
            return true;
        } else if(evt.target instanceof MenuItem) {
            if (((Menu) ((MenuItem) evt.target).getParent()).
➡getLabel().equals("File")) {
                return handleFileEvent(evt);
            } else if (((Menu) ((MenuItem) evt.target).getParent()).
➡getLabel().equals("Edit")) {
                return handleEditEvent(evt);
            } else if (((Menu) ((MenuItem) evt.target).getParent()).
➡getLabel().equals("Display")) {
                return handleDisplayEvent(evt);
            } else if (((Menu) ((MenuItem) evt.target).getParent()).
➡getLabel().equals("Help")) {
                return handleHelpEvent(evt);
            }
        } else if (evt.target instanceof Checkbox) {
            return handleCheckbox(evt, (Checkbox) evt.target);
        }
          return super.handleEvent(evt);      // Let parent handle event
    }
```

```
// main method used to start application
public static void main(String args[]){
    // Verify that there is a filename to attempt to load show
    if (args.length <= 0) {
        System.out.println("Usage: java SlideShow filename.");
        System.exit(0);
    }
    // Create instance of this object
    SlideShow ss = new SlideShow(args);
    ss.setTitle("Slide Show");          // Set the title of the frame
    ss.pack();                          // Pack components
    Dimension d;
    d = Toolkit.getDefaultToolkit().getScreenSize();
    ss.resize(d.width, d.height);
    ss.show();                          // Display the frame
}
}
```

The Final Version of **SlideShow**

Referring back to the design, you can see that the completed modification includes all the changes listed. All the new objects have been added. The modifications to existing objects have been completed. The menu items listed in the design now appear and function on the working application. For easy reference, the application is available on the CD-ROM that accompanies this book. Also, each class-level object has its own section in this chapter, so you can refer to them individually for reference if necessary.

The SlideShow application with its modifications represents a real-world development project. Adding the features in this chapter should have given you insight into how simple applications can evolve into large projects over time.

Testing and Debugging

Testing is even more crucial for application upgrades than it is for the initial release. At this point, your users are accustomed to the way the original application operates and do not want any surprise changes. Your thorough testing should ensure that no such surprises occur. The users will also be paying careful attention to the places where the application has changed. Again, your tests should make sure they see what they are expecting.

To test an upgrade thoroughly, create a completely new set of tests. Document these tests for the same reasons that you documented the test plan for the original application. In addition to testing the new features, you should also run the tests from the initial installation. This verifies that all the features originally provided still work.

It is useful to have a separate directory to run tests. This keeps the results from being confused with those of a previous test. Wait until all the modifications for a release are completed before beginning testing. Just as with new development, perform all testing before correcting problems.

The remainder of this section provides a brief set of tests for each change implemented.

Testing the Build-and-Save Capability

The build-and-save capability affects several portions of the application. Tests must be provided for all the new features. The first set of questions deals with the options added to the menu:

- Does the Edit menu appear on the menu bar?
- Is the Cut option available on the Edit menu?
- Is the Copy option available on the Edit menu?
- Is the Paste option present but dimmed on the Edit menu when the program first starts?
- Is the Insert option available on the Edit menu?
- Is the Save option available on the File menu?
- After a slide is copied with the Copy option, is the Paste option available?
- After a slide is cut with the Cut option, is the Paste option available?

In addition to verifying that the option appears correctly on the menu, you need to make sure that the application saves work correctly:

- Does the Save option produce a File dialog box and allow the user to save a file?
- Can the user load a file that has been saved in a prior session?

The next set of questions focuses on correct functioning of the Cut, Copy, Paste, and Insert options.

- Do the picture and text disappear from the screen when the Cut option is selected?
- Are the picture and text inserted prior to the current picture when the Paste option is selected after the Cut option?
- Do the picture and text remain on the screen when the Copy option is selected?
- Are the picture and text inserted prior to the current picture and text when the Paste option is selected after the Copy option?
- Does the Insert option bring up a File dialog box?
- Does the File dialog box from the Insert option allow you to select a `.gif` file to load?
- When a file is selected in the File dialog box from the Insert option, do the picture and text load into the show prior to the current slide?

Testing the Check Boxes

Build-and-save has the longest test plan because it is changed so extensively. The check boxes do not take as long to verify. However, care must still be taken to verify the interaction between the check boxes and the menu. Suggested test questions include the following:

- When the Slides box is cleared, is the display of pictures hidden?
- When the Text box is cleared, is the display of text hidden?
- When the Slides box is checked, are the pictures displayed again?
- When the Text box is checked, is the text displayed again?
- When the Slides box is checked, is the No Slides menu option unchecked?
- When the Slides box is cleared, is the No Slides menu option checked?
- When the Text box is checked, is the No Text menu option unchecked?
- When the Text box is cleared, is the No Text menu option checked?
- When the Slides box is checked, is the No Slides menu option unchecked?
- When the No Slides menu option is checked, is the Slides box cleared?
- When the No Slides menu option is cleared, is the Slides box checked?
- When the No Text menu option is checked, is the Text box cleared?
- When the No Text menu option is cleared, is the Text box checked?

Testing the Capability to Read Multiple Files

Compared with the first two changes, the test plan for the capability to read multiple files is quite short. Test questions include the following:

- When the command line contains a list of two or more files to load, are they visible in the program?
- When the command line contains only one file, is it correctly loaded into the program?

Testing the Continuous-Play Capability

To test the continuous-play feature, you need to verify both the start and stop of continuous play. The questions to ask follow:

- When the AutoPlay button is selected, are new slides displayed on a four-second interval?
- When the Stop button is selected, does the screen remain on the same slide?

Testing the Number of Possible Slides

Changing the number of slides that can be held internally will not result any obvious changes to the application. However, it is still important to verify that the change accomplished what is needed. The test plan for this modification is simply

- Can a show containing more than 20 slides be loaded into the program?

Summary

This chapter covers several ideas relating to the modification of existing applications. Various upgrades to the SlideShow application have been developed to serve as examples of how applications can be modified and to further demonstrate the capabilities and limitations of the Java language.

At this point you should be comfortable with reading and understanding existing Java code. You should be able to create new classes by extending existing classes and adding features. You have covered most of the techniques involved in building Java applications and can create your own intermediate applets and applications. You are ready to move on to building advanced applets and applications.

VII

Advanced
Issues

20

Designing and Implementing Advanced Applets

Java is much more than a tool for animating objects. Whether you are on a corporate intranet or the Internet, you can use Java to solve your real-world business problems today. This chapter takes you step by step through the development of an advanced applet called SpreadSheet.

SpreadSheet is an amazing applet that implements a full-featured spreadsheet in less than 900 lines of code, using many of the advanced features of the Java programming language. Whereas previous chapters focus primarily on programming concepts, this chapter's emphasis is on design concepts. The design of your applet is the key to its power and reusability. Examining the SpreadSheet applet should give you a better understanding of using text and graphics, manipulating text strings, using mathematical formulas, and processing user input.

Project Development and Planning

Creating quick solutions for problems is what most programmers and Web administrators do every day. However, quick solutions usually are not the best ones. If problems occur or you must modify the hack later, far too often you spend more time trying to rework your quick solution than it would have taken to develop the program the right way in the first place. As you begin to develop more advanced applets, you should take the time to develop and plan them carefully.

Planning involves determining the steps necessary to complete the project. After you plot out the steps that will take you through project completion, you can group the steps into phases. The duration of each phase should be relevant to the size and complexity of the applet you are developing. Although you may be able to develop and implement an intermediate applet in a single day, more advanced projects are developed and implemented over a period of days, weeks, or months. Most projects include six phases: requirements, specification/analysis, planning, design, implementation, and testing.

> **Note:** Because some phases are dependent on others, usually you should perform each phase in order. However, you can sometimes combine phases to suit the needs of the project you are developing. For the SpreadSheet applet, I combined the requirements, specification, and planning phases into a general phase called development and planning.

The Requirements Phase

The first step in the *requirements phase* is to develop a list of project needs by examining the purpose, scope, and audience of the project. Then you identify your reasonable expectations for the project. Finally, you translate these needs, goals, and purposes into project requirements.

The *purpose statement* should describe what type of applet you are creating and why you are creating it. The *scope* of the project relates to its size and functionality. The *target user* is the person or group for whom you are developing the applet. Often you will have primary and secondary target users.

> **Tip:** If you have not created a project folder, you should create one now. The project folder, generally kept in both paper and electronic form, will hold everything related to the project. The paper form of the folder can be a three-ring binder or notepad, and the electronic version can reside on your hard drive as a directory.

The purpose, scope, and target user for the `SpreadSheet` applet are defined as follows:

- Purpose: A spreadsheet that can be used interactively on the corporate intranet or the Internet.
- Scope: An advanced applet with many features.
- Target user: Employees in the customer service division and customers who want to perform spreadsheet calculations prior to making buy/sell decisions.

Now make a list of project constraints. Key constraints for most projects include duration, budget, and size. The project's duration is usually constrained by deadlines or milestones you must meet; its budget is usually constrained by the amount of time and money you have to invest in the project; and the size is usually constrained by user requirements, performance issues, and the budget as well. The initial constraints for the `SpreadSheet` applet are

- Project duration: 8–10 days
- Project budget: 25–40 hours
- Project size: Less than 1,000 lines

Now that you know the issues that are driving the development of the project, you can develop a list of needs for the project. Project needs include personnel, computer hardware and software, financial resources, and supplies. For the `SpreadSheet` applet, the list of needs is small:

- A computer with the Java Developer's Kit installed on it
- A Java-capable Web browser
- Disk space on hard drive
- A floppy disk to back up the project
- Daily time investment

The Specification/Analysis Phase

During the *specification/analysis phase*, you determine the inner workings of the applet. You can do this in a traditional manner through specification diagrams such as data-flow diagrams or state-transition diagrams, or you can simply define the necessary objects and the flow of data among them. The methodology you use during this phase will depend largely on the type of applet you are developing, the modeling tools you are using, and the development philosophy at your organization.

For the SpreadSheet applet, I borrowed some of the concepts used in structured analysis. Preliminary modeling in structured analysis is done in the *environmental model*, which helps you define the interfaces between your applet and the user. The environmental model includes three key components:

- Statement of purpose—Provides management with a brief description of the applet.
- Context diagram—Provides an overview of the interaction between the applet and outside entities.
- Event list—Provides a complete list of events that can occur and to which the applet must respond.

The great thing about the environmental model is that its components can be modified to meet the needs of just about any type of project. The first step in using this model is to define a purpose statement for the project. Because the statement of purpose is intended for management, it usually is no more than one paragraph. The brief statement of purpose defined in the "The Requirements Phase" section is expanded on for management use as follows:

- Statement of Purpose: The purpose of the SpreadSheet applet is to help customer service personnel and clients work through complex financial matters that require spreadsheet calculations. The spreadsheet includes advanced features that make it useful for solving formula-based math issues, such as summing rows and columns.

The second step in using the environmental model is to create a context diagram that defines the external entities with which the applet interacts. As with most applets, a Web browser or external viewer acts as an intermediary between the user and the applet. The level of detail you use in the context diagram is up to you. For complex applets, you might want to depict each class object that the main object interacts with on this diagram as well.

Looking Ahead: For the SpreadSheet applet, I chose not to develop a context diagram. For an example of a context diagram, see the section titled "Defining the Necessary Objects" in Chapter 21, "Designing and Implementing Advanced Applications."

Instead of developing a context diagram for the SpreadSheet applet, let's take a preliminary look at the objects needed on the applet's primary frame. Break down the applet frame into regions, such as a title bar, menu bar, display areas, and input areas. You can then break these objects down into their main components.

For the SpreadSheet applet, the main regions on the frame are a title bar, an input area, and a display area made up of the rows and columns of the spreadsheet. These rows and columns are, in turn, made up of individual cells.

To aid the design process, you can create a diagram that depicts the location of these objects on the applet's primary frame. Figure 20.1 shows the preliminary design of the SpreadSheet applet's primary frame.

Figure 20.1.
Sketching the objects for the
SpreadSheet *applet's*
primary frame.

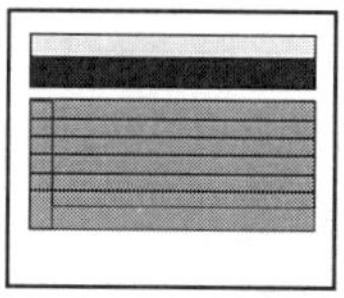

The final step in using the environmental model is to create an event list, a list of events the applet should support. You will use this list to help define objects for the applet. In general, most events that occur in applets are user driven. However, the type of applet you are developing ultimately determines the type of events in your list.

Applets by their nature as Web-published programs have a common set of events related to the core methods of the Applet class. These events are handled explicitly by the applet when defined in the applet or implicitly by the Applet class when not defined in the applet. Common events for applets include the following:

- Initializing the applet
- Starting the applet
- Running applet threads
- Painting the applet
- Updating the applet
- Destroying the applet when finished

Most events for a spreadsheet are initiated when a user enters data, such as a label for a row or column, a mathematical formula, or a value for a cell. Because applets are published on the Web, events can also be triggered by parameters set in the HTML document used to display the applet. Events for the SpreadSheet applet include the following:

1. Initializing the applet
2. Accepting and processing parameter values

3. Starting the applet with default values

4. Running applet threads

5. Performing calculations

6. Creating the spreadsheet

7. Painting the spreadsheet

8. Accepting and process user input

9. Updating the spreadsheet

10. Destroying the applet when finished.

Now that you have completed the environmental model for your applet, you can go on to more detailed modeling. Here's where you translate the event list into the actual data flow between objects. The data flow should include input and output to key objects. The type of data models you use will depend primarily on the type and complexity of the applet you are developing.

The Planning Phase

In the *planning phase*, you take the requirements and specifications developed in the previous phases and determine the steps necessary to complete the project and how long each step will take. Use the resulting schedule to define the necessary milestones, goals, and time allocations to take the project through to completion.

The plans for a small project could be basic—for example, a list of 15 steps with deadlines for completion of each step. In advanced projects, there could be hundreds of project steps, with multiple steps being performed simultaneously, or a handful of steps, with each step being performed one after the other. Some steps would be dependent on other steps, meaning they could not be started until certain aspects of the project were completed. Other steps would not be dependent on any other steps and could be performed at any time during the project's development.

The planning phase can be a reality check for project constraints and requirements. For example, after you plan each step of the project you discover that it will take at least five weeks to complete the project, yet management's deadline for project completion is 30 days. In this case, you may have to renegotiate the deadline, hire additional team members, or eliminate certain time-intensive parts of the project.

Project Design

You design the layout of the project in detail during the *design phase*. Because applets include a common set of objects as well as unique objects, applet design is slightly different from application design. In most applets, the primary frame and associated objects are initialized in the `init()` method and drawn on the frame using the `paint()` method. Before the applet can be used, it must be started using the `start()` method. You can use threads if you use the `run()` method.

When the applet frame must be updated, the `update()` method is usually called. When users move to a different page or otherwise terminate the applet, the applet must be stopped and cleaned out of memory. The `stop()` method is responsible for stopping the applet, and the `destroy()` method is responsible for cleaning up after the applet.

Although most of these common objects can be called implicitly by the browser that displays the applet, you still should determine how these objects will be used and called by your applet. After you have identified the common objects, reexamine the primary frame components and event list developed in the specification phase. Each frame component and event should translate into an object you will need in the finished applet.

These objects can be grouped into object categories, such as functions and user interfaces. The user interface enables users to manipulate the primary frame of the applet. For applets, the primary frame and the user interface are usually created in the `init()` method or by methods that the `init()` method calls. Both the primary frame and the user interface should have attributes that make them easy to use, read, and understand.

As you design the primary frame and user interface in detail, keep the following attributes in mind:

- Initial frame size
- Color of the frame and borders
- Color, size, and font of text on the frame
- Location of the user interface
- Location of the menu bar
- Style of the title bar
- Size of the display area

Also keep in mind the main objects used on frame, which were identified in the specification phase. For the `SpreadSheet` applet, key objects on the primary frame include a title bar, an input area, and a display area. Following the top-down methodology of object-oriented design, you should now create a high-level design for each of these objects.

The `SpreadSheet` applet's title bar object is quite simple. It accepts an input parameter for the font type used to display the title text and displays the title centered on the frame.

The input area enables the user to enter new data for the current cell, which implies that you need a method to determine the current cell. Although the method used to display the input area is not complex, everything that happens after the user enters data into the input area is. At this stage, you should determine the data types the input area accepts and how the applet will determine the data type.

Generally, spreadsheets accept three types of data: labels, values, and formulas. Because the SpreadSheet applet is made for viewing on the Web, it accepts a fourth data type as well: URLs. The SpreadSheet applet determines the data type by a single character that proceeds the input value: Values are identified with the letter v, formulas with the letter f, labels with the letter l, and URLs with the letter u.

You will need objects to process the input. The main object should parse the input values and perform specific actions related to the data type. At this point, you do not have to determine these actions; however, you should note that you will need at least one object to handle each data type.

The most complex objects for data types are those that process formulas. To get a better understanding of how the applet will work, you might want to break down the formula object or at least determine the types of formulas the object will process. The SpreadSheet applet accepts formulas that use addition, subtraction, multiplication, and division. When the applet has finished processing the formula, you will need a method to recalculate values for cells that use formulas.

The next object you should examine is the display area. It contains the rows and columns of the spreadsheet, which are made up of individual cells. You will need a method to create the cells. To determine how many cells to create and ultimately how many rows and columns the spreadsheet should have, either initialize the spreadsheet to a default size or let the spreadsheet size be updated as needed.

One way to allow the spreadsheet to be updated is to accept parameter values. The SpreadSheet applet accepts parameters for font size, base font type, number of columns, number of rows, and initial values for cells. Because the user can update data on the spreadsheet, you also need a method to update the cells. Each of these parameter values will need an associated container that holds its values in the applet.

Now that you have identified the major objects used in the applet, you can create a list of these objects. As you implement each object in the next phase, you can check the object off the list to be sure that you account for all the major functions of the applet. Here's the list:

- `init()` method
- `paint()` method
- `start()` method
- `run()` method
- `stop()` method
- `destroy()` method
- Title bar
- Input area
- Display area
- Rows and columns

- Cells
- Method to determine the current cell
- Method to process data types
- Method to process formulas
- Method to recalculate values for cells
- Method to create and display the cells
- Method to update the cells

After determining most of the objects for the applet, you can go on to more detailed design. Here you should work out the interaction between objects and determine the arguments that objects will accept and pass. When you are comfortable with the design of the applet and can visualize the flow of data from object to object, you can begin the implementation phase. The next section provides a detailed look at how the SpreadSheet applet is transformed from a concept to a completed applet.

The Implementation Phase

The implementation phase is when you actually create the project you have developed. This phase is often the longest and usually involves teams of programmers who implement and integrate the source code. Usually, each programming team is responsible for creating a specific set of objects with related functionality, such as the user interface or file I/O. After these object sets are created, they are integrated into the applet.

In implementing the applet, start with the top-level objects, which usually relate to the user interface and the display, and work toward the lowest-level objects, which usually perform the key functions that the applet requires. The sections that follow demonstrate how to build the SpreadSheet applet.

Containers for the Objects Used in the **SpreadSheet** Applet

Containers create instances of the objects identified in the design phase so the objects can be used throughout the applet. The containers used in most applets include the low-level objects used as placeholders for parameter values. To create a container, you use instance variables. Most instance variable declarations follow the main class declaration.

The containers used in the SpreadSheet applet are shown in Listing 20.1. As you can see, there is a container for each of the parameter values identified in the design phase. Other containers hold values for key objects in the spreadsheet. Some of these objects define spreadsheet attributes with initial values.

Listing 20.1. Initial containers for the **SpreadSheet** applet.

```
public class SpreadSheet extends Applet {
    //container to hold the parameter value for title text
    String            title;
    //container to hold the parameter value for base font
    String            bfont;
    //container to hold the parameter value for title font
    String            tfont;
    //container for the inputfont object
    Font              inputFont;
    //container for the title font object
    Font              titleFont;
    //container for the cell color object
    Color             cellColor;
    //container for the input area's color object
    Color             inputColor;
    //container for the parameter value for font size
    int               fontSize;
    //container for the cell width object
    int               cellWidth;
    //container for the cell height object
    int               cellHeight;
    //container for the title height object
    int               titleHeight;
    //container for the row label width object
    int               rowLabelWidth;
    //container for the status object
    boolean           isStopped = false;
    //container for the update object
    boolean           fullUpdate = true;
    //container for the rows object
    int               rows;
    //container for the columns object
    int               columns;
    //container for the current key object
    int               currentKey = -1;
    //container for the selected row object
    int               selectedRow = -1;
    //container for the selected column object
    int               selectedColumn = -1;
    //container for the input area
    SpreadSheetInput  inputArea;
    //container for the individual cells
    Cell              cells[][];
    //container for the current cell
    Cell              current = null;
```

Initializing the Primary Frame

Before you implement the primary frame of an applet, you should carefully consider the type and style of the document with which the applet will be used. If you do not already have an HTML document in which you want to display the applet, you should design one. Depending on the type and style of the HTML document, you might want to make some changes to the design of your applet's interface. You also might want to place additional restrictions on the size of the applet.

For example, if your applet will be used on the corporate home page, you might want to mesh the style of the applet with the existing style of the home page or modify the style of both the applet and the home page so they work well together. Most conflicts between the home page style and the applet style relate to

- The colors used in the applet
- The display size of the applet in pixels
- The file size of the applet in kilobytes
- The appropriateness of the applet for the page

As you add features to the applet's frame window, keep these concepts in mind. Key features for the SpreadSheet applet's primary frame, identified in the design phase, are a title bar, an input area, and a display area. Earlier, you should have also identified key attributes for the primary frame, such as the initial frame size, the color of the frame and borders, and the style of the title bar.

Figure 20.2 shows how the SpreadSheet applet looks when completed and displayed in an HTML document. By the end of this chapter, you will be able to create this document.

The SpreadSheet applet's primary frame is initialized in the init() method. Because the SpreadSheet applet's init() method is fairly complex, it is broken down here into a series of steps.

Figure 20.2.
The main screen of the SpreadSheet *applet.*

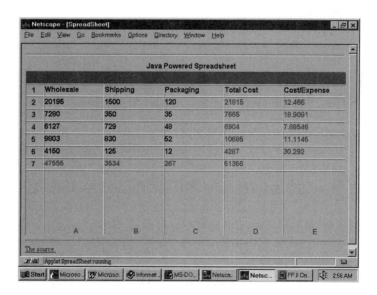

Step 1: Initializing Values

The first step is to initialize containers for the necessary objects. As shown in Listing 20.2, two local containers are used for the method. The first container, rs, is a multipurpose read string holding parameter values. The second, fs, is a string used to hold the value for the font size parameter. The init() method is synchronized to prevent more than one thread from executing the method at the same time. In this way, the entire method is locked when it is being used by a thread.

After initializing the containers, initialize the color of active cells to white and set the color of the input area to blue. You can change this color value to anything you like. For example, to change the color value to yellow, use the following:

```
cellColor = Color.yellow;
```

Tip: Although you could use a parameter value to set the color for the active cell and the input area, keep in mind that Color is an object. You would have to convert the string you obtain using the getParameter() method to an instance of the Color object.

Listing 20.2. The first section of the init() method.

```
public synchronized void init() {
    String rs;
    String fs;

    cellColor = Color.white;
    inputColor = new Color(100, 100, 225);
```

Step 2: Using Parameter Values

The getParameter() method is used to read values for key attributes of the spreadsheet set in the <PARAM> tag of the applet's HTML document. If no parameter value is set by the publisher, a default value is used. Similarly, your applets should set default values for all input parameters.

As shown in Listing 20.3, the first parameter the SpreadSheet applet checks for is the font size. If no font size is set in the <PARAM> tag, it is set to 10. If the <PARAM> tag contains a setting for the font size, the string read with the getParameter() method is converted to an integer using the Integer.parseInt() method, which you will use to convert all parameter values that you plan to manipulate as numbers.

The fontSize parameter value is used to set key spreadsheet attributes proportional to the font size. Keeping the size of objects used in the spreadsheet proportional to the current font size is essential to the readability and usability of the applet. The current font size affects every major display aspect of the spreadsheet, including the height and width of cells in the spreadsheet, the width of row labels, the height of the area used for titles, the font size used for titles, the position of the title, the position of row and column headers, the size of the input area, and the position of text in the input area.

For this reason, throughout the SpreadSheet applet, you will see the size of objects set proportional to the fontSize object. You can use this technique in your applets to keep the display consistent with the current font size.

The next parameter values the SpreadSheet applet checks for are the base font type and the title font type. Using these values, initialize the inputFont and titleFont objects. The default value for both font types, Courier, is used when no parameter value is set in the <PARAM> tag. When selecting a default font type, you should use one that is widely available on most systems, such as Courier, Helvetica, Times Roman, or System.

The applet also checks for a title for the spreadsheet. If no parameter value is set, the title is set to Spreadsheet.

The final parameter values the applet checks for are the number of rows and columns to be used in the spreadsheet. These must be integer values, so the string read using the getParameter() method is converted to an integer using the parseInt() method.

Listing 20.3. Getting and using parameter values.

```
    fs = getParameter("fontsize");
    if (fs == null) {
        fontSize = 10;
    } else {
        fontSize = Integer.parseInt(fs);
    }

cellWidth = fontSize * 10;
cellHeight = fontSize * 2;
titleHeight = fontSize * 2;
rowLabelWidth = fontSize * 3;
    bfont = getParameter("basefont");
    if (bfont == null) {
        bfont = "Courier";
    }
    inputFont = new Font(bfont, Font.PLAIN, fontSize);

    tfont = getParameter("titlefont");
    if (tfont == null) {
        tfont = "Courier";
    }
    titleFont = new Font(tfont, Font.BOLD, (fontSize + 2));

    title = getParameter("title");
    if (title == null) {
        title = "Spreadsheet";
    }
    rs = getParameter("rows");
    if (rs == null) {
```

continues

Listing 20.3. continued

```
        rows = 9;
    } else {
        rows = Integer.parseInt(rs);
    }
    rs = getParameter("columns");
    if (rs == null) {
        columns = 5;
    } else {
        columns = Integer.parseInt(rs);
    }
```

Step 3: Initializing the Spreadsheet

Initializing an object as complex as a spreadsheet requires careful forethought, especially when its size can be dynamically updated using parameter values. To reduce the difficulty of this task, you could set the spreadsheet to a predetermined size, such as nine rows and five columns. Then, after you understand the way the spreadsheet is built, you could modify the code to allow the size of the spreadsheet to be updated as needed.

To create the spreadsheet, determine the number of cells needed. Then initialize the cells to default values and attributes. One way to handle this is to build an array of an array. The first array holds the row index. The second array holds the column index. Together, these indexes point to a particular cell in the spreadsheet.

To make it easier to set initial values for each cell using parameter values, the spreadsheet applet assumes each column is ordered alphabetically and each row is ordered numerically. Thus, the index value a1 points to the cell in column 1, row 1, and the value b4 points to the cell in column 2, row 4. Because Java integers begin with 0, you might be wondering what happened to values for column 0. All cells in column 0 are used to hold values for row headers. Similarly, all cells in row 0 are used to hold values for column headers. This way, when you create a spreadsheet with the parameter value for rows set to 3 and columns set to 4, you get a spreadsheet with 3 rows and 4 columns.

As shown in Listing 20.4, reading the parameter values for cells from the HTML document is accomplished with two conditional loops. The first loop continues until the row count is reached, and the second continues until the column count is reached. Within the second loop, the index values for the row and column are used to build an array of arrays.

Each new cell is created as an instance of the Cell object. Included in each new cell are parameters for the background color of the cell; the color of text in the cell; the width and height of the cell; an array containing the cell's index, such as a1 or b4; and a value associated with the cell as read by the getParameter() method. Following the logic of the cell-building loops, the following parameter values could be used:

```
<PARAM NAME=a1 value="1Wholesale">
<PARAM NAME=a2 value="v20195">
<PARAM NAME=a3 value="v7280">
<PARAM NAME=a4 value="v6127">
<PARAM NAME=a5 value="v9803">
<PARAM NAME=a6 value="v4150">
<PARAM NAME=a7 value="fA2+(A3/A4)">
```

If you do not set a value for a particular cell in the spreadsheet, the setUnparsedValue() method is called to build a value for the Cell object. Just as the setUnparsedValue() method is called to add default values for undefined cells, the cell values provided to the Cell object are parsed as well. This parsing takes place in the Cell class.

Listing 20.4. Initializing the spreadsheet.

```
cells = new Cell[rows][columns];
char l[] = new char[1];
for (int i=0; i < rows; i++) {
    for (int j=0; j < columns; j++) {

        cells[i][j] = new Cell(this,
                               Color.lightGray,
                               Color.black,
                               cellColor,
                               cellWidth - (fontSize/4),
                               cellHeight - (fontSize/4));
        l[0] = (char)((int)'a' + j);
        rs = getParameter("" + new String(l) + (i+1));
        if (rs != null) {
            cells[i][j].setUnparsedValue(rs);
        }
    }
}
}
```

Step 4: Sizing the Spreadsheet

Sizing a complex structure on the applet frame is a difficult task. You do not want your key objects to be larger than the frame or placed off the frame and thus off the screen. However, you do want the objects to fill the frame if possible. The best way to build the structure within your frame is to base it on the actual dimensions of the frame by creating a dimension object with the current size values and then allocating this area proportionally to each object as necessary.

Although this is the best way to size the objects, you do not always have this luxury and may have to size objects on the basis of some other constraint. The font size is a constraint in the SpreadSheet applet simply because you must be able to view the data in the cells no matter the font size.

The inputArea for the SpreadSheet applet is created as a new instance of the SpreadSheetInput object. The size of the inputArea is based on the current width minus two pixels, and its height is based on the current height minus two pixels.

The spreadsheet is then resized on the basis of the width and height of all component objects of the spreadsheet. As noted earlier, these objects are sized proportional to the fontSize object. The code used to initialize the input area and size the spreadsheet is shown in Listing 20.5.

Listing 20.5. Sizing the spreadsheet.

```
    Dimension d = size();
    inputArea = new SpreadSheetInput(null, this, d.width - 2, cellHeight - 2,
                                 inputColor, Color.white);
    resize(columns * cellWidth + rowLabelWidth,
          ((rows + 1) * cellHeight) + cellHeight + titleHeight);
}
```

Determining the State of the Applet

After initializing the applet, implement the other common applet methods if necessary. Usually, your applet does not have to explicitly call the start(), stop(), and destroy() methods. You can better determine the behavior of your applet if you define these methods.

The SpreadSheet applet uses the start() and stop() methods to determine the state of the applet. When the applet is active, the boolean value isStopped is set to false; when inactive, the boolean value isStopped is set to true. The value isStopped is used later in the applet to stop it from repainting itself before exiting.

The destroy method is used to clean up after you halt the applet. If you have processes that could be active even after the applet exits, terminate them in your applet's destroy() method. Examples include any connections you made to remote hosts or documents you were accessing.

The start(), stop(), and destroy() methods for the SpreadSheet applet are shown in Listing 20.6.

Listing 20.6. The state of the applet.

```
public void start() {
    isStopped = false;
}
public void stop() {
    isStopped = true;
}
public void destroy() {
    for (int i=0; i < rows; i++) {
        for (int j=0; j < columns; j++) {
            if (cells[i][j].type == Cell.URL) {
                cells[i][j].updaterThread.stop();
            }
        }
    }
}
```

Running Applet Threads

The task of running applet threads is handled by the `run()` method. As shown in Listing 20.7, the `run()` method for the `SpreadSheet` applet is fairly lengthy and is handled in a separate class called `CellUpdater` that extends the `Thread` class. By extending the `Thread` class, the applet can use Java's multithreading capabilities to accept input from the token stream and display the data in the spreadsheet. This allows cells of the spreadsheet to be dynamically updated based on data coming from an input stream.

The function of the `while` loop in the `CellUpdater` class is to read string tokens passed from the input stream. As long as there are tokens to read, the `run()` method continues through the `while` loop. This causes the applet to call the `setTransientValue` method, which in turn sets a transient value flag. Before continuing the loop, the `repaint()` method is called to update the frame. When there are no more tokens to read, the `dataStream` object is closed and the `run()` method waits for the next token to be passed.

To use this threading feature of the `SpreadSheet` applet, define a cell as a URL type and specify the URL path to the document you want to read on the input stream.

Listing 20.7. Running and updating the applet.

```
class CellUpdater extends Thread {

    Cell          target;
    InputStream dataStream = null;
    StreamTokenizer tokenStream;

    public CellUpdater(Cell c) {
        super("cell updater");
        target = c;
    }

    public void run() {

        try {
            dataStream = new URL(target.app.getDocumentBase(),
                            target.getValueString()).openStream();
            tokenStream = new StreamTokenizer(dataStream);
            tokenStream.eolIsSignificant(false);

            while (true) {
                switch (tokenStream.nextToken()) {
                case tokenStream.TT_EOF:
                    dataStream.close();
                    return;
                default:
                    break;
                case tokenStream.TT_NUMBER:
                    target.setTransientValue((float)tokenStream.nval);
```

continues

Listing 20.7. continued

```
                    if (! target.app.isStopped && ! target.paused) {
                        target.app.repaint();
                    }
                    break;
                }
                try {
                    Thread.sleep(2000);
                } catch (InterruptedException e) {
                    break;
                }
            }
        } catch (IOException e) {
            return;
        }
    }
}
```

Painting the Frame

After you have initialized the spreadsheet, you must display it. This is usually done by means of the `paint()` method, which draws all the objects added during the initialization phase. As discussed in "Step 4: Sizing the Spreadsheet," the objects should be sized according to the dimensions of the frame or a key constraint such as the font size. You should also paint the objects in the order they are to be added to the frame.

The `SpreadSheet` applet uses many interesting techniques to place objects precisely on the frame. As shown in Listing 20.8, centering the title horizontally in the title area involves five steps:

1. Obtaining the dimension of the frame
2. Determining the pixel length of the title on the basis of the current font
3. Subtracting the length of the title from the width of the frame
4. Adding in a factor that accounts for differences in font size
5. Dividing the result by 2

The value you obtain by doing this is the x coordinate for the beginning of the title. You also need a y coordinate for the title. Because the height of the title area is relative to the font size used, the font size is used to help determine this coordinate.

Next, the `paint()` method draws the input area by simply filling a rectangle with a color based on the value of the `inputColor` object. The starting location for the upper-left corner of the input area is determined by moving vertically down the height of one cell. The width of the input area is set to the width of the frame, and the height is set to the height of one cell.

Finally, the paint() method draws the individual cells. To create them, use a series of draws. The first adds the horizontal lines for rows using the draw3DRect method of the Graphics class. As the 3D lines are drawn to the frame, blue numerals representing the row numbers are added as appropriate. The second draw adds the vertical lines for columns, again using the draw3DRect method. As the 3D lines are drawn to the frame, red letters representing the column letters are added as appropriate. Finally, data is added to the cells by painting the values associated with a cell precisely within the rectangles created by the previous draws.

The last section of code in the paint() method, although only a few lines, is important to the spreadsheet. The line of code using the draw3DRect() method draws a 3D line above the input area and on the left side of the frame. The next-to-last line calls the paint() method of the inputArea class, which ensures that the data associated with the currently selected cell is painted to the input area.

Listing 20.8. Painting the frame.

```
public synchronized void paint(Graphics g) {

    int i, j;
    int cx, cy;
    char l[] = new char[1];

    Dimension d = size();

    //draws the title on the frame
    g.setFont(titleFont);
    i = g.getFontMetrics().stringWidth(title);
    g.drawString((title == null) ? "Spreadsheet" : title,
                 (d.width - i + (fontSize*3/2)) / 2, (fontSize*3/2));

    //draws the input area on the frame
    g.setColor(inputColor);
    g.fillRect(0, cellHeight, d.width, cellHeight);

    //draws the lines for rows using 3d effect
    //adds row numbering in blue
    g.setFont(titleFont);
    for (i=0; i < rows+1; i++) {
        cy = (i+2) * cellHeight;
        g.setColor(getBackground());
        g.draw3DRect(0, cy, d.width, 2, true);
        if (i < rows) {
            g.setColor(Color.blue);
            g.drawString("" + (i+1), fontSize, cy + (fontSize *3/2));
        }
    }

    //draws the lines for columns using 3d effect
    //adds column alphas in red
    g.setColor(Color.red);
    for (i=0; i < columns; i++) {
        cx = i * cellWidth;
```

continues

Listing 20.8. continued

```
        g.setColor(getBackground());
        g.draw3DRect(cx + rowLabelWidth,
                    2 * cellHeight, 1, d.height, true);
        if (i < columns) {
            g.setColor(Color.red);
            l[0] = (char)((int)'A' + i);
            g.drawString(new String(l),
                        cx + rowLabelWidth + (cellWidth / 2),
                        d.height - 3);
        }
    }

    //paints the cell data
    for (i=0; i < rows; i++) {
        for (j=0; j < columns; j++) {
            cx = (j * cellWidth) + 2 + rowLabelWidth;
            cy = ((i+1) * cellHeight) + 2 + titleHeight;
            if (cells[i][j] != null) {
                cells[i][j].paint(g, cx, cy);
            }
        }
    }

    g.setColor(getBackground());
    //draws a 3d line for the input area and to the left side of the frame
    g.draw3DRect(0, titleHeight, d.width, d.height - titleHeight, false);
    //paints the data of the current cell to the input area
    inputArea.paint(g, 1, titleHeight + 1);
}
```

Updating the Applet's Frame

When changes occur in the applet, you must repaint the applet's frame using the `repaint()` method of the `Applet` class. If you recall earlier discussions on repainting the applet's frame, you probably know that the `repaint()` method calls the `update()` method of the `Applet` class, which in turn clears the screen and calls the `paint()` method. The `paint` method then draws in the applet's frame.

Clearing and then drawing the frame produces a noticeable flicker. To reduce it, usually it's best to override the `update()` method of the `Applet` class. You do this by defining an `update()` method in your applet that does not clear the frame at all before painting it and, if possible, clears only the parts of the screen that have changed.

Listing 20.9 shows the `update()` method for the `SpreadSheet` applet. This method uses a boolean value called `full update` to determine whether to repaint the whole frame or just a portion of it. When only a portion must be repainted, the appropriate section is redrawn. The partial update occurs when the user selects a cell and the applet places the data associated with the cell in the input area and redraws the cell with a white background. When the entire applet frame needs to be updated, the `update()` method calls the `paint()` method directly without clearing the frame first.

Listing 20.9. Updating the frame.

```java
public void update(Graphics g) {
    if (! fullUpdate) {
        int cx, cy;

        g.setFont(titleFont);
        for (int i=0; i < rows; i++) {
            for (int j=0; j < columns; j++) {
                if (cells[i][j].needRedisplay) {
                    cx = (j * cellWidth) + (fontSize*2) + rowLabelWidth;
                    cy = ((i+1) * cellHeight) + (fontSize*2) + titleHeight;
                    cells[i][j].paint(g, cx, cy);
                }
            }
        }
    } else {
        paint(g);
        fullUpdate = false;
    }
}
```

Handling Events in the Applet

Updates to the SpreadSheet applet are driven by the occurrence of user events, such as keypresses and mouse button clicks. As discussed in previous chapters, events are usually handled with either the action() method or the handleEvent() method. The action() method of the Components class is the preferred way to handle a limited number of events. The handleEvent method of the Event class is the preferred way to handle multiple or complex series of events.

When an applet has only a few possible events that deal with the mouse or keypresses, you can call more direct methods that eliminate the necessity of nested if or case statements to check event type. These methods, like the action() method, are members of the Component class. Table 20.1 lists these events.

Table 20.1. Direct event handling with Component class methods.

Method	Description	Called with Values
keyDown()	Called if a key is pressed	keyDown(Event evt, int x)
keyUp()	Called if a key is released	keyUp(Event evt, int x)
mouseDown()	Called if the mouse button is down	mouseDown(Event evt, int x, int y)
mouseDrag()	Called if the mouse moves while a button is pressed	mouseDrag(Event evt, int x, int y)

continues

Table 20.1. continued

Method	Description	Called with Values
mouseEnter()	Called when the mouse enters the component	mouseEnter(Event evt, int x, int y)
mouseExit()	Called when the mouse exits the component	mouseExit(Event evt, int x, int y)
mouseMove()	Called if the mouse moves while no buttons are pressed	mouseMove(Event evt, int x, int y)
mouseUp()	Called if the mouse button is up	mouseUp(Event evt, int x, int y)

The SpreadSheet applet uses two of these direct methods to check for events: mouseDown and keyDown. The handling of these events is shown in Listing 20.10.

When a user moves the mouse pointer over a cell and selects it by clicking the mouse button, the applet determines the exact cell the user selected based on the position of the mouse in the spreadsheet. As you can see from Listing 20.10, finding the selected cell is a lot of work.

The first conditional loop ensures that the y coordinate of the mouse pointer is in a valid section of the spreadsheet. If the y coordinate is less than the combined height of the title and input area, the selected row is set to -1. The nested if loop sets the value for the current cell to null when the user clicks the mouse button when the pointer is in the title area and the deselect method is called.

The second conditional loop ensures that the x coordinate of the mouse pointer is in a valid section of the spreadsheet. If the x coordinate is less than the width of the row label, the selected row is set to -1. The nested if loop sets the value for the current cell to null when the user clicks the mouse button when the pointer is in the row label area and the deselect method is called.

Next, the method determines the column/row coordinate for the selected cell. If the selected cell is greater than the number of rows or columns in the spreadsheet, the value for the current cell is set to null and the deselect method is called. If the column/row coordinate for the selected cell is valid, the value of the selected cell is displayed in the input area and the select() method is called to paint the current cell with a white background.

The final event checked for is a keypress. As long as a valid cell is selected, any character key you press on the keyboard is displayed in the input area. When you press Enter and a valid cell is selected, the value from the input area replaces the value of the current cell and the entire spreadsheet is updated. This is all handled by setting fullUpdate to true and calling the keyDown() method, which actually does the work of updating the spreadsheet as necessary.

You can use similar techniques to determine the selected object in your applets as well. The key is to narrow the valid range by eliminating areas of the frame that cannot be selected, such as the title bar, rows with header labels, and columns with header labels. When you narrow the selection area, you can determine the specific object the user selected.

Listing 20.10. Handling applet events.

```
public boolean mouseDown(Event evt, int x, int y) {
      Cell cell;

      //ensures the y coordinate of the mouse pointer
      //is not in the title/input area
      if (y < (titleHeight + cellHeight)) {
         selectedRow = -1;
         if (y <= titleHeight && current != null) {
            current.deselect();
            current = null;
         }
         return true;
      }
      //ensures the x coordinate of the mouse pointer
      //is not in the row label area
      if (x < rowLabelWidth) {
         selectedRow = -1;
         if (current != null) {
            current.deselect();
            current = null;
         }
         return true;
      }

      //determines the row of the selected cell
      selectedRow = ((y - cellHeight - titleHeight) / cellHeight);

      //determines the column of the selected cell
      selectedColumn = (x - rowLabelWidth) / cellWidth;

      //ensures the row and column coordinate is valid
      if (selectedRow >= rows ||
         selectedColumn >= columns) {
         selectedRow = -1;
         if (current != null) {
            current.deselect();
            current = null;
         }
      }

      //if the row-column coordinate is valid place the selected cell's value
      //in the input area
      } else {
         cell = cells[selectedRow][selectedColumn];
         inputArea.setText(new String(cell.getPrintString()));
         if (current != null) {
            current.deselect();
         }
```

continues

Listing 20.10. continued

```
            current = cell;
            current.select();
            requestFocus();
            fullUpdate = true;
            repaint();
        }
        return true;
    }

    //determine if a key is pressed
    public boolean keyDown(Event evt, int key) {
        fullUpdate=true;
        inputArea.keyDown(key);
        return true;
    }
}
```

Updating the Current Cell's Value

User events drive changes in the spreadsheet. When a cell's value is changed, the spreadsheet must be updated to reflect this. As noted in the "Handling Events in the Applet" section in this chapter, the keyDown() method is called to handle the update. One of the high-level objects keyDown calls is the setCurrentValue() method of the SpreadSheet class, which takes the current value of the input area and assigns it to the active cell.

Two versions of the setCurrentValue() method are defined in the applet: The first sets values for floating-point numbers, and the second sets values for strings. This is a good example of overloading a method to handle multiple types of input. Listing 20.11 shows the code for updating the current cell's value.

Listing 20.11. Updating the current cell's value.

```
public void setCurrentValue(float val) {
    if (selectedRow == -1 || selectedColumn == -1) {
        return;
    }
    cells[selectedRow][selectedColumn].setValue(val);
    repaint();
}

public void setCurrentValue(int type, String val) {
    if (selectedRow == -1 || selectedColumn == -1) {
        return;
    }
    cells[selectedRow][selectedColumn].setValue(type, val);
    repaint();
}
```

Handling Formulas

The SpreadSheet class is responsible for most of the high-level functions of the applet. To complete this class, you need methods for calculating formulas and evaluating formulas.

Before the spreadsheet is displayed, the recalculate() method is called to convert any formulas the spreadsheet may have to numeric values. Without a call to this method, the spreadsheet makes no calculations, and the formula is displayed in the cell instead of the numeric value. To ensure that both the numeric value and the formula are available to the user, the SpreadSheet applet stores the formula and the value in separate buffers.

As you can see from Listing 20.12, the recalculate() method goes through each cell in the spreadsheet checking for the cell type FORMULA. If a cell contains a formula, the formula is evaluated using the evaluateFormula() method. The values returned from the evaluateFormula() method are passed to the setRawValue() method.

Listing 20.12. Calculating formula values.

```
public void recalculate() {
    int     i,j;

    //System.out.println("SpreadSheet.recalculate");
    for (i=0; i < rows; i++) {
        for (j=0; j < columns; j++) {
            if (cells[i][j] != null && cells[i][j].type == Cell.FORMULA) {
                cells[i][j].setRawValue(evaluateFormula(cells[i][j].parseRoot));
                cells[i][j].needRedisplay = true;
            }
        }
    }
    repaint();
}
```

The SpreadSheet applet has the capability to parse formulas with basic math functions like addition, subtraction, multiplication, and division by examining formula nodes. Nodes are defined in the applet as class-level objects that have a left value, an operand, and a right value.

The evaluateFormula() method shown in Listing 20.13 examines formula nodes looking for operands, values, and cell references. Many computer science majors will recognize the simple algorithm used to evaluate spreadsheet formulas as an *expression tree*. A simple recursive process is then used to evaluate the nodes of the tree. Values associated with these node components are returned to the setRawValue() method, which displays the numeric value of the cell as a string.

Tip: Recursion on trees is one of the basic algorithms in the programmer's toolkit. If this is the first time you have encountered an expression tree algorithm, take the time to learn how this is done. Start by examining the `evaluateFormula()` method and then examine the `parseFormula()` and `parseValue()` methods of the `Cell` class. You may be surprised at the number of uses for this algorithm.

Listing 20.13. Evaluating formulas.

```
public float evaluateFormula(Node n) {
    float    val = 0.0f;

    if (n == null) {
        return val;
    }
    switch (n.type) {
      case Node.OP:
        val = evaluateFormula(n.left);
        switch (n.op) {
          case '+':
            val += evaluateFormula(n.right);
            break;
          case '*':
            val *= evaluateFormula(n.right);
            break;
          case '-':
            val -= evaluateFormula(n.right);
            break;
          case '/':
            val /= evaluateFormula(n.right);
            break;
        }
        break;
      case Node.VALUE:
        return n.value;
      case Node.CELL:
        if (n == null) {
        } else {
            if (cells[n.row][n.column] == null) {
            } else {
                return cells[n.row][n.column].value;
            }
        }
    }

    return val;
}
```

Creating Cells

The next class-level object in the spreadsheet is the `Cell` object, which is responsible for maintaining the attributes of a cell. Listing 20.14 shows the declarations for the `Cell` object's containers.

When new instances of the `Cell` class are created during the initialization of the frame, the `Cell` method is called and the initial attributes for the cell are set. These attributes include the background color, the foreground color, the color to use when the cell is selected, and the width and height of the cell. Other attributes of the cell are set to default values or are based on the value associated with each cell as read by the `getParameter()` method.

Listing 20.14. Containers for the `Cell` object.

```
class Cell {

    public static final int VALUE = 0;    //initializes the VALUE container
    public static final int LABEL = 1;    //initializes the LABEL container
    public static final int URL   = 2;    //initializes the URL container
    public static final int FORMULA = 3;   //initializes the FORMULA container
    Node        parseRoot;   //sets the node for the cell
    boolean     needRedisplay;   //used to determine the need for redisplay
    boolean selected = false;    //used to determine whether cell is selected
    boolean transientValue = false;   //tracks need to set transient value
    public int  type = Cell.VALUE;    //sets the cell type
    String      valueString = "";    //initializes the value string
    String      printString = "v";   //initiliazes the print string
    float       value;   //container for a float called value
    Color       bgColor;   //container for the background color
    Color       fgColor;   //container for the foreground color
    Color       highlightColor;   //container for cell color when selected
    int         width;   //container for the width of the cell
    int         height;    //container for the height of the cell
    SpreadSheet app;     //container for the SpreadSheet object
    CellUpdater updaterThread;    //container for the CellUpdater object
    boolean     paused = false;     //used to determine if paused
```

Preparing Cells for Display

After the containers for `Cell` objects are initialized, a series of methods, shown in Listing 20.15, prepare the cell for display.

The `Cell()` method is called with values for the key attributes of the cell; it then associates these values with the `Cell` object. All cells of the spreadsheet must have a type, `valueString`, and `printString` associated with them. The first character of the value read by the `getParameter()` method character is used to set the cell type. The `valueString` excludes the first character and is used in calculations. The `printString` contains the value of the cell as it should be displayed to the input area when the cell is selected.

The setUnparsedValue() method sets the cell type. If the first character is a v, the type is set to VALUE; if it is an l, the type is set to LABEL; if it is a u, the type is set to URL; and if it is an f, the type is set to FORMULA.

setValue() is an overloaded method that builds the valueString and printString objects of all cells. The first version of the method accepts string values and, depending on cell type, calls associated methods. The second version accepts floating-point values and is called only when the cell type is VALUE. This overloaded method in turn calls the setRawValue() method that converts the floating-point value it is passed to a String object.

The setTransientValue() method sets a transient value associated with the cell. This value is set only when a number is passed through the token stream.

Listing 20.15. Preparing the cell for display.

```java
//sets attributes for the Cell objects as passed
public Cell(SpreadSheet app,
            Color bgColor,
            Color fgColor,
            Color highlightColor,
            int width,
            int height) {
    this.app = app;
    this.bgColor = bgColor;
    this.fgColor = fgColor;
    this.highlightColor = highlightColor;
     this.width = width;
       this.height = height;
       needRedisplay = true;
   }

    //sets the valueString by converting the numeric value of the cell to a string
    public void setRawValue(float f) {
        valueString = Float.toString(f);
        value = f;
    }

    //sets the cell type for values, formulas, labels and URLs
    public void setUnparsedValue(String s) {
        switch (s.charAt(0)) {
          case 'v':
            setValue(Cell.VALUE, s.substring(1));
            break;
          case 'f':
            setValue(Cell.FORMULA, s.substring(1));
            break;
          case 'l':
            setValue(Cell.LABEL, s.substring(1));
            break;
          case 'u':
            setValue(Cell.URL, s.substring(1));
            break;
        }
    }
}
```

```
//sets the printString by prepending a type indicator to the valueString
public void setValue(float f) {
    setRawValue(f);
    printString = "v" + valueString;
    type = Cell.VALUE;
    paused = false;
    app.recalculate();
    needRedisplay = true;
}

//sets the printString by prepending a type indicator to the valueString
public void setValue(int type, String s) {

    paused = false;
    if (this.type == Cell.URL) {
        updaterThread.stop();
        updaterThread = null;
    }

    valueString = new String(s);
    this.type = type;
    needRedisplay = true;
    switch (type) {
      case Cell.VALUE:
        setValue(Float.valueOf(s).floatValue());
        break;
      case Cell.LABEL:
        printString = "l" + valueString;
        break;
      case Cell.URL:
        printString = "u" + valueString;
        updaterThread = new CellUpdater(this);
        updaterThread.start();
        break;
      case Cell.FORMULA:
        parseFormula(valueString, parseRoot = new Node());
        printString = "f" + valueString;
        break;
    }
    app.recalculate();
}

//sets a transient value flag
public void setTransientValue(float f) {
    transientValue = true;
    value = f;
    needRedisplay = true;
    app.recalculate();
}
```

Utility Methods

Four utility methods, shown in Listing 20.16, handle low-level tasks for Cell objects: The getPrintString()method returns the value of the printString associated with the cell; the getValueString()method returns the value of the valueString associated with the cell; the select()method sets flags to highlight the cell when the frame is next painted; and the deselect() method sets flags to reset the cell's background to its original color when the frame is next painted.

Listing 20.16. Utility methods of the Cell class.

```
public String getPrintString() {
    return printString;
}
public String getValueString() {
    return valueString;
}
public void select() {
    selected = true;
    paused = true;
}
public void deselect() {
    selected = false;
    paused = false;
    needRedisplay = true;
}
```

Parsing Formulas

Parsing formulas associated with a cell is a difficult task handled by two methods: parseFormula and parseValue. These two methods take cell formulas apart piece by piece by examining formula nodes. As you examine Listing 20.17, study the algorithm that builds and dissects the nodes. Recall that modes are defined in the applet as class-level objects that have a left value, an operand, and a right value. (See the section "Handling Formulas" for a listing of valid operands and how they are used.)

The values associated with a node can be either implicit or explicit. Explicit node values are numbers that you want to add, multiply, divide, or subtract. Implicit values are numbers associated with a particular cell. Reference implicit values in formulas using the column/row coordinate of the cell.

A node that has only a left value for it is still valid. Using these concepts of nodes, the basic syntax for formulas is

```
value
value operand value
```

where each instance of *value* can be an actual value or a reference to a particular cell of the spreadsheet, such as

```
A2 * 4
```

or

```
A2 + B2
```

To allow for more complex formulas, the parseFormula and parseValue methods allow you to define subformulas for the right-hand value of the original node using parentheses. Because subformulas are treated as nodes, they also can have a left value, an operand, and a right value. You can continue to nest subformulas as long as you follow the concept of nodes. Using subformulas, you can create formulas with the following syntax:

```
value operand (value operand value)
value operand (value operand (value operand value))
```

You can continue to nest subformulas as long as you follow the basic node structure of value oper-
and value. As discussed earlier, the algorithm that makes this work is a recursive procedure on an expression tree.

Listing 20.17. Parsing formulas.

```
/**
 * Parse a spreadsheet formula. The syntax is defined as:
 *
 * formula -> value
 * formula -> value op value
 * value -> '(' formula ')'
 * value -> cell
 * value -> <number>
 * op -> '+' | '*' | '/' | '-'
 * cell -> <letter><number>
 */
public String parseFormula(String formula, Node node) {
    String subformula;
    String restFormula;
    float value;
    int length = formula.length();
    Node left;
    Node right;
    char op;

    if (formula == null) {
        return null;
    }
    subformula = parseValue(formula, node);
    if (subformula == null || subformula.length() == 0) {
        //System.out.println("Parse succeeded");
        return null;
    }
    if (subformula == formula) {
        return formula;
    }

    // parse an operator and then another value
    switch (op = subformula.charAt(0)) {
      case 0:
        return null;
      case ')':
        return subformula;
      case '+':
```

Listing 20.17. continued

```
          case '*':
          case '-':
          case '/':
            restFormula = subformula.substring(1);
            subformula = parseValue(restFormula, right=new Node());
            if (subformula != restFormula) {
                left = new Node(node);
                node.left = left;
                node.right = right;
                node.op = op;
                node.type = Node.OP;
                return subformula;
            } else {
                return formula;
            }
        default:
            return formula;
        }
}
public String parseValue(String formula, Node node) {

    char     c = formula.charAt(0);
    String   subformula;
    String   restFormula;
    float    value;
    int      row;
    int      column;

    restFormula = formula;
    if (c == '(') {
        restFormula = formula.substring(1);
        subformula = parseFormula(restFormula, node);
        if (subformula == null ||
            subformula.length() == restFormula.length()) {
            return formula;
        } else if (! (subformula.charAt(0) == ')')) {
            return formula;
        }
        restFormula = subformula;
    } else if (c >= '0' && c <= '9') {
        int i;

        try {
            value = Float.valueOf(formula).floatValue();
        } catch (NumberFormatException e) {
            return formula;
        }
        for (i=0; i < formula.length(); i++) {
            c = formula.charAt(i);
            if ((c < '0' || c > '9') && c != '.') {
                break;
            }
        }
        node.type = Node.VALUE;
        node.value = value;
        restFormula = formula.substring(i);
```

```
        //                          " rest = " + restFormula);
        return restFormula;
    } else if (c >= 'A' && c <= 'Z') {
        int i;

        column = c - 'A';
        restFormula = formula.substring(1);
        row = Float.valueOf(restFormula).intValue();
        for (i=0; i < restFormula.length(); i++) {
            c = restFormula.charAt(i);
            if (c < '0' || c > '9') {
                break;
            }
        }
        node.row = row - 1;
        node.column = column;
        node.type = Node.CELL;
        if (i == restFormula.length()) {
            restFormula = null;
        } else {
            restFormula = restFormula.substring(i);
            if (restFormula.charAt(0) == 0) {
                return null;
            }
        }
    }

    return restFormula;
}
```

Painting Cells

The `paint()` method of the `Cell` class sets the colors for spreadsheet cells. If the selected flag is set, the background color of the cell is set to the value associated with the `highlightColor` object—white. If it is not set, the background color of the cell is set to the value associated with the `bgColor` object—gray. When the background color is set, the rectangle associated with the cell is painted.

When new cell objects are created, the `fgcolor` attribute is set to black. This attribute is used to set the font color for each cell. If the cell type is `VALUE` or `LABEL`, the font color is set to black; if the cell type is `FORMULA`, it is set to red; and if the cell type is `URL`, it is set to blue. When the color for data associated with a cell is set, the data is drawn to the frame using the `drawString()` method. Listing 20.18 shows the `paint()` method of the `Cell` class.

Listing 20.18. Painting cells.

```
public void paint(Graphics g, int x, int y) {
    if (selected) {
        g.setColor(highlightColor);
    } else {
        g.setColor(bgColor);
```

continues

Listing 20.18. continued

```
        }
        g.fillRect(x, y, width - 1, height);
        if (valueString != null) {
            switch (type) {
              case Cell.VALUE:
              case Cell.LABEL:
                g.setColor(fgColor);
                break;
              case Cell.FORMULA:
                g.setColor(Color.red);
                break;
              case Cell.URL:
                g.setColor(Color.blue);
                break;
            }
            if (transientValue){
                g.drawString("" + value, x, y + (height / 2) + 5);
            } else {
                if (valueString.length() > 14) {
                    g.drawString(valueString.substring(0, 14),
                                 x, y + (height / 2) + 5);
                } else {
                    g.drawString(valueString, x, y + (height / 2) + 5);
                }
            }
        }
        needRedisplay = false;
    }
}
```

Building the Node Object

You use the Node class of the SpreadSheet applet to build the nodes used in formulas. As you can see in Listing 20.19, nodes are not complex objects, and building a node is rather easy when you understand that all nodes have a left value, an operand, and a right value associated with them.

To track the types of values associated with nodes, three static variables are used: The OP variable is set for operands, the VALUE variable is set for numeric values, and the CELL variable is set for references to cell objects.

The Node class includes an overloaded method called Node(). The first version of the Node() method builds a generic node that is used when parsing subformulas. The second version is used when parsing formulas.

Listing 20.19. Building nodes.

```
class Node {

    //set for node components that are operands
    public static final int OP = 0;
    //set for node components that are values
    public static final int VALUE = 1;
    //set for node components that are cell references
    public static final int CELL = 2;

    int         type;
    Node        left;    //the lefthand value for the node
    Node        right;   //the righthand value for the node
    int         row;    //the row coordinate of the selected cell
    int         column;   //the column coordinate of the selected cell
    float       value;   //the current value
    char        op;    //the operand +, -, /, *

    public Node() {
        left = null;
        right = null;
        value = 0;
        row = -1;
        column = -1;
        op = 0;
        type = Node.VALUE;
    }
    public Node(Node n) {
        left = n.left;
        right = n.right;
        value = n.value;
        row = n.row;
        column = n.column;
        op = n.op;
        type = n.type;
    }
}
```

Building the Input Area

The input area is the final object needed in the SpreadSheet applet. Although it could have been built using a simple textField object, a more advanced approach is to build an input area that behaves and looks exactly as you want it to.

Note: You will find that there are many times when control over the behavior and style of the input area is needed in an advanced applet. To do this, you must build your own input area.

When building your own input area, there are many things you should consider. Most are obvious and relate to why you wanted to create your own input area in the first place. Style considerations include the following:

- The size of the input area
- The color of the background
- The font type, size, and color of text input

Behavior considerations include the following:

- How the input area is activated
- What the accepted key values are
- Whether any input must be parsed
- What the maximum length of the input is
- Whether the Enter key causes the applet to update its display

Two class-level objects are used to build the input area for the SpreadSheet applet: SpreadSheetInput and InputField.

The `SpreadSheetInput` Class

The SpreadSheetInput class, shown in Listing 20.20, extends the InputField class, which is defined next. The class includes two fairly basic methods.

The SpreadSheetInput() method passes the values with which it was called to the InputField class. The selected() method calls the setCurrentValue method with the appropriate parameters so the value of the input area can be passed back to the currently selected cell. Thus, the cell is updated when the user makes a change and presses Enter.

Listing 20.20. The **SpreadSheetInput** class.

```
class SpreadSheetInput extends InputField {

    public SpreadSheetInput(String initValue,
                            SpreadSheet app,
                            int width,
                            int height,
                            Color bgColor,
                            Color fgColor) {
        super(initValue, app, width, height, bgColor, fgColor);
    }

    public void selected() {
        float f;

        switch (sval.charAt(0)) {
          case 'v':
            try {
```

```
        f = Float.valueOf(sval.substring(1)).floatValue();
        ((SpreadSheet)app).setCurrentValue(f);
      } catch (NumberFormatException e) {
        System.out.println("Not a float...");
      }
      break;
    case 'l':
      ((SpreadSheet)app).setCurrentValue(Cell.LABEL, sval.substring(1));
      break;
    case 'u':
      ((SpreadSheet)app).setCurrentValue(Cell.URL, sval.substring(1));
      break;
    case 'f':
      ((SpreadSheet)app).setCurrentValue(Cell.FORMULA, sval.substring(1));
      break;
    }
  }
}
```

The `InputField` Class

As you can see in Listing 20.21, the `InputField` class is more complex than the `SpreadSheetInput` class, primarily because the `InputField` object defines the style and behavior of the input area.

The first section of the `InputField` class initializes containers that determine the style of the input area and limit its behavior. The maximum number of characters the input area accepts is 50. Each character entered into the input area is stored in an array. When the user adds characters to the input area by either selecting a cell or entering data, the array grows. When the user deletes characters, the array shrinks.

The `InputField()` method is called to set the attributes for the input area. In the unlikely case that the method is called with an initial value set, the string buffer is set to this value.

The `setText()` method updates the input area when a cell is selected or when text is entered or deleted by reading the string buffer character by character. The `paint()` method overrides the `paint()` method of the applet class and draws values to the input area.

The heart of this class is the event handler. As with other event handlers in the `SpreadSheet` applet, this one checks for events directly using methods of the `Component` class. Here, the `keyDown` event is checked to determine when a key is pressed.

The `keyDown()` method converts the value of the pressed key to an integer and then checks for three specific key types using their integer values. The integer value of the delete key is 8. When the Delete key is pressed, one character is deleted from the `buffer[]` array. The integer value of the Enter key is 10. When the Enter key is pressed, the current value of the `buffer[]` array is passed back to the cell. This happens behind the scenes after the empty `selected()` method of the `InputField` class is called. By default, the `keyDown()` method stores the value of any keypress other than Delete or Enter to the `buffer[]` array.

Listing 20.21. The **InputField** class.

```
class InputField {
    int         maxchars = 50;    //the maximum characters for the input field
    int         cursorPos = 0;    //index to the current cursor position
    Applet      app;   //instance of the applet object
    String      sval;    //container for string values
    char        buffer[];   //an array of characters up to maxchars in length
    int         nChars;    //the number of characters in the input area
    int         width;   //width of the input area
    int         height;   //height of the input area
    Color       bgColor;   //background color of the input area
    Color       fgColor;   //font color for text in the input area

    public InputField(String initValue, Applet app, int width, int height,
                    Color bgColor, Color fgColor) {
        this.width = width;
        this.height = height;
        this.bgColor = bgColor;
        this.fgColor = fgColor;
        this.app = app;
        buffer = new char[maxchars];
        nChars = 0;
        if (initValue != null) {
            initValue.getChars(0, initValue.length(), this.buffer, 0);
            nChars = initValue.length();
        }
        sval = initValue;
    }
    public void setText(String val) {
        int i;

        for (i=0; i < maxchars; i++) {
            buffer[i] = 0;
        }
        sval = new String(val);
        if (val == null) {
            sval = "";
            nChars = 0;
            buffer[0] = 0;
        } else {
            sval.getChars(0, sval.length(), buffer, 0);
            nChars = val.length();
            sval = new String(buffer);
        }
    }

    public void paint(Graphics g, int x, int y) {
        g.setColor(bgColor);
        g.fillRect(x, y, width, height);
        if (sval != null) {
            g.setColor(fgColor);
            g.drawString(sval, x, y + (height / 2) + 3);
        }
    }

    public void keyDown(int key) {
        if (nChars < maxchars) {
            switch (key) {
```

```
          case 8: // delete
            --nChars;
            if (nChars < 0) {
               nChars = 0;
            }
            buffer[nChars] = 0;
            sval = new String(new String(buffer));
            break;
          case 10: // return
            selected();
            break;
          default:
            buffer[nChars++] = (char)key;
            sval = new String(new String(buffer));
            break;
        }
      }
      app.repaint();
    }
    public void selected() {
    }
}
```

The Complete Applet

Listing 21.22 shows the complete code for the SpreadSheet applet. Although you can go straight to the CD-ROM and access the complete source code, typing it in line by line forces you to study each line of code.

Listing 21.22. The SpreadSheet applet.

```
/*
 * @(#)SpreadSheet.java 1.17 95/03/09 Sami Shaio
 *
 * Copyright (c) 1994-1995 Sun Microsystems, Inc. All Rights Reserved.
 *
 * Permission to use, copy, modify, and distribute this software
 * and its documentation for NON-COMMERCIAL or COMMERCIAL purposes and
 * without fee is hereby granted.
 * Please refer to the file http://java.sun.com/copy_trademarks.html
 * for further important copyright and trademark information and to
 * http://java.sun.com/licensing.html for further important licensing
 * information for the Java (tm) Technology.
 *
 * Modified for Peter Norton's Guide to Programming Java by William R. Stanek
 * 21 March 1996
 * @version 2.02
 *
 * These modifications include:
 *
 * Added parameter support for publisher defined title fonts, base fonts
```

continues

Listing 21.22. continued

```
* for columns and rows, and font sizes.
* Updated the title, column and row positions/sizes to make them dynamic and
* thus support publisher defined font types and sizes.
* Changed display characteristics.
* Eliminates a display bug.
* Adds comment descriptions to methods
* Streamlined some class objects
*
* SUN MAKES NO REPRESENTATIONS OR WARRANTIES ABOUT THE SUITABILITY OF
* THE SOFTWARE, EITHER EXPRESS OR IMPLIED, INCLUDING BUT NOT LIMITED
* TO THE IMPLIED WARRANTIES OF MERCHANTABILITY, FITNESS FOR A
* PARTICULAR PURPOSE, OR NON-INFRINGEMENT. SUN SHALL NOT BE LIABLE FOR
* ANY DAMAGES SUFFERED BY LICENSEE AS A RESULT OF USING, MODIFYING OR
* DISTRIBUTING THIS SOFTWARE OR ITS DERIVATIVES.
*
* THIS SOFTWARE IS NOT DESIGNED OR INTENDED FOR USE OR RESALE AS ON-LINE
* CONTROL EQUIPMENT IN HAZARDOUS ENVIRONMENTS REQUIRING FAIL-SAFE
* PERFORMANCE, SUCH AS IN THE OPERATION OF NUCLEAR FACILITIES, AIRCRAFT
* NAVIGATION OR COMMUNICATION SYSTEMS, AIR TRAFFIC CONTROL, DIRECT LIFE
* SUPPORT MACHINES, OR WEAPONS SYSTEMS, IN WHICH THE FAILURE OF THE
* SOFTWARE COULD LEAD DIRECTLY TO DEATH, PERSONAL INJURY, OR SEVERE
* PHYSICAL OR ENVIRONMENTAL DAMAGE ("HIGH RISK ACTIVITIES").  SUN
* SPECIFICALLY DISCLAIMS ANY EXPRESS OR IMPLIED WARRANTY OF FITNESS FOR
* HIGH RISK ACTIVITIES.
*/

import java.applet.Applet;
import java.awt.*;
import java.io.*;
import java.lang.*;
import java.net.*;

public class SpreadSheet extends Applet {
    //container to hold the parameter value for title text
    String          title;
    //container to hold the parameter value for base font
    String          bfont;
    //container to hold the parameter value for title font
    String          tfont;
    //container for the inputfont object
    Font            inputFont;
    //container for the title font object
    Font            titleFont;
    //container for the cell color object
    Color           cellColor;
    //container for the input area's color object
    Color           inputColor;
    //container for the parameter value for font size
    int             fontSize;
    //container for the cell width object
    int             cellWidth;
    //container for the cell height object
    int             cellHeight;
    //container for the title height object
    int             titleHeight;
    //container for the row label width object
    int             rowLabelWidth;
```

```
    //container for the status object
boolean              isStopped = false;
    //container for the update object
boolean              fullUpdate = true;
    //container for the rows object
int                  rows;
    //container for the columns object
int                  columns;
    //container for the current key object
int                  currentKey = -1;
    //container for the selected row object
int                  selectedRow = -1;
    //container for the selected column object
int                  selectedColumn = -1;
    //container for the input area
SpreadSheetInput     inputArea;
    //container for the individual cells
Cell                 cells[][];
    //container for the current cell
Cell                 current = null;

public synchronized void init() {
    String rs;
    String fs;

    cellColor = Color.white;
    inputColor = new Color(100, 100, 225);

    fs = getParameter("fontsize");
    if (fs == null) {
        fontSize = 10;
    } else {
        fontSize = Integer.parseInt(fs);
    }

cellWidth = fontSize * 10;
cellHeight = fontSize * 2;
titleHeight = fontSize * 2;
rowLabelWidth = fontSize * 3;

    bfont = getParameter("basefont");
    if (bfont == null) {
        bfont = "Courier";
    }
    inputFont = new Font(bfont, Font.PLAIN, fontSize);

    tfont = getParameter("titlefont");
    if (tfont == null) {
        tfont = "Courier";
    }
    titleFont = new Font(tfont, Font.BOLD, (fontSize + 2));

    title = getParameter("title");
    if (title == null) {
        title = "Spreadsheet";
    }
    rs = getParameter("rows");
```

continues

Listing 21.22. continued

```
            if (rs == null) {
                rows = 9;
            } else {
                rows = Integer.parseInt(rs);
            }
            rs = getParameter("columns");
            if (rs == null) {
                columns = 5;
            } else {
                columns = Integer.parseInt(rs);
            }
            cells = new Cell[rows][columns];
            char l[] = new char[1];
            for (int i=0; i < rows; i++) {
                for (int j=0; j < columns; j++) {

                    cells[i][j] = new Cell(this,
                                        Color.lightGray,
                                        Color.black,
                                        cellColor,
                                        cellWidth - (fontSize/4),
                                        cellHeight - (fontSize/4));
                    l[0] = (char)((int)'a' + j);
                    rs = getParameter("" + new String(l) + (i+1));
                    if (rs != null) {
                        cells[i][j].setUnparsedValue(rs);
                    }
                }
            }

            Dimension d = size();
            inputArea = new SpreadSheetInput(null, this, d.width - 2,
                    cellHeight - 2, inputColor, Color.white);
            resize(columns * cellWidth + rowLabelWidth,
                    ((rows + 1) * cellHeight) + cellHeight + titleHeight);
        }

    public void setCurrentValue(float val) {
        if (selectedRow == -1 || selectedColumn == -1) {
            return;
        }
        cells[selectedRow][selectedColumn].setValue(val);
        repaint();
    }

    public void stop() {
        isStopped = true;
    }

    public void start() {
        isStopped = false;
    }

    public void destroy() {
        for (int i=0; i < rows; i++) {
            for (int j=0; j < columns; j++) {
                if (cells[i][j].type == Cell.URL) {
```

```
                    cells[i][j].updaterThread.stop();
                }
            }
        }
    }

    public void setCurrentValue(int type, String val) {
        if (selectedRow == -1 || selectedColumn == -1) {
            return;
        }
        cells[selectedRow][selectedColumn].setValue(type, val);
        repaint();
    }

    public void update(Graphics g) {
        if (! fullUpdate) {
            int cx, cy;

            g.setFont(titleFont);
            for (int i=0; i < rows; i++) {
                for (int j=0; j < columns; j++) {
                    if (cells[i][j].needRedisplay) {
                        cx = (j * cellWidth) + (fontSize*2) + rowLabelWidth;
                        cy = ((i+1) * cellHeight) + (fontSize*2) + titleHeight;
                        cells[i][j].paint(g, cx, cy);
                    }
                }
            }
        } else {
            paint(g);
            fullUpdate = false;
        }
    }

    public void recalculate() {
        int    i,j;

        //System.out.println("SpreadSheet.recalculate");
        for (i=0; i < rows; i++) {
            for (j=0; j < columns; j++) {
                if (cells[i][j] != null && cells[i][j].type == Cell.FORMULA) {
                    cells[i][j].setRawValue(evaluateFormula
        ➥(cells[i][j].parseRoot));
                    cells[i][j].needRedisplay = true;
                }
            }
        }
        repaint();
    }

    public float evaluateFormula(Node n) {
        float    val = 0.0f;

        //System.out.println("evaluateFormula:");
        //n.print(3);
        if (n == null) {
            //System.out.println("Null node");
```

continues

Listing 21.22. continued

```
                return val;
        }
        switch (n.type) {
          case Node.OP:
            val = evaluateFormula(n.left);
            switch (n.op) {
              case '+':
                val += evaluateFormula(n.right);
                break;
              case '*':
                val *= evaluateFormula(n.right);
                break;
              case '-':
                val -= evaluateFormula(n.right);
                break;
              case '/':
                val /= evaluateFormula(n.right);
                break;
            }
            break;
          case Node.VALUE:
            //System.out.println("=>" + n.value);
            return n.value;
          case Node.CELL:
            if (n == null) {
                //System.out.println("NULL at 192");
            } else {
                if (cells[n.row][n.column] == null) {
                    //System.out.println("NULL at 193");
                } else {
                    //System.out.println("=>" + cells[n.row][n.column].value);
                    return cells[n.row][n.column].value;
                }
            }
        }

        //System.out.println("=>" + val);
        return val;
    }

    public synchronized void paint(Graphics g) {

        int i, j;
        int cx, cy;
        char l[] = new char[1];

        Dimension d = size();

        //draws the title on the frame
        g.setFont(titleFont);
        i = g.getFontMetrics().stringWidth(title);
        g.drawString((title == null) ? "Spreadsheet" : title,
                    (d.width - i + (fontSize*3/2)) / 2, (fontSize*3/2));

        //draws the input area on the frame
        g.setColor(inputColor);
        g.fillRect(0, cellHeight, d.width, cellHeight);
```

```
        //draws the lines for rows using 3d effect
        //adds row numbering in blue
        g.setFont(titleFont);
        for (i=0; i < rows+1; i++) {
            cy = (i+2) * cellHeight;
            g.setColor(getBackground());
            g.draw3DRect(0, cy, d.width, 2, true);
            if (i < rows) {
                g.setColor(Color.blue);
                g.drawString("" + (i+1), fontSize, cy + (fontSize *3/2));
            }
        }

        //draws the lines for columns using 3d effect
        //adds column alphas in red
        g.setColor(Color.red);
        for (i=0; i < columns; i++) {
            cx = i * cellWidth;
            g.setColor(getBackground());
            g.draw3DRect(cx + rowLabelWidth,
                        2 * cellHeight, 1, d.height, true);
            if (i < columns) {
                g.setColor(Color.red);
                l[0] = (char)((int)'A' + i);
                g.drawString(new String(l),
                            cx + rowLabelWidth + (cellWidth / 2),
                            d.height - 3);
            }
        }

        //paints the cell data
        for (i=0; i < rows; i++) {
            for (j=0; j < columns; j++) {
                cx = (j * cellWidth) + 2 + rowLabelWidth;
                cy = ((i+1) * cellHeight) + 2 + titleHeight;
                if (cells[i][j] != null) {
                    cells[i][j].paint(g, cx, cy);
                }
            }
        }

        g.setColor(getBackground());
        //draws a 3d line for the input area and to the left side of the frame
        g.draw3DRect(0, titleHeight, d.width, d.height - titleHeight, false);
        //paints the data of the current cell to the input area
        inputArea.paint(g, 1, titleHeight + 1);
    }

    public boolean mouseDown(Event evt, int x, int y) {
        Cell cell;
//ensures the y coordinate of the mouse pointer
        //is not in the title/input area
        if (y < (titleHeight + cellHeight)) {
            selectedRow = -1;
            if (y <= titleHeight && current != null) {
                current.deselect();
```

continues

Listing 21.22. continued

```
                        current = null;
                }
                return true;
        }
//ensures the x coordinate of the mouse pointer
        //is not in the row label area
        if (x < rowLabelWidth) {
            selectedRow = -1;
            if (current != null) {
                current.deselect();
                current = null;
            }
            return true;
        }

        //determines the row of the selected cell
        selectedRow = ((y - cellHeight - titleHeight) / cellHeight);

        //determines the column of the selected cell
        selectedColumn = (x - rowLabelWidth) / cellWidth;

        //ensures the row and column coordinate is valid
        if (selectedRow >= rows ||
            selectedColumn >= columns) {
            selectedRow = -1;
            if (current != null) {
                current.deselect();
                current = null;
            }

        //if the row-column coordinate is valid place the selected cells value
        //in the input area
        } else {
            cell = cells[selectedRow][selectedColumn];
            inputArea.setText(new String(cell.getPrintString()));
            if (current != null) {
                current.deselect();
            }
            current = cell;
            current.select();
            requestFocus();
            fullUpdate = true;
            repaint();
        }
        return true;
    }

    //determine if a key is pressed
    public boolean keyDown(Event evt, int key) {
        fullUpdate=true;
        inputArea.keyDown(key);
        return true;
    }
}

class CellUpdater extends Thread {
    Cell        target;
```

```
        InputStream dataStream = null;
        StreamTokenizer tokenStream;

        public CellUpdater(Cell c) {
            super("cell updater");
            target = c;
        }

        public void run() {
            try {
                dataStream = new URL(target.app.getDocumentBase(),
                                  target.getValueString()).openStream();
                tokenStream = new StreamTokenizer(dataStream);
                tokenStream.eolIsSignificant(false);

                while (true) {
                    switch (tokenStream.nextToken()) {
                    case tokenStream.TT_EOF:
                        dataStream.close();
                        return;
                    default:
                        break;
                    case tokenStream.TT_NUMBER:
                        target.setTransientValue((float)tokenStream.nval);
                        if (! target.app.isStopped && ! target.paused) {
                            target.app.repaint();
                        }
                        break;
                    }
                    try {
                        Thread.sleep(2000);
                    } catch (InterruptedException e) {
                        break;
                    }
                }
            } catch (IOException e) {
                return;
            }
        }
    }
}

class Cell {
    public static final int VALUE = 0;    //initializes the VALUE container
    public static final int LABEL = 1;    //initializes the LABEL container
    public static final int URL   = 2;    //initializes the URL container
    public static final int FORMULA = 3;  //initializes the FORMULA container
    Node        parseRoot;  //sets the node for the cell
    boolean     needRedisplay;  //used to determine the need for redisplay
    boolean selected = false;    //used to determine whether cell is selected
    boolean transientValue = false;    //tracks need to set transient value
    public int  type = Cell.VALUE;    //sets the cell type
    String      valueString = "";    //initializes the value string
    String      printString = "v";    //initiliazes the print string
    float       value;    //container for a float called value
    Color       bgColor;    //container for the background color
    Color       fgColor;    //container for the foreground color
    Color       highlightColor;    //container for cell color when selected
```

continues

Listing 21.22. continued

```
int         width;    //container for the width of the cell
int         height;   //container for the height of the cell
SpreadSheet app;      //container for the SpreadSheet object
CellUpdater updaterThread;  //container for the CellUpdater object
boolean     paused = false;    //used to determine if paused

public Cell(SpreadSheet app,
            Color bgColor,
            Color fgColor,
            Color highlightColor,
            int width,
            int height) {
    this.app = app;
    this.bgColor = bgColor;
    this.fgColor = fgColor;
    this.highlightColor = highlightColor;
    this.width = width;
    this.height = height;
    needRedisplay = true;
}

public void setRawValue(float f) {
    valueString = Float.toString(f);
    value = f;
}
public void setValue(float f) {
    setRawValue(f);
    printString = "v" + valueString;
    type = Cell.VALUE;
    paused = false;
    app.recalculate();
    needRedisplay = true;
}

public void setTransientValue(float f) {
    transientValue = true;
    value = f;
    needRedisplay = true;
    app.recalculate();
}

public void setUnparsedValue(String s) {
    switch (s.charAt(0)) {
      case 'v':
        setValue(Cell.VALUE, s.substring(1));
        break;
      case 'f':
        setValue(Cell.FORMULA, s.substring(1));
        break;
      case 'l':
        setValue(Cell.LABEL, s.substring(1));
        break;
      case 'u':
        setValue(Cell.URL, s.substring(1));
        break;
    }
}
```

```java
/**
 * Parse a spreadsheet formula. The syntax is defined as:
 *
 * formula -> value
 * formula -> value op value
 * value -> '(' formula ')'
 * value -> cell
 * value -> <number>
 * op -> '+' | '*' | '/' | '-'
 * cell -> <letter><number>
 */
public String parseFormula(String formula, Node node) {
    String subformula;
    String restFormula;
    float value;
    int length = formula.length();
    Node left;
    Node right;
    char op;

    if (formula == null) {
        return null;
    }
    subformula = parseValue(formula, node);
    //System.out.println("subformula = " + subformula);
    if (subformula == null || subformula.length() == 0) {
        //System.out.println("Parse succeeded");
        return null;
    }
    if (subformula == formula) {
        //System.out.println("Parse failed");
        return formula;
    }

    // parse an operator and then another value
    switch (op = subformula.charAt(0)) {
      case 0:
        //System.out.println("Parse succeeded");
        return null;
      case ')':
        //System.out.println("Returning subformula=" + subformula);
        return subformula;
      case '+':
      case '*':
      case '-':
      case '/':
        restFormula = subformula.substring(1);
        subformula = parseValue(restFormula, right=new Node());
        //System.out.println("subformula(2) = " + subformula);
        if (subformula != restFormula) {
            //System.out.println("Parse succeeded");
            left = new Node(node);
            node.left = left;
            node.right = right;
            node.op = op;
            node.type = Node.OP;
```

continues

Listing 21.22. continued

```
                //node.print(3);
                return subformula;
            } else {
                //System.out.println("Parse failed");
                return formula;
            }
        default:
            //System.out.println("Parse failed (bad operator): " + subformula);
            return formula;
        }
    }

    public String parseValue(String formula, Node node) {
        char    c = formula.charAt(0);
        String  subformula;
        String  restFormula;
        float   value;
        int     row;
        int     column;

        //System.out.println("parseValue: " + formula);
        restFormula = formula;
        if (c == '(') {
            //System.out.println("parseValue(" + formula + ")");
            restFormula = formula.substring(1);
            subformula = parseFormula(restFormula, node);
            //System.out.println("rest=(" + subformula + ")");
            if (subformula == null ||
                subformula.length() == restFormula.length()) {
                //System.out.println("Failed");
                return formula;
            } else if (! (subformula.charAt(0) == ')')) {
                //System.out.println("Failed (missing parentheses)");
                return formula;
            }
            restFormula = subformula;
        } else if (c >= '0' && c <= '9') {
            int i;

            //System.out.println("formula=" + formula);
            try {
                value = Float.valueOf(formula).floatValue();
            } catch (NumberFormatException e) {
                //System.out.println("Failed (number format error)");
                return formula;
            }
            for (i=0; i < formula.length(); i++) {
                c = formula.charAt(i);
                if ((c < '0' || c > '9') && c != '.') {
                    break;
                }
            }
            node.type = Node.VALUE;
            node.value = value;
            //node.print(3);
            restFormula = formula.substring(i);
            //System.out.println("value= " + value + " i=" + i +
```

```
            //                        " rest = " + restFormula);
        return restFormula;
    } else if (c >= 'A' && c <= 'Z') {
        int i;

        column = c - 'A';
        restFormula = formula.substring(1);
        row = Float.valueOf(restFormula).intValue();
        //System.out.println("row = " + row + " column = " + column);
        for (i=0; i < restFormula.length(); i++) {
            c = restFormula.charAt(i);
            if (c < '0' || c > '9') {
                break;
            }
        }
        node.row = row - 1;
        node.column = column;
        node.type = Node.CELL;
        //node.print(3);
        if (i == restFormula.length()) {
            restFormula = null;
        } else {
            restFormula = restFormula.substring(i);
            if (restFormula.charAt(0) == 0) {
                return null;
            }
        }
    }
}

    return restFormula;
}


public void setValue(int type, String s) {
    paused = false;
    if (this.type == Cell.URL) {
        updaterThread.stop();
        updaterThread = null;
    }

    valueString = new String(s);
    this.type = type;
    needRedisplay = true;
    switch (type) {
      case Cell.VALUE:
        setValue(Float.valueOf(s).floatValue());
        break;
      case Cell.LABEL:
        printString = "l" + valueString;
        break;
      case Cell.URL:
        printString = "u" + valueString;
        updaterThread = new CellUpdater(this);
        updaterThread.start();
        break;
      case Cell.FORMULA:
        parseFormula(valueString, parseRoot = new Node());
```

continues

Listing 21.22. continued

```
                printString = "f" + valueString;
                break;
        }
        app.recalculate();
    }

    public String getValueString() {
        return valueString;
    }

    public String getPrintString() {
        return printString;
    }

    public void select() {
        selected = true;
        paused = true;
    }
    public void deselect() {
        selected = false;
        paused = false;
        needRedisplay = true;
    }
    public void paint(Graphics g, int x, int y) {
        if (selected) {
            g.setColor(highlightColor);
        } else {
            g.setColor(bgColor);
        }
        g.fillRect(x, y, width - 1, height);
        if (valueString != null) {
            switch (type) {
              case Cell.VALUE:
              case Cell.LABEL:
                g.setColor(fgColor);
                break;
              case Cell.FORMULA:
                g.setColor(Color.red);
                break;
              case Cell.URL:
                g.setColor(Color.blue);
                break;
            }
            if (transientValue){
                g.drawString("" + value, x, y + (height / 2) + 5);
            } else {
                if (valueString.length() > 14) {
                    g.drawString(valueString.substring(0, 14),
                                 x, y + (height / 2) + 5);
                } else {
                    g.drawString(valueString, x, y + (height / 2) + 5);
                }
            }
        }
        needRedisplay = false;
    }
}
```

```
class Node {
    //set for node components that are operands
    public static final int OP = 0;
    //set for node components that are values
    public static final int VALUE = 1;
    //set for node components that are cell references
    public static final int CELL = 2;

    int        type;
    Node       left;    //the lefthand value for the node
    Node       right;   //the righthand value for the node
    int        row;     //the row coordinate of the selected cell
    int        column;  //the column coordinate of the selected cell
    float      value;   //the current value
    char       op;   //the operand +, -, /, *

    public Node() {
        left = null;
        right = null;
        value = 0;
        row = -1;
        column = -1;
        op = 0;
        type = Node.VALUE;
    }
    public Node(Node n) {
        left = n.left;
        right = n.right;
        value = n.value;
        row = n.row;
        column = n.column;
        op = n.op;
        type = n.type;
    }
    public void indent(int ind) {
        for (int i = 0; i < ind; i++) {
            System.out.print(" ");
        }
    }
    public void print(int indentLevel) {
        char l[] = new char[1];
        indent(indentLevel);
        System.out.println("NODE type=" + type);
        indent(indentLevel);
        switch (type) {
          case Node.VALUE:
            System.out.println(" value=" + value);
            break;
          case Node.CELL:
            l[0] = (char)((int)'A' + column);
            System.out.println(" cell=" + new String(l) + (row+1));
            break;
          case Node.OP:
            System.out.println(" op=" + op);
            left.print(indentLevel + 3);
            right.print(indentLevel + 3);
```

continues

Listing 21.22. continued

```
                break;
        }
    }
}

class InputField {
    int         maxchars = 50;    //the maximum characters for the input field
    int         cursorPos = 0;    //index to the current cursor position
    Applet      app;    //instance of the applet object
    String      sval;    //container for string values
    char        buffer[];    //an array of characters up to maxchars in length
    int         nChars;    //the number of characters in the input area
    int         width;    //width of the input area
    int         height;    //height of the input area
    Color       bgColor;    //background color of the input area
    Color       fgColor;    //font color for text in the input area

    public InputField(String initValue, Applet app, int width, int height,
                        Color bgColor, Color fgColor) {
        this.width = width;
        this.height = height;
        this.bgColor = bgColor;
        this.fgColor = fgColor;
        this.app = app;
        buffer = new char[maxchars];
        nChars = 0;
        if (initValue != null) {
            initValue.getChars(0, initValue.length(), this.buffer, 0);
            nChars = initValue.length();
        }
        sval = initValue;
    }

    public void setText(String val) {
        int i;

        for (i=0; i < maxchars; i++) {
            buffer[i] = 0;
        }
        sval = new String(val);
        if (val == null) {
            sval = "";
            nChars = 0;
            buffer[0] = 0;
        } else {
            sval.getChars(0, sval.length(), buffer, 0);
            nChars = val.length();
            sval = new String(buffer);
        }
    }

    public void paint(Graphics g, int x, int y) {
        g.setColor(bgColor);
        g.fillRect(x, y, width, height);
        if (sval != null) {
            g.setColor(fgColor);
            g.drawString(sval, x, y + (height / 2) + 3);
```

```
            }
        }
    public void keyDown(int key) {
        if (nChars < maxchars) {
            switch (key) {
              case 8: // delete
                --nChars;
                if (nChars < 0) {
                    nChars = 0;
                }
                buffer[nChars] = 0;
                sval = new String(new String(buffer));
                break;
              case 10: // return
                selected();
                break;
              default:
                buffer[nChars++] = (char)key;
                sval = new String(new String(buffer));
                break;
            }
        }
        app.repaint();
    }
    public void selected() {
    }
}

class SpreadSheetInput extends InputField {
    public SpreadSheetInput(String initValue,
                            SpreadSheet app,
                            int width,
                            int height,
                            Color bgColor,
                            Color fgColor) {
        super(initValue, app, width, height, bgColor, fgColor);
    }

    public void selected() {
        float f;

        switch (sval.charAt(0)) {
          case 'v':
            try {
                f = Float.valueOf(sval.substring(1)).floatValue();
                ((SpreadSheet)app).setCurrentValue(f);
            } catch (NumberFormatException e) {
                System.out.println("Not a float...");
            }
            break;
          case 'l':
            ((SpreadSheet)app).setCurrentValue(Cell.LABEL, sval.substring(1));
            break;
          case 'u':
            ((SpreadSheet)app).setCurrentValue(Cell.URL, sval.substring(1));
            break;
          case 'f':
```

continues

Listing 21.22. continued

```
            ((SpreadSheet)app).setCurrentValue(Cell.FORMULA, sval.substring(1));
            break;
        }
    }
}
```

Putting the **SpreadSheet** Applet to Use

To use the SpreadSheet applet, you need to create an HTML document that calls the applet. The document can be as simple or as complex as you want it to be. The code for a simple HTML document that causes the SpreadSheet applet to use default values is shown in Listing 20.23. This document is shown in Figure 20.3.

Listing 20.23. A simple HTML document using the **SpreadSheet** applet.

```
<HTML>
<HEAD>
<TITLE>Default SpreadSheet</TITLE>
</HEAD>
<BODY>
<APPLET CODE="SpreadSheet.class" WIDTH=400 HEIGHT=250>
</APPLET>
</BODY>
</HTML>
```

Figure 20.3.

A document using the SpreadSheet *applet's default settings.*

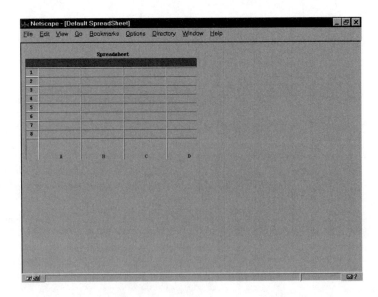

Although your HTML document does not have to set parameter values for the spreadsheet, the best way to see how the applet behaves is to experiment with parameter values. Listing 20.24 shows how an advanced spreadsheet was built using the SpreadSheet applet. This document is shown earlier in this chapter as Figure 20.2.

Listing 20.24. A more advanced example using the SpreadSheet applet.

```
<HTML>
<HEAD>
<TITLE>SpreadSheet</TITLE>
</HEAD>
<BODY>
<HR>
<APPLET CODE="SpreadSheet.class" WIDTH=750 HEIGHT=400>
<PARAM NAME=title value="Java Powered Spreadsheet">
<PARAM NAME=columns value="5">
<PARAM NAME=rows value="7">
<PARAM NAME=fontsize value="14">
<PARAM NAME=basefont value="TimesRoman">
<PARAM NAME=titlefont value="Helvetica">
<PARAM NAME=a1 value="lWholesale">
<PARAM NAME=a2 value="v20195">
<PARAM NAME=a3 value="v7280">
<PARAM NAME=a4 value="v6127">
<PARAM NAME=a5 value="v9803">
<PARAM NAME=a6 value="v4150">
<PARAM NAME=a7 value="fA2+(A3+(A4+(A5+A6)))">
<PARAM NAME=b1 value="lShipping">
<PARAM NAME=b2 value="v1500">
<PARAM NAME=b3 value="v350">
<PARAM NAME=b4 value="v729">
<PARAM NAME=b5 value="v830">
<PARAM NAME=b6 value="v125">
<PARAM NAME=b7 value="fB2+(B3+(B4+(B5+B6)))">
<PARAM NAME=c1 value="lPackaging">
<PARAM NAME=c2 value="v120">
<PARAM NAME=c3 value="v35">
<PARAM NAME=c4 value="v48">
<PARAM NAME=c5 value="v52">
<PARAM NAME=c6 value="v12">
<PARAM NAME=c7 value="fC2+(C3+(C4+(C5+C6)))">
<PARAM NAME=d1 value="lTotal Cost">
<PARAM NAME=d2 value="fA2+(B2+C2)">
<PARAM NAME=d3 value="fA3+(B3+C3)">
<PARAM NAME=d4 value="fA4+(B4+C4)">
<PARAM NAME=d5 value="fA5+(B5+C5)">
<PARAM NAME=d6 value="fA6+(B6+C6)">
<PARAM NAME=d7 value="fD2+(D3+(D4+(D5+D6)))">
<PARAM NAME=e1 value="lCost/Expense">
<PARAM NAME=e2 value="fA2/(B2+C2)">
<PARAM NAME=e3 value="fA3/(B3+C3)">
<PARAM NAME=e4 value="fA4/(B4+C4)">
<PARAM NAME=e5 value="fA5/(B5+C5)">
<PARAM NAME=e6 value="fA6/(B6+C6)">
```

continues

Listing 21.24. continued

```
</APPLET>
<HR>
<A HREF="SpreadSheet.java">The source.</A>
</BODY>
</HTML>
```

Summary

After completing this chapter, you should have a good understanding of how to develop advanced applets using the Java programming language. Although you may be able to develop and implement some applets in a single day, more advanced projects are developed and implemented over a period of days, weeks, or months. Most advanced projects include six phases: requirements, specification/analysis, planning, design, implementation, and testing.

The SpreadSheet applet developed in this chapter has many characteristics of advanced applets. Now that you have examined it, you should have a better understanding of using text and graphics, manipulating text strings, using mathematical formulas, and processing user input.

21

Designing and Implementing Advanced Applications

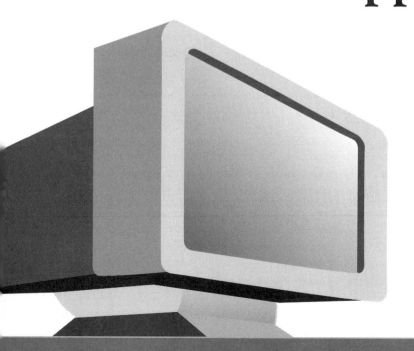

Java is a programming language that knows no bounds. Just as you can create advanced applications in other programming languages, you can do so in Java as well. This chapter takes you step by step through the development of an advanced application called Jompanion.

Jompanion is a companion editor for Java programming that includes many features found in advanced applications. Whereas previous chapters have focused primarily on programming concepts, this chapter focuses on design concepts. The design of your application's interface tells the user a lot about the program itself. Well-designed applications feature friendly graphical interfaces complete with pull-down menus, choice menus, and pop-up windows.

Because the Jompanion editor has a well-thought-out design, it is the perfect example for illustrating design issues. The editor also includes a complete set of advanced functions that you can use in just about any application you create.

Project Development and Planning

Although you can often create a small application on a whim, you should create advanced applications only with careful forethought. The more complex the project, the more involved your planning should be. For most projects, planning involves mapping out the steps necessary to complete the project on paper. For very complex projects you might want to use a project-management tool such as Microsoft Project to make the planning process easier.

Each step is generally allocated a time period, such as six days for planning or eight days for implementation. Some steps are dependent on other steps, meaning they cannot be started until other aspects of the project are completed. Other steps are not dependent on any other steps and can be performed at any time during the project's development. Therefore, when you map out the steps necessary to complete the project, you should always note which steps are dependent on others and which are independent.

After you plot out the steps that will take you through project completion, you can group the steps into phases that form the software development life cycle for the application. Generally, most projects include six phases:

- **Requirements phase:** This phase is when you determine project needs by first examining the purpose, scope, and audience of the project and then evaluating your reasonable expectations for the project. Finally, you translate these needs, goals, and purposes into project requirements.

- **Specification/Analysis phase:** During this phase, you determine the inner workings of the application. You can do this in a traditional manner, through specification diagrams such as data flow diagrams or state transition diagrams, or you can simply write out the programming logic. You should also define the necessary objects and the functions they will perform.

- **Planning phase:** During the planning phase, you take the requirements and specifications developed in the previous phases and plot out the steps necessary to complete the project.

- **Design phase:** The design phase is when you design the layout of the project in more detail than you did in the specification phase. For example, you might create outlines for classes and methods.

- **Implementation phase:** During the implementation phase, you actually create the project you have developed. This phase often takes the longest period of time.

- **Testing phase:** During the testing phase, you ensure the project performs as it was designed. Ideally, testing is an ongoing phase throughout the development of the project. In fact, when you complete each phase you should verify the materials you have generated.

The duration of each phase should be relevant to the size and complexity of the application you are developing. You might be able to develop and implement a project with limited scope in a single day, but for more advanced projects this process can take days, weeks, or months.

Although each phase should be performed in order, you can sometimes combine phases if it suits your needs. For Jompanion, I combined the requirements, specification, and planning phases into a general phase called development and planning.

Determining Requirements

When you begin a new project, the first thing you should do is develop a list of project needs. If you have not created a project folder, you should do so now. The *project folder* will hold everything related to the project. Generally, your project folder will have both a paper and an electronic form. The paper form of the folder can be a three-ring binder or a note pad. The electronic version of the folder should reside on your hard drive as a directory.

To help you develop a list of project requirements, you should first identify the purpose, scope, and target user for the application. Your *purpose statement* should describe the type of application you are creating and why you are creating it. The *scope* of the project relates to its size and functionality. The *target user* is the person or group for whom you are developing the application.

Often you will have primary and secondary target users. The primary target users are those who will use the application. The secondary target users are those who may purchase or review the application. For example, although children would use an educational application, adults would purchase it. The children using the application would want it to be fun. The adults buying the application would want it to help the children learn.

The purpose, scope, and target user for Jompanion are defined as follows:

Purpose:

A companion editor for Java programming

Scope:

An advanced application with many features

Target user:

Anyone who plans to do Java programming and wants an easy-to-use text editor.

Next, make a list of constraints for the project. Constraints that apply to most projects include duration, size, and budget. Normally, you will specify the duration of the project if you have a deadline. When you have a set amount of time or money to invest in the project, you will want to constrain the budget. You might also want to limit the size of the application, especially if performance and memory use are a concern. The initial constraints for Jompanion are

Project duration:

No more than 2 weeks

Project size:

25–50KB

Project budget:

40–50 hours

After you have determined the project constraints, you can develop a list of needs. Project needs include personnel, computer hardware and software, financial resources, and supplies. For Jompanion, the list of needs is small:

- A computer with the Java Developer's Kit installed on it
- Disk space on hard drive
- Floppy disks to back up the project
- Daily time investment

Defining the Necessary Objects

After determining project requirements, you should create an overview of the inner workings of the application by defining the necessary objects and the flow of data between the objects. The way you map out the objects and their flow will largely depend on the type of application you are developing, the modeling tools you are using, and the development philosophy at the organization where you work. For Jompanion, I borrowed some of the concepts used in structured analysis.

Preliminary modeling in structured analysis is done in the *environmental model*, which helps you define the interfaces between your application and the user. The environmental model includes three key components:

- Statement of purpose—Provides a brief description of the application for the management staff.

- Context diagram—Provides an overview of the interaction between the application and outside entities.

- Event list—Provides a complete list of events that can occur and to which the application must respond.

You will find that the components of the environmental model are useful for most projects and can be modified to suit almost any type of project. Earlier I defined a brief statement of purpose for Jompanion. I expanded upon it for use by management as follows:

Statement of Purpose:

The purpose of the Jompanion text editor is to be a companion editor for Java development. The editor includes advanced features that make it useful for development, but it uses minimal system resources.

The *context diagram* defines the external entities with which the application interacts. You will find that the more complex the system, the more useful the diagram. As you can see in Figure 21.1, the only entities Jompanion interacts with are the user and the file system.

Figure 21.1.
Context diagram for Jompanion.

The most useful component of the environmental model is the *event list*. The event list for Jompanion provides a complete list of events it should support. You use this list to help you define objects for your application. Events for Jompanion include

- Create a new file
- Open a file
- Save current file
- Save current file with a new name
- Find a keyword or phrase
- Replace a keyword or phrase with another keyword or phrase
- Replace all occurrences of a keyword or phrase with another keyword or phrase
- Cut text and save to a buffer

- Copy text and save to a buffer
- Paste text from the buffer
- Change font type
- Change font size
- Provide help or overview information
- Inform user when errors occur
- Allow user to resize the window if necessary
- Quit or exit the editor

After you develop the environmental model for your application, you can go on to more detailed modeling. This is when you translate the event list into data flow, input, and output. Whether you use data-flow diagrams, state-transition diagrams, petri nets, or some other type of data models will primarily depend on the type of application you are developing.

Plotting the Project to Completion

After you have modeled the project, you can plan it. The first thing you should do in the planning stage is work out a schedule for the project. The schedule does not have to be absolute, however; the best schedules are flexible and include the necessary milestones, goals, and time allocations to take the project through to completion.

The purpose of the schedule is to get you thinking about the project. Plotting the project to completion helps you visualize the finished project and transforms it from an abstract idea to something more tangible and doable. The schedule for Jompanion is based on the materials developed in earlier stages of the project.

After you develop a schedule, reevaluate the project specifications. Are the constraints, needs, and functionality determined earlier realistic given the timetable you have developed? If the answer is yes, you can go on to designing the project.

If the answer is no, carefully review the project and see what you can modify. Sometimes this might mean going back to management and asking for more time. Other times it might mean postponing the development of nonessential functions.

Project Design

During the *design phase*, you use the preliminary materials developed in the previous phases to design the application. Because Java is an object-oriented language, it seems logical that you use object-oriented design methodology to create Java applications. The goal of object-oriented design is to determine the objects in an application and then to design the application in terms of those objects.

If you take a close look at the event list developed earlier in the section titled "Defining the Necessary Objects," you should see that it translates into a series of objects needed in the application. Start by grouping the events into object categories, such as functions and user interfaces. Then consider which object groups should be added to the main window. For Jompanion, these objects include a menu bar, choice menus, a text area, and the file you are editing. There must be containers for these objects in the application.

You also need to allow users to manipulate the main window of the application. In most applications, this is a feature of the method that displays the window. This method should describe either the attributes of the window or the call functions that describe those attributes. Some of the attributes you should consider for the main window of any application include

- Initial screen size
- Color of the screen and borders
- Color, size, and font type of text on the screen
- Location of window-manipulation mechanisms
- Style of the title bar
- Location of the menu bar
- Size of the text area

The next object to design is a menu bar with several menus. You can determine the type of menus by grouping the functions of the editor into common categories, as shown in Table 21.1.

Table 21.1. The **MenuBar** object.

Object	Component
Menu bar	File menu
	Edit menu
	About menu

Each menu component contains *menu items*, which are objects that perform specific operations. These operations are driven by the events defined earlier in this chapter and help to define the methods needed in the application. Table 21.2 shows these operations.

Table 21.2. Menu functions.

Object	Menu Item	Purpose
File menu	New	Create a new file
	Open	Open a file

continues

Table 21.2. continued

Object	Menu Item	Purpose
	Save	Save current file
	Save As	Save current file with a new name
	Exit	Exit the editor
Edit menu	Find	Find a keyword or phrase
	Replace	Replace a keyword or phrase
	Replace All	Replace all occurrences of a keyword or phrase
	Cut	Cut text and save to a buffer
	Copy	Copy text and save to a buffer
	Paste	Paste text from the buffer
About menu	About	Provide help or overview information

In Java, events the user can cause by clicking a mouse button are generally called *action events*. A set of related events, called *key actions*, are events that occur when the user presses a key. As you design the application, you should consider mapping certain key actions to events. To make the Jompanion editor easier to use, I decided to map most events to the function keys, thus letting the user press a function key to initiate an event. Table 21.3 shows how I mapped the function keys to events.

Table 21.3. Mapping key actions to events.

Function Key	Related Event
F1	Open
F2	Save
F3	Save As
F4	Find
F5	Replace
F6	Replace All
F7	Cut
F8	Copy
F9	Paste

The next two objects in the application are the choice menus that allow users to select the size and type of the font. (See Table 21.4.) When a user makes a selection, all text in the current document is displayed in the new font type or size.

Table 21.4. Choice menus.

Selection Menu	Selection Menu Choices
Font Type	Courier
	System
	Helvetica
	Times Roman
Font Size	6
	7
	8
	9
	. . .
	24

So far, I have accounted for all but two of the events specified earlier, but the application still lacks a mechanism to inform users when errors occur. Most applications display errors in pop-up windows, which sounds like a good idea. This revelation, however, leads to the question of where in the application other pop-up windows might be needed and what purpose they will serve. Pop-up windows that display information or accept user input are generally called *dialog boxes*; Table 21.5 shows the list of dialog boxes to be used in the Jompanion application.

Table 21.5. Dialog boxes for Jompanion.

Dialog Box	Description
Error	Informs the user when an error occurs
Find	Lets the user enter search text
Help	Displays quick keys for the editor
Open File	Allows the user to open a file
Replace	Lets the user enter text to search for and the text with which to replace it
Replace All	Lets the user replace all occurrences of a word or phrase
Save File	Allows the user to save a file

Now that you have identified the major objects used in the application, you can create a list of them. As you implement each object in the next phase, you can check off the object from the list to be sure that you have accounted for all the major functions of the application.

Key Object List:

- About dialog box
- About menu item
- Choice menu for font size
- Choice menu for font type
- Copy menu item
- Cut menu item
- Error dialog box
- Exit menu item
- `File` object
- Find dialog box
- Find menu item
- Main window
- Menu bar
- New menu item
- Open File dialog box
- Open menu item
- Paste menu item
- Replace All dialog box
- Replace All menu item
- Replace dialog box
- Replace menu item
- Save As menu item
- Save File dialog box
- Save menu item
- Text-editing area

After mapping out most of the objects and events for the application, you can go on to more detailed design. Here you should work out the interaction between objects and determine the arguments objects will accept and pass. When you are comfortable with the design of the application and can visualize the flow of data from object to object, you can begin the implementation phase. The next section provides a detailed description of how Jompanion was transformed from a concept to a completed application.

Project Implementation

In the *implementation phase*, you create the source code for the project. For most advanced projects, this phase is actually a combined phase involving teams of programmers who implement and integrate the source code. Generally, each programming team is responsible for creating a specific set of objects with related functionality, such as the user interface or file I/O. After these object sets are created, they are integrated into the application.

The Java programming language shakes up this methodology by allowing programming teams to focus on higher-level functions, which can cut hundreds of hours off any advanced project. As you saw in the "Project Design" section, the Jompanion editor is a fairly advanced project, especially when you consider it has a completely graphical user interface. If Jompanion were programmed in C, the source code would easily run 10,000+ lines. Thanks to the class libraries in the Java API, the source code for Jompanion is just over 800 lines.

The sections that follow show you how to build the Jompanion editor following the design I have described. Step by step, each of the objects identified in the design is implemented. As with any program created in an object-oriented programming language, the key objects identified in the design phase need containers so they can be used throughout the program. The next section details those containers.

Containers for the Objects

One purpose of the design phase is to help you identify objects needed in the application. In the source code, you must create an instance of these objects before you can use them. You do this by declaring containers for the objects as instance variables. Most instance-variable declarations follow the main class declaration.

Whenever you use instance variables, you should try to determine if initial or default values are needed. In Jompanion, 20 of the key containers follow the Jompanion class declaration:

```
//container for the editing window in the application
  TextArea textArea;
  //container for the choice menu for font type
  //container for the size of the font as a string
  String fontSize;
  //container for the name of the current font
  String fontName = "Courier";
  //container for the size of the font as a number
  int fontNumeric = 12;

  Choice fontChoice;
  //container for the choice menu for font size
  Choice sizeChoice;
  //container for the file object
  private String fileName = null;
  //container for the about dialog box
```

```
    private AboutDialog aboutDialog = null;
    //container for the error dialog box
    private ErrorDialog errorDialog = null;
    //container for the find dialog box
    private FindDialog findDialog = null;
    //container for the replace dialog box
    private ReplaceDialog replaceDialog = null;
    //container for the replace all dialog box
    private ReplaceAllDialog replaceAllDialog = null;
    //container for the open file dialog box
    private FileDialog openDialog;
    //container for the save file dialog box
    private FileDialog saveDialog;
    //container for the about menu item
    private MenuItem aboutMenuItem;
    //container for the copy menu item
    private MenuItem copyMenuItem;
    //container for the cut menu item
    private MenuItem cutMenuItem;
    //container for the exit menu item
    private MenuItem exitMenuItem;
    //container for the find menu item
    private MenuItem findMenuItem;
    //container for the new menu item
    private MenuItem newMenuItem;
    //container for the open menu item
    private MenuItem openMenuItem;
    //container for the paste menu item
    private MenuItem pasteMenuItem;
    //container for the replace all menu item
    private MenuItem replaceAllMenuItem;
    //container for the replace menu item
    private MenuItem replaceMenuItem;
    //container for the save as menu item
    private MenuItem saveAsMenuItem;
    //container for the save menu item
```

Naturally, a text editor needs objects associated with the direct manipulation of text. Although the objects associated with the menus and dialog boxes are used to display the graphical user interface, they do not directly manipulate the text. You have already identified the key functions for manipulating text; now all you need to do is define containers to hold the objects used to manipulate text. These containers include the following:

```
//container for the text you are copying
  String copyString = "";
  //container for the text you are searching for
  String findString = "";
  //container for the text you are replacing the search text with
  String replaceString = "";
  //container for the size of the font as a string
  String fontSize = "";
  //container for the name of the current font
  String fontName = "Courier";
  //container for the size of the font as a number
```

Building the Main Window

The way you design and implement the main window of your application is extremely important. Users do not want to stare at a screen with colors that hurt their eyes, nor do they want to go through three or four menu levels to perform core functions such as copying text or opening a file. Users also do not like applications that are frustrating to use. For this reason, your main window should

- Be visually appealing
- Provide quick access to all major functions of the application
- Be friendly and logically organized

As you add features to the application's main window, you should keep these concepts in mind. The key features for Jompanion's main window were identified in the design phase, including a menu bar, two choice menus, a text area, and a file object. Earlier, you should have also identified key attributes for the main window, such as the color of the background and text, the initial font type and size, and the size of the window.

The Jompanion() method shown in Listing 21.1 sets up the main window for the Jompanion editor. A call to super places the title bar on the window. The background color is set to white. The font size and type are set to the default values for the fontName and fontNumeric objects.

Listing 21.1. The **Jompanion()** method.

```
/**
 * This method Adds all the essential object interfaces to the application
 * and displays the application as well.
 */
  public Jompanion() {

    super("Jompanion
    ➥Written by William R. Stanek (c) 1996");

    setBackground(Color.white);
    setFont(new Font(fontName, Font.PLAIN, fontNumeric));

    AddMenu();
    AddChoice();
    AddTextArea();
    AddDialog();

    Dimension d;
    d = Toolkit.getDefaultToolkit().getScreenSize();
    resize(d.width, d.height);

    show();
    textArea.requestFocus();
  }
```

Next, the key objects are added to the screen by calling their associated methods. You should always call these objects in the order you want them to be placed on the screen. The AddMenu() method adds the menu bar to the window. The AddChoice() method adds the two choice menus to the window. The AddTextArea() method adds the text area to the window. The AddDialog() method sets up the file I/O dialog box for File objects.

After the key objects are constructed, the window size is set to the current screen size. This is done by obtaining the dimensions for the user's screen and then resizing the main window to the screen size. You can also use this technique to set the initial window size proportional to the user's screen size. The final step is to display the main window. Figure 21.2 shows Jompanion's main window.

Figure 21.2.
Jompanion's main window.

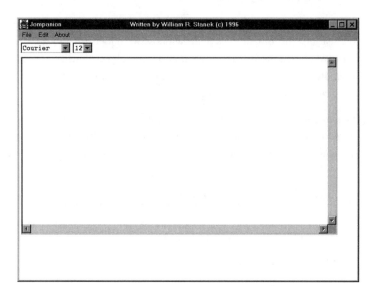

Adding the Menu Bar with Pull-down Menus

The first step in creating the objects used in Jompanion's main window is to build the menu bar. The menu bar contains pull-down menus from which users can make selections. Although you can put as many pull-down menus as you want on a single menu bar, you should try to limit the number of pull-down menus to 10 or less. By the same token, you should also try to limit the number of menu items on any single pull-down menu.

When determining the number of items for a menu, keep in mind that you should balance the length of the menus if possible. A good rule of thumb is to limit menu items to roughly two times the number of menus. Thus, instead of building a menu bar with three pull-down menus and roughly 30 menu items per pull-down, you could create a menu bar with seven pull-down menus and roughly 14 menu items per pull-down.

As shown in Listing 21.2, the menu bar for Jompanion was created by logically grouping the necessary functions of the editor into three menus. The first menu, called File, contains file-related menu items. The second menu, Edit, contains all the editing functions. The third menu, About, contains a menu item that provides information on function-key assignments. Although you should try to balance the length of items in menus, for some menus like Jompanion's About menu it doesn't make sense to add other items to the menu.

To make the menu more readable and quicker to scan, menu items should be logically grouped and ordered into subcategories as well. You can separate subcategories in a pull-down menu using the addSeparator() method, which adds a graphical rule to the menu that serves to visually separate categories of menu items. Jompanion's File menu is divided into three subcategories of file-related functions with two separators. Similarly, the Edit menu is divided into two subcategories of editing functions with one separator.

After all menus and menu items are added to the menu bar, the menu bar is set for display using the setMenuBar()method. Keep in mind that the menu bar is not actually displayed until the show() method is invoked. Figure 21.3 shows Jompanion with the Edit menu activated.

Listing 21.2. Adding the menu bar.

```
/**
 * Menu Creation Routines:
 * File: New, Open (F1), Save (F2), Save As (F3), Exit
 * Edit: Find (F4), Replace (F5), Replace All (F6),
 *       Cut (F7), Copy (F8), Paste (F9)
 * About: About Jompanion
 */

  private void AddMenu() {

    Menu menu;
    MenuBar menuBar = new MenuBar();
    //Sets up the File menu
    menu = new Menu("File");
    newMenuItem = new MenuItem("New");
    menu.add(newMenuItem);
    openMenuItem = new MenuItem("Open  (F1)");
    menu.add(openMenuItem);
    menu.addSeparator();
    saveMenuItem = new MenuItem("Save  (F2)");
    menu.add(saveMenuItem);
    saveAsMenuItem = new MenuItem("Save As  (F3)");
    menu.add(saveAsMenuItem);
    menu.addSeparator();
    exitMenuItem = new MenuItem("Exit");
    menu.add(exitMenuItem);
    menuBar.add(menu);
    //sets up the Edit menu
    menu = new Menu("Edit");
    findMenuItem = new MenuItem("Find  (F4)");
```

continues

Listing 21.2. continued

```
    menu.add(findMenuItem);
    replaceMenuItem = new MenuItem("Replace  (F5)");
    menu.add(replaceMenuItem);
    replaceAllMenuItem = new MenuItem("ReplaceAll  (F6)");
    menu.add(replaceAllMenuItem);
    menu.addSeparator();
    cutMenuItem = new MenuItem("Cut  (F7)");
    menu.add(cutMenuItem);
    copyMenuItem = new MenuItem("Copy  (F8)");
    menu.add(copyMenuItem);
    pasteMenuItem = new MenuItem("Paste  (F9)");
    menu.add(pasteMenuItem);
    menuBar.add(menu);
    //sets up the About menu
    menu = new Menu("About");
    aboutMenuItem = new MenuItem("About Jompanion");
    menu.add(aboutMenuItem);
    menuBar.add(menu);
    setMenuBar(menuBar);
  }
```

Figure 21.3.
Jompanion's Edit menu.

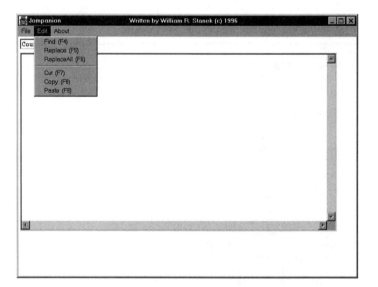

Adding the Choice Menus

The second step in creating the objects used in Jompanion's main window is to create the two choice menus identified in the design phase. Unlike menus that are added to an application via a menu bar, choice menus are added as individual objects. Although you could group the choice menus on a panel, the choice menus used in Jompanion are added directly to the main window. This is done by declaring instances of the Choice() method for the fontChoice and fontSize menu objects, adding items to the menus, and then using the add() method to add the choice menus to the main window.

> **Tip:** If you have not set the layout for the current window, the choice menus will not display. Although you could set the layout in Jompanion's `addChoice()` method, the layout is currently set in the `addText()` method. Either way, the choice menus and the text area are placed onto the screen with the same layout.

When you design a choice menu, you should use clear organization. Notice in Listing 21.3 that Jompanion uses both an alphabetic and a numeric list. Generally, choice menus with alphabetic lists should be in alphabetic order, and choice menus with numeric lists should be in numeric order.

Listing 21.3. Adding the choice menus.

```
/**
 * AddChoice creates the choice boxes for font type and size.
 * Once the choice boxes are built, they are added to the application.
 */
 private void AddChoice() {

   //set up choice box for font type
   fontChoice = new Choice();
   fontChoice.addItem("Courier");
   fontChoice.addItem("Helvetica");
   fontChoice.addItem("System");
   fontChoice.addItem("TimesRoman");
   fontChoice.select(0);
   add(fontChoice);

   //set up choice box for font size
   sizeChoice = new Choice();
   sizeChoice.addItem("8");
   sizeChoice.addItem("10");
   sizeChoice.addItem("12");
   sizeChoice.addItem("14");
   sizeChoice.addItem("16");
   sizeChoice.addItem("18");
   sizeChoice.addItem("20");
   sizeChoice.addItem("22");
   sizeChoice.addItem("24");
   sizeChoice.addItem("26");
   sizeChoice.addItem("28");
   sizeChoice.addItem("30");
   sizeChoice.select(2);
   add(sizeChoice);
   }
```

You should always set appropriate default values that mirror the initial settings for the application, especially when the menu affects the screen display. If the default values are not set, the first choice in the menu is displayed. The default value for the `fontChoice` menu object in Jompanion is set to Courier, and the default value for the `fontSize` menu object is set to 12. These defaults mirror the initial settings for font type and font size specified in the variable declarations. The `select()` method is used to set the default value.

Adding the Text Area

The third step in creating the objects used in Jompanion's main window is to build the text area. This is done using the `TextArea()` method. Because the `TextArea()` method only allows you to set the size of the text area in terms of rows and columns, the optimal size of the text area is difficult to determine and ultimately depends on the display mode of the end-user's computer and the font type and size being used.

Jompanion sets the size of the text area to 24 rows and 80 columns. For users with a 640×480 display mode or a 13" Macintosh screen, 24 rows by 80 columns is probably a good size for the text area. However, this means that the text area will not fill the screen on computer systems with larger display modes. Because the text area is for editing and previewing text files, the boolean value `SetEditable` is set to `true` before the text area is displayed.

The method in Jompanion that calls the `TextArea()` method is called `AddTextArea`, which is defined as follows:

```
/**
 * AddTextArea creates the text area for your edit sessions.
 */
 private void AddTextArea() {
   setLayout(new FlowLayout(FlowLayout.LEFT));
   textArea = new TextArea(24, 80);
   textArea.setEditable(true);
   add(textArea);
 }
```

Adding `File` Objects

The final step in creating the objects used in Jompanion's main window is to initialize the dialog boxes for opening and saving files. This is done by creating new instances of `FileDialog`. The first dialog box is set with a value of `LOAD`, which allows the user to open files using the `FileDialog` method and its associated pop-up window. The second dialog box is set with a value of `SAVE`, which allows the user to save files using the `FileDialog` method and its associated pop-up window.

The method in Jompanion that calls the `FileDialog()` method is called `AddDialog` and is defined as follows:

```
/**
 * AddDialog initializes the dialog boxes for opening and saving files.
 */
 private void AddDialog() {
   openDialog = new FileDialog(this, "Open File",FileDialog.LOAD);
   saveDialog = new FileDialog(this, "Save File",FileDialog.SAVE);
 }
```

Setting the Wheels in Motion

Although the Jompanion() method builds the main window and calls the methods that add objects to the window, it is not the method that sets the whole application in motion. This task is handled by the main() method, which is the first method invoked when any application starts. The purpose of Jompanion's main() method is to call the Jompanion() method.

To increase the functionality of the application as a whole, you can allow the application to accept a filename as a parameter. For this reason, Jompanion's main() method lets you pass the name of a file you want to open when the application starts. In addition to being able to open a file in the current directory simply by entering the filename, you can also specify the path to the file when you invoke Jompanion from the command line.

The code for the main() method follows:

```
//the main method of the application invokes the Jompanion method
public static void main(String args[]) {
  Jompanion n = new Jompanion();
  if (args.length == 1)
    if (n.read(args[0])) n.fileName = args[0];
  }
}
```

All events that occur after the application starts and the main window displays are user driven. *User-driven events* occur when the user makes a selection on a menu, presses a function key, or causes an error.

Handling Events

The best way to handle events in applications is with the handleEvent() method. Most of the events that your application handles should have been identified when you created the event list during the design phase. Normally, appropriate actions for each of these events should be defined in your application's handleEvent() method. However, two particular events—error handling and window resizing—are generally not handled at this level. Because error handling is particular to a class or method, events related to errors are usually handled at a lower level. Because window resizing is particular to each window used in the application, window resizing is also handled at a lower level.

Updating the font type and font size based on a choice menu involves converting argument values. For font type, the value of the argument related to the target event is converted to a string. The string contains the name of the font the user selected and is used as an input value for the Font() method. Converting the font size is a bit more tricky. First, a string called fontSize is set to the value of the target argument; then the string is converted to an integer value using the parseInt() method. Because this method throws an exception, the exception is checked for and corrected if it occurs.

The handleEvent() method plays a crucial role in the behavior of your application. If there is a flaw in your event-handling logic, your program will not behave as you expect. The first draft of Jompanion's handleEvent method for events related to font type and size contains a logic flaw that causes the font setting to not get updated as you would expect. Because the values for font type and font size are set in separate if...then statements in the code that follows, the application forgets the value of the current fontName object when you set value for the fontSize object and forgets the value of the current fontSize object when you set the value for the fontName object:

```
if(event.target == fontChoice) {
            String fontName = event.arg.toString();
            textArea.setFont(new Font(fontName, Font.PLAIN, fontNumeric));
            }
        if(event.target == sizeChoice) {
            String fontSize = event.arg.toString();
            try {
                fontNumeric = Integer.parseInt(fontSize);

              } catch (NumberFormatException e) {
                fontNumeric = 12;      // If error occurs set font size to 12
              }
            textArea.setFont(new Font(fontName, Font.PLAIN, fontNumeric));
            }
```

The logic flaw is corrected by setting the fontName and fontSize values in the same if...then statement, as shown in the code sample that follows. To do this, the two related events are combined using a logical or. Thus when the user makes a selection on either choice menu, the values for both the fontName object and fontSize object are set:

```
if(event.target == fontChoice ¦¦ event.target == sizeChoice){
            String fontName = event.arg.toString();
            textArea.setFont(new Font(fontName, Font.PLAIN, fontNumeric));
            String fontSize = event.arg.toString();
            try {
                fontNumeric = Integer.parseInt(fontSize);

              } catch (NumberFormatException e) {
                fontNumeric = 12;      // If error occurs set font size to 12
              }
            textArea.setFont(new Font(fontName, Font.PLAIN, fontNumeric));
            }
```

Jompanion's event list includes 16 items. Except for error handling and window resizing, each of these events is handled by the method shown in Listing 21.4. When a user closes the main window, the WINDOW_DESTROY event occurs and the program exits. When a user makes a selection from a pull-down or choice menu, an ACTION_EVENT event occurs. If the event is an instance of a MenuItem object, a method that corresponds to the selected menu item is called, such as cut() or paste(). If the value associated with the event is an instance of fontChoice or fontSize, a new font type or size is set for the text area. When a user presses a key, a KEY_ACTION event occurs, and the method associated with the key is called.

Listing 21.4. Handling events from the menu bar.

```java
/**
 * Handle Events:
 * Event.WINDOW_DESTROY: ensures clean exit
 * Event.ACTION_EVENT: Events from menu and choice boxes
 * Event.KEY_ACTION: Press function keys
 */

  public boolean handleEvent(Event event) {
    switch(event.id) {
      case Event.WINDOW_DESTROY:
        System.exit(0);
      case Event.ACTION_EVENT:
        if(event.target instanceof MenuItem) {
          if(event.target == aboutMenuItem) showAboutDialog();
          else if(event.target == copyMenuItem) copy();
          else if(event.target == cutMenuItem) cut();
          else if(event.target == exitMenuItem) System.exit(0);
          else if(event.target == findMenuItem) showFindDialog();
          else if(event.target == newMenuItem) startNewWindow();
          else if(event.target == openMenuItem) openFile();
          else if(event.target == pasteMenuItem) paste();
          else if(event.target == replaceAllMenuItem) showReplaceAllDialog();
          else if(event.target == replaceMenuItem) showRepDialog();
          else if(event.target == saveAsMenuItem) saveAsFile();
          else if(event.target == saveMenuItem) saveOpenedFile();
        }
        if(event.target == fontChoice || event.target == sizeChoice){
            String fontName = event.arg.toString();
            textArea.setFont(new Font(fontName, Font.PLAIN, fontNumeric));
            String fontSize = event.arg.toString();
            try {
                fontNumeric = Integer.parseInt(fontSize);

              } catch (NumberFormatException e) {
                fontNumeric = 12;      // If error occurs set font size to 12
            }
            textArea.setFont(new Font(fontName, Font.PLAIN, fontNumeric));
          }
      return(true);
        if(event.target == fontChoice || event.target == sizeChoice){
            String fontName = event.arg.toString();
            textArea.setFont(new Font(fontName, Font.PLAIN, fontNumeric));
            String fontSize = event.arg.toString();
            try {
                fontNumeric = Integer.parseInt(fontSize);

              } catch (NumberFormatException e) {
                fontNumeric = 12;      // If error occurs set font size to 12
            }
            textArea.setFont(new Font(fontName, Font.PLAIN, fontNumeric));
          }
      case Event.KEY_ACTION:
        if(event.key == Event.F1) openFile();
        else if (event.key == Event.F2) saveOpenedFile();
        else if (event.key == Event.F3) saveAsFile();
```

continues

Listing 21.4. continued

```
        else if (event.key == Event.F4) showFindDialog();
        else if (event.key == Event.F5) showRepDialog();
        else if (event.key == Event.F6) showReplaceAllDialog();
        else if (event.key == Event.F7) cut();
        else if (event.key == Event.F8) copy();
        else if (event.key == Event.F9) paste();
    }
    return(false);
}
```

Building the Utility Functions

At the heart of your application is a core set of functions, called *utility functions*, that perform most of the real work. These functions manipulate the text, graphics, audio, video, or other objects used by your application. For Jompanion, there are two sets of core functions.

The first set of core functions relates to text manipulation. The cut() method allows the user to cut selected text and place it in the buffer. This is done by setting a string equal to the value of the selected text and then calling the replaceText method of the textArea class. The values passed to the replaceText method tell it to replace the selected text from start to finish with an empty value, which effectively cuts the text from the current editing session. If you do not set a buffer, your cut() method is nothing more than the Delete key on the user's keyboard.

To update the text area after the cut, the requestFocus() method is called. The cut() method follows:

```
//cuts selected text and places it on the buffer
public void cut() {
  copyString = textArea.getSelectedText();
  textArea.replaceText("", textArea.getSelectionStart(),
                                  textArea.getSelectionEnd());
  textArea.requestFocus();
  }
```

The second core function allows the user to copy selected text to the buffer. This is done simply by setting a string equal to the value of the selected text. The copy() method follows:

```
//copies selected text to the buffer
public void copy() {
  copyString = textArea.getSelectedText();
  textArea.requestFocus();
  }
```

The third core function allows the user to paste text from the buffer. Before you paste an object to the current window, you should check to make sure the object is in the buffer. This is done in the past() method by making sure the length of the copyString object—the buffer—is greater than zero. If the copyString is set to a value, the insertText method of the textArea class is called. The values passed to the insertText method tell it to add the buffer text at the current cursor location.

The paste() method follows:

```
//pastes text from the buffer to the screen
  public void paste() {
    if (copyString.length() > 0)
      textArea.insertText(copyString,
textArea.getSelectionStart());
    textArea.requestFocus();
  }
```

The next set of core functions relates to file I/O. The openFile() method allows the user to open a text file. This is done by displaying the openDialog box initialized earlier as an instance of fileDialog. When the user enters a filename, the method checks the validity of the filename and then calls Jompanion's read() method. If the file is successfully read, a value is set for the fileName variable and the file is displayed in the text area. The openFile() method follows:

```
//method for opening files with a specified name
  private void openFile() {
    String filename;
    openDialog.show();
    filename = openDialog.getFile();
    if (filename != null) {
      filename = check(filename);
      if (read(filename)) fileName = filename;
    }
    textArea.requestFocus();
  }
```

The Save menu item allows the user to save a currently opened file. For this reason, the next file I/O function depends on a value being set for the fileName variable, which means the user opened a file and it is in the editing window. If this value is not set, the saveOpenedFile() method invokes the showErrorDialog to inform the user that he has made an error. If this value is set, the saveOpenedFile() method writes the file to the disk. The code for the method is as follows:

```
//method saves a file you opened previously.
  //method produces error if you did not open a file previously.
  public void saveOpenedFile() {
    if (fileName == null) {
      showErrorDialog("You did not previously open a file. Use Save As.");
    } else {
      write(fileName);
      textArea.requestFocus();
    }
  }
```

When the user selects the Save As menu item, the saveAsFile() method is called. This method allows the user to save the current editing session to a named file. To do this, the user enters a name for the file in the saveDialog box initialized earlier as an instance of fileDialog. Provided that a filename is entered and is valid for the system, the current editing session is saved by calling Jompanion's write() method. The code for the saveAsFile() method follows:

```
//method saves the file you are currently editing
  private void saveAsFile() {
    String filename;
```

```
      saveDialog.show();
      filename = saveDialog.getFile();
      if (filename != null) {
        filename = check(filename);
        if (write(filename)) fileName = filename;
      }
      textArea.requestFocus();
    }
```

When the user selects the New menu item, the `startNewWindow()` method is called. There are several ways you could start a new window. One way would be to clear the current editing window, as this method does:

```
  //creates a new editing session by deleting any previous text
  private void startNewWindow() {
    fileName = null;
    textArea.setText("");
    textArea.requestFocus();
  }\
```

The problem with clearing the current window is that the user could possibly lose hours of work simply by selecting the wrong menu item. Therefore, a better way to start a new window is to invoke a new instance of the `Jompanion()` method, which actually does create a new window. This is done as follows:

```
  //creates a new editing session by deleting any previous text
  private void startNewWindow() {
    Jompanion n = new Jompanion();
  }
```

Handling File I/O

After opening a File dialog box that allows the user to open or save text files, Jompanion checks the validity of the filename and then invokes related methods for reading and writing files. Jompanion's `read()` and `write()` methods extend corresponding methods in the `java.io` package and return a boolean value that indicates success or failure.

Appropriately, a method called `check` is used to check the validity of filenames. Although the method currently only checks for a bug that appends erroneous characters to the end of the filename, you could easily modify this method to always save files with a particular extension, such as `.java` or `.txt`. The `check()` method follows:

```
//method checks the validity of file names and specifically for a bug
  //fixes the error if it occurs
  private String check(String filename) {
    if (filename.endsWith(".*.*")) {
      filename = filename.substring(0, filename.length()-4);
    }
    return(filename);
  }
```

Jompanion's `read()` method, shown in Listing 21.5, reads data input from the buffered input stream one line at a time. Provided that the line contains text, the `read()` method reads the line, inserts a null character at the end of the line, and continues to read until it reaches the end of the file. When the end of the file is reached, the file is closed and the `read()` method returns the boolean value `true` to the caller.

Listing 21.5. The `read()` method.

```
//method handles reading files from the file system
private boolean read(String filename) {

    String line;
    FileInputStream in = null;
    DataInputStream dataIn = null;
    BufferedInputStream bis = null;
    StringBuffer buffer = new StringBuffer();

    try {
      in = new FileInputStream(filename);
      bis = new BufferedInputStream(in);
      dataIn = new DataInputStream(bis);
    } catch(Throwable e) {
      showErrorDialog("Can't open \""+filename+"\"");
      return(false);
    }

    try {
      while ((line = dataIn.readLine()) != null) {
        buffer.append(line + "\n");
      }
      in.close();
      textArea.setText(buffer.toString());
    } catch(IOException e) {
      showErrorDialog("Can't read \""+filename+"\"");
      return(false);
    }

    return(true);
  }
```

This method catches two errors that occur in different stages of the read process. The first error occurs when Jompanion cannot open the file; the second occurs when Jompanion cannot read a line in the open file. In either case, `read()` calls the `showErrorDialog` object, passes it an appropriate error message, and returns the boolean value `false` to the caller.

Jompanion's `write()` method, shown in Listing 21.6, is very different from the `read()` method. As long as there are characters to read from the text area, the `write()` method writes to a named output file. When the end of the file is reached, the output file is closed and the `write()` method returns the boolean value `true` to the caller.

The `write()` method catches two errors that occur in different stages of the read process. The first error occurs when Jompanion cannot open the output stream file; the second occurs when Jompanion cannot read a line from the text area and write it to the output file. In either case, `write()` calls the `showErrorDialog` object, passes it an appropriate error message, and returns the boolean value `false` to the caller.

Listing 21.6. The `write()` method.

```
//method handles writing files to the file system
private boolean write(String filename) {

  FileOutputStream os = null;

  try {
    os = new FileOutputStream(filename);
  } catch (Throwable e) {
    showErrorDialog("Can't write \""+filename+"\"");
    return(false);
  }

  try {
    String s = textArea.getText();
    int len = s.length();
    for (int i=0; i<len; i++) {
        os.write(s.charAt(i));
    }
    os.close();
  } catch(IOException e) {
    showErrorDialog("Can't write \""+filename+"\"");
    return(false);
  }

  return(true);
}
```

Displaying the Dialog Boxes

As you have probably noticed, the previous sections have not covered the methods for finding and replacing text or for displaying the related dialog boxes. Following the top-down design structure used in Jompanion, you should create the user interface before creating the methods that actually do the work of finding and replacing text. For an advanced project, the best way to create the user interface for dialog boxes is in two stages. First, you create methods that show the dialog boxes; then you create classes or methods that build the dialog boxes.

If you refer back to Jompanion's `handleEvent()` method, you will see that when a user selects a menu item, methods that show the related dialog boxes are called directly if appropriate. Jompanion uses five dialog boxes in all. The dialog boxes for find, replace, replace all, and about are called directly when a user selects a related item from a pull-down menu or presses an appropriate function key. The error dialog box is invoked only when an error occurs.

As you can see in Listing 21.7, the methods for displaying the dialog boxes are very similar. The showFindDialog() method checks to make sure it was not called with a null value. If it was, it does not display the dialog box. Otherwise, it checks to see if text is selected in the editing window, uses the selected text as the initial string for the find, and then creates a new instance of Jompanion's FindDialog class.

Listing 21.7. Displaying the dialog boxes.

```
/**
 * Show Dialog Boxes
 * Find, Replace, Replace All, About, and Error
 */

  //displays the find dialog box which has one input field.
  //Currently selected text is placed in the input field.
  public void showFindDialog() {
    if (findDialog != null) findDialog.dispose();
    String sel = textArea.getSelectedText();
    if (sel.length() > 0) findString = sel;
    findDialog = new FindDialog(this, findString);
    findDialog.show();
    findDialog.setFocus();
  }

  //displays the replace dialog box which has two input fields.
  //Currently selected text is placed in the find input field.
  //Previously searched and replaced text is placed in the input field.
  public void showRepDialog() {
    if (replaceDialog != null) replaceDialog.dispose();
    String sel = textArea.getSelectedText();
    if (sel.length() > 0) findString = sel;
    replaceDialog = new ReplaceDialog(this, findString,
replaceString);
    replaceDialog.show();
    replaceDialog.setFocus();
  }

  //displays the replace all dialog box which has two input fields.
  //Currently selected text is placed in the find input field.
  //Previously searched and replaced text is placed in the input field.
  public void showReplaceAllDialog() {
    if (replaceAllDialog != null) replaceAllDialog.dispose();
    String sel = textArea.getSelectedText();
    if (sel.length() > 0) findString = sel;
    replaceAllDialog = new ReplaceAllDialog(this, findString,
replaceString);
    replaceAllDialog.show();
    replaceAllDialog.setFocus();
  }

  //displays the about dialog box
  private void showAboutDialog() {
    if (aboutDialog != null) aboutDialog.dispose();
    aboutDialog = new AboutDialog(this);
```

continues

Listing 21.7. continued

```
    aboutDialog.show();
}

//displays the error dialog box and the current error
public void showErrorDialog(String message) {
    if (errorDialog != null) errorDialog.dispose();
    errorDialog = new ErrorDialog(this, message);
    errorDialog.show();
}
```

Although the `showReplaceDialog()` and `showReplaceAllDialog()` methods behave similarly, you should note that new instances of their related classes are passed two strings: `findString` and `replaceString`. Because the `findString` and `replaceString` objects are declared in the `Jompanion` class and are not access restricted, they are accessible to any of the methods and classes in Jompanion. This allows text placed in these strings to be buffered, which provides additional functionality for the user.

When the user finds text using the Find dialog box, the find string is buffered. If the user later selects Replace or Replace All from the Edit menu, the current value of the find string is placed on the appropriate line of the dialog box. However, because the `showReplaceDialog()` and the `showReplaceAllDialog()` methods check for selected text and assign this value to the `findString` object, currently selected text always replaces any previously buffered value for the `findString` object.

Similarly, Jompanion remembers the value of the `replaceString` object, which makes it easier to follow a single replace with a replace all. You should consider using buffers in your applications as well.

Because the `showAboutDialog()` and the `showErrorDialog()` methods do not allow the user to manipulate objects, they are set up differently. The `showAboutDialog()` method simply creates a new instance of Jompanion's `AboutDialog` class and displays it. The `showErrorDialog()` method creates a new instance of Jompanion's `ErrorDialog` class. The string passed to the `ErrorDialog` class contains a message related to the error that occurred.

Building the Dialog Boxes

Because the objects that build Jompanion's dialog boxes contain several methods and discrete functionality, I created them as class-level objects. Declaring these objects within class structures provides the added advantage of reducing the overhead associated with the dialog boxes until they are actually needed and making it easier to handle the distinct functionality of each dialog box.

The `FindDialog` Class

The `FindDialog` class, shown in Listing 21.8, is the first of five related classes that extend the `Dialog` class of the AWT package. The purpose of the `FindDialog` class is to build the Find dialog box, handle related events, and set the focus of the editing window. These three functions are controlled by separate methods. Figure 21.4 shows Jompanion with the Find dialog box active.

Figure 21.4.
Jompanion's Find dialog box.

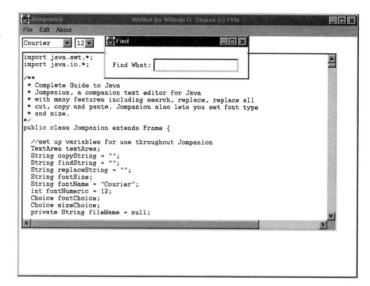

Listing 21.8. The `FindDialog` class.

```
/**
 * The FindDialog Class sets up the find dialog box
 * and handles related events.
 */
class FindDialog extends Dialog {

  Jompanion parent;
  TextField textField;

  public FindDialog(Jompanion parent, String text) {

    super(parent, "Find", true);
    setBackground(Color.white);
    this.parent = parent;

    Panel p;
    p = new Panel();
    Label l;
    l = new Label("Find What:");
    p.setLayout(null);
    l.reshape(0,25,110,30);
    p.add(l);
```

continues

Listing 21.8. continued

```
    textField = new TextField(text);
    textField.reshape(111,25,200,30);
    p.add(textField);

    add("Center", p);

    Dimension d;
    d = parent.size();
    reshape(200,50,340,100);
    setResizable(false);
}

public boolean handleEvent(Event event) {
    switch(event.id) {
      case Event.WINDOW_DESTROY:
        dispose();
        parent.textArea.requestFocus();
        return(true);
      case Event.ACTION_EVENT:
        if(event.target == textField) {
          dispose();
          if (textField.getText().length() > 0) {
            parent.setFindString(textField.getText());
            parent.findText();
            parent.textArea.requestFocus();
            return(true);
          }
        } else {
          parent.showErrorDialog("Find Error");
          parent.textArea.requestFocus();
          return(true);
        }
    }
    return(false);
}

public void setFocus() {
    textField.requestFocus();
    textField.select(0, textField.getText().length());
}
}
```

As you design your own dialog boxes for your applications, you should consider carefully their style, size, and placement. Generally, the dialog box should have a style that makes it easy to use and read. Its size should be appropriate for the contents of the box and should rarely display at more than half of the current screen size. The dialog box should also display in an appropriate location, such as centered on the current window.

The `FindDialog()` method builds the dialog box as a panel with a single text field labeled with the keywords `Find What`. The style of the Find dialog box is controlled by setting the background color, positioning the label and the text area within the panel so it is easy to read and use, and defining the layout. The size of the Find dialog box is set so that it is just large enough to display the label and the text area. Finally, the dialog box is placed so that it is displayed in the upper portion of the window and to the right of the pull-down menus. To ensure the user cannot resize the dialog box, the boolean value for the `setResizable()` method is set to `false`.

The `handleEvent()` method handles two events: the closing of the dialog box and the pressing of the Enter key with the cursor in the text field. When the user closes the dialog box, the `WINDOW_DESTROY` event occurs and the Find dialog box is closed. Because text fields are a single line of text, pressing the Enter key within the text field causes an `ACTION_EVENT` to occur. To process the related event, check for a target event that is an instance of the `TextField` object. In this class, the instance of the `TextField` object is declared as `textField`.

When an event related to object `textField` occurs, the `handleEvent()` method checks the validity of the input by checking the length of the text in the text field to ensure it is greater than zero. If the length is greater than zero, the `findText()` method of the parent class is called. Otherwise, an error occurs and an appropriate message is displayed by calling the `showErrorDialog()` method of the parent.

Note: Even when the user presses Enter and leaves the text field empty, the length of the text field is greater than zero. This is because the carriage-return and line-feed characters are generally associated with the Enter key. Therefore, it is virtually impossible for an error to occur. (However, a well-designed program checks for all possible errors and handles them appropriately if they occur.)

The final method declared in the `FindDialog` class is the `setFocus()` method. This method shows the location of the text the user searched for and then selects the search text—an easy way to highlight the results of the find.

The `ReplaceDialog` Class

Although the design of the `ReplaceDialog` class is very similar to that of the `FindDialog` class, the `ReplaceDialog` class is more complex because it uses multiple input fields. (See Listing 21.9.) The logic used to handle events from multiple text fields is extremely important. If your logic is not precise, the application will not behave as you expect. Figure 21.5 shows Jompanion with the Replace dialog box active.

Figure 21.5.
Jompanion's Replace
dialog box.

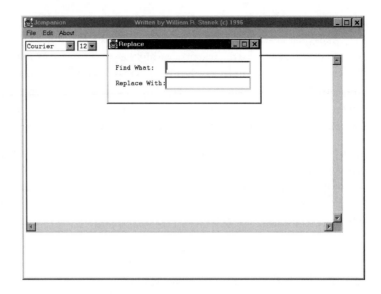

Listing 21.9. The `ReplaceDialog` class.

```
/**
 * The ReplaceDialog Class sets up the replace dialog box
 * and handles related events.
 */
class ReplaceDialog extends Dialog {

  Jompanion parent;
  TextField fromField, toField;

  public ReplaceDialog(Jompanion parent, String fromString, String
toString) {

    super(parent, "Replace", true);
    setBackground(Color.white);
    this.parent = parent;

    Panel p;
    p = new Panel();
    Label l;
    l = new Label("Find What:");
    p.setLayout(null);

    l.reshape(0,25,130,30);
    p.add(l);

    fromField = new TextField(fromString);
    fromField.reshape(131,25,200,30);
    p.add(fromField);

    l = new Label("Replace With:");
    l.reshape(0,60,130,30);
    p.add(l);
```

```
      toField = new TextField(toString);
      toField.reshape(131,60,200,30);
      p.add(toField);

      add("Center", p);

      Dimension d;
      d = parent.size();
      reshape(200,50,360,150);
      setResizable(false);
    }

  public boolean handleEvent(Event event) {
    switch(event.id) {
      case Event.WINDOW_DESTROY:
        dispose();
        parent.textArea.requestFocus();
        return(true);
      case Event.ACTION_EVENT:
        if(event.target == fromField) {
          toField.requestFocus();
          return(true);
        } else if(event.target == toField) {
          dispose();
          if (fromField.getText().length() > 0) {
            parent.setFindString(fromField.getText());
            parent.setReplaceString(toField.getText());
            parent.replaceText();
            parent.textArea.requestFocus();
            return(true);
          }
        } else {
          parent.showErrorDialog("Replace Error");
          parent.textArea.requestFocus();
          return(true);
        }
    }
    return(false);
  }

  public void setFocus() {
    fromField.requestFocus();
    fromField.select(0, fromField.getText().length());
  }
}
```

The ReplaceDialog class declares two instances of the TextField object that tell the application where to search from and the point to search to. The fromField object allows the user to input search text. The toField object allows the user to input the replacement text.

Before the handleEvent() method processes the events related to these fields, it checks the name of the field in which the user pressed Enter. If the event is related to the fromField object, the focus is reset to the toField object, which allows the user to press Enter to get to the next input field. If the event is related to the toField object and the length of the input text is greater than zero, the replaceText() method of the parent class is called. Otherwise, an error occurs and an appropriate message is displayed by calling the showErrorDialog() method of the parent.

> **Tip:** When you use multiple text fields for input values that are dependent on each other, you should always reset the focus to the next field until the user is in the final input field. When the user is in the final input field, you should then process all input values.

The `ReplaceAllDialog` Class

The `ReplaceAllDialog` class is shown in Listing 21.10. This class is almost identical to the `ReplaceDialog` class, but there is one important difference in the way this class functions. Instead of replacing a single instance of the search text, the `ReplaceAllDialog` class replaces all instances of the search text.

The programming trick used to accomplish this involves changing only a single line of the original `ReplaceDialog` class. The line of code reading

```
parent.replaceText();
```

is changed to

```
while (parent.replaceText()) ;
```

The new line of code says that while the `replaceText()` method returns a `true` value, continue to loop. Therefore, as long as the `replaceText()` method finds occurrences of the search text, the search text is replaced.

Listing 21.10. The `ReplaceAllDialog` class.

```
/**
 * The ReplaceAllDialog Class sets up the dialog box for replacing
 * all occurrences of a word or phrase and handles related events.
 */
class ReplaceAllDialog extends Dialog {

  Jompanion parent;
  TextField fromAllField, toAllField;

  public ReplaceAllDialog(Jompanion parent, String fromAllString, String
toAllString) {

    super(parent, "Replace All", true);
    setBackground(Color.white);
    this.parent = parent;

    Panel p;
    p = new Panel();
    Label l;
    l = new Label("Find All:");
    p.setLayout(null);
```

```
      l.reshape(0,25,130,30);
      p.add(l);

      fromAllField = new TextField(fromAllString);
      fromAllField.reshape(131,25,200,30);
      p.add(fromAllField);

      l = new Label("Replace With:");
      l.reshape(0,60,130,30);
      p.add(l);

      toAllField = new TextField(toAllString);
      toAllField.reshape(131,60,200,30);
      p.add(toAllField);

      add("Center", p);

      Dimension d;
      d = parent.size();
      reshape(200,50,360,150);
      setResizable(false);
    }

  public boolean handleEvent(Event event) {
    switch(event.id) {
      case Event.WINDOW_DESTROY:
        dispose();
        parent.textArea.requestFocus();
        return(true);
      case Event.ACTION_EVENT:
        if(event.target == fromAllField) {
          toAllField.requestFocus();
          return(true);
        } else if(event.target == toAllField) {
          dispose();
          if (fromAllField.getText().length() > 0) {
            parent.setFindString(fromAllField.getText());
            parent.setReplaceString(toAllField.getText());
            while (parent.replaceText()) ;
            parent.textArea.requestFocus();
            return(true);
          }
        } else {
          parent.showErrorDialog("Replace All Error");
          parent.textArea.requestFocus();
          return(true);
        }
    }
    return(false);
  }

  public void setFocus() {
    fromAllField.requestFocus();
    fromAllField.select(0, fromAllField.getText().length());
  }
}
```

The **AboutDialog** Class

The purpose of the AboutDialog class (shown in Listing 21.11) is to build the About dialog box, which displays the mapping of the function keys. The About dialog box is designed so that it can be placed in the bottom of the viewing area for easy reference. For this reason, the height of the box is set to 120 pixels and the width of the box is set to 640 pixels. A grid layout is used to align the nine entries for function keys into easy-to-read columns. To ensure the entries are logically ordered when viewed, they are organized by column in the code. Figure 21.6 shows Jompanion with the About dialog box active.

Listing 21.11. The **AboutDialog** class.

```
/**
 * The AboutDialog Class sets up the dialog box that displays
 * information about Jompanion and handles related events
 */
class AboutDialog extends Dialog {

  Jompanion parent;

  public AboutDialog(Jompanion parent) {
    super(parent, "Jompanion from the Complete Guide to Java", true);
    setBackground(Color.white);
    this.parent = parent;

    Panel p;
    p = new Panel();
    p.setLayout(new GridLayout(3, 3));
    p.add(new Label("F1 - Open Files"));
    p.add(new Label("F4 - Find"));
    p.add(new Label("F7 - Cut"));
    p.add(new Label("F2 - Save"));
    p.add(new Label("F5 - Replace"));
    p.add(new Label("F8 - Copy"));
    p.add(new Label("F3 - Save As"));
    p.add(new Label("F6 - Replace All"));
    p.add(new Label("F9 - Paste"));
    add("Center", p);

    Dimension d;
    d = parent.size();
    reshape(50,440,640,120);
    setResizable(false);
  }

  public boolean handleEvent(Event event) {
    switch(event.id) {
      case Event.WINDOW_DESTROY:
        dispose();
        parent.textArea.requestFocus();
        return(true);
    }
    return(false);
  }
}
```

Figure 21.6.

Jompanion's About dialog box.

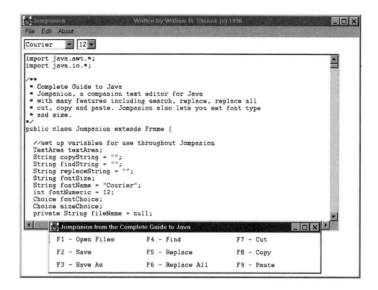

The `ErrorDialog` Class

The purpose of the `ErrorDialog` class is to build a dialog box that displays errors. (See Listing 21.12.) To ensure the dialog box gets the reader's immediate attention, it has a yellow background and a bold font.

Listing 21.12. The `ErrorDialog` class.

```
/**
 * The ErrorDialog Class sets up the dialog box that displays
 * errors to the user and handles the closing of the window
 */
class ErrorDialog extends Dialog {

  Jompanion parent;
  String message;

  public ErrorDialog(Jompanion parent, String message) {
    super(parent, "Error", true);
    setBackground(Color.yellow);
    this.parent = parent;
    this.message = message;

    Panel p;
    p = new Panel();
    p.add(new Label(message));
    p.setFont(new Font("System", Font.BOLD, 12));
    add("Center", p);

    Dimension d;
    d = parent.size();
```

continues

Listing 21.12. continued

```
    reshape(200,50,420,100);
    setResizable(false);
  }

  public boolean handleEvent(Event event) {
    switch(event.id) {
      case Event.WINDOW_DESTROY:
        dispose();
        parent.textArea.requestFocus();
        return(true);
    }
    return(false);
  }
}
```

Text-Manipulation Objects

Now that the user interface for finding and replacing text is built, you can define the associated text-manipulation objects. As with other parts of the application, it is easiest if you start with the basic objects and work to the advanced objects. As Listing 21.13 shows, Jompanion includes two basic text-manipulation objects and two advanced ones.

Listing 21.13. Text-manipulation objects.

```
//sets the find string
public void setFindString(String str) {
  findString = str;
}

//sets the replace string
public void setReplaceString(String str) {
  replaceString = str;
}

//handles the search for text in the find input field
public void findText() {

  String s;
  int spoint, index;

  textArea.requestFocus();
  if (findString.length() == 0) return;

  s = textArea.getText();
  if (s.length() == 0) return;

  spoint = textArea.getSelectionEnd();
  index = s.substring(spoint).indexOf(findString);
```

```
    if (index >= 0) {
      int i = spoint + index;
      textArea.select(i, i + findString.length());
    }
  }

  //handles replacing text
  public boolean replaceText() {
    String s;
    int spoint, index;

    textArea.requestFocus();
    if (findString.length() == 0) return(false);

    s = textArea.getText();
    if (s.length() == 0) return(false);

    spoint = textArea.getSelectionStart();
    index = s.substring(spoint).indexOf(findString);
    if (index >= 0) {
      int i = spoint + index;
      int j = i + findString.length();
      textArea.replaceText(replaceString, i, j);
      textArea.select(i, i+replaceString.length());
      return(true);
    }
    return(false);
  }
```

The purpose of the setFindString() and setReplaceString() methods is simply to set a value for the find and replace strings. These functions are created as separate methods so they can be called from wherever they are needed in the application.

The findText()method is called by the FindDialog class. The purpose of this method is to search for text entered in the Find input field by setting an index point within the document and searching forward through the document until the next instance of the text is found. The getSelectionEnd() method is used to determine the starting location of the index point. By placing the index after the current occurrence of the search text, the user can select text and then find the next occurrence of the selected text. If the index point was placed before the currently selected text using the getSelectionStart()method, the application would consider the currently selected text as the next occurrence of the search text, which is flawed logic.

The replaceText() method is called by both the ReplaceDialog class and the ReplaceAllDialog class. The purpose of this method is to search for text entered in the find input field and replace it with text in the replace input field. To ensure a currently selected occurrence of the find text is replaced, the index point for the start of the search is set with the getSelectionStart() method. If the index point was placed after the currently selected text using the getSelectionEnd() method, the application would never replace an instance of the currently selected text, which is flawed logic.

The Complete Project

Although Jompanion is a fairly advanced application, its sound design helped to ensure that the development and implementation of the project went smoothly. Listing 21.14 shows the complete code for the Jompanion application. Although typing in the code line by line forces you to study each line of code, you can go straight to the CD-ROM and access the complete source code if you choose.

Listing 21.14. The finished application.

```java
import java.awt.*;
import java.io.*;

/**
 * Peter Norton's Guide to Java Programming
 * Jompanion, a companion text editor for Java
 * with many features including search, replace, replace all
 * cut, copy and paste. Jompanion also lets you set font type
 * and size.
 */
public class Jompanion extends Frame {

  //set up variables for use throughout Jompanion

  //container for the editing window in the application
  TextArea textArea;
  //container for the choice menu for font type

  //container for the size of the font as a string
  String fontSize;
  //container for the name of the current font
  String fontName = "Courier";
  //container for the size of the font as a number
  int fontNumeric = 12;
  Choice fontChoice;
  //container for the choice menu for font size
  Choice sizeChoice;
  //container for the file object
  private String fileName = null;
  //container for the about dialog box
  private AboutDialog aboutDialog = null;
  //container for the error dialog box
  private ErrorDialog errorDialog = null;
  //container for the find dialog box
  private FindDialog findDialog = null;
  //container for the replace dialog box
  private ReplaceDialog replaceDialog = null;
  //container for the replace all dialog box
  private ReplaceAllDialog replaceAllDialog = null;
  //container for the open file dialog box
  private FileDialog openDialog;
  //container for the save file dialog box
  private FileDialog saveDialog;
  //container for the about menu item
  private MenuItem aboutMenuItem;
  //container for the copy menu item
```

```java
   private MenuItem copyMenuItem;
   //container for the cut menu item
   private MenuItem cutMenuItem;
   //container for the exit menu item
   private MenuItem exitMenuItem;
   //container for the find menu item
   private MenuItem findMenuItem;
   //container for the new menu item
   private MenuItem newMenuItem;
   //container for the open menu item
   private MenuItem openMenuItem;
   //container for the paste menu item
   private MenuItem pasteMenuItem;
   //container for the replace all menu item
   private MenuItem replaceAllMenuItem;
   //container for the replace menu item
   private MenuItem replaceMenuItem;
   //container for the save as menu item
   private MenuItem saveAsMenuItem;
   //container for the save menu item
   private MenuItem saveMenuItem;
/**
 * This method Adds all the essential object interfaces to the application
 * and displays the application as well.
 */
   public Jompanion() {

      super("Jompanion
      ➥Written by William R. Stanek (c) 1996");

      setBackground(Color.white);
      setFont(new Font(fontName, Font.PLAIN, fontNumeric));

      AddMenu();
      AddChoice();
      AddTextArea();
      AddDialog();

      Dimension d;
      d = Toolkit.getDefaultToolkit().getScreenSize();
      resize(d.width, d.height);

      show();
      textArea.requestFocus();
   }

/**
 * Menu Creation Routines:
 * File: New, Open (F1), Save (F2), Save As (F3), Exit
 * Edit: Find (F4), Replace (F5), Replace All (F6),
 *       Cut (F7), Copy (F8), Paste (F9)
 * About: About Jompanion
 */

   private void AddMenu() {

      Menu menu;
      MenuBar menuBar = new MenuBar();
```

continues

Listing 21.14. continued

```
    //Sets up the File menu
    menu = new Menu("File");
    newMenuItem = new MenuItem("New");
    menu.add(newMenuItem);
    openMenuItem = new MenuItem("Open  (F1)");
    menu.add(openMenuItem);
    menu.addSeparator();
    saveMenuItem = new MenuItem("Save  (F2)");
    menu.add(saveMenuItem);
    saveAsMenuItem = new MenuItem("Save As  (F3)");
    menu.add(saveAsMenuItem);
    menu.addSeparator();
    exitMenuItem = new MenuItem("Exit");
    menu.add(exitMenuItem);
    menuBar.add(menu);

    //sets up the Edit menu
    menu = new Menu("Edit");
    findMenuItem = new MenuItem("Find  (F4)");
    menu.add(findMenuItem);
    replaceMenuItem = new MenuItem("Replace  (F5)");
    menu.add(replaceMenuItem);
    replaceAllMenuItem = new MenuItem("ReplaceAll  (F6)");
    menu.add(replaceAllMenuItem);
    menu.addSeparator();
    cutMenuItem = new MenuItem("Cut  (F7)");
    menu.add(cutMenuItem);
    copyMenuItem = new MenuItem("Copy  (F8)");
    menu.add(copyMenuItem);
    pasteMenuItem = new MenuItem("Paste  (F9)");
    menu.add(pasteMenuItem);
    menuBar.add(menu);

    //sets up the About menu
    menu = new Menu("About");
    aboutMenuItem = new MenuItem("About Jompanion");
    menu.add(aboutMenuItem);
    menuBar.add(menu);

    setMenuBar(menuBar);
  }

/**
 * AddChoice creates the choice boxes for font type and size.
 * Once the choice boxes are built, they are added to the application.
 */
  private void AddChoice() {

    //set up choice box for font type
    fontChoice = new Choice();
    fontChoice.addItem("Courier");
    fontChoice.addItem("Helvetica");
    fontChoice.addItem("System");
    fontChoice.addItem("TimesRoman");
    fontChoice.select(0);
    add(fontChoice);
```

```
          //set up choice box for font size
          sizeChoice = new Choice();
          sizeChoice.addItem("8");
          sizeChoice.addItem("10");
          sizeChoice.addItem("12");
          sizeChoice.addItem("14");
          sizeChoice.addItem("16");
          sizeChoice.addItem("18");
          sizeChoice.addItem("20");
          sizeChoice.addItem("22");
          sizeChoice.addItem("24");
          sizeChoice.addItem("26");
          sizeChoice.addItem("28");
          sizeChoice.addItem("30");
          sizeChoice.select(2);
          add(sizeChoice);
          }

/**
 * AddTextArea creates the text area for your edit sessions.
 */
  private void AddTextArea() {
    setLayout(new FlowLayout(FlowLayout.LEFT));
    textArea = new TextArea(24, 80);
    textArea.setEditable(true);
    add(textArea);
  }

/**
 * AddDialog adds the dialog boxes for opening and saving files.
 */
  private void AddDialog() {
    openDialog = new FileDialog(this, "Open File",FileDialog.LOAD);
    saveDialog = new FileDialog(this, "Save File",FileDialog.SAVE);
  }


/**
 * Handle Events:
 * Event.WINDOW_DESTROY: ensures clean exit
 * Event.ACTION_EVENT: Events from menu and choice boxes
 * Event.KEY_ACTION: Press function keys
 */

  public boolean handleEvent(Event event) {
    switch(event.id) {
      case Event.WINDOW_DESTROY:
        System.exit(0);
      case Event.ACTION_EVENT:
        if(event.target instanceof MenuItem) {
          if(event.target == aboutMenuItem) showAboutDialog();
          else if(event.target == copyMenuItem) copy();
          else if(event.target == cutMenuItem) cut();
          else if(event.target == exitMenuItem) System.exit(0);
          else if(event.target == findMenuItem) showFindDialog();
          else if(event.target == newMenuItem) startNewWindow();
          else if(event.target == openMenuItem) openFile();
```

continues

Listing 21.14. continued

```
        else if(event.target == pasteMenuItem) paste();
        else if(event.target == replaceAllMenuItem) showReplaceAllDialog();
        else if(event.target == replaceMenuItem) showRepDialog();
        else if(event.target == saveAsMenuItem) saveAsFile();
        else if(event.target == saveMenuItem) saveOpenedFile();
        }
        if(event.target == fontChoice || event.target == sizeChoice){
            String fontName = event.arg.toString();
            textArea.setFont(new Font(fontName, Font.PLAIN, fontNumeric));
            String fontSize = event.arg.toString();
            try {
                fontNumeric = Integer.parseInt(fontSize);

              } catch (NumberFormatException e) {
                fontNumeric = 12;      // If error occurs set font size to 12
            }
            textArea.setFont(new Font(fontName, Font.PLAIN, fontNumeric));
            }
      return(true);
    case Event.KEY_ACTION:
      if(event.key == Event.F1) openFile();
      else if (event.key == Event.F2) saveOpenedFile();
      else if (event.key == Event.F3) saveAsFile();
      else if (event.key == Event.F4) showFindDialog();
      else if (event.key == Event.F5) showRepDialog();
      else if (event.key == Event.F6) showReplaceAllDialog();
      else if (event.key == Event.F7) cut();
      else if (event.key == Event.F8) copy();
      else if (event.key == Event.F9) paste();
    }
    return(false);
  }

/**
 * Utility Functions:
 * Copy, Cut, Paste
 * Open file, SaveAs, Save
 * New
 */

  //cuts selected text and places it on the buffer
  public void cut() {
    copyString = textArea.getSelectedText();
    textArea.replaceText("", textArea.getSelectionStart(),
                                      textArea.getSelectionEnd());
    textArea.requestFocus();
    }

  //copies selected text to the buffer
  public void copy() {
    copyString = textArea.getSelectedText();
    textArea.requestFocus();
  }

  //pastes text from the buffer to the screen
  public void paste() {
    if (copyString.length() > 0)
```

```
      textArea.insertText(copyString,
textArea.getSelectionStart());
      textArea.requestFocus();
  }

  //method for opening files with a specified name
  private void openFile() {
    String filename;
    openDialog.show();
    filename = openDialog.getFile();
    if (filename != null) {
      filename = check(filename);
      if (read(filename)) fileName = filename;
    }
    textArea.requestFocus();
  }

  //method saves the file you are currently editing
  private void saveAsFile() {
    String filename;
    saveDialog.show();
    filename = saveDialog.getFile();
    if (filename != null) {
      filename = check(filename);
      if (write(filename)) fileName = filename;
    }
    textArea.requestFocus();
  }

  //method saves a file you opened previously.
  //method produces error if you did not open a file previously.
  public void saveOpenedFile() {
    if (fileName == null) {
      showErrorDialog("You did not previously open a file. Use Save As.");
    } else {
      write(fileName);
      textArea.requestFocus();
    }
  }

  //creates a new editing session by deleting any previous text
  private void startNewWindow() {
    fileName = null;
    textArea.setText("");
    textArea.requestFocus();
  }

/**
 * Show Dialog Boxes
 * Find, Replace, Replace All, About, and Error
 */

  //displays the find dialog box which has one input field.
  //Currently selected text is placed in the input field.
  public void showFindDialog() {
    if (findDialog != null) findDialog.dispose();
    String sel = textArea.getSelectedText();
```

continues

Listing 21.14. continued

```
      if (sel.length() > 0) findString = sel;
      findDialog = new FindDialog(this, findString);
      findDialog.show();
      findDialog.setFocus();
  }

  //displays the replace dialog box which has two input fields.
  //Currently selected text is placed in the find input field.
  //Previously searched and replaced text is placed in the input field.
  public void showRepDialog() {
     if (replaceDialog != null) replaceDialog.dispose();
     String sel = textArea.getSelectedText();
     if (sel.length() > 0) findString = sel;
     replaceDialog = new ReplaceDialog(this, findString,
replaceString);
     replaceDialog.show();
     replaceDialog.setFocus();
  }

  //displays the replace all dialog box which has two input fields.
  //Currently selected text is placed in the find input field.
  //Previously searched and replaced text is placed in the input field.
  public void showReplaceAllDialog() {
     if (replaceAllDialog != null) replaceAllDialog.dispose();
     String sel = textArea.getSelectedText();
     if (sel.length() > 0) findString = sel;
     replaceAllDialog = new ReplaceAllDialog(this, findString,
replaceString);
     replaceAllDialog.show();
     replaceAllDialog.setFocus();
  }

  //displays the about dialog box
  private void showAboutDialog() {
     if (aboutDialog != null) aboutDialog.dispose();
     aboutDialog = new AboutDialog(this);
     aboutDialog.show();
  }

  //displays the error dialog box and the current error
  public void showErrorDialog(String message) {
     if (errorDialog != null) errorDialog.dispose();
     errorDialog = new ErrorDialog(this, message);
     errorDialog.show();
  }

  //method handles reading files from the file system
  private boolean read(String filename) {

     String line;
     FileInputStream in = null;
     DataInputStream dataIn = null;
     BufferedInputStream bis = null;
     StringBuffer buffer = new StringBuffer();

     try {
       in = new FileInputStream(filename);
```

```
      bis = new BufferedInputStream(in);
      dataIn = new DataInputStream(bis);
    } catch(Throwable e) {
      showErrorDialog("Can't open \""+filename+"\"");
      return(false);
    }

    try {
      while ((line = dataIn.readLine()) != null) {
        buffer.append(line + "\n");
      }
      in.close();
      textArea.setText(buffer.toString());
    } catch(IOException e) {
      showErrorDialog("Can't read \""+filename+"\"");
      return(false);
    }

    return(true);
}

//method handles writing files to the file system
private boolean write(String filename) {

  FileOutputStream os = null;

  try {
    os = new FileOutputStream(filename);
  } catch (Throwable e) {
    showErrorDialog("Can't write \""+filename+"\"");
    return(false);
  }

  try {
    String s = textArea.getText();
    int len = s.length();
    for (int i=0; i<len; i++) {
       os.write(s.charAt(i));
    }
    os.close();
  } catch(IOException e) {
    showErrorDialog("Can't write \""+filename+"\"");
    return(false);
  }

  return(true);
}

//method checks the validity of file names and specifically for a bug
//fixes the error if it occurs
private String check(String filename) {
  if (filename.endsWith(".*.*")) {
    filename = filename.substring(0, filename.length()-4);
  }
  return(filename);
}
```

continues

Listing 21.14. continued

```java
//sets the find string
public void setFindString(String str) {
  findString = str;
}

//sets the replace string
public void setReplaceString(String str) {
  replaceString = str;
}

//handles the search for text in the find input field
public void findText() {

  String s;
  int spoint, index;

  textArea.requestFocus();
  if (findString.length() == 0) return;

  s = textArea.getText();
  if (s.length() == 0) return;

  spoint = textArea.getSelectionEnd();
  index = s.substring(spoint).indexOf(findString);
  if (index >= 0) {
    int i = spoint + index;
    textArea.select(i, i + findString.length());
  }
}

//handles replacing text
public boolean replaceText() {
  String s;
  int spoint, index;

  textArea.requestFocus();
  if (findString.length() == 0) return(false);

  s = textArea.getText();
  if (s.length() == 0) return(false);

  spoint = textArea.getSelectionStart();
  index = s.substring(spoint).indexOf(findString);
  if (index >= 0) {
    int i = spoint + index;
    int j = i + findString.length();
    textArea.replaceText(replaceString, i, j);
    textArea.select(i, i+replaceString.length());
    return(true);
  }
  return(false);
}

//the main method of the application invokes the Jompanion method
public static void main(String args[]) {
  Jompanion n = new Jompanion();
```

```
      if (args.length == 1)
        if (n.read(args[0])) n.fileName = args[0];
   }
}

/**
 * The FindDialog Class sets up the find dialog box
 * and handles related events.
 */
class FindDialog extends Dialog {

  Jompanion parent;
  TextField textField;

  public FindDialog(Jompanion parent, String text) {

    super(parent, "Find", true);
    setBackground(Color.white);
    this.parent = parent;

    Panel p;
    p = new Panel();
    Label l;
    l = new Label("Find What:");
    p.setLayout(null);
    l.reshape(0,25,110,30);
    p.add(l);

    textField = new TextField(text);
    textField.reshape(111,25,200,30);
    p.add(textField);

    add("Center", p);

    Dimension d;
    d = parent.size();
    reshape(200,50,340,100);
    setResizable(false);
  }

  public boolean handleEvent(Event event) {
    switch(event.id) {
      case Event.WINDOW_DESTROY:
        dispose();
        parent.textArea.requestFocus();
        return(true);
      case Event.ACTION_EVENT:
        if(event.target == textField) {
          dispose();
          if (textField.getText().length() > 0) {
            parent.setFindString(textField.getText());
            parent.findText();
            parent.textArea.requestFocus();
            return(true);
          }
        } else {
          parent.showErrorDialog("Find Error");
```

continues

Listing 21.14. continued

```
                parent.textArea.requestFocus();
                return(true);
            }
        }
        return(false);
    }

    public void setFocus() {
        textField.requestFocus();
        textField.select(0, textField.getText().length());
    }
}

/**
 * The ReplaceDialog Class sets up the replace dialog box
 * and handles related events.
 */
class ReplaceDialog extends Dialog {

    Jompanion parent;
    TextField fromField, toField;

    public ReplaceDialog(Jompanion parent, String fromString, String
toString) {

        super(parent, "Replace", true);
        setBackground(Color.white);
        this.parent = parent;

        Panel p;
        p = new Panel();
        Label l;
        l = new Label("Find What:");
        p.setLayout(null);

        l.reshape(0,25,130,30);
        p.add(l);

        fromField = new TextField(fromString);
        fromField.reshape(131,25,200,30);
        p.add(fromField);

        l = new Label("Replace With:");
        l.reshape(0,60,130,30);
        p.add(l);

        toField = new TextField(toString);
        toField.reshape(131,60,200,30);
        p.add(toField);

        add("Center", p);

        Dimension d;
        d = parent.size();
        reshape(200,50,360,150);
        setResizable(false);
    }
```

```
    public boolean handleEvent(Event event) {
      switch(event.id) {
        case Event.WINDOW_DESTROY:
          dispose();
          parent.textArea.requestFocus();
          return(true);
        case Event.ACTION_EVENT:
          if(event.target == fromField) {
            toField.requestFocus();
            return(true);
          } else if(event.target == toField) {
            dispose();
            if (fromField.getText().length() > 0) {
              parent.setFindString(fromField.getText());
              parent.setReplaceString(toField.getText());
              parent.replaceText();
              parent.textArea.requestFocus();
              return(true);
            }
          } else {
            parent.showErrorDialog("Replace Error");
            parent.textArea.requestFocus();
            return(true);
          }
      }
      return(false);
    }

  public void setFocus() {
    fromField.requestFocus();
    fromField.select(0, fromField.getText().length());
  }
}

/**
 * The ReplaceAllDialog Class sets up the dialog box for replacing
 * all occurrences of a word or phrase and handles related events.
 */
class ReplaceAllDialog extends Dialog {

  Jompanion parent;
  TextField fromAllField, toAllField;

  public ReplaceAllDialog(Jompanion parent, String fromAllString, String
toAllString) {

    super(parent, "Replace All", true);
    setBackground(Color.white);
    this.parent = parent;

    Panel p;
    p = new Panel();
    Label l;
    l = new Label("Find All:");
    p.setLayout(null);
```

continues

Listing 21.14. continued

```java
        l.reshape(0,25,130,30);
        p.add(l);

        fromAllField = new TextField(fromAllString);
        fromAllField.reshape(131,25,200,30);
        p.add(fromAllField);

        l = new Label("Replace With:");
        l.reshape(0,60,130,30);
        p.add(l);

        toAllField = new TextField(toAllString);
        toAllField.reshape(131,60,200,30);
        p.add(toAllField);

        add("Center", p);

        Dimension d;
        d = parent.size();
        reshape(200,50,360,150);
        setResizable(false);
    }

    public boolean handleEvent(Event event) {
        switch(event.id) {
            case Event.WINDOW_DESTROY:
                dispose();
                parent.textArea.requestFocus();
                return(true);
            case Event.ACTION_EVENT:
                if(event.target == fromAllField) {
                    toAllField.requestFocus();
                    return(true);
                } else if(event.target == toAllField) {
                    dispose();
                    if (fromAllField.getText().length() > 0) {
                        parent.setFindString(fromAllField.getText());
                        parent.setReplaceString(toAllField.getText());
                        while (parent.replaceText()) ;
                        parent.textArea.requestFocus();
                        return(true);
                    }
                } else {
                    parent.showErrorDialog("Replace All Error");
                    parent.textArea.requestFocus();
                    return(true);
                }
        }
        return(false);
    }
    public void setFocus() {
        fromAllField.requestFocus();
        fromAllField.select(0, fromAllField.getText().length());
    }
}
```

```java
/**
 * The AboutDialog Class sets up the dialog box that displays
 * information about Jompanion and handles related events
 */
class AboutDialog extends Dialog {

  Jompanion parent;

  public AboutDialog(Jompanion parent) {
    super(parent, "Jompanion from the Complete Guide to Java", true);
    setBackground(Color.white);
    this.parent = parent;

    Panel p;
    p = new Panel();
    p.setLayout(new GridLayout(3, 3));
    p.add(new Label("F1 - Open Files"));
    p.add(new Label("F4 - Find"));
    p.add(new Label("F7 - Cut"));
    p.add(new Label("F2 - Save"));
    p.add(new Label("F5 - Replace"));
    p.add(new Label("F8 - Copy"));
    p.add(new Label("F3 - Save As"));
    p.add(new Label("F6 - Replace All"));
    p.add(new Label("F9 - Paste"));
    add("Center", p);

    Dimension d;
    d = parent.size();
    reshape(50,440,640,120);
    setResizable(false);
  }

  public boolean handleEvent(Event event) {
    switch(event.id) {
      case Event.WINDOW_DESTROY:
        dispose();
        parent.textArea.requestFocus();
        return(true);
    }
    return(false);
  }
}

/**
 * The ErrorDialog Class sets up the dialog box that displays
 * errors to the user and handles the closing of the window
 */
class ErrorDialog extends Dialog {

  Jompanion parent;
  String message;

  public ErrorDialog(Jompanion parent, String message) {
    super(parent, "Error", true);
    setBackground(Color.yellow);
    this.parent = parent;
```

continues

Listing 21.14. continued

```
    this.message = message;

    Panel p;
    p = new Panel();
    p.add(new Label(message));
    p.setFont(new Font("System", Font.BOLD, 12));
    add("Center", p);

    Dimension d;
    d = parent.size();
    reshape(200,50,420,100);
    setResizable(false);
  }

  public boolean handleEvent(Event event) {
    switch(event.id) {
      case Event.WINDOW_DESTROY:
        dispose();
        parent.textArea.requestFocus();
        return(true);
    }
    return(false);
  }
}
```

After you understand how the application works, you should try your hand at upgrading it. Some of the additional features you may want to add to Jompanion include

- Using the dim() method to dim functions that are currently inaccessible, such as the Cut, Copy, and Paste menu items that cannot be used until the user selects text. You could implement this upgrade by checking the length of the selected text. A length greater than zero means the user has selected text. A length of zero or less means no text is selected.

- Add more menu items, such as a Close menu item to the File menu and a Help menu item to the About menu. You could create a menu item to close the current file. One way to do this is to simply clear the text area. However, you should check the text area to determine if there is data the user might want to save before the window is cleared. To add a Help menu item, you should develop methods to display and build the dialog box.

- Support for more keys, such as Page Down and Page Up. In addition to support for function keys F1 to F12, Java can also check for other types of keys including Shift; Alt; Ctrl; Meta; Home; End; Page Up; Page Down; and the left-arrow, right-arrow, up-arrow, and down-arrow keys. You can add support for these keys by adding events to Jompanion's handleEvent() method and creating methods that handle the events. Methods that change the current position in the text area can be set by moving the current focus within the document.

- Multilevel undo, such as being able to undo a replace all. To implement multilevel undo, you first need to create an array that stores the index to the location of the change within the document and the string that was changed at that location.

Note: The Meta key is used primarily on Sun UNIX workstations. On a Windows 95–compatible keyboard, this key would be your Windows key.

Summary

Developing advanced applications involves careful planning. For most projects, planning involves mapping out the steps necessary to complete the project and allocating a time period for implementing each step. After you plot out the steps that will take you through project completion, you can group the steps into phases. These phases form the software development life cycle for the application.

A top-down methodology was used to develop and implement the Jompanion editor. Using this type of methodology, high-level objects are developed before the low-level ones. For Jompanion, the first step in design and implementation involved developing the main window. After the main window was developed, you looked at the next level of objects and so on, working your way to the low-level objects that performed the actual manipulation of text. In following this design approach, you used sound object-oriented design techniques and should now be ready to create your own advanced applications in Java.

22

Integrating Native Programs and Libraries

Although Java has many advantages, it is a relatively new programming language compared with C, C++, or Smalltalk. These and other existing languages provide some features not yet available in Java. Also, many useful applications written in other languages are in use in businesses today. Programmers can use Java in more applications if they can include existing code written in other languages.

Despite the advantages of leveraging existing code, any time multiple languages are used in a single application there is more complexity. For example, it is necessary to create code to translate information between the two different languages. This code will make some Java methods available to other languages and will make the functions from other languages available to Java. Data as well as functions can be transferred between languages.

Why and When to Use Native Methods with Java Applications

Before explaining how to include native methods in your Java code, this section provides a little more detail on when such methods are appropriate. Part of the power of Java is its platform independence. Code compiled on one platform can be run on any platform with a Java interpreter. This advantage is lost, however, as soon as native methods are used.

Even if the native method can be compiled on every platform where the application is desired, there is still the additional cost of maintaining multiple versions of the compiled code. With native methods, the application will run only on platforms with the same operating system, and the dynamic library used to store the native methods must be transferred along with the application. Given these restrictions, there are still times when you will find it appropriate to use code written in a different language.

When the code you want to use already exists in another language, it may be faster to integrate the existing code with a new Java application than to rewrite it in Java. This is especially true with large, complex applications. It also may be appropriate to use Java as the front-end interface. Such an application would leave the number-crunching or back-end interface in the existing language. This combination would enable a programmer to develop a graphical user interface for applications currently run with a text-based interface. The users would have the advantage of a graphical interface while the code for the remainder of the application was still being rewritten.

When the features you need cannot yet be done with Java, it certainly makes sense to use native methods. This is true even if you have to create several different libraries for different platforms. Examples of this situation include recording audio in applications or displaying images in a format other than GIF or JPEG. Of course, if you are using native methods for this reason, it is also worthwhile to contact the Java development team to let them know what features you want. If there is sufficient interest in a particular feature, it will probably be added to the Java API.

Accessing a device on the machine that Java does not recognize is another reason for employing native code. There are many new peripherals being developed, and many of them have device drivers specific to a particular platform. To access these devices, you most likely will need to link dynamic libraries specific to the platform where the device is installed.

The final reason for using native methods in Java applications is speed. Even after optimizing your Java code to achieve as much speed as possible, native methods may still run faster. This is particularly true if they can access properties in the hardware, additional processors, or video boards, which Java does not use.

Using C Programs

The C language is considered first because this language is so prevalent. There is a large body of existing C code that has been tested over time and that many businesses may be reluctant to rewrite.

In fact, the use of C is so extensive that the Java Developer's Kit includes a tool just to create header files for linking C programs into Java applications. This tool is called javah and is used to create the header files for the example shown here.

The first topic in this section describes how to write a new C program to work with a Java application. The next topic reviews how to modify an existing C program to access it through Java. Although the two topics are closely related, creating new code is a longer, more complex process than modifying existing code.

Creating New C Programs for Use with Java Applications

The SumGraph application is used to illustrate how to create new code for use with Java by rewriting the ASum class so that the sum is calculated in C rather than in Java. This is an extreme example in that the calculations could easily be done in Java, but it serves to illustrate how a Java class can be used to encapsulate calculations done in other code. It also shows how parameters can be transferred between Java and other languages.

Step 1: Create the Java Class

The first step is to create a Java class that declares a native method. The previous Java class for ASum appeared as follows:

```
class ASum {
int theSum;
```

```
public ASum() {theSum = 0;}      // Constructor set instance variable to 0
public void incSum(int toAdd) {
theSum = theSum + toAdd;      // Add to instance variable
}
public int getSum(){
return theSum;      // Return the value of the instance variable
}
}
```

This example explains how to modify it so that the calculations currently done in the incSum() method are done in a C routine. The new incSum method appears as

```
public native void incSum(int toAdd);
```

Although the method definition for incSum has been replaced with a call to a native method, the method operates as before. It updates the class variable theSum by adding the value in the input variable to the value already stored in theSum.

You must add one more feature to the class. Because the class is using a native function, Java must be certain that the library containing that function has been loaded into the runtime environment. Java does this using a *class initializer*. A class initializer starts with the keyword static followed by braces that surround the methods called when the class is loaded. The modified code for ASum that calls a native C method appears as follows:

```
class ASum {
   int theSum;

   public ASum() {theSum = 0;}      // Constructor set instance variable to 0
   public native void incSum(int toAdd);
   public int getSum(){
      return theSum;            // Return the value of the instance variable
   }
      static {
         System.loadLibrary("sum_in_c");
      }
}
```

The loadLibrary() method that replaces the method body loads a dynamic library. The string passed to it is the name of the library containing the C function that the method will use. This method looks for the library along the library path. On UNIX systems, the library path is specified in the environmental variable LD_LIBRARY_PATH. On Windows systems, the environmental variable PATH is used to search for DLL libraries. The directory where the executable is stored is also checked for DLLs.

An alternate form is the System.load() method, which loads a library based on a complete pathname. If you use this form, you can include libraries that are not part of the library path in your application.

The loadLibrary() method is part of the System class. All the components of the System class are static, so it cannot be instantiated or subclassed. It is, however, a useful class. In the nongraphical examples, this class is used to supply an output stream that displays on the user's command line.

Here, the System class is used to load a dynamic library. The System class also can be accessed to run the garbage collector, obtain parameters, or get the current time.

The new ASum class is called from within the Java application. The call remains exactly as it was in earlier examples. The class is stored in the file ASum.java and compiled just like any other class. The command is

```
javac ASum.java
```

When the class has been compiled and the .class file has been created, the header files needed to create the C code can be generated.

Step 2: Generate Header and Stub Files

The next step is to use the .class file generated by the Java compiler to create the header file required by the C compiler. The header file can be automatically generated by the javah tool. The header file defines a C structure to depict ASum. It also contains the function definition for the implementation of the incSum method.

To run javah against your class file and create the ASum.h file, type the following at the command line:

```
javah ASum
```

Be certain before running javah that the CLASSPATH environmental variable has been set to point to the classes.zip file. If it is not set, the javah program will return an error.

If everything is set correctly, the javah tool will place the ASum.h file in the same directory as the .class file. The contents of the file on a Windows 95/NT–based machine are as follows:

```
/* DO NOT EDIT THIS FILE - it is machine generated */
#include <native.h>
/* Header for class ASum */

#ifndef _Included_ASum
#define _Included_ASum

typedef struct ClassASum {
    long theSum;
} ClassASum;
HandleTo(ASum);

#ifdef __cplusplus
extern "C" {
#endif
__declspec(dllexport) void ASum_incSum(struct HASum *,long);
#ifdef __cplusplus
}
#endif
#endif
```

The header file defines a structure, `ClassASum`, that contains the instance variables in the Java class `ASum`. In this case there is only one instance variable, but it is important to the application. After the instance variable structure, the header file provides a check for a C++ compiler. If a C++ compiler is used, you must define the C function as `extern`. This prevents the C++ compiler from modifying the function name.

The definition for the C function is generated as part of the header file. The function is expected to be part of a DLL export and is declared as such. The function returns a `void` and takes two parameters: an instance of the structure just defined and the value passed to the method from the caller.

The name of the C function is `ASum_incSum`. The `javah` tool created this function name by combining the class name and the name of the Java method. If the class were part of a package, the package name would have been prefixed to the function name as well.

In addition to the header file, interfacing between Java and C requires a stubs file that translates the parameters and return values between the two programming languages. The stubs file is also automatically generated using the `javah` tool. To create a stubs file, type the following at the command line:

```
javah -stubs ASum
```

The resulting file is `ASum.c`, and it contains the following code:

```
/* DO NOT EDIT THIS FILE - it is machine generated */
#include <StubPreamble.h>

/* Stubs for class ASum */
/* SYMBOL: "ASum/incSum(I)V", Java_ASum_incSum_stub */
__declspec(dllexport) stack_item *Java_ASum_incSum_stub
➥(stack_item *_P_,struct execenv *_EE_) {
extern void ASum_incSum(void *,long);
(void) ASum_incSum(_P_[0].p,((_P_[1].i)));
return _P_;
}
```

The `ASum.c` file is compiled and linked when the C code is linked.

Step 3: Write the C Program

The C function must include the signature generated with `javah`. There are three included header files in the C code that follows. The header file `StubPreamble.h` is included to provide information to the C code to enable it to interact with the Java runtime system. This header file should be included in any C code that is being linked to Java. The header file generated earlier with `javah` is included in the C code to provide the function declaration. The last header file included is the standard I/O header file.

The following code is saved in the file `ASumInC.c`:

```
#include <StubPreamble.h>
#include "ASum.h"
#include <stdio.h>
```

```
void ASum_incSum(struct HASum *this,long addend) {
    long currentSum;
    currentSum = unhand(this)->theSum;
    unhand(this)->theSum = currentSum + addend
}
```

The next section explains how to compile and link the C program on both UNIX and Windows platforms.

Step 4: Compile and Link the C Program

Before attempting to compile the C source code, be sure the directory containing the Java `include` file `StubPreamble.h` is in your `include` path. If it is not, extend the `include` path as part of the compiler command.

The correct command to compile the C code and link a dynamic library depends on the system on which you are compiling. For a Windows system with Visual C++ version 2.0, the command is

```
cl ASum.c ASumInC.c -FeASum.dll -MD -LD javai.lib
```

The library `javai.lib` must be the last argument to the C compiler. You may also need to update the library path so the linker can locate this library. The command to do so is

```
set LIB=%JAVAHOME%\lib;%LIB%
```

where `JAVAHOME` is the installation directory for Java.

For a UNIX system, the command to compile and link is

```
cc -G ASum.c ASumInC.c -o libASum.so
```

Now that your program is compiled and linked, you can use the `java` class to start the program as you would any other Java application.

Running the Program

Running an application with a native method is no different than running any other Java application. If the environment has been set up correctly, the native method is transparent to the user. The command to run the example is still

```
java SumGraph
```

The program should perform as it has throughout the chapter. If a `NullPointerException` appears when the application is run, make sure the library path is set. In Windows, the library path is the same as your `PATH` variable. In UNIX C shell, the path is set using the command

```
setenv LD_LIBRARY_PATH mylibrarypath
```

If an `UnsatisfiedLinkError` message is encountered, it indicates that the library path is set but does not include the library that was just created for this example. In Windows, extend the `PATH` using

```
PATH = %PATH%;C:\path_to_dll_file
```

In UNIX C shell, extend the library path using

```
setenv LD_LIBRARY_PATH mylibrarypath
```

Using Existing C Programs

The previous section explained in detail how to create a new C program and include it in your Java application. The steps to include an existing C program are similar. Therefore, this section only highlights the key differences.

If you already have C code to link into a Java program, you just need to create the hooks in the Java classes to access your C functions. The important, and difficult, task is to make sure the header files generated by the Java compiler match the declaration of the existing C functions.

To create structures accessible to both your C code and your Java code, use the `unhand()` function in the C code. You may want to create an interface layer, which does the `unhand` and puts the result in a separate structure known only to the C code.

There are several useful functions available for accessing Java from within C. Java methods may be executed from within C code using the following function:

```
long execute_java_dynamic_method(ExecEnv *e, Hobject *ojb,
char *method_method_name, char*method_signature, ...);
```

To have the C code throw a Java exception when control returns to Java, use this function:

```
SignalError(0, JAVAPKG "NameOfExceptionClass","ExceptionMessage");
```

Peter's Principle: When including native code in a Java application, it is worth giving some consideration to freeing memory allocated in the native method. If the native method does not use `alloc` to reserve memory, this is not a concern. Unfortunately, most complex applications will make some use of memory-allocation functions. This memory must be freed at some point.

Java's garbage collector will not automatically reclaim memory allocated in native methods; you must write a native method to free the memory allocated in a native method. However, you can call the method used to free the memory from within your Java class using the `dispose()` method. This method is automatically called when your instance is garbage collected. In this way you can be assured that memory allocated by native methods in association with a specific instance of a class is freed when that instance is discarded.

Using Programming Languages Other Than C

There is a large body of C programs currently in use in the business and scientific worlds, so it is expected that most of the code linked to Java will be C code. However, there are many other languages in use, and algorithms coded in those languages also can be linked to Java.

C++ Programs

C++ code is the next-easiest language to link into a Java application. Although you do not need to create C functions to call your C++ code, you do need to surround your C++ code with extern "C". This will enable you to reference the C++ functions by the names used in the source file. The following is a simple example of using extern "C":

```
extern "C" {
    void HelloWorld(void) {
    cout << "Hello, world.\n";
    } // end HelloWorld
}      // end extern "C"
```

If you do not use extern "C" in your C++ code, the compiler will modify the names and the linker will not be able to resolve the references. You may also run into some type conflicts, which can be handled using wrapper functions. However, accessing C++ functions from Java is usually no more complicated than accessing C. Therefore, you can follow the same steps outlined previously to link C++ code into Java applications. To recap:

1. Create the Java class with appropriate references for use with native functions.

2. Generate header and stub files.

3. Write or modify the C++ program for use with Java.

4. Compile and link the C++ program.

Programs in Other Languages

Any program compiled into a dynamically loadable library can be linked into a Java program. The advantage using of C/C++ is the availability of Java tools that create the appropriate header and stub files. If you are linking in other languages, you must create these files manually.

To incorporate other languages easily, consider linking the code from that language into a C program and then linking the C code to Java. The additional overhead of going through the extra compile is offset by the advantage of having the Java compiler create the header and stub files.

Microsoft has recently announced support for the Java language. The new ActiveX controls, formerly known as OLE controls, will make many full-featured components available to Java developers. These components can be incorporated into Java applications and applets. It would then be possible to include a Microsoft application such as Excel in a Java application.

As you include features from other languages in your applications, it is important to remember that these features are not available on every platform. If you are developing for a specific target audience, this may not be a problem. Many corporate information-systems groups believe in keeping all desktop platforms standardized. Developing in this environment means you can use any native tools that are considered part of the corporate standard. However, if you want your application to be truly portable, stay with objects defined and supported as part of the Java Developer's Kit.

One final word of caution involves dynamically loadable libraries. Be very certain that the names you provide for your libraries do not conflict with other library names the user may have installed already. The functions compiled in your libraries also must have unique names. If the names are not unique, the Java application risks interfering with applications already installed on the user's system.

The fact that Java uses a combination of the package, class, and method names to create the interface function names should help to ensure uniqueness. If you notice any problems with other applications after installing a Java application that calls native methods, remove the dynamic library installed with the Java application. If the other applications then perform normally, modify the names of the functions in the dynamic library installed with the Java application to resolve the conflict.

Summary

Your Java applications can access native methods written in other programming languages, such as C/C++. The Java Developer's Kit includes a tool called `javah` that you can use to create header files for linking C programs into Java applications, which makes C the easiest language to integrate with Java.

C++ code is the next-easiest language to link into a Java application. All you need to do is surround your C++ code with `extern "C"`. You can link programs written in other programming languages into your Java applications as long as the program is compiled into a dynamically linked library, yet for ease of integration you will probably want to link the code into a C program and then link the C code to Java.

23

Advanced Debugging and Troubleshooting

Sometimes your code will compile just fine but will not run properly. As you begin to develop advanced applets and applications, this will happen more frequently. Instead of spending days poring over thousands of lines of code trying to pinpoint problem areas, you should spend an hour with a tool called the Java debugger. Use it whenever you have problems in your source code that you cannot solve without a little help.

Debugging code after a successful compile is quite different from debugging code that will not compile, primarily because of the type of errors you will come across at this stage of troubleshooting. When your program will not compile, the errors mostly relate to syntax, such as missing semicolons or bad references to objects. However, when your program does not run the way you expect or displays errors during execution of the code, the errors mostly relate to the program's logic, such as calling the wrong method or using a variable set to the wrong value.

Although the Java debugger is quite useful for debugging code interactively, sometimes you do not want to do that. For those times, a debugging utility called `HelpDebug` can be used to help debug your code using a noninteractive means. For this reason, this chapter covers both interactive and noninteractive debugging.

Advanced troubleshooting requires more logic than concept. Therefore, this chapter takes you step by step through the debugging process as it demonstrates how to use the Java debugger.

Starting the Java Debugger

Anyone who has ever programmed in C/C++ knows that a good debugger can quite literally save the day. The Java debugger works much like the other debuggers you may have used to debug your C or C++ code. You invoke it from the command line. The name of the command-line program is `jdb`, which stands for Java debugger. When invoked, the debugger uses the Debugger API—`sun.tools.debug`—to help you troubleshoot problems in your code.

You can invoke the debugger from the command line in one of two ways: The first way to start a `jdb` session is to pass it the name of your Java class file without the `.class` extension, and the second is to attach it to a Java interpreter or applet viewer.

As with other tools in the Java Developer's Kit, the debugger allows you to use command-line options. These options depend on the way you use the debugger. If you use it directly, any options you specify on the command line are passed on to the interpreter the debugger invokes, so you can use any of the interpreter options when you start the debugger directly.

When you attach the debugger to an interpreter session, you are limited to three options: `-host`, `-password`, and `-classpath`. The `-host` option sets the name of the host machine on which the interpreter session is running. The `-password` option sets the password and enables you to attach the debugger to a particular session. The `-classpath` option lets you specify a path for your class files that overrides the default or current `CLASSPATH` setting. Because this option takes precedence, you should set it to include the current directory, the location of your personal or third-party class files, and the location of the Java API classes.

> **Tip:** To aid the debugging process, compile your code with the -g option of the Java compiler. This option tells the Java compiler to generate debugging tables. Although debugging tables are not useful for troubleshooting syntax problems, they are useful for troubleshooting logic problems. Generally, you will use these tables to browse local variables on the stack.

Starting the Debugger Directly

To start a debugging session directly, usually you would pass it the name of your Java class file without the .class extension by typing the following at the command line:

```
jdb classname
```

where classname is the name of the class file that starts the program you want to debug.

When you start the debugger directly, it in turn starts the Java interpreter with any parameters you passed on the command line. Afterward, the debugger loads the specified class file.

> **Note:** For the JDK version 1.0 or later, the debugger expects you to be on a networked host. If you are not, you may see the following error message or a similar one:
> ```
> java.net.UnknownHostException
>         at java.net.InetAddress.getLocalHost(InetAddress.java:276)
>         at sun.tools.debug.RemoteDebugger.<init>(RemoteDebugger.java:61)
>         at sun.tools.ttydebug.TTY.<init>(TTY.java:1263)
>         at sun.tools.ttydebug.TTY.main(TTY.java:1387)
> ```
> To clear up this problem, start a browser session that connects your computer to the Internet. Then you should be able to start the debugger.

Attaching the Debugger to a Current Interpreter Session

Although most programmers prefer to invoke the debugger directly, you can also attach a debugging session to an interpreter that is already running. To do this, start the Java interpreter with the -debug option. When you use this option, the interpreter displays a password that must be used when starting the debugging session.

Note: Because the password is randomly allocated by session, you can use it only for the applet or application currently running on your system.

Here are the steps you should follow to attach the debugger to an interpreter:

1. Start the interpreter with the `-debug` option, such as

   ```
   java -debug classname
   ```

   where `classname` is the name of the class file that starts the application.

2. Invoke the debugger with the session password:

   ```
   jdb -host hostname -password session_password
   ```

   where `hostname` is the hostname of your computer and `session_password` is the password provided by the interpreter.

Note: When you start the Java interpreter or applet viewer with the `-debug` option under JDK version 1.0, they both check for the hostname and local Internet address of your system. If you are not on a networked host, you may see the following error message or a similar one:

```
java.net.UnknownHostException
        at java.net.InetAddress.getLocalHost(InetAddress.java:276)
        at sun.tools.debug.RemoteDebugger.<init>(RemoteDebugger.java:61)
        at sun.tools.ttydebug.TTY.<init>(TTY.java:1263)
        at sun.tools.ttydebug.TTY.main(TTY.java:1387)
```

To clear up this problem, start a browser session that connects your computer to the Internet. Then you should be able to start the interpreter or applet viewer with the `-debug` option.

Attaching the Debugger to an Applet Viewer Session

The final way to use the debugger is to attach it to an applet viewer session by starting the applet viewer with the `-debug` option.

Here are the steps you would follow to attach the debugger to the applet viewer:

1. Start the applet viewer with the `-debug` option, such as

   ```
   appletviewer -debug document.html
   ```

   where `document.html` is the name of the HTML document with a valid `<APPLET>` tag.

2. Run the applet using the `run` command of the debugger.

Troubleshooting the Code with the Debugger

After you start the debugger, an input prompt appears. You can enter commands directly to the debugger at this prompt. One of the most useful commands is `help`, which lists all the commands the debugger recognizes. The help listing for the debugger follows:

```
Initializing jdb…
> help

** command list **
threads [threadgroup]      -- list threads
thread <thread id>         -- set default thread
suspend [thread id(s)]     -- suspend threads (default: all)
resume [thread id(s)]      -- resume threads (default: all)
where [thread id] ¦ all    -- dump a thread's stack
threadgroups               -- list threadgroups
threadgroup <name>         -- set current threadgroup

print <id> [id(s)]         -- print object or field
dump <id> [id(s)]          -- print all object information

locals                     -- print all local variables in current stack frame

classes                    -- list currently known classes
methods <class id>         -- list a class's methods

stop in <class id>.<method> -- set a breakpoint in a method
stop at <class id>:<line>  -- set a breakpoint at a line
up [n frames]              -- move up a thread's stack
down [n frames]            -- move down a thread's stack
clear <class id>:<line>    -- clear a breakpoint
step                       -- execute current line
cont                       -- continue execution from breakpoint

catch <class id>           -- break for the specified exception
ignore <class id>          -- ignore when the specified exception

list [line number]         -- print source code
use [source file path]     -- display or change the source path

memory                     -- report memory usage
gc                         -- free unused objects

load classname             -- load Java class to be debugged
run <class> [args]         -- start execution of a loaded Java class
!!                         -- repeat last command
help (or ?)                -- list commands
exit (or quit)             -- exit debugger
```

The sections that follow examine how many of these options are used to debug your code.

Examining Threads

The debugger includes a group of useful commands for examining threads. All Java programs have at least one thread of execution.

The `threads` command lists all the threads in use and their status. The type and number of threads running on the system vary according to the threads used by your system, how you start the debugger, and the threads used by your Java program. When you start the debugger directly, no Java program is running, and few threads are running on your system.

To follow along with this debugging session, start the debugger for use with the Jompanion editor developed in Chapter 21, "Designing and Implementing Advanced Applications." To do this, change to the directory containing the class files for Jompanion and type the following:

```
jdb Jompanion
```

Your system should display output similar to this:

```
Initializing jdb...
0x13a41e0:class(Jompanion)
>
```

> **Note:** The greater-than sign (>) is the input prompt for the debugger.

At this point in the debugging session, the Jompanion application is not running; I have merely invoked a session with the debugger. To examine the threads currently running on your system, type `threads` at the debugger input prompt. On a Windows 95 system using JDK 1.0, the following threads run whenever you start the debugger:

```
> threads
Group system:
  1. (java.lang.Thread)0x13931f8            Finalizer thread cond. waiting
  2. (java.lang.Thread)0x1393918            Debugger agent    running
  3. (sun.tools.debug.BreakpointHandler)0x13a2668 Breakpoint
➥handler cond. waiting
Group main:
  4. (java.lang.Thread)0x13930a0 main running
```

The output from the `threads` command tells you a lot about the threads running on your system. As you can see, each thread is listed by threadgroup and is numbered consecutively. This number is the ID of the thread. Following the thread ID is the class associated with the thread, its name, and its status.

Using the ID number, you can set the default thread using the `thread` command. To switch to the main thread, type the following:

```
>thread 4
```

When you do this, the input prompt changes to this:

```
main[1]
```

The new prompt, `main[1]`, tells you the current thread is the thread named `main`. All commands typed at the input prompt are taken in context of this thread. However, because no Java program is running on your system now, the debugger essentially behaves the same. To switch to the debugger agent thread, type its ID at the input prompt, like this:

```
main[1] thread 2
```

When you do this, the input prompt changes to this:

```
Debugger agent[1]
```

To start the application from within the debugging session, type `run` at the debugger input prompt. The following output should display in your command area:

```
> run
run Jompanion
running ...
main[1]
```

Now that a program is running, the `main[1]` prompt references the main thread of your program—in this case, Jompanion's main thread. Using the `threads` command, you can check the threads running in the context of the main thread. As you can see from the following listing, the threadgroup and threads are different when a program is running:

```
main[1] threads
Group Jompanion.main:
  1. (java.lang.Thread)0x13a6738      AWT-Win32          running
  2. (java.lang.Thread)0x13a6790      AWT-Callback-Win32 running
  3. (sun.awt.ScreenUpdater)0x13a6a38 Screen Updater     cond. waiting
main[1]
```

The three threads listed previously are all the threads running in the context of the current thread. Obviously, there are more threads running on your system, and you may be wondering what happened to the threads the debugger is running. To see all the threads running on your system, change to the system threadgroup and then type the `threads` command:

```
main[1] threadgroup system
main[1] threads
Group system:
  1. (java.lang.Thread)0x13931f8                   Finalizer thread   cond. waiting
  2. (java.lang.Thread)0x1393918                    Debugger agent    running
  3. (sun.tools.debug.BreakpointHandler)0x13a2668
➥Breakpoint handler cond. waiting
Group main:
  4. (java.lang.Thread)0x13930a0 main cond. waiting
Group Jompanion.main:
  5. (java.lang.Thread)0x13a6738      AWT-Win32          running
  6. (java.lang.Thread)0x13a6790      AWT-Callback-Win32 running
  7. (sun.awt.ScreenUpdater)0x13a6a38 Screen Updater     cond. waiting
main[1]
```

To analyze the behavior of your program when certain threads are stopped, use the `suspend` command. Although this command is more useful when you have multiple background threads, it is used here to stop the `Screen Updater` thread of the Jompanion application. After stopping a thread, you can check its status using the `threads` command. Here's how:

```
main[1] suspend 7
main[1] threads
Group system:
 1. (java.lang.Thread)0x13931f8              Finalizer thread    cond. waiting
 2. (java.lang.Thread)0x1393918              Debugger agent     running
 3. (sun.tools.debug.BreakpointHandler)0x13a2668
↪Breakpoint handler cond. waiting
Group main:
 4. (java.lang.Thread)0x13930a0 main cond. waiting
Group Jompanion.main:
 5. (java.lang.Thread)0x13a6738      AWT-Win32           running
 6. (java.lang.Thread)0x13a6790      AWT-Callback-Win32 running
 7. (sun.awt.ScreenUpdater)0x13a6a38 Screen Updater       suspended
main[1]
```

After testing the behavior of your application with the thread suspended, you will usually want to restart the thread and go on to test the behavior of your application with other threads suspended. To restart a thread, use the `resume` command.

Examining Methods and Classes

By examining the methods and classes used in your program, you can learn more about the behavior of your program, verify that sections of the code are being executed as you expect, and pinpoint problem areas in the code. The debugger provides many ways to examine methods and classes. However, before you can do so, you need to start a debugging session.

This section demonstrates how to attach the debugger to a running application. To follow along, change to the directory containing the Jompanion class files and start the Jompanion application using the interpreter as follows:

```
java -debug Jompanion
```

Your system should display a password to be used with the debugger, such as the following:

```
Agent password=52d2zj
```

If your password is `52d2zj`, you now open a new command window and type this:

```
jdb -password 52d2zj
```

Your system should display output similar to the following:

```
Initializing jdb...
>
```

Now that your debugging session is started, you can examine the classes and methods. To list the classes the debugger currently knows about, use the debugger's `classes` command. If you use this command for Jompanion, the output from the debugger is similar to the following abbreviated listing:

```
> classes
** classes list **
0x1393008:class(java.lang.Thread)
0x1393018:class(java.lang.Object)
0x1393098:class(java.lang.Class)
0x1393028:class(java.lang.String)
0x1393038:class(java.lang.ThreadDeath)
0x1393048:class(java.lang.Error)
0x13932f0:class(Jompanion)
0x1393300:class(java.awt.Frame)
0x1393310:class(java.awt.Window)
0x1393320:class(java.awt.Container)
0x1393330:class(java.awt.Component)
0x1393ab0:class(java.awt.BorderLayout)
0x1393af8:class(java.awt.Color)
0x1393b70:class(java.awt.Font)
0x1393bd0:class(java.awt.MenuBar)
0x1393be0:class(java.awt.MenuComponent)
0x1393c08:class(sun.tools.java.ClassPath)
0x1393c18:class(java.io.File)
0x1393c60:class(sun.tools.java.ClassPathEntry)
0x1393cd0:class(sun.tools.zip.ZipFile)
0x1393d00:class(java.io.RandomAccessFile)
0x1393d70:class(java.util.Vector)
0x1393d90:class(java.awt.Menu)
0x1393da0:class(java.awt.MenuItem)
0x1393e90:interface(sun.tools.zip.ZipConstants)
0x1393ee0:class(sun.tools.zip.ZipEntry)
0x1393f30:interface(java.awt.peer.MenuBarPeer)
0x1394088:interface(java.awt.peer.FramePeer)
0x1394098:class(java.awt.Choice)
0x13940c0:interface(java.awt.peer.ChoicePeer)
0x13942d0:class(java.awt.FlowLayout)
0x13949a0:class(java.awt.TextArea)
0x13949b0:class(java.awt.TextComponent)
0x13949e0:interface(java.awt.peer.TextComponentPeer)
0x1394a08:class(java.awt.FileDialog)
0x1394a18:class(java.awt.Dialog)
0x1394a88:class(java.awt.Toolkit)
0x1395878:class(sun.awt.win32.MToolkit)
0x1398038:class(java.awt.Dimension)
0x1398050:class(sun.awt.win32.MFramePeer)
0x1398db8:class(sun.awt.win32.MPanelPeer)
0x1398dc8:class(sun.awt.win32.MCanvasPeer)
0x1398dd8:class(sun.awt.win32.MComponentPeer)
0x139df48:class(java.awt.Rectangle)
0x139df60:class(java.awt.Insets)
0x139e148:class(sun.awt.win32.MMenuBarPeer)
0x139e168:class(sun.tools.debug.BreakpointHandler)
0x139e1a0:class(sun.tools.debug.BreakpointQueue)
0x139e1e8:class(java.net.Socket)
0x139e220:class(sun.awt.win32.MMenuPeer)
```

```
0x139e230:class(sun.awt.win32.MMenuItemPeer)
0x139e2d0:class(sun.awt.win32.MChoicePeer)
0x139e300:class(sun.awt.win32.MTextAreaPeer)
0x139e330:interface(java.awt.peer.ContainerPeer)
0x139e340:interface(java.awt.peer.WindowPeer)
0x139e350:class(sun.awt.win32.Win32FontMetrics)
0x139e360:class(java.awt.FontMetrics)
0x139e3a8:interface(java.awt.peer.TextAreaPeer)
0x139e3d8:class(sun.awt.ScreenUpdater)
0x139e410:class(sun.awt.ScreenUpdaterEntry)
0x139e468:class(sun.awt.win32.Win32Graphics)
0x139e478:class(java.awt.Graphics)
>
```

As you can see, the list of classes known to the debugger includes all classes used by both the debugger and the program you are debugging. You can use the methods command to see the methods in any class shown in the classes list. To see a list of methods in the Jompanion class, type the following:

```
> methods Jompanion
```

The debugger output should be similar to the following:

```
void AddDialog()
boolean handleEvent(Event)
void cut()
void copy()
void paste()
void openFile()
void saveAsFile()
void saveOpenedFile()
void startNewText()
void showFindDialog()
void showRepDialog()
void showReplaceAllDialog()
void showAboutDialog()
void showErrorDialog(String)
boolean read(String)
boolean write(String)
String check(String)
void setFindString(String)
void setReplaceString(String)
void findSelectedText()
void findText()
void replaceSelectText()
boolean replaceText()
void main(String[])
```

When you know the methods for a particular class, you can debug the method using breakpoints and steps. When the program you are debugging reaches a breakpoint, execution of the program stops. You can then step through the program line by line to examine what happens when the program executes specific lines within the method.

> **Warning:** When your program reaches a breakpoint, all execution of the program stops. If the program occupies the entire screen when you hit the breakpoint, your workstation may lock up. To avoid this, resize the application or applet's frame so you can access the command area with the active debugging session.

To set a breakpoint, use the `stop` command and reference the method you want to put the breakpoint in at the class level. For example, to place a breakpoint in the `copy` method of the Jompanion class, you would reference the method as `Jompanion.copy`, like this:

```
> stop in Jompanion.copy
Breakpoint set in Jompanion.copy
```

When the breakpoint is reached, program execution stops. You can then examine the stack of the current thread using the `where` command or step through the method line by line using the `step` command. A useful command to use as you step through the program is `list`, which shows the current execution point in the program.

To cause Jompanion to reach the breakpoint set in the `copy` method, use the `copy` command to copy selected text in the text area. The debugger should print out the following:

```
Breakpoint hit: Jompanion.copy (Jompanion:244)
AWT-Callback-Win32[1]
```

This output tells you the method that reached the breakpoint is called `Jompanion.copy`, the parent program is called Jompanion, and the line number where the breakpoint was reached is 244. Notice that on the Windows system used in the example, the prompt changed to `AWT-Callback-Win32[1]`, which is the current thread. All commands issued to the debugger with this new prompt are in the context of the `AWT-Callback-Win32` thread.

Using the `where` command, you can see what the stack looks like:

```
AWT-Callback-Win32[1] where
  [1] Jompanion.copy (Jompanion:244)
  [2] Jompanion.handleEvent (Jompanion:187)
  [3] java.awt.Component.postEvent (Component:838)
  [4] java.awt.MenuComponent.postEvent (MenuComponent:94)
  [5] java.awt.MenuComponent.postEvent (MenuComponent:94)
  [6] java.awt.MenuComponent.postEvent (MenuComponent:94)
  [7] sun.awt.win32.MMenuItemPeer.action (MMenuItemPeer:50)
AWT-Callback-Win32[1]
```

The stack shows you a picture of the steps the program took to get to the breakpoint. In this case, you selected a menu item, which posted an event that must be handled by the event handler. The event handler in turn called the `copy` method, and the breakpoint was reached. You can move up and down the stack using the `up` and `down` commands.

Other breakpoint-related commands include `cont`, used to continue execution of the program after the breakpoint; `resume`, used to resume execution of the current thread; and `clear`, used to clear a breakpoint.

> **Note:** Keep in mind that the Java stack is organized according to the last in, first out methodology (LIFO). Because the last item in the stack is the first to pop off it when execution resumes, you need to read the stack in reverse order. Therefore, to trace the path to the current event in time order, start at the bottom of the stack and work to the top.

Using the `list` command, you can see exactly where you are in the source code:

```
AWT-Callback-Win32[1] list
240           textArea.requestFocus();
241           }
242
243           //copies selected text to the buffer
244    =>     public void copy() {
245              copyString = textArea.getSelectedText();
246              textArea.requestFocus();
247           }
248
AWT-Callback-Win32[1]
```

The output of the `list` command tells you where you are in the program. In the previous listing, the program stopped on line number 244. You can then step through the current method line by line using the `step` command.

Examining Instance Variables

By examining the instance variables in your program, you can check their values and ensure that they are set within the ranges you expect. Generally, you will want to check the status of instance variables at a specific point during the program's execution, so it's a good idea to set a breakpoint in a method whose instance variables you want to check. Before you can examine methods and classes used in your application, you need to start a debugging session.

This section demonstrates how to attach the debugger to an applet. If you want to follow along, change to the directory containing the `ScrollText` class files. (The `ScrollText` applet was created in Chapter 15, "Creating Java-Powered Web Presentations with Applets.") Next, create a new HTML document or use an existing one that references the `ScrollText` applet, such as the following:

```
<HTML>
<HEAD>
<TITLE>ScrollText Applet</TITLE>
</HEAD>
<BODY>
<APPLET CODE="ScrollText.class" WIDTH=500 HEIGHT=300>
```

```
</APPLET>
</BODY>
</HTML>
```

Then start the ScrollText applet with the applet viewer:

```
appletviewer -debug ScrollText
```

Your system should display output similar to the following:

```
appletviewer -debug test.html
Initializing jdb...
0x13a41e0:class(sun.applet.AppletViewer)
>
```

Finally, start the ScrollText applet using the run command:

```
> run
```

Your system should display output similar to the following:

```
run sun.applet.AppletViewer test.html
running ...
main[1]
```

Now that the applet is started, you can use the dump command to check the status of a specified object's instance variables:

```
main[1] dump ScrollText
ScrollText = 0x13a7ea8:class(ScrollText) {
    superclass = 0x13a7eb8:class(java.applet.Applet)
    loader = null
    interfaces:
        0x13a2f70:interface(java.lang.Runnable)

    static final LayoutManager panelLayout = (java.awt.FlowLayout)0x13a7738
}
```

The dump listing tells you many things about the state of the class or object to which it relates. For the ScrollText class, the dump tells you the superclass is java.applet.Applet, the loader is null, the applet uses the runnable interface, and the layout setting is for FlowLayout. Provided that local variables are used in your program and are available, you can also check the status of local variables using the locals command:

```
main[1] locals
Local variables and arguments:
  this = ScrollText[3000,3000,0x0,layout=java.awt.FlowLayout]
```

You can set a breakpoint in the applet to check instance variables related to a specific method at a given point in time. Because the scroll method plays a key role in how the ScrollText applet works, it's a good idea to check variables in this method. First, place the breakpoint; then dump the variable you want to check, as in the following:

```
main[1] stop in ScrollText.scroll
Breakpoint set in ScrollText.scroll
main[1]
```

```
Breakpoint hit: ScrollText.scroll (ScrollText:83)
Thread-2[1] dump dist
this.dist = -480
```

Using the cont command, you can resume execution of the program. Then, when the next breakpoint is reached, you can dump the variable you want to check again, as in the following:

```
Thread-2[1] cont
Thread-2[1]
Breakpoint hit: ScrollText.scroll (ScrollText:83)
Thread-2[1] dump dist
this.dist = -481
```

Identifying Trouble with the Code

Debugging your code is not a straightforward process, so there are many ways to do it. There are two key methods used by Java programmers; one is highly interactive and one is mostly noninteractive. Just as you use the debugger to provide a highly interactive way to find out the status of variables and what the program is doing at a particular line of code, you can use the program itself to tell you what it's doing at any given time in a primarily noninteractive way simply by inserting print statements at key points in the logic of the program.

By adding print statements to key methods, you can ensure that the methods are executing. You can check the sequence of events that lead to the method being called and which methods are called after the method executes. Usually, this type of print statement simply echoes the name of the method being executed, as in the following:

```
System.out.println("In the run method.");
```

By placing print statements in conditional loops, you can see what conditions are met on the basis of the current state of the program. You can then alter the program's state and see if other conditions of the loop are met. Usually, this type of print statement simply echoes the condition you are checking for, as in the following:

```
System.out.println("No parameter, using default.");
```

By placing print statements before or after values associated with a variable are changed, you can ensure the value associated with the variable is what you expect it to be when called and after the change occurs. Usually, this type of print statement describes the variable and displays the value, such as

```
System.out.println("The location parameter is set to: " + x);
```

After you use this mostly noninteractive method of debugging for a while, you may see why many programmers prefer it. The key concept is that you insert the print statements to help you debug and then either comment them out or delete them before you provide the finished version of the program.

The only bad thing about this method of debugging is that tracking the print statements that display to your screen is sometimes difficult, especially if your command window doesn't have a scroll feature. To make this style of debugging easier, you may want to create a utility to aid the debugging process, such as a window that displays all your debugging messages in reverse time order so you always see the most current messages but also have access to all previous messages.

Putting your debugging messages in a more usable and trackable format is exactly what the HelpDebug application shown in Listing 23.1 does. The application creates a window to which you can pass input and thus log your debugging information. The heart of the application is an overloaded method called out. The first version of the out method enables you to pass strings that you want displayed in the debugging window, the second enables you to display values associated with objects, and the final version enables you to pass values associated with integers.

Listing 23.1. The **HelpDebug** application.

```
/**
 * The Complete Guide to HelpDebug Application
 * This application creates a window to log debugging information.
 */

import java.applet.Applet;
import java.awt.*;
import java.util.*;


public class HelpDebug extends Frame {
    TextArea textArea;

    void out(String str) {
        textArea.insertText(str + '\n',0);
    }

    void out(Object obj) {
        textArea.insertText(String.valueOf(obj) + '\n',0);
    }

    void out(int x) {
        textArea.insertText("The value of the integer is:" + x + '\n',0);
    }


    HelpDebug() {

        super("HelpDebug Output Window");
        pack();
        reshape(200,0,300,300);
        show();

        textArea = new TextArea();
        textArea.setText("[New Debug Session]");
        setLayout(new BorderLayout());
        add("Center",textArea);
    }
```

continues

Listing 23.1. continued

```
    public boolean handleEvent(Event e) {

        if (e.id == Event.WINDOW_DESTROY) {
        dispose();
         return true;
        }
        else return super.handleEvent(e);

    }
}
```

Before you can use the HelpDebug application, type in and compile the code or access the source code for the application on the CD-ROM. Then you need to let your application or applet know the HelpDebug application exists by doing the following:

1. Import the HelpDebug class:

   ```
   import HelpDebug;
   ```

2. Create a container for the debug object:

   ```
   HelpDebug debug;
   ```

3. Create an instance of the HelpDebug object in the main() method of an application or the init() method of an applet:

   ```
   debug = new HelpDebug();
   ```

When your program can access HelpDebug, you can direct your debugging output to the HelpDebug application itself. You do this by calling the out() method of the object you created in step 3, like this:

```
debug.out("The height parameter as read in is:" + hs);
```

To show you how to use this method of debugging and gain practice with the HelpDebug class, I'll modify the ScrollText applet. I'll do this by directing debugging statements to HelpDebug's out() method. As you examine the modified applet shown in Listing 23.2, look at how the debugging statements are added, where they are added, and what they output.

Listing 23.2. The modified **ScrollText** applet with debugging.

```
import java.awt.Graphics;
import java.awt.Font;
import HelpDebug;

/**
 * The Complete Guide to Java ScrollText Applet with Debugging information
 * This applet is used to scroll a text banner across the screen
 * The applet takes TEXT, WIDTH, and HEIGHT as parameters.
 */
```

```java
public class ScrollText extends java.applet.Applet implements Runnable {

    int h;                          // Height of applet in pixels
    int w;                          // Width of applet in pixels
    char separated[];               // Output string in array form
    String s = null;                // Input string containing display text
    String hs = null;               // Input string containing height
    String ws = null;               // Input string containing width
    Thread ScrollThread = null;        // Thread to control processing
    int speed=35;                   // Length of delay in milliseconds
    boolean threadSuspended = false;
    int dist;
    HelpDebug debug;        //container for the debug object


/* Setup width, height, and display text */
public void init() {
    debug = new HelpDebug();
    ws = getParameter ("width");
    debug.out("The width parameter as read in is:" + ws);
    hs = getParameter ("height");
    debug.out("The height parameter as read in is:" + hs);
    if (ws == null){          // Read width as input
        w = 150;              // If not found use default
    } else {
        w = Integer.parseInt(ws); // Convert input string to integer
    }
    if (hs == null){          // Read height as input
        h = 50;               // If not found use default
    } else {
        h = Integer.parseInt (hs); // Convert input string to integer
    }
    resize(w,h);              // Set font based on height
    setFont(new Font("TimesRoman",Font.BOLD,h - 6));
    s = getParameter("text");// Read input text, if null use default
    if (s == null) {
        s = " The Java ScrollText Applet at work.";
        debug.out("No text parameter, using default");
    }

    separated =  new char [s.length()];
    s.getChars(0,s.length(),separated,0);
 }

/* Start new thread to run applet */
public void start() {
    if(ScrollThread == null)
    {
    debug.out("Thread is null");
        ScrollThread = new Thread(this);
        ScrollThread.start();
    }
}

/* End thread containing applet */
public void stop() {
    debug.out("In the stop method.");
    ScrollThread = null;
```

continues

Listing 23.2. continued

```java
    }

// While applet is running pause then scroll text
public void run() {
    debug.out("In the run method.");
    while (ScrollThread != null) {
    try {Thread.sleep(speed);} catch (InterruptedException e){}
    scroll();
    }
    ScrollThread = null;
}

// Scroll text by determining new location to draw text and redrawing
synchronized void scroll () {
    debug.out("In the scroll method.");
    dist--;                  // Move string to left
    debug.out(dist);
    // If string has disappeared to the left, move back to right edge
    if (dist + ((s.length()+1)*(h *5 / 11)) == 0){
    dist=w;
}
    repaint();
}

// Redraw string at given location
public void paint(Graphics g) {
    g.drawChars(separated, 0, s.length(), dist,4 *h / 5);
}

// Suspend thread when mouse is pushed, resume when pushed again
public boolean mouseDown(java.awt.Event evt, int x, int y) {
    debug.out("Detected mouseDown event");
        if (threadSuspended) {
            debug.out("Resuming Thread…");
            ScrollThread.resume();
        }
        else {
            debug.out("Stopping Thread…");
            ScrollThread.suspend();
        }
        threadSuspended = !threadSuspended;
    return true;
    }
}
```

Before you can use the modified applet, you have to type in and compile the source code or access the source code for the modified applet on the CD-ROM. You also need to create an HTML document that displays the applet, such as the one shown in Listing 23.3. This document is also available on the CD-ROM.

Listing 23.3. The HTML document used to display the applet.

```
<HTML>
<HEAD>
<TITLE>Applet for Debugging</TITLE>
</HEAD>
<BODY>
<APPLET CODE="ScrollText.class" WIDTH=500 HEIGHT=300>
<PARAM NAME=TEXT VALUE="Applet Debugging Example…">
</APPLET>
</BODY>
</HTML>
```

After creating the necessary files, you can run the applet using the applet viewer or your Web browser. Figure 23.1 shows the applet and the debugging window. Note that the debugging output displayed in the HelpDebug window is in reverse time order, which ensures that the most current debugging information is always displayed at the top of the window.

Figure 23.1.
Using the HelpDebug *application.*

Summary

Debugging logic problems in your code is more difficult than debugging syntax problems. Therefore, you need a set of advanced tools to aid the debugging process. When you want to debug your code in a highly interactive way, use the Java debugger. The Java debugger is one of the most advanced tools in the Java Developer's Kit and, as such, has many useful features for debugging your code. When you want to debug your code in a mostly noninteractive way, you may want to use print statements and possibly a utility that helps you track them. The HelpDebug utility presented in this chapter is designed to help you do just that.

24

The Java Virtual Machine

Throughout this book, I have referenced the Java Virtual Machine and the mysterious bytecodes it reads. Without the Java Virtual Machine, Java would not be architecture neutral and you would not be able to run Java programs on platforms running different operating systems. To understand the Java Virtual Machine, you need to examine its basic parts, the objects it uses, and the bytecodes that make it work.

Introducing the Virtual Machine

Using an interpreter, all Java programs are compiled to an intermediate level called *bytecode*. You can run the compiled bytecode on any computer with the Java runtime environment installed on it. The runtime environment consists of the virtual machine and its supporting code.

The Java interpreter translates bytecode into sets of instructions the computer can understand. Because the bytecode is in an intermediate form, there is only a slight delay caused by the translation.

The difficult part of creating Java bytecode is that the source code is compiled for a machine that does not exist. This machine is called the *Java Virtual Machine*, and it exists only in the memory of your computer. Fooling the Java compiler into creating bytecode for a nonexistent machine is only one-half of the ingenious process that makes Java architecture neutral. The Java interpreter must also make your computer and the bytecode file believe they are running on a real machine. It does this by acting as the intermediary between the Virtual Machine and your real machine.

The Basic Parts of the Java Virtual Machine

Creating a Virtual Machine within your computer's memory banks requires building every major function of a real computer down to the very environment within which programs operate. For our purposes here, we'll break down these functions into seven basic parts:

- A set of registers
- A stack
- An execution environment
- A garbage-collected heap
- A constant pool
- A method storage area
- An instruction set

Registers

The *registers* of the Java Virtual Machine are similar to the registers in your computer. However, because the Virtual Machine is stack based, its registers are not used for passing or receiving arguments. In Java, registers hold the machine's state and are updated after each line of bytecode is executed to maintain that state. The following four registers hold the state of the virtual machine:

- frame, the reference frame, contains a pointer to the execution environment of the current method.
- optop, the operand top, contains a pointer to the top of the operand stack and is used to evaluate arithmetic expressions.
- pc, the program counter, contains the address of the next bytecode to be executed.
- vars, the variable register, contains a pointer to local variables.

All these registers are 32 bits wide and are allocated immediately. This is possible because the compiler knows the size of the local variables and operand stack and because the interpreter knows the size of the execution environment.

The Stack

The Java Virtual Machine uses an *operand stack* to supply parameters to methods and operations, and to receive results back from them. All bytecode instructions take operands from the stack, operate on them, and return results to the stack. Like registers in the virtual machine, the operand stack is 32 bits wide.

The operand stack follows the last-in first-out (LIFO) methodology and expects the operands on the stack to be in a specific order. For example, the isub bytecode instruction expects two integers to be stored on the top of the stack, which means that the operands must have been pushed there by the previous set of instructions. isub pops the operands off the stack, subtracts them, and then pushes the results back onto the stack.

In Java, integers are a primitive data type. Each primitive data type has unique instructions that tell it how to operate on operands of that type. For example, the lsub bytecode is used to perform long integer subtraction, the fsub bytecode is used to perform floating-point subtraction, and the dsub bytecode is used to perform long integer subtraction. Because of this, it is illegal to push two integers onto the stack and then treat them as a single long integer. However, it is legal to push a 64-bit long integer onto the stack and have it occupy two 32-bit slots. Aren't you glad the Java compiler checks the rules for you as it compiles your program?

Each method in your Java program has a stack frame associated with it. The *stack frame* holds the state of the method with three sets of data: the method's local variables, the method's execution environment, and the method's operand stack. Although the sizes of the local variable and execution environment data sets are always fixed at the start of the method call, the size of the operand stack changes as the method's bytecode instructions are executed. Because the Java stack is 32 bits wide, 64-bit numbers are not guaranteed to be 64-bit aligned.

The Execution Environment

The *execution environment* is maintained within the stack as a data set and is used to handle dynamic linking, normal method returns, and exception generation. To handle dynamic linking, the execution environment contains symbolic references to methods and variables for the current method and current class. These symbolic calls are translated into actual method calls through dynamic linking to a symbol table.

Whenever a method completes normally, a value is returned to the calling method. The execution environment handles normal method returns by restoring the registers of the caller and incrementing the program counter of the caller to skip the method call instruction. Execution of the program then continues in the calling method's execution environment.

If execution of the current method completes normally, a value is returned to the calling method. This occurs when the calling method executes a return instruction appropriate to the return type.

If the calling method executes a return instruction that is not appropriate to the return type, the method throws an exception or an error. Errors that can occur include dynamic linkage failure, such as a failure to find a class file, or runtime errors, such as a reference outside the bounds of an array. When errors occur, the execution environment generates an exception. (See Chapter 8, "Tying It All Together: Threads, Exceptions, and More," for a discussion of exception handling.)

The Garbage-Collected Heap

Each program running in the Java runtime environment has a *garbage-collected heap* assigned to it. Because instances of class objects are allocated from this heap, another word for the heap is the *memory allocation pool*. By default, the heap size is set to 1MB on most systems.

Although the heap is set to a specific size when you start a program, it can grow—for example, when new objects are allocated. To ensure that the heap does not get too large, objects that are no longer in use are automatically deallocated or garbage-collected by the Java Virtual Machine.

Java performs automatic garbage collection as a background thread. Each thread running in the Java runtime environment has two stacks associated with it: The first stack is used for Java code; the second is used for C code. Memory used by these stacks draws from the total system memory pool.

Whenever a new thread starts execution, it is assigned a maximum stack size for Java code and for C code. By default on most systems, the maximum size of the Java code stack is 400KB and the maximum size of the C code stack is 128KB.

If your system has memory limitations, you can force Java to perform more aggressive cleanup and thus reduce the total amount of memory used. To do this, reduce the maximum size of the Java and C code stacks. If your system has lots of memory, you can force Java to perform less aggressive cleanup, thus reducing the amount of background processing. To do this, increase the maximum size of the Java and C code stacks.

The Constant Pool

Each class in the heap has a *constant pool* associated with it. Because constants do not change, they are usually created at compile time. Items in the constant pool encode all the names used by any method in a particular class. The class contains a count of how many constants exist and an offset that specifies where a particular listing of constants begins within the class description.

All information associated with a constant follows a specific format based on the type of the constant. For example, *class-level constants* are used to represent a class or an interface and have the following format:

```
CONSTANT_Class_info {
    u1 tag;
    u2 name_index;
}
```

where `tag` is the value of `CONSTANT_Class` and the `name_index` provides the string name of the class. The class name for `int[][]` is `[[I`. The class name for `Thread[]` is `[Ljava.lang.Thread;`.

The Method Area

Java's *method area* is similar to the compiled code areas of the runtime environments used by other programming languages. It stores bytecode instructions that are associated with methods in the compiled code and the symbol table the execution environment needs for dynamic linking. Any debugging or additional information that might need to be associated with a method is stored in this area as well.

The Bytecode Instruction Set

Although programmers prefer to write code in a high-level format, your computer cannot execute this code directly, which is why you must compile Java programs before you can run them. Generally, compiled code is either in a machine-readable format called *machine language* or in an intermediate-level format such as the assembly language or Java bytecode.

The bytecode instructions used by the Java Virtual Machine resemble Assembler instructions. If you have ever used Assembler, you know that the instruction set is streamlined to a minimum for the sake of efficiency and that tasks, such as printing to the screen, are accomplished using a series of instructions. For example, the Java language allows you to print to the screen using a single line of code, such as

```
System.out.println("Hello world!");
```

At compile time, the Java compiler converts the single-line print statement to the following bytecode:

```
0 getstatic #6 <Field java.lang.System.out Ljava/io/PrintStream;>
3 ldc #1 <String "Hello world!">
5 invokevirtual #7 <Method java.io.PrintStream.println(Ljava/lang/String;)V>
8 return
```

The JDK provides a tool for examining bytecode called the *Java class file disassembler*. As you will see later in this chapter, you can run the disassembler by typing javap at the command line or by starting a graphical disassembler that you got with a third-party toolkit.

Because the bytecode instructions are in such a low-level format, your programs execute at nearly the speed of programs compiled to machine language. All instructions in machine language are represented by byte streams of 0s and 1s. In a low-level language, byte streams of 0s and 1s are replaced by suitable mnemonics, such as the bytecode instruction isub. As with the assembly language, the basic format of a bytecode instruction is

```
<operation> <operands(s)>
```

Therefore, an instruction in the bytecode instruction set consists of a 1-byte opcode specifying the operation to be performed, and zero or more operands that supply parameters or data that will be used by the operation.

Examining Bytecode

If you are familiar with how intermediate-level languages like Assembler are used, you should see the true beauty of Java. Here's a language that allows you to compile the source code to a machine-independent, intermediate form that will execute nearly as quickly as if it were fully compiled.

To allow you to examine bytecode instructions, the JDK includes a tool called the *Java class file disassembler*. The name of this tool is somewhat deceptive: You can use it to look at the internals of Java class files, but you cannot disassemble a compiled class file to create a Java source file.

You can use the disassembler for several purposes:

- To gain quick insight into how a class works.
- To see how a class uses system resources.
- To check your import statements and dependencies

Two versions of the disassembler are included in the JDK. The first version, javap, is optimized for normal use and has only limited debugging capabilities. The second version, javap_g, is optimized for debugging and is intended for use with the Java debugger.

You run the Java disassembler from the command line and pass it the name of your Java class file without the .class extension. If you invoke the disassembler with no options, it outputs the name of the file you compiled the class file from and abbreviated declarations for public variables, methods, and classes. If you created the FirstApplet program in Chapter 23, "Advanced Debugging and Troubleshooting," you can use javap to disassemble the applet by changing to the directory with the compiled class file and typing the following:

```
javap FirstApplet
```

The output to your screen should be similar to this:

```
Compiled from FirstApplet.java
public class FirstApplet extends java.applet.Applet {
    java.awt.Image NewImage;
    public void init();
    public void paint(java.awt.Graphics);
    public FirstApplet();
}
```

Although the output looks rather terse, it is extremely useful. From this output, you can see all public fields and the basic structure of the program at a glance. This gives you a fair idea of how the program actually works. You can also see exactly where Java needs fully qualified paths to classes and what those paths are. The previous example shows that FirstApplet uses three classes in the Java API:

```
java.applet.Applet
```

```
java.awt.Image
```

```
java.awt.Graphics
```

Beginning Java programmers can use the output of javap as a guide to see if they are importing too many classes. To check this, compare which classes are actually used to the classes you are importing. You can also use javap to clean up your code. Using the fully qualified class names, you could rewrite the FirstApplet program so that it does not need import statements. Because the Java compiler no longer has to search the namespace for specific class instances, this new version of FirstApplet compiles slightly faster than the old version. The new version of FirstApplet follows:

```
public class FirstApplet extends java.applet.Applet {
java.awt.Image NewImage;

  public void init() {
      resize(300,300);
      NewImage = getImage(getCodeBase(),"New.gif");
  }

  public void paint(java.awt.Graphics g) {
```

```
              g.drawImage(NewImage,50,50,this);
              play(getCodeBase(),"New.au");
    }

}
```

You can use the -v option to get verbose output from the disassembler. Verbose output gives you some idea of the stacks, local variables, and arguments used by the program. If you use this option on the FirstApplet program by typing

```
javap -v FirstApplet
```

the output to your screen should be similar to this:

```
Compiled from FirstApplet.java
public class FirstApplet extends java.applet.Applet {
    java.awt.Image NewImage;
    public void init();
/* Stack=4, Locals=1, Args_size=1 */
    public void paint(java.awt.Graphics);
/* Stack=5, Locals=2, Args_size=2 */
    public FirstApplet();
/* Stack=1, Locals=1, Args_size=1 */
}
```

You can use the -p and -c options to get more information about a program. The -p option specifies that you want javap to print out private and protected variables, methods, and classes in addition to the public ones. You use the -c option to disassemble compiled code to bytecode instructions.

Note: You can use the Java disassembler to examine the bytecode instructions of any Java class file.

Bytecode instructions are useful when you want to see exactly what the Java Virtual Machine is doing when it runs the bytecode. However, bytecode instructions do not resemble your original source code. In fact, they more closely resemble an assembler program. For example, the four-line paint() method of FirstApplet is displayed in bytecode as the following:

```
Method void paint(java.awt.Graphics)
   0 aload_1
   1 aload_0
   2 getfield #12 <Field FirstApplet.NewImage Ljava/awt/Image;>
   5 bipush 50
   7 bipush 50
   9 aload_0
  10 invokevirtual #8 <Method java.awt.Graphics.drawImage(Ljava/awt/Image;
➥IILjava/awt/image/ImageObserver;)Z>
  13 pop
  14 aload_0
  15 aload_0
  16 invokevirtual #9 <Method java.applet.Applet.getCodeBase()Ljava/net/URL;>
  19 ldc #2 <String "New.au">
  21 invokevirtual #7 <Method java.applet.Applet.play
```

```
➥(Ljava/net/URL;Ljava/lang/String;)V>
24 return
```

The entire listing of bytecode instructions for the `FirstApplet.class` file is shown in Listing 24.1.

Listing 24.1. Bytecode for `FirstApplet`.

```
Compiled from FirstApplet.java
public class FirstApplet extends java.applet.Applet {
    java.awt.Image NewImage;
    public void init();
    public void paint(java.awt.Graphics);
    public FirstApplet();

Method void init()
   0 aload_0
   1 sipush 300
   4 sipush 300
   7 invokevirtual #11 <Method java.applet.Applet.resize(II)V>
  10 aload_0
  11 aload_0
  12 aload_0
  13 invokevirtual #9 <Method java.applet.Applet.getCodeBase()Ljava/net/URL;>
  16 ldc #1 <String "New.gif">
  18 invokevirtual #10 <Method java.applet.Applet.getImage
     ➥(Ljava/net/URL;Ljava/lang/String;)Ljava/awt/Image;>
  21 putfield #12 <Field FirstApplet.NewImage Ljava/awt/Image;>
  24 return

Method void paint(java.awt.Graphics)
   0 aload_1
   1 aload_0
   2 getfield #12 <Field FirstApplet.NewImage Ljava/awt/Image;>
   5 bipush 50
   7 bipush 50
   9 aload_0
  10 invokevirtual #8 <Method java.awt.Graphics.drawImage(Ljava/awt/Image;
     ➥IILjava/awt/image/ImageObserver;)Z>
  13 pop
  14 aload_0
  15 aload_0
  16 invokevirtual #9 <Method java.applet.Applet.getCodeBase()Ljava/net/URL;>
  19 ldc #2 <String "New.au">
  21 invokevirtual #7 <Method java.applet.Applet.play
     ➥(Ljava/net/URL;Ljava/lang/String;)V>
  24 return

Method FirstApplet()
   0 aload_0
   1 invokenonvirtual #6 <Method java.applet.Applet.<init>()V>
   4 return

}
```

As you can see from the previous examples, when you compile a Java program the compiler translates each line of high-level code into multiple lines of low-level instructions. These instructions are organized by the key class-level and method objects.

In the sections that follow, I examine the bytecode instruction set to give you a firm understanding of both the Java Virtual Machine and Java bytecode.

You can also use the disassembler to create minimal C header files. To do this, you use the -h option. If you generate a header file for FirstApplet using javap, you will find that the resulting output is very different from the output generated by javah. For this reason, you should really use the javap tool for what it was designed for and not to generate C header files.

Other useful options are -classpath and -verify. The -classpath option lets you override the default and current CLASSPATH setting. If the program you are disassembling makes use of any classes that are not stored in the current directory, you should either set the CLASSPATH environment variable or use the -classpath option. The -verify option lets you validate the Java class file. The general message you will get if the class file is valid is

```
Class classname succeeds
```

The command-line syntax for the disassembler is

```
javap [options] classname
```

or

```
javap [options] classname1 classname2 classname3 …
```

The disassembler takes these options:

Option	Description
-c	Disassembles compiled code to bytecode instructions
-classpath	Overrides the default or current CLASSPATH environment variable setting
-h	Creates a minimal C header file
-p	Displays private and protected variables, methods, and classes in addition to the public ones
-v	Displays verbose output and gives you some idea of the stacks, local variables, and arguments used by the program
-verify	Validates the Java class file

A Walk-through of the Instruction Set

The instruction set walkthrough that follows should help you understand how the Java Virtual Machine uses bytecode instructions. As you read this section, keep in mind that each instruction in the bytecode instruction set consists of a 1-byte opcode specifying the operation to be performed, and zero or more operands that supply parameters or data that will be used by the operation. Most bytecode instructions take as an operand a numeric value, an object name, or both, such as

```
bipush 50
```

or

```
getfield #12 <Field FirstApplet.NewImage Ljava/awt/Image;>
```

Knowing this, you can key in on the most important aspect of the bytecode instruction set: understanding how the instruction affects the stack. For this reason, along with a brief description of what a bytecode instruction does, I present a text picture of the operand stack before and after the operation associated with a bytecode instruction is performed, such as the following example:

Stack	
Before	**After**
.	value
.	.
.	.
	.

or

Stack	
Before	**After**
v2	result
v1	.
.	.
.	.
.	

The first stack drawing shows that the `bipush` instruction expects no operands to be on the top of the stack but does push a value onto the stack. The second drawing shows that the `iadd` instruction expects two operands—v1 and v2—to be on the top of the stack. These values are in turn popped off the stack and operated on to produce the result, and the result is pushed back onto the top of the stack.

Note: After v1 and v2 are operated on, only the result is pushed back on the stack. The variables have served their purpose.

Bytecode instructions that do not affect control flow simply execute and advance the program counter register so that it points to the address of the next bytecode instruction. Otherwise, the program counter is advanced over any operand bytes so that it points to the next bytecode in sequence. In the sections that follow, references to `byte1`, `byte2`, and so on, refer to the bytes following the opcode.

Tip: To better understand the walkthrough of the bytecode instruction set that follows, you might want to disassemble some of the class files you created as you read this book. You can also disassemble any of the class files on the CD-ROM.

Pushing Constants onto the Stack

One of the most basic tasks of the virtual machine is to push constants onto the stack. The next section looks at instructions that are used to do this.

bipush

Meaning: Push a 1-byte signed integer.

Description: The first byte following the opcode, `byte1`, is interpreted as a signed 8-bit value. This value is expanded to a 32-bit integer and pushed onto the operand stack.

Stack	
Before	**After**
.	value
.	.
.	.
	.

sipush

Meaning: Push a 2-byte signed integer.

Description: The first and second byte following the opcode, `byte1` and `byte2`, are assembled into a signed 16-bit value. This value is expanded to a 32-bit integer and pushed onto the operand stack.

Stack	
Before	**After**
.	item
.	.
.	.
	.

ldc1

Meaning: Push item from constant pool.

Description: `byte1` is used as an unsigned 8-bit index into the constant pool of the current class. After the item at that index is resolved, it is pushed onto the stack.

Stack	
Before	**After**
.	item
.	.
.	.
	.

> **Note:** This bytecode instruction throws an `OutOfMemoryError` if a `String` object is being pushed and there is not enough memory to allocate space for it.

ldc2

Meaning: Push 2-byte item from constant pool.

Description: `byte1` and `byte2` are used to construct an unsigned 16-bit index into the constant pool of the current class. After the item at that index is resolved, it is pushed onto the stack.

Stack	
Before	**After**
.	item
.	.
.	.
	.

> **Note:** This bytecode instruction throws an `OutOfMemoryError` if a `String` object is being pushed and there is not enough memory to allocate space for it.

ldc2w

Meaning: Push long or double from constant pool.

Description: `byte1` and `byte2` are used to construct an unsigned 16-bit index into the constant pool of the current class. After the two-word constant at that index is resolved, it is pushed onto the stack.

Stack	
Before	**After**
.	constant-word2
.	constant-word1
.	.
	.
	.

> **Note:** This bytecode instruction throws an `OutOfMemoryError` if a `String` object is being pushed and there is not enough memory to allocate space for it.

aconst_null

Meaning: Push a null object reference.

Description: This bytecode pushes a null object reference onto the stack.

Stack	
Before	**After**
.	null
.	.
.	.
	.

iconst_m1

Meaning: Push the integer constant -1.

Description: This bytecode pushes the integer constant -1 onto the stack.

Stack	
Before	**After**
.	-1
.	.
.	.
	.

iconst_<C>

Meaning: Push the integer constant <C>.

Description: This bytecode pushes an integer constant onto the stack. There are six associated bytecodes, one for each of the integers 0–5: iconst_0, iconst_1, iconst_2, iconst_3, iconst_4, and iconst_5.

Stack	
Before	**After**
.	<C>
.	.
.	.
	.

lconst_<LC>

Meaning: Push the long integer constant <LC>.

Description: This bytecode pushes a long integer constant onto the stack. There are two associated bytecodes, one for each of the integers 0–1: lconst_0 and lconst_1.

Stack	
Before	**After**
.	<lc>-word2
.	<lc>-word1
.	.
	.
	.

fconst_<F>

Meaning: Push the single-precision floating-point number <F>.

Description: This bytecode pushes a single-precision floating-point number onto the stack. There are three associated bytecodes, one for each of the integers 0–2: fconst_0, fconst_1, and fconst_2.

Stack	
Before	**After**
.	<f>
.	.
.	.
	.

dconst_<D>

Meaning: Push the double-precision floating-point number <D>.

Description: This bytecode pushes a double-precision floating-point number onto the stack. There are two associated bytecodes, one for each of the integers 0–1: dconst_0 and dconst_1.

Stack	
Before	**After**
.	<d>-word2
.	<d>-word1
.	.
	.
	.

Loading Local Variables onto the Stack

iload

Meaning: Load integer from local variable.

Description: The value of the local variable in the current Java frame is pushed onto the operand stack. This value must be of type integer.

Stack	
Before	**After**
.	value
.	.
.	.
	.

iload_<1>

Meaning: Load integer from local variable with specific index.

Description: The value of the local variable <1> in the current Java frame is pushed onto the operand stack. This value must be of type integer. There are four of these bytecodes, one for each of the integers 0–3: iload_0, iload_1, iload_2, and iload_3.

Stack	
Before	**After**
.	value
.	.
.	.
	.

lload

Meaning: Load long integer from local variable.

Description: The values of the local variables word1 and word2 in the current Java frame are pushed onto the operand stack. These values together must form a long integer.

Stack	
Before	**After**
.	value-word2
.	value-word1
.	.
	.
	.

lload_<1>

Meaning: Load long integer from local variable with specific index.

Description: The values of the local variables <1> and <1>+1 in the current Java frame are pushed onto the operand stack. These values together must form a long integer. There are four of these bytecodes, one for each of the integers 0–3: lload_0, lload_1, lload_2, and lload_3.

Stack	
Before	**After**
.	value-word2
.	value-word1
.	.
	.
	.

fload

Meaning: Load single float from local variable.

Description: The value of the local variable in the current Java frame is pushed onto the operand stack. This value must be a single-precision floating-point number.

Stack	
Before	**After**
.	value
.	.
.	.
	.

fload_<1>

Meaning: Load single float from local variable with specific index.

Description: The value of the local variable <1> in the current Java frame is pushed onto the operand stack. This value must be a single-precision floating-point number. There are four of these bytecodes, one for each of the integers 0–3: fload_0, fload_1, fload_2, and fload_3.

Stack	
Before	**After**
.	value
.	.
.	.
	.

dload

Meaning: Load double float from local variable.

Description: The values of the local variables word1 and word2 in the current Java frame are pushed onto the operand stack. These values together must form a double-precision floating-point number.

Stack	
Before	**After**
.	value-word2
.	value-word1
.	.
	.
	.

dload_<1>

Meaning: Load double float from local variable with specific index.

Description: The values of the local variables <1> and <1>+1 in the current Java frame are pushed onto the operand stack. These values together must form a double-precision floating-point number. There are four of these bytecodes, one for each of the integers 0–3: dload_0, dload_1, dload_2, and dload_3.

Stack	
Before	**After**
.	value-word2
.	value-word1
.	.
	.
	.

aload

Meaning: Load object reference from local variable.

Description: The value of the local variable in the current Java frame is pushed onto the operand stack. This value must contain a return address or be a reference to an object or array.

Stack	
Before	**After**
.	value
.	.
.	.
	.

aload_<l>

Meaning: Load object reference from local variable with specific index.

Description: The value of the local variable <l> in the current Java frame is pushed onto the operand stack. This value must contain a return address or be a reference to an object or array. There are four of these bytecodes, one for each of the integers 0–3: aload_0, aload_1, aload_2, and aload_3.

Stack	
Before	**After**
.	value
.	.
.	.
	.

Storing Stack Values into Local Variables

istore

Meaning: Store integer into local variable.

Description: Local variable in the current Java frame is set to a value. This value must be an integer.

Stack	
Before	**After**
value	.
.	.
.	.
.	

istore_<l>

Meaning: Store integer into local variable with specific index.

Description: Local variable <l> in the current Java frame is set to a value. This value must be an integer. There are four of these bytecodes, one for each of the integers 0–3: istore_0, istore_1, istore_2, and istore_3.

Stack	
Before	**After**
value	.
.	.
.	.
.	

lstore

Meaning: Store long integer into local variable.

Description: Local variables word1 and word2 in the current Java frame are set to a value. This value must be a long integer.

Stack	
Before	**After**
value-word2	.
value-word1	.
.	.
.	
.	

lstore_<l>

Meaning: Store long integer into local variable with specific index.

Description: Local variables <l> and <l>+1 in the current Java frame are set to a value. This value must be a long integer. There are four of these bytecodes, one for each of the integers 0–3: lstore_0, lstore_1, lstore_2, and lstore_3.

Stack	
Before	**After**
value-word2	.
value-word1	.
.	.
.	
.	

fstore

Meaning: Store single float into local variable.

Description: Local variable in the current Java frame is set to a value. This value must be a single-precision floating-point number.

Stack	
Before	**After**
value	.
.	.
.	.
.	

fstore_<l>

Meaning: Store single float into local variable with specific index.

Description: Local variable <l> in the current Java frame is set to a value. This value must be a single-precision floating-point number. There are four of these bytecodes, one for each of the integers 0–3: lstore_0, lstore_1, lstore_2, and lstore_3.

Stack	
Before	**After**
value	.
.	.
.	.
.	

dstore

Meaning: Store double-precision floating-point number into local variable.

Description: Local variables word1 and word2 in the current Java frame are set to a value. The value must be a double-precision floating-point number.

Stack	
Before	**After**
value-word2	.
value-word1	.
.	.
.	
.	

dstore_<1>

Meaning: Store double float into local variable with specific index.

Description: Local variables <1> and <1>+1 in the current Java frame are set to a value. The value must be a double-precision floating-point number. There are four of these bytecodes, one for each of the integers 0–3: dstore_0, dstore_1, dstore_2, and dstore_3.

Stack	
Before	**After**
value-word2	.
value-word1	.
.	.
.	
.	

astore

Meaning: Store object reference into local variable.

Description: Local variable at the index in the current Java frame is set to a value. The value must be a return address or a reference to an object.

Stack	
Before	**After**
value	.
.	.
.	.
.	

astore_<1>

Meaning: Store object reference into local variable with specific index.

Description: Local variable <1> in the current Java frame is set to a value. The value must be a return address or a reference to an object. There are four of these bytecodes, one for each of the integers 0–3: astore_0, astore_1, astore_2, and astore_3.

Stack	
Before	**After**
value	.
.	.
.	.
.	

`iinc`

Meaning: Increment local variable by constant.

Description: Local variable at `byte1` in the current Java frame must contain an integer. Its value is incremented by the value `byte2`, where `byte2` is treated as a signed 8-bit quantity.

Stack	
Before	**After**
.	.
.	.
.	.

Handling Arrays

`newarray`

Meaning: Allocate new array.

Description: A new array of a specific array type, capable of holding `size` elements, is allocated. The result is a reference to the new object. Allocation of an array large enough to contain `size` items of the specific array type is attempted and all elements of the array are initialized to `0`.

Stack	
Before	**After**
size	result
.	.
.	.
.	.

`size` represents the number of elements in the new array and must be an integer. The result is stored with an internal code that indicates the type of array to allocate. Possible values for the type of array are as follows: `T_BOOLEAN(4)`, `T_CHAR(5)`, `T_FLOAT(6)`, `T_DOUBLE(7)`, `T_BYTE(8)`, `T_SHORT(9)`, `T_INT(10)`, and `T_LONG(11)`.

> **Note:** A `NegativeArraySizeException` is thrown if `size` is less than `0`. An `OutOfMemoryError` is thrown if there is not enough memory to allocate the array.

`anewarray`

Meaning: Allocate new array of objects.

Description: A new array of the indicated class type and capable of holding `size` elements is allocated. The result is a reference to the new object. Allocation of an array large enough to contain `size` elements of the given class type is attempted and all elements of the array are initialized to null.

Stack	
Before	**After**
size	result
.	.
.	.
.	.

size represents the number of elements in the new array and must be an integer. `byte1` and `byte2` are used to construct an index into the constant pool of the current class. When the item at that index is resolved, the resulting entry must be a class.

> **Note:** A `NegativeArraySizeException` is thrown if size is less than 0. An `OutOfMemoryError` is thrown if there is not enough memory to allocate the array.

The `anewarray` instruction is used to create a single-dimension array. For example, the declaration `new Thread[7]` generates the following bytecode instructions:

```
bipush 7
anewarray <Class "java.lang.Thread">
```

The `anewarray` instruction can also be used to create the outermost dimension of a multidimensional array. For example, the array declaration `new int[6][]` generates the following bytecode instructions:

```
bipush 6
anewarray <Class "[I">
```

multianewarray

Meaning: Allocate new multidimensional array.

Description: A new multidimensional array of a specific array type is allocated. The number of dimensions in the array is determined by `sizeN`. The value of `sizeN` represents the number of elements in the new array and must be an integer. `byte1` and `byte2` are used to construct an index in the constant pool of the current class. The item at that index is resolved and the resulting entry must be an array class of one or more dimensions.

Stack	
Before	**After**
size1	result
size2	.
...	.
sizeN	.
.	
.	
.	

> **Note:** A `NegativeArraySizeException` is thrown if `sizeN` is less than 0. An `OutOfMemoryError` is thrown if there is not enough memory to allocate the array.

arraylength

Meaning: Get length of array.

Description: The length of the array is determined and replaces aref on the top of the stack. The aref must be a reference to an array object.

Stack	
Before	**After**
aref	length
.	.
.	.
.	.

Note: A NullPointerException is thrown if the aref is null.

iaload

Meaning: Load integer from array.

Description: The integer value at the array index is retrieved and pushed onto the top of the stack. The aref must be a reference to an array of integers; likewise, the index into the array must be an integer.

Stack	
Before	**After**
index	value
aref	.
.	.
.	.
.	

Note: A NullPointerException is thrown if aref is null. An ArrayIndexOutOfBoundsException is thrown if the array index is not within the bounds of the array.

laload

Meaning: Load long integer from array.

Description: The long integer value at the array index is retrieved and pushed onto the top of the stack. The aref must be a reference to an array of long integers; likewise, the index into the array must be an integer.

Stack	
Before	**After**
index	value-word2
aref	value-word1
.	.
.	.
.	.

faload

Meaning: Load single float from array.

Description: The single-precision floating-point number at the array `index` is retrieved and pushed onto the top of the stack. The `aref` must be a reference to an array of single-precision floating-point numbers, and the index into the array must be an integer.

Stack	
Before	**After**
index	value
aref	.
.	.
.	.
.	

daload

Meaning: Load double float from array.

Description: The double-precision floating-point number at the array `index` is retrieved and pushed onto the top of the stack. The `aref` must be a reference to an array of double-precision floating-point numbers, and the index into the array must be an integer.

Stack	
Before	**After**
index	value-word2
aref	value-word1
.	.
.	.
.	.

aaload

Meaning: Load object reference from array.

Description: The object reference at the array `index` is retrieved and pushed onto the top of the stack. The `aref` must be a reference to an array of object references, and the index into the array must be an integer.

Stack	
Before	**After**
index	value
aref	.
.	.
.	.
.	

baload

Meaning: Load signed byte from array.

Description: The signed byte value at the array `index` is retrieved, expanded to an integer, and pushed onto the top of the stack. The `aref` must be a reference to an array of signed byte values, and the index into the array must be an integer.

Stack	
Before	**After**
index	value
aref	.
.	.
.	.
.	

caload

Meaning: Load character from array.

Description: The character value at the array index is retrieved, expanded to an integer, and pushed onto the top of the stack. The aref must be a reference to an array of character values, and the index into the array must be an integer.

Stack	
Before	**After**
index	value
aref	.
.	.
.	.
.	

saload

Meaning: Load short integer from array.

Description: The short integer value at the array index is retrieved, expanded to an integer, and pushed onto the top of the stack. The aref must be a reference to an array of short integer values and the index into the array must be an integer.

Stack	
Before	**After**
index	value
aref	.
.	.
.	.
.	

iastore

Meaning: Store into integer array.

Description: An integer value is popped off the stack and stored in the array at the index. The aref must be a reference to an array of integer values, and the index into the array must be an integer as well.

Stack	
Before	**After**
value	.
index	.
aref	.
.	
.	
.	

lastore

Meaning: Store into long integer array.

Description: A long integer value is popped off the stack and stored in the array at the index. The arrayref must be a reference to an array of long integer values, and the index into the array must be an integer.

Stack	
Before	**After**
value-word2	.
value-word1	.
index	.
arrayref	
.	
.	
.	

fastore

Meaning: Store into single float array.

Description: A single-precision floating-point number is popped off the stack and stored in the array at the index. The arrayref must be a reference to an array of single-precision floating-point numbers, and the index into the array must be an integer.

Stack	
Before	**After**
value	.
index	.
arrayref	.
.	
.	
.	

dastore

Meaning: Store into double float array.

Description: A double-precision floating-point number is popped off the stack and stored in the array at the index. The arrayref must be a reference to an array of double-precision floating-point numbers, and the index into the array must be an integer.

Stack	
Before	**After**
value-word2	.
value-word1	.
index	.
arrayref	
.	
.	
.	

aastore

Meaning: Store into object reference array.

Description: An object reference is popped off the stack and stored in the array at the index. The arrayref must be a reference to an array of objects, and the index into the array must be an integer.

Stack	
Before	**After**
value	.
index	.
arrayref	.
.	
.	
.	

bastore

Meaning: Store into signed byte array.

Description: An integer is popped off the stack, converted to a signed byte, and stored in the array at the index. The arrayref must be a reference to an array of signed bytes, and the index into the array must be an integer. If the integer value is too large to be a signed byte, it is truncated.

Stack	
Before	**After**
value	.
index	.
arrayref	.
.	
.	
.	

castore

Meaning: Store into character array.

Description: An integer is popped off the stack, converted to a character, and stored in the array at the `index`. The `arrayref` must be a reference to an array of characters and the index into the array must be an integer. If the integer value is too large to be a character, it is truncated.

Stack	
Before	**After**
value	.
index	.
arrayref	.
.	
.	
.	

sastore

Meaning: Store into short array.

Description: An integer is popped off the stack, converted to a short integer, and stored in the array at the `index`. The `aref` must be a reference to an array of short integers, and the index into the array must be an integer. If the integer value is too large to be a short integer, it is truncated.

Stack	
Before	**After**
value	.
index	.
aref	.
.	
.	
.	

Note: Now that you are familiar with bytecode instructions, I will only provide descriptions as necessary.

Handling the Stack

nop

Meaning: Do nothing.

Stack	
Before	**After**
.	.
.	.
.	.

pop

Meaning: Pop the top word from the stack.

Stack	
Before	**After**
any	.
.	.
.	.
.	

pop2

Meaning: Pop the top two words from the stack.

Stack	
Before	**After**
any1	.
any2	.
.	.
.	.
.	

dup

Meaning: Duplicate the top word on the stack.

Stack	
Before	**After**
any	any
	any
.	.
.	.
.	.

dup2

Meaning: Duplicate the top two words on the stack.

Stack	
Before	**After**
any1	any1
any2	any2
.	any1
.	any2
.	.
	.
	.

dup_x1

Meaning: Duplicate the top word on the stack and insert a copy two words down in the stack.

Stack	
Before	**After**
any1	any1
any2	any2
.	any1
.	.
.	.
	.

dup2_x1

Meaning: Duplicate the top two words on the stack and insert the copies two words down in the stack.

Stack	
Before	**After**
any1	any1
any2	any2
any3	any3
.	any1
.	any2
.	.
	.
	.

dup_x2

Meaning: Duplicate the top word on the stack and insert the copy three words down in the stack.

Stack	
Before	**After**
any1	any1
any2	any2
any3	any3
.	any1
.	.
.	.
	.

dup2_x2

Meaning: Duplicate the top two words on the stack and insert the copies three words down in the stack.

Stack	
Before	**After**
any1	any1
any2	any2
any3	any3
any4	any4
.	any1
.	any2
.	.
	.
	.

swap

Meaning: Swap the top two elements on the stack.

Stack	
Before	**After**
any1	any2
any2	any1
.	.
.	.
.	.

Performing Arithmetic

Bytecode arithmetic is performed at a very basic level. In general, values are popped off the stack, an arithmetic function is performed, and the result of the operation is placed back on the stack, which effectively replaces the original values. To perform the bytecode arithmetic correctly, both values must be of the same type.

Addition

In bytecode addition, two values are popped off the stack and added; then the sum is placed back on the stack.

iadd

Meaning: Integer add.

Stack	
Before	**After**
v2	result
v1	.
.	.
.	.
.	

ladd

Meaning: Long integer add.

Stack	
Before	**After**
v2-word2	result-word2
v2-word1	result-word1
v1-word2	.
v1-word1	.
.	.
.	
.	

fadd

Meaning: Single-precision floating-point add.

Stack	
Before	**After**
v2	result
v1	.
	.
.	.
.	
.	

dadd

Meaning: Double-precision floating-point add.

Stack	
Before	**After**
v2-word2	result-word2
v2-word1	result-word1
v1-word2	.
v1-word1	.
.	.
.	
.	

Subtraction

In bytecode subtraction, two values are popped off the stack, the second value is subtracted from the first, and the result is placed back on the stack.

isub

Meaning: Integer subtract.

Stack	
Before	**After**
v2	result
v1	.
.	.
.	.
.	

lsub

Meaning: Long integer subtract.

Stack	
Before	**After**
v2-word2	result-word2
v2-word1	result-word1
v1-word2	.
v1-word1	.
.	.
.	
.	

fsub

Meaning: Single-precision floating-point subtract.

Stack	
Before	**After**
v2	result
v1	.
.	.
.	.
.	

dsub

Meaning: Double-precision floating-point subtract.

Stack	
Before	**After**
v2-word2	result-word2
v2-word1	result-word1
v1-word2	.
v1-word1	.
.	.
.	
.	

Multiplication

In bytecode multiplication, the values are popped off the stack and multiplied; then the product is placed back on the stack.

imul

Meaning: Integer multiply.

Stack	
Before	**After**
v2	result
v1	.
.	.
.	.
.	

lmul

Meaning: Long integer multiply.

Stack	
Before	**After**
v2-word2	result-word2
v2-word1	result-word1
v1-word2	.
v1-word1	.
.	.
.	
.	

fmul

Meaning: Single-precision floating-point multiply.

Stack	
Before	**After**
v2	result
v1	.
.	.
.	.
.	

dmul

Meaning: Double-precision floating-point multiply.

Stack	
Before	**After**
v2-word2	result-word2
v2-word1	result-word1
v1-word2	.
v1-word1	.
.	.
.	
.	

Division

In bytecode division, two values are popped off the stack, the first value is divided by the second value, and the quotient is placed back on the stack. The result is truncated to the nearest integer.

> **Note:** For integers, shorts, and long integers, an attempt to divide by zero results in an `ArithmeticException`. For floating-point numbers, an attempt to divide by zero results in the quotient being not a number. If you remember NAN from calculus, you'll know that it's immeasurable and will distort your results. The Virtual Machine can check for NAN values using bytecodes that perform comparisons.

`idiv`

Meaning: Integer divide.

Stack	
Before	**After**
v2	result
v1	.
.	.
.	.
.	

`ldiv`

Meaning: Long integer divide.

Stack	
Before	**After**
v2-word2	result-word2
v2-word1	result-word1
v1-word2	.
v1-word1	.
.	.
.	
.	

`fdiv`

Meaning: Single-precision floating-point divide.

Stack	
Before	**After**
v2	result
v1	.
.	.
.	.
.	

ddiv

Meaning: Double-precision floating-point divide.

Stack	
Before	**After**
v2-word2	result-word2
v2-word1	result-word1
v1-word2	.
v1-word1	.
.	.
.	
.	

Remainders

To get a remainder for division operations on integers and long integers, two values are popped off the stack, the first value is divided by the second value, and the remainder is placed back on the stack. The result is always truncated to the nearest integer. Therefore, to get a quotient and a remainder, two division operations are done by the compiler.

> **Note:** For integers, shorts, and long integers, an attempt to divide by zero results in an `ArithmeticException`.

irem

Meaning: Integer remainder.

Stack	
Before	**After**
v2	result
v1	.
.	.
.	.
.	

lrem

Meaning: Long integer remainder.

To get a remainder for division operations on floating-point numbers, two values are popped off the stack. The first value is divided by the second value and then multiplied by the second value. The product is subtracted from the first value, and the result is placed back on the stack. The result always rounds to the nearest integer, with a tie going to the even number.

Stack	
Before	**After**
v2-word2	result-word2
v2-word1	result-word1
v1-word2	.
v1-word1	.
.	.
.	
.	

Note: For floating-point numbers, an attempt to divide by zero results in the quotient being not a number.

frem

Meaning: Single-precision floating-point remainder.

Stack	
Before	**After**
v2	result
v1	.
.	.
.	.
.	

drem

Meaning: Double-precision floating-point remainder.

Stack	
Before	**After**
v2-word2	result-word2
v2-word1	result-word1
v1-word2	.
v1-word1	.
.	.
.	
.	

Negation

In bytecode negation, a value is popped off the stack and negated, and the result is placed back on the stack.

ineg

Meaning: Integer negate.

Stack	
Before	**After**
value	result
.	.
.	.
.	.

lneg

Meaning: Long integer negate.

Stack	
Before	**After**
value-word2	result-word2
value-word1	result-word1
.	.
.	.
.	.

fneg

Meaning: Single-precision floating-point negate.

Stack	
Before	**After**
value	result
.	.
.	.
.	.

dneg

Meaning: Double-precision floating-point negate.

Stack	
Before	**After**
value-word2	result-word2
value-word1	result-word1
.	.
.	.
.	.

Logical Instructions

Logical instructions include operations to shift values and perform logical AND, logical OR, or logical XOR. To perform logical functions, both values must be of the same type.

Shifting Values

When values are left-shifted, the sign of the value is not affected. However, when values are right-shifted, the sign of the value can be affected. For this reason, values are right-shifted in one of two ways: with the sign extension (called *arithmetic shifting*) or without the sign extension (called *logical* or *unsigned shifting*).

For right arithmetic shifting, the first value is generally shifted by the amount indicated by the low 6 bits of the second value. For right logical shifting, the first value is generally shifted by the amount indicated by the low 5 bits of the second value.

ishl

Meaning: Integer shift left.

Stack	
Before	**After**
v2	result
v1	.
.	.
.	.
.	

ishr

Meaning: Integer arithmetic shift right.

Stack	
Before	**After**
v2	result
v1	.
.	.
.	.
.	

iushr

Meaning: Integer logical shift right.

Stack	
Before	**After**
v2	result
v1	.
.	.
.	.
.	

lshl

Meaning: Long integer shift left.

Stack	
Before	**After**
v2	result-word2
v1-word2	result-word1
v1-word1	.
.	.
.	.
.	

lshr

Meaning: Long integer arithmetic shift right.

Stack	
Before	**After**
v2	result-word2
v1-word2	result-word1
v1-word1	.
.	.
.	.
.	

lushr

Meaning: Long integer logical shift right.

Stack	
Before	**After**
v2-word2	result-word2
v2-word1	result-word1
v1-word2	.
v1-word1	.
.	.
.	
.	

Logical AND

For logical AND, two values are popped off the stack and replaced on the stack by their bitwise logical AND. A logical AND is also called the *conjunction* of the values.

iand

Meaning: Integer boolean AND.

Stack	
Before	**After**
v2	result
v1	.
.	.
.	.
.	

land

Meaning: Long integer boolean AND.

Stack	
Before	**After**
v2-word2	result-word2
v2-word1	result-word1
v1-word2	.
v1-word1	.
.	.
.	
.	

Logical OR

For logical OR, two values are popped off the stack and replaced on the stack by their bitwise logical OR. A logical OR is also called the *disconjunction* of the values.

ior

Meaning: Integer boolean OR.

Stack	
Before	**After**
v2	result
v1	.
.	.
.	.
.	

lor

Meaning: Long integer boolean OR.

Stack	
Before	**After**
v2-word2	result-word2
v2-word1	result-word1
v1-word2	.
v1-word1	.
.	.
.	
.	

Logical XOR

For logical XOR, two values are popped off the stack and replaced on the stack by their bitwise logical XOR. A logical XOR is also called an *exclusive disconjunction* of the values.

ixor

Meaning: Integer boolean XOR.

Stack	
Before	**After**
v2	result
v1	.
.	.
.	.
.	

lxor

Meaning: Long integer boolean XOR.

Stack	
Before	**After**
v2-word2	result-word2
v2-word1	result-word1
v1-word2	.
v1-word1	.
.	.
.	
.	

Handling Conversions

Conversions in the Java Virtual Machine are handled by a specific set of bytecode instructions. As you know, Java allows you to convert from one type of value to another either implicitly or explicitly. When a conversion occurs, such as an integer to single-precision floating-point, one of these bytecodes is used.

Note: If the conversion is to a type of smaller bit width, truncation may occur. There is no notification when truncation occurs.

i2l

Meaning: Integer-to-long integer conversion.

Stack	
Before	**After**
value	result-word2
.	result-word1
.	.
.	.
	.

i2f

Meaning: Integer to single float.

Stack	
Before	**After**
value	result
.	.
.	.
.	.

i2d

Meaning: Integer to double float.

Stack	
Before	**After**
value	result-word2
.	result-word1
.	.
.	.
	.

l2i

Meaning: Long integer to integer.

Stack	
Before	**After**
value-word2	result
value-word1	.
.	.
.	.
.	

l2f

Meaning: Long integer to single float.

Stack	
Before	**After**
value-word2	result
value-word1	.
.	.
.	.
.	

l2d

Meaning: Long integer to double float.

Stack	
Before	**After**
value-word2	result-word2
value-word1	result-word1
.	.
.	.
.	.

f2i

Meaning: Single float to integer.

Stack	
Before	**After**
value	result
.	.
.	.
.	.

f2l

Meaning: Single float to long integer.

Stack	
Before	**After**
value	result-word2
.	result-word1
.	.
.	.
	.

f2d

Meaning: Single float to double float.

Stack	
Before	**After**
value	result-word2
.	result-word1
.	.
.	.
	.

d2i

Meaning: Double float to integer.

Stack	
Before	**After**
value-word2	result
value-word1	.
.	.
.	.
.	

d2l

Meaning: Double float to long integer.

Stack	
Before	**After**
value-word2	result-word2
value-word1	result-word1
.	.
.	.
.	.

d2f

Meaning: Double float to single float.

Stack	
Before	**After**
value-word2	result
value-word1	.
.	.
.	.
.	

int2byte

Meaning: Integer to signed byte.

Stack	
Before	**After**
value	result
.	.
.	.
.	.

int2char

Meaning: Integer to char.

Stack	
Before	**After**
value	result
.	.
.	.
.	.

int2short

Meaning: Integer to short.

Stack	
Before	**After**
value	result
.	.
.	.
.	.

Control Transfer Instructions

Instructions that transfer control are a big part of any language structure. In the Java bytecode instruction set, control transfer is handled by instructions that perform branching, comparisons, and movement to and from subroutines.

Unconditional Branching

One way to transfer control is with *unconditional branching*. The Virtual Machine handles this type of branching with the bytecodes discussed in this section.

goto

Meaning: Branch.

Description: Execution proceeds at the signed 16-bit offset from the address of this instruction. The offset is constructed from byte1 and byte2.

Stack	
Before	**After**
.	.
.	.
.	.

goto_w

Meaning: Branch always for wide index.

Description: Execution proceeds at the signed 32-bit offset from the address of this instruction. The offset is constructed from byte1, byte2, byte3, and byte4.

Stack	
Before	**After**
.	.
.	.
.	.

Handling Subroutines and Breakpoints

Instructions that jump to a subroutine push the return address onto the stack. This address is retrieved from a local variable.

jsr

Meaning: Jump subroutine.

Description: Execution proceeds at the signed 16-bit offset from the address of this instruction. The offset is constructed from byte1 and byte2. The address of the instruction immediately following the current instruction is pushed onto the stack to provide a return address from the subroutine.

Stack	
Before	**After**
.	return-address
.	.
.	.
	.

jsr_w

Meaning: Jump subroutine for wide index.

Description: Execution proceeds at the signed 32-bit offset from the address of this instruction. The offset is constructed from byte1, byte2, byte3, and byte4. The address of the instruction immediately following the current instruction is pushed onto the stack to provide a return address from the subroutine.

Stack	
Before	**After**
.	return-address
.	.
.	.
	.

ret

Meaning: Return from subroutine.

Description: Local variable in the current Java frame must contain a return address. The contents of the local variable are written into the program counter.

Stack	
Before	**After**
.	.
.	.
.	.

ret_w

Meaning: Return from subroutine for wide index.

Description: Local variable in the current Java frame must contain a return address. The contents of the local variable are written into the program counter.

Stack	
Before	**After**
.	.
.	.
.	.

breakpoint

Meaning: Breakpoint.

Description: Stop and pass control to breakpoint handler.

Stack	
Before	**After**
.	.
.	.
.	.

Conditional Branching

Branching instructions check for a specific value. If the value is as expected, execution proceeds at an offset from the address of the current instruction. Otherwise, execution proceeds to the next instruction.

ifeq

Meaning: Branch if equal.

Stack	
Before	**After**
value	.
.	.
.	.
.	

ifnull

Meaning: Branch if null.

Stack	
Before	**After**
value	.
.	.
.	.
.	

iflt

Meaning: Branch if less than.

Stack	
Before	**After**
value	.
.	.
.	.
.	

ifle

Meaning: Branch if less than or equal.

Stack	
Before	**After**
value	.
.	.
.	.
.	

ifne

Meaning: Branch if not equal.

Stack	
Before	**After**
value	.
.	.
.	.
.	

ifnonnull

Meaning: Branch if not null.

Stack	
Before	**After**
value	.
.	.
.	.
.	

ifgt

Meaning: Branch if greater than.

Stack	
Before	**After**
value	.
.	.
.	.
.	

ifge

Meaning: Branch if greater than or equal.

Stack	
Before	**After**
value	.
.	.
.	.
.	

`if_icmpeq`

Meaning: Branch if integers v1 and v2 are equal.

Stack	
Before	**After**
v2	.
v1	.
.	.
.	
.	

`if_icmpne`

Meaning: Branch if integers v1 and v2 are not equal.

Stack	
Before	**After**
v2	.
v1	.
.	.
.	
.	

`if_icmplt`

Meaning: Branch if integer v1 is less than integer v2.

Stack	
Before	**After**
v2	.
v1	.
.	.
.	
.	

`if_icmpgt`

Meaning: Branch if integer v1 is greater than integer v2.

Stack	
Before	**After**
v2	.
v1	.
.	.
.	
.	

if_icmple

Meaning: Branch if integer v1 less than or equal to integer v2.

Stack	
Before	**After**
v2	.
v1	.
.	.
.	
.	

if_icmpge

Meaning: Branch if integer v1 greater than or equal to integer v2.

Stack	
Before	**After**
v2	.
v1	.
.	.
.	
.	

if_acmpeq

Meaning: Branch if object references equal.

Stack	
Before	**After**
v2	.
v1	.
.	.
.	
.	

if_acmpne

Meaning: Branch if object references not equal.

Stack	
Before	**After**
v2	.
v1	.
.	.
.	
.	

Comparisons

Comparison instructions compare two values. If v1 is less than v2, the value -1 is pushed onto the stack. If the values are equal, the value 0 is pushed onto the stack. If v1 is greater than v2, the value +1 is pushed onto the stack.

For floating-point numbers, if either v1 or v2 is not a number, the value -1 is pushed onto the stack for the first pair of bytecodes and the value +1 is pushed onto the stack for the second pair of bytecodes. The process of checking for the infamous not-a-number problem is handled by performing two comparisons. The first comparison checks for the value -1, and the second checks for the value +1.

lcmp

Meaning: Long integer compare.

Stack	
Before	**After**
v2-word1	result
v2-word1	.
v1-word2	.
v1-word1	.
.	
.	
.	

fcmpl

Meaning: Single-precision floating-point number compare; return -1 if v1 or v2 is not a number.

Stack	
Before	**After**
v2	result
v1	.
.	.
.	.
.	

dcmpl

Meaning: Double-precision floating-point number compare; return -1 if v1 or v2 is not a number.

Stack	
Before	**After**
v2-word2	result
v2-word1	.
v1-word2	.
v1-word1	.
.	
.	
.	

fcmpg

Meaning: Single-precision floating-point number compare; return +1 if v1 or v2 is not a number.

Stack	
Before	**After**
v2	result
v1	.
.	.
.	.
.	

dcmpg

Meaning: Double-precision floating-point number compare; return +1 if v1 or v2 is not a number.

Stack	
Before	**After**
v2-word2	result
v2-word1	.
v1-word2	.
v1-word1	.
.	
.	
.	

Returning from Methods

Returns are handled in one of two ways by bytecode instructions: return (void) or return (normal). *Void returns* are used to back out cleanly from the previous method. Thus, all values on the operand stack are discarded and the interpreter then returns control to its caller. *Normal returns* are used to proceed normally with execution and push a value associated with the previous method onto the stack. After the return value is pushed onto the stack, any other values on the operand stack are discarded and the interpreter then returns control to its caller.

Note: Java's operand stack is not contiguous like the operand stacks you may be familiar with from programming in other languages. Because each method has its own section of the operand stack, when the operand stack for the method is discarded, only the section related to the method is cleared out.

return

Meaning: Return (void) from method.

Stack	
Before	**After**
.	
.	
.	

ireturn

Meaning: Return integer from function.

Stack	
Before	**After**
value	
.	
.	
.	

lreturn

Meaning: Return long integer from function.

Stack	
Before	**After**
value-word2	
value-word1	
.	
.	
.	

freturn

Meaning: Return single float from function.

Stack	
Before	**After**
value	
.	
.	
.	

dreturn

Meaning: Return double float from function.

Stack	
Before	**After**
value-word2	
value-word1	
.	
.	
.	

areturn

Meaning: Return object reference from function.

Stack	
Before	**After**
value	
.	
.	
.	

Table Jumping

In Java, complex addressing is handled using *jump tables*. These jump tables are accessed with index switches or key lookups.

tableswitch

Meaning: Access jump table by index and jump.

Stack	
Before	**After**
index	.
.	.
.	.
.	

Description: Immediately after the `tableswitch` instruction, padding consisting of 0–3 zeros is inserted so that the next byte begins at an address that is a multiple of four. A series of offsets follows the padding. These offsets are signed 4-byte quantities and consist of a default offset, a low offset, and a high offset, followed by additional `high` - `low` + 1 offsets. These additional offsets are treated as a 0–based jump table.

The `index` the offsets point to must be an integer. If the `index` is less than the low offset or greater than the high offset, the default offset is added to the address of the current instruction. Otherwise, the low offset is subtracted from the index, and the element at the position `index` - `low offset` in the jump table is extracted and added to the address of the current instruction.

lookupswitch

Meaning: Access jump table by key match and jump.

Stack	
Before	**After**
key	.
.	.
.	.
.	

Description: Immediately after the `lookupswitch` instruction, padding consisting of 0–3 zeros is inserted so that the next byte begins at an address that is a multiple of four. A series of pairs of offsets follows the padding. These offsets are signed 4-byte quantities. The first item in the pair is the default offset, and the second item in the pair gives the number of pairs that follow. The additional pairs consist of a match and an offset.

The integer `key` on the stack is then compared against each of the matches. If the `key` is equal to one of the matches, the offset is added to the address of the current instruction. If the `key` does not match any of the matches, the default offset is added to the address of the current instruction.

Manipulating Object Fields

Java manipulates two types of fields: dynamic and static. Whereas dynamic fields change, static fields do not. These fields are manipulated using simple `get` and `put` mechanisms.

Putting Fields

The `put` mechanism uses `byte1` and `byte2` to construct an index into the constant pool of the current class. The item at the index is a field reference to a class name and a field name, which is resolved to a field block pointer that has both the field width and the field offset. The field at the offset from the start of the object referenced is set to the value on the top of the stack.

> **Note:** A `NullPointerException` is generated if the referenced object is null. For static fields, an `IncompatibleClassChangeError` is thrown if the specified field is a static field.

putfield

Meaning: Set 32-bit field in object.

Stack	
Before	**After**
value	.
oref	.
.	.
.	
.	

putfield

Meaning: Set 64-bit field in object.

Stack	
Before	**After**
value-word2	.
value-word1	.
oref	.
.	
.	
.	

putstatic

Meaning: Set 32-bit static field in class.

Stack	
Before	**After**
value	.
.	.
.	.
.	

putstatic

Meaning: Set 64-bit static field in class.

Stack	
Before	**After**
value-word2	.
value-word1	.
.	.
.	
.	

Getting Fields

The `get` mechanism uses `byte1` and `byte2` to construct an index into the constant pool of the current class. The item at the index is a field reference to a class name and a field name, which is resolved to a field block pointer that has both the field width and the field offset. The value at the offset replaces the object reference on the top of the stack.

> **Note:** A `NullPointerException` is generated if the referenced object is null. For static fields, an `IncompatibleClassChangeError` is thrown if the specified field is a static field.

getfield

Meaning: Fetch 32-bit field from object.

Stack	
Before	**After**
oref	value
.	.
.	.
.	.

getfield

Meaning: Fetch 64-bit field from object.

Stack	
Before	**After**
oref	value-word2
.	value-word1
.	.
.	.
	.

getstatic

Meaning: Get 32-bit static field from class.

Stack	
Before	**After**
.	value
.	.
.	.
	.

getstatic

Meaning: Get 64-bit static field from class.

Stack	
Before	**After**
.	value-word2
.	value-word1
.	.
	.
	.

Invoking Methods

Method invocation is a complex process. To invoke a method, the operand stack must contain a reference to an object and some number of arguments. The object reference is used as a pointer to the object's method table, which contains the method signature. The method signature is guaranteed to exactly match one of the method signatures in the table. The arguments byte1 and byte2 are used to construct an index into the constant pool of the current class, which contains the complete method signature.

The result of the lookup is an index into the method table of the named class. This index is used with the referenced object's dynamic type to look in the method table of that type, where a pointer to the method block for the matched method is found. The method block indicates the type of method, such as native or synchronized, and the number of arguments expected on the operand stack.

The object reference and arguments are popped off the method's operand stack and become the initial values of the local variables of the new method. Execution continues with the first instruction of the new method.

> **Note:** The monitor associated with the referenced object is entered if the method is marked as synchronized. A `NullPointerException` is thrown if the object reference on the operand stack is null. A `StackOverflowError` is thrown if a stack overflow is detected during the method invocation.

invokevirtual

Meaning: Invoke method based on runtime type.

Stack	
Before	**After**
[[argN]	.
[...]	.
[arg2]	.
[arg1]]	
oref	
.	
.	
.	

invokenonvirtual

Meaning: Invoke method based on compile-time type.

Stack	
Before	**After**
[[argN]	.
[...]	.
[arg2]	.
[arg1]]	
oref	
.	
.	
.	

invokestatic

Meaning: Invoke a class (static) method.

Stack	
Before	**After**
[[argN]	.
[...]	.
[arg2]	.
[arg1]]	
.	
.	
.	

invokeinterface

Meaning: Invoke interface method.

Stack	
Before	**After**
[[argN]	.
[...]	.
[arg2]	.
[arg1]]	
oref	
.	
.	
.	

Note: Unlike `invokevirtual` and `invokenonvirtual`, the method block does not indicate the number of available arguments. This number is taken from the bytecode.

Exception Handling

Because exception handling is a major feature of the Java programming language, you might be surprised to learn that exceptions are handled with a single bytecode instruction. When exceptions occur, the object thrown must be a reference to an object of the subclass `Throwable`, and the current Java stackframe is searched for the most recent `catch` clause that catches exceptions of this class or a superclass of this class. When a matching `catch` clause is found, the program counter is reset to the address indicated by the `catch` clause and execution continues from there. When no appropriate `catch` clause is found, that frame is popped and the object is rethrown. If a `catch` clause is then found, the clause will contain the location of the code for the exception, the program counter is reset to that location, and execution continues. Otherwise, the frame is popped and the object is rethrown.

Note: A `NullPointerException` is thrown instead if the referenced object is null.

athrow

Meaning: Throw exception or error.

Stack	
Before	**After**
oref	?
.	
.	
.	

Miscellaneous Object Operations

Several miscellaneous object operations are grouped together here.

new

Meaning: Create new object.

Description: byte1 and byte2 are used to construct an index into the constant pool of the current class, which must be a class name that can be resolved to a class pointer. A new instance of that class is then created, and a reference to the object is pushed on the stack.

Stack	
Before	**After**
.	oref
.	.
.	.
	.

checkcast

Meaning: Make sure object is of given type.

Description: Determines whether the referenced object can be cast to be a reference to an object of another class. A null object reference can be cast to any class. Otherwise, the referenced object must be an instance of the expected class or one of its superclasses. byte1 and byte2 are used to construct an index into the constant pool of the current class, which is presumed to be a class name that can be resolved to a class pointer.

Stack	
Before	**After**
oref	oref
.	.
.	.
.	.

Note: A ClassCastException is thrown if the referenced object cannot be cast to the expected class.

instanceof

Meaning: Determine if an object is of given type and return result.

Description: Determines whether the referenced object can be cast to be a reference to an object of the expected class. This instruction will overwrite the object reference with 1 if the object is an instance of the expected class or one of its superclasses. Otherwise, the object reference is overwritten by 0.

Stack	
Before	**After**
oref	result
.	.
.	.
.	.

Monitors

Monitors are used to obtain exclusive access to a referenced object using a lock. Because a single thread can have multiple locks on a single object, careful checks are performed before granting an exclusive lock. Likewise, checks are done before releasing a lock. The locking and unlocking process is handled with monitors.

To *lock* an object, the monitor checks the object's status. When the object is not locked by another thread, an *exclusive lock* is obtained. When another thread already has the object locked, the current thread waits until the object is unlocked.

When the lock on the object is released, the monitor checks to see if this is the last lock that this thread has on the object. If it is, then other threads waiting for the object are allowed to gain access to and possibly lock the object.

> **Note:** A `NullPointerException` is thrown instead if the referenced object is null.

monitorenter

Meaning: Enter monitored region of code.

Stack	
Before	**After**
oref	.
.	.
.	.
.	

monitorexit

Meaning: Exit monitored region of code.

Stack	
Before	**After**
oref	.
.	.
.	.
.	

Breaking Down the Class File Format

Source files are organized by object, and so are compiled source files in bytecode. When you compile source code, the Java compiler places each class in its own file. This class file represents a single object that is in turn made up of smaller objects.

By breaking down the objects used in the compiled class files, you can gain a better understanding of how the Java Virtual Machine works. For this reason, this section examines the class file format and formats for related objects, including methods, method signatures, fields, and attributes.

To ensure that Java programs are portable to any computer platform, the compiled files with the .class extension must follow a specific format. This format is known as the .class *file format*. Because Java interfaces are essentially abstract classes, the .class file format is also used for Java classes and Java interfaces.

At its most basic level, the .class file format is represented by streams of 8-bit bytes, which means that all 16-bit and 32-bit values are constructed by reading in two or four 8-bit bytes, respectively. As with assembly language, the byte order of 16-bit and 32-bit values is extremely important. Therefore, in order to accurately reconstruct a 16-bit or 32-bit value, bytes must be stored either in low-byte order or high-byte order.

Low-byte order places the entire 16-bit or 32-bit value in one contiguous stream. Although it seems logical to store a byte stream in low-byte order, not all computers store bytes in this manner. In fact, many computers follow the high-byte order, where the highest 8 or 16 bits are stored first.

In assembly language it is perfectly acceptable to read assembly code in high-byte order on one platform and low-byte order on another platform. However, because Java can be used across multiple platforms with disparate operating systems and architecture, it was not enough to simply use the byte order specific to the local machine. For this reason, all byte streams are stored in high-byte order.

> **Note:** Other terms for high-byte order are *network order* and *big-endian order*. If you want to read or write files in this format, you can use the java.io.DataInput and java.io.DataOutput interfaces.

Listing 24.2 shows the top-level format of class files. C programmers may recognize this format as being similar to the structures used in C. However, unlike a C struct, each field in the structure is represented without padding or alignment, and arrays may contain elements of various sizes. The types u1, u2, and u4 represent an unsigned 1-, 2-, or 4-byte value, respectively.

Listing 24.2. The .class file structure format.

```
ClassFile {
 u4 magic;
 u2 minor_version;
 u2 major_version;
 u2 constant_pool_count;
 cp_info constant_pool[constant_pool_count - 1];
 u2 access_flags;
```

continues

Listing 24.2. continued

```
u2 this_class;
u2 super_class;
u2 interfaces_count;
u2 interfaces[interfaces_count];
u2 fields_count;
field_info fields[fields_count];
u2 methods_count;
method_info methods[methods_count];
u2 attributes_count;
attribute_info attributes[attribute_count];
}
```

All fields listed in the .class files follow a specific variable-length format. (See Listing 24.3.) The type u2 represents an unsigned 2-byte value.

Listing 24.3. Field formats.

```
field_info {
u2 access_flags;
u2 name_index;
u2 signature_index;
u2 attributes_count;
attribute_info  attributes[attribute_count];
}
```

All methods listed in the .class files follow a specific variable-length format as well. (See Listing 24.4.) Again, the type u2 represents an unsigned 2-byte value.

Listing 24.4. Method formats.

```
method_info {
u2 access_flags;
u2 name_index;
u2 signature_index;
u2 attributes_count;
attribute_info  attributes[attribute_count];
}
```

The final format for .class files pertains to attributes. All attributes have the format shown in Listing 24.5. The types u1, u2, and u4 represent an unsigned 1-, 2-, or 4-byte value, respectively.

Listing 24.5. Attribute formats.

```
GenericAttribute_info {
u2 attribute_name;
u4 attribute_length;
u1 info[attribute_length];
}
```

Signatures

Each object in the class file has a specific *signature*. Signatures are strings representing a type of method, field, or array.

The signature for a field represents the value of a function's argument or the value of a variable. The following syntax structure generates the series of bytes that form the signature of a field:

```
<field_signature> ::= <field_type>

<field_type> ::= <base_type>¦<object_type>¦<array_type>

<base_type> ::= B¦C¦D¦F¦I¦J¦S¦Z

<object_type> ::= L<fullclassname>;

<array_type> ::= [<optional_size><field_type>

<optional_size> ::= [0-9]*
```

The base type value determines the base type of the field as a B (byte), C (character), D (double), F (float), I (integer), J (long integer), S (short integer), or Z (boolean).

The signature for return type represents the return value from a method. In the following code line, the character V indicates that the method returns no value:

```
<return_signature> ::= <field_type> ¦ V
```

The signature for an argument represents an argument passed to a method and is represented by the following:

```
<argument_signature> ::= <field_type>
```

Finally, the signature for a method represents the arguments the method expects and the value the method returns. Method signatures are represented by

```
<method_signature> ::= (<arguments_signature>) <return_signature>

<arguments_signature>: := <argument_signature>*
```

To put these rules to use, you can build a method signature for an arbitrary method. For example, let's create a method called construct() in the class your.package.constructors. This method takes four arguments, two integers, a boolean, and a two-dimensional array of characters. Then the method signature is

```
(II[[C)Lyour.package.constructors.constructor;
```

Complete method signatures are usually prefixed by the name of the method or the full package name to the class level followed by a forward slash and the name of the method. Therefore, the complete method signature for the construct() method would look like this:

```
your_package_constructors/constructor(II[[C)Lyour.package.
➥constructors.constructor;
```

Summary

The Java Virtual Machine exists only in the memory of your computer. Reproducing a machine within your computer's memory requires seven key objects: a set of registers, a stack, an execution environment, a garbage-collected heap, a constant pool, a method storage area, and a mechanism to tie it all together. This mechanism is the bytecode instruction set.

To examine bytecode, you can use the Java class file disassembler, `javap`. By examining bytecode instructions in detail, you gain valuable insight into the inner workings of the Java Virtual Machine and Java itself. Each bytecode instruction performs a specific function of extremely limited scope, such as pushing an object onto the stack or popping an object off the stack. Combinations of these basic functions represent the complex high-level tasks defined as statements in the Java programming language. As amazing as it seems, sometimes dozens of bytecode instructions are used to carry out the operation specified by a single Java statement. When you use these bytecode instructions with the seven key objects of the virtual machine, Java gains its platform independence and becomes the most powerful and versatile programming language in the world.

VIII

Appendixes

Java API
Table
Reference

Table A.1 shows the objects in the `java.applet` package. The objects in this package are specific to applets.

Table A.1. `java.applet` package API reference.

Interfaces	Classes
AppletContext	Applet
AppletStub	
AudioClip	

Table A.2 shows the objects in the `java.awt` package. The package contains the objects used to create Java's powerful GUI elements such as pop-up windows, scrollbars, menus, and much more.

Table A.2. `java.awt` package API reference.

Interfaces	Classes	Exceptions	Error
LayoutManager	BorderLayout	AWTException	AWTError
MenuContainer	Button		
	Canvas		
	CardLayout		
	Checkbox		
	CheckboxGroup		
	CheckboxMenuItem		
	Choice		
	Color		
	Component		
	Container		
	Dialog		
	Dimension		
	Event		
	FileDialog		
	FlowLayout		
	Font		

Interfaces	Classes	Exceptions	Error
	FontMetrics		
	Frame		
	Graphics		
	GridBagConstraints		
	GridBagLayout		
	GridLayout		
	Image		
	Insets		
	Label		
	List		
	MediaTracker		
	Menu		
	MenuBar		
	MenuComponent		
	MenuItem		
	Panel		
	Point		
	Polygon		
	Rectangle		
	Scrollbar		
	TextArea		
	TextComponent		
	TextField		
	Toolkit		
	Window		

Table A.3 shows the objects in the `java.awt.image` package. This package contains objects that deal with the graphical user interface as a single screen image, which includes the complete window used by your Java program.

Table A.3. `java.awt.image` package API reference.

Interfaces	Classes
ImageConsumer	ColorModel
ImageObserver	CropImageFilter
ImageProducer	DirectColorModel
	FilteredImageSource
	ImageFilter
	IndexColorModel
	MemoryImageSource
	PixelGrabber
	RGBImageFilter

Table A.4 shows the objects in the `java.awt.peer` package. This package provides platform-dependent graphics for the screen image, which is the complete window used by your Java program.

Table A.4. `java.awt.peer` package API reference.

Interfaces
ButtonPeer
CanvasPeer
CheckboxMenuItemPeer
CheckboxPeer
ChoicePeer
ComponentPeer
ContainerPeer
DialogPeer
FileDialogPeer
FramePeer
LabelPeer
ListPeer
MenuBarPeer
MenuComponentPeer
MenuItemPeer
MenuPeer

Interfaces
PanelPeer
ScrollbarPeer
TextAreaPeer
TextComponentPeer
TextFieldPeer
WindowPeer

Table A.5 shows the objects in the `java.io` package. This package contains objects used in handling the input and output between Java and any device on your computer system.

Table A.5. `java.io` package API reference.

Interfaces	Classes	Exceptions
DataInput	BufferedInputStream	EOFException
DataOutput	BufferedOutputStream	FileNotFoundException
FilenameFilter	ByteArrayInputStream	IOException
	ByteArrayOutputStream	InterruptedIOException
	DataInputStream	UTFDataFormatException
	DataOutputStream	
	File	
	FileDescriptor	
	FileInputStream	
	FileOutputStream	
	FilterInputStream	
	FilterOutputStream	
	InputStream	
	LineNumberInputStream	
	OutputStream	
	PipedInputStream	
	PipedOutputStream	
	PrintStream	
	PushbackInputStream	

continues

Table A.5. continued

Interfaces	Classes	Exceptions
	RandomAccessFile	
	SequenceInputStream	
	StreamTokenizer	
	StringBufferInputStream	

Table A.6 shows the objects in the `java.lang` package. This package contains the objects that define the fundamental elements of Java and is imported by default into each class at compile time.

Table A.6. `java.lang` package API reference.

Interfaces	Classes	Exceptions	Error
Cloneable	Boolean	ArithmeticException	AbstractMethodError
Runnable	Character	ArrayIndexOutOfBoundsException	ClassCircularityError
	Class	ArrayStoreException	ClassFormatError
	ClassLoader	ClassCastException	Error
	Compiler	ClassNotFoundException	IllegalAccessError
	Double	CloneNotSupportedException	IncompatibleClassChangeError
	Float	Exception	InstantiationError
	Integer	IllegalAccessException	InternalError
	Long	IllegalArgumentException	LinkageError
	Math	IllegalMonitorStateException	NoClassDefFoundError
	Number	IllegalThreadStateException	NoSuchFieldError
	Object	IndexOutOfBoundsException	NoSuchMethodError
	Process	InstantiationException	OutOfMemoryError
	Runtime	InterruptedException	StackOverflowError
	SecurityManager	NegativeArraySizeException	ThreadDeath
	String	NoSuchMethodException	UnknownError
	StringBuffer	NullPointerException	UnsatisfiedLinkError
	System	NumberFormatException	VerifyError
	Thread	RuntimeException	VirtualMachineError
	ThreadGroup	SecurityException	
	Throwable	StringIndexOutOfBoundsException	

Table A.7 shows the objects in the `java.net` package. This package contains the objects that interact with network protocols.

Table A.7. `java.net` package API reference.

Interfaces	Classes	Exceptions
ContentHandlerFactory	ContentHandler	MalformedURLException
SocketImplFactory	DatagramPacket	ProtocolException
URLStreamHandlerFactory	DatagramSocket	SocketException
	InetAddress	UnknownHostException
	ServerSocket	UnknownServiceException
	Socket	
	SocketImpl	
	URL	
	URLConnection	
	URLEncoder	
	URLStreamHandler	

Table A.8 shows the objects in the `java.util` package. This package contains objects used for system utilities.

Table A.8. `java.util` package API reference.

Interfaces	Classes	Exceptions
Enumeration	BitSet	EmptyStackException
Observer	Date	NoSuchElementException
	Dictionary	
	Hashtable	
	Observable	
	Properties	
	Random	
	Stack	
	StringTokenizer	
	Vector	

Table A.9 shows the objects in the sun.tools.debug package. The objects in this package are used for debugging Java programs with a client application such as the Java debugger.

Table A.9. sun.tools.debug package API reference.

Interfaces	Classes	Exceptions
DebuggerCallback	RemoteArray	NoSessionException
	RemoteBoolean	NoSuchFieldException
	RemoteByte	NoSuchLineNumberException
	RemoteChar	
	RemoteClass	
	RemoteDebugger	
	RemoteDouble	
	RemoteField	
	RemoteFloat	
	RemoteInt	
	RemoteLong	
	RemoteObject	
	RemoteShort	
	RemoteStackFrame	
	RemoteStackVariable	
	RemoteString	
	RemoteThread	
	RemoteThreadGroup	
	RemoteValue	
	StackFrame	

B

Java Terminology

abstract modifier   A modifier used to create *template classes*.

abstract class   A template class that contains such things as variable declarations and methods, but cannot contain code for creating new instances.

applet   Code that requires an external program to provide an interface to the user. Web browsers and the Java Developer's Kit (JDK) applet viewer are examples of interfaces that support applets.

applet viewer   A program that allows you to view an applet directly without a Java-enabled browser. You will find this program in the Java Developer's Kit.

application   Stand-alone program that can be run directly from the command line.

argument   A parameter that is passed to a method when it is called.

array   A single- or multidimensional group of variables.

available() method   A method used to determine if some amount of data is ready to be read without blocking in the input stream. This method is found in the following `java.io` classes: `InputStream`, `FilterInputStream`, `BufferedInputStream`, `ByteArrayInputStream`, and `PushbackInputStream`.

binary operator   An operator that acts on two values and returns one value.

block   A section of code beginning and ending with curly braces `{}`. The statements are grouped so they can be used together to accomplish a certain task or so that they can be executed when a particular condition is met.

boolean   A data type that can be either `true` or `false`.

boolean literal   A literal declared with the keywords `true` or `false`.

catch   Code that realizes an exception has occurred and deals with it appropriately. See also `try`.

char data type   A 16-bit unsigned integer that represents a Unicode value.

character literal   A single character value.

class   Made up of objects that are not all exactly alike but have enough similar characteristics that they can be grouped together.

class library   A set of classes. See also *package*.

class variable   A variable that is available to all instances of a class.

close() method   A method used to close an output stream that an application or applet no longer needs. This method is found in the following `java.io` classes: `OutputStream` and `FilterOutputStream`.

conditional expression   An expression that executes one of several sections of code based on a conditional test.

constructor   A special method used in the initialization of an object.

data type   Defines the kind of data that can be stored in a variable.

declaration statement   A statement that declares a variable or a line of code. Most declaration statements end with a semicolon.

double data type   A double-precision, 64-bit long, floating-point number used as a variable.

exception   Java's method of handling errors.

expression   Performs computations.

final   A modifier that indicates an object is fixed and cannot be changed.

finally   Used to perform any necessary cleanup if an exception occurs. The `finally` statement ensures that a section of code will be run.

float data type   Designates a single-precision, 32-bit long, floating-point number as a variable.

floating-point literal   Represents a number that has a decimal point, such as 3.7.

friendly   A term used to describe the default access control for methods of a particular class in which the class itself, subclasses, and classes in the same package can call the method.

flush() method   A method that is used to force any data buffered for the output stream to be written to the output device. This method is found in the following `java.io` classes: `OutputStream`, `FilterOutputStream`, `BufferedOutputStream`, and `DataOutputStream`.

keyword   A reserved word that can be used only as it is assigned in Java. Here is a complete list of reserved words in Java:

abstract	false	new	throw
boolean	final	null	transient
break	finally	operator	true
byte	float	outer	try
byvalue	for	package	var
case	future	private	void
cast	generic	protected	while
catch	goto	public	
char	if	rest	
class	implements	return	
const	import	short	
continue	inner	static	
default	instance of	super	
do	int	switch	
double	interface	synchronized	
else	long	this	
extends	native	threadsafe	

identifier   A Java reserved word or title given to variables, classes, and methods.

import statement   A statement that is used to include a class to be searched for in a particular package.

inheritance   A methodology whereby the code that was developed for one use can be extended for use elsewhere without having to actually make a copy of the code.

init() method   A method that is only called the first time an applet is loaded into a viewer. It is used to initialize data. The method is in the `java.applet.Applet` class.

input stream   A data stream that is accepted and processed by a process looking for incoming data.

instance   One specific object within the class of objects.

instance variable   A variable particular to an instance of a class.

integer   A whole number, such as 1 and 5280.

integer literal   A literal that can be decimal (base 10), octal (base 8), or hexadecimal (base 16).

interface   Used to define the structure of a set of methods that will be implemented by classes yet to be designed and coded.

literal   Represents data in Java. It is based on character and number representations. The types of literals are *integer, floating-point, boolean, character,* and *string.*

main() method   A method that must be defined in every Java application. When a Java application is invoked, the Java compiler looks for the method named `main` and begins execution there.

mark() method   Used to mark a point in an input stream to which it may be necessary to return at a later time. This method is found in the following `java.io` classes: `InputStream`, `FilterInputStream`, and `BufferedInputStream`.

method   A function that reports back a status.

modifier   Used to alter certain aspects of classes. Modifiers are specified in the declaration of a class before the class name.

native   Methods implemented in a platform-dependent language, such as C or C++.

new   The command in Java that creates a new instance of a reference data type.

null   No value is assigned to a variable.

operator   A symbol used for arithmetic and logical operations.

output stream   A data stream that is generated by a producer process.

package   To group together a variety of classes and/or interfaces that perform similar functions.

primitive data type   A data type that can have only one value at a time and is the simplest built-in form of data within Java.

private   A modifier that specifies only the current class can call this method or variable. When you use this modifier, you are excluding subclasses of the class as well.

private protected   A modifier is a special combination of private and protected access modifiers. This modifier specifies that only the class in which the method or variable is defined can call the method or variable, and does not exclude subclasses of the class, which can access the method.

protected   A modifier that specifies that only classes in the current package in which the method or variable is defined can call the method. This allows access for objects that are part of the same application, but not to other applications.

read() method   The method an application actually uses to read data from a stream. This method is found in the following `java.io` classes: `InputStream`, `FilterInputStream`, `BufferedInputStream`, `DataInputStream`, `ByteArrayInputStream`, and `PushbackInputStream`.

reserved word   A word that can be used only as it is assigned in Java.

separator   Divides code into segments.

single inheritance   The concept that a class can only have one superclass.

skip() method   The method used to bypass part of an input stream. `skip` is used to move quickly through a stream by skipping a fixed number of bytes. This method is found in the following `java.io` classes: `InputStream`, `FilterInputStream`, `BufferedInputStream`, and `ByteArrayInputStream`.

start() method   The method that is called after the `init()` method the first time an applet is loaded into a viewer or if an applet has been suspended and must be restarted. The method is in the `java.applet.Applet` class.

statement   Any line or lines of code ending in a semicolon. Statements may be an expression, a method call, or a declaration.

static modifier   A modifier that is used to specify a method that can be declared only once. No subclasses are allowed to implement a method of the same name.

static variable   A variable that exists in only one location and is globally accessible by all instances of a class. See also *class variable*.

stop() method   A method that is called whenever an applet needs to be stopped or suspended. The method is in the `java.applet.Applet` class.

stream   Allows a Java application to communicate with files, networks, devices, other applications, and even among threads within the same application.

string literal   A sequence of characters enclosed in double quotes, such as `"This is a string literal"`.

subclass   Extends the superclass and creates a new variation of the class. Inherits the characteristics of the preceding class.

super   A reference to the superclass. It is often used as a shortcut or explicit way to reference a member in the superclass of the current class.

superclass   The top-level class of every application.

template classes   Classes that are normally used to provide a superclass for other classes.

this   Allows the current instance of a variable to be explicitly referenced.

thread   Provides Java with the capability to have a single application easily run multiple concurrent code execution.

token   The basic elements of the Java language. At compile time, the `javac` compiler takes the code and pulls out these basic building blocks for further processing.

try   Executes a block of code that may generate (*throw*) an exception. See also `catch`.

unary operator   An operator that manipulates a single value.

void   A special return type in Java. `void` indicates that there is no return type of any kind. This is used for methods that have no need to return anything to the calling program, or that only modify method arguments or global variables.

write() method   The method an application actually uses to write data to a stream. This method is found in the following `java.io` classes: `OutputStream`, `FilterOutputStream`, `BufferedOutputStream`, `DataOutputStream`, and `ByteArrayOutputStream`.

Index

Get Café at a Special Price

Symantec® Café™ contains the latest Java Developer's Kit and many exciting new features and tools:

- Debug your Java applets with Symantec's new integrated Visual Java Debugger
- View the class relationships and their methods with the Hierarchy Editor
- Navigate your classes and edit your class methods with the Class Editor

Go to our Web page and check out the latest version of Café:

`http://www.symantec.com/lit/dev/javaindex.html`

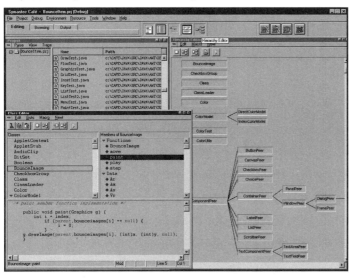

Symantec Café includes a heirarchy editor that displays the relationships of both the Java source classes and your custom classes. You can zoom in on any class and see its data and methods.

State Sales/Use Tax

In the following states, add sales/use tax: CO–3%; GA, LA, NY–4%; VA–4.5%; KS–4.9%; AZ, IA, IN, MA, MD, OH, SC, WI–5%; CT, FL, ME, MI, NC, NJ, PA, TN–6%; CA, IL, TX–6.25%; MN, WA–6.5%; DC–5.75%.

Please add local tax for: AZ, CA, FL, GA, MO, NY, OH, SC, TN, TX, WA, WI.

Order Information:

- Please allow 2–4 weeks for processing your order.
- Please attach the order form with your payment.
- No P.O. boxes and no C.O.D.s accepted.
- Order form good in the U.S. only.
- If you are tax-exempt, please include exemption certificate or letter with tax-exempt number.
- Resellers not eligible.
- Offer not valid with any other promotion.
- One copy per product, per order.
- Special offer expires 12/31/96.

HTML & CGI Unleashed

— *John December & Mark Ginsburg*

Targeted to professional developers who need a detailed guide and have a basic understanding of programming, *HTML & CGI Unleashed* provides a complete, detailed reference to developing Web information systems. Covers the full range of tools—HTML, CGI, Perl C, editing and conversion programs, and more—and how to create commercial-grade Web applications. Perfect for the developer who will be designing, creating, and maintaining a Web presence for a company or large institution. Covers the World Wide Web.

Price: $49.99 USA/$67.99 CDN   User Level: Accomplished - Expert
ISBN: 0-672-30745-6   864 pages

The Internet Unleashed 1996

— *Barron, Ellsworth, Savetz, et al.*

The Internet Unleashed 1996 is designed to help the newcomer get up and running on the Internet and to serve as a reference for the more experienced user. It shows readers how to take advantage of all the Net has to offer for business, education, libraries, and government. CD-ROM contains both starter software and advanced tools. The only book that includes the experience of over 40 of the world's top Internet experts. New edition is updated with expanded coverage of Web publishing, Internet business, Internet multimedia and virtual reality, Internet security, Java, and more.

*Price: $49.99 USA/$67.99 CDN   User Level: New - Casual -
                                                    Accomplished - Expert*

ISBN: 1-57521-041-X   1,456 pages

The World Wide Web Unleashed 1996

— *John December & Neil Randall*

The World Wide Web Unleashed 1996 is designed to be the only book a reader will need to help him get on the World Wide Web and continue to guide him as he becomes more experienced. CD-ROM includes starter software such as Netscape, Mosaic, and advanced tools. Describes how to connect to the World Wide Web and get the most out of popular browsers. Shows readers how to explore the Web's amazing world of electronic art museums, online magazines, virtual malls, and video music libraries.

*Price: $49.99 USA/$67.99 CDN   User Level: New - Casual -
                                                    Accomplished - Expert*

ISBN: 1-57521-040-1   1,440 pages

Web Site Construction Kit for Windows NT

— *Christopher L.T. Brown & Scott Zimmerman*

Web Site Construction Kit for Windows NT provides readers with everything they need to set up, develop, and maintain a Web site with Windows NT. It teaches the ins and outs of planning, installing, configuring, and administering a Windows NT–based Web site for an organization, and includes detailed instructions on how to use the software on the included CD-ROM to develop the Web site's content—HTML pages, CGI scripts, image maps, and so on. Teaches how to install, configure, and administer a Windows NT Web server. Covers ways to develop a Web site's content with HTML pages and CGI scripts.

Price: $49.99 USA/$67.99 CDN   User Level: Casual - Accomplished
ISBN: 1-57521-047-9   400 pages

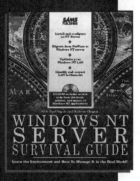

Windows NT Server Survival Guide

— Rick Sant'Angelo & Nadeem Chagtai

Joining the popular *Survival Guide* series, this book is a necessary tool for every system administrator implementing an NT network. It gives in-depth coverage of the latest and most complex features of NT networking, including steps to configure a heterogeneous system and procedures on implementing the BackOffice suite of NT Server–based products. Included CD-ROM contains a Workgroup Help Desk application, demonstration files, exotic logon scripts, and more. Step-by-step instructions cover every detail, including some advanced NT features. Explore the NT Server—its features, capabilities, and requirements. Covers latest version.

Price: $55.00 USA/$74.95 CDN   User Level: Accomplished
ISBN: 0-672-30860-6   996 pages

Web Publishing Unleashed

— William Stanek, Gregory Stenstrom, & Rich Tuttle

Web Publishing Unleashed includes sections on how to organize and plan your information, design pages, and become familiar with hypertext and hypermedia. Choose from a range of applications and technologies, including Java, SGML, VRML, and the newest HTML and Netscape extensions. The CD-ROM contains software, templates, and examples to help you become a successful Web publisher. Teaches how to convey information on the Web using the latest technologies—including Java. Readers learn how to integrate multimedia and interactivity into their Web publications.

Price: $49.99 USA/$67.99 CDN   User Level: Casual - Expert
ISBN: 1-57521-051-7   1,000 pages

Java Unleashed

— Michael Morrison, et al.

Java Unleashed is the ultimate guide to the year's hottest new Internet technologies—the Java language and the HotJava browser from Sun Microsystems. This is a complete programmer's reference and a guide to the hundreds of exciting ways Java is being used to add interactivity to the World Wide Web. Includes a helpful and informative CD-ROM. Shows readers how Java and HotJava are being used across the Internet.

Price: $49.99 USA/$67.99 CDN   User Level: Casual - Accomplished - Expert
ISBN: 1-57521-049-5   1,000 pages

Teach Yourself JavaScript in a Week

— Arman Danesh

Teach Yourself JavaScript in a Week is the easiest way to learn how to create interactive Web pages with JavaScript, Netscape's Java-like scripting language. It is intended for non-technical people, and will be equally of value to users on the Macintosh, Windows, and UNIX platforms. Teaches how to design and create attention-grabbing Web pages with JavaScript and how to add interactivity to Web pages.

Price: $39.99 USA/$53.99 CDN   User Level: Accomplished - Expert
ISBN: 1-57521-073-8   450 pages

Creating Web Applets with Java

— *David Gulbransen & Ben Rawlin*

Creating Web Applets with Java is the easiest way to learn how to integrate Java applets into Web pages. Java applets can be used for everything from spicing up a Web page's presentation to running sophisticated applications. This book is designed for the non-programmer who wants to use or customize preprogrammed Java applets with a minimum of trouble. Teaches the easiest way to incorporate the power of Java in a Web page and the basics of Java applet programming. CD-ROM included.

Price: $39.99 USA/$53.99 CDN   *User Level: Casual - Accomplished*
ISBN: 1-57521-070-3   500 pages

Developing Professional Java Applets

— *Casey Hopson & Stephen E. Ingram*

Developing Professional Java Applets is a reference for the professional programmer who needs to develop real-world, business-oriented Java applets—not just animations and games. This book assumes a basic familiarity with Java and gets right down to the business of applying Java to professional development. It is a comprehensive guide to developing professional Java applets. Teaches how to create new Java applets for business, research, and education. Filled with extensive examples of real-world Java applets. CD-ROM included.

Price: $49.99 USA/$67.99 CDN   *User Level: Accomplished - Expert*
ISBN: 1-57521-083-5   600 pages

Java Developer's Guide

— *Jamie Jaworski*

Java is one of the major growth areas for developers on the World Wide Web. It brings with it the capability to download and run small applications called applets from a Web server. *Java Developer's Guide* teaches developers everything they need to know to effectively develop Java applications. CD-ROM includes source code from the book and valuable utilities. Covers the Java interface, VRML extensions, security, and more. Explores new technology and future trends of Java development.

Price: $49.99 USA/$67.99 CDN   *User Level: Accomplished - Expert*
ISBN: 1-57521-069-X   1,000 pages

Teach Yourself Web Publishing with HTML 3.2 in 14 Days, Professional Reference Edition

— *Laura Lemay*

This is the updated edition of Lemay's previous bestseller, *Teach Yourself Web Publishing with HTML in 14 Days, Premier Edition*. In it readers will find all the advanced topics and updates—including adding audio, video, and animation—to Web page creation. Explores the use of CGI scripts, tables, HTML 3.0, the Netscape and Internet Explorer extensions, Java applets and JavaScript, and VRML.

Price: $59.99 USA/$81.95 CDN   *User Level: New - Casual - Accomplished*
ISBN: 1-57521-096-7   1,104 pages

Teach Yourself Java in Café in 21 Days

— Laura Lemay, et al.

Teach Yourself Java in Café in 21 Days steps you through all you need to learn to add interactivity to your static Web pages with Café, the first set of visual tools for the fast development of Java applets. You learn the fundamental concepts of the fully featured project-management system, as well as the basics of applet design and Web page integration. Gives you a thorough understanding of Café, including the graphical debugger for powerful source-level debugging, Café Studio for editing Java application resources, the ProjectExpress and AppExpress wizards, the incremental parser technology for Java programs, the class editor, and the professional programmer's editor. Covers Java and Café 1.2. CD-ROM included.

Price: $39.99 USA/$56.95 CDN   User Level: Accomplished - Expert
ISBN: 1-57521-157-2   614 pages

Windows NT 4 Web Development

— Sanjaya Hettihewa

Windows NT and Microsoft's newly developed Internet Information Server are making it easier and more cost-effective to set up, manage, and administer a good Web site. Because the Windows NT environment is relatively new, there are few books on the market that adequately discuss its full potential. *Windows NT 4 Web Development* addresses that potential by providing information on all key aspects of server setup, maintenance, design, and implementation. CD-ROM contains valuable source code and powerful utilities. Teaches how to incorporate new technologies in your Web site. Covers Java, JavaScript, Internet Studio, and VBScript.

Price: $59.99 USA/$84.95 CDN   User Level: Accomplished - Expert
ISBN: 1-57521-089-4   900 pages

Tricks of the Java Programming Gurus

— Glenn Vanderburg, et al.

This book is a guide for the experienced Java programmer who wants to take his Java skills beyond simple animations and applets. Shows how to streamline Java code, how to achieve unique results with undocumented tricks, and how to add advanced-level functions to your existing Java programs. CD-ROM includes all the source code from the book. Skilled Java professionals show how to improve garbage collection before and after compilation for improved performance. Provides a fast-paced guide to advanced Java programming.

Price: $49.99 USA/$70.95 CDN   User Level: Accomplished - Expert
ISBN: 1-57521-102-5   750 pages

Teach Yourself Java in 21 Days

— Laura Lemay, et al.

Introducing the first, best, and most detailed guide to developing applications with the hot new Java language from Sun Microsystems. CD-ROM includes the Java Developer's Kit. Provides detailed coverage of the hottest new technology on the World Wide Web. Includes coverage of browsing Java applications with Netscape and other popular Web browsers.

Price: $39.99 USA/$53.99 CDN   User Level: Accomplished - Expert
ISBN: 1-57521-030-4   500 pages

Add to Your Sams.net Library Today
with the Best Books for Internet Technologies

ISBN	Quantity	Description of Item	Unit Cost	Total Cost
0-672-30737-5		The World Wide Web Unleashed, Second Edition	$39.99	
0-672-30714-6		The Internet Unleashed, Second Edition	$35.00	
1-57521-047-9		Web Site Construction Kit for Windows NT (Book/CD-ROM)	$49.99	
1-57521-051-7		Web Publishing Unleashed (Book/CD-ROM)	$49.99	
1-57521-049-5		Java Unleashed (Book/CD-ROM)	$49.99	
1-57521-073-8		Teach Yourself JavaScript in a Week (Book/CD-ROM)	$39.99	
1-57521-083-5		Developing Professional Java Applets (Book/CD-ROM)	$49.99	
1-57521-069-X		Java Developer's Guide (Book/CD-ROM)	$49.99	
1-57521-096-7		Teach Yourself Web Publishing with HTML 3.2 in 14 Days, Professional Reference Edition (Book/CD-ROM)	$59.99	
1-57521-133-5		Professional Java Programming Kit (3 Books/4 CDs)	$129.99	
1-57521-089-4		Windows NT 4 Web Development (Book/CD-ROM)	$59.99	
1-57521-030-4		Teach Yourself Java in 21 Days (Book/CD-ROM)	$39.99	
		Shipping and Handling: See information below.		
		TOTAL		

Shipping and Handling: $4.00 for the first book, and $1.75 for each additional book. If you need to have it NOW, we can ship product to you in 24 hours for an additional charge of approximately $18.00, and you will receive your item overnight or in two days. Overseas shipping and handling adds $2.00. Prices subject to change. Call between 9:00 a.m. and 5:00 p.m. EST for availability and pricing information on latest editions.

201 W. 103rd Street, Indianapolis, Indiana 46290

1-800-428-5331 — Orders   1-800-835-3202 — FAX   1-800-858-7674 — Customer Service

Book ISBN 1-57521-088-6

What's on
the Disc

The companion CD-ROM contains all the source code and project files developed by the authors, plus an assortment of evaluation versions of third-party tools. The disc is designed to be explored using a browser program. Using the browser, you can view information concerning products and companies, and install programs with a single click of the mouse. To run the Guide to the CD-ROM, here's what to do:

Windows 95 Installation Instructions

> **Note:** If you have the AutoPlay feature of Windows 95 enabled, the Guide to the CD-ROM program will start automatically. If you have disabled the AutoPlay feature, please follow the instructions below.

1. Insert the CD-ROM into your CD-ROM drive.
2. From the Windows 95 desktop, double-click on the My Computer icon.
3. Double-click on the icon representing your CD-ROM drive.
4. Double-click on the icon titled `Cdguide.exe` to run the Guide to the CD-ROM program.

Windows NT Installation Instructions

1. Insert the CD-ROM into your CD-ROM drive.
2. From File Manager or Program Manager, choose Run from the File menu.
3. Type `<drive>\cdguide` and press Enter, where `<drive>` corresponds to the drive letter of your CD-ROM. For example, if your CD-ROM is drive D:, type `D:\CDGUIDE` and press Enter.
4. Follow the onscreen instructions in the Guide to the CD-ROM program.

Macintosh Installation Instructions

1. Insert the CD-ROM into your CD-ROM drive.
2. When an icon for the CD appears on the desktop, open the disc by double-clicking on its icon.
3. Double-click on the icon named Guide to the CD-ROM and follow the directions that appear.